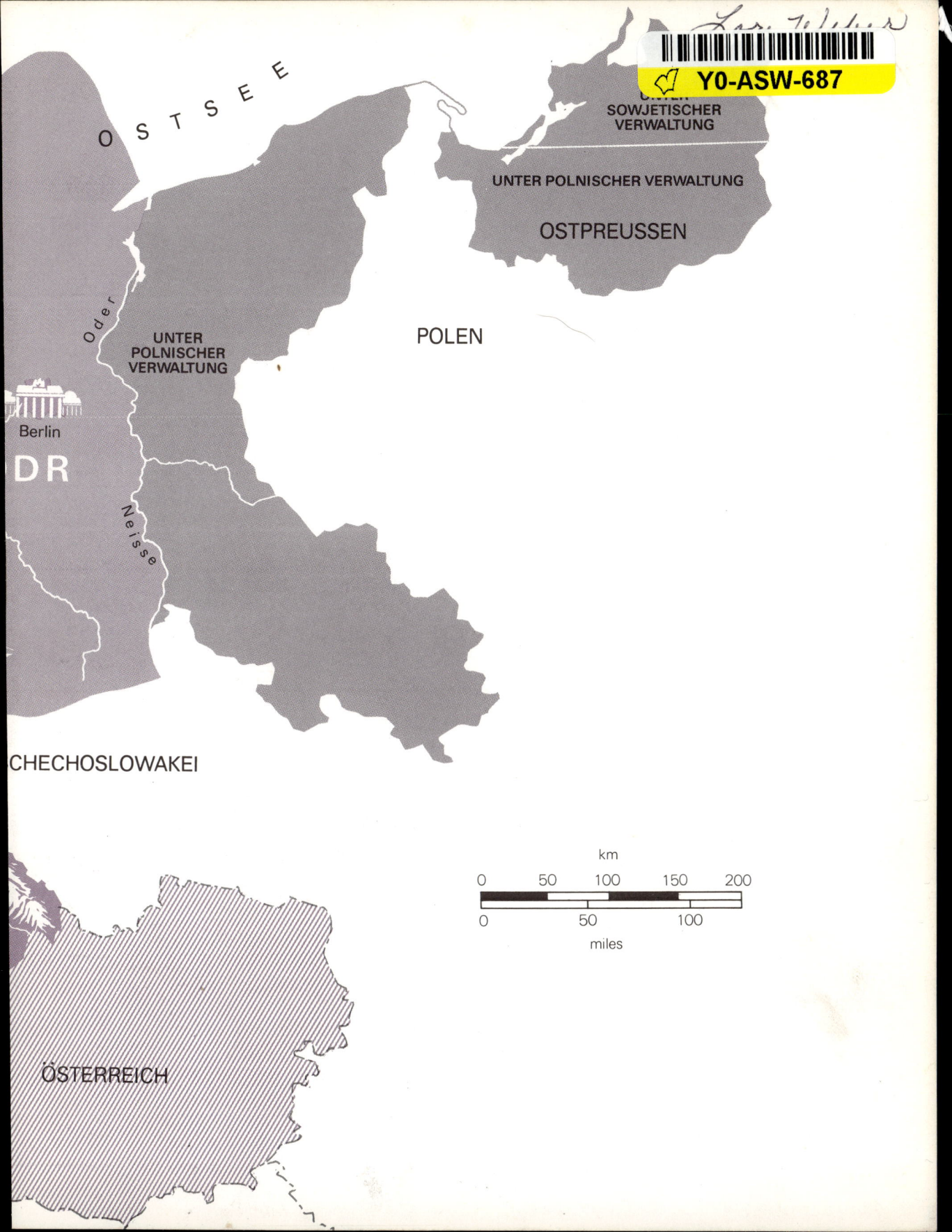

**CONTEMPORARY
GERMAN**

CONTEMPORARY GERMAN SECOND EDITION

Hans-Heinrich Wängler
University of Colorado

Robert L. Kyes
University of Michigan

George A. C. Scherer
*Late Professor of Modern Languages,
University of Colorado*

McGraw-Hill Book Company
*New York   St. Louis   San Francisco   Düsseldorf   Johannesburg   Kuala Lumpur   London
Mexico   Montreal   New Delhi   Panama   Rio de Janeiro   Singapore   Sydney   Toronto*

CONTEMPORARY GERMAN

Copyright © 1966, 1971 by McGraw-Hill, Inc. All rights reserved. Printed in the United States of America. No part of this publication may be reproduced, stored in a retrieval system, or transmitted, in any form or by any means, electronic, mechanical, photocopying, recording, or otherwise, without the prior written permission of the publisher.

Library of Congress Catalog Card Number 77-96243

07-067661-5

1234567890 VHVH 7987654321

This book was set in Monophoto Times with Univers, and was printed on permanent paper and bound by Von Hoffmann Press, Inc. The designer was Elliot Epstein; the drawings were done by Kenneth Longtemps. The editors were Samuel B. Bossard and Viola Sperka. Robert R. Laffler supervised production.

CONTENTS

Preface, **xi**
To the Student, **xv**
List of Abbreviations, **xx**

Unit 1 Dialog: **Hans und seine Tante Inge** • Sounds similar to English sounds • Directed Dialog • Question and answer patterns • Verb forms • Sentence types • Spelling • Listening: sound discrimination   1

Unit 2 Dialog: **Die Sonne scheint so schön** • Sounds different from English sounds • Directed Dialog • Question and answer patterns • Position of the dependent infinitive • Sentence structure • The predicate • Negators • Spelling • Syllabication • Listening: sound discrimination   29

Unit 3 Dialog: **Im Vorlesungsraum (Anfang)** • The **l**- and **r**-sounds • Question and answer patterns • Position of the dependent infinitive • Some question-words • Dependent clause structure • Position of the finite verb • Spelling • Listening: **Hans und Tante Inge; Fräulein Schneider und Herr Held**   55

Unit 4 Dialog: **Im Vorlesungsraum (Schluß)** • Vowel practice • Question and answer patterns • The definite article • Dependent infinitives • Compound nouns • Spelling • Punctuation • Listening: narrative   75

Unit 5 Dialog: **Der Unfall am Schillerplatz (Anfang)** • Unfamiliar consonant combinations • Personal pronoun subjects • The alphabet • Spelling • Capitalization • Punctuation • Listening: **Hans und Heike; Rolf und Inge**   95

Unit 6 Dialog: **Der Unfall am Schillerplatz (Schluß)** • Cardinal and ordinal numbers • Dates • Consonant combinations • The glottal stop • Position of the finite verb • Notes on adjectives • Spelling • Punctuation • Listening: **Ein Unfall; Fräulein Schneider und Herr Held**   117

Unit 7 Dialog: **In der Stadtbahn (Anfang)** • Telling time • Present tense verb forms • Dependent clauses • Separable and inseparable prefixes • Reading: **Tante Ilse liest die Zeitung** 139

Unit 8 Dialog: **In der Stadtbahn (Schluß)** • Some time and travel expressions • Masculine-feminine noun pairs • Some difficult little words • Present tense forms of irregular verbs • Imperative verb forms • Listening: **Frau Hartmann und Herr Schneider; Heike, Peter, und Uwe** 161

Unit 9 Dialog: **Der neue Hut (Anfang)** • Possessive adjectives • Identification expressions • Gender of nouns • Cases • Limiting adjectives in the nominative and accusative cases • Uses of the nominative and accusative cases • Spelling • Reading: **Haben Sie schon ein Sparbuch?** 183

Unit 10 Dialog: **Der neue Hut (Schluß)** • Prices • Neuter noun suffixes **-chen** and **-lein** • Noun plurals • Direct object pronouns • Personal pronouns in the nominative and accusative cases • Prepositions with the accusative case • Questions with **wer, wen, was** • Listening: **Lilo und Peter** 205

Unit 11 Dialog: **Der Schrank aus der Kiste (Anfang)** • Days of the week • Times of day • Months • Seasons • The dative case • Limiting adjectives and personal pronouns in the nominative, accusative, and dative cases • Noun endings in the dative case • Uses of the dative case • Reading: **Im Buchgeschäft** 227

Unit 12 Dialog: **Der Schrank aus der Kiste (Schluß)** • Directions • Germany's neighbors • Prepositions with the dative case • Contractions • Questions with **wem** • **Nach Hause, zu Hause** • Listening: **Deutschland und seine Nachbarländer** 247

Unit 13 Dialog: **Susi deckt den Mittagstisch (Anfang)** • Dependent infinitives with and without **zu** • The future tense • The modal auxiliaries • The verbs **sehen, helfen,** and **lassen** with dependent infinitives • Reading: **Gegen Mittag** 271

Unit 14   Dialog: **Susi deckt den Mittagstisch (Schluß)** • The verb **wissen** • Accusative/dative prepositions • **Wo-** and **da-**compounds • **Wo, wohin, woher** • Listening: **Susi und Vater; Herr und Frau Schneider**   291

Unit 15   Dialog: **Ein Krankenbesuch (Anfang)** • Some more time expressions • Position of time adverbs • Weak, strong, and irregular verbs • The past participle • The present perfect tense • Word order with the present perfect tense • Use of the present perfect tense • Reading: **Mein Onkel Richard**   317

Unit 16   Dialog: **Ein Krankenbesuch (Schluß)** • The suffix **-los** • The prefix **-un** • Idiomatic use of the present tense • The present participle • **Um zu, ohne zu, (an)statt zu** • Anticipatory **da**-compounds • Listening: **Heinz und Rolf**   347

Unit 17   Dialog: **Am Verkaufsstand (Anfang)** • The suffix **-ung** • Limiting adjectives and personal pronouns in the nominative, accusative, dative, and genitive cases • Noun endings in the genitive case • Uses of the genitive case • Questions with **wer, wen, wem,** and **wessen** • Reading: **Köln am Rhein**   365

Unit 18   Dialog: **Am Verkaufsstand (Schluß)** • Verbs ending in **-ieren** • Descriptive adjectives • Weak and strong adjective declensions • Adjectival nouns • Comparison of adjectives and adverbs • Uses of the positive, comparative, and superlative degrees • Idiomatic uses of **gern** • Apposition • Listening: **Der Festzug kommt**   389

Unit 19   Recombination reading: **Ein Student hat es gut** • Review of long and short vowels • Inference: words similar to English; German **pf** — English *p*   423

Unit 20   Dialog: **Ein unverhofftes Wiedersehen (Anfang)** • The past tense • Use of the past tense • Principal parts of strong and irregular verbs • The past perfect tense • Listening: **Käthe und Renate**   435

Unit 21   Dialog: **Ein unverhofftes Wiedersehen (Schluß)** • Verb-noun pairs • Reflexive verbs • **Einander** • Irregular imperatives • Coordinating and subordinating conjunctions • Reading: **Werner Bäckers Vater**   457

viii   CONTENTS

Unit 22   Reading: **Kleine Einführung in das ,,Sie''-Problem** • Review of umlaut sounds, long and short vowels, and diphthongs • Inference: words similar to English; German **z** — English *c*; German **k, ck** — English *c*; German **z, tz** — English *t*   481

Unit 23   Dialog: **Das Treffen bei Familie Kellner (Anfang)** • Infinitive as noun • The demonstrative adjective **der** • The demonstrative pronoun **der** • Relative pronouns • Structure of the relative clause • Some notes on nouns • Listening: **Heinrich Kellner, Kiel, Poststraße 34**   493

Unit 24   Dialog: **Das Treffen bei Familie Kellner (Schluß)** • Separable prefixes • The dependent infinitive with **zu** • The double infinitive • The verbs **hören, helfen, lassen,** and **sehen** • Future of probability • Reading: **Heinrich und Renate**   517

Unit 25   Reading: **Von deutschen Schulen** • Review of long and short vowels, diphthongs, and fricatives • Inference: words similar to English; German **d** — English *th*; German words of foreign origin spelled with **th**   539

Unit 26   Dialog: **Die Klassenreise (Anfang)** • Inseparable prefixes • The passive voice • Summary of functions of **werden** • **Ein**-words as pronouns • Before and after • Listening: **Anja und Sabine**   553

Unit 27   Dialog: **Die Klassenreise (Schluß)** • Agents of passive verbs • Subjectless passives • Substitutes for the passive voice • The passive with dative objects • The perfect infinitive • Reading: **Schloß Augustusburg bei Köln**   577

Unit 28   Reading: **Der Lehrerberuf in Deutschland** • Review of fricatives, long and short vowels, and diphthongs • Inference: words similar to English; German **t** — English *d*   599

Unit 29   Dialog: **Was wäre, wenn . . . (Anfang)** • **Ge**-prefix nouns • The subjunctive mood • Present subjunctive II forms • Past subjunctive II • The **würde**-alternatives • Summary of subjunctive II tenses • Some uses of subjunctive II: wishes contrary to fact; politeness; modals • Listening: **Der Wirtschaftskommentar**   611

CONTENTS ix

Unit 30   Dialog: **Was wäre, wenn... (Schluß)** • Other uses of subjunctive II: **als ob, als wenn**; wishes introduced by verbs of wishing; conditional sentences • Omission of **wenn** and **ob** • Reading: **Theater in Deutschland**   635

Unit 31   Reading: **Der Ehemann aus der Zeitung** • **Bekanntschaften** • **Deutschland — Reiseland** • Review of **l**- and **r**-sounds • Inference: meaning from context   661

Unit 32   Grammar: Indirect discourse • Subjunctive I • Tense forms of subjunctive I • Subjunctive I in indirect discourse • Subjunctive II in indirect discourse • Preferred forms • Other uses of subjunctive I • The indefinite pronoun **man** • Descriptive adjectives after expressions of indefinite quantity • Word order: basic sentence structure; the predicate; order of adverbs; order of objects; order of objects in relation to adverbs; variations; position of negatives; **nichts, gar nichts**, and **kein** as direct objects • The suffix **-heit** • The suffix **-keit** • The suffix **-schaft** • Other feminine suffixes • Inference: meaning from context   677

Unit 33   Reading: **Vom Geist unserer Zeit: Rekorde, Rekorde!** • **Fortschritt oder der Weg nach oben** • Review of **l**- and **r**-sounds, consonants and consonant clusters, vowel quality and quantity • Inference: meaning from context • Some sets of adverbs, adjectives, and prepositions   697

Unit 34   Reading: **Die Zimmervermieterin** • **Eigener Herd ist Goldes wert** • **Herr und Frau Neureich** • **Fanny** by Jo Hanns Rösler • Oral sentences • Inference: meaning from context • Syllabication   711

Unit 35   Reading: **Wolfgang Borchert (1921–1947)** • **Das Brot** by Wolfgang Borchert • **Der Stiftzahn oder Warum mein Vetter keine Rahmbonbon mehr ißt** by Wolfgang Borchert   727

Glossary, **741**

Index, **773**

PREFACE

A foreign language course must provide the student with the ability to comprehend the spoken language and its written representation, together with the ability to express himself in speaking and in writing. These four skills — listening, reading, speaking, and writing — must become automatic and must ultimately be free of any dependence on translation, on the conscious application of grammatical principles, or on the conscious recall of memorized sentences. The goal of such a program should not be translation, grammatical analysis, or memorization for its own sake. The goal should be *communication in the foreign language*.

Contemporary German has been designed to lead the student to a beginning proficiency in listening, reading, speaking, and writing. It is the culmination of several years of formal and informal experimentation with linguistically oriented materials, and has benefited from publications in the fields of psychology, pedagogy, learning theory, and linguistics, as well as from the first-hand experience of hundreds of teachers and thousands of students.

First of all, on the most elementary level, the German language is approached as a network of habits — habits of perception, habits of articulation, habits of inflection, and habits of order. The student's first task is to master these habits. Once they have become automatic, however, and can be accomplished without conscious thought, analysis, or recall, the student is led toward relatively free and fluent expression. The closer the student comes to this stage, the more his own aptitudes, desires, and motivations will determine his success, and the less will be the control exerted upon him by the text.

Audiolingual Approach. Although reading and writing are carefully cultivated throughout the book, the fundamental approach is through the spoken German language. The Dialogs introduce the basic audiolingual material and accordingly must be memorized by the students and "performed" aloud. New grammatical patterns are dealt with initially as spoken exercises. Audiolingual work continues in the Reading units in the form of simple questions and answers and in a systematic review of German phonology.

Graded Phonology. The entire sound system of Standard German is incorporated in the first six units. The sounds are distributed in such a way that the easier ones precede the more difficult ones. Unit 1 includes German sounds that cause little difficulty to speakers of most varieties of American English; either they are so similar to corresponding English sounds that they require no special attention at all, or they involve only minor articulatory adjustments. Unit 2 presents German sounds that are quite different from the sounds of American English and therefore require major adjustments and deliberate attention, both in articulation and in perception. Unit 3 introduces the German **l-** and **r-**sounds. Unit 4 gives further attention to the German **r-**sounds and to the sounds introduced in Unit 2. Units 5 and 6 deal with consonant combinations that are unfamiliar to the American and therefore require particular attention and practice.

The articulation of the German sound is described, contrasted with similar English sounds, and finally drilled in contrast to related German sounds. The sounds are reviewed in the Reading units, beginning with Unit 19.

Grammar. The student's attention is focused on those aspects of German inflection and order that differ significantly from those of English. The drills concentrate on these differences, while the grammatical explanations present the German patterns as parts of a unified, internally consistent system. The grammatical statements are intended to clarify, organize, and systematize what the student is learning through drills.

Dialogs. Most of the units are introduced by means of a short Dialog. The Dialogs portray meaningful confrontations between two or three persons; care has been taken to avoid the usual "tourist" situations, as well as the usual stereotypes. The tone is deliberately humorous, often ironic, and sometimes not without a hint of irritation on the part of one or more of the participants. These also serve as the vehicle for the introduction of new vocabulary and new grammatical patterns (and, in Units 1 to 6, new sounds and sound-combinations); they should therefore be committed to memory. A translation accompanies each Dialog; the English lines are the natural conversational equivalents of the German and do not attempt to provide a literal rendition of every single German word. The notes on vocabulary and grammar, to the right of the English sentences, clarify those features which might confuse the student. These are for home study; they are provided in order that the teacher will not have to spend valuable class time explaining simple grammatical details.

Supplements. The Supplement following each Dialog presents additional new vocabulary and at the same time focuses attention on the specific grammatical patterns that are drilled in the Audiolingual Drills. The student should become thoroughly familiar with the sentences of the Supplements.

Immediate Reinforcement. Much of the material in this book is designed in such a way that the student can work with it easily in private study. The slider provided with the book can be used to convert the drills into a simple "teaching machine;" the student is advised to make constant use of it while practicing the drills alone, in order to check the correctness of his responses immediately. This of course places much responsibility on the student himself; if he has difficulty working a particular drill, or must constantly peek under the slider to get the answer, then he should restudy the corresponding Grammar sections, perhaps even review the Dialog and Supplement, and then try the drill again.

Tapes. The Dialogs, Supplements, Audiolingual Drills, Listening Practices, and reading selections from the Reading units, as well as the phonological exercises of Units 1 to 6, are recorded on tape. The Dialogs, Supplements, and Drills are done in a three-stage format: stimulus — pause for student response — confirmation. The student should go through these in the language laboratory, but he should not refer to his book while in the laboratory; time spent with the tapes should be devoted *only* to listening and speaking. Experience indicates that laboratory practice is most effective when done in frequent (i.e. daily) but short (twenty- or thirty-minute) periods, rather than during a single weekly marathon session, and that the student should practice only those drills for which he has been adequately prepared beforehand — either by the teacher in the classroom or by private study with the slider, or both. The purpose of the tapes is to provide the student with all the oral practice he needs in order to achieve automatic control of the patterns.

Reading. Reading receives a steadily increasing amount of attention throughout the book. At first the student reads only what he has already memorized; he simply recognizes the written representation of what has been learned audiolingually. In Unit 7 a short Reading Practice appears; from that point on, Reading Practices alternate with Listening Practices. Starting with Unit 19, every third unit is constructed around a reading selection rather than around a conversation. The reading selections that occur up through Unit 19 contain only familiar vocabulary and grammatical patterns, but these are combined in different ways and in different contexts. From Unit 22 on, however, new vocabulary is introduced in the readings. Many of these new items are easy cognates, loanwords, and the like. Those which are not so easy to recognize are glossed for the student on the facing page — with a familiar German term if one is available, but in English otherwise.

The technique of guessing the meanings of new words is encouraged and deliberately cultivated. It is facilitated by the intentionally low density of new words, and it is practiced in the Inference exercises.

Step-by-Step Writing. The principles that govern German orthography are deliberately introduced early, in order to help the student make sense of the German sound-to-letter relationships. Although quite different from those of English, these relationships are relatively consistent and therefore useful to the student. Writing begins with simple copying and blank-filling, progresses to the arrangement of given words and phrases to form German sentences, then advances to the slightly more complicated Dehydrated Sentences in which the student must supply missing words and grammatical forms, and moves gradually to paragraph writing and story writing. Although quite rigid at first, controls are gradually removed as the student becomes more and more linguistically independent. Translation exercises (English to German) are employed only when a specific German pattern differs from the equivalent English pattern to a considerable degree, and it is deemed desirable to bring that difference to the student's attention.

Instructor's Handbook. A detailed *Instructor's Handbook* accompanies *Contemporary German*. Because of the radical departure of this course from traditionally oriented courses, suggestions on teaching procedures and the construction of appropriate tests may be helpful. The *Instructor's Handbook* may also be helpful for orienting those long-neglected members of our profession: the new teaching assistants and associates.

The Revised Edition. The gratifying results achieved by so many teachers of so many different backgrounds, using *Contemporary German*, confirm the correctness of the design and approach of this book. The basic design and approach therefore remain unchanged, although the format has undergone considerable alteration. The Dialog Units, beginning with Unit 3, have been divided into two units each, resulting in a total of thirty-five units, compared to the first edition's twenty-three. It is hoped that this rearrangement has resulted in a somewhat tighter organization and will enable the teacher to deal with smaller, more compact amounts of material at a given time. Some of the Audiolingual Drills have been shortened or omitted, and new ones have been added. We have added reference numbers to the Drills so that the student can refer quickly to the appropriate Grammar sections. The Grammar sections have been rewritten in order to bring them into closer alignment with the Drills, and some material on syntax has been added. To give greater attention to the "passive skills" of reading and listening, short Listening Practices and Reading Practices have been added, together with simple questions to check comprehension and stimulate discussion. Writing sections now appear from the very beginning and include a variety of kinds of exercises; including this material within the text has thus rendered a separate workbook unnecessary. Questions on the reading selections in the Reading units have been simplified and increased in number, but answers are not provided as they were in the first edition; the student should have little difficulty in formulating his own answers to them. The reading selections have been modified somewhat in terms of vocabulary and grammar, and the notes expanded. The principal parts of strong and irregular verbs are given in the Glossary, rather than in one of the Grammar sections.

In preparing the revision of *Contemporary German* we have been guided by the suggestions of many, many teachers. We acknowledge a debt of gratitude to them all and wish to thank them warmly for their time and effort, and for giving us the benefit of their experience and insight.

Hans-Heinrich Wängler
Robert L. Kyes

TO THE STUDENT

Many people who enter into the study of a second language do so with (1) great enthusiasm and (2) a lot of notions about what language is, how it functions, and what is involved in learning a second language. We welcome the former and wish to take full advantage of it; the latter, however, may be detrimental to one's progress, since many of these notions are — to be quite plain about it — false. Perhaps your first task, then, should be to get rid of some common, erroneous notions that might make learning German more difficult than it has to be.

The German language and intelligence. The idea that only the very smart students can possibly learn German has been around for as long as German has been taught as a foreign language in this country, which is quite a long time. This idea is probably the result of the way that languages used to be taught, rather than of the complexity of the language itself. After all, German children learn to speak German just as easily as American children learn to speak English, and German children are no more intelligent, on the average, than American children.

German and English. A popular misconception about foreign languages is that they differ from English only in that they use different words to say the same thing. This leads to the notion that learning a foreign language involves mainly learning a list of words and their "English meanings." Other differences between the languages — differences in word order, in inflection, etc. — are regarded as strange little quirks that reflect the peculiarities of the speakers of the foreign language, and are all lumped together under "idioms." It is closer to the truth, however, to think of German and English as being *totally* different from each other in *all* respects. They are used by completely different cultures and thus embrace completely different ideas, concepts, and values. They reflect the world of their speakers in entirely different ways. Even though we may translate the German word **Freund** with English *friend*, the German means something by **Freund** that is quite different from what the American means by *friend*. Furthermore, the languages are pronounced differently — American English with an "American accent" and German with a "German accent." Words are formed and varied in different ways, depending on different things. Phrases and sentences are constructed and changed in different ways, according to principles that are not at all the same in the two languages. There are things that you can say in English, but that you simply cannot say in German, and vice versa. This is just the way languages are; each one follows its own rules, and the rules are different for all languages.

Language and grammar. Back in the old days one of the favorite techniques used in the language class was the memorization and recitation of rules of grammar. This may not have been very interesting, but it certainly gave the students a feeling of accomplishment. What they were learning was not the language, however; they were simply learning *about* the language. The memorization of rules can result in only one thing: a list of memorized rules! Knowledge of abstract principles does not ensure that one can apply those principles. Just as a knowledge of music theory does not make one a competent pianist, so the knowledge of German grammar does not make one a speaker of German. In this course, the goal is *the ability to use German*, not knowledge about

German. Your primary activity — in class and outside of class — will be *using* the language. The rules are not ends in themselves. They are justified only when they can help you acquire active control of the language, or some part of it, quickly and efficiently. This is the intended function of the Grammar sections in this book.

Reading and translating. Students used to have to spend a lot of time translating their foreign language texts into English. The class hour was often spent reading translations and listening to the teacher lecture on any grammatical points that happened to come up. But reading and translating are not the same. They involve two different processes. When you translate from German to English, you actually convert a string of German words — which may or may not mean anything to you, depending on how well you know German in the first place — into a string of English words. You accomplish this by bringing to bear upon that German string whatever pertinent information you can find in your German-English dictionary, plus whatever pertinent information you can find in your German reference grammar. Then you read the English sentence, and the message comes across. The goal of translating, then, is not to read German; it is rather to remove oneself from the German and get back into good old understandable English. It also gives practice in dictionary-thumbing and index-using. But our interest is not in dictionaries or in indices — it is in the German language itself. What you must learn to do is not translate into English, but read the German text and know what it means *in German* with little or no recourse to English. Translating is at times a useful device in learning a foreign language, but it is not one of our goals. We provide translations of the Dialogs and the Supplements, and there are even some translation exercises in the Writing sections — but these all have specific functions and do not alter the fact that translation is not one of the skills that you are being taught.

Questions you shouldn't ask. Every language follows its own rules and functions in its own unique way. It is the result of uncounted centuries of historical development, during which time ordinary people learned it, used it, and passed it on to their children, rarely if ever giving any thought to it. When you encounter a new sound, word, or pattern in German that differs from what you are accustomed to in English, it may seem quite natural to ask: "Why do they say it that way in German?" The question may seem natural, but the answer is not; the answers to such questions may simply not exist, or they may be rooted in the history of the language ("They say it that way because that's how their parents and grandparents said it"), or they may be so complicated and abstract that they could be of little interest to anyone but a linguist. The question "Why do they say it that way in German?" is about as relevant as the question "Why is water wet?" It just is! To go into the matter any more deeply would be to miss the whole point, namely, that water *is* wet, or that that *is* the way they say it in German.

So much for some popular misconceptions about languages, language-learning, and German. It might also be helpful to have some positive suggestions with regard to this book and how it can be used to best advantage.

The use of imitation. Children love to imitate the people and things that they observe around them. They spend hours at it and take utter delight in it. This is good; they learn a lot that way. Adults, on the other hand, are not such willing imitators. Imitating somebody else requires that

they step out of the roles they have built up for themselves over the years, in which they feel secure and confident, and most adults are, quite understandably, reluctant to do this. This is unfortunate, from the standpoint of learning a second language, because imitation is a very effective device. Because it is so effective, it is exploited in nearly all modern language courses — and it is used here as well. You have two models to imitate: your teacher and the voices recorded on tape. Both your teacher and the tape will be producing noises that may strike you as strange, outlandish, or even impossible — but these all belong to the German way of speaking, and you will have to learn to produce them correctly. The only way to achieve this is to imitate the model as closely as possible. Don't be embarrassed — all your classmates are in the same boat, and it will be the best imitators who learn most quickly and most accurately.

The use of practice. Mastery of the language is not accomplished by merely imitating, however. Correct imitation is only a necessary beginning. You must learn to produce the sounds, words, and sentence patterns of German at will, even when there is no model around for you to imitate. The sounds, words, and patterns that you repeat after your teacher, or after the recorded voice, must become completely effortless; their production must become a matter of *habit* for you. This takes practice. The Dialogs, Supplements, Audiolingual Drills, and other exercises have been recorded on tape for the purpose of giving you all the practice you want or need, on all the sounds and patterns introduced in this book. It is not enough to read about the German language, or to understand how it works in the abstract, or even to be a good mimic — you have to be able to *use* the language, and this comes only with practice. It is suggested that this practice be done in short periods — say twenty or thirty minutes — and at frequent intervals.

The use of generalizations. Children learn best from observation and imitation. Adults have at least one advantage over children, however — they can learn also from explanation and instruction. Learning by imitation is effective, but it is also rather inefficient; it requires a lot of time, much trial and error, and a tremendous amount of motivation. The adult can avoid much of this trial and error, as well as the disadvantages of inconstant motivation, and thus increase his efficiency, by learning something about the principles that govern particular patterns and formations. Your learning of German will progress fastest if you combine practice (the Audiolingual Drills) with conscious understanding (the Grammar sections). Before going through a set of drills, then, you should read the corresponding explanations. Study them again after having gone through the drills once or twice, and then do the drills again.

Dialogs. Most of the units begin with a Dialog. Since the Dialog contains examples of the new sounds, words, and grammatical patterns that are to be learned in the unit, you should memorize the entire Dialog. This is easy, once you become accustomed to it. Your teacher will help you get started with this in class. Then you should practice it with the recording until you are certain that your control of the pronunciation is perfect. In order to know what you are saying, read the translations facing the Dialog. The notes to the right will help to clarify new or puzzling forms. Test your control of the Dialog by practicing it with another student; try switching parts, and play around with the sentences by varying them somewhat.

Supplements. The sentences of the Supplement represent a midpoint between the Dialog and the Audiolingual Drills, and they introduce additional new vocabulary. They are based on patterns that occur in the Dialog, but serve to focus your attention more clearly on the specific grammatical feature that is to be treated in detail in the drills. You should practice these until you can repeat them rapidly and effortlessly, and study the translations and notes.

Directed Dialogs. Part A of the Audiolingual Drills is called the Directed Dialog. For the most part it is taken directly from the sentences of the Dialog itself; you are told what to say, and then you say it. This helps solidify your command of the new Dialog sentences, and at the same time it gives you practice in replying to what somebody else says. Your teacher will help you with these in class at first. As you become familiar with the technique, you will be expected to prepare these without your teacher's help. Practice them with the recordings, and go through them with the slider. Again, two or more students can practice these together. You should bring this drill to the point where you can give a reply immediately, without any hesitation or fumbling about.

Audiolingual Drills. These are designed to give you abundant opportunity to learn through practice the basic grammatical patterns of German sentences. There are four kinds: some simply require that you *repeat* the recorded sentence; some require the *replacement* of one word by another; others involve major *structural changes* in the sentence; and some ask for a suitable *answer* of your own creation. In the first three kinds of drills, your replies are rigidly controlled, i.e. only one reply is possible; in the fourth, however, you are "on your own" to make up anything that makes sense. Of course, to make sense it must be understandable to someone else, and to be understandable it has to be grammatically correct. Your teacher will help you with these drills as long as you require help; when you become familiar with the various procedures and have a fairly good control of German pronunciation, the drills will be left more and more to you. You must practice these drills — with the recordings and also with your book and slider — until you can go through them rapidly without making any mistakes. Also, in conjunction with the drills, study the corresponding Grammar sections. Avoid spending long periods of time on the drills; your memory will serve you better if you work on them often, but briefly.

Listening Practices and Reading Practices. Each Dialog unit ends with a Listening Practice or a Reading Practice. The Listening Practices are recorded on tape and are intended to be listened to in your language laboratory. The Reading Practices appear in the book. These exercises contain only those words and patterns that you have already learned in different contexts or (in the second half of the book) some words that you should be able to guess from context. The selections are solely for passive understanding; you will not have to translate them, nor will it be necessary to subject them to grammatical analysis, nor will you be required to memorize them.

Reading Units. Beginning with Unit 19, every third unit is built around a reading selection rather than around a conversation. The readings are simple at first, containing only known vocabulary and patterns, but gradually they become more complex and new words are introduced. New words are glossed on the page facing the text; if you already know a German term that might explain the meaning of a new word, then that German term is used — otherwise an English translation is provided. You should make a deliberate effort to avoid putting these selections into English. The following suggestions may help you in preparing the reading assignments:

1. Read through the entire selection as quickly as you can. Read every word, but do not bother checking the notes on the facing page, even for new words. Do not stop to puzzle over constructions that you don't understand.

2. Read the passage a second time, slowly and carefully. Study the notes on the right in order to understand the meaning and function of new words or complex grammatical constructions. Try to guess the meanings of new words that aren't glossed in the notes; do not look them up in the Glossary except as a last resort.

3. Your third reading should also be slow and careful. Make a deliberate attempt to remember those words and constructions that you had to look up earlier. Underline the ones that cause you difficulty, and come back to them later for review; ask your teacher about the forms that seem to defy understanding.

4. Having gone through the selection three times, see how many of the questions you can answer without looking up the answers in the text. Most of the questions are simple, and the answers that they require are also simple. Be original in your answers, though; don't merely parrot the text.

5. The fifth stage in preparing a reading selection is simply a memory-refresher. Shortly before your German class meets, read through the passage again quickly. By now you should not have to re-check any of the new words; but if you have forgotten one, look it up in the notes again.

It is preferable to keep these five stages separate in time, allowing at least an hour or two to elapse between any two.

How to study for tests. Your teacher is interested in how well you can handle the language, not in how many words you can translate in a minute, or how quickly you can untangle complicated constructions that you have never seen before, or how well you remember the rules of grammar. You should therefore expect to be asked to *produce German* on your tests and quizzes. There are many ways of doing this — blank fill-ins, questions and answers, rewriting sentences according to instructions, making up sentences using given words, supplying missing sentences in a conversation, etc. You will be able to do these things only if you have practiced doing them beforehand. This means that *constant* effort and attention on your part are essential. Last-minute cramming is of questionable value in any course; in a foreign language course it is utterly futile.

LIST OF ABBREVIATIONS

abbr.	abbreviation	neg.	negative
acc.	accusative	neut.	neuter
act.	active	nom.	nominative
adj.	adjective, adjectival	p.	participle
adv.	adverb	pass.	passive
alt.	alternative	perf.	perfect
aux.	auxiliary	pl.	plural
coll.	colloquial	pos.	positive
compar.	comparative	poss.	possessive
conj.	conjunction	pp.	past participle
coord.	coordinating	pred.	predicate
dat.	dative	prep.	preposition
dim.	diminutive	pres.	present
fem.	feminine	pron.	pronoun
fut.	future	refl.	reflexive
gen.	genitive	rel.	relative
imper.	imperative	sg.	singular
inf.	infinitive	subj.	subjunctive
interj.	interjection	subord.	subordinating
intrans.	intransitive	superl.	superlative
lit.	literally	trans.	transitive
masc.	masculine		

Unit 1

DIALOG

Hans und seine Tante Inge

ˌhans ˈunt zaɪnə tantə ˈɪŋə

1 **Hans:** Es ist heiß heute, Tante Inge.

ˌhans ɛs ɪst ˈhaɪs hɔɪtə tantə ɪŋə

2 **Tante Inge:** Ja, mein Junge, du kannst Eis kaufen.

tantə ˈɪŋə ˌjaː maɪn jʊŋə duː kanst ˈaɪs kaufən

3 **Hans:** Danke, du bist nett.

ˌdaŋkə duː bɪst ˈnɛt

4 **Tante Inge:** Da ist ein Eismann.

ˌdɑː ɪst aɪn ˈaɪsman

Hans and His Aunt Inge   die Tante

1   It's hot today, Aunt Inge.   sein (es ist)

2   Yes, my boy, you can buy some ice cream.   **der Junge** boy   **jung** young · **du** *familiar pronoun of address* · **können (du kannst)** · **das Eis**

3   Thanks, you're nice.   sein (du bist)

4   There's an ice-cream man.   **der Eismann**   das Eis + der Mann

4   UNIT 1 · DIALOG

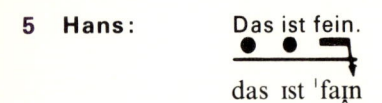

5   **Hans:**   Das ist fein.
                     das ɪst ˈfaɪn

6   **Tante Inge:** Was nimmst du?
                     vas ˈnɪmst du:

7   **Hans:**   Nuß-Eis, bitte, das schmeckt am besten.
                     ˈnus aɪs ˌbɪtə ˌdas ʃmɛkt am ˈbɛstən

8   **Tante Inge:** Meinst du?
                     ˈmaɪnst du:

9   **Hans:**   Bestimmt! Nimmst du kein Eis?
                     bəˈʃtɪmt   nɪmst du: kaɪn aɪs

10 **Tante Inge:** Nein, danke.
                     naɪn ˈdaŋkə

11 **Hans:**   Hast du Angst?
                     hast du: ˈaŋst

12 **Tante Inge:** Ißt deine Mutti denn Eis?
                     ɪst daɪnə ˈmuti dɛn aɪs

13 **Hans:**   Nein, Mutti ißt nie Eis.
                     naɪn ˌmuti ɪst ˈni: aɪs

14 **Tante Inge:** Siehst du?
                     ˈzi:st du:

5	That's fine.	
6	What are you going to have?	**nehmen (du nimmst)** take, get, have
7	Walnut ice cream, please; it tastes best.	**das Nuß-Eis die Nuß** walnut, nut + **das Eis · schmecken (das schmeckt) · gut** good **am besten** best
8	Do you think so?	**meinen (du meinst)** think, say, mean
9	Sure. Aren't you going to have any ice cream?	**kein** no, not any
10	No, thanks.	
11	Are you afraid?	**Angst haben** be afraid **haben (du hast)** have **die Angst** fear, anxiety
12	Tell me, does your mother eat ice cream?	**essen (sie ißt) · die Mutti** Mommy, *from* **die Mutter** mother · **denn** *gives the question a slight emphasis*
13	No, Mommy never eats ice cream.	
14	You see?	**sehen (du siehst)**

15 Hans: Ist Eis denn Gift?

ɪst ˌaɪs dɛn ˈgɪft

16 Tante Inge: Kauf dein Eis, mein Kind!

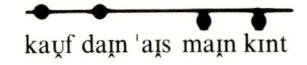

kaʊf daɪn ˈaɪs maɪn kɪnt

SUPPLEMENT

1 Es ist heiß heute.

ɛs ɪst ˈhaɪs hɔɪtə

2 Ist es heiß heute?

ɪst ɛs ˈhaɪs hɔɪtə

3 Hans sagt, es ist heiß heute.

hans zɑːkt ɛs ɪst ˈhaɪs hɔɪtə

4 Tante Inge ist nett.

tantə ɪŋə ɪst ˈnɛt

5 Ist Tante Inge nett?

ɪst tantə ɪŋə ˈnɛt

6 Hat Tante Inge Angst?

hat tantə ɪŋə ˈaŋst

7 Ja, Tante Inge hat Angst.

jaː tantə ɪŋə hat ˈaŋst

15 Well, is ice cream poison?   **das Gift**

16 Buy your ice cream, my child!   **kaufen (kauf** *imper.***) · das Kind**

---

1 It's hot today.

2 Is it hot today?

3 Hans says it's hot today.   **sagen (er sagt)**

4 Aunt Inge is nice.

5 Is Aunt Inge nice?

6 Is Aunt Inge afraid?   **haben (sie hat)**

7 Yes, Aunt Inge is afraid.

UNIT 1 · SUPPLEMENT

8 Nimmt Tante Inge Eis?
   nɪmt tantə ɪŋə aɪs

9 Nein, Tante Inge nimmt kein Eis.
   naɪn tantə ɪŋə nɪmt ˈkaɪn aɪs

10 Das Kind kauft Eis.
   das kɪnt kaʊft ˈaɪs

11 Kauft das Kind Eis?
   kaʊft das kɪnt ˈaɪs

12 Kann Hans Eis kaufen?
   kan hans ˈaɪs kaʊfən

13 Was kann Hans kaufen?
   was kan hans ˈkaʊfən

14 Hans kann Eis kaufen.
   hans kan ˈaɪs kaʊfən

15 Iß dein Eis, Hans!
   ɪs daɪn ˈaɪs hans

8   Is Aunt Inge having ice cream?   **nehmen (sie nimmt)**

9   No, Aunt Inge isn't having any ice cream.

10 The child buys (is buying) ice cream.   **kaufen (es kauft)**

11 Is the child buying ice cream?

12 Can Hans buy (some) ice cream?   **können (er kann)**

13 What can Hans buy?

14 Hans can buy some ice cream.

15 Eat your ice cream, Hans!   **essen (iß** *imper.***)**

PHONOLOGY

No two languages are alike. Every language has its own *vocabulary* or set of words, its own *grammar* or way of arranging forms meaningfully, and its own *phonology* or way of pronouncing its meaningful forms. The vocabulary, grammar, and phonology of one language are different from the vocabulary, grammar, and phonology of all other languages. In learning German, then, you not only will acquire a substantial portion of German vocabulary and learn how to form meaningful German sentence patterns; you must also learn how to pronounce German words and sentences using German sounds. If you try to speak German using the sounds of English, then no one — not even your teacher — will be able to understand you very well. You have to learn to speak German with a German accent — which is the way the Germans do it!

Unit 1 includes only those German sounds that correspond closely to sounds of American English. Despite the similarities, however, there are slight but important differences between these German sounds and their English counterparts.

The first step in acquiring an excellent pronunciation of a new language is to be able to hear the new sounds accurately; only then will it be possible for you to provide an accurate imitation of the foreign pronunciation. The human ear is not a microphone; it does not accurately record every feature of every sound that falls upon it. Therefore, we all tend to hear new speech sounds subjectively, identifying them with sounds that are already familiar to us — the sounds of our native language — and perceiving them as the nearest familiar equivalents. For this reason it is imperative that the relevant differences between sounds that seem similar in the two languages be understood and heard. After you have understood the relevant difference between two sounds and have learned to hear this difference, then you will have to practice imitating the new sound until it becomes easy for you. The procedure is as follows:

1. Learn what the differences are.
2. Learn to recognize these differences when you hear them.
3. Imitate the new sounds correctly.
4. Practice the new sounds until their pronunciation is automatic.

An awareness of these four steps is essential throughout the entire course.

In the discussions that follow, the sounds of German are described and contrasted with the sounds of American English, and with similar but different German sounds. The descriptions are not intended to serve as a substitute for listening practice, but as explanations of how the new sounds that you will be hearing are formed. A mirror will be helpful in checking the position of lips and tongue as you work on the new pronunciations.

The accompanying diagram will also aid you in locating the various parts of the mouth, tongue, and throat in the descriptions that follow. The symbols used are adapted from those of the International Phonetic Alphabet. Unlike the letters of the ordinary English or German alphabet, each symbol stands for one and only one sound. Thus the *i*-sound of **bitte** is written phonetically [ɪ], and the vowel of **die**, **siehst**, or **ihm** is written [i:]. The following devices will also be used:

[ ]   always enclose phonetic symbols.

:   following the phonetic symbol for a vowel sound, as in [i:], indicates that the sound is long.

‿   beneath a symbol, as in [aɪ̯], signifies that the sound goes with the previous element to form a diphthong, rather than the beginning of a new syllable.

ˈ   preceding a syllable above the line, as in [ˈaɪ̯sman], indicates loud stress on that syllable. Below the line [ˌ] it indicates medium stress.

8   Is Aunt Inge having ice cream?   **nehmen (sie nimmt)**

9   No, Aunt Inge isn't having any ice cream.

10 The child buys (is buying) ice cream.   **kaufen (es kauft)**

11 Is the child buying ice cream?

12 Can Hans buy (some) ice cream?   **können (er kann)**

13 What can Hans buy?

14 Hans can buy some ice cream.

15 Eat your ice cream, Hans!   **essen (iß** *imper.***)**

PHONOLOGY

No two languages are alike. Every language has its own *vocabulary* or set of words, its own *grammar* or way of arranging forms meaningfully, and its own *phonology* or way of pronouncing its meaningful forms. The vocabulary, grammar, and phonology of one language are different from the vocabulary, grammar, and phonology of all other languages. In learning German, then, you not only will acquire a substantial portion of German vocabulary and learn how to form meaningful German sentence patterns; you must also learn how to pronounce German words and sentences using German sounds. If you try to speak German using the sounds of English, then no one — not even your teacher — will be able to understand you very well. You have to learn to speak German with a German accent — which is the way the Germans do it!

Unit 1 includes only those German sounds that correspond closely to sounds of American English. Despite the similarities, however, there are slight but important differences between these German sounds and their English counterparts.

The first step in acquiring an excellent pronunciation of a new language is to be able to hear the new sounds accurately; only then will it be possible for you to provide an accurate imitation of the foreign pronunciation. The human ear is not a microphone; it does not accurately record every feature of every sound that falls upon it. Therefore, we all tend to hear new speech sounds subjectively, identifying them with sounds that are already familiar to us — the sounds of our native language — and perceiving them as the nearest familiar equivalents. For this reason it is imperative that the relevant differences between sounds that seem similar in the two languages be understood and heard. After you have understood the relevant difference between two sounds and have learned to hear this difference, then you will have to practice imitating the new sound until it becomes easy for you. The procedure is as follows:

1. Learn what the differences are.
2. Learn to recognize these differences when you hear them.
3. Imitate the new sounds correctly.
4. Practice the new sounds until their pronunciation is automatic.

An awareness of these four steps is essential throughout the entire course.

In the discussions that follow, the sounds of German are described and contrasted with the sounds of American English, and with similar but different German sounds. The descriptions are not intended to serve as a substitute for listening practice, but as explanations of how the new sounds that you will be hearing are formed. A mirror will be helpful in checking the position of lips and tongue as you work on the new pronunciations.

The accompanying diagram will also aid you in locating the various parts of the mouth, tongue, and throat in the descriptions that follow. The symbols used are adapted from those of the International Phonetic Alphabet. Unlike the letters of the ordinary English or German alphabet, each symbol stands for one and only one sound. Thus the *i*-sound of **bitte** is written phonetically [ɪ], and the vowel of **die**, **siehst**, or **ihm** is written [i:]. The following devices will also be used:

[ ] always enclose phonetic symbols.

: following the phonetic symbol for a vowel sound, as in [i:], indicates that the sound is long.

˯ beneath a symbol, as in [aɪ̯], signifies that the sound goes with the previous element to form a diphthong, rather than the beginning of a new syllable.

ˈ preceding a syllable above the line, as in [ˈaɪ̯sman], indicates loud stress on that syllable. Below the line [ˌ] it indicates medium stress.

. beneath the symbol for the *r*-sound [ʀ] indicates a reduction to weaker articulation, sometimes even suggesting the quality of a vowel.

˛ beneath a vowel symbol indicates relative laxness and openness; it is used only with English vowels.

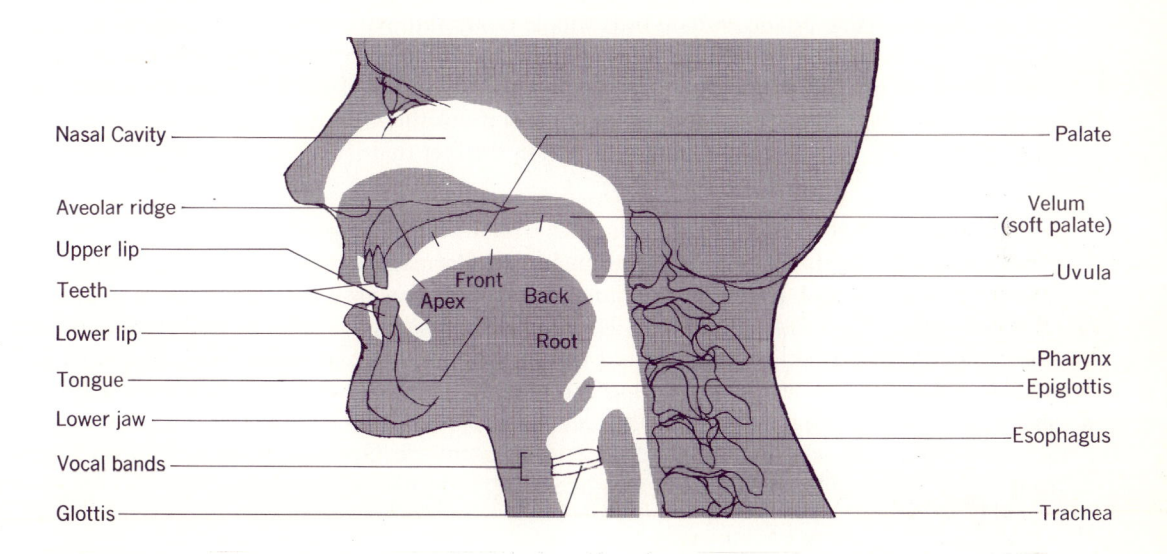

Diagram of the vocal tract with labels:
- Nasal Cavity
- Aveolar ridge
- Upper lip
- Teeth
- Lower lip
- Tongue
- Lower jaw
- Vocal bands
- Glottis
- Palate
- Velum (soft palate)
- Uvula
- Pharynx
- Epiglottis
- Esophagus
- Trachea
- Front, Apex, Back, Root (tongue regions)

The sounds in Unit 1

	Vowels		Closest English counterpart				Consonants		Closest English counterpart		
[iː]	s **ieh** st	[ziːst]	[i̞]	b *ea* st	[bi̞st]	[p]	**P**apa	[ˈpapa]	[p]	*p*apa	[ˈpapʌ]
[ɪ]	b **i** tte	[ˈbɪtə]	[ɪ]	b *i* t	[bɪt]	[b]	**b** ist	[bɪst]	[b]	*b* it	[bɪt]
[uː]	d **u**	[duː]	[u̞]	d *o*	[du̞]	[t]	**T** an **t** e	[ˈtantə]	[t]	*t* ip	[tɪp]
[ʊ]	M **u** tti	[ˈmʊti]	[ʊ]	p *u* t	[pʊt]	[d]	**d** anke	[ˈdaŋkə]	[d]	*d* ot	[dɑt]
[ɛ]	n **e** tt	[nɛt]	[ɛ]	n *e* t	[nɛt]	[k]	**k** ein	[kai̯n]	[k]	*k* ey	[kɪi̯]
[ə]	Tant **e**	[ˈtantə]	[ʌ]	sof *a*	[ˈsoʊ̯fʌ]	[g]	**G** ift	[gɪft]	[g]	*g* ift	[gɪft]
[ɑː]	j **a**	[jɑː]				[f]	**f** ein	[fai̯n]	[f]	*f* ine	[fai̯n]
[a]	**T a** nte	[ˈtantə]	[ɑ̯]	kn *o* t	[nɑ̯t]	[v]	**w** as	[vas]	[v]	*v* ery	[ˈvɛrɪi̯]
[ai̯]	**Ei** s	[ai̯s]	[ai̯]	*i* ce	[ai̯s]	[s]	da **s**	[das]	[s]	hou *s* e	[haʊ̯s]
[ɔi̯]	h **eu** te	[ˈhɔi̯tə]	[ɔi̯]	b *oy*	[bɔi̯]	[z]	**s** eine	[ˈzai̯nə]	[z]	*z* oo	[zuʊ̯]
[aʊ̯]	k **au** f	[kaʊ̯f]	[aʊ̯]	h *ou* se	[haʊ̯s]	[ʃ]	**sch** meckt	[ʃmɛkt]	[ʃ]	*sh* oe	[ʃuʊ̯]
						[j]	**j** a	[jɑː]	[j]	*y* ear	[jɪr]
						[h]	**h** eiß	[hai̯s]	[h]	*h* ouse	[haʊ̯s]
						[m]	**m** ein	[mai̯n]	[m]	*m* ine	[mai̯n]
						[n]	**n** ein	[nai̯n]	[n]	*n* i *n* e	[nai̯n]
						[ŋ]	Ju **ng** e	[ˈjuŋə]	[ŋ]	si *ng*	[sɪŋ]

Vowels

An important difference between the German and English vowel systems is that the length, or duration, of the vowels is significant in German but not in English. The English sounds that are often called "long vowels" are actually diphthongs, or combinations of a vowel and an off-glide. The so-called "short vowels" of English are comparatively pure; that is, they generally lack the diphthongal off-glide and are thus simple monophthongs. The English diphthongs may be quite short, as in *light*, or long, as in *lied*. The English monophthongs may likewise be either short, as in *kit*, or relatively long, as in *kid* or *kin*. The vowel of *bet* [ɛ] is traditionally called "short *e*," and the vowel of *bait* [eɪ] "long *a*" in spite of the fact that both are approximately equal in duration. The important difference lies in the fact that [ɛ] is a monophthong and [eɪ] a diphthong.

In articulating the [eɪ] of *bait*, the tongue moves from its initial [e]-position upward and forward in the direction of the [ɪ]-position. In pronouncing the German long vowels, however, the tongue remains in one position. The beginning language student can easily recognize the diphthongal nature of "long *i*" as in *write*, "long *a*" as in *rate*, "long *o*" as in *wrote*, as well as the obvious diphthongs [ɔɪ] in *boy*, [aɪ] in *buy*, and [aʊ] in *bout*. However, the movements of the tongue are smaller in the "long *e*" [ɪi] of *theme*, and the "long *u*" [ʊu] of *blue*. Although Americans are hardly aware of these slight off-glides, they are very apparent to the German ear and are among the most telling characteristics of the "American accent" in German. In some English words "long *u*" has an on-glide as well as an off-glide [jʊu], as in *few, beauty, university*. This on-glide is lacking in German.

While learning to pronounce the German vowels, then, remember that the long vowels as well as the short vowels are relatively pure monophthongs. Make the short vowels very short and the long vowels very long—about three times as long as the short ones. In pronouncing German vowels, the tip of the tongue has direct contact with the lower front teeth far more frequently than is the case with American vowels.

Another difference between German and American vowels is that German vowels, especially the long ones, are pronounced with a greater degree of muscular tension than are the American vowels; therefore they often sound somewhat exaggerated to American ears. German short vowels are relatively less tense than German long vowels, so the two groups may be described as *long-tense* versus *short-lax*. Furthermore the long vowels—with the exception of the *a*-vowels—are pronounced with the tongue relatively closer to the roof of the mouth than are the short vowels. An even more complete description of the two groups of vowels, then, is *long-tense-close* versus *short-lax-open*. For the sake of brevity we shall usually use the terms *long* and *short* to refer to the two groups.

When a German vowel has the tense and close quality of the long vowels, as in **sieht**, but the syllable in which it occurs is not stressed, as in the second syllable of **Mutti**, then that vowel is short. Unstressed vowels in German are always short, regardless of their relative closeness or tenseness. Accordingly, such a vowel is transcribed without the symbol for length. The *i*-sound in **Mutti** is thus written [i], not [i:].

Terms used in describing the vowels:

long — short	long or short duration
tense — lax	pronounced with relatively tense or relaxed tongue muscles
high — mid — low	pronounced with some part of the tongue high in the mouth, between high and low, or low in the mouth
close — open	pronounced with a relatively small or large opening between the tongue and the roof of the mouth (mainly by varying the position of the tongue)
front — central — back	pronounced with the tongue raised in the front (the part behind the tip), center, or back

The high front vowels [i:] and [ɪ]

German [i:] is higher and more tense than the corresponding sound in American English (*beat*). The front of the tongue, the part just behind the tip, is raised so that it is close to the roof of the mouth. It must be clearly contrasted with [ɪ], which is much shorter, less tense, and more open.

Listen to the difference between the German long and short high front vowels and their English counterparts:

German [i:]	*English* [ɪj]	*German* [ɪ]	*English* [ɪ]
nie	knee	bin	bin
bieten	beaten	mit	mitt
Biest	beast	List	list
Ski	she	Fisch	fish
schien	sheen	nimmt	limped

Now practice the pronunciation of the high front vowels [i:] and [ɪ] by repeating the following words:

[i:] *long - tense - close*		[ɪ] *short - lax* - open*	
nie	[ni:]	ist	[ɪst]
siehst	[zi:st]	bist	[bɪst]
die	[di:]	nimmst	[nɪmst]
ihn	[i:n]	bestimmt	[bəˈʃtɪmt]
bieten	[ˈbi:tən]	bitte	[ˈbɪtə]

---

* "Lax" when applied to German vowels is not nearly so "lax" as when applied to English vowels.

Practice making the contrast between the two high front vowels by repeating the following pairs of words:

[iː]	[ɪ]
ihn	in
ihm	im
bieten	bitten
Biest	bist
schief	Schiff

The mid front vowel [ɛ]

Compared to its English counterpart [ɛ], German [ɛ] is shorter and somewhat tenser. It is never lengthened or drawled.

Listen to the difference between the German mid front vowel [ɛ] and English [ɛ]:

German [ɛ]	*English* [ɛ]
nett	net
West	vest
denn	den
Ebbe	ebb
Speck	speck

Now practice pronouncing the German mid front vowel [ɛ] by repeating the following words:

[ɛ] *short - lax - open*

nett	[nɛt]
es	[ɛs]
denn	[dɛn]
besten	[ˈbɛstən]

The mid central vowel [ə]

German [ə] occurs only in unstressed syllables. It resembles most closely the unstressed vowel [ʌ] of such English words as so*fa*, *a*bout. In American English, however, this vowel may also be stressed, as in c*u*t, b*u*t, *u*p. German [ə], like other unstressed vowels of German, is always very short. Compared to English [ʌ], German [ə] is pronounced with the tongue further forward and a bit higher. The only exception is when the unstressed [ə] occurs before an *r*-sound in the same syllable; this will be explained in Unit 3.

Practice pronouncing the German mid central vowel [ə] by repeating the following words:

[ə] *short, unstressed, clearly different from* [a] *and* [ɛ]

heute	[ˈhɔɪtə]
Tante	[ˈtantə]
danke	[ˈdaŋkə]
bitte	[ˈbɪtə]
Junge	[ˈjuŋə]

The high back vowels [uː] *and* [ʊ]

The German [uː] is pronounced with more rounding and protrusion of the lips than is English [uu̯], and the tongue is drawn further back in the mouth. It must be clearly contrasted with [ʊ], which is short and is pronounced with less lip rounding than [uː], but still more than in English.

Listen to the difference between the German long and short high back vowels and their English counterparts:

German [uː]	*English* [uu̯]		*German* [ʊ]	*English* [ʊ]
du	do		Buchse	books
Schuh	shoe		Putz	puts
tun	tune		Luchs	looks
Mut	moot		Busch	bush
Spuk	spook			

Now practice pronouncing the high back vowels [uː] and [ʊ] by repeating the following words:

[uː] *long - tense - close*			[ʊ] *short - lax - open*	
du	[duː]		Nuß	[nʊs]
gut	[guːt]		muß	[mʊs]
nun	[nuːn]		Mutti	[ˈmʊti]
tun	[tuːn]		Junge	[ˈjuŋə]
Schuh	[ʃuː]		und	[ʊnt]

Practice making the contrast between the two high back vowels [uː] and [ʊ] by repeating the following pairs of words:

[uː]	[ʊ]
Mus	muß
spuken	spucken
Buße	Busse
Muhme	Mumme
Huhne	Hunne

The low back and front vowels [ɑ:] *and* [a]

The two German *a*-sounds differ both in length and in vowel quality. [ɑ:] is long and is pronounced with the mouth relatively wide open and the back of the tongue slightly raised. [a] is short and is pronounced with a smaller opening of the mouth. It is more lax than [ɑ:], but is still tenser than the corresponding English vowel [ə] as in c *o* mma.

Listen to the difference between the German low vowels and their English counterpart (Note: not all Americans use the vowel [ə] in the words listed below):

German [ɑ:]	*English* [ɑ]	*German* [a]	*English* [ə]
Tag	tock	hackt	hocked
mahnt	mont	hat	hot
naht	knot	fand	font
Kahn	con	dann	Don

Practice pronouncing the low vowels [ɑ:] and [a] by repeating the following words:

[ɑ:] *long - open - back*		[a] *short - close - front*	
ja	[jɑ:]	Tante	[ˈtantə]
da	[dɑ:]	Hans	[hans]
haben	[ˈhɑ:bən]	danke	[ˈdaŋkə]
Abend	[ˈɑ:bənt]	das	[das]
Nase	[ˈnɑ:zə]	Angst	[aŋst]
		hast	[hast]

Practice making the contrast between the low vowels [ɑ:] and [a] by repeating the following pairs of words:

[ɑ:]	[a]
Bahn	Bann
Haken	Hacken
Kahn	kann
Saat	satt
kam	Kamm

It is of greatest importance to make a clear contrast between the long and short German vowels. Pronounce the following words, giving the short vowels one beat and the long ones three, and do not diphthongize the long vowels!

short - lax	long - tense
Hans	ja
und	du
nimmst	nie
kannst	da
Nuß	du
ist	siehst

How many beats do the vowels of the stressed syllables in the following words receive?

Tante, Inge, nett, ist, nie, Gift, da, es, Nuß, ja, das, du, siehst, danke, bestimmt, du, Mutti, schmeckt

The diphthongs [aɪ̯] [ɔɪ̯] [aʊ̯]

The German diphthongs sound crisper than the corresponding English diphthongs. The first vowel element is always short in German and always has the emphasis. The off-glide is articulated more softly than the initial element. German diphthongs are never lengthened or drawled.

Listen and compare the German diphthongs with their English counterparts:

German [aɪ̯]	*English* [aɪ̯]		*German* [aʊ̯]	*English* [aʊ̯]
fein	fine		Bau	bough
Eis	ice		Maus	mouse
nein	nine		kau	cow
dein	dine			

German [ɔɪ̯]	*English* [ɔɪ̯]
neu	annoy
Heu	ahoy
Leute	loiter

Practice the pronunciation of the German diphthongs by repeating the following words:

[aɪ̯] *quick transition from a short but energetically articulated* [a] *toward a short and much weaker* [ɪ]

Eis	[aɪ̯s]
heiß	[haɪ̯s]
fein	[faɪ̯n]
nein	[naɪ̯n]
ein	[aɪ̯n]

[ɔɪ̯] *quick transition from a short, strongly articulated* [ɔ] *(almost as in* **bought** *when pronounced very short)* toward a short, weaker* [ɪ]

deutsch	[dɔɪ̯tʃ]
heute	[ˈhɔɪ̯tə]
neun	[nɔɪ̯n]
neu	[nɔɪ̯]
Beute	[ˈbɔɪ̯tə]

[au̯] *quick transition from short, strongly articulated* [a] *toward a short, weaker* [ʊ]

kaufen	[ˈkau̯fən]
Haus	[hau̯s]
Maus	[mau̯s]
aus	[au̯s]
Tau	[tau̯]

Practice repeating the following pairs of words:

[aɪ̯]	[ɔɪ̯]		[aɪ̯]	[au̯]
heiß	Heuß		Eis	aus
nein	neun		Mais	Maus
Hai	Heu		heiß	Haus

Consonants

Voiced versus voiceless

One of the fundamental distinctions among German consonants is the voiced-voiceless contrast. A voiced sound is one whose articulation is characterized in part by the audible vibration of the vocal cords. A voiceless sound lacks this audible vibration. If you cover your ears and pronounce the word *zeal,* you can feel your vocal cords vibrating for the *z*-sound, creating a buzzing sensation in your ears; but if you pronounce *seal* instead, you will note that there is no vibration for the *s*-sound. The first is a voiced [z], the second a voiceless [s].

The stops [p] [t] [k] [b] [d] [g]

The sounds [p] [t] [k] [b] [d] [g] are called *stops,* because in producing them we stop the flow of air through the mouth at some point. We hold it briefly, then release it. The release of the voiceless stops [p] [t] [k] is usually accompanied by a noticeable puff of air, especially when the stops are in initial position followed by a vowel, or between vowels, or in final position. This puff of air is called *aspiration.* The voiced stops [b] [d] [g] are never aspirated.

* A more detailed description of [ɔ] will be given in Unit 2.

Stops between vowels or at the end of a word are more strongly articulated in German than in English.

Practice pronouncing the following words, making sure that the aspiration of the voiceless stops is clearly audible:

Angst	[aŋst]	kannst	[kanst]
bist	[bɪst]	nett	[nɛt]
bestimmt	[bəˈʃtɪmt]	nimmst	[nɪmst]
Gift	[gɪft]	schmeckt	[ʃmɛkt]
ist	[ɪst]		

In final position or before **-t** or **-st** the voiceless stops [p] [t] [k] may be represented by the letters **b d g** in German spelling. The voiced stops [b] [d] [g] do not occur in final position or before final **-t** or **-st** in German.

ab	[ap]	Hand	[hant]
weg	[vɛk]	Kind	[kɪnt]
Tag	[tɑ:k]	gibt	[gi:pt]
und	[ʊnt]	gibst	[gi:pst]
Hund	[hʊnt]		

At the beginning of a word or between vowels, however, the letters **b d g** always represent the voiced stops.

bestimmt	[bəˈʃtɪmt]	danke	[ˈdaŋkə]
bitte	[ˈbɪtə]	da	[dɑ:]
besten	[ˈbɛstən]	baden	[ˈbɑ:dən]
Abend	[ˈɑ:bənt]	Gift	[gɪft]
du	[du:]	Wagen	[ˈvɑ:gən]

The fricatives [f] [s] [ʃ] [v] [z] [j]

The sounds [f] [s] [ʃ] [v] [z] [j] are called *fricatives*. In pronouncing them, we force a stream of air through a narrow opening in the mouth so that audible friction is produced. The fricatives [f] [s] [ʃ] are voiceless; [v] [z] [j] are voiced.

German [f] and [v] are so similar to their English counterparts that their articulation needs no special treatment here. [f] is usually represented by the letter **f**, and [v] by **w**. Both are also sometimes spelled **v**.

fein	[faɪn]	was	[vas]
kauf	[kaʊf]	wie	[vi:]
Gift	[gɪft]	weg	[vɛk]

[s] is the symbol for the voiceless *s*-sound. It is represented chiefly by the letter **s** at the end of a word or syllable, and also by **ss** or **ß**. The sound [s] does not occur initially.

das	[das]	Hans	[hans]
was	[vas]	Nuß	[nʊs]
Eis	[aɪs]	wissen	[ˈvɪsən]

[z] is the symbol for the voiced counterpart of [s]. It is spelled only **s** and occurs only before a vowel at the beginning of a word or syllable.

Sonne	[ˈzɔnə]	seine	[ˈzaɪnə]
so	[zoː]	diese	[ˈdiːzə]
siehst	[ziːst]		

Practice making the contrast between the voiced [z] and voiceless [s] by repeating the following pairs of words:

[z]	[s]
Nase	nasse
Hasen	hassen
Gase	Gasse
Wiesen	wissen
Muse	Muße

[ʃ] is the symbol for a voiceless fricative quite similar to the English *sh*-sound. In German it is pronounced with the lips more rounded and protruding and with a deeper groove along the center of the tongue than is the case with the English counterpart. The German [ʃ] is spelled **s** when followed by **p** or **t** at the beginning of a word or syllable; otherwise it is spelled **sch**.

Practice pronouncing the German [ʃ] by repeating the following words. Round your lips and make a deep groove in your tongue.

schade	[ˈʃɑːdə]	Tasche	[ˈtaʃə]
schmeckt	[ʃmɛkt]	Mensch	[mɛnʃ]
Schuh	[ʃuː]	bestimmt	[bəˈʃtɪmt]

The combinations **sp** and **st** are pronounced [sp] and [st], however, when they come at the end of a word or syllable.

bist	[bɪst]	Angst	[aŋst]
nimmst	[nɪmst]	siehst	[ziːst]
meinst	[maɪnst]	besten	[ˈbɛstən]

Practice making the distinction between [ʃ] and [s] by repeating the following words:

[ʃ]	[s]
Masche	Masse
Tasche	Tasse
mischen	missen
Busch	Bus

[j] is pronounced in German with distinct friction sound. The oral passage is narrower than for the English *y*-sound of *year* or *yes*, and the air is forced between the front of the tongue (the part behind the tip) and the roof of the mouth with greater energy.

ja	[jɑ:]		Juni	[ˈjuːni]
Junge	[ˈjʊŋə]			

AUDIOLINGUAL DRILLS

A. Directed Dialog

Begin each statement with **Hans sagt,** . . . .

Example:
Es ist heiß heute.
Hans sagt, es ist heiß heute.

Tante Inge ist nett.
Hans sagt, Tante Inge ist nett.

Das ist fein.
Hans sagt, das ist fein.

Nuß-Eis schmeckt am besten.
Hans sagt, Nuß-Eis schmeckt am besten.

Tante Inge hat Angst.
Hans sagt, Tante Inge hat Angst.

Mutti ißt nie Eis.
Hans sagt, Mutti ißt nie Eis.

Eis ist kein Gift.
Hans sagt, Eis ist kein Gift.

B. Affirmative Answer Pattern (*See Grammar* §§1.1, 1.2)

Answer the questions in the affirmative by beginning with **Ja,** . . . and reversing the order of subject and verb.

Example:
Ist es heiß heute?
Ja, es ist heiß heute.

Kann Hans Eis kaufen?
Ja, Hans kann Eis kaufen.

Ist Tante Inge nett?
Ja, Tante Inge ist nett.

Ist das ein Eismann?
Ja, das ist ein Eismann.

Ist das fein?
Ja, das ist fein.

Kauft das Kind Eis?
Ja, das Kind kauft Eis.

Nimmt Hans Nuß-Eis?
Ja, Hans nimmt Nuß-Eis.

Schmeckt das am besten?
Ja, das schmeckt am besten.

Hat Tante Inge Angst?
Ja, Tante Inge hat Angst.

Ist es heiß heute?
Ja, es ist heiß heute.

C. Negative Answer Pattern (*See Grammar* §1.2)

Answer the questions in the negative by beginning with **Nein,** . . . and using **kein** as in the pattern provided.

Example:
Nimmt Tante Inge Eis?
Nein, Tante Inge nimmt kein Eis.

Kauft Tante Inge Eis?
Nein, Tante Inge kauft kein Eis.

Ißt Mutti Eis?
Nein, Mutti ißt kein Eis.

Kauft Mutti Eis?
Nein, Mutti kauft kein Eis.

Ist Eis Gift?
Nein, Eis ist kein Gift.

Nimmt Tante Inge Eis?
Nein, Tante Inge nimmt kein Eis.

D. Question Pattern (*See Grammar* §1.2)

Change the statements into questions by reversing the order of subject and verb.

Example:
Es ist heiß heute.
Ist es heiß heute?

Hans kann Eis kaufen.
Kann Hans Eis kaufen?

Tante Inge ist nett.
Ist Tante Inge nett?

Das ist ein Eismann.	Tante Inge nimmt kein Eis.
Ist das ein Eismann?	Nimmt Tante Inge kein Eis?
Das ist fein.	Tante Inge hat Angst.
Ist das fein?	Hat Tante Inge Angst?
Hans kauft Eis.	Mutti ißt nie Eis.
Kauft Hans Eis?	Ißt Mutti nie Eis?
Das Kind nimmt Nuß-Eis.	Eis ist kein Gift.
Nimmt das Kind Nuß-Eis?	Ist Eis kein Gift?
Das schmeckt am besten.	Es ist heiß heute.
Schmeckt das am besten?	Ist es heiß heute?

GRAMMAR

1.1 Verb Forms

The *infinitive* form of a verb is the form that appears in the dictionary. The English verb forms *buy, see, think* may function as infinitives. German infinitives end in **-en** or **-n**: **kaufen**, **nehmen**, **sehen**, **meinen**, **sein**.

The *stem* of a German verb is what is left after the infinitive ending has been removed. Stems of the verbs listed above are **kauf-**, **nehm-**, **seh-**, **mein-**, **sei-**.

A *finite* form of a verb consists of a stem plus a personal ending, that is, an ending that agrees with the subject in terms of number (singular or plural) and person (first, second, or third). Finite verb forms that occur in the dialog are **ist**, **kannst**, **bist**, **nimmst**, **schmeckt**, **meinst**, **hast**, **ißt**, **siehst**, **kauf**. Except for **kauf** each of these forms consists of a stem plus the personal ending **-st** or **-t**.

1.2 German Sentence Types

The most important functional unit in a language is the *sentence*. In German, as in English, a sentence may symbolize either a *condition* or an *action*. It may place this condition or action in past time, present time, or future time, and may also indicate whether the condition or action is real, possible, necessary, desirable, or questionable. Within the context of a given situation, then, a sentence performs a particular *function* such as asserting, wishing, ordering, asking, etc. This function is signaled by the sentence's *form*.

German sentences occur in many different forms and variations; yet all of them can be related directly to three basic communicative functions. They are:

1. To assert something about a condition or an action (*statement*):

Da ist ein Eismann.

2. To elicit a condition or an action (*command*):

Kauf dein Eis, mein Kind!

3. To elicit information from the person or persons addressed (*question*):

Was nimmst du?   Meinst du?

The formal criteria that signal these three basic functions in German are *word order* and *intonation*. These two criteria are independent of each other, and together they provide the formal clues to the function of a sentence. They are significant in the following ways:

1. The feature of word order that serves to signal the basic function of a sentence is *the position of the finite verb*.

2. The feature of intonation that serves to signal the basic function of a sentence is *the rise or fall in pitch of the voice at the end of a sentence*.

German *statements* are formally signaled by the following combination of features:

Word order: finite verb in second position
Intonation: pitch of the voice falls at end of sentence

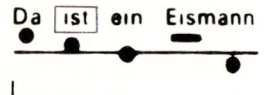

Da ist ein Eismann

German *commands* are formally signaled by:

Word order: finite verb in first position
Intonation: pitch of the voice falls

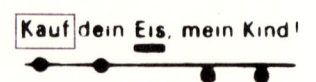

Kauf dein Eis, mein Kind!

German *questions* have two possible forms, depending on whether the speaker desires a simple *yes* or *no* for an answer (yes-no questions) or wants additional information such as *who*, *why*, *how*, etc. (word questions). A third type of question will be discussed later.

Word questions are signaled by:

Word order: finite verb in second position
Intonation: pitch of the voice falls

Was nimmst du?

In terms of word order and intonation alone, this form is identical to that of the statement. The important formal difference between the word question and the statement is the presence of the *question-word* at the beginning of the word question.

The German *yes-no question* has the features:

Word order: finite verb in first position
Intonation: pitch of the voice rises

Meinst du?

WRITING

A. German Orthography

The German spelling system reflects German pronunciation with a fairly high degree of consistency. If you know how to pronounce a German word, then you can be reasonably certain as to how to spell it; conversely, if you know how a German word is spelled, then you can be fairly sure of its pronunciation. It is therefore highly profitable for the student of German to acquaint himself with the relatively few principles that govern the relationship between German spelling and German pronunciation.

Both groups of German vowels — the long vowels and the short vowels — are represented by the same letters in German orthography. The letter **u**, for example, stands for long [uː] in **du** and for short [ʊ] in **Mutti**. There is nothing in the vowel letter itself to indicate whether the sound that it represents is long or short, tense or lax, close or open. The distinction is usually signaled by some other feature, however.

1. If the vowel letter stands at the end of a stressed syllable, then it represents the long vowel:

   j a [jaː]   d u [duː]
   d a [daː]

2. If two or more consonant letters follow a single vowel letter in the same syllable, then that vowel letter usually represents a short vowel:

   H a ns [hans]   h a st   [hast]
   u nd   [ʊnt]   A ngst   [aŋst]
   i st   [ɪst]   G i ft   [gɪft]
   b i st [bɪst]   K i nd   [kɪnt]

3. If a single vowel letter is followed by a doubled consonant letter such as **tt**, **nn**, **mm**, or by the combination **ck**, then the vowel letter represents a short vowel. Doubling a consonant letter has nothing to do with the pronunciation of the consonant; it indicates only that the preceding vowel is short:

n e tt	[nɛt]	n i mmst	[nɪmst]
M a nn	[man]	b i tte	[ˈbɪtə]
k a nnst	[kanst]	schm e ckt	[ʃmɛkt]

4. If a single vowel letter is followed by a single consonant letter in a one-syllable word, then the vowel letter may stand for the short vowel:

e s	[ɛs]	N u ß	[nʊs]
d a s	[das]	a m	[am]
w a s	[vas]	h a t	[hat]

5. There are some letters in German that may be used to signal length of a preceding vowel. The two that are most frequently used in this function are **h** and **e**. If either one of these follows a vowel letter directly, then it serves only to show that the preceding vowel is long and *does not* represent the *h*-sound or an *e*-sound. The letter **e** most commonly occurs in association with a preceding **i** (**ie**), but **h** occurs with all vowel letters (**ih**, **eh**, **ah**, **oh**, **uh**, as well as with combinations, such as **ieh**):

| n ie | [niː] | n eh men | [ˈneːmən] |
| s ieh st | [ziːst] | s eh en | [ˈzeːən] |

6. The combinations of letters **ei**, **au**, and **eu** represent the diphthongs [aɪ̯], [aʊ̯] and [ɔɪ̯], respectively. Since there are no quantitative distinctions among the German diphthongs, the manner in which a following consonant is spelled is not relevant to the pronunciation of the diphthong:

E i s	[aɪ̯s]	k au fen	[ˈkaʊ̯fən]
h ei ß	[haɪ̯s]	m ei nst	[maɪ̯nst]
k au f	[kaʊ̯f]	k au ft	[kaʊ̯ft]
s ei ne	[ˈzaɪ̯nə]		

B. Writing Practice

Arrange the words and phrases in such a way as to form German statements.

Example:
Es / heiß heute / ist.
Es ist heiß heute.

1 Du / nett / bist.
2 Nuß-Eis / am besten / schmeckt.
3 Du / kein Eis / nimmst.
4 Du / Angst / hast.
5 Mutti / kein Eis / ißt.
6 Eis / kein Gift / ist.

Arrange the words and phrases to form German commands:

7 dein Eis / Kauf!
8 Nuß-Eis / Kauf!
9 kein Eis / Kauf!
10 dein Eis / Iß!
11 kein Eis / mein Kind / Iß!

Arrange the words and phrases to form German word questions:

12 du / Was / ißt?
13 du / nimmst / Was?
14 du / Was / siehst?
15 Tante Inge / kauft / Was?
16 Mutti / Was / ißt?
17 sagt / Was / Hans?

Arrange the words and phrases to form German yes-no questions:

18 es / heiß heute / Ist?
19 du / Eis kaufen / Kannst?
20 du / Nuß-Eis / Nimmst?
21 das / am besten / Schmeckt?
22 du / kein Eis / Ißt?
23 Angst / Hast / du?
24 Eis / Mutti / Ißt?

Now read your sentences aloud, paying close attention to correct intonation. Be prepared to provide English equivalents for your German sentences.

LISTENING PRACTICE

Number a sheet of paper from 1 to 20. Then listen to the taped voice. The speaker will pronounce twenty pairs of words containing sounds that were introduced in Unit 1. You decide whether the two words of a pair are *the same* or *different*, and indicate this on your numbered sheet of paper by writing *S* or *D* opposite the appropriate number.

Example:
bieten   bieten   (You write *S*, because the two words sound the same.)
bieten   bitten   (You write *D*, because the two words sound different.)

Unit 2

DIALOG

Die Sonne scheint so schön

di: ˈzɔnə ʃaɪnt zo: ʃøːn

1 **Uwe:** Guten Tag, Heike. Wie geht's?

uːvə guːtən tɑːk ˈhaɪkə viː ˈgeːts

2 **Heike:** Tag, Uwe. Gut, danke.

haɪkə tɑːk ˈuːvə ˈguːt daŋkə

3 **Uwe:** Was tust du heute nachmittag?

vas tuːst duː hɔɪtə ˈnɑːxmɪtɑːk

4 **Heike:** Ich muß Geige üben.

ɪç mus ˈgaɪgə yːbən

UNIT 2 · DIALOG

The Sun Is Shining So Beautifully

scheinen (sie scheint)

1 Hello, Heike. How are you?

gut (guten Tag *acc.***)** good   **der Tag** day ·
Heike (*girl's name*) · **gehen (es geht)** go
geht's = geht es

2 Hi, Uwe. Fine, thanks.

Uwe (*boy's name*)

3 What are you doing this afternoon?

tun (du tust) · **heute** today   **heute nachmittag** this afternoon

4 I have to practice the violin.

müssen (ich muß) · **die Geige**

UNIT 2 · DIALOG

5 **Uwe:** Tüchtig, tüchtig, Mädchen! Ich sehe dich schon auf dem Podium stehen!
ˈtʏçtɪç ˈtʏçtɪç mɛːtçən ɪç zeːə dɪç ʃoːn aʊ̯f deːm ˈpoːdiʊm ʃteːən

6 **Heike:** Spotte nicht, Geige üben macht Spaß.
ˈʃpɔtə nɪçt ˌɡaɪ̯ɡə yːbən maxt ˈʃpaːs

7 **Uwe:** Auch wenn die Sonne so schön scheint?
ˌaʊ̯x vɛn diː ˈzɔnə zoː ʃøːn ʃaɪ̯nt

8 **Heike:** Was tust du denn heute nachmittag?
vas tuːst ˈduː dɛn hɔɪ̯tə naːxmɪtaːk

9 **Uwe:** Ich gehe zum Baden.
ˌɪç geːə tsʊm ˈbaːdən

10 **Heike:** Eine hübsche Sache! Das möchte ich auch.
aɪ̯nə ˌhʏpʃə ˈzaxə das mœçtə ɪç ˈaʊ̯x

11 **Uwe:** Komm doch mit!
kɔm dɔx ˈmɪt

12 **Heike:** Abgemacht! Wann bist du bei uns?
ˈapɡəmaxt ˌvan bɪst duː ˈbaɪ̯ ʊns

13 **Uwe:** So gegen fünf.
ˌzoː ɡeːɡən ˈfʏnf

14 **Heike:** Ob die Sonne dann noch scheint?
ɔp diː ˈzɔnə dan nɔx ʃaɪ̯nt

5	Just keep at it! I already see you standing on the stage.	**tüchtig** hardworking, efficient, able; smart, clever · **das Mädchen** · **sehen (ich sehe)** · **du (dich** *acc.*) · **das Podium (dem Podium** *dat.*) · **stehen** stand *inf.*
6	Don't be sarcastic. Violin practice is fun.	**spotten (spotte** *imper.*) mock, ridicule · **machen** make · **der Spaß** fun **macht Spaß** is fun
7	Even when the sun is shining so beautifully?	**auch** also **wenn** when, whenever, if *subord. conj.* **auch wenn** even when, even if
8	Tell me, what are you doing this afternoon?	
9	I'm going swimming.	**gehen (ich gehe)** · **zum = zu + dem** to the · **das Baden (zum Baden** *dat.*) *infinitive used as noun*
10	A fine thing. I'd like to do that too.	**hübsch (hübsche)** fine, pretty · **die Sache** · **mögen (möchte** *a subjunctive form meaning* would like to**)**
11	Why don't you come along?	**mitkommen (komm ... mit** *imper.*) come along · **doch** *softens the command, making it rather a request or invitation:* Do come along! *or* Well, come along!
12	O.K. When will you be at our place?	**abmachen (abgemacht** *pp.*) settle · **bei uns** *dat.* at our place, with us
13	Around five.	**so** about · **gegen** around, toward
14	I wonder if the sun will still be shining then.	**ob** if, whether *subord. conj.* · **dann** then · **noch** still, yet

15 Uwe: Heute bestimmt. Doch was ist nun mit dem Üben?
ˌhɔɪtə bəˈʃtɪmt dɔx ˌvas ɪst nuːn mɪt deːm ˈyːbən

16 Heike: Üben sagst du? Siehst du nicht, wie schön die Sonne scheint?
ˈyːbən zaːkst duː ˌziːst duː nɪçt viː ʃøːn diː ˈzɔnə ʃaɪnt

17 Uwe: Oh, oh, ich sehe dich doch noch nicht auf dem Podium stehen!
ˌoː oː ɪç zeːə dɪç ˈdɔx nɔx nɪçt aʊ̯f deːm poːdium ʃteːən

SUPPLEMENT

1 Wie scheint die Sonne?
ˌviː ʃaɪnt diː ˈzɔnə

2 Die Sonne scheint schön.
diː ˌzɔnə ʃaɪnt ˈʃøːn

3 Wo sieht Uwe Heike schon stehen?
ˌvoː ziːt uːvə haɪkə ʃoːn ˈʃteːən

4 Uwe sieht Heike schon auf dem Podium stehen.
ˌuːvə ziːt haɪkə ʃoːn aʊ̯f deːm ˈpoːdium ʃteːən

5 Ist das Mädchen tüchtig?
ɪst das mɛːtçən ˈtʏçtɪç

15	Today, of course. But then what about the practicing?	**bestimmt** certain(ly), without a doubt · **doch** *here a coordinating conjunction* but · **das Üben (dem Üben** *dat.*) *infinitive used as a noun*
16	Practicing you say? Don't you see how beautifully the sun is shining?	**sagen (du sagst)** · **wie** *here a subordinating conjunction*
17	Oh, oh! I don't see you standing on the stage yet, after all!	**noch nicht** not yet · **doch** (*stressed*) after all

---

1	How is the sun shining?	
2	The sun is shining beautifully.	
3	Where does Uwe already see Heike standing?	**wo** where (*location*) · **sehen (er sieht)**
4	Uwe already sees Heike standing on the stage.	
5	Is the girl hardworking?	

6 Ja, das Mädchen ist tüchtig.

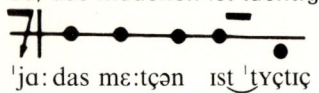

ˈjaː das mɛːtçən ɪst ˈtʏçtɪç

7 Wohin geht Uwe heute nachmittag?

voːhɪn geːt ˌuːvə hɔɪ̯tə ˈnaːxmɪtaːk

8 Uwe geht heute nachmittag zum Baden.

ˌuːvə geːt hɔɪ̯tə naːxmɪtaːk tsuːn ˈbaːdən

9 Was möchte Heike auch tun?

ˌvas mœçtə haɪ̯kə ˈau̯x tuːn

10 Heike möchte auch zum Baden gehen.

haɪ̯kə mœçtə ˈau̯x tsum baːdən geːən

11 Kommt das Mädchen mit?

kɔmt das mɛːtçən ˈmɪt

12 Ja, das Mädchen kommt mit.

ˈjaː das mɛːtçən kɔmt ˈmɪt

6   Yes, the girl is hardworking.

7   Where is Uwe going this afternoon? **wohin** where, to what place (*destination*)

8   Uwe is going swimming this afternoon.

9   What would Heike like to do too? **mögen (sie möchte)**

10 Heike would like to go swimming too.

11 Is the girl coming along? **mitkommen (sie kommt . . . mit)**

12 Yes, the girl is coming along.

PHONOLOGY

In Unit 2 you are encountering some German sounds that are quite unlike any of the sounds of English. You must therefore learn them as entirely new sounds. Practice pronouncing them in isolation, in words and sentences, and consciously compare them with the English sounds that are most similar to them. Remember: before you can pronounce these sounds correctly, you have to know how they differ from their closest English counterparts as well as how they differ from similar German sounds. Otherwise you might spend several hours practicing the wrong pronunciation — and then you'll have to start all over again.

New sounds in Unit 2

Vowels

[e:]	s e he	[ˈzeːə]
[ɛ:]	M ä dchen	[ˈmɛːtçən]
[o:]	s o	[zoː]
[ɔ]	o b	[ɔp]
[ø:]	sch ö n	[ʃøːn]
[œ]	m ö chte	[ˈmœçtə]
[y:]	ü ben	[ˈyːbən]
[ʏ]	f ü nf	[fʏnf]

Consonants

[ç]	ich	[ɪç]
[x]	doch	[dɔx]

The mid front vowels [e:] and [ɛ:]

German [e:] is quite different from its closest English counterpart, a diphthong [ɛɪ] as in *day, wade, gain*. The German [e:] is to be pronounced with the lips tensed and spread, and with the tongue so strongly arched that only a very narrow space remains between the tongue and the palate. The sound thus produced is so much closer and more tense than the English "long *a*" [ɛɪ] that it may be mistaken by the American student for the high front [i:]; thus **leben** *to live* may be confused with **lieben** *to love*. The German vowel is a pure monophthong and therefore should not be diphthongized; tongue and jaw should remain in one position during its articulation. This can easily be checked with a mirror.

Listen to the difference between German [e:] and English [ɛɪ]:

German [e:]	*English* [ɛɪ]
geh	gay
dem	dame
Beet	bait
wen	vain

Practice pronouncing the mid front [e:] by repeating the following words:

[eː] *long - tense - close*

geht's	[geːts]
gehe	[ˈgeːə]
sehe	[ˈzeːə]
stehen	[ˈʃteːən]
dem	[deːm]
gegen	[ˈgeːgən]

Practice making the distinction between mid front [eː] and high front [iː] by repeating the following pairs of words:

[eː]	[iː]
gebt	gibt
wegen	wiegen
Steg	stieg
denen	dienen
beten	bieten

Practice making the contrast between long [eː] and short [ɛ] by repeating the following pairs of words:

[eː]	[ɛ]
den	denn
beten	Betten
Weg	weg
Steg	steck

Although most lax open German vowels are short, [ɛː] is lax, open, and long. It should be distinguished from close [eː] in quality and from short [ɛ] in length.

Practice pronouncing long-lax-open [ɛː] by repeating the following words:

[ɛː] *long - lax - open*

Mädchen	[ˈmɛːtçən]
Käse	[ˈkɛːzə]
sägen	[ˈzɛːgən]
spät	[ʃpɛːt]

Many Germans actually use tense close [eː] in place of lax open [ɛː], although the "official pronunciation" of German prescribes that a difference be made between the two. The long-lax-open [ɛː] is invariably spelled with the letter **ä**.

The mid back vowels [o:] and [ɔ]

Both [o:] and [ɔ] differ markedly from the corresponding sounds of American English. As is the case with all German long tense vowels, everything about the [o:] seems exaggerated to the American. The vowel lacks the off-glide characteristic of the English [oʊ] in *road, flow, home*. The lips are more pursed and rounded than in English, and the position of the tongue, jaw, and lips does not change during the pronunciation of the vowel. A mirror will help you check your pronunciation.

Listen to the difference between German [o:] and English [oʊ]:

German [o:]	*English* [oʊ]
Boot	boat
Sohn	zone
schon	shone
floh	flow

Practice pronouncing long [o:] by repeating the following words:

[o:] *long - tense - close*

Podium	[ˈpo:diʊm]
so	[zo:]
schon	[ʃo:n]
wo	[vo:]
oh	[o:]
oben	[ˈo:bən]

German [ɔ] is short, lax, and open. It differs from English [ɑ] *nod* and [ʌ] *bud* in that it is shorter, further back, and somewhat higher, and is pronounced with rounded lips. It differs from the vowel of English *caught, pawn, raw* [ɔ] (some American dialects have [ɑ] in these words) in that it is slightly higher and much shorter.

Listen to the difference between German [ɔ] and similar vowels of American English:

German [ɔ]	*English* [ɑ]	*German* [ɔ]	*English* [ɔ]
komm	calm	oft	off
Hopp	hop	offen	often
blond	blond	Kost	cost
		Dogma	dogma

German [ɔ]	*English* [ʌ]
komm	come
Bonn	bun
hofft	huffed

Practice pronouncing the short [ɔ] by repeating the following words:

[ɔ] *short - lax - open*

Sonne	[ˈzɔnə]
komm	[kɔm]
spotte	[ˈʃpɔtə]
doch	[dɔx]
ob	[ɔp]
noch	[nɔx]

The umlaut vowels [y:] [ʏ] [ø:] [œ]

The umlaut vowels [y:] [ʏ] [ø:] [œ] may be regarded as combinations of the articulations of two different vowels. The tongue assumes the position characteristic of [i:], [ɪ], [e:], or [ɛ], while the lips are rounded as for [u:], [ʊ], [o:], or [ɔ], respectively. If you start by pronouncing a sustained [i:] [ɪ] [e:] [ɛ], and then press your cheeks forward, causing the lips to be rounded as for [u:] [ʊ] [o:] [ɔ], while attempting to continue to say [i:] [ɪ] [e:] [ɛ], you will approach the correct vowel qualities for [y:] [ʏ] [ø:] [œ].

Lip position (silent)		*Tongue position (aloud)*		
[u:]	+	[i:]	>	[y:]
[ʊ]	+	[ɪ]	>	[ʏ]
[o:]	+	[e:]	>	[ø:]
[ɔ]	+	[ɛ]	>	[œ]

Practice in this way until you acquire the correct vowel quality, listening carefully and checking your lip position in a mirror.

[y:] *long - tense - close*   [ʏ] *short - lax - open*

üben	[ˈy:bən]	tüchtig	[ˈtʏçtɪç]
Düse	[ˈdy:zə]	fünf	[fʏnf]
kühn	[ky:n]	hübsch	[hʏpʃ]
müde	[ˈmy:də]	Küste	[ˈkʏstə]
Süden	[ˈzy:dən]	küssen	[ˈkʏsən]
Bühne	[ˈby:nə]	müssen	[ˈmʏsən]
typisch	[ˈty:pɪʃ]	Hütte	[ˈhʏtə]

Practice each word with [i:], followed by its corresponding word with rounded lips for [y:].

[i:] *unrounded*   [y:] *rounded*

diese	Düse
Biene	Bühne
sieden	Süden

Practice each word with [ɪ], followed by its corresponding word with lips rounded for [ʏ].

[ɪ] *unrounded*	[ʏ] *rounded*
Kissen	küssen
Kiste	Küste
missen	müssen

Practice the following pairs, making the [y:] very long and the [ʏ] very short.

[y:]	[ʏ]
Hüte	Hütte
Wüste	wüßte
Füßen	Füssen

Practice the pronunciation of long [ø:] and short [œ] by repeating the following words:

[ø:] *long - tense - close*		[œ] *short - lax - open*	
schön	[ʃø:n]	möchte	[ˈmœçtə]
böse	[ˈbø:zə]	können	[ˈkœnən]
König	[ˈkø:nɪç]	öffnen	[ˈœfnən]
mögen	[ˈmø:gən]	Köpfe	[ˈkœpfə]
töten	[ˈtø:tən]	könnte	[ˈkœntə]
Söhne	[ˈzø:nə]	Stöcke	[ˈʃtœkə]
Öfen	[ˈø:fən]		

Practice pronouncing first [e:], then rounding the lips and pronouncing [ø:].

[e:] *unrounded*	[ø:] *rounded*
Besen	Bösen
Sehne	Söhne
Hefe	Höfe
beten	böten

Practice pronouncing first [ɛ], then rounding the lips and pronouncing [œ].

[ɛ] *unrounded*	[œ] *rounded*
Mächte	möchte
kennen	können
stecke	Stöcke
kennte	könnte
Becken	Böcken

The fricatives [x] *and* [ç]

There are two voiceless fricatives in German that are quite different from the fricatives of English: [x] and [ç]. Both are spelled **ch**. When **ch** follows one of the vowels **a**, **o**, **u**, or **au**, then it represents [x]; when it follows anything else, in the same syllable, it represents [ç]. There are some words, however, in which the combination of **ch** with **s** represents [ks] rather than [xs]; this will be shown in Unit 6.

[x] is formed in the same area in the mouth as the stop [k]. In pronouncing [x], however, do not completely stop off the air stream as in forming [k] but, instead, leave a narrow slit between the tongue and the roof of the mouth to allow the air to pass through. Start by pronouncing a strongly aspirated [ak]; then release the stop very slowly, forcing breath through the opening that is formed. This will produce [akx]. Then try to pronounce [ax] without forming the stop [k].

Your natural tendency will probably be to substitute your [k] for the German [x]. This has to be avoided, because it can result in a word that means something other than what you might have intended. If you pronounce the word **Nacht** [naxt] *night* with [k] instead of [x], then the word will come out as **nackt** [nakt] *naked*.

Practice pronouncing the voiceless fricative [x] by repeating the following words:

[x] *voiceless fricative*

auch	[aʊx]
noch	[nɔx]
macht	[maxt]
nachmittag	[ˈnɑːxmɪtɑːk]
doch	[dɔx]
abgemacht	[ˈapɡəmaxt]
Buch	[buːx]
Nacht	[naxt]

Now practice making the distinction between [x] and [k] by repeating the following pairs of words:

[x] *fricative*   [k] *stop*

doch	Dock
pochen	Pocken
Nacht	nackt
mach	mag
Macht	Magd
sachte	sagte
taucht	taugt

[ç] is a voiceless counterpart to [j], but is pronounced with stronger friction. If you can pronounce the German [j], then you can pronounce [ç] by placing your tongue and lips in the [j] position and forcing air through the opening between the tongue and palate without voicing.

Practice the pronunciation of the voiceless fricative [ç]:

[ç] *voiceless fricative*

ich	[ɪç]
dich	[dɪç]
mich	[mɪç]
sich	[zɪç]
Mädchen	[ˈmɛːtçən]
möchte	[ˈmœçtə]
tüchtig	[ˈtʏçtɪç]

Americans have a tendency to mistake [ç] for [ʃ]. The English [ʃ] is produced with a relatively shallow groove running lengthwise along the center of the tongue, through which the air passes. The German [ʃ] has a deeper groove, however. The English groove is sometimes so shallow that it resembles the slit of the German [ç], whereas in German the two sounds are kept strictly apart. German [ʃ] is further characterized by lip rounding, while [ç] is not.

Practice the contrast between the two fricatives [ç] and [ʃ]:

[ç] *lips spread, shallow tongue slit*	[ʃ] *lips rounded, deep tongue groove*
Männchen	Menschen
wichen	wischen
Gicht	Gischt
selig	seelisch
mich	misch
keuche	keusche

The following vowel chart shows the relative positions of the vowels. The terms used are explained in Unit 1.

		Front	Central	Back
High	long - close - tense	[iː] [yː]		[uː]
	short - open - lax	[ɪ] [ʏ]		[ʊ]
Mid	long - close - tense	[eː] [øː]	[ə]	[oː]
	short - open - lax	[ɛ][1] [œ]		[ɔ]
Low			[a]	[ɑː]

Note that the short, lax vowels are relatively near the center of the diagram and the long, tense vowels are relatively far from the center.

[1] [ɛː], of course, is open but long.

AUDIOLINGUAL DRILLS

A. Directed Dialog

Begin each statement with **Hans sagt,** . . . .

Example:
Die Sonne scheint so schön.
Hans sagt, die Sonne scheint so schön.

Heike muß Geige üben.
Hans sagt, Heike muß Geige üben.

Das Mädchen ist tüchtig.
Hans sagt, das Mädchen ist tüchtig.

Uwe sieht Heike auf dem Podium stehen.
Hans sagt, Uwe sieht Heike auf dem Podium stehen.

Geige üben macht Spaß.
Hans sagt, Geige üben macht Spaß.

Uwe geht heute nachmittag zum Baden.
Hans sagt, Uwe geht heute nachmittag zum Baden.

Das ist eine hübsche Sache.
Hans sagt, das ist eine hübsche Sache.

Heike möchte auch zum Baden gehen.
Hans sagt, Heike möchte auch zum Baden gehen.

Das Mädchen kommt mit.
Hans sagt, das Mädchen kommt mit.

Uwe ist gegen fünf bei uns.
Hans sagt, Uwe ist gegen fünf bei uns.

Die Sonne scheint gegen fünf bestimmt noch.
Hans sagt, die Sonne scheint gegen fünf bestimmt noch.

Die Sonne scheint so schön.
Hans sagt, die Sonne scheint so schön.

B. Affirmative Answer Pattern

Answer the questions in the affirmative by beginning with **Ja,** . . . and changing the order of subject and verb.

Example:
Scheint die Sonne schön?
Ja, die Sonne scheint schön.

Muß Heike Geige üben?
Ja, Heike muß Geige üben.

Ist das Mädchen tüchtig?
Ja, das Mädchen ist tüchtig.

Macht Geige üben Spaß?
Ja, Geige üben macht Spaß.

Geht Uwe zum Baden?
Ja, Uwe geht zum Baden.

Ist das eine hübsche Sache?
Ja, das ist eine hübsche Sache.

Möchte Heike auch zum Baden gehen?
Ja, Heike möchte auch zum Baden gehen.

Kommt Heike mit?
Ja, Heike kommt mit.

Ist Uwe gegen fünf bei uns?
Ja, Uwe ist gegen fünf bei uns.

Scheint die Sonne dann noch?
Ja, die Sonne scheint dann noch.

Scheint die Sonne schön?
Ja, die Sonne scheint schön.

C. Question Pattern

Change the statements into questions by changing the order of subject and verb.

Example:
Die Sonne scheint schön.
Scheint die Sonne schön?

Heike muß Geige üben.
Muß Heike Geige üben?

Das Mädchen ist tüchtig.
Ist das Mädchen tüchtig?

Geige üben macht Spaß.
Macht Geige üben Spaß?

Uwe geht zum Baden.
Geht Uwe zum Baden?

Heike möchte auch zum Baden gehen.
Möchte Heike auch zum Baden gehen?

Das Mädchen kommt mit.
Kommt das Mädchen mit?

Uwe ist gegen fünf bei uns.
Ist Uwe gegen fünf bei uns?

Die Sonne scheint dann noch.
Scheint die Sonne dann noch?

Die Sonne scheint schön.
Scheint die Sonne schön?

D. Position of the Dependent Infinitive (*See Grammar* §§2.1, 2.2)

Change the verb to its infinitive form and shift it to last position, and insert **möchte** as in the example.

Example:
Heike übt Geige.
Heike möchte Geige üben.

Uwe geht zum Baden.
Uwe möchte zum Baden gehen.

Heike geht auch zum Baden.
Heike möchte auch zum Baden gehen.

Das Mädchen kommt mit.
Das Mädchen möchte mitkommen.

Hans kauft Nuß-Eis.
Hans möchte Nuß-Eis kaufen.

Tante Inge nimmt kein Eis.
Tante Inge möchte kein Eis nehmen.

Heike übt heute Geige.
Heike möchte heute Geige üben.

E. Negative Answer Pattern (*See Grammar* §2.3)

Answer the questions in the negative by beginning with **Nein, . . .** and inserting **nicht** as in the example.

Example:
Ist das Mädchen tüchtig?
Nein, das Mädchen ist nicht tüchtig.

Scheint die Sonne schön?
Nein, die Sonne scheint nicht schön.

Geht Uwe zum Baden?
Nein, Uwe geht nicht zum Baden.

Kommt das Mädchen mit?
Nein, das Mädchen kommt nicht mit.

Ist Uwe bei uns?
Nein, Uwe ist nicht bei uns.

Sieht Heike, wie die Sonne scheint?
Nein, Heike sieht nicht, wie die Sonne scheint.

Schmeckt Nuß-Eis am besten?
Nein, Nuß-Eis schmeckt nicht am besten.

F. Questions and Answers

Although specific answers are provided, correct variations of these are not only possible but also desirable.

Example:
Wie scheint die Sonne?
Die Sonne scheint schön.

Was muß Heike tun?
Heike muß Geige üben.

Wie ist das Mädchen?
Das Mädchen ist tüchtig.

Wo sieht Uwe Heike schon stehen?
Uwe sieht Heike schon auf dem Podium stehen.

Wohin geht Uwe?
Uwe geht zum Baden.

Was möchte Heike auch tun?
Heike möchte auch zum Baden gehen.

Kommt das Mädchen mit?
Ja, das Mädchen kommt mit.

Wann ist Uwe bei Heike?
Uwe ist gegen fünf bei Heike.

Scheint die Sonne dann noch?
Ja, die Sonne scheint dann bestimmt noch.

GRAMMAR

2.1 German Sentence Structure

The typical simple sentence in German consists of a subject and a predicate. The subject may be a pronoun:

Du bist nett.
Ich muß Geige üben.

The subject may be a noun:

Eis ist kein Gift.
Heike muß Geige üben.

It may also be a phrase consisting of two or more words:

Die Sonne scheint so schön.   **Geige üben** macht Spaß.
Hans und seine Tante Inge kaufen Nuß-Eis.

The predicate is that part of the sentence which is not the subject. Like the subject it may consist of a single word or of several words:

Die Sonne **scheint**.   Du **bist nett**.
Meinst du?   Heike **möchte auch zum Baden gehen**.

2.2 The German Predicate

In Unit 1 we saw that the position of the finite verb is crucial in determining the basic function of a German sentence. For purposes of the following discussion, we shall leave the finite verb in second position and treat only simple independent statements. This is entirely arbitrary; we could just as easily choose to put the verb first and talk about yes-no questions.

In its simplest form the predicate consists of a single finite verb:

Die Sonne **scheint**.

It often happens, however, that the finite verb requires the presence of some additional element in the sentence in order for its meaning to be clear and complete. This is true, for example, of the English words:

John would like ....

Without some additional element, such as *tomatoes* or *to go swimming*, the meaning is not at all complete. This is also true of German. The words:

Du bist ....   Heike muß Geige ....
Das ist ....

are quite meaningless as they stand; something must be added to tell what *you are*, what *that is*, and what it is that *Heike has to* do with her violin:

Du bist **nett**.   Heike muß Geige **üben**.
Das ist **fein**.

The phrases **bist nett**, **ist fein**, and **muß ... üben** are all *verb phrases*. A verb phrase consists of a finite verb (**bist**, **ist**, **muß**, etc.) plus some other element closely associated with that finite verb. These *associated elements* stand at the end of their clause, regardless of whether the finite verb occurs in first position or second position, and also regardless of the length of the clause.

The associated element in a verb phrase — the part that has to stand last — may be any one of several things. You have encountered the following kinds of associated elements thus far:

1. *Predicate adjectives*   Es ist **heiß**.
   Du bist **nett**.
   Das Mädchen ist **tüchtig**.

2. *Predicate nouns*   Es ist **kein Gift**.

3. *Certain adverbial expressions*   Heike kommt **mit**.
   Uwe geht **zum Baden**.

4. *Infinitives*   Hans kann Nuß-Eis **kaufen**.
   Ich muß Geige **üben**.
   Was möchte Heike auch **tun**?
   Heike möchte auch zum Baden **gehen**.
   Ich sehe dich schon auf dem Podium **stehen**.

Elements that do not belong to the verb phrase fill the space between the finite verb and the associated element, as long as they do not stand in first position (to be discussed in Unit 6). The verb phrase may thus be — and usually is — "split in half" by other elements such as adverbs of time, direct and indirect objects, the subject if it does not stand in first position, and verb-negators such as **nicht**, **nie**. The order of these intervening elements is regulated by principles that will be introduced in subsequent units.

2.3 Negators *kein, nicht,* and *nie*

The word **kein** is an adjective. It modifies nouns and, in doing so, negates them. It conveys the meaning *no, not any, not*:

Eis *ice cream* — kein Eis *no (not) ice cream*   Gift *poison* — kein Gift *no (not) poison*

The word **nicht**, on the other hand, is an adverb. Whereas **kein** negates only the following noun, **nicht** may negate the entire sentence. Its normal position is between the finite verb and the associated element, as close to the latter as possible:

Es ist nicht heiß.
It isn't hot.

Das Mädchen ist nicht tüchtig.
The girl isn't hardworking.

Die Sonne scheint heute nachmittag nicht schön.
The sun isn't shining beautifully this afternoon.

Uwe geht nicht zum Baden.
Uwe isn't going swimming.

Das Mädchen kommt nicht mit.
The girl isn't coming along.

Nuß-Eis schmeckt nicht am besten.
Walnut ice cream doesn't taste best.

The adverb **nie** *never* behaves in a manner similar to **nicht**:

Uwe geht nie zum Baden.
Uwe never goes swimming.

Mutti ißt nie Nuß-Eis.
Mommy never eats walnut ice cream.

WRITING

A. German Orthography

1 In Unit 1 (Writing §A.4) it was stated that a single vowel letter followed by a single consonant letter, in a one-syllable word, may represent a short vowel. New examples of this are:

o b   [ɔp]   m u ß   [mʊs]
m i t [mɪt]   z u m   [tsʊm]

New words that do not follow this pattern — i.e. one-syllable words with a long vowel followed by a single consonant letter — are:

sch o n [ʃoːn]   Sp a ß   [ʃpɑːs]
d e m   [deːm]   n u n   [nuːn]

2 Vowel letters followed by **ch** in the majority of cases represent short vowels:

i ch	[ɪç]	S **a** che	[ˈzaxə]
t **ü** chtig	[ˈtʏçtɪç]	m **a** cht	[maxt]
d **i** ch	[dɪç]	d **o** ch	[dɔx]
n **i** cht	[nɪçt]	n **o** ch	[nɔx]
m **ö** chte	[ˈmœçtə]		

The single exception so far is the form **nach-** in **nachmittag** [ˈnɑːxmɪtɑːk].

Since the diphthongs [aɪ̯] [au̯] [ɔɪ̯] do not have short counterparts, the above statement does not apply to them, i.e. it would be incorrect to conclude that they get shortened before **ch**.

B. Syllabication

The German rules of syllabication are quite different from those of English. The two words **baden** and *bathing*, for example, each consist of two syllables. The German word **baden** is divided between the vowel and consonant: **ba-den**. The English word *bathing*, however, is divided between the stem and the suffix: *bath-ing*.

1 If a single consonant letter stands between two vowels, that consonant letter belongs with the following syllable:

gu-ten
Hei-ke
heu-te
Gei-ge
se-he
ste-hen

2 In the words above, the vowel of the first syllable stands in final position within its own syllable; the letter accordingly represents the long vowel, since stressed vowels in syllable-final position are long:

g **u** -ten	[ˈguːtən]	g **e** -gen	[ˈgeːgən]
s **e** -he	[ˈzeːə]	P **o** -di-um	[ˈpoːdiʊm]
st **e** -hen	[ˈʃteːən]		

3 The combination **ch** represents a single consonant, usually [ç] or [x]. If **ch** stands between two vowels, the division comes before the **ch**:

Sa-che [ˈzaxə]

Even though the vowel of the first syllable thus comes to stand in last position in its own syllable, it is short; this is often the case before [x].

4 Double consonant letters between vowels are divided between the preceding and following syllables. The preceding vowel is always short:

Son-ne [ˈzɔnə]   Mut-ti [ˈmʊti]
spot-te [ˈʃpɔtə]

5   If two or more different consonant letters stand between two vowels, then the last consonant letter (or group of letters, if the sound is spelled by a combination such as **ch**, **sch**, etc.) goes with the following syllable. The preceding stressed vowel is nearly always short:

dan-ke	[ˈdaŋkə]	hüb-sche	[ˈhypʃə]
tüch-tig	[ˈtʏçtɪç]	möch-te	[ˈmœçtə]

The vowel of the preceding stressed syllable is long, however, in **Mäd-chen** [ˈmɛːtçən].

6   Many words of two or more syllables are made up of a stem plus an inflectional ending such as **-e**, **-en**, etc. The above rules of syllabication apply to such words:

schö-ne   gu-ten
Ta-ge   hüb-sche

In the first three examples, the vowel letter stands last in its own syllable and thus represents a long vowel. If the ending **-e**, **-en**, etc. is removed, then the vowel remains long even though the syllable ends in a consonant:

| schön | [ʃøːn] | gut | [guːt] |
| Tag | [tɑːk] | | |

7   Conversely, many one-syllable words are made up of a stem plus an ending:

tust = tu + st   sagst = sag + st

If such words are based on forms with long vowels, then the long vowel is retained in spite of the fact that the syllable may have several consonant letters in final position. Thus:

tun [tuːn] → tust [tuːst]   sagen [ˈzɑːgən] → sagst [zɑːkst]

8   German compound words are divided between the constituents of the compounds, without regard to vowel length or number of consonant letters:

Eis-mann   mit-kommen
nach-mittag

If a constituent of a compound word should itself contain more than one syllable, then the rules stated above apply to the syllabication of that constituent:

nach-mit-tag   mit-kom-men

C. Writing Practice: Vowel Quantity

Copy each of the following words. In each case determine whether the vowel of the stressed syllable is long or short, and identify the orthographic feature that indicates this.

Sonne, so, wie, geht's, danke, was, du, sehe, spotte, wenn, stehen, die, denn, das, gehe, komm, mit, wann, fünf, bist, auch, bestimmt, scheint, Kind

D. Writing Practice: Sentences

Arrange the elements to form statements:

1 die Sonne / so schön / scheint .
2 ich / muß / üben / Geige .
3 ich / sehe / stehen / dich / auf dem Podium .
4 ich / zum Baden / gehe .
5 Heike / zum Baden / möchte / gehen .
6 das Mädchen / nicht / tüchtig / ist .

Arrange the elements to form commands:

7 dein Eis / kauf !
8 nicht / spotte !
9 doch / mit / komm !
10 kein Eis / iß !

Arrange the elements to form word questions:

11 heute nachmittag / du / tust / was ?
12 du / wann / bei uns / bist ?
13 was / mit dem Üben / ist ?
14 die Sonne / wie / scheint ?
15 heute / wohin / Uwe / geht ?
16 Heike / möchte / tun / was ?

Arrange the elements to form yes-no questions:

17 Heike / muß / üben / Geige ?
18 Geige üben / Spaß / macht ?
19 die Sonne / schön / scheint ?
20 du / siehst / nicht ?
21 Uwe / zum Baden / heute nachmittag / geht ?
22 das Mädchen / mit / kommt ?

Read your sentences aloud, paying close attention to correct pronunciation and intonation. Be ready to give English equivalents for the German sentences you have written.

LISTENING PRACTICE

Number a sheet of paper from 1 to 24. Listen to the taped voice, and indicate whether the two words of each pair are the same (*S*) or different (*D*).

Unit 3

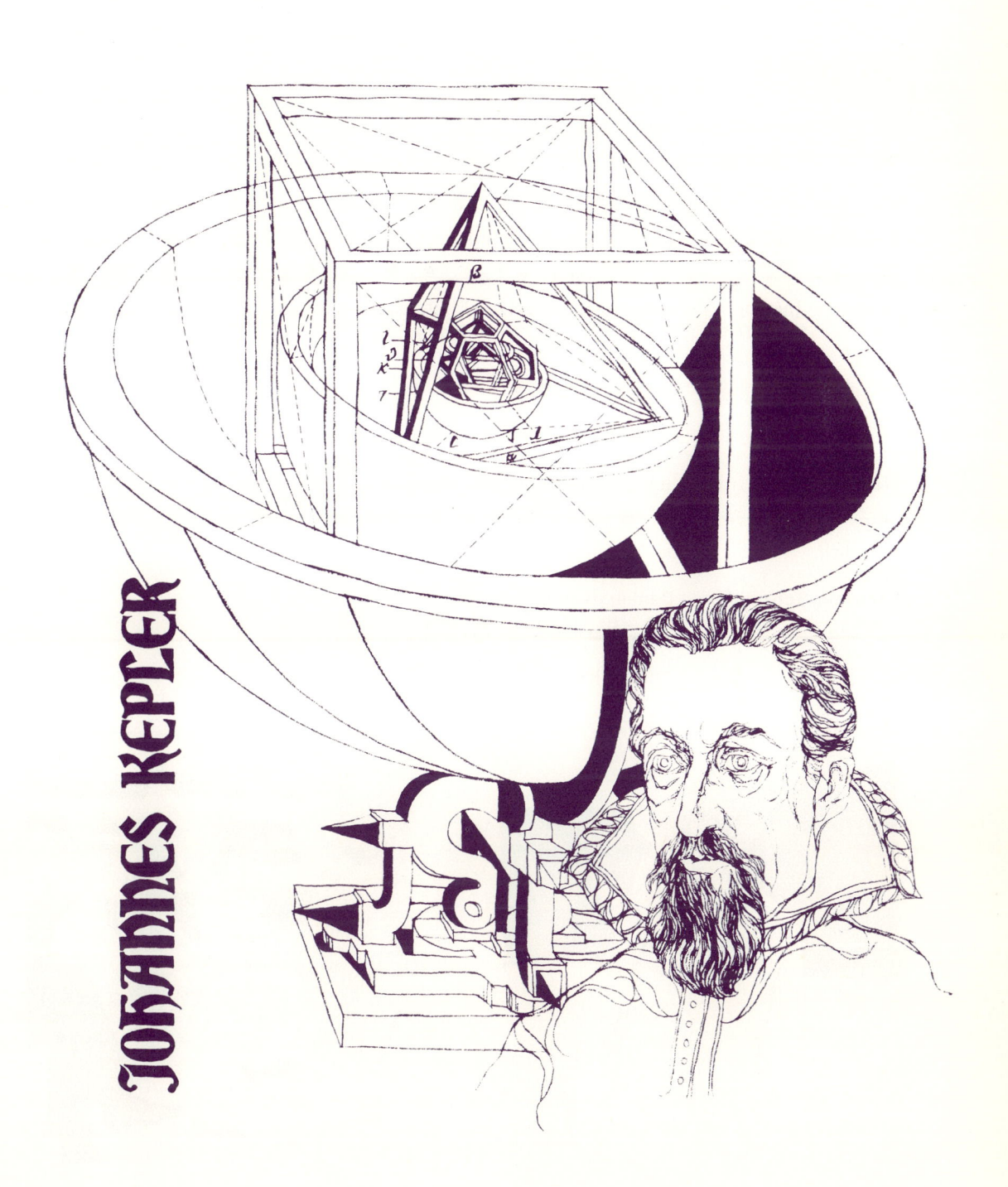

JOHANNES KEPLER

DIALOG

Im Vorlesungsraum (Anfang)

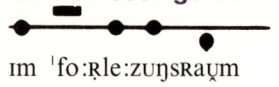

ɪm ˈfoːʀleːzuŋsʀaʊ̯m

1 **Fräulein Schneider:** Entschuldigen Sie, soll hier nicht Professor Müller die ,,Einführung in die

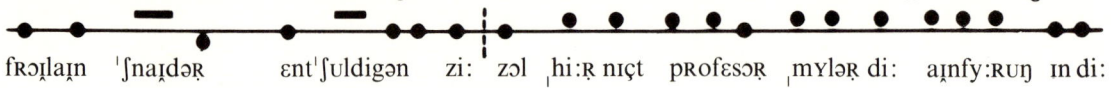

fʀɔɪ̯laɪ̯n ˈʃnaɪ̯dəʀ ɛntˈʃuldigən ziː zɔl ˌhiːʀ nɪçt pʀɔfɛsɔʀ ˌmʏləʀ diː aɪ̯nfyːʀuŋ ɪn diː

Philosophie'' lesen?

filozoˈfiː leːzən

2 **Herr Held:** Ich glaube schon, jedenfalls warte ich auch darauf.

hɛʀ hɛlt ɪç glaʊ̯bə ˈʃoːn jeːdənfals vaʀtə ɪç ˈaʊ̯x daʀaʊ̯f

3 **Fräulein Schneider:** Danke, dann bleibe ich hier.

daŋkə dan blaɪ̯bə ɪç ˈhiːʀ

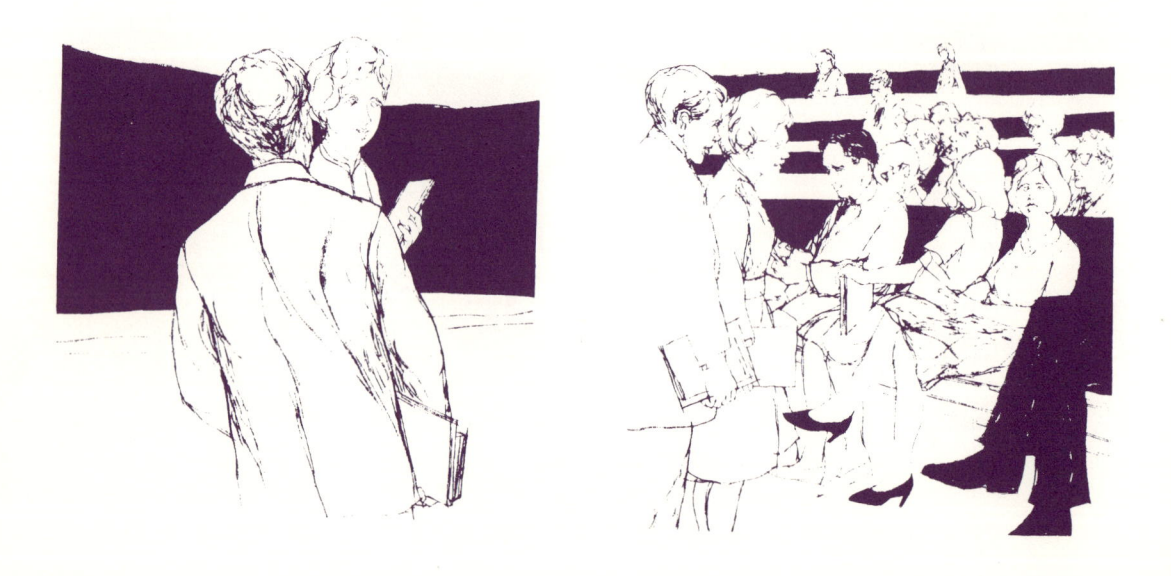

In the Lecture Hall (Beginning)

im = in + dem · der Vorlesungsraum (im Vorlesungsraum *dat.*) **die Vorlesung** lecture + **der Raum** hall, room · **der Anfang**

1 Excuse me. Isn't Professor Müller supposed to give the "Introduction to Philosophy" here?

das Fräulein Miss; young lady · **der Schneider** tailor   *German names will be translated here as a matter of interest* · **entschuldigen (entschuldigen Sie** *imper.*) excuse · **Sie** you *standard pronoun of address; it must be expressed in the imperative* · **sollen (er soll)** · **der Müller** miller · **lesen** read; give a lecture

2 I believe so. At any rate, that's what I'm waiting for, too.

Herr Mr.; gentleman · **der Held** hero · **glauben (ich glaube)** · **warten auf (ich warte darauf)** wait for · **darauf = da + r + auf** for it

3 Thanks, then I'll stay here.

bleiben (ich bleibe)

4 **Herr Held:** Der Platz hier ist noch frei. Ist dies Ihre erste Vorlesung?

deːʁ plats hiːʁ ɪst nɔx 'fʁaɪ ɪst diːs iːʁə 'eːʁstə foːʁleːzuŋ

5 **Fräulein Schneider:** Ja, aller Anfang ist schwer.

'jaː alɐʁ anfaŋ ɪst 'ʃveːʁ

6 **Herr Held:** Ach, das ist nur ein Sprichwort.

ɑːx das ɪst nuːʁ aɪn 'ʃpʁɪçvɔʁt

7 **Fräulein Schneider:** Aber ich glaube daran.

ɑːbɐʁ ɪç 'ɡlaʊ̯bə dɑʁan

8 **Herr Held:** Ich finde im Gegenteil: Aller Anfang ist leicht.

ɪç fɪndə ɪm 'ɡeːɡəntaɪ̯l alɐʁ anfaŋ ɪst 'laɪ̯çt

9 **Fräulein Schneider:** Ist das Ihr Ernst?

ɪst das iːʁ 'ɛʁnst

10 **Herr Held:** Warum nicht? Warten Sie nur ab!

vɑːʁʊm 'nɪçt vaʁtən ziː nuːʁ 'ap

(Forsetzung folgt)

SUPPLEMENT

1 Fragen Sie, worauf Fräulein Schneider wartet!

ˌfʁɑːɡən ziː voːʁaʊ̯f fʁɔɪ̯laɪ̯n ʃnaɪ̯dɐʁ 'vaʁtət

4	The seat here is still free. Is this your first lecture?	**Ihr (Ihre)** *possessive adjective form of* **Sie** · **erst (erste)**
5	Yes. The first step is always hard.	**all (aller)** every, all
6	Oh, that's only a proverb.	**das Sprichwort sprich** (*from* **sprechen** speak) + **das Wort** word
7	But I believe in it.	**glauben an** believe in · **daran** = **da** + **r** + **an**
8	I find on the contrary: the first step is always easy.	**finden (ich finde)** · **das Gegenteil (im Gegenteil** *dat.*) **gegen** against + **der** (*or* **das**) **Teil** part
9	Are you serious?	**Ihr** your · **der Ernst** earnestness, seriousness
10	Why not? Just wait and see!	**abwarten (warten Sie ab** *imper.*) wait and see
	(To be continued)	**die Fortseztung** continuation · **folgen (sie folgt)** follow

---

1	Ask what Miss Schneider is waiting for.	**fragen (fragen Sie** *imper.*) · **worauf** = **wo** + **r** + **auf** for what? · **warten (sie wartet)**

2 Worauf wartet Fräulein Schneider?
voːraʊf ˈvartət frɔɪlaɪn ʃnaɪdər

3 Antworten Sie, daß sie auf die Vorlesung wartet!
ˌantvɔrtən ziː das ziː aʊf diː ˈfoːrleːzuŋ vartət

4 Sie wartet auf die Vorlesung.
ziː vartət aʊf diː ˈfoːrleːzuŋ

5 Sagen Sie, daß Herr Held auch darauf wartet!
ˌzaːgən ziː das hɛr hɛlt ˈaʊx daraʊf vartət

6 Herr Held wartet auch darauf.
hɛr hɛlt vartət ˈaʊx daraʊf

7 Fragen Sie, ob dies Fräulein Schneiders erste Vorlesung ist!
ˌfraːgən ziː ɔp diːs frɔɪlaɪn ʃnaɪdərs ˈeːrstə foːrleːzuŋ ɪst

8 Ist dies Fräulein Schneiders erste Vorlesung?
ɪst diːs frɔɪlaɪn ʃnaɪdərs ˈeːrstə foːrleːzuŋ

9 Fragen Sie, woran Fräulein Schneider glaubt!
ˌfraːgən ziː voːran frɔɪlaɪn ʃnaɪdər ˈglaʊpt

10 Woran glaubt Fräulein Schneider?
voːran ˈglaʊpt frɔɪlaɪn ʃnaɪdər

11 Sagen Sie, daß sie an das Sprichwort glaubt.
ˌzaːgən ziː das ziː an das ˈʃprɪçvɔrt glaʊpt

2   What is Miss Schneider waiting for?

3   Answer that she is waiting for the lecture.   **antworten (antworten Sie** *imper.***)**

4   She is waiting for the lecture.

5   Say that Mr. Held is waiting for it too.   **sagen (sagen Sie** *imper.***)**

6   Mr. Held is waiting for it too.

7   Ask if this is Miss Schneider's first lecture.

8   Is this Miss Schneider's first lecture?

9   Ask what Miss Schneider believes in.   **glauben (sie glaubt)** · **woran = wo +
                                                         r + an** in what?

10 What does Miss Schneider believe in?

11 Say that she believes in the proverb.

12 Sie glaubt an das Sprichwort.

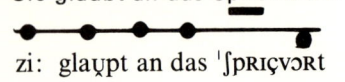

zi: glaʊpt an das ˈʃpRɪçvɔRt

12 She believes in the proverb.

PHONOLOGY

New sounds in Unit 3

[l] soll   [zɔl]
[ʀ] warum [vaːˈʀum]
[r] warum [vaːˈrum]

The substitution of the American *l-* and *r-* sounds for the German l- and r-sounds is one of the most obnoxious features of an American accent in German. Both languages spell these sounds with the same letters; this tends to obscure the fact that they are phonetically quite different, and may suggest to the unwary student that they are somehow "the same." Although substitution of the American *l-* and *r-*sounds in German will rarely lead to misunderstanding or confusion (as is the case with [x] and [k], or with [ç] and [ʃ]), they strike the native speaker of German as strange, comical, or irritating.

The sound [l]

In pronouncing the German [l], the lips are moderately spread, and the tip and front edge of the tongue are in contact with the inner surfaces of the upper front teeth or the alveolar ridge (the bony ridge just behind the upper front teeth). So far, this is just like the English pronunciation. For the German [l], however, the back of the tongue is flat. The English *l*-sound is sometimes pronounced this way, as in the words *million, silly, trilling*; but usually the back of the tongue is arched upward toward the velum (soft palate) just as in articulating the vowel [uː], while the tip of the tongue remains pressed against the upper teeth or the alveolar ridge. This is called a *velarized l*; its phonetic symbol is [ɫ]. The German [l] is never velarized; the back of the tongue lies flat, resulting in a "bright" or "clear" quality.

Listen to the difference between English [ɫ] and German [l]:

English [ɫ]	*German* [l]
hell	hell
lie	leih
low	Lohe
pull	Pulle
feel	viel
plots	Platz

Practice pronouncing the German [l] by repeating the following words:

lesen	['le:zən]	viel	[fi:l]
liest	[li:st]	soll	[zɔl]
leicht	[laɪçt]	voll	[fɔl]
los	[lo:s]		
		eigentlich	['aɪgəntlıç]
alle	['alə]	hoffentlich	['hɔfəntlıç]
alte	['altə]	endlich	['ɛntlıç]
also	['alzo]		
sollen	['zɔlən]	bleiben	['blaɪbən]
helfen	['hɛlfən]	glauben	['glaʊbən]
Held	[hɛlt]	Platz	[plats]

The sounds [R] and [r]

The American *r*-sound functions as a vowel in such words as *bird, thirty, hurt,* and as a consonant or semivowel in initial and, in some parts of the country, also in final position. The German [R] and [r], however, are *trills* in initial position, between vowels, and sometimes also in final position.

The [r] is an alveolar trill; it is produced by holding the tip of the tongue lightly against the alveolar ridge so that it flutters when air is forced through. Youngsters make this sound when they imitate police whistles, motor noises, etc. [R] is a uvular trill, produced by raising the back of the tongue up toward the uvula (the fleshy appendage dangling down from the soft palate at the back of the mouth) and forcing air through so that the uvula flutters. Both of these trills are prevalent and acceptable. The [R] is preferable, however, for two reasons: it is the more frequent pronunciation, especially in German cities, and, once you have mastered it, you will be less likely to replace it with your English *r*-sound.

The German sound that [R] is most similar to is the voiceless fricative [x], the differences being that [R] is voiced and it is a trill. The English sound it comes closest to is the sound you make when gargling. The tip of the tongue remains in contact with the inner surfaces of the lower front teeth. The back of the tongue is raised gently upward toward the uvula, but the throat must be relaxed in order to allow the fluttering movement to occur. Begin the articulation of [R] softly and easily, without too much pressure or breath. Practice the following articulations, making the [R] as long as you can:

1.
ra	[Rɑ:]	re	[Re:]
rau	[Raʊ]	ri	[Ri:]
ro	[Ro:]	rö	[Rø:]
ru	[Ru:]	rü	[Ry:]
reu	[Rɔɪ]		

2 ara   [ɑːʀɑː]   are   [ɑːʀeː]
   arau [ɑːʀaʊ̯]   ari   [ɑːʀiː]
   aro   [ɑːʀoː]   arö   [ɑːʀøː]
   aru   [ɑːʀuː]   arü   [ɑːʀyː]
   areu [ɑːʀɔɪ̯]

3 ara   [ɑːʀɑː]   uru   [uːʀuː]
   ere   [eːʀeː]   örö   [øːʀøː]
   iri   [iːʀiː]   ürü   [yːʀyː]
   oro   [oːʀoː]

4 ar   [ɑːʀ]   ur   [uːʀ]
   er   [eːʀ]   ör   [øːʀ]
   ir   [iːʀ]   ür   [yːʀ]
   or   [oːʀ]

There are several varieties of the German uvular [ʀ]. Initially, and before vowels, this **r**-sound is a distinct voiced uvular trill:

richtig	[ˈʀɪçtɪç]	daran	[dɑˈʀan]
Ruhe	[ˈʀuːə]	darauf	[dɑˈʀaʊ̯f]
Rolf	[ʀɔlf]	warum	[vɑˈʀʊm]
Fräulein	[ˈfʀɔɪ̯laɪ̯n]	studieren	[ʃtuˈdiːʀən]
frei	[fʀaɪ̯]	Sprichwort	[ˈʃpʀɪçvɔrt]

Following a short vowel the uvular trill is somewhat reduced. In the speech of many persons it may be reduced to a single tap or to a uvular fricative:

| Ernst | [ɛʀnst] | warten | [ˈvaʀtən] |
| Herr | [hɛʀ] | | |

Further reduction in the articulation of the uvular [ʀ] occurs following long vowels or diphthongs. This distinctly reduced [ʀ] is designated as [ʁ]:

der	[deːʁ]	nur	[nuːʁ]
hier	[hiːʁ]	Vorlesung	[ˈfoːʁleːzʊŋ]
ihr	[iːʁ] *but* ihre [ˈiːʀə]		

Distinguish:

Jahr	ja	vier	Vieh
sehr	See	Ohr	oh
wir	wie	Kur	Kuh

An even greater degree of reduction is found in final syllables following [ə]:

aber	[ˈɑːbəʀ]	Müller	[ˈmʏləʀ]
Bruder	[ˈbʀuːdəʀ]	Eltern	[ˈɛltəʀn]
dieser	[ˈdiːzəʀ]		

Distinguish:

dieser	diese	mancher	manche
ihrer	ihre	jener	jene
roter	rote	jeder	jede
Lehrer	lehre		
bitter	bitte		

The degree of reduction, which may lead to complete vocalization of [ʀ], depends upon the level of speech and the speech situation. In classical drama performed by good actors, the stage tradition does not permit reduction of [ʀ] beyond a single tap of the uvula. When [əʀ] has been reduced to a vowel sound, its pronunciation is still kept distinct from [ə], so that **dieser** does not rhyme with **diese**.

The student should not attempt to acquire the various degrees of reduction until he has first mastered the correct articulation of [ʀ] in all positions. The reason for this is that the native speech habits of Americans will probably interfere with the characteristic reductions of [ʀ], sounds which do not exist in English. For the sake of practice, too, it is desirable to articulate [ʀ] in all positions as a voiced uvular trill. In rapid speech, then, the reductions characteristic of German will come about naturally.

The sound of the other German **r** is produced by a vibration of the tip of the tongue against the alveolar ridge. Like [ʀ], [r] is voiced. The stages of reduction of the [r] are less clearly defined than those of [ʀ], although the degree of vibration depends upon the position of [r] in the word as well as upon factors of accent and expression. In unstressed final position (and sometimes in unstressed intervocalic position), [r] becomes a tap or a flap rather than a trill, i.e. the tongue touches the alveolar ridge only once.

The exercises for [ʀ] can also be used for perfecting the sound of [r].

AUDIOLINGUAL DRILLS

A. Directed Dialog

Fragen Sie, wo Fräulein Schneider ist!
Wo ist Fräulein Schneider?

Antworten Sie, daß sie im Vorlesungsraum ist!
Sie ist im Vorlesungsraum.

Sagen Sie, daß Herr Held auch im Vorlesungsraum ist!
Herr Held ist auch im Vorlesungsraum.

Fragen Sie, worauf Fräulein Schneider wartet!
Worauf wartet Fräulein Schneider?

Sagen Sie, daß sie auf die Vorlesung wartet!
Sie wartet auf die Vorlesung.

Fragen Sie, ob Herr Held auch darauf wartet!
Wartet Herr Held auch darauf?

Sagen Sie, daß er auch darauf wartet!
Er wartet auch darauf.

Fragen Sie, ob der Platz hier noch frei ist!
Ist der Platz hier noch frei?

Antworten Sie, daß der Platz hier noch frei ist!
Der Platz hier ist noch frei.

Fragen Sie, ob dies Fräulein Schneiders erste Vorlesung ist!
Ist dies Fräulein Schneiders erste Vorlesung?

Fragen Sie, woran Fräulein Schneider glaubt!
Woran glaubt Fräulein Schneider?

Antworten Sie, daß sie an das Sprichwort glaubt!
Sie glaubt an das Sprichwort.

Sagen Sie, daß sie daran glaubt!
Sie glaubt daran.

B. Affirmative Answer Pattern

Answer the questions in the affirmative by beginning with **Ja,** . . . and reversing the order of subject and verb.

Example:
Wartet Fräulein Schneider auf die Vorlesung?
Ja, Fräulein Schneider wartet auf die Vorlesung.

Wartet Herr Held auch darauf?
Ja, Herr Held wartet auch darauf.

Bleibt Fräulein Schneider hier?
Ja, Fräulein Schneider bleibt hier.

Ist der Platz hier noch frei?
Ja, der Platz hier ist noch frei.

Ist dies Fräulein Schneiders erste Vorlesung?
Ja, dies ist Fräulein Schneiders erste Vorlesung.

Ist aller Anfang schwer?
Ja, aller Anfang ist schwer.

Ist das nur ein Sprichwort?
Ja, das ist nur ein Sprichwort.

Glaubt Fräulein Schneider daran?
Ja, Fräulein Schneider glaubt daran.

C. Negative Answer Pattern (*See Grammar* §2.3)

Answer the questions in the negative by beginning with **Nein, . . .**, reversing the order of subject and verb, and inserting **nicht** as in the example.

Example:
Wartet Fräulein Schneider auf die Vorlesung?
Nein, Fräulein Schneider wartet nicht auf die Vorlesung.

Wartet Herr Held darauf?
Nein, Herr Held wartet nicht darauf.

Bleibt Fräulein Schneider hier?
Nein, Fräulein Schneider bleibt nicht hier.

Ist der Platz frei?
Nein, der Platz ist nicht frei.

Ist dies Fräulein Schneiders erste Vorlesung?
Nein, dies ist nicht Fräulein Schneiders erste Vorlesung.

Ist aller Anfang schwer?
Nein, aller Anfang ist nicht schwer.

Glaubt Fräulein Schneider daran?
Nein, Fräulein Schneider glaubt nicht daran.

D. Position of the Dependent Infinitive (*See Grammar* §2.2)

Insert **kann**, change the finite verb to its infinitive form, and place the infinitive in last position.

Example:
Ich warte darauf.
Ich kann darauf warten.

Herr Held glaubt daran.
Herr Held kann daran glauben.

Fräulein Schneider bleibt hier.
Fräulein Schneider kann hier bleiben.

Aller Anfang ist leicht.
Aller Anfang kann leicht sein.

Ich warte jetzt ab.
Ich kann jetzt abwarten.

Ich warte auf die Vorlesung.
Ich kann auf die Vorlesung warten.

E. Questions and Answers

Wo ist Fräulein Schneider?
Sie ist im Vorlesungsraum.

Und wo ist Herr Held?
Er ist auch im Vorlesungsraum.

Worauf wartet Herr Held?
Er wartet auf die Vorlesung.

Wartet Fräulein Schneider auch darauf?
Ja, sie wartet auch darauf.

Was soll Professor Müller lesen?
Er soll die „Einführung in die Philosophie" lesen.

Woran glaubt Fräulein Schneider?
Sie glaubt an das Sprichwort.

Glaubt Herr Held auch daran?
Nein, er glaubt nicht daran.

GRAMMAR

3.1 Some Question-Words

The German question-words that you have learned thus far are:

wie	*how?*	Wie geht's?
wo	*where?*	Wo ist Fräulein Schneider?
wann	*when?*	Wann bist du bei uns?
was	*what?*	Was nimmst du?
warum	*why?*	Warum nicht?
worauf	*for what?*	Worauf wartet Fräulein Schneider?
woran	*in what?*	Woran glaubt Fräulein Schneider?

The last two—**worauf** and **woran**—are compound words made up of **wo** *where* plus a preposition **auf**, **an**, with the consonant [R] inserted between the two parts. At one time this sort of compounding was quite common in English, giving forms like *wherewith, whereby, wherefore, whereon,* etc. These have a rather archaic ring in English nowadays, but the analogous formations in German are very much in use. The answer to a question introduced by such a **wo**-compound will generally contain the preposition that appears in the compound, plus an object:

Wor| auf |wartet Fräulein Schneider?
Sie wartet | auf | **die Vorlesung**.

Wor| an |glaubt Fräulein Schneider?
Sie glaubt | an | **das Sprichwort**.

3.2 Dependent Clause Structure

In Units 1 and 2 we discussed the position of the finite verb in German statements, word questions, commands, and yes-no questions. The sentences under consideration were simple one-clause sentences with the finite verb in first or second position. Such sentences are called *independent clauses*. The term independent means simply that the clause is not grammatically bound to some other clause. A clause that is grammatically bound to some other one is called a *dependent clause*. Examples of dependent clauses in English are:

I know *that he'll be here at five*. *That smoking is harmful* is a well-known fact.
He asked *if we'd seen his hat*. Can you tell me *where the phone is*?

German dependent clauses are marked by two features:

1. The finite verb is in last position.

2. The clause is introduced by a subordinating conjunction (**daß**, **wenn**, **ob**, and others), or by a question-word (**wie**, **wo**, **wann**, **was**, **warum**, **worauf**, **woran**, and others), or by a relative pronoun (to be taken up in Unit 23).

Note that both of these features are present in each of the following dependent clauses:

Fragen Sie, **wo** Fräulein Schneider ist .

Sagen Sie, **daß** Herr Held auf die Vorlesung wartet .

Siehst du nicht, **wie** schön die Sonne scheint ?

Ob die Sonne dann noch scheint ?

3.3 Position of the Finite Verb: Summary

In commands and yes-no questions the finite verb stands in first position.

In statements and word questions the finite verb stands in second position.

In dependent clauses the finite verb stands in last position.

There are certain words that may stand at the beginning of a German sentence or clause without counting as first-position elements, and therefore have no effect on the order of words in the following clause. This is true of such words as **ja**, **nein**, **danke**, **ach**, and a small set of words called *coordinating conjunctions*, of which you have learned **aber** and **doch**. Compare the following:

Verb second   Uwe ⟨geht⟩ heute nachmittag zum Baden.
Uwe is going swimming this afternoon.

Aber Uwe ⟨geht⟩ heute nachmittag zum Baden.
But Uwe is going swimming this afternoon.

Ja, Uwe ⟨geht⟩ heute nachmittag zum Baden.
Yes, Uwe is going swimming this afternoon.

Verb first   ⟨Kommt⟩ Heike auch mit?
Is Heike coming along too?

Aber ⟨kommt⟩ Heike auch mit?
But is Heike coming along too?

Verb last   Auch wenn die Sonne so schön ⟨scheint⟩?
Even when the sun is shining so beautifully?

Ja, wenn die Sonne so schön ⟨scheint⟩.
Yes, if the sun is shining so beautifully.

WRITING

A. German Orthography

1 The German voiced fricative [v] is most often spelled **w**. Voiceless [f] is often represented by **f**:

w arten   [ˈvaʀtən]   **f** rei   [fʀaɪ̯]
sch **w** er [ʃveːʀ]   **f** inde   [ˈfɪndə]

The voiceless fricative [f] is also spelled **v**, however:

V orlesung   [ˈfoːʀleːzʊŋ]

2 New one-syllable words that end in a consonant, yet whose vowel is long (contrary to the general pattern stated in Unit 1, Writing §A.4), are:

n u r   [nuːʀ]   v o r   [foːʀ]

Even when **vor** is attached to another word as a prefix, the vowel remains long:

die V o rlesung   [ˈfoːʀleːzʊŋ]

3 The diphthong [ɔɪ] in German is represented not only by the spelling **eu**, but also rather frequently by **äu**:

h **eu** te   [ˈhɔɪtə]   das Fr **äu** lein   [ˈfʀɔɪlaɪn]

B. Writing Practice

Arrange the elements to form statements:

1 ich / darauf / warte .
2 ich / hier / bleibe .
3 aber / ich / daran / glaube .
4 der Professor / soll / lesen / die „Einführung in die Philosophie" .
5 Fräulein Schneider / muß / warten / auf die Vorlesung .
6 Herr Held / nicht / daran / glaubt .
7 Nuß-Eis / nicht / am besten / schmeckt .
8 Nein / aller Anfang / nicht / ist / leicht .

Arrange the elements to form commands:

9   Sie / warten / ab !
10 Sie / entschuldigen !
11 daran / Sie / glauben !
12 Nuß-Eis / Sie / kaufen !
13 zum Baden / gehen / Sie !
14 nicht / spotte !
15 mit / komm !

Arrange the elements to form word questions:

16 Fräulein Schneider / glaubt / woran ?
17 Herr Held / wartet / worauf ?
18 du / was / tust ?
19 der Eismann / wo / ist ?
20 die Sonne / wie / scheint ?
21 du / im Vorlesungsraum / bist / wann ?

Arrange the elements to form yes-no questions:

22 Hans / kann / kaufen / Nuß-Eis ?
23 Heike / möchte / gehen / zum Baden ?
24 der Professor / soll / warten / im Vorlesungsraum ?
25 sie / wartet / darauf ?
26 er / glaubt / an das Sprichwort ?
27 die Sonne / heute nachmittag / scheint ?

Read your sentences aloud, paying close attention to correct intonation, and be prepared to give their English equivalents.

LISTENING PRACTICE

Listen to the two taped conversations: **Hans und Tante Inge** and **Fräulein Schneider und Herr Held**. Then, on the basis of sentence patterns that you have already learned, formulate answers to the following questions.

A. Hans und Tante Inge

1 Was tut Professor Wolf heute nachmittag?
2 Kann Professor Wolf zum Baden gehen?
3 Warum kann er nicht zum Baden gehen?

B. Fräulein Schneider und Herr Held

1 Worauf wartet Fräulein Schneider?
2 Was tut Herr Held?
3 Ist Professor Müller gut?

Unit 4

DIALOG

Im Vorlesungsraum (Schluß)

1 Fräulein Schneider: Eigentlich kann es nun endlich losgehen.

ˌaɪgəntlɪç kan ɛs nuːn ɛntlɪç ˈloːsgeːn

2 Herr Held: Alle Vorlesungen beginnen erst um viertel nach voll.

ˌalə foːʀleːzuŋən bəgɪnən eːʀst um fɪʀtəl ˈnɑːx fɔl

3 Fräulein Schneider: Ach ja, mein Bruder hat es mir erzählt.

ɑx ˈjɑː maɪn ˈbʀuːdəʀ hat ɛs miːʀ ɛʀtsɛːlt

4 Herr Held: Studiert Ihr Bruder auch Philosophie?

ʃtudiːʀt iːʀ bʀuːdəʀ ˈaʊx filozofiː

In the Lecture Hall (Conclusion)   **der Schluß**

1. Actually, it can start any time now.

   eigentlich actually, really · **endlich** finally, at last · **losgehen** start   **los** loose *and the idea of motion* + **gehen** go

2. Lectures don't begin until a quarter after.

   all (alle) · **die Vorlesung**, *pl.* **die Vorlesungen** · **beginnen (sie beginnen)** · **erst** *adverb with time expression* not until · **um** *with time expression* at · **das Viertel** quarter · **voll** whole; *here* the full hour

3. Oh yes, my brother told me that.

   der Bruder · **ich (mir** *dat.*) · **erzählen (er hat . . . erzählt** he has told) tell

4. Is your brother studying philosophy too?

   studieren (er studiert) study *at a university*; *otherwise* study *is* **lernen**

5 Fräulein Schneider: Nein, er studiert Jurisprudenz.

naɪn eːʀ ʃtudiːʀt juːʀɪspʀu'dɛnts

6 Herr Held: Da kann er Ihnen also nicht viel helfen?

dɑː kan eːʀ iːnən alzoː nɪçt fiːl 'hǝlfən

7 Fräulein Schneider: Vielleicht doch. Die älteren Studenten haben alle viel Erfahrung.

fiːlaɪçt 'dɔx diː ˌɛltəʀən ʃtudɛntən hɑːbən alə fiːl ɛʀ'fɑːʀʊŋ

8 Herr Held: Das stimmt! Und nicht nur im Studieren!

das 'ʃtɪmt ʊnt ˌnɪçt nuːʀ ɪm ʃtuˈdiːʀən

9 Fräulein Schneider: Da kommt Professor Müller.

ˌdɑː kɔmt pʀɔfɛsɔʀ 'mylǝʀ

10 Herr Held: Also, es geht endlich los. Hoffentlich liest er nicht so langweilig

alzoː ɛs geːt ɛntlɪç 'loːs hɔfəntlɪç liːst eːʀ nɪçt zoː laŋvaɪ̯lɪç

wie der alte Professor Wolf.

viː deːʀ altə pʀɔfɛsɔʀ 'vɔlf

5	No, he's studying law.	**die Jurisprudenz**
6	So then he can't help you much?	**da** then; there, here · **Sie (Ihnen** *dat.*) · **also** so, well; therefore
7	But maybe he can. The older students all have lots of experience.	**vielleicht** maybe · **doch** *stressed* on the contrary · **alt (älteren)** · **der Student,** *pl.* **die Studenten** university student · **die Erfahrung**
8	That's true! And not only in study!	**stimmen (es stimmt)** be correct · **das Studieren (im Studieren** *dat.*) *infinitive used as noun*
9	There comes Professor Müller.	
10	So, it's finally starting. Let's hope he's not as boring as old Professor Wolf.	**losgehen (es geht ... los)** · **hoffentlich** it is to be hoped, I hope, let's hope · **lesen (er liest)** · **langweilig** tedious, boring **lang** long + **weilig** (*from* **die Weile** while, length of time) · **der alte Professor Wolf** old Professor Wolf *The definite article is sometimes used with names.*

SUPPLEMENT

1 Fragen Sie, wann die Vorlesung beginnt!
 ˌfrɑːgən ziː ˈvan diː foːʀleːzuŋ bəˈgɪnt

2 Wann beginnt die Vorlesung?
 van bəˈgɪnt diː foːʀleːzuŋ

3 Fragen Sie, ob der Bruder viel helfen kann!
 ˌfrɑːgən ziː ɔp deːʀ bʀuːdəʀ fiːl ˈhɛlfən kan

4 Kann der Bruder viel helfen?
 kan deːʀ bʀuːdəʀ fiːl ˈhɛlfən

5 Sagen Sie, daß es endlich losgeht.
 ˌzɑːgən ziː das ɛs ɛntlɪç ˈloːsgeːt

6 Es geht endlich los.
 ɛs geːt ɛntlɪç ˈloːs

1 Ask when the lecture begins.　　　　　　**beginnen (sie beginnt)**

2 When does the lecture begin?

3 Ask if the brother can help much.

4 Can the brother help much?

5 Say that it's finally starting.

6 It's finally starting.

UNIVERSITAS SARAVIENSIS

PERSONAL- UND VORLESUNGSVERZEICHNIS

SOMMERSEMESTER 1970

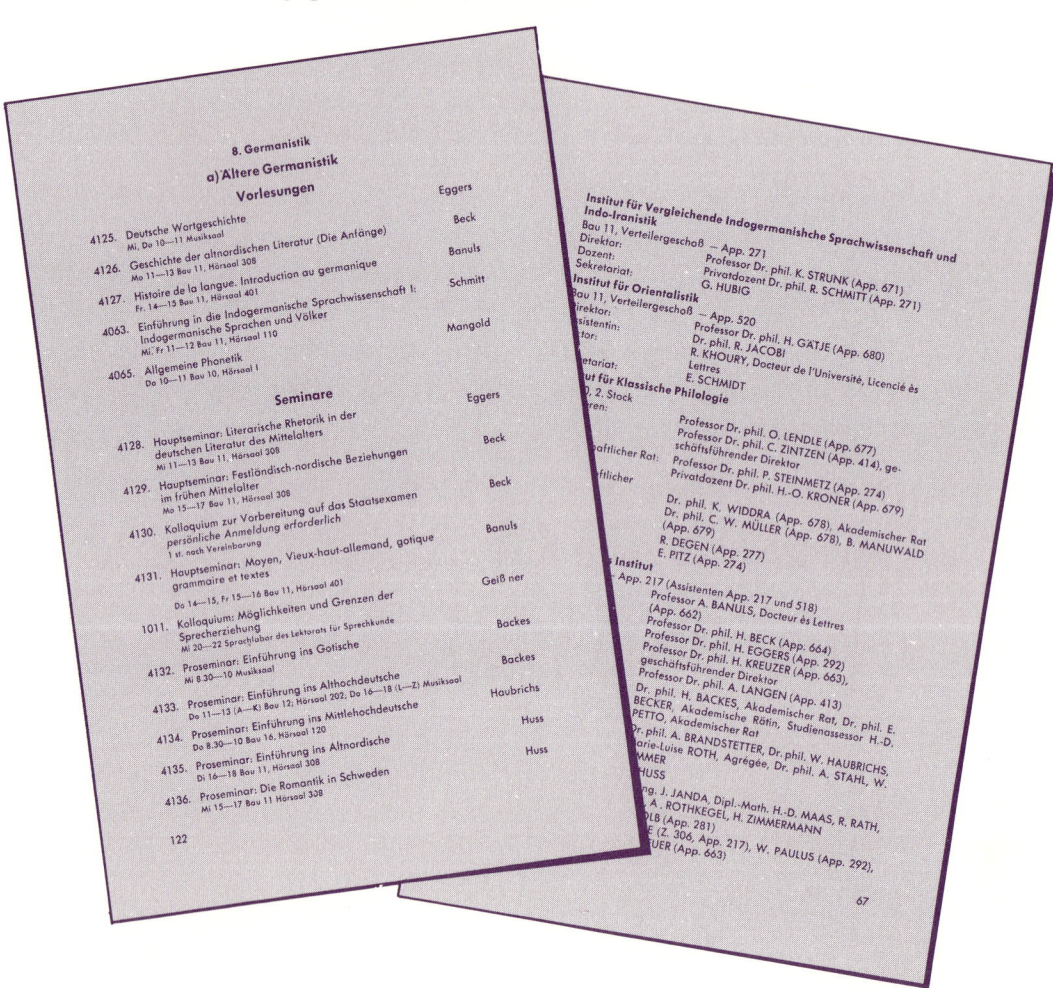

UNIVERSITÄT DES SAARLANDES

PHONOLOGY

In many varieties of American English there are restrictions on the occurrence of certain vowels before [r]. Many speakers of American English rhyme such words as *hurry—furry*, *Mary—merry*, *nearer—mirror*. In German, however, all vowels—the long ones as well as the short ones—may occur before [ʀ], and the long-short contrast is maintained in that position. Thus **Herr** and **Heer** do not rhyme; the first is pronounced with [ɛ], the second with [e:].

Practice pronouncing long and short vowels before [ʀ] by repeating the following pairs of words:

Short vowel	*Long vowel*
Herr	Heer
wirr	wir
irr	ihr
Bord	bohrt

Practice making the distinction between unstressed [ə] and [əʀ]:

[ə]	[əʀ]
bitte	bitter
diene	Diener
fliege	Flieger
diese	dieser
eine	einer
fahre	Fahrer

Practice distinguishing between the following pairs of vowels. Make the short vowels very short and the long ones very tense; do not diphthongize the long vowels.

[ø:]	[œ]		[y:]	[ʏ]
Höhle	Hölle		Hüte	Hütte
blöke	Blöcke		kühnste	Künste
Röslein	Rößlein		Flüge	flügge
Schöße	schösse		Wüste	wüßte
			fühlen	füllen
			Düne	dünne

Make a clear distinction in quality between the vowels in the following words:

[y:]	[ø:]		[ʏ]	[œ]
Flüge	flöge		Hülle	Hölle
grüße	Größe		München	Mönchen
führe	Föhre		Flüsse	flösse
lügen	lögen		rücke	Röcke
			bücken	Böcken
			Schüsse	schösse

[eː]	[iː]		[oː]	[uː]
legen	liegen		Tor	Tour
Lehen	liehen		vor	fuhr
fehlen	fielen		trog	trug
denen	dienen		bog	Bug
segen	siegen		flog	Flug
Gebet	Gebiet		zog	Zug

AUDIOLINGUAL DRILLS

A. Directed Dialog

Sagen Sie, daß es nun endlich losgehen kann!
Es kann nun endlich losgehen.

Fragen Sie, wann die Vorlesung beginnt!
Wann beginnt die Vorlesung?

Antworten Sie, daß die Vorlesung erst um viertel nach voll beginnt!
Die Vorlesung beginnt erst um viertel nach voll.

Fragen Sie, was Herr Held studiert!
Was studiert Herr Held?

Sagen Sie, daß er Philosophie studiert!
Er studiert Philosophie.

Sagen Sie, daß Fräulein Schneider auch Philosophie studiert!
Fräulein Schneider studiert auch Philosophie.

Fragen Sie, was Fräulein Schneiders Bruder studiert!
Was studiert Fräulein Schneiders Bruder?

Antworten Sie, daß er Jurisprudenz studiert!
Er studiert Jurisprudenz.

Sagen Sie, daß er hoffentlich helfen kann!
Er kann hoffentlich helfen.

Sagen Sie, daß die älteren Studenten alle viel Erfahrung haben!
Die älteren Studenten haben alle viel Erfahrung.

Fragen Sie, wie der alte Professor Wolf liest!
Wie liest der alte Professor Wolf?

Antworten Sie, daß er langweilig liest!
Er liest langweilig.

Sagen Sie, daß es endlich losgeht!
Es geht endlich los.

B. Affirmative Answer Pattern

Answer the questions in the affirmative:

Kann es endlich losgehen?
Ja, es kann endlich losgehen.

Beginnen alle Vorlesungen erst um viertel nach voll?
Ja, alle Vorlesungen beginnen erst um viertel nach voll.

Hat der Bruder es erzählt?
Ja, der Bruder hat es erzählt.

Studiert der Bruder auch Philosophie?
Ja, der Bruder studiert auch Philosophie.

Kann er viel helfen?
Ja, er kann viel helfen.

Haben die älteren Studenten viel Erfahrung?
Ja, die älteren Studenten haben viel Erfahrung.

Geht es endlich los?
Ja, es geht endlich los.

Liest Professor Müller langweilig?
Ja, Professor Müller liest langweilig.

C. Negative Answer Pattern

Answer the questions in the negative:

Kann es losgehen?
Nein, es kann nicht losgehen.

Hat der Bruder es erzählt?
Nein, der Bruder hat es nicht erzählt.

Kann der Bruder helfen?
Nein, der Bruder kann nicht helfen.

Haben die älteren Studenten viel Erfahrung?
Nein, die älteren Studenten haben nicht viel Erfahrung.

Liest Professor Müller langweilig?
Nein, Professor Müller liest nicht langweilig.

D. The Definite Article (*See Grammar* §§4.1–4.3)

1 Substitute the new masculine (**der**) noun:

Hier ist der Bruder. **Eismann**
Hier ist der Eismann. **Junge**
Hier ist der Junge. **Platz**
Hier ist der Platz. **Student**
Hier ist der Student. **Vorlesungsraum**
Hier ist der Vorlesungsraum.

2 Substitute the new feminine (**die**) noun:

Wo ist die Geige? **Mutti**   Wo ist die Vorlesung? **Sonne**
Wo ist die Mutti? **Tante**   Wo ist die Sonne? **Nuß**
Wo ist die Tante? **Vorlesung**   Wo ist die Nuß?

3 Substitute the new neuter (**das**) noun:

Da ist das Eis. **Fräulein**   Da ist das Podium. **Mädchen**
Da ist das Fräulein. **Kind**   Da ist das Mädchen. **Sprichwort**
Da ist das Kind. **Podium**   Da ist das Sprichwort.

4 Substitute the new noun with the correct form of the definite article:

Wo ist der Professor? **Tante**   Wo ist die Mutti? **Mädchen**
Wo ist die Tante? **Kind**   Wo ist das Mädchen? **Student**
Wo ist das Kind? **Platz**   Wo ist der Student? **Fräulein**
Wo ist der Platz? **Eis**   Wo ist das Fräulein? **Junge**
Wo ist das Eis? **Geige**   Wo ist der Junge? **Vorlesung**
Wo ist die Geige? **Mutti**   Wo ist die Vorlesung?

E. Dependent Infinitives

Insert **muß** in the following sentences. Change the given finite verb to an infinitive and place it in last position:

Es geht los.
Es muß losgehen.

Die Vorlesung beginnt jetzt.
Die Vorlesung muß jetzt beginnen.

Ich helfe Ihnen.
Ich muß Ihnen helfen.

Professor Wolf liest langweilig.
Professor Wolf muß langweilig lesen.

Studiert Fräulein Schneider Philosophie?
Muß Fräulein Schneider Philosophie studieren?

Wartet Herr Held darauf?
Muß Herr Held darauf warten?

F. Questions and Answers

Was kann endlich losgehen?
Die Vorlesung kann endlich losgehen.

Wann beginnen alle Vorlesungen?
Alle Vorlesungen beginnen um viertel nach voll.

Was studiert Fräulein Schneider?
Sie studiert Philosophie.

Und was studiert Herr Held?
Er studiert auch Philosophie.

Studiert Fräulein Schneiders Bruder Philosophie?
Nein, er studiert Jurisprudenz.

Kann der Bruder viel helfen?
Ja, er kann hoffentlich viel helfen.

Haben die älteren Studenten viel Erfahrung?
Ja, die älteren Studenten haben viel Erfahrung.

Wie liest der alte Professor Wolf?
Er liest langweilig.

GRAMMAR

4.1 The Definite Article

The definite article in English is *the*. The German definite article has three basic forms: **der**, **die**, **das**. Any German noun will typically occur with one of these forms but not the other two, i.e. **der Junge** (never **die** or **das**), **die Vorlesung** (never **der** or **das**), and **das Kind** (never **der** or **die**). German nouns may thus be divided into three groups, traditionally called *genders*, determined by which of the three forms of the article is used. Nouns that occur with the form **der** are called masculine nouns, and they belong to the masculine gender. Nouns that occur with **die** are called feminine nouns, and those with **das** are called neuter nouns. Do not look for any kind of logical or biological basis for these three genders; there is none. You must learn the correct form of the article with every new noun you learn, as though the article and noun were one expression. The basic form of the article for all plural nouns, regardless of gender, is **die**.

Masculine	der Bruder	*Neuter*	das Kind
	der Anfang		das Sprichwort
Feminine	die Tante	*Plural*	die Studenten
	die Geige		die Vorlesungen
			die Kinder

4.2 Word-Formation

In both English and German there are many compound words, i.e. words that are made up of parts that can also occur alone as separate words. English compounds are often composed of elements of Latin or Greek origin, e.g. *motorcycle, sexennial, ideograph, thyroarytenoid*. German compounds, however, are almost always made up of common German words. German schoolchildren rarely have to look a word up in the dictionary because they can usually figure out the meaning of even very long words, on the basis of the meanings of their constituent parts. The word **Lebensversicherungsgesellschaft**, for example, is easy to understand when you see that it is composed of three very common nouns: **Leben** *life*, **Versicherung** *insurance*, and **Gesellschaft** *company*. Even scientific names are combinations of ordinary terms. **Wasserstoff** *hydrogen* is simply **Wasser** *water* plus **Stoff** *matter, substance*. The addition of **Kohle** *carbon* gives **Kohlenwasserstoff** *carbohydrate*. When a word is coined for a new invention, the Germans usually do not turn to Greek or Latin for an appropriate name, but to the resources of their own language. **Roll**, from **rollen** *roll*, and **Treppe** *stairway* together form **Rolltreppe** *escalator*. **Welt** *world, universe* and **Raum** *space* and **Fahrer** *driver* combine to form **Weltraumfahrer** *astronaut*.

Such words are very common in German. This means that, with the knowledge of a comparatively small number of constituent elements, it is possible to determine the meanings of many compound words. In addition, there are many related words that can be recognized easily once the derivational systems are understood. In these sections on word-formation a number of the more common derivational patterns will be treated. This will make it possible for you to increase your German vocabulary more rapidly and to identify and remember compound words more easily.

Compound nouns

The gender of a compound noun is determined by the gender of its last constituent; **Vorlesungsraum** takes the definite article **der**, because the last constituent is **der Raum**, and similarly

Lebensversicherungsgesellschaft takes **die**, because the last part of the compound is **die Gesellschaft**.

das Eis ice, ice cream + **der Mann** man = **der Eismann** iceman, ice-cream man
die Nuß nut, walnut + **das Eis** ice cream = **das Nuß-Eis** walnut ice cream
die Vorlesung lecture + **der Raum** hall, room, space = **der Vorlesungsraum** lecture hall

A connective **-s** or **-es** appears in some compounds: **Vorlesungsraum, Lebensversicherungsgesellschaft**.

In English some compound nouns are written as one word (*classroom*), some are hyphenated (*secretary-treasurer*), and others are written with spaces between the parts (*lecture hall, walnut ice cream, life insurance company*). German compound nouns are nearly always written as one word, without spaces or hyphens between the constituents. **Nuß-Eis** is a rare exception.

4.3 Definite Articles of Nouns, Units 1 to 4

Masculine	*Feminine*
der Anfang	die Angst
der Bruder	die Einführung
der Eismann	die Erfahrung
der Ernst	die Geige
der Held	die Jurisprudenz
der Herr	die Mutti
der Junge	die Nuß
der Mann	die Philosophie
der Müller	die Sache
der Platz	die Sonne
der Professor	die Tante
der Raum	die Vorlesung, *pl.* die Vorlesungen
der Schneider	die Weile
der Spaß	
der Student, *pl.* die Studenten	
der Tag	
der Teil*	
der Vorlesungsraum	
der Wolf	

* **Das Teil** also occurs, but rarely. In some compounds it is treated as neuter: **das Gegenteil**.

Neuter

das Baden	das Nuß-Eis
das Eis	das Podium
das Fräulein	das Sprichwort
das Gegenteil	das Studieren
das Gift	das Üben
das Kind	das Viertel
das Mädchen	das Wort

WRITING

A. The Comma

Grammatical units such as phrases, clauses, and sentences are often signaled in speech by such features as stress, intonation, rhythm, tempo, or pauses. Although these features may be essential to the correct interpretation of a spoken utterance, they are generally disregarded by the English and German writing systems. These writing systems do provide a few devices that are helpful in this regard. A period, for example, may signify falling intonation which in turn conveys the meaning "end of utterance." A question mark may signal rising intonation (yes-no questions) or falling intonation (word question), in either case meaning "end of utterance, answer expected."

In English the *comma* is generally — although certainly not exclusively — associated with a pause in speech. In German, however, it is primarily associated with grammatical units. It is conditioned not so much by the phonological feature "pause" as by certain kinds of grammatical boundaries. Whether or not a spoken German utterance has a pause at a certain point has absolutely nothing to do with whether a comma should be written at that point.

In German, a comma is used to mark the boundary between a main (independent) clause and a dependent clause. There is no pause associated with such a boundary.

Fragen Sie, worauf Fräulein Schneider wartet.
Antworten Sie, daß sie auf die Vorlesung wartet.
Sagen Sie, daß Herr Held auch darauf wartet.
Siehst du nicht, wie schön die Sonne scheint?

Two main clauses within the same sentence are separated by a comma. In speech, a pause occurs at the clause boundary.

Entschuldigen Sie, soll hier nicht Professor Müller die „Einführung in die Philosophie" lesen?
Ich glaube schon, jedenfalls warte ich auch darauf.

An initial element like **ja**, **nein**, **danke**, **ach** is followed by a comma.

Ja, Heike muß Geige üben.   Danke, dann bleibe ich hier.
Nein, Mutti ißt nie Eis.   Ach, das ist nur ein Sprichwort.

A comma is used to set off the name of the person addressed. There is no pause here.

Es ist heiß heute, Tante Inge.   Guten Tag, Heike.

In English it is customary to place a comma after an initial adverb or adverbial phrase, especially if the meaning of the sentence could be ambiguous without it. German does not use the comma in this way. Compare:

Eigentlich kann es nun losgehen.   Jedenfalls warte ich auch darauf.
Actually, it can start any time now.   At any rate, that's what I'm waiting for, too.

B. German Orthography

Two new spellings that do not conform to the observations presented in previous units concerning the representation of vowel length are:

V **ie** rtel   [ˈfɪʀtəl]   *short* [ɪ] *is spelled* **ie**
e rst   [eːʀst]   *long* [eː] *is followed by more than one consonant letter*

C. Writing Practice: Punctuation

Copy the sentences and insert commas, periods, and question marks:

1 Sagen Sie daß die Vorlesung beginnt
2 Fragen Sie wann Uwe zum Baden geht
3 Antworten Sie daß er Geige üben muß
4 Fragen Sie ob die Sonne scheint
5 Wenn die Sonne scheint geht Uwe zum Baden
6 Kann ich Eis kaufen
7 Kann ich Eis kaufen wenn es heiß ist
8 Die Sonne scheint
9 Die Sonne scheint aber ich muß Geige üben
10 Es ist heiß heute Tante Inge
11 Ist es heiß heute Tante Inge
12 Glauben Sie daran Fräulein Schneider
13 Guten Tag Herr Professor
14 Wie geht's Heike
15 Danke gut
16 Ja ich komme mit
17 Ach die Sonne scheint nicht
18 Also es geht los
19 Hoffentlich liest er nicht langweilig
20 Eigentlich muß ich warten
21 Jedenfalls kaufe ich kein Nuß-Eis
22 Heute nachmittag kann er Ihnen helfen

D. Writing Practice: Sentences

Arrange the elements to form statements:

1 es / kann / losgehen / nun endlich .
2 mein Bruder / hat / erzählt / es mir .
3 er / kann / helfen / Ihnen / nicht viel .
4 die älteren Studenten / viel Erfahrung / haben .
5 es / endlich / los / geht .
6 hoffentlich / er / nicht / langweilig / liest .

Arrange the elements to form commands:

7 Sie / erzählen / es mir !
8 Sie / warten / nur / ab !
9 Sie / lesen / nicht so langweilig !
10 mit / komm / doch !
11 es mir / erzähl !

Arrange the elements to form word questions:

12 Professor Müller / wo / ist ?
13 glauben / Sie / woran ?
14 Fräulein Schneider / wartet / warum ?
15 es / losgehen / kann / wann ?
16 Ihr Bruder / studiert / was ?
17 liest / der alte Professor / wie ?
18 Herr Held / worauf / wartet ?
19 die Vorlesung / beginnt / wann ?

Arrange the elements to form yes-no questions:

20 es / kann / losgehen / nun endlich ?
21 alle Vorlesungen / beginnen / erst um viertel nach voll ?
22 der Bruder / hat / erzählt / es Ihnen ?
23 er / kann / helfen / Ihnen ?
24 das / stimmt ?
25 es / geht / los / endlich ?
26 Fräulein Schneider / muß / warten / auch darauf ?
27 Tante Inge / mit / kommt ?
28 er / langweilig / liest ?
29 Professor Wolf / soll / lesen / heute ?

Read your sentences aloud, paying close attention to correct intonation, and be able to provide an English equivalent for each.

LISTENING PRACTICE

Listen to the narrative on tape; then answer the following questions.

1 Wo warten Fräulein Schneider und Herr Held?
2 Wohin geht Inge Schneider heute nachmittag?
3 Warum möchte Hans Held auch mitkommen?
4 Kann Hans Held mitkommen?

Unit 5

DIALOG

Der Unfall am Schillerplatz (Anfang)

deːʀ ˌunfal am ˈʃilɐʀplats

1 **Rolf:** Mensch, da, kannst du sehen?

ʀɔlf   mɛnʃ   ˈdaː kanst du ˈzeːən

2 **Günther:** Ich sehe nichts. Was läufst du denn plötzlich?

gyntɐʀ   ɪç zeːə ˈnɪçts vas ˈlɔɪfst duː dɛn plœtsliç

3 **Rolf:** Da hinten an der Kreuzung! Der Milchwagen rutscht!

daː ˌhɪntən an deːʀ ˈkʀɔɪtsuŋ deːʀ ˈmɪlçvaːgən ʀutʃt

4 **Günther:** Tatsächlich, jetzt kippt die alte Kiste sogar noch um.

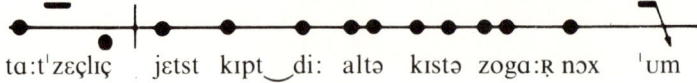

taːtˈzɛçlɪç   jɛtst kɪpt diː altə kɪstə zogaːʀ nɔx ˈum

The Accident at Schiller Square
(Beginning)

am = **an** + **dem** · **der Schillerplatz (am Schillerplatz** *dat.*) **Schiller** *a German poet* + **der Platz** square; place

1 Man, there, can you see?

der Mensch man, human being

2 I don't see a thing. Why are you suddenly running, anyway?

nichts nothing · **was** what; why · **laufen (du läufst)**

3 Over there at the crossing. The milk truck is skidding.

hinten in the distance; behind · **die Kreuzung (der Kreuzung** *dat.*) · **der Milchwagen die Milch** milk + **der Wagen** truck, car

4 So it is; now the old crate's even tipping over.

tatsächlich actual(ly), real(ly) · **umkippen (sie kippt ... um)** tip over · **sogar** even **sogar noch** even

5 **Rolf:** Klatsch, da liegt der ganze Salat auf der Straße!
ˈklatʃ ˌdɑː liːkt deːʁ gantsə zalɑːt aʊ̯f deːʁ ˈʃtʁɑːsə

6 **Günther:** Da lachst du noch? Die ganze Milch schwappt über die Straße!
dɑː ˈlaxst duː nɔx diː gantsə ˌmɪlç ʃvapt yːbəʁ diː ˈʃtʁɑːsə

7 **Rolf:** Klar, das macht doch nichts. Der Milchmann ist bestimmt versichert.
ˈklɑːʁ das ˈmaxt dɔx nɪçts deːʁ mɪlçman ɪst bəˌʃtɪmt fɛʁˈzɪçɐʁt

8 **Günther:** Aber was ist da rechts bei der Laterne?
ɑːbəʁ vas ɪst dɑː ˌʁɛçts baɪ̯ deːʁ laˈtɛʁnə

9 **Rolf:** Da liegt eine alte Frau. Schnell, die Sache ist ernst.
dɑː liːkt aɪ̯nə altə ˈfʁaʊ̯ ˈʃnɛl ˌdiː zaxə ɪst ˈɛʁnst

Nichts wie hin! Wir müssen ihr helfen.

10 **Günther:** nɪçts viː ˈhɪn viːʁ mʏsən iːʁ ˈhɛlfən

(Fortsetzung folgt)

SUPPLEMENT

The subject pronouns er, sie, es, and pl. sie

1 Warum läuft Rolf?
vɑːʁʊm ˈlɔɪ̯ft ʁɔlf

5 Crash! The whole mess is lying there on the street.	**liegen (er liegt)** · **ganz (ganze)** whole; all · **der Salat** salad · **die Straße (der Straße** *dat.***)**

6 And you think it's funny? All the milk is splashing over the street.	**da** about it; there · **lachen (du lachst)** laugh · **schwappen (sie schwappt)**

7 Sure, but it doesn't really matter. The milkman is certainly insured.	**das macht nichts** that doesn't matter, that's all right · **der Milchmann die Milch + der Mann**

8 But what's that over there to the right, near the streetlight?	**die Laterne (der Laterne** *dat.***)** streetlight; lantern, lamp

9 An old woman is lying there. Quick! The thing is serious.	**die Frau** woman; Mrs.

10 Let's get over there. We've got to help her.	**wie** as, how, like *conj.* · **hin** to that place, in that direction · **müssen (wir müssen)** · **sie (ihr** *dat.***)**

(To be continued)

---

1 Why is Rolf running?	**laufen (er läuft)**

2 Er muß helfen.

eːʀ mus ˈhɛlfən

3 Wo ist der Student?

voː ɪst deːʀ ʃtuˈdɛnt

4 Er ist im Vorlesungsraum.

eːʀ ɪst ɪm ˈfoːʀleːzuŋsʀaʊ̯m

5 Wo ist der Unfall?

voː ɪst deːʀ ˈunfal

6 Er ist am Schillerplatz.

eːʀ ɪst am ˈʃɪləʀplats

7 Ist Tante Inge nett?

ɪst tantə ɪŋə ˈnɛt

8 Ja, sie ist nett.

ˌjaː ziː ɪst ˈnɛt

9 Ist die Frau alt?

ɪst diː fʀaʊ̯ ˈalt

10 Ja, sie ist alt.

ˌjaː ziː ɪst ˈalt

2 He has to help.   müssen (er muß)

3 Where is the student?

4 He's in the lecture hall.

5 Where is the accident?

6 It's at Schiller Square.

7 Is Aunt Inge nice?

8 Yes, she's nice.

9 Is the woman old?

10 Yes, she's old.

11 Ist die Kreuzung rutschig?

ɪst di: kʀɔɪtsuŋ ˈʀutʃɪç

12 Ja, sie ist rutschig.

ˌjɑ: zi: ɪst ˈʀutʃɪç

13 Wo ist das Kind?

vo: ɪst das ˈkɪnt

14 Es ist auf der Straße.

ɛs ɪst aʊ̯f de:ʀ ˈʃtʀɑ:sə

15 Stimmt das alte Sprichwort?

ˈʃtɪmt das altə ʃpʀɪçvɔʀt

16 Nein, es stimmt nicht.

ˌnaɪn ɛs ʃtɪmt ˈnɪçt

17 Sind Rolf und Günther am Schillerplatz?

zɪnt ʀɔlf unt gyntəʀ am ˈʃɪləʀplats

18 Ja, sie sind am Schillerplatz.

ˌjɑ: zi: zɪnt am ˈʃɪləʀplats

19 Wo sind die Studenten?

vo: zɪnt di: ʃtuˈdɛntən

11 Is the crossing slippery?

12 Yes, it's slippery.

13 Where is the child?

14 It's on the street.

15 Is the old proverb true?

16 No, it isn't true.

17 Are Rolf and Günther at Schiller Square?

18 Yes, they're at Schiller Square.

19 Where are the students?

20 Sie sind im V̲o̲r̲l̲e̲s̲u̲n̲g̲sraum.

zi: zınt ım ˈfoːʁleːzuŋsraʊ̯m

21 Wann beg̲i̲n̲n̲en die Vorlesungen?

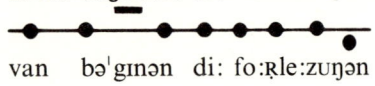

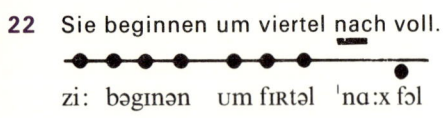

van bəˈgınən diː foːʁleːzuŋən

22 Sie beginnen um viertel n̲a̲c̲h voll.

ziː bəgınən ʊm fırtəl ˈnɑːx fɔl

20 They're in the lecture hall.

21 When do the lectures begin?

22 They begin at a quarter after the hour.

PHONOLOGY

Consonant combinations

In Units 1 to 4 you learned the sounds of German that differ from the sounds of English. The differences between the German and English sound systems do not end there, however; there are also differences in the ways in which the two languages combine their sounds. Practice the German combinations by repeating the words below.

[ts] occurs in English in the middle of words (Betsy) and at the end of words (cats); in German it also occurs initially

ganz	[gants]
heizen	[ˈhaɪtsən]
Katze	[ˈkatsə]
jetzt	[jɛtst]
Zimmer	[ˈtsɪmər]
Zahl	[tsɑːl]
Zeit	[tsaɪt]
zum	[tsʊm]

The combination [ts] is spelled z or tz; do not confuse it with [z] or [s], spelled s

[ts]	[z] or [s]
Zeit	seit
Zahl	Saal
Zoo	so
Katze	Kasse
heizen	heißen

[tʃ] *occurs in English and in German, but there is a difference between the English and German pronunciation of the* [ʃ] *sound*

deutsch	[dɔɪtʃ]
Klatsch	[klatʃ]
rutschige	[ˈRʊtʃigə]
Cello	[ˈtʃɛlo]
Tscheche	[ˈtʃɛçə]

[ʃt] *occurs medially and finally in English* (fishtail, wished); *in German it may also occur initially*

Straße	[ˈʃtRɑːsə]
Student	[ʃtuˈdɛnt]
studiert	[ʃtuˈdiːRt]
stimmt	[ʃtɪmt]

[ʃp] *occurs initially in German, but not in English*

Spaß	[ʃpɑːs]
Sprichwort	[ˈʃpRɪçvɔRt]

The following combinations do not occur in English at all:

[çt]			[xt]	
nicht	[nɪçt]		Nacht	[naxt]
Licht	[lɪçt]		macht	[maxt]
Pflicht	[pflɪçt]		sucht	[zuːxt]
leicht	[laɪçt]		Docht	[dɔxt]
möchte	[ˈmœçtə]		locht	[lɔxt]

[xt] *should not be confused with* [kt]

[xt]	[kt]
Nacht	nackt
locht	lockt
taucht	taugt

[xs] *should not be confused with* [ks]

[xs]	[ks]		[çts]	
(des) Dachs	(der) Dachs		nichts	[nɪçts]
(du) wachst	(du) wachst		rechts	[Rɛçts]
(du) lachst	(der) Lachs		rücksichtslos	[ˈRʏkzɪçtslos]
(des) Buchs	(der) Buchs(-baum)			

[xts]

| nachts | [naxts] |

[çst]

sprichst	[ʃpRıçst]
wichst	[vıçst]
reichst	[Raɪçst]
weichst	[vaɪçst]

Combinations with [l] and [R]:

[pl]

Platz	[plats]
Platzwunde	[ˈplatsvʊndə]
plötzlich	[ˈplœtslıç]

[kl]

klar	[klɑːR]
Klatsch	[klatʃ]
klein	[klaɪn]
Klapperschlange	[ˈklapəRʃlaŋə]

[pR] *and* [bR]

Professor	[pRoˈfɛsɔR]
Problem	[pRoˈbleːm]
Bruder	[ˈbRuːdəR]
bringen	[ˈbRıŋən]

[tR] *and* [dR]

tragen	[ˈtRɑːgən]
trinken	[ˈtRıŋkən]
dran	[dRan]
drei	[dRaɪ]

[kR] *and* [gR]

krank	[kRaŋk]
Krieg	[kRiːk]
groß	[gRoːs]
Grund	[gRʊnt]

[xst]

lachst	[laxst]
wachst	[vaxst]
machst	[maxst]
suchst	[zuːxst]

[ʃR]

| schreiben | [ˈʃRaɪbən] |
| Schrei | [ʃRaɪ] |

[fR]

| Fräulein | [ˈfRɔɪlaɪn] |
| frei | [fRaɪ] |

AUDIOLINGUAL DRILLS

A. Directed Dialog

Fragen Sie, wo der Unfall ist!
Wo ist der Unfall?

Antworten Sie, daß er am Schillerplatz ist!
Er ist am Schillerplatz.

Sagen Sie, daß Günther nichts sieht!
Günther sieht nichts.

Sagen Sie, daß Rolf plötzlich läuft!
Rolf läuft plötzlich.

Fragen Sie, warum er plötzlich läuft!
Warum läuft er plötzlich?

Antworten Sie, daß der Milchwagen rutscht!
Der Milchwagen rutscht.

Sagen Sie, daß die alte Kiste sogar noch umkippt!
Die alte Kiste kippt sogar noch um.

Sagen Sie, daß der ganze Salat auf der Straße liegt!
Der ganze Salat liegt auf der Straße.

Sagen Sie, daß die ganze Milch über die Straße schwappt!
Die ganze Milch schwappt über die Straße.

Sagen Sie, daß das doch nichts macht!
Das macht doch nichts.

Fragen Sie, warum das nichts macht!
Warum macht das nichts?

Antworten Sie, daß der Milchmann bestimmt versichert ist!
Der Milchmann ist bestimmt versichert.

Fragen Sie, was da rechts bei der Laterne ist!
Was ist da rechts bei der Laterne?

Sagen Sie, daß da eine alte Frau liegt!
Da liegt eine alte Frau.

Fragen Sie, ob die Sache ernst ist!
Ist die Sache ernst?

B. Noun-Pronoun Agreement (*See Grammar* §5.3)

1 Substitute the correct pronoun subject for the noun subject.

Example:
Der Junge kauft Eis.
Er kauft Eis.

Der Milchwagen rutscht.
Er rutscht.

Die Kiste kippt um.
Sie kippt um.

Der Mann ist versichert.
Er ist versichert.

Die Straße ist gut.
Sie ist gut.

Die Laterne ist da hinten.
Sie ist da hinten.

Das Eis schmeckt gut.
Es schmeckt gut.

Die Sonne scheint schön.
Sie scheint schön.

Uwe geht zum Baden.
Er geht zum Baden.

Die Vorlesungen beginnen um viertel nach voll.
Sie beginnen um viertel nach voll.

Der Platz ist noch frei.
Er ist noch frei.

Das Kind ist tüchtig.
Es ist tüchtig.

Fräulein Schneider und Herr Held sind Studenten.
Sie sind Studenten.

2 Answer the questions in the affirmative by beginning with **Ja,** ... and substitute the correct pronoun for the subject.

Example:
Scheint die Sonne schön?
Ja, sie scheint schön.

Liegt die Frau da?
Ja, sie liegt da.

Ist der Milchmann versichert?
Ja, er ist versichert.

Sind die Studenten im Vorlesungsraum?
Ja, sie sind im Vorlesungsraum.

Beginnt die Vorlesung jetzt?
Ja, sie beginnt jetzt.

Wartet der Student darauf?
Ja, er wartet darauf.

Liest Professor Wolf langweilig?
Ja, er liest langweilig.

Glaubt Tante Inge daran?
Ja, sie glaubt daran.

Schmeckt das Eis gut?
Ja, es schmeckt gut.

3 Answer the questions in the negative by beginning with **Nein,** ... and inserting **nicht** before the adjective. Also, substitute the correct pronoun for the subject.

Example:
Ist Professor Wolf nett?
Nein, er ist nicht nett.

Ist die Frau alt?
Nein, sie ist nicht alt.

Ist Heike tüchtig?
Nein, sie ist nicht tüchtig.

Schmeckt das Eis gut?
Nein, es schmeckt nicht gut.

Ist die Straße gut?
Nein, sie ist nicht gut.

Ist der Milchmann versichert?
Nein, er ist nicht versichert.

Sind die Vorlesungen langweilig?
Nein, sie sind nicht langweilig.

Ist das Sprichwort alt?
Nein, es ist nicht alt.

Ist die Vorlesung schwer?
Nein, sie ist nicht schwer.

C. Questions and Answers

Wo ist der Unfall?
Er ist am Schillerplatz.

Warum läuft Rolf plötzlich?
Der Milchwagen rutscht.

Kippt der Milchwagen um?
Ja, er kippt sogar noch um.

Was liegt auf der Straße?
Der ganze Salat liegt auf der Straße.

Was schwappt über die Straße?
Die ganze Milch schwappt über die Straße.

Ist der Milchmann versichert?
Ja, er ist bestimmt versichert.

Wo liegt die alte Frau?
Sie liegt auf der Straße.

Ist der Unfall ernst?
Ja, er ist ernst.

GRAMMAR

5.1 Word-Formation

Compound nouns

gegen against + **das Teil** part = **das Gegenteil** opposite
die Milch milk + **der Mann** man = **der Milchmann** milkman
die Milch + **der Wagen** truck, car, wagon = **der Milchwagen** milk truck
Schiller name of a German writer + **der Platz** square; place = **der Schillerplatz** Schiller Square
sprich *from* **sprechen** speak + **das Wort** word = **das Sprichwort** saying, proverb

5.2 Definite Articles of New Nouns

Masculine	*Feminine*
der Klatsch	die Frau
der Mann	die Kiste
der Mensch	die Kreuzung
der Milchmann	die Laterne
der Platz	die Milch
der Salat	die Straße
der Schillerplatz	
der Unfall	
der Wagen	

5.3 Subject Forms of the Personal Pronouns

	Singular		*Plural*	
1st person	ich	I	wir	we
2nd person	du	you	ihr	you
3rd person	er	he, it	sie	they
	sie	she, it		
	es	it		
2nd person standard (singular and plural)	Sie	you		

Ordinarily Germans use **du** (familiar singular) and **ihr** (familiar plural) with people whom they address by their first names, such as members of the family, close friends, and children. They also use these forms when speaking to animals and to a deity. The standard form of address is **Sie** (note the capital **S**!). Like the English pronoun *you*, it is used to address a single person or several persons. The familiar **du** and **ihr** imply closeness or intimacy, while the standard **Sie** does not. The verb form used with **Sie** is the same as that used with the 3rd person plural:

sie sagen   they say   **Sie sagen**   you say

A more detailed explanation of the socially correct usage of **du**, **ihr** versus **Sie** will be given in Unit 22.

A pronoun of the 3rd person must agree in *number* and *gender* with the noun it replaces.

Masculine	**Der Platz** ist frei. **Er** ist frei.	*Neuter*	**Das Eis** schmeckt gut. **Es** schmeckt gut.
Feminine	**Die Vorlesung** beginnt jetzt. **Sie** beginnt jetzt.		

Plural **Die Vorlesungen** sind langweilig. **Die älteren Studenten** haben viel Erfahrung.
Sie sind langweilig. **Sie** haben viel Erfahrung.

If a neuter noun refers to a person (**das Kind**, **das Mädchen**, **das Fräulein**), the pronoun that replaces the neuter noun may be neuter **es**; more often, however, the pronoun is determined by the sex of the person being referred to.

Ist das Mädchen tüchtig?—Ja, **es** ist tüchtig.
Ja, **sie** ist tüchtig.

WRITING

A. The German Alphabet

a	[ɑ:]	u	[u:]
b	[be:]	v	[faʊ]
c	[tse:]	w	[ve:]
d	[de:]	x	[ɪks]
e	[e:]	y	[ˈʏpsilɔn]
f	[ɛf]	z	[tsɛt]
g	[ge:]		
h	[hɑ:]	ä	[ɛ:] oder [ɑ:]-Umlaut
i	[i:]	ö	[ø:] oder [o:]-Umlaut
j	[jɔt]	ü	[y:] oder [u:]-Umlaut
k	[kɑ:]		
l	[ɛl]	ei, ai	[aɪ]
m	[ɛm]		
n	[ɛn]	au	[aʊ]
o	[o:]		
p	[pe:]	eu, äu	[ɔɪ]
q	[ku:]		
r	[ɛʀ], [ɛr]	ch	[tseˈhɑ:]
s	[ɛs]	ß	[ɛsˈtsɛt]
t	[te:]		

B. Capitalization

1 All nouns are capitalized, no matter where they appear in a sentence: **der Unfall**, **die Milch**, **das Sprichwort**.

2   All forms of the pronoun **Sie** *you* and the possessive adjective **Ihr** *your* are capitalized: **Entschuldigen Sie, ist das Ihr Ernst?**

3   Unless it is the first word in a sentence, the pronoun **ich** *I* is not capitalized: **Das möchte ich auch.**

4   In titles, only the first word and the nouns are capitalized: **Die Sonne scheint so schön.**

C. The Use of ß and ss

The letter **ß** is used instead of **ss** under certain conditions:

1   After a long vowel or a diphthong: **die Straße**.
2   Before a consonant: **du ißt** (but **essen**).
3   At the end of a word or syllable: **die Nuß, ich muß** (but **müssen**).
4   But **ß** is not used between vowels if the preceding vowel is short: **müssen, der Professor, essen**.

D. The Comma

You saw in Unit 4 (Writing §A) that two independent clauses in the same sentence are separated by a comma, and that a comma in this function is associated with a pause in speech. Both the comma and a pause occur in:

Ich glaube schon, jedenfalls warte ich auch darauf.

The same is true of independent clauses connected by a coordinating conjunction (**aber**, **und**, and others):

Heike übt Geige, und Hans geht zum Baden.

If two independent clauses in the same sentence have either a subject or a finite verb in common, then they are not separated by a comma. A pause will normally not occur between two such clauses. In the sentence:

Sie gehen zum Baden und kaufen Eis.

the two clauses have a common subject **Sie**. Accordingly, no comma is placed between **Baden** and **und**. Compare:

Sie gehen zum Baden, und **wir** kaufen Eis.

E. Writing Practice: Punctuation

Copy the sentences and insert commas, periods, and question marks:

1 Die Sonne scheint und Heike geht zum Baden
2 Wenn die Sonne scheint geht Uwe auch zum Baden
3 Gehst du zum Baden auch wenn die Sonne nicht scheint
4 Der Wagen rutscht und kippt um
5 Plötzlich läuft Rolf aber Günther sieht nichts
6 Eine alte Frau liegt da und wir müssen ihr helfen
7 Rolf sieht die alte Frau und läuft plötzlich
8 Professor Müller kommt um viertel nach voll und liest langweilig
9 Ich bleibe hier und warte darauf
10 Fräulein Schneider glaubt an das Sprichwort aber Herr Held sagt daß aller Anfang leicht ist

F. Writing Practice: Pronouns

Write answers in the affirmative or negative, as directed, and substitute the correct pronoun for the noun subject. Pay close attention to punctuation:

1 Kauft der Junge Eis?   Ja
2 Rutscht der Milchwagen?   Nein
3 Kippt die alte Kiste um?   Ja
4 Ist der Eismann versichert?   Ja
5 Ist die Laterne da hinten?   Nein
6 Schmeckt Nuß-Eis am besten?   Ja
7 Scheint die Sonne heute nachmittag?   Ja
8 Geht Uwe zum Baden?   Ja
9 Kommt Heike mit?   Nein
10 Gehen Hans und Uwe zum Baden?   Nein
11 Beginnen alle Vorlesungen jetzt?   Ja
12 Ist der Platz noch frei?   Ja
13 Ist das Kind tüchtig?   Nein
14 Sind die Studenten auf dem Podium?   Ja
15 Liest Professor Wolf langweilig?   Nein
16 Glaubt Fräulein Schneider daran?   Nein
17 Wartet die Frau auf die Vorlesung?   Ja
18 Studiert Fräulein Schneiders Bruder auch Philosophie?   Ja

Read your answers aloud, paying close attention to correct intonation. Be able to give an English equivalent for each of your sentences.

LISTENING PRACTICE

Listen to the two taped conversations; then answer the following questions.

A. **Hans und Heike**

1. Was sieht Heike?
2. Was fragt Hans?
3. Was müssen Hans und Heike tun?

B. **Rolf und Inge**

1. Worauf wartet Rolf?
2. Wohin geht Inge?
3. Warum kommt Rolf auch mit?

Unit 6

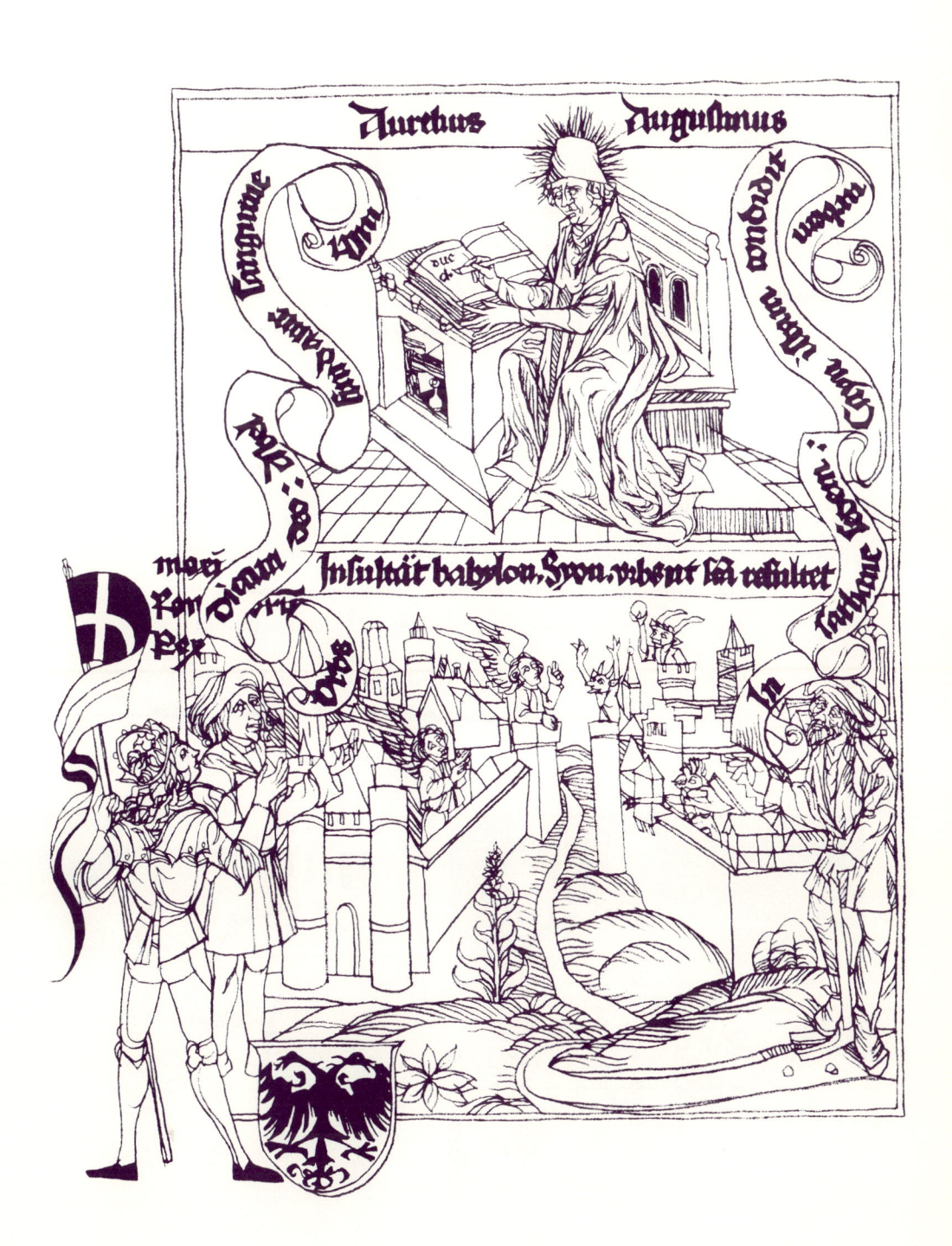

DIALOG

Der Unfall am Schillerplatz (Schluß)

1 Rolf: Gott sei Dank, es ist nicht allzu schlimm!

   gɔt zaɪ ˈdaŋk ɛs ɪst nɪçt altsuː ˈʃlɪm

2 Günther: Schlimm genug! Die Frau hat eine Platzwunde am Kopf!

   ʃlɪm gəˈnuːk diː fʀaʊ hat aɪnə ˌplatsvʊndə am ˈkɔpf

3 Rolf: Sie hat noch den Angstschweiß auf der Stirn!

   ziː hat nɔx deːn ˈaŋstʃvaɪs aʊf deːʀ ʃtɪʀn

4 Günther: Und dem rücksichtslosen Fahrer ist nichts passiert!

   ʊnt deːm ʀʏkzɪçtsloːzən ˌfaːʀəʀ ɪst ˈnɪçts pasiːʀt

5 Rolf: Quatsch, rücksichtslos! Dies ist eine ganz schlechte, rutschige Straße.

   kvatʃ ˈʀʏkzɪçtsloːs diːs ɪst aɪnə gants ʃlɛçtə ʀʊtʃɪgə ˈʃtʀaːsə

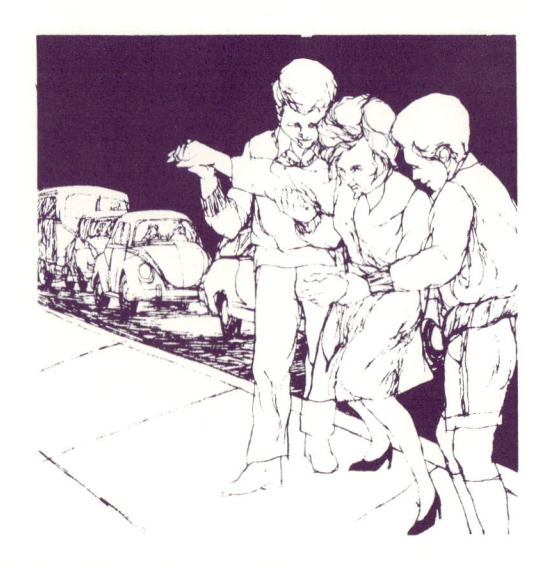

The Accident at Schiller Square
(Conclusion)

1 Thank goodness, it isn't too bad. — **der Gott** God; god · **sein (er sei** *subj.*)

2 Bad enough! The woman has a bad cut on her head. — **die Platzwunde** platz (*from* **platzen** burst) + **die Wunde** wound · **der Kopf (am Kopf** *dat.*) *The definite article is generally used instead of a possessive adjective with parts of the body.*

3 She still has the sweat of fear on her forehead! — **der Angstschweiß (den Angstschweiß** *acc.*) **die Angst** + **der Schweiß** sweat, perspiration · **die Stirn (der Stirn** *dat.*)

4 And nothing happened to the careless driver! — **rücksichtslos** careless · **der Fahrer** driver **(dem rücksichtslosen Fahrer** *dat.*) · **passieren (ist . . . passiert** happened)

5 Careless, my eye! This is a very bad, slippery street. — **der Quatsch** baloney, nonsense *slang* · **ganz** very; completely *adv.* · **schlecht (schlechte) rutschig (rutschige)**

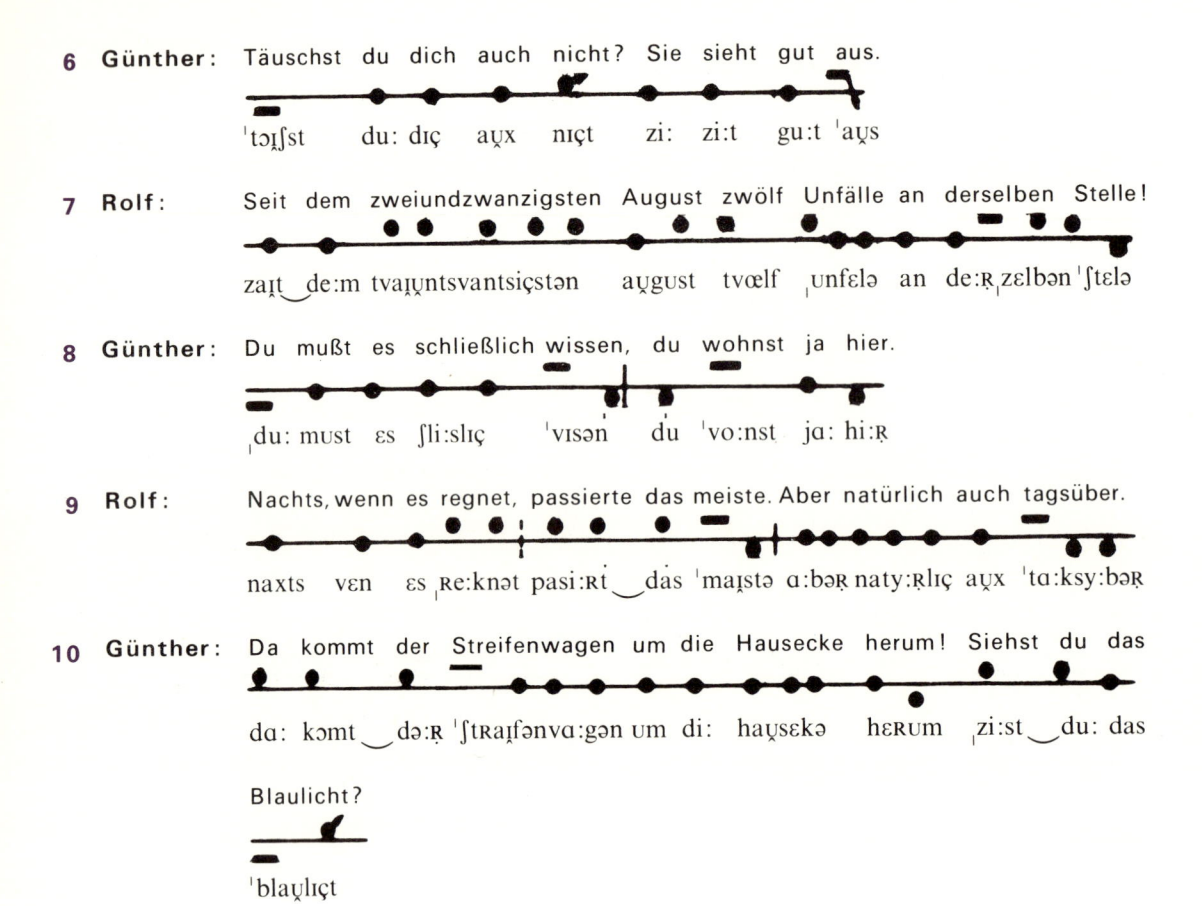

6 Günther: Täuschst du dich auch nicht? Sie sieht gut aus.
ˈtɔɪ̯st du: dɪç au̯x nɪçt zi: zi:t gu:t ˈau̯s

7 Rolf: Seit dem zweiundzwanzigsten August zwölf Unfälle an derselben Stelle!
zaɪ̯t de:m tvaɪ̯ʊntsvantsɪçstən au̯gust tvœlf ˌunfɛlə an de:ʀˌzɛlbən ˈʃtɛlə

8 Günther: Du mußt es schließlich wissen, du wohnst ja hier.
ˌdu: must ɛs ʃli:slɪç ˈvɪsən du ˈvo:nst ja: hi:ʀ

9 Rolf: Nachts, wenn es regnet, passierte das meiste. Aber natürlich auch tagsüber.
naxts vɛn ɛs ˌʀe:knət pasi:ʀt das ˈmaɪ̯stə a:bəʀ naty:ʀlɪç au̯x ˈta:ksy:bəʀ

10 Günther: Da kommt der Streifenwagen um die Hausecke herum! Siehst du das
da: kɔmt de:ʀ ˈʃtʀaɪ̯fənva:gən um di: hau̯sɛkə hɛʀum ˌzi:st du: das

Blaulicht?
ˈblau̯lɪçt

6 Aren't you mistaken, though? It looks all right.

täuschen (du täuschst) deceive · **dich** yourself *acc.* · **aussehen (sie sieht ... aus)** look, appear

7 Since the twenty-second of August twelve accidents at the same place!

der August (seit dem 22. August *dat.*) · **die Stelle (an derselben Stelle** *dat.*) place · **der Unfall,** *pl.* **die Unfälle**

8 You really ought to know; after all, you live here.

müssen (du mußt) · **schließlich** really, after all; finally · **wohnen (du wohnst)** · **ja** after all; yes, indeed

9 At night, when it's raining, most of it happens. But naturally during the day, too.

regnen (es regnet) rain · **das meiste** the most, most of it · **passieren (es passiert)**

10 There comes the patrol car around the corner of the building. Do you see the blue light?

der Streifenwagen streifen patrol + **der Wagen** · **die Hausecke das Haus** house, building + **die Ecke** corner · **das Blaulicht blau** blue + **das Licht** light

SUPPLEMENT

Cardinal numbers

0	null	[nʊl]		21	einundzwanzig	[ˈaɪnʊntsvantsɪç]
1	eins	[aɪns]		22	zweiundzwanzig	
2	zwei	[tsvaɪ]		23	dreiundzwanzig	
3	drei	[dʀaɪ]		24	vierundzwanzig	
4	vier	[fiːʀ]		25	fünfundzwanzig	
5	fünf	[fʏnf]		26	sechsundzwanzig	
6	sechs	[zɛks]		27	siebenundzwanzig	
7	sieben	[ˈziːbən]		28	achtundzwanzig	
8	acht	[axt]		29	neunundzwanzig	
9	neun	[nɔɪn]				
10	zehn	[tseːn]				
11	elf	[ɛlf]				
12	zwölf	[tsvœlf]		10	zehn	
13	dreizehn	[ˈdʀaɪtseːn]		20	zwanzig	
14	vierzehn	[ˈfɪʀtseːn]		30	dreißig	[ˈdʀaɪsɪç]
15	fünfzehn	[ˈfʏnftseːn]		40	vierzig	[ˈfɪʀtsɪç]
16	sechzehn	[ˈzɛçtseːn]		50	fünfzig	[ˈfʏnftsɪç]
17	siebzehn	[ˈziːptseːn]		60	sechzig	[ˈzɛçtsɪç]
18	achtzehn	[ˈaxtseːn]		70	siebzig	[ˈziːptsɪç]
19	neunzehn	[ˈnɔɪntseːn]		80	achtzig	[ˈaxtsɪç]
20	zwanzig	[ˈtsvantsɪç]		90	neunzig	[ˈnɔɪntsɪç]

100	hundert, einhundert	[ˈhʊndəʀt], [ˈaɪnhʊndəʀt]
101	hunderteins	[hʊndəʀtˈaɪns]
110	hundertzehn	
200	zweihundert	
300	dreihundert	
	usw. (und so weiter)	

1 000	tausend, eintausend	[ˈtaʊzənt], [ˈaɪntaʊzənt]
1 000 000	eine Million	[aɪnə mɪliˈoːn]
1 000 000 000	eine Milliarde	[aɪnə mɪliˈaʀdə]

Ordinal numbers

der 1.	der erste	[deːʀ ˈeːʀstə]	der 14.	der vierzehnte
der 2.	der zweite	[deːʀ ˈtsvaɪ̯tə]	der 15.	der fünfzehnte
der 3.	der dritte	[deːʀ ˈdʀɪtə]	der 16.	der sechzehnte
der 4.	der vierte		der 17.	der siebzehnte
der 5.	der fünfte		der 18.	der achtzehnte
der 6.	der sechste		der 19.	der neunzehnte
der 7.	der siebte		der 20.	der zwanzigste
der 8.	der achte		der 21.	der einundzwanzigste
der 9.	der neunte		der 22.	der zweiundzwanzigste
der 10.	der zehnte		der 30.	der dreißigste
der 11.	der elfte		der 40.	der vierzigste
der 12.	der zwölfte		der 100.	der hundertste
der 13.	der dreizehnte		der 1 000.	der tausendste

Numbers and dates

1   Zehn und zwei ist zwölf.

2   Vier mal fünf ist zwanzig.

3   Sechs durch zwei ist drei.

4   Fünfzehn weniger fünf ist zehn.

5   Heute ist der erste August.

6   Heute ist der zweite August.

7   Heute ist der dritte August.

1   Ten and two are twelve.

2   Four times five is twenty.

3   Six divided by two is three.

4   Fifteen minus five is ten.

5   Today is the first of August.

6   Today is the second of August.

7   Today is the third of August.

8   Heute ist der siebte August.

9   Heute ist der sechzehnte August.

10 Heute ist der siebzehnte August.

11 Heute ist der zwanzigste August.

12 Heute ist der dreißigste August.

13 Er kommt am ersten August.

14 Er kommt am zweiten August.

15 Er kommt am dritten August.

16 Er kommt am siebten August.

17 Er kommt am sechzehnten August.

18 Er kommt am siebzehnten August.

19 Er kommt am zwanzigsten August.

20 Er kommt am dreißigsten August.

21 Er kommt am letzten August.

8   Today is the seventh of August.

9   Today is the sixteenth of August.

10 Today is the seventeenth of August.

11 Today is the twentieth of August.

12 Today is the thirtieth of August.

13 He is coming on the first of August.　　　　**erst (am ersten** *dat.***)**

14 He is coming on the second of August.

15 He is coming on the third of August.

16 He is coming on the seventh of August.

17 He is coming on the sixteenth of August.

18 He is coming on the seventeenth of August.

19 He is coming on the twentieth of August.

20 He is coming on the thirtieth of August.

21 He is coming on the last day of August.　　**letzt (am letzten** *dat.***)** last

PHONOLOGY

Consonant combinations

[pf] *occurs medially in such English words as* hopeful *or* cupful. *In German this combination occurs in all positions, including initially*

Kopf	[kɔpf]
Schnupfen	[ˈʃnʊpfən]
Apfel	[ˈapfəl]
Pferd	[pfeːʀt]
Pfarrer	[ˈpfaʀəʀ]

[pf] *must be distinguished from* [f]

Pferd	fährt
Pfahl	fahl
Pfund	Fund
Pfarrer	Fahrer
Pfeil	feil
stopfen	Stoffen

[ʃst] *is a combination that does not occur in English*

täuschst	[tɔɪʃst]
wischst	[vɪʃst]
zischst	[tsɪʃst]
fischst	[fɪʃst]
mischst	[mɪʃst]

[tsv] *occurs initially in German, but not in English*

zwölf	[tsvœlf]
zwei	[tsvaɪ]
zwanzig	[ˈtsvantsɪç]
zwischen	[ˈtsvɪʃən]
Zweifel	[ˈtsvaɪfəl]

[kv] *occurs initially in German, but not in English*

Quittung	[ˈkvɪtuŋ]
Quelle	[ˈkvɛlə]
Qual	[kvɑːl]
quer	[kveːʀ]
bequem	[bəˈkveːm]

Glottal stop

In initial position in a syllable, German vowels are pronounced in three different ways:

1. With aspiration, which is indicated with the letter h: **h**eiß, **h**elfen, **h**at. This parallels English: *h*ot, *h*elp, *h*as (but not: hour, heir, honor).
2. With a smooth onset, which occurs when a vowel begins an unstressed syllable: seh **e**n, Podi **u**m. This parallels English: see *i*ng, the *a* ter.
3. With abrupt onset (glottal stop), which occurs when a vowel begins a stressed syllable: **a**lt, **Ei**nführung, **ü**ben. The smooth onset is applied in English even in initial position of stressed syllables, so that *an old ox* can sound like one word: *anoldox*. This should not happen in German. The expression **ein alter Ochse** should be spoken and heard as three words [aɪn ˈaltəʀ ˈɔksə] because the abrupt onset automatically separates the words. In English

the abrupt onset is used in such cases only if the speaker is being especially careful for one reason or another.

The abrupt onset in German is more common in the north than in the south of the German-speaking area.

Pronounce the following phrases in English and German, using the abrupt onset in the German only:

an old lady	splashes over
eine alte Frau	schwappt über
an accident	buy your ice cream
ein Unfall	kauf dein Eis
his Aunt Inge	
seine Tante Inge	

It is a good idea to exaggerate the contrast between the aspirated onset and the abrupt onset with glottal stop because meaning could depend on this contrast:

halt	'alt	hin	'in
Hans	'ans	Hund	'und
her	'er	Verhalten	ver'alten
heiß	'Eis		

AUDIOLINGUAL DRILLS

A. Directed Dialog

Fragen Sie, ob es nicht allzu schlimm ist!
Ist es nicht allzu schlimm?

Sagen Sie, daß es schlimm genug ist!
Es ist schlimm genug.

Fragen Sie, was die Frau am Kopf hat!
Was hat die Frau am Kopf?

Antworten Sie, daß sie eine Platzwunde am Kopf hat!
Sie hat eine Platzwunde am Kopf.

Fragen Sie, was sie auf der Stirn hat!
Was hat sie auf der Stirn?

Sagen Sie, daß sie noch den Angstschweiß auf der Stirn hat!
Sie hat noch den Angstschweiß auf der Stirn.

Fragen Sie, was dem rücksichtslosen Fahrer passiert ist!
Was ist dem rücksichtslosen Fahrer passiert?

Antworten Sie, daß dem rücksichtslosen Fahrer nichts passiert ist!
Dem rücksichtslosen Fahrer ist nichts passiert.

Fragen Sie, wie die Straße ist!
Wie ist die Straße?

Sagen Sie, daß dies eine ganz schlechte, rutschige Straße ist!
Dies ist eine ganz schlechte, rutschige Straße.

Fragen Sie, wann das meiste passiert!
Wann passiert das meiste?

Antworten Sie, daß nachts, wenn es regnet, das meiste passiert!
Nachts, wenn es regnet, passiert das meiste.

Fragen Sie, ob tagsüber nichts passiert!
Passiert tagsüber nichts?

Fragen Sie, ob der Streifenwagen um die Hausecke herumkommt!
Kommt der Streifenwagen um die Hausecke herum?

Sagen Sie, daß der Streifenwagen um die Hausecke herumkommt!
Der Streifenwagen kommt um die Hausecke herum.

Fragen Sie, ob Rolf das Blaulicht sieht!
Sieht Rolf das Blaulicht?

B. Numbers (*See Grammar* §6.3)

1 Begin each sentence with the new number and complete the problem:

Null und zwei ist zwei. **eins**
Eins und zwei ist drei. **zwei**
Zwei und zwei ist vier. **drei**
Drei und zwei ist fünf. **vier**
Vier und zwei ist sechs. **fünf**
Fünf und zwei ist sieben. **sechs**
Sechs und zwei ist acht. **sieben**
Sieben und zwei ist neun. **acht**

Acht und zwei ist zehn. **zehn**
Zehn und zwei ist zwölf. **elf**
Elf und zwei ist dreizehn. **fünfzehn**
Fünfzehn und zwei ist siebzehn. **sechzehn**
Sechzehn und zwei ist achtzehn. **achtzehn**
Achtzehn und zwei ist zwanzig. **zwanzig**
Zwanzig und zwei ist zweiundzwanzig.

2 Begin each sentence with the new number and complete the problem:

Ein mal zwei ist zwei.	**zwei**	Fünf mal zwei ist zehn.	**sieben**
Zwei mal zwei ist vier.	**drei**	Sieben mal zwei ist vierzehn.	**zehn**
Drei mal zwei ist sechs.	**vier**	Zehn mal zwei ist zwanzig.	**siebzehn**
Vier mal zwei ist acht.	**fünf**	Siebzehn mal zwei ist vierunddreißig.	

3 Begin each sentence with the new number and complete the problem:

Vier durch zwei ist zwei.	**sechs**	Sechsundzwanzig durch zwei ist dreizehn.	
Sechs durch zwei ist drei.	**acht**		**dreißig**
Acht durch zwei ist vier.	**zehn**	Dreißig durch zwei ist fünfzehn.	**sechzig**
Zehn durch zwei ist fünf.	**sechsundzwanzig**	Sechzig durch zwei ist dreißig.	

4 Begin each sentence with the new number and complete the problem:

Zwanzig weniger zwei ist achtzehn. **neunzehn**
Neunzehn weniger zwei ist siebzehn. **achtzehn**
Achtzehn weniger zwei ist sechzehn. **siebzehn**
Siebzehn weniger zwei ist fünfzehn. **sechzehn**
Sechzehn weniger zwei ist vierzehn. **drei**
Drei weniger zwei ist eins.

5 Substitute the ordinal form of the new number:

Heute ist der zehnte August. **neun**
Heute ist der neunte August. **sechs**
Heute ist der sechste August. **eins**
Heute ist der erste August. **drei**
Heute ist der dritte August. **sieben**
Heute ist der siebte August. **sechzehn**
Heute ist der sechzehnte August. **zwanzig**
Heute ist der zwanzigste August. **einundzwanzig**
Heute ist der einundzwanzigste August. **dreißig**
Heute ist der dreißigste August.

6 Substitute the ordinal form of the new number:

Er kommt am vierten August. **acht**
Er kommt am achten August. **zehn**
Er kommt am zehnten August. **elf**
Er kommt am elften August. **eins**
Er kommt am ersten August. **drei**
Er kommt am dritten August. **dreizehn**
Er kommt am dreizehnten August. **zwanzig**
Er kommt am zwanzigsten August.

C. Position of the Finite Verb (*See Grammar* §6.4)

7 Repeat the sentences with the adverbial element in first position. The finite verb must always be the second element.

Example:
Der Unfall ist am Schillerplatz.
Am Schillerplatz ist der Unfall.

Rolf läuft plötzlich.
Plötzlich läuft Rolf.

Die Milch schwappt über die Straße.
Über die Straße schwappt die Milch.

Eine alte Frau liegt da.
Da liegt eine alte Frau.

Das meiste passiert nachts.
Nachts passiert das meiste.

Der Streifenwagen kommt um die Ecke.
Um die Ecke kommt der Streifenwagen.

Ich glaube nicht daran.
Daran glaube ich nicht.

Heike steht auf dem Podium.
Auf dem Podium steht Heike.

8 Restate each sentence by beginning with **Wenn es regnet**, ... and placing the finite verb of the main clause right after **regnet**.

Example:
Das meiste passiert.
Wenn es regnet, passiert das meiste.

Die Straße ist schlimm.
Wenn es regnet, ist die Straße schlimm.

Der Wagen rutscht.
Wenn es regnet, rutscht der Wagen.

Die alte Kiste kippt um.
Wenn es regnet, kippt die alte Kiste um.

Professor Wolf kommt nicht.
Wenn es regnet, kommt Professor Wolf nicht.

Heike muß Geige üben.
Wenn es regnet, muß Heike Geige üben.

9 Restate each sentence by beginning with **Wenn die Sonne scheint**, ... and placing the finite verb of the main clause right after **scheint**:

Wir gehen zum Baden.
Wenn die Sonne scheint, gehen wir zum Baden.

Die Straße sieht gut aus.
Wenn die Sonne scheint, sieht die Straße gut aus.

Nuß-Eis schmeckt am besten.
Wenn die Sonne scheint, schmeckt Nuß-Eis am besten.

Ich bleibe hier.
Wenn die Sonne scheint, bleibe ich hier.

Professor Müller liest langweilig.
Wenn die Sonne scheint, liest Professor Müller langweilig.

D. Noun-Pronoun Agreement (*See Grammar* §5.3)

10   Answer the questions in the affirmative, using the correct pronoun subject:

Ist der Unfall schlimm?
Ja, er ist schlimm.

Sind Unfälle schlimm?
Ja, sie sind schlimm.

Ist die Kreuzung rutschig?
Ja, sie ist rutschig.

Ist das Blaulicht am Streifenwagen?
Ja, es ist am Streifenwagen.

Hat die Frau eine Platzwunde?
Ja, sie hat eine Platzwunde.

Sieht die Straße gut aus?
Ja, sie sieht gut aus.

11   Answer the questions in the negative, using the correct pronoun subject:

Ist der Unfall schlimm?
Nein, er ist nicht schlimm.

Sind die Vorlesungen gut?
Nein, sie sind nicht gut.

Ist das Kind tüchtig?
Nein, es ist nicht tüchtig.

Sieht die Frau gut aus?
Nein, sie sieht nicht gut aus.

Ist der Platz frei?
Nein, er ist nicht frei.

Ist die Platzwunde schlimm?
Nein, sie ist nicht schlimm.

Ist die Laterne da hinten?
Nein, sie ist nicht da hinten.

E. Questions and Answers

Was hat die Frau am Kopf?
Sie hat eine Platzwunde am Kopf.

Wie sieht die Straße aus?
Sie sieht gut aus.

Was hat sie noch auf der Stirn?
Sie hat noch den Angstschweiß auf der Stirn.

Ist der Fahrer rücksichtslos?
Nein, er ist nicht rücksichtslos.

Was ist dem Fahrer passiert?
Dem Fahrer ist nichts passiert.

Passiert das meiste tagsüber?
Nein, das meiste passiert nachts.

Was kommt um die Hausecke herum?
Der Streifenwagen kommt um die Hausecke herum.

Wo sind Rolf und Günther?
Sie sind am Schillerplatz.

GRAMMAR

6.1 Word-Formation

Compound nouns

die Angst fear, anxiety + **der Schweiß** sweat = **der Angstschweiß** cold sweat of fear
blau blue + **das Licht** light = **das Blaulicht** blue light
das Haus house, building + **die Ecke** corner = **die Hausecke** corner of the house, building
platz *from* **platzen** burst + **die Wunde** wound = **die Platzwunde** open wound, bad cut
streifen patrol + **der Wagen** car = **der Streifenwagen** patrol car, police car

6.2 Definite Articles of New Nouns

Masculine

der Angstschweiß
der August
der Dank
der Fahrer
der Gott
der Kopf
der Quatsch
der Schweiß
der Streifenwagen
der Unfall, *pl.* die Unfälle

Feminine

die Ecke
die Hausecke
die Milliarde
die Million
die Platzwunde
die Stelle
die Stirn
die Wunde

Neuter

das Blaulicht
das Haus
das Licht

6.3 Numbers

German, like English, makes use of two kinds of numbers: cardinal numbers, for counting things (*one, two, three*), and ordinal numbers, for designating one thing in a series (*first, second, third*). Since the German numbers are presented in the Supplement above, they will not be listed again here; we shall merely point out a few irregularities.

1. The stem **sieben** is reduced to **sieb-** in forming the various derivatives: **sieb-zehn**, **sieb-zig**, **sieb-te**.

2. The ordinal stems corresponding to **eins**, **drei**, and **acht** are **erst-**, **dritt**, and **acht-** respectively. In all other numbers from *two* through *nineteen* the ordinal suffix **-t-** is added to the cardinal stem: **vier-t-**, **neun-t-**, **dreizehn-t-**. From *twenty* on up, the ordinal suffix is **-st-**: **zwanzig-st-**, **vierunddreißig-st-**, **hundert-st-**.

3. Notice how the pronunciation changes in the following:

[ks] in **sechs** [zɛks] and **sechste** [ˈzɛkstə], but [ç] in **sechzehn** [ˈzɛçtseːn] and **sechzig** [ˈzɛçtsɪç]

[iː] in **vier** [fiːʀ] and **vierte** [ˈfiːʀtə], but [ɪ] in **vierzehn** [ˈfɪʀtseːn] and **vierzig** [ˈfɪʀtsɪç]

6.4 More on the Position of the Finite Verb

The finite verb in German may stand in one of three positions. It stands in first position in yes-no questions and in commands:

 Siehst du das Blaulicht?

 Kauf dein Eis, mein Kind!

 Warten Sie nur ab!

It stands last in dependent clauses:

Siehst du nicht, wie schön die Sonne scheint ?

Nachts, wenn es regnet , passiert das meiste.

Fragen Sie, warum er plötzlich läuft !

Tante Inge sagt, daß Hans Nuß-Eis kaufen kann

It stands in second position in word questions and statements:

Was boxed(läufst) du denn plötzlich?

Wo boxed(ist) die alte Frau?

Was boxed(tust) du heute nachmittag?

Sie boxed(hat) noch den Angstschweiß auf der Stirn.

Du boxed(wohnst) ja hier.

Die älteren Studenten boxed(haben) viel Erfahrung.

In an independent statement the first element may be the subject, as in the last three examples above. But an independent statement may also begin with some element other than the subject; the finite verb remains in second position, and the subject then follows the finite verb:

Das boxed(möchte) ich auch.

Dem rücksichtslosen Fahrer boxed(ist) nichts passiert.

Da boxed(kommt) Professor Wolf.

Eigentlich boxed(kann) es nun losgehen.

Dann boxed(bleibe) ich hier.

Wenn es regnet, boxed(passiert) das meiste.

The first element may thus be a direct object (**das**), an indirect object (**dem rücksichtslosen Fahrer**), an adverb (**da**, **eigentlich**, **dann**), or even a dependent clause (**wenn es regnet**).

Recall that words like **danke**, **nein**, **ja** and coordinating conjunctions such as **aber** and **und** do not count as sentence elements, and accordingly have no effect on the position of the finite verb in a following clause:

Danke, dann boxed(bleibe) ich hier.

Ja, ich boxed(warte) darauf.

Aber ich boxed(glaube) daran.

Und dem rücksichtslosen Fahrer boxed(ist) nichts passiert.

The movability of sentence elements like subjects, objects, adverbs, and to an extent dependent clauses makes it possible to vary a German sentence considerably without changing its basic structure. As long as the finite verb is in second position and the first element is not a question-word, a statement remains a statement. The following sentences are merely variations of a single pattern; they share the same structure and are all statements:

1. Ich $\boxed{\text{gehe}}$ heute mit Uwe zum Baden.

2. Heute $\boxed{\text{gehe}}$ ich mit Uwe zum Baden.

3. Mit Uwe $\boxed{\text{gehe}}$ ich heute zum Baden.

4. Zum Baden $\boxed{\text{gehe}}$ ich heute mit Uwe.

In spite of the fact that these sentences have the same basic structure, however, they all have different meanings. The differences arise not through structural changes, as would be the case if we were to change the position of the finite verb, but rather through a shifting of emphasis or focus of attention.

1 The first sentence:

Ich gehe heute mit Uwe zum Baden.

has what we may call a "neutral" arrangement of elements: subject, finite verb, and then the remaining elements. The main stress in the sentence falls on the first syllable of the word **Baden**. The sentence may be regarded as an answer to the question: **Was tust du heute?**

2 If the speaker wishes to focus attention on some particular element in the sentence, then he may place that element in first position and shift the main sentence stress to it. The subject then goes after the finite verb. Thus the second sentence:

Heute gehe ich mit Uwe zum Baden.

with main stress on **heute**, clearly contrasts the time *today* with other times like *tomorrow, day after tomorrow,* etc. It answers the question: **Wann gehst du mit Uwe zum Baden?**

3 The third sentence:

Mit Uwe gehe ich heute zum Baden.

with main stress on **Uwe**, focuses attention on Uwe as against other people with whom one might have gone swimming. It answers the question: **Mit wem** (with whom) **gehst du heute zum Baden?**

4 The last sentence:

Zum Baden gehe ich heute mit Uwe.

with stress on **Baden**, answers the question: **Wohin gehst du heute mit Uwe?** It contrasts *swimming* with other possible activities.

6.5 Notes on Adjectives

The declension of descriptive adjectives will be treated in full in Unit 18. A few adjectives are used earlier, usually in the nominative case. The following rules apply:

1. A predicate adjective never has an ending added:

   Es ist heiß.
   Du bist nett.
   Der Platz hier ist frei.
   Der Milchmann ist versichert.
   Die Sache ist ernst.

2. When a descriptive adjective precedes a noun, it always has an ending. In the nominative singular, an adjective used with a **der**-word or with an inflected **ein**-word ends in **-e**. **Der, die, das; dieser, diese, dieses; jener, jene, jenes**, etc. are **der**-words. **Eine, meine, keine**, etc. are inflected **ein**-words; that is, they have the ending **-e** added to the basic form:

   der alt **e** Professor Wolf
   die alt **e** Kiste
   das klein **e** Kind
   der ganz **e** Salat
   die ganz **e** Milch
   eine hübsch **e** Sache
   eine ganz schlecht **e**, rutschig **e** Straße

WRITING

A. The Comma

In Unit 4 (Writing §A) you saw that a comma is used in German to separate a main clause from a dependent clause and that the boundary between two such clauses is normally not marked by a pause in speech. The comma is thus not associated with a pause in:

Wenn es regnet, passiert das meiste.
Wenn die Sonne scheint, gehen wir zum Baden.
Wenn du nett bist, kannst du Eis kaufen.

In these examples the dependent clause precedes the main clause. The dependent clause may also follow the main clause, however, in which case the above remarks still apply:

Das meiste passiert, wenn es regnet.
Wir gehen zum Baden, wenn die Sonne scheint.
Du kannst Eis kaufen, wenn du nett bist.

A third possibility is that the dependent clause may occur embedded within the main clause. Such embedded dependent clauses are preceded and followed by commas. A pause is normally associated with the second (following) comma, but not with the first (preceding):

Nachts, wenn es regnet, passiert das meiste.
Wir gehen, wenn die Sonne scheint, zum Baden.

B. Writing Practice: Punctuation

Copy the sentences and insert commas, periods, and question marks:

1. Wenn es regnet gehen wir nicht zum Baden
2. Sagt er daß die Sonne scheint
3. Du kannst mitkommen wenn du nett bist
4. Du mußt es wissen wenn du hier wohnst
5. Nachts wenn es regnet bleiben wir hier
6. Wenn die Sonne scheint sieht die Straße gut aus
7. Tagsüber passiert das meiste
8. Tagsüber wenn es heiß ist gehen wir zum Baden

C. Writing Practice: Finite Verb Position

Write sentences to answer the following questions. Place the suggested answer in first position for emphasis. Also, change the noun subject to the corresponding pronoun:

1. Wann kippt die alte Kiste um?   Jetzt
2. Wo liegt der ganze Salat?   Auf der Straße
3. Wo liegt die alte Frau?   Bei der Laterne
4. Wann passiert das meiste?   Nachts
5. Wo wohnen Herr und Frau Schneider?   Hier
6. Wo ist der Unfall?   Am Schillerplatz
7. Wann geht Inge zum Baden?   Wenn die Sonne scheint
8. Wann kann Hans Nuß-Eis kaufen?   Wenn es heiß ist

D. Writing Practice: Dependent Clauses

Rewrite the sentences as dependent clauses after the given introductory phrase:

1. Er sieht nichts.   Er sagt, daß _____.
2. Kannst du sehen?   Er fragt, ob _____.
3. Der Wagen rutscht plötzlich.   Er sagt, daß _____.

4 Warum läuft Rolf so schnell? Sie fragt, warum _____.
5 Ist die Sache ernst? Sie fragt, ob _____.
6 Was hat die alte Frau am Kopf? Wir fragen, was _____.
7 Dies ist eine rutschige Straße. Er sagt, daß _____.
8 Heike möchte zum Baden gehen. Sie sagen, daß _____.
9 Kann Hans Eis kaufen? Sie fragt, ob _____.
10 Es kann jetzt losgehen. Sie sagt, daß _____.

E. Writing Practice: Numbers

Write out the following expressions in German:

1 $3 + 3 = 6$
2 $10 \div 2 = 5$
3 $7 \times 4 = 28$
4 $32 - 12 = 20$
5 $13 + 17 = 30$
6 $24 \div 12 = 2$
7 $1 \times 1 = 1$
8 $1 - 1 = 0$
9 $8 + 3 = 11$
10 $7 \times 10 = 70$

LISTENING PRACTICE

Listen to the taped exercises; then answer the following questions.

A. Ein Unfall

1 Wo ist der Streifenwagen?
2 Was ist passiert?
3 Ist die Sache ernst?
4 Was ist ein Krankenwagen?

B. Fräulein Schneider und Herr Held

1 Was fragt Fräulein Schneider?
2 Ist dies Fräulein Schneiders erste Vorlesung?
3 Was kann Herr Held tun?

Unit 7

Albrecht Dürer

DIALOG

In der Stadtbahn (Anfang)

1 **Ilse:** Wo bist du, Peter, der Zug kommt!

2 **Peter:** Hier, ich kaufe noch schnell eine Zeitung.

3 **Ilse:** Ist das so eilig? Es steht doch immer dasselbe darin.

4 **Peter:** Ich bitte dich, wie kannst du so etwas sagen!

5 **Ilse:** Ich empfinde es jedenfalls so.

On the Commuter Train (Beginning)

die Stadtbahn (der Stadtbahn *dat.***) die Stadt** city + **die Bahn** railway; road; track, course

1 Where are you, Peter? The train is coming!

2 Here. I'm buying a newspaper quickly before we go.

kaufen (ich kaufe) · **noch** still, yet; *in this context* before we go · **die Zeitung**

3 Is that so urgent? There's always the same thing in it anyway.

eilig urgent; quick · **stehen (es steht** there is, there stands) stand · **doch** anyway, after all · **darin = da + r + in**

4 Please! How can you say such a thing!

bitten (ich bitte) ask, request · **so** so, thus **etwas** something; somewhat; some **so etwas** such a thing, something like that

5 Anyway, that's how I feel.

empfinden (ich empfinde) feel, perceive · **jedenfalls** anyway, in any case

6 **Peter:** Du hast eben nicht genug Interesse an Tagesfragen.

7 **Ilse:** Das kann schon sein. Ist das so schlimm?

8 **Peter:** Vielleicht, ich erkläre dir das mal.

9 **Ilse:** Aber nicht jetzt, hier läuft nämlich unser Zug ein.

10 **Peter:** Schon gut, steigen wir ein!

(Fortsetzung folgt)

SUPPLEMENT

Present tense of glauben, empfinden, and lesen

The verb **glauben**:

Ich glaube nicht daran.
Du glaubst nicht daran.
Er glaubt nicht daran.
Sie glaubt nicht daran.
Es glaubt nicht daran.

Wir glauben nicht daran.
Ihr glaubt nicht daran.
Sie glauben nicht daran.
Glauben Sie nicht daran, Herr Held?

The verb **empfinden** with a vowel sound after the stem in all forms:

Ich empfinde es auch so.
Du empfindest es auch so.
Er empfindet es auch so.
Sie empfindet es auch so.
Es empfindet es auch so.

Wir empfinden es auch so.
Ihr empfindet es auch so.
Sie empfinden es auch so.
Empfinden Sie es auch so, Professor Wolf?

6	You just don't have enough interest in current events.	**das Interesse · die Tagesfrage,** *pl.* **die Tagesfragen der Tag** day + **die Frage** question
7	That may be, all right. Is that so bad?	**schon** already; all right
8	Perhaps. I'll explain it to you sometime.	**erklären (ich erkläre)** explain · **du** (*dir dat.*) · **mal** once, sometime; just
9	But not now. You see, our train is pulling in.	**einlaufen (er läuft ... ein)** come in, arrive · **nämlich** you see; that is to say; namely
10	All right, let's get on.	**einsteigen (steigen wir ... ein** *imper.***)** get on

(To be continued)

The verb **lesen** with changes in **du liest** and **er, sie, es liest**:

Ich lese häufig die Zeitung.
Du liest häufig die Zeitung.
Er liest häufig die Zeitung.
Sie liest häufig die Zeitung.
Es liest häufig die Zeitung.
Wir lesen häufig die Zeitung.
Ihr lest häufig die Zeitung.
Sie lesen häufig die Zeitung.
Lesen Sie häufig die Zeitung, Herr Professor?

Telling time

1	(6.00 Uhr)	Es ist sechs Uhr.	1		It's six o'clock.
2	(6.05 Uhr)	Es ist fünf Minuten nach sechs.	2		It's five minutes after six.
3		Es ist fünf nach sechs.	3		It's five after six.
4		Es ist sechs Uhr fünf.	4		It's six five.
5	(6.15 Uhr)	Es ist fünfzehn Minuten nach sechs.	5		It's fifteen minutes after six.
6		Es ist fünfzehn nach sechs.	6		It's fifteen after six.
7		Es ist sechs Uhr fünfzehn.	7		It's six fifteen.
8		Es ist viertel nach sechs.	8		It's a quarter after six.
9		Es ist viertel sieben.	9		(It's a quarter of the way to seven.)
10	(6.30 Uhr)	Es ist sechs Uhr dreißig.	10		It's six thirty.
11		Es ist halb sieben.	11		(It's half the way to seven.)
12	(6.35 Uhr)	Es ist sechs Uhr fünfunddreißig.	12		It's six thirty-five.
13		Es ist fünfundzwanzig Minuten vor sieben.	13		It's twenty-five minutes to seven.
14		Es ist fünf nach halb sieben.	14		(It's five after half the way to seven.)
15	(6.45 Uhr)	Es ist sechs Uhr fünfundvierzig.	15		It's six forty-five.
16		Es ist viertel vor sieben.	16		It's a quarter to seven.
17		Es ist dreiviertel sieben.	17		(It's three quarters of the way to seven.)

Uhr o'clock   **die Uhr** clock, watch

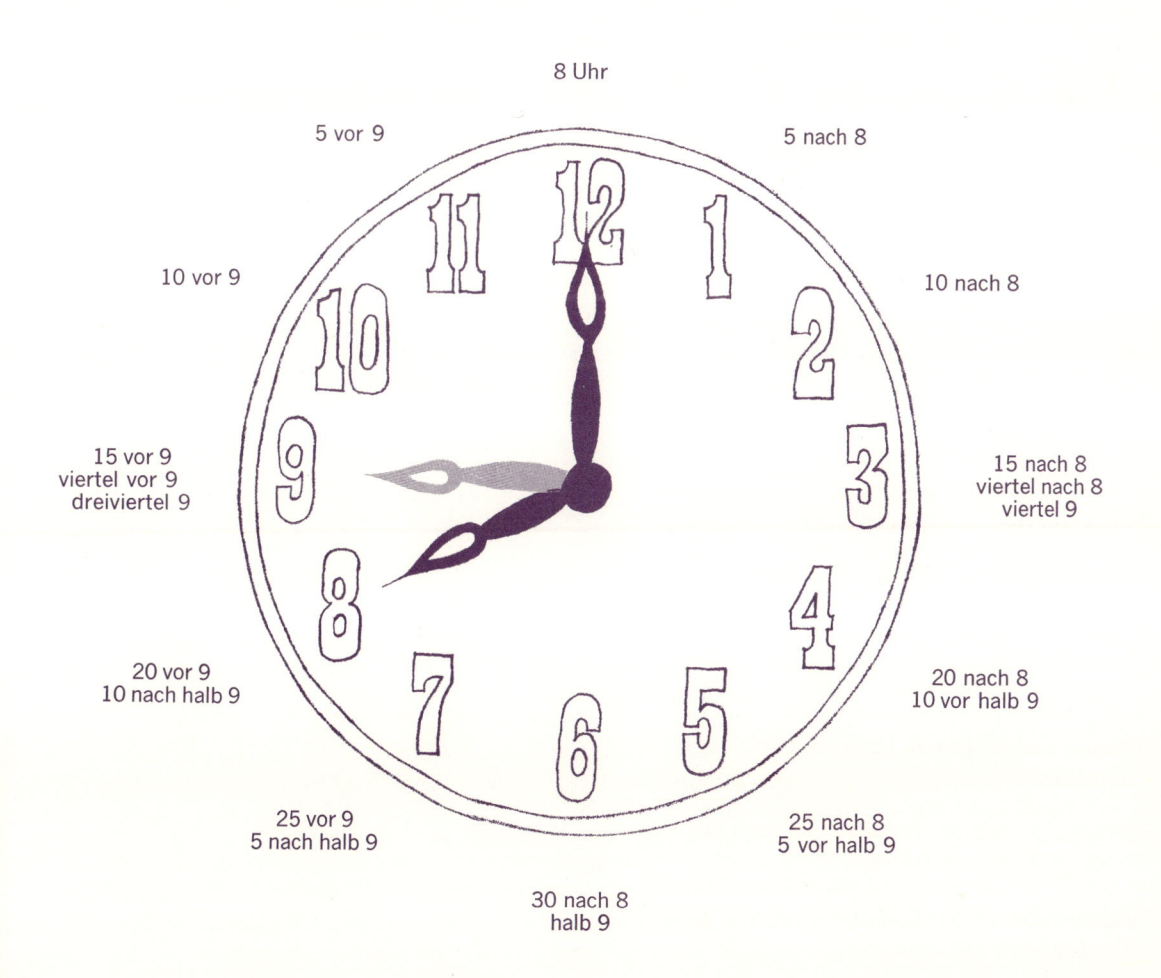

8 Uhr

5 vor 9   5 nach 8

10 vor 9   10 nach 8

15 vor 9   15 nach 8
viertel vor 9   viertel nach 8
dreiviertel 9   viertel 9

20 vor 9   20 nach 8
10 nach halb 9   10 vor halb 9

25 vor 9   25 nach 8
5 nach halb 9   5 vor halb 9

30 nach 8
halb 9

AUDIOLINGUAL DRILLS

A. Directed Dialog

Fragen Sie, worauf Ilse und Peter warten!
Worauf warten Ilse und Peter?

Antworten Sie, daß sie auf den Zug warten!
Sie warten auf den Zug.

Sagen Sie, daß der Zug kommt!
Der Zug kommt.

Fragen Sie, was Peter noch schnell kauft!
Was kauft Peter noch schnell?

Sagen Sie, daß er noch schnell eine Zeitung kauft!
Er kauft noch schnell eine Zeitung.

Fragen Sie, ob das so eilig ist!
Ist das so eilig?

Fragen Sie, wie Ilse so etwas sagen kann!
Wie kann Ilse so etwas sagen?

Sagen Sie, daß sie es jedenfalls so empfindet!
Sie empfindet es jedenfalls so.

Sagen Sie, daß sie eben nicht genug Interesse an Tagesfragen hat!
Sie hat eben nicht genug Interesse an Tagesfragen.

Fragen Sie, ob das so schlimm ist!
Ist das so schlimm?

Sagen Sie, daß es vielleicht schlimm ist!
Es ist vielleicht schlimm.

Sagen Sie, daß der Zug jetzt einläuft!
Der Zug läuft jetzt ein.

Fragen Sie, ob Ilse und Peter einsteigen!
Steigen Ilse und Peter ein?

Sagen Sie, daß sie schnell einsteigen!
Sie steigen schnell ein.

B. Present Tense Verb Forms (See Grammar §7.3)

Substitute the new subject and change the verb form accordingly:

1 The verb **kaufen** *buy*:

Ich kaufe nie Nuß-Eis.   **wir**
Wir kaufen nie Nuß-Eis.   **du**
Du kaufst nie Nuß-Eis.   **ihr**
Ihr kauft nie Nuß-Eis.   **die Studenten**

Die Studenten kaufen nie Nuß-Eis.   **er**
Er kauft nie Nuß-Eis.   **das Kind**
Das Kind kauft nie Nuß-Eis.   **ich**
Ich kaufe nie Nuß-Eis.

2 The verb **warten** *wait* with a vowel sound after the stem in all forms:

Mein Bruder wartet auch darauf.   **du**
Du wartest auch darauf.   **Hans und Inge**
Hans und Inge warten auch darauf.   **der Eismann**
Der Eismann wartet auch darauf.   **wir**
Wir warten auch darauf.   **ihr**
Ihr wartet auch darauf.   **ich**
Ich warte auch darauf.   **die Frau**
Die Frau wartet auch darauf.

3 The verb **lesen** *read* with changes in **du liest** and **er, sie, es liest**:

Wir lesen die Zeitung.   **Peter**
Peter liest die Zeitung.   **ihr**
Ihr lest die Zeitung.   **ich**
Ich lese die Zeitung.   **Hans und Heike**

Hans und Heike lesen die Zeitung.   **du**
Du liest die Zeitung.   **Ilse**
Ilse liest die Zeitung.   **wir**
Wir lesen die Zeitung.

C. Dependent Clauses (See Grammar §7.4)

4 Change the independent clauses to dependent clauses by introducing them with **Er sagt, daß** . . . .

Example:
Es ist heiß.
Er sagt, daß es heiß ist.

Hans kauft Nuß-Eis.
Er sagt, daß Hans Nuß-Eis kauft.

Uwe geht zum Baden.
Er sagt, daß Uwe zum Baden geht.

Aller Anfang ist schwer.
Er sagt, daß aller Anfang schwer ist.

Er glaubt daran.
Er sagt, daß er daran glaubt.

Professor Müller liest langweilig.
Er sagt, daß Professor Müller langweilig liest.

Die Frau liegt auf der Straße.
Er sagt, daß die Frau auf der Straße liegt.

Peter kauft eine Zeitung.
Er sagt, daß Peter eine Zeitung kauft.

Immer dasselbe steht darin.
Er sagt, daß immer dasselbe darin steht.

Dies ist eine schlechte Straße.
Er sagt, daß dies eine schlechte Straße ist.

Du hast kein Interesse an Tagesfragen.
Er sagt, daß du kein Interesse an Tagesfragen hast.

D. Separable Prefixes (*See Grammar* §7.5)

5 Change the following sentences to direct questions by dropping **Sie fragt, ob** . . . .

Example:
Sie fragt, ob es jetzt losgeht.
Geht es jetzt los?

Sie fragt, ob der Milchwagen umkippt.
Kippt der Milchwagen um?

Sie fragt, ob die Straße schlimm aussieht.
Sieht die Straße schlimm aus?

Sie fragt, ob der Zug hier einläuft.
Läuft der Zug hier ein?

Sie fragt, ob Peter nun einsteigt.
Steigt Peter nun ein?

Sie fragt, ob Fräulein Schneider noch abwartet.
Wartet Fräulein Schneider noch ab?

Sie fragt, ob Heike heute mitkommt.
Kommt Heike heute mit?

6 Change the sentences to direct questions by dropping the introductory phrase and beginning with the question-word.

Example:
Hans fragt, wann es losgeht.
Wann geht es los?

Günther fragt, warum der Milchwagen umkippt.
Warum kippt der Milchwagen um?

Rolf fragt, wie die Platzwunde aussieht.
Wie sieht die Platzwunde aus?

Herr Held fragt, wann der Zug einläuft.
Wann läuft der Zug ein?

Die Frau fragt, wo Herr Hartmann einsteigt.
Wo steigt Herr Hartmann ein?

Tante Inge fragt, warum du einsteigst.
Warum steigst du ein?

Uwe fragt, warum Heike nicht mitkommt.
Warum kommt Heike nicht mit?

7 Change the questions to dependent clauses by beginning with **Wir fragen,** . . . .

Example:
Wann geht es los?
Wir fragen, wann es losgeht.

Warum kippt der Milchwagen um?
Wir fragen, warum der Milchwagen umkippt.

Wie sieht die Straße aus?
Wir fragen, wie die Straße aussieht.

Wann läuft der Zug ein?
Wir fragen, wann der Zug einläuft.

Warum kommt Heike nicht mit?
Wir fragen, warum Heike nicht mitkommt.

Wo steigst du ein?
Wir fragen, wo du einsteigst.

Warum wartet Fräulein Schneider noch ab?
Wir fragen, warum Fräulein Schneider noch abwartet.

E. Noun-Pronoun Agreement (*See Grammar* §5.3)

8 Answer in the affirmative and change the noun subject to a pronoun:

Läuft unser Zug jetzt ein?
Ja, er läuft jetzt ein.

Ist die Zeitung alt?
Ja, sie ist alt.

Sind die Tagesfragen ernst?
Ja, sie sind ernst.

Kommt der Streifenwagen um die Hausecke herum?
Ja, er kommt um die Hausecke herum.

9 Answer in the negative and change the noun subject to a pronoun:

Ist die Stadtbahn da hinten?
Nein, sie ist nicht da hinten.

Steigen Herr und Frau Hartmann ein?
Nein, sie steigen nicht ein.

Sieht der Unfall schlimm aus?
Nein, er sieht nicht schlimm aus.

Ist das Blaulicht hübsch?
Nein, es ist nicht hübsch.

F. Questions and Answers

Worauf warten Ilse und Peter?
Sie warten auf den Zug.

Was macht Peter noch schnell?
Er kauft noch schnell eine Zeitung.

Was fragt Ilse?
Sie fragt, ob das so eilig ist.

Was sagt sie über die Zeitung?
Sie sagt, es steht immer dasselbe darin.

Was sagt Peter über Ilse?
Er sagt, sie hat nicht genug Interesse an Tagesfragen.

Was fragt Ilse nun?
Sie fragt, ob das so schlimm ist.

Was läuft jetzt ein?
Der Zug läuft jetzt ein.

Was tun Ilse und Peter dann?
Sie steigen dann ein.

GRAMMAR

7.1 Word-Formation

Compound nouns

die Stadt city + **die Bahn** railway; road; track, course = **die Stadtbahn** commuter train
der Tag day + **die Frage** question = **die Tagesfrage** current issue

7.2 Definite Articles of New Nouns

Masculine

der Tag
der Zug

Feminine

die Bahn
die Frage
die Minute, *pl.* die Minuten
die Stadt
die Stadtbahn
die Tagesfrage, *pl.* die Tagesfragen
die Zeitung

Neuter

das Interesse

7.3 The Present Tense

Present tense verb forms

1. The present tense forms of German verbs are made by adding personal endings to the verb stem. Most German verbs take the following endings:

	Singular	Plural
1st person	e	en
2nd person	st	t
3rd person	t	en
2nd person standard		en

Thus the verb **sagen** *say* has the present tense forms:

    ich sage   wir sagen
    du sagst   ihr sagt
er, sie, es sagt   sie, Sie sagen

2. If the verb stem ends in **d** or **t**, then an **e** [ə] is inserted between the stem and the endings **-st** and **-t**:

    ich wart e   wir wart en
    du wart e st   ihr wart e t
er, sie, es wart e t   sie, Sie wart en

This **e** [ə] is also inserted between the stem and the endings **-st** and **-t** if the stem ends in a combination of a stop or fricative plus **m** or **n**:

regnen *rain*   es regnet
atmen *breathe* du atmest
öffnen *open*   ihr öffnet
zeichnen *draw* er zeichnet

If the stem ends in [s] or [z] (spellings: **s, ss, ß, z**), then the 2nd person singular ending is **-t** instead of **-st**:

du lies t
du muß t
du iß t

If the verb stem ends in **ss** (**müssen, essen**), the spelling becomes **ß** before the consonant **t**.

3. The stem vowel of the verb **lesen** *read* changes in the 2nd and 3rd persons singular; the forms are:

    ich lese   wir lesen
    du l ie st   ihr lest
er, sie, es l ie st sie, Sie lesen

There are other verbs that have similar changes. The changes are not predictable — i.e. you can't tell by looking at the infinitive whether a verb has a vowel change — so you have to learn them as individual items. Along with **lesen** *read* remember the forms **du liest**, **er liest**.

Uses of present tense

The present tense in German has a range of functions that overlap but do not completely coincide with those of the English present tense.

1 The present tense is commonly used in German, as in English, to indicate the immediate present time:

   Da kommt der Streifenwagen um die Hausecke herum.
   There comes the patrol car around the corner of the building.

   Hier läuft unser Zug ein.
   Our train is pulling in here.

   Es geht endlich los.
   It's finally starting.

2 The German present tense is often used with reference to future time, just as the English present progressive may be used with future meaning. This is much more common in German, however, than in English.

   Was tust du denn heute nachmittag?
   Tell me, what are you doing (going to do) this afternoon?

   Ich gehe zum Baden.
   I'm going (going to go) swimming.

   Wann bist du bei uns?
   When will you be at our place?

3 The present tense is used in both languages in a timeless sense, that is, to state a fact or opinion that has no temporal limitation:

   Mutti ißt nie Eis.
   Mommy never eats ice cream.

   Es steht doch immer dasselbe darin.
   There's always the same thing in it anyway.

   Zwei und zwei ist vier.
   Two and two are four.

4 The present tense may be used in German to indicate that an action or condition began in the past and is still going on in the present. The meaning is equivalent to that of the English present

or present perfect progressive. In this function, the verb is modified by an adverb or adverbial phrase that points back into past time, often with **schon**. In Unit 16 this will be treated in greater detail.

Ich kenne Sie schon lange.
I have known you for a long time.

Er wohnt schon seit dem zweiundzwanzigsten August hier.
He's been living here since the twenty-second of August.

5   Most English verbs may undergo certain modifications in the present tense. Among these modifications are the *emphatic* modification with *do*, *does* plus an infinitive, and the *progressive* modification with *am*, *is*, *are* plus a verb with the suffix *-ing*. There are other possible modifications, but right now we are concerned with these two only.

No modification   The train comes at five.

Emphatic   The train does come at five.

Progressive   The train is coming at five.

Most English verbs actually require such modification when they are used in questions or in negative expressions:

 Is the train coming at five?

 Does the train come at five?

(*but not:* Comes the train at five?)

The train is n't coming at five.

The train does n't come at five.

(*but not:* The train comes n't at five.)

German verbs have no such emphatic or progressive modification. There is no special German verb construction similar to *is coming* or *does come*; or, to put it differently, the three English forms *comes, is coming, does come* are all equivalent to the one German verb form **kommt**:

The train comes at five.
The train is coming at five. ⟶ Der Zug kommt um fünf.
The train does come at five.

Is the train coming at five? ⟶ Kommt der Zug um fünf?
Does the train come at five?

The train isn't coming at five. ⟶ Der Zug kommt nicht um fünf.
The train doesn't come at five.

7.4 Dependent Clauses

A dependent clause in German has been defined (Grammar §3.2) as a clause in which the first word is a subordinating conjunction, a question-word, or a relative pronoun, *and* the finite verb is in last position. Such clauses are "dependent" in the sense that they usually modify some word in an adjacent main clause (**wenn es regnet** modifies **nachts** in: **Nachts, wenn es regnet, passiert das meiste**), or they fulfill some vital grammatical function within the main clause itself (**daß es heiß ist** is the direct object of **sagt** in: **Hans sagt, daß es heiß ist**).

Recall that a German verb phrase may be a two-part construction consisting of (1) a finite verb plus (2) an associated element such as an infinitive, a predicate adjective, a predicate noun, or certain adverbial expressions (Grammar §2.2). In a main clause the associated element stands in last position:

Hans kann Eis **kaufen**.   Kommt das Mädchen **mit**?
Die Sache ist nicht allzu **schlimm**.

In a dependent clause, however, the finite verb occupies last position; it therefore follows an associated element:

... daß Hans Eis **kaufen kann**.   ... daß das Mädchen **mitkommt**.
... daß die Sache nicht allzu **schlimm ist**.

7.5 Verb Prefixes

There are two kinds of verb prefixes in German: unstressed prefixes and stressed prefixes.

Unstressed	*Stressed*
be'ginnen	'mitkommen
emp'finden	'aussehen
ent'schuldigen	'einlaufen
er'klären	'umkippen

Stressed (separable) prefixes

Under certain conditions, stressed prefixes become separated from the stem of the verb; this property has earned for them the name *separable prefixes*. Separable — i.e. stressed — prefixes are included among the associated elements mentioned above, together with infinitives, predicate adjectives, etc., and stand at the end of a main clause. A verb together with its separable prefix is therefore to be regarded as a two-part phrase (finite verb plus associated element) rather than as a single word that sometimes comes apart. All this leads us to observe that the last position in a main clause is reserved for:

1. Predicate adjectives
2. Predicate nouns
3. Infinitives
4. Separable prefixes

As examples of the latter we have:

Heike kommt heute nachmittag **mit**.
Die Straße sieht gut **aus**.

Der Zug läuft jetzt **ein**.
Jetzt kippt die alte Kiste **um**.

If the verb should occur as an infinitive, then the infinitive stands in last position and is attached to the separable prefix:

Heike möchte heute nachmittag **mitkommen**.
Die Straße soll gut **aussehen**.

Der Zug muß jetzt **einlaufen**.
Jetzt kann die alte Kiste **umkippen**.

If the clause is a dependent one, then the finite verb stands in last position and is attached to the separable prefix:

Hans sagt, daß Heike heute nachmittag **mitkommt**.
Peter sagt, daß die Straße gut **aussieht**.

Ilse sagt, daß der Zug jetzt **einläuft**.
Günther sagt, daß die alte Kiste **umkippt**.

To summarize:

If the verb is in first position or in second position, then the separable prefix is separated from the verb stem and stands in last position.

If the verb stands in last position, then the separable prefix is attached to the verb stem, and they stand together at the end of the clause.

Unstressed (inseparable) prefixes

Unstressed prefixes are never separated from their verb stems, regardless of where the verb stands; for this reason they are called *inseparable* prefixes.

Die Vorlesung **beginnt** jetzt.
Die Vorlesung soll jetzt **beginnen**.
Fragen Sie, ob die Vorlesung jetzt **beginnt**.

Ich **empfinde** es jedenfalls so.
Ich muß es jedenfalls so **empfinden**.
Ich sage, daß ich es jedenfalls so **empfinde**.

7.6 Telling Time

The German word corresponding to *o'clock* is **Uhr**. Thus:

Es ist zwei **Uhr**.
It's two *o'clock*.

Ist es schon ein **Uhr**?
Is it one *o'clock* already?

Just as the word *o'clock* is often omitted in English, so may the German word **Uhr** be left unexpressed. Note, however, that **ein Uhr** *one o'clock* then becomes **eins** *one* (not **ein**):

Es ist schon eins.
It's already one.

Ist es schon zwölf?
Is it already twelve?

The number of minutes *after* the hour is expressed with the preposition **nach**. The number of minutes *before* or *to* the hour is expressed with **vor**. The word **Minuten** *minutes* is often omitted, as in English.

zehn **vor** acht
zehn Minuten **vor** acht ⟶ ten (minutes) *to* eight
zehn Minuten **vor** acht Uhr

zwanzig **nach** drei
zwanzig Minuten **nach** drei ⟶ twenty (minutes) *after* three
zwanzig Minuten **nach** drei Uhr

drei Uhr zwanzig   three twenty

When we refer to *half hours* in English, we use the preceding hour as the point of reference:

6:30   *six* thirty (thirty minutes past the hour of six)

In German the point of reference is the following full hour:

6.30   halb **sieben** (halfway to the hour of seven)

Similarly:

6.45   dreiviertel **sieben** (three quarters of the way to the hour of seven)
9.15   viertel **zehn** (one quarter of the way to the hour of ten)

WRITING

A. Word Copying

The common written representations of German sounds are given in the exercises that follow. Additional spellings can occur, however, especially in words of foreign origin. Copy the words in boldface. Note that all nouns are capitalized.

1   The sound [s] is represented in spelling by **s**, **ss**, or **ß**:

Es ist heiß.
Du kannst Eis kaufen.
Nuß-Eis, bitte.

Was tust du denn?
Du mußt es wissen.
Was ist passiert?

2   The sound [aɪ] is represented chiefly by **ei** in spelling:

Hans und **seine** Tante Inge.
Es ist **heiß**.
Du kannst **Eis** kaufen.

Das ist **fein**.
Meinst du?
Kauf **dein Eis**!

3 The sound [i:] is represented in spelling chiefly by **i**, **ie**, **ih**, and **ieh**. Note that standard forms of address (**Sie**, **Ihr**, **Ihnen**) are capitalized:

Mutti nimmt **nie** Eis.
Die Sonne scheint.
Warten **Sie** nur ab!

Ist das **Ihr** Ernst?
Da kann er **Ihnen** helfen.
Na, **siehst** du?

4 The sound [ɪ] is almost always represented by **i** followed by two or more consonants. A few short words like **mit**, **hin**, **in**, **im** are exceptions to the two-consonant rule:

Es **ist** heiß, Tante **Inge**.
Du **bist** nett.
Ist Eis denn **Gift**?

Nuß-Eis, **bitte**.
Nimmst du kein Eis?
Komm **mit**!

5 The sound [t] is represented chiefly by **t**, **tt**, **dt** and by **d** when this letter is final in a word or syllable:

Du **bist nett**.
Nuß-Eis, **bitte**.
In der **Stadtbahn**.

Kauf dein Eis, mein **Kind**!
Hans **und** seine **Tante** Inge.
Es **geht endlich** los.

6 The sound [v] is represented chiefly by **w**:

Was nimmst du?
Wie geht's?
Wann bist du bei uns?

Wo ist Heike?
Wohin geht **Uwe**?
Der alte Professor **Wolf**.

7 The sound [ʃ] is represented by **sch** and by **s** when the **s** is followed by **t** or **p** in initial position in a stressed syllable:

Das **schmeckt** am besten.
Das **stimmt**.
Heute **bestimmt**.

Es ist **Spaß**.
Uwe **spottet**.
Wo **steht** Heike **schon**?

8 The sound [j] is represented chiefly by **j**:

Du wohnst **ja** hier.
Ilse empfindet es **jedenfalls** so.
Jedenfalls stimmt das.

Er kippt **jetzt** um.
Er studiert **Jurisprudenz**.
Ja, mein **Junge**.

9 The sound [ɔɪ] is represented chiefly by **eu** or **äu**:

Es ist heiß **heute**.
Fräulein Schneider.
Was **läufst** du?

Da hinten an der **Kreuzung**.
Warum **läuft** Rolf?
Ilse spricht **häufig** von Ihnen.

10 The sound [z] is represented in spelling chiefly by **s** before vowels:

Hans und **seine** Tante Inge.
Na, **siehst** du?
Die **Sonne** scheint.

Ich **sehe** dich.
Also, es geht los.
Die **Sache** ist ernst.

B. Present Tense Verb Forms

Copy the sentences, inserting the correct present tense form of the verb given in parentheses:

1 Ich _____ an das Sprichwort. (glauben)
2 _____ du es so? (empfinden)
3 Peter _____ die Zeitung. (lesen)
4 Hans und Inge _____ Nuß-Eis. (kaufen)
5 _____ Sie auf die Vorlesung? (warten)
6 Ihr _____ die Zeitung. (lesen)
7 Wir _____ nicht daran. (glauben)
8 Herr Held _____ eine Zeitung. (kaufen)
9 _____ ihr auf Professor Wolf? (warten)
10 _____ du die Zeitung? (lesen)
11 Heike _____ es auch so. (empfinden)
12 Er _____ auch darauf. (warten)

C. Dependent Clauses and Separable Prefixes

Arrange the elements to form meaningful German sentences:

1 die Straße / aussieht / nicht gut .
2 der Wagen / herumkommt / um die Ecke .
3 losgeht / es / jetzt ?
4 umkippt / die alte Kiste / sogar noch ?
5 mitkommst / du ?
6 unser Zug / einläuft / nämlich .
7 Heike / abwartet / noch .
8 Inge fragt, ob / aller Anfang / ist / schwer .
9 Herr Held sagt, daß / er / glaubt / daran .
10 Siehst du nicht, wie / schön / scheint / die Sonne ?
11 Er fragt, warum / die alte Frau / liegt / auf der Straße .
12 Wissen Sie, ob / Professor Müller / liest / langweilig ?
13 Sie sagt, daß / Inge / einsteigt / jetzt .
14 Peter antwortet, daß / der Milchwagen / umkippt / sogar noch .
15 Günther glaubt, daß / die Straße / aussieht / gut .
16 Mein Bruder fragt, ob / du / kannst / mitkommen .
17 Heike sagt, daß / sie / muß / einsteigen / jetzt .
18 Glauben Sie, daß / es / soll / losgehen / eigentlich ?

D. Telling Time

Write German sentences to correspond to the following English sentences:

1 It's six o'clock.
2 It's seven minutes after five.
3 Is it already ten to three?
4 It's (a) quarter after two.
5 Is it already half past three?

READING PRACTICE

The following paragraph is made up of words, phrases, and sentence patterns that you have learned in the dialogs and practiced in the audiolingual drills and writing exercises. Read the paragraph through rapidly several times, silently and aloud, and try consciously to comprehend its meaning without translating it into English.

Tante Ilse liest die Zeitung

Es ist schon viertel nach sechs. Tante Ilse wartet noch auf die Zeitung. Schließlich kommt die Zeitung, und Tante Ilse liest sie. Sie hat nämlich viel Interesse an Tagesfragen. Heute liest Tante Ilse, daß ein Unfall in der Stadtbahn passiert ist. Professor Schneider steigt in die Stadtbahn ein, aber plötzlich läuft ein Junge um ihn herum. Der Professor rutscht—und schon liegt er. Gott sei Dank ist es nicht allzu schlimm. Der Professor hat eine Platzwunde an der Stirn, aber dem rücksichtslosen Jungen ist nichts passiert.

Unit 8

DIALOG

In der Stadtbahn (Schluß)

1 **Ilse:** Rat mal, Peter, wen ich sehe! Dort sitzt meine Freundin Lilo!

2 **Peter:** Wer? Oh, die Lilo! Ist denn heute der Dreizehnte?

3 **Ilse:** Du brauchst gar nicht zu spotten, Lilo ist sehr nett.

4 **Peter:** Na, wenn man an deine Erzählungen über sie denkt!

5 **Ilse:** Hallo, Lilo, kennst du eigentlich meinen Mann?

6 **Lilo:** Nein. Guten Morgen, Herr Hartmann. Schön, daß ich Sie endlich kennenlerne.

7 **Peter:** Ich kenne Sie schon lange. Ilse spricht häufig von Ihnen.

On the Commuter Train (Conclusion)

1 Peter, just guess who I see! My friend Lilo is sitting over there!

raten (rat *imper.*) · **wer (wen** *acc.*) · **sitzen (sie sitzt)** · **die Freundin** (female) friend   **der Freund** (male) friend · **Lilo** *nickname for* **Liselotte**

2 Who? Oh, Lilo! Tell me, is today the thirteenth?

3 You don't have to be so sarcastic. Lilo is very nice.

brauchen (du brauchst) · **gar** quite, very **gar nicht** not at all

4 Well, if one thinks of your stories about her!

wenn *subord. conj.* · **denken an (man an . . . denkt)** think of · **die Erzählung,** *pl.* **die Erzählungen**

5 Hello, Lilo; you don't really know my husband, do you?

kennen (du kennst) know · **mein (meinen Mann** *acc.*)

6 No. Good morning, Mr. Hartmann. Nice to meet you finally.

kennenlernen meet, become acquainted with, get to know   **kennen** + **lernen** learn

7 I've known you for a long time. Ilse often speaks of you.

schon *Present tense with* **schon** *may indicate an action or state begun in the past and still continuing in the present* · **lange** *adv.* for a long time

8 **Lilo:** Oh, wenn Sie es so meinen, dann kenne ich Sie vielleicht noch besser!

9 **Peter:** Dann sind wir also alte Bekannte!

10 **Ilse:** Na, ihr beiden braucht nicht gleich zu übertreiben.

SUPPLEMENT

Present tense of haben and sein

The irregular verb **haben**:

Ich habe keine Angst.
Du hast keine Angst.
Er hat keine Angst.
Sie hat keine Angst.
Es hat keine Angst.
Wir haben keine Angst.
Ihr habt keine Angst.
Sie haben keine Angst.
Haben Sie keine Angst, Frau Hartmann?

The irregular verb **sein**:

Ich bin versichert.
Du bist versichert.
Er ist versichert.
Sie ist versichert.
Es ist versichert.
Wir sind versichert.
Ihr seid versichert.
Sie sind versichert.
Sind Sie versichert, Fräulein Schneider?

Time and travel expressions

1 Wie spät ist es?

2 Wieviel Uhr ist es?

3 Wann fährt der Zug ab?

4 Der Zug fährt um vier Uhr ab.

5 Von wo fährt der Zug ab?

8 Oh, if you mean it that way, then maybe I know you even better!

9 So then we're old acquaintances.

10 Well, you two don't have to overdo it right away!

kennen (ich kenne) · **gut** good **besser** better   **am besten** best

sein (wir sind)

beide (beiden) two, both · **brauchen (ihr braucht)** · **übertreiben** overdo it, exaggerate   **über** over + **treiben** drive; do

STÄDTEVERBINDUNGEN
Von Berlin Zool Garten nach

	Lübeck	③ 2. Kl 25.40, 1. Kl 36.40 ② 2. Kl 42.20, 1. Kl 64.40
ab	Zug Nr	an	Bemerkungen
Ⓑ 6.27	D 116	13.36	←NEU ✕ Ⓤ Hannover
✕ 7.38	D 112	16.23	✕ Ⓤ Hann Ⓤ Hamburg
8.00	D 166	14.52	✕ Ⓤ Hamburg
10.31	D 110	18.56	✕ Ⓤ Hann Ⓤ Hamburg
13.39	D 198	21.55	✕ Ⓤ Hann Ⓤ Hamburg
14.57	D 164	23.54	✕ Ⓤ Han TEE Ⓤ Hamb
17.08	D 118	0.25	✕ Ⓤ Hannover 🚋
✕ 21.45	D 120	6.48	🛏 Ⓤ Hann Ⓤ Hamb
23.36	D 1394	7.56	Ⓤ Hann Ⓤ Hamb

	Mainz	① 2. Kl 49.40, 1. Kl 72.80 ② 2. Kl 57.20, 1. Kl 85.40
6.27	D 116	16.42	Ⓤ Han Ⓤ Frankf ✕ bis Han
7.38	D 112	18.36	✕ Ⓤ Hann Ⓤ Frankfurt
10.31	D 110	20.51	✕ Ⓤ Hann ✕ Ⓤ Frankf
✕ 11.57	D 218	21.09	✕ Ⓤ Frankfurt
13.39	D 198	22.25	✕ Ⓤ Hann Ⓤ Frankfurt
22.17	D 202	7.56	🛏 🍴 Ⓤ Frankfurt

	Mannheim	① 2. Kl 52.40, 1. Kl 77.20 ② 2. Kl 26.20, 1. Kl 93.00
6.27	D 116	17.41	✕ Ⓤ Hann Ⓤ Frankf
7.38	D 112	18.59	✕ Ⓤ Hannover TEE
Ⓐ 10.31	D 110	20.53	✕ Ⓤ Hannover F
10.31	D 110	22.13	✕ Ⓤ Han Ⓤ Frkf Ⓤ Heidbg
11.57	D 218	22.18	✕
13.39	D 198	23.09	✕ Ⓤ Hann Ⓤ Frankfurt
22.17	D 202	8.41	🛏 🍴 Ⓤ Frankfurt

1 How late is it?

2 What time is it?

3 When does the train leave?

4 The train is leaving at four o'clock.

5 From where does the train leave?

wieviel how much, how many

abfahren (fährt . . . ab) leave, depart **fahren** go, travel

um at (*with time expressions*)

6   Der Zug fährt von Nürnberg ab.

7   Der Zug fährt um vier Uhr von Nürnberg ab.

8   Er fährt über Ulm nach München.

9   Um wieviel Uhr kommt der Zug an?

10 Der Zug kommt um zwei Uhr fünf an.

11 Wo kommt der Zug an?

12 Der Zug kommt in Kassel an.

13 Der Zug kommt um zwei Uhr fünf in Kassel an.

14 Herr Hartmann steigt in Kiel ein.

15 Herr Hartmann steigt in Hannover aus.

6 The train leaves from Nuremberg.

7 The train leaves from Nuremberg at four o'clock.

8 It goes to Munich by way of Ulm.   **über** by way of (*with travel expressions*)

9 At what time does the train arrive?   **ankommen (kommt ... an)** arrive

10 The train arrives at 2:05.

11 Where does the train arrive?

12 The train arrives in Kassel.

13 The train arrives in Kassel at 2:05.

14 Mr. Hartmann is getting on in Kiel.   **einsteigen (er steigt ... ein)**

15 Mr. Hartmann is getting off in Hanover.   **aussteigen (er steigt ... aus)**

AUDIOLINGUAL DRILLS

A. Directed Dialog

Fragen Sie, wen Ilse sieht!
Wen sieht Ilse?

Fragen Sie, wer dort sitzt!
Wer sitzt dort?

Sagen Sie, daß Ilses Freundin Lilo dort sitzt!
Ilses Freundin Lilo sitzt dort.

Fragen Sie, ob heute der Dreizehnte ist!
Ist heute der Dreizehnte?

Antworten Sie, daß Peter gar nicht zu spotten braucht!
Peter braucht gar nicht zu spotten.

Sagen Sie, daß Lilo sehr nett ist!
Lilo ist sehr nett.

Sagen Sie, daß Peter an Ilses Erzählungen über sie denkt!
Peter denkt an Ilses Erzählungen über sie.

Fragen Sie, ob Lilo eigentlich Ilses Mann kennt!
Kennt Lilo eigentlich Ilses Mann?

Antworten Sie, daß Lilo Ilses Mann endlich kennenlernt!
Lilo lernt Ilses Mann endlich kennen.

Sagen Sie, daß Peter Lilo schon lange kennt!
Peter kennt Lilo schon lange.

Fragen Sie, ob Ilse häufig von Lilo spricht!
Spricht Ilse häufig von Lilo?

Antworten Sie, daß sie häufig von Lilo spricht!
Sie spricht häufig von Lilo.

Sagen Sie, daß Lilo Ilses Mann vielleicht noch besser kennt!
Lilo kennt Ilses Mann vielleicht noch besser.

Sagen Sie, daß sie also alte Bekannte sind!
Sie sind also alte Bekannte.

Sagen Sie, daß Peter es nicht zu übertreiben braucht!
Peter braucht es nicht zu übertreiben.

B. Present Tense Verb Forms (*See Grammar* §8.4)

Substitute the new subject and change the verb form accordingly:

1 The irregular verb **haben** *have*:

Wir haben viel Erfahrung.   **Lilo**
Lilo hat viel Erfahrung.   **ihr**
Ihr habt viel Erfahrung.   **ich**
Ich habe viel Erfahrung.   **Ilse und Peter**

Ilse und Peter haben viel Erfahrung.   **du**
Du hast viel Erfahrung.   **wir**
Wir haben viel Erfahrung.

2 The irregular verb **sein** *be*:

Ich bin um fünf bei Heike.   **wir**
Wir sind um fünf bei Heike.   **du**
Du bist um fünf bei Heike.   **ihr**
Ihr seid um fünf bei Heike.   **er**

Er ist um fünf bei Heike.   **die Studenten**
Die Studenten sind um fünf bei Heike.   **ich**
Ich bin um fünf bei Heike.

3 The verb **sprechen** *speak* with changes in **du sprichst** and **er spricht**:

Wir sprechen über Lilo.   **ihr**
Ihr sprecht über Lilo.   **du**
Du sprichst über Lilo.   **ich**
Ich spreche über Lilo.   **Herr Held**

Herr Held spricht über Lilo.   **die Studenten**
Die Studenten sprechen über Lilo.   **wir**
Wir sprechen über Lilo.

4 The verb **helfen** *help* with changes in **du hilfst** and **er hilft**:

Er hilft Fräulein Schneider.   **wir**
Wir helfen Fräulein Schneider.   **du**
Du hilfst Fräulein Schneider.   **ihr**
Ihr helft Fräulein Schneider.   **Inge und Lilo**

Inge und Lilo helfen Fräulein Schneider.   **ich**
Ich helfe Fräulein Schneider.   **er**
Er hilft Fräulein Schneider.

5 The verb **nehmen** *take* with changes in **du nimmst** and **er nimmt**:

    Das Kind nimmt kein Eis.   **ihr**   Wir nehmen kein Eis.   **ich**
    Ihr nehmt kein Eis.   **du**   Ich nehme kein Eis.   **das Kind**
    Du nimmst kein Eis.   **die Studenten**   Das Kind nimmt kein Eis.
    Die Studenten nehmen kein Eis.   **wir**

6 The verb **essen** *eat* with changes in **du ißt** and **er ißt**:

    Wir essen Nuß-Eis.   **du**   Ihr eßt Nuß-Eis.   **ich**
    Du ißt Nuß-Eis.   **Hans und Inge**   Ich esse Nuß-Eis.   **wir**
    Hans und Inge essen Nuß-Eis.   **er**   Wir essen Nuß-Eis.
    Er ißt Nuß-Eis.   **ihr**

7 The verb **fahren** *travel* with changes in **du fährst** and **er fährt**:

    Sie fahren heute nach München.   **du**   Das Mädchen fährt heute nach München.
    Du fährst heute nach München.   **ich**   **ihr**
    Ich fahre heute nach München.   **wir**   Ihr fahrt heute nach München.
    Wir fahren heute nach München.   **die Studenten**
            das Mädchen   Die Studenten fahren heute nach München.

8 The verb **laufen** *run* with changes in **du läufst** and **er läuft**:

    Wir laufen schnell.   **er**   Du läufst schnell.   **ich**
    Er läuft schnell.   **Rolf und Günther**   Ich laufe schnell.   **er**
    Rolf und Günther laufen schnell.   **ihr**   Er läuft schnell.
    Ihr lauft schnell.   **du**

9 The verb **raten** *guess* with changes in **du rätst** and **er rät**:

    Ich rate es nicht.   **wir**   Ihr ratet es nicht.   **die Studenten**
    Wir raten es nicht.   **er**   Die Studenten raten es nicht.   **ich**
    Er rät es nicht.   **ihr**   Ich rate es nicht.

C. Imperative Verb Forms (See Grammar §8.5)

10 Change the indicative statements to **Sie**-imperatives by placing the finite verb first. The form **sind** must be changed to **seien**:

Example:
Sie kaufen Nuß-Eis.
Kaufen Sie Nuß-Eis!

Sie bleiben hier.
Bleiben Sie hier!

Sie essen Nuß-Eis.
Essen Sie Nuß-Eis!

Sie warten ab.
Warten Sie ab!

Sie kommen heute nachmittag mit.
Kommen Sie heute nachmittag mit!

Sie lesen nicht so langweilig.
Lesen Sie nicht so langweilig!

Sie sind um sieben bei uns.
Seien Sie um sieben bei uns!

Sie sehen die alte Frau.
Sehen Sie die alte Frau!

Sie sehen, wie schön die Sonne scheint.
Sehen Sie, wie schön die Sonne scheint!

Sie übertreiben nicht.
Übertreiben Sie nicht!

11 Change the indicative statements to **wir**-imperatives by placing the finite verb first. Change **sind** to **seien**:

Wir kaufen Nuß-Eis.
Kaufen wir Nuß-Eis!

Wir denken an deine Erzählungen.
Denken wir an deine Erzählungen!

Wir gehen heute nachmittag zum Baden.
Gehen wir heute nachmittag zum Baden!

Wir sind um acht Uhr bei Heike.
Seien wir um acht Uhr bei Heike!

Wir warten auf die Vorlesung.
Warten wir auf die Vorlesung!

Wir laufen schnell.
Laufen wir schnell!

12 Change the indicative statements to **ihr**-imperatives by deleting the pronoun **ihr**:

Ihr geht heute zum Baden.
Geht heute zum Baden!

Ihr steigt in Ulm aus.
Steigt in Ulm aus!

Ihr kauft noch schnell eine Zeitung.
Kauft noch schnell eine Zeitung!

Ihr eßt kein Nuß-Eis.
Eßt kein Nuß-Eis!

Ihr wartet noch ab.
Wartet noch ab!

Ihr seid um drei bei uns.
Seid um drei bei uns!

13 Change from indicative statements to **du**-imperatives by deleting both the pronoun **du** and the verb ending. Change **bist** to **sei**:

Du gehst heute zum Baden.
Geh heute zum Baden!

Du kaufst noch schnell eine Zeitung.
Kauf noch schnell eine Zeitung!

Du kommst um neun Uhr an.
Komm um neun Uhr an!

Du glaubst an das Sprichwort.
Glaub an das Sprichwort!

Du steigst in Kassel aus.
Steig in Kassel aus!

Du bist nett, mein Kind.
Sei nett, mein Kind!

Du hilfst Fräulein Schneider.
Hilf Fräulein Schneider!

Du sprichst nicht so schnell.
Sprich nicht so schnell!

Du nimmst kein Nuß-Eis.
Nimm kein Nuß-Eis!

Du ißt dein Eis, mein Kind.
Iß dein Eis, mein Kind!

Du liest die Zeitung.
Lies die Zeitung!

Du siehst, wie schön die Sonne scheint.
Sieh, wie schön die Sonne scheint!

14 Change the indicative statements to **du**-imperatives. Delete the pronoun **du** and the verb ending, but keep the connecting **e**:

Du spottest nicht, Uwe.
Spotte nicht, Uwe!

Du wartest darauf, Heike.
Warte darauf, Heike!

Du antwortest.
Antworte!

15 Change the indicative statements to **du**-imperatives. Delete the pronoun **du** and the verb ending, and change the stem vowel to that of the infinitive:

Du läufst nicht so langsam.
Lauf nicht so langsam!

Du fährst um sieben Uhr ab.
Fahr um sieben Uhr ab!

Du rätst, wen ich sehe.
Rat, wen ich sehe!

Du fährst schnell um die Ecke.
Fahr schnell um die Ecke!

D. Time and Travel (*See Grammar* §8.6)

16 Answer the questions as directed, using pronouns wherever possible:

Wieviel Uhr ist es? **8.00**
Es ist acht Uhr.

Wie spät ist es? **3.30**
Es ist halb vier.

Um wieviel Uhr kommt der Zug an? **8.30**
Er kommt um halb neun an.

Wann fährt der Zug ab? **10.00**
Er fährt um zehn Uhr ab.

Wo steigt Herr Hartmann ein? **Ulm**
Er steigt in Ulm ein.

Wo steigt Fräulein Schneider aus?
                                   München
Sie steigt in München aus.

Von wo fährt der Zug ab? **Hamburg**
Er fährt von Hamburg ab.

Wo kommt der Zug an? **Nürnberg**
Er kommt in Nürnberg an.

Wann läuft unser Zug ein? **6.00**
Er läuft um sechs Uhr ein.

E. Questions and Answers

Wer sitzt dort?
Ilses Freundin Lilo sitzt dort.

Wie spottet Peter?
Er fragt, ob heute der Dreizehnte ist.

Was sagt Ilse über Lilo?
Sie sagt, daß Lilo sehr nett ist.

Woran denkt Peter?
Er denkt an Ilses Erzählungen über Lilo.

Kennt Lilo Ilses Mann schon?
Nein, sie kennt Ilses Mann noch nicht.

Spricht Ilse häufig von Peter?
Ja, sie spricht häufig von Peter.

Was sind Lilo und Peter?
Sie sind alte Bekannte.

Was brauchen Lilo und Peter nicht gleich zu tun?
Sie brauchen nicht gleich zu übertreiben.

GRAMMAR

8.1 Word-Formation

Masculine-feminine noun pairs

Many masculine nouns that refer to people or animals have corresponding feminine forms with the suffix **-in**. Thus the feminine counterpart of **der Freund** is **die Freundin** *girl friend*. Some feminine forms have an umlaut: **der Wolf**, **die Wölfin**.

der Fahrer	**die Fahrerin** woman driver
der Freund	**die Freundin** girl friend
der Gott	**die Göttin** goddess
der Held	**die Heldin** heroine
der Professor	**die Profesˈsorin** woman professor
der Schneider	**die Schneiderin** woman tailor, dressmaker
der Student	**die Studentin** co-ed
der Wolf	**die Wölfin** she-wolf

8.2 Definite Articles of New Nouns

Masculine	*Feminine*
der Dreizehnte	die Erzählung, *pl.* die Erzählungen
der Morgen	die Freundin

8.3 Some Difficult Little Words

There are several words in German which, in addition to having relatively concrete and easily definable meanings, are often used to express subtle shades of attitude on the part of the speaker which are not at all easy to define. Although not essential to the grammatical structure of a sentence, these words are often important in communicating clearly and unambiguously a particular meaning. Although English has its share of such words, they do not match those of German very closely; they are rarely mutually translatable. Note how the following sentences differ in meaning, depending on the presence or absence of "little" words:

It's raining.
Why, it's raining.

Do you believe that?
Do you *really* believe that?

He's a student.
So he's a student.

Come by around five.
Do come by around five.

That's fine.
That's *just* fine.

The following list contains a few of these difficult little words, plus a few others that are easily confused:

also thus, so; therefore, consequently, then

Also, es geht endlich los.
Dann sind wir also alte Bekannte.
Dann kann er Ihnen also nicht viel helfen.

da there; then; so, in that case

Da ist ein Eismann.
Da kommt Professor Müller.
Da lachst du noch!
Da kann er Ihnen also nicht viel helfen.

doch *When stressed, implies a refutation:* Oh yes it is! Oh no it isn't! Oh yes you did! etc.

Ich sehe dich doch noch nicht auf dem Podium stehen!
Vielleicht doch!

doch *When unstressed with an imperative verb, implies gentle urging:* do!

Komm doch mit!

doch *When unstressed in a statement or question:* after all, but, nevertheless

Das macht doch nichts.
Es steht doch immer dasselbe darin.
Doch was ist nun mit dem Üben?

eigentlich really, actually, to tell the truth

Eigentlich kann es nun endlich losgehen.
Kennst du eigentlich meinen Mann?

ja yes; indeed, to be sure, after all *Indicates that the speaker regards his statement as being common knowledge*

Ja, aller Anfang ist schwer.
Du wohnst ja hier.

na well

Na, wenn man an deine Erzählungen über sie denkt!

noch still, yet **noch nicht** not yet

Ob die Sonne dann noch scheint?
Der Platz hier ist noch frei.
Ich sehe dich doch noch nicht auf dem Podium stehen.

nun now

Doch was ist nun mit dem Üben?
Eigentlich kann es nun endlich losgehen.

nur only, just

Ach, das ist nur ein Sprichwort.
Warten Sie nur ab!

erst *(adj.)* first

Ist dies Ihre erste Vorlesung?

erst *(adv.) with expression of time* not until, no sooner than

Alle Vorlesungen beginnen erst um viertel nach voll.

schon already; so *Also used with a present tense verb to indicate that the action or state began in the past and is still going on*
schon gut good, all right

Ich sehe dich schon auf dem Podium stehen.
Das kann schon sein.
Ich glaube schon.
Schon gut, steigen wir ein!
Ich kenne Sie schon lange.

dann then, at that time

Ob die Sonne dann noch scheint?

denn anyway; tell me *Used in questions to indicate mild surprise or lively interest*

Ist Eis denn Gift?
Was tust du denn heute nachmittag?
Ist denn heute der Dreizehnte?

wo where, at what place *direct or indirect question-word*

Wo ist der Unfall?
Fragen Sie, wo der Unfall ist!

wer who *direct or indirect question-word*

Wer sitzt dort?
Fragen Sie, wer dort sitzt!

wann when, at what time *direct or indirect question-word*

wenn if; when, whenever *subord. conj.* (not a question-word)

Wann bist du bei uns?
Fragen Sie, wann die Vorlesung beginnt!

Auch wenn die Sonne so schön scheint?
Nachts, wenn es regnet, passiert das meiste.

Na, wenn man an deine Erzählungen über sie denkt!

8.4 Present Tense Verb Forms: Irregular Verbs

1. A German finite verb must agree with its subject in both person and number. If the subject is 1st person singular, then the verb must be 1st person singular also. If the subject is 2nd person plural, then the form of the verb must likewise be 2nd person plural. This agreement between subject and verb is indicated primarily by the ending that is attached to the verb stem. In some verbs, however, it is further shown by a change in the vowel of the verb stem. The vowel change occurs *only* in the 2nd and 3rd persons singular, and in only a few verb stems (about five dozen). So far you have encountered the following:

essen: du i ßt, er i ßt
helfen: du h i lfst, er h i lft
nehmen: du n i mmst, er n i mmt
sprechen: du spr i chst, er spr i cht

laufen: du l äu fst, er l äu ft

lesen: du l ie st, er l ie st
sehen: du s ie hst, er s ie ht
fahren: du f ä hrst, er f ä hrt
raten: du r ä tst, er r ä t

2. In Grammar §7.3 you saw that, if a verb stem ends in **d** or **t** or certain consonant combinations, a connecting vowel **e** [ə] is inserted between the stem and the endings **-st** and **-t**: **du wartest, es empfindet, ihr antwortet**. To this rule we must now add a condition, in order to account for the forms of **raten** and several others like it, namely: if the verb stem ends in **d** or **t** *and* if the stem vowel changes in the 2nd and 3rd persons singular, then the 2nd singular ending is **-st** and the 3rd singular form has no ending at all. This explains the forms:

ich rate   wir raten
du rätst   ihr ratet
er, sie, es rät   sie, Sie raten

Remember that both conditions must be present for these endings:

1. The stem ends in **d** or **t**, *and*
2. There is a vowel change in the 2nd and 3rd persons singular.

3   The present tense forms of **sein** and **haben** are as follows:

ich bin	wir sind	ich habe	wir haben
du bist	ihr seid	du hast	ihr habt
er, sie, es ist	sie, Sie sind	er, sie, es hat	sie, Sie haben

8.5 Imperative Verb Forms

German commands are characterized by (1) the finite verb occurring in first position and (2) falling intonation (see Grammar §1.2):

Sagen Sie, daß der Zug kommt!
Steigen wir ein!

Kauf dein Eis, mein Kind!
Spotte nicht!

The finite verb in a German command, in addition to standing in first position, must also be in the *imperative verb form*. There are four imperative forms: the 2nd person standard (**Sie**-imperative), the 1st person plural (**wir**-imperative), the 2nd person plural familiar (**ihr**-imperative), and the 2nd person singular familiar (**du**-imperative).

1 *Second person standard* (**Sie**-*imperative*). The 2nd person standard imperative form of **sein** *be* is **seien**. For all other verbs the 2nd person standard imperative form is identical to the form of the indicative. The imperative verb stands first and is followed immediately by the pronoun **Sie**.

Warten Sie nur ab!
Just wait and see!

Kommen Sie doch mit!
Why don't you come along?

Entschuldigen Sie!
Excuse me.

Seien Sie um fünf bei uns!
Be at our place at five.

2 *First person plural* (**wir**-*imperative*). The 1st person plural imperative form of **sein** is **seien**. For all other verbs, the **wir**-imperative form is identical to the indicative. The verb stands first and is followed by the pronoun **wir**. The construction is equivalent in meaning to English "Let us . . . ."

Steigen wir ein!
Let's get on.

Gehen wir doch zum Baden!
Let's go swimming.

Seien wir doch nett!
Let's be nice.

3 *Second person plural familiar* (**ihr**-*imperative*). The **ihr**-imperative verb is identical in form to the indicative. The pronoun **ihr** is not expressed, unless the speaker wishes to add special emphasis

to the persons whom he is addressing; in this case it follows the finite verb and receives the main sentence stress.

Sagt das nicht!
Don't say that!

Seid um fünf bei uns!
Be at our place at five.

Kommt doch mit!
Why don't you come along?

Antwortet!
Answer me!

Spottet nicht!
Don't be sarcastic.

Kommt **ihr** mit!
You come along!

4   *Second person singular familiar* (**du**-*imperative*). The pronoun **du** is not expressed in a 2nd person singular familiar command, except for special emphasis:

Kauf dein Eis, mein Kind!
Buy your ice cream, my child.

Komm **du** mit!
You come along!

Spotte nicht!
Don't be sarcastic.

As you see in the examples above, there is sometimes an ending **-e** attached to the stem, and sometimes no ending at all. The presence or absence of this **-e** is governed by the following principles:

a. Verbs whose stem vowel changes from an **e**-sound to an **i**-sound in the 2nd and 3rd persons singular *have no ending* in the **du**-imperative form. The same is true of the verb **sein**:

Infinitive	d u -*indicative*	d u -*imperative*
helfen	du hilfst	hilf
sehen	du siehst	sieh
nehmen	du nimmst	nimm
lesen	du liest	lies
sein	du bist	sei

b. Verbs that require the connecting **-e-** in the indicative take the ending **-e** in the **du**-imperative:

spotten	du spottest	spotte
warten	du wartest	warte
antworten	du antwortest	antworte
finden	du findest	finde

c. Verbs not included in the above two groups generally occur without the ending **-e**, except in very slow or solemn speech and very formal writing. Thus:

kommen	du kommst	komm
kaufen	du kaufst	kauf
glauben	du glaubst	glaub
haben	du hast	hab
laufen	du läufst	lauf

Furthermore, verbs that have a stem vowel change from an **e**-sound to an **i**-sound in the 2nd and 3rd persons singular indicative also have this change in the **du**-imperative. Other verbs have no vowel change in the imperative. Thus:

sehen	du siehst	sieh
lesen	du liest	lies
nehmen	du nimmst	nimm

But the vowel change does not appear in the **du**-imperative in verbs like:

laufen	du läufst	lauf
fahren	du fährst	fahr
raten	du rätst	rat

The word **doch** is often used with the imperative to furnish a tone of earnest though polite solicitation. It has the effect of changing what would otherwise be an order into a suggestion:

Kaufen Sie eine Zeitung!
Buy a newspaper.

Kaufen Sie doch eine Zeitung!
Why don't you buy a newspaper?
Do buy a newspaper!

8.6 Some Time and Travel Expressions

1 There are several ways to ask what time it is in German. Among them are:

Wieviel Uhr ist es?
What time is it?

Wie spät ist es?
How late is it?

2 In telling time, the German preposition **um** is equivalent to English *at*:

Er kommt **um** drei Uhr.
He's coming *at* three o'clock.

Um wieviel Uhr mußt du Geige üben?
At what time do you have to practice the violin?

Die Vorlesung beginnt **um** viertel nach zwei.
The lecture begins *at* quarter past two.

The preposition **gegen** with a time expression means *about, around, approximately, along toward*:

Uwe ist **gegen** fünf bei uns.
Uwe will be at our place *around* five.

3 In the description of a journey that involves going from one city to another, the place of origin is indicated by the preposition **von** *from* and the destination usually by **nach** *to, toward*. The phrase *by way of* is equivalent to German **über**. Thus:

Der Zug fährt **von** Nürnberg ab.
The train leaves *from* Nuremberg.

Der Zug fährt **über** Ulm.
The train is going *by way of* Ulm.

Wir fahren **nach** München.
We're going *to* Munich.

Location within a particular geographical place is expressed by the preposition **in**. As in English, the definite article is usually not used:

Der Zug kommt **in** Kassel an.
The train arrives *in* Kassel.

WRITING

A. Present Tense Verb Forms

Copy the sentences and insert the correct present tense form of the verb given in parentheses:

1 _____ du Nuß-Eis? (nehmen)
2 Er _____ heute nach München. (fahren)
3 Ihr Bruder _____ viel Erfahrung. (haben)
4 Die Studenten _____ Ihnen. (helfen)
5 _____ Lilo meinen Mann? (kennen)
6 Peter, wo _____ du? (sein)
7 Lilo _____ das Sprichwort. (erklären)
8 Günther _____ plötzlich über die Straße. (laufen)
9 Wann _____ ihr bei uns? (sein)
10 Tante Inge _____ kein Eis. (essen)
11 Peter _____ nicht, wo es ist. (raten)
12 _____ ihr Interesse an Tagesfragen? (haben)
13 Du _____ nicht gleich zu übertreiben. (brauchen)
14 Ilse und Peter _____ häufig von Ihnen. (sprechen)
15 _____ du es auch so? (empfinden)

B. Imperative Verb Forms

Use each of the following expressions to write four commands: 1st person plural, 2nd person standard, 2nd person plural familiar, and 2nd person singular familiar. Insert **doch**.

Example:
zum Baden gehen
Gehen wir doch zum Baden!
Gehen Sie doch zum Baden!
Geht doch zum Baden!
Geh doch zum Baden!

1. eine Zeitung kaufen
2. nicht so langsam sprechen
3. auf die Vorlesung warten
4. an das Sprichwort glauben
5. nicht übertreiben
6. um zwei Uhr dort sein
7. von Ulm abfahren
8. in Berlin aussteigen

C. Time and Travel Expressions

Write German sentences to correspond to the given English sentences:

1. At what time are you leaving?
2. We leave at two o'clock.
3. From where does the train leave?
4. It leaves from Stuttgart.
5. Where do we get off?
6. I'm getting off in Kassel.
7. The train goes by way of Kassel to Hamburg.
8. When do you arrive?
9. The train pulls in around half past three.
10. Are you going to get on in Kassel?
11. I'm getting on in Munich.
12. Does the train go to Ulm?

D. Word Order

Arrange the elements to form meaningful German sentences:

1. Es ist schön, daß / ich / kennenlerne / Sie .
2. Ich weiß nicht, wie / du / kannst / sagen / so etwas .
3. Um wieviel Uhr / einläuft / der Zug ?
4. Fragen Sie, ob / Herr Hartmann / ankommt / gegen sieben .
5. Wissen Sie, wann / beginnt / die Vorlesung ?
6. Wir / einsteigen / um elf Uhr zwanzig .
7. Sie / brauchen / zu spotten / nicht .
8. Du / brauchst / zu übertreiben / nicht .

9 Ich kenne Sie besser, wenn / Sie / meinen / es so .
10 Dann / wir / sind / alte Bekannte .
11 Um zwei Uhr / unser Zug / abfährt / von Stuttgart .
12 Wenn / man / denkt / an deine Erzählungen !

LISTENING PRACTICE

Listen to the recorded conversations; then answer the following questions.

A. **Frau Hartmann und Herr Schneider**
1 Was fragt Frau Hartmann?
2 Um wieviel Uhr fährt ihr Zug ab?
3 Wohin fährt sie?

B. **Heike, Peter und Uwe**
1 Wen sehen Peter und Heike?
2 Wie sieht Uwe aus?
3 Wer lernt wen kennen?

Unit 9

Hans Holbein

DIALOG

Der neue Hut (Anfang)

1 **Frau Wegner:** Schau mal, Heinz, dieser Hut ist doch unmöglich!

2 **Herr Wegner:** Warum? Ich finde ihn noch sehr schön, Christa.

3 **Frau Wegner:** Aber die Form ist doch vollkommen unmodern!

4 **Herr Wegner:** Vielleicht, aber du kannst nicht jeden Monat einen Hut kaufen.

5 **Frau Wegner:** Jeden Monat! Ich habe diesen Hut schon ein Jahr!

6 **Herr Wegner:** Jedenfalls geht der Monat zu Ende. Mein Geld ist fast alle.

7 **Frau Wegner:** Dein Geld? Du meinst: unser Geld!

8 **Herr Wegner:** Das macht keinen Unterschied. Das Geld ist knapp.

The New Hat (Beginning)

        neu (neue)

1 Just look, Heinz, this hat is really impossible.

2 Why? I think it's still very nice, Christa.

        finden think; find · **er (ihn** *acc.***)**

3 But the shape is really completely out of style.

4 Maybe so, but you can't buy a hat every month.

        der Monat (jeden Monat *acc.***) · einen Hut** *acc.*

5 Every month! I've had this hat for a year!

        diesen Hut *acc.* · **das Jahr (ein Jahr** *acc.***)**

6 Anyway, the month is coming to an end. My money is almost gone.

        gehen go; walk · **das Ende** · **das Geld** · **alle** *adv.* all gone, at an end

7 Your money? You mean our money!

8 That doesn't make any difference. We're low on money.

        der Unterschied (keinen Unterschied *acc.***) · knapp** scarce

9 **Frau Wegner:** Ich habe ja auch noch ein Sparbuch.

10 **Herr Wegner:** Dein Sparbuch ist deine Sache. Davon kannst du meinetwegen jede Woche einen Hut kaufen!

(Fortsetzung folgt)

SUPPLEMENT

Possessive adjectives

1 Das ist mein Zug. (ich)

2 Das ist dein Zug. (du)

3 Das ist sein Zug. (er, es)

4 Das ist ihr Zug. (sie *sg.*)

5 Das ist unser Zug. (wir)

6 Das ist euer Zug. (ihr)

7 Das ist ihr Zug. (sie *pl.*)

8 Das ist Ihr Zug, Herr Hartmann. (Sie)

Identification expressions

9 Es ist die Zeitung.

10 Es sind die Zeitungen.

11 Das ist die Zeitung.

9   Well, I still have a savings account, you know.   **das Sparbuch** savings account book   **spar** (*from* **sparen** save) + **das Buch** book

10 Your savings account is your affair. For all I care you can buy a hat out of it every week.   **die Sache** affair; thing; matter · **davon** = **da** + **von** from it, out of it; from there · **meinetwegen** for all I care, as far as I'm concerned · **die Woche (jede Woche** *acc.*)

(To be continued)

---

1   That's my train.

2   That's your train.

3   That's his (its) train.

4   That's her train.

5   That's our train.

6   That's your train.

7   That's their train.

8   That's your train, Mr. Hartmann.

9   It's the newspaper.

10 It's the newspapers.

11 That's the newspaper.

12 Das sind die Zeitungen.

13 Dies ist die Zeitung.

14 Dies sind die Zeitungen.

12   Those are the newspapers.

13   This is the newspaper.

14   These are the newspapers.

AUDIOLINGUAL DRILLS

A. Directed Dialog

Fragen Sie, ob Frau Wegners Hut unmöglich ist!
Ist Frau Wegners Hut unmöglich?

Antworten Sie, daß Herr Wegner ihn noch sehr schön findet!
Herr Wegner findet ihn noch sehr schön.

Sagen Sie, daß die Form doch vollkommen unmodern ist!
Die Form ist doch vollkommen unmodern.

Sagen Sie, daß Frau Wegner nicht jeden Monat einen Hut kaufen kann!
Frau Wegner kann nicht jeden Monat einen Hut kaufen.

Fragen Sie, ob Frau Wegner diesen Hut schon ein Jahr hat!
Hat Frau Wegner diesen Hut schon ein Jahr?

Antworten Sie, daß sie ihn schon ein Jahr hat!
Sie hat ihn schon ein Jahr.

Sagen Sie, daß der Monat zu Ende geht!
Der Monat geht zu Ende.

Sagen Sie, daß das Geld knapp ist!
Das Geld ist knapp.

Fragen Sie, ob es auch Frau Wegners Geld ist!
Ist es auch Frau Wegners Geld?

Antworten Sie, daß es auch Frau Wegners Geld ist!
Es ist auch Frau Wegners Geld.

Fragen Sie, ob das einen Unterschied macht!
Macht das einen Unterschied?

Antworten Sie, daß das keinen Unterschied macht!
Das macht keinen Unterschied.

Fragen Sie, ob Frau Wegner auch noch ein Sparbuch hat!
Hat Frau Wegner auch noch ein Sparbuch?

Antworten Sie, daß sie auch noch ein Sparbuch hat!
Sie hat auch noch ein Sparbuch.

Sagen Sie, daß sie davon jede Woche einen Hut kaufen kann!
Sie kann davon jede Woche einen Hut kaufen.

B. Der-Words, Nominative Case (*See Grammar §§9.4–9.6*)

The **der**-words are: **der** *the*, **dieser** *this*, **jeder** *each*, **jener** *that*, **mancher** *many* (*a*), **solcher** *such*, and **welcher** *which?*

1 Repeat the following sentences:

Dieser Platz ist frei.
Diese Form ist unmodern.
Dieses Haus ist alt.
Diese Unfälle sind schlimm.

Mancher Professor ist langweilig.
Jede Vorlesung ist gut.
Jenes Mädchen ist tüchtig.
Solche Unfälle sind schlimm.
Welcher Fahrer ist rücksichtslos?

2 Substitute the new noun or **der**-word as indicated.

Example:
Dieser Platz ist gut.   **Eis**
Dieses Eis ist gut.   **jener**
Jenes Eis ist gut.   **Straße**
Jene Straße ist gut.

Manche Straße ist gut.   **Sprichwort**
Manches Sprichwort ist gut.   **dieser**
Dieses Sprichwort ist gut.   **Erzählungen**
Diese Erzählungen sind gut.   **welcher?**
Welche Erzählungen sind gut?   **Kreuzung**
Welche Kreuzung ist gut?   **jeder**
Jede Kreuzung ist gut.   **Mensch**
Jeder Mensch ist gut.   **der**

Der Mensch ist gut.   **Vorlesung**
Die Vorlesung ist gut.   **jener**
Jene Vorlesung ist gut.   **Licht**
Jenes Licht ist gut.   **welcher?**
Welches Licht ist gut?   **Studenten**
Welche Studenten sind gut?   **solcher**
Solche Studenten sind gut.

C. *Der*-Words, Accusative Case (*See Grammar* §§9.5, 9.7)

3 Substitute the provided accusative form of the new **der**-word:

Sie kauft den Hut. **diesen**
Sie kauft diesen Hut. **jenen**
Sie kauft jenen Hut. **jeden**
Sie kauft jeden Hut. **welchen?**
Sie kauft welchen Hut?

Er liest die Zeitung. **diese**
Er liest diese Zeitung. **jede**
Er liest jede Zeitung. **manche**
Er liest manche Zeitung. **welche?**
Er liest welche Zeitung?

Sie erklärt das Sprichwort. **jedes**
Sie erklärt jedes Sprichwort. **dieses**
Sie erklärt dieses Sprichwort. **jenes**
Sie erklärt jenes Sprichwort. **welches?**
Sie erklärt welches Sprichwort?

Wir kennen die Erzählungen. **solche**
Wir kennen solche Erzählungen. **diese**
Wir kennen diese Erzählungen. **manche**
Wir kennen manche Erzählungen. **welche?**
Wir kennen welche Erzählungen?

4 Substitute the new element:

Ich kenne diesen Mann. **Erzählung**
Ich kenne diese Erzählung. **mancher**
Ich kenne manche Erzählung. **Sprichwort**
Ich kenne manches Sprichwort. **jeder**
Ich kenne jedes Sprichwort. **Straße**
Ich kenne jede Straße. **der**
Ich kenne die Straße. **Haus**
Ich kenne das Haus. **jener**

Ich kenne jenes Haus. **Bruder**
Ich kenne jenen Bruder. **dieser**
Ich kenne diesen Bruder. **Studenten**
Ich kenne diese Studenten. **solcher**
Ich kenne solche Studenten. **Erzählungen**
Ich kenne solche Erzählungen. **welcher?**
Ich kenne welche Erzählungen?

D. *Ein*-Words, Nominative Case (*See Grammar* §§9.5, 9.6)

The **ein**-words are **ein** *a*, **kein** *no, not a*, and the possessive adjectives **mein** *my*, **dein** *your*, **sein** *his, its*, **ihr** *her*, **unser** *our*, **euer** *your*, **ihr** *their*, and **Ihr** *your*.

5 Substitute the new **ein**-word:

Das ist ein Wagen. **kein**
Das ist kein Wagen. **mein**
Das ist mein Wagen. **dein**
Das ist dein Wagen.

Das ist eine Geige. **seine**
Das ist seine Geige. **ihre**
Das ist ihre Geige. **unsere**
Das ist unsere Geige.

Mein Geld ist knapp. **dein**
Dein Geld ist knapp. **sein**
Sein Geld ist knapp. **ihr**
Ihr Geld ist knapp.

Deine Vorlesungen sind langweilig. **ihre**
Ihre Vorlesungen sind langweilig. **unsere**
Unsere Vorlesungen sind langweilig. **eure**
Eure Vorlesungen sind langweilig.

6 Substitute the new possessive adjective or noun as indicated.

Example:
Dein Platz ist dort.   **Geige**
Deine Geige ist dort.   **euer**
Eure Geige ist dort.   **Vorlesungen**
Eure Vorlesungen sind dort.

Sein Bruder ist hier.   **Tante**
Seine Tante ist hier.   **unser**
Unsere Tante ist hier.   **Sparbuch**
Unser Sparbuch ist hier.   **euer**
Euer Sparbuch ist hier.   **Straße**
Eure Straße ist hier.   **dein**
Deine Straße ist hier.   **Hut**
Dein Hut ist hier.   **mein**
Mein Hut ist hier.   **Geige**
Meine Geige ist hier.   **ihr**

Ihre Geige ist hier.   **Zeitung**
Ihre Zeitung ist hier.   **unser**
Unsere Zeitung ist hier.   **Bruder**
Unser Bruder ist hier.   **euer**
Euer Bruder ist hier.   **Freundin**
Eure Freundin ist hier.   **ihr**
Ihre Freundin ist hier.   **Erzählungen**
Ihre Erzählungen sind hier.   **sein**
Seine Erzählungen sind hier.

7 Substitute **ein**, **kein**, or a noun as indicated:

Das ist keine Kreuzung.   **ein**
Das ist eine Kreuzung.   **Sparbuch**
Das ist ein Sparbuch.   **kein**
Das ist kein Sparbuch.   **Freundin**
Das ist keine Freundin.   **ein**

Das ist eine Freundin.   **Hut**
Das ist ein Hut.   **Laterne**
Das ist eine Laterne.   **kein**
Das ist keine Laterne.

E. *Ein*-Words, Accusative Case (*See Grammar* §§9.5, 9.7)

8 Substitute the provided accusative form of the new **ein**-word:

Ich sehe einen Zug.   **keinen**
Ich sehe keinen Zug.   **meinen**
Ich sehe meinen Zug.   **euren**
Ich sehe euren Zug.   **ihren**
Ich sehe ihren Zug.

Er hat meine Geige.   **deine**
Er hat deine Geige.   **eine**
Er hat eine Geige.   **unsere**
Er hat unsere Geige.   **seine**
Er hat seine Geige.

Sie nimmt ihr Sparbuch.   **euer**
Sie nimmt euer Sparbuch.   **sein**
Sie nimmt sein Sparbuch.   **dein**
Sie nimmt dein Sparbuch.   **unser**
Sie nimmt unser Sparbuch.

Wir kennen eure Erzählungen.   **ihre**
Wir kennen ihre Erzählungen.   **keine**
Wir kennen keine Erzählungen.   **seine**
Wir kennen seine Erzählungen.   **deine**
Wir kennen deine Erzählungen.

9 Substitute the new element as indicated:

Sieht er meine Geige?	**ein**	Sieht er ihren Milchmann?	**Freundin**
Sieht er eine Geige?	**Licht**	Sieht er ihre Freundin?	**unser**
Sieht er ein Licht?	**kein**	Sieht er unsere Freundin?	**Kind**
Sieht er kein Licht?	**Zug**	Sieht er unser Kind?	**euer**
Sieht er keinen Zug?	**sein**	Sieht er euer Kind?	**Straße**
Sieht er seinen Zug?	**Frau**	Sieht er eure Straße?	**ihr**
Sieht er seine Frau?	**dein**	Sieht er ihre Straße?	**Studenten**
Sieht er deine Frau?	**Milchmann**	Sieht er ihre Studenten?	**unser**
Sieht er deinen Milchmann?	**ihr**	Sieht er unsere Studenten?	

F. *Der*-Words and *ein*-Words, Nominative and Accusative Cases

10 Answer the questions with the subject **Ich** . . . or **Das** . . . , the verb provided, and the correct case form of the suggested answer.

Example:
Was ist das? **mein Wagen**
Das ist mein Wagen.

Was sehen Sie? **ein Hut**
Ich sehe einen Hut.

Was ist das? **ihr Zug**
Das ist ihr Zug.

Was sehen Sie? **der Zug**
Ich sehe den Zug.

Was ist das? **sein Sparbuch**
Das ist sein Sparbuch.

Was haben Sie? **unser Sparbuch**
Ich habe unser Sparbuch.

Was ist das? **dein Hut**
Das ist dein Hut.

Was kaufen Sie? **dieser Hut**
Ich kaufe diesen Hut.

Was ist das? **euer Geld**
Das ist euer Geld.

Was nehmen Sie? **das Geld**
Ich nehme das Geld.

Was ist das? **ein Platz**
Das ist ein Platz.

Was sehen Sie? **jeder Platz**
Ich sehe jeden Platz.

Wer ist das? **unser Milchmann**
Das ist unser Milchmann.

Wen sehen Sie? **Ihr Milchmann**
Ich sehe Ihren Milchmann.

Was ist das? **der Streifenwagen**
Das ist der Streifenwagen.

Was lesen Sie? **solche Zeitungen**
Ich lese solche Zeitungen.

Was finden Sie?   **ihre Geige**
Ich finde ihre Geige.

Wer ist das?   **unsere Tante**
Das ist unsere Tante.

Wen kennen Sie?   **der Professor**
Ich kenne den Professor.

Was kennen Sie?   **manches Sprichwort**
Ich kenne manches Sprichwort.

G. Identification Expressions (*See Grammar* §9.8)

11 Answer the questions with the nouns or names provided.

Example:
Wer ist es?   Uwe
Es ist Uwe.   Uwe und Heike
Es sind Uwe und Heike.

Wer ist es?   **Uwe**
Es ist Uwe.   **Uwe und Heike**
Es sind Uwe und Heike.   **eine Frau**
Es ist eine Frau.   **die Studenten**
Es sind die Studenten.

Wer ist das?   **Hans**
Das ist Hans.   **Hans und Tante Inge**
Das sind Hans und Tante Inge.
　　　　　　　　　mein Bruder
Das ist mein Bruder.
　　　　　　Herr und Frau Hartmann
Das sind Herr und Frau Hartmann.

Was ist das?   **die Zeitung**
Das ist die Zeitung.   **seine Erzählungen**
Das sind seine Erzählungen.
　　　　　　　　　　　unser Sparbuch
Das ist unser Sparbuch.   **die Vorlesungen**
Das sind die Vorlesungen.

Wer ist dies?   **meine Frau**
Dies ist meine Frau.   **unsere Studenten**
Dies sind unsere Studenten.
　　　　　　　　　Fräulein Schneider
Dies ist Fräulein Schneider.
　　　　　　　　　Peter und Lilo
Dies sind Peter und Lilo.

H. Questions and Answers

Was sagt Frau Wegner über ihren Hut?
Sie sagt, daß er unmöglich ist.

Wie findet Herr Wegner den Hut?
Er findet ihn noch sehr schön.

Wie findet Frau Wegner die Form?
Sie findet sie vollkommen unmodern.

Was kann Frau Wegner nicht jeden Monat tun?
Sie kann nicht jeden Monat einen Hut kaufen.

Wie lange hat sie den Hut schon?
Sie hat ihn schon ein Jahr.

Was geht zu Ende?
Der Monat geht zu Ende.

Was ist fast alle?
Das Geld ist fast alle.

Was hat Frau Wegner noch?
Sie hat noch ihr Sparbuch.

Ist das Sparbuch Frau Wegners Sache?
Ja, es ist ihre Sache.

Was kann sie davon jede Woche kaufen?
Sie kann davon jede Woche einen Hut kaufen.

GRAMMAR

9.1 Word-Formation

Compound noun

spar *from* **sparen** save + **das Buch** book = **das Sparbuch** savings account book

9.2 Definite Articles of New Nouns

Masculine	*Feminine*	*Neuter*
der Hut	die Form	das Ende
der Monat	die Woche	das Geld
der Unterschied		das Jahr
		das Sparbuch

9.3 Grammatical Gender of Nouns

English pronouns are masculine, feminine, or neuter, depending on the biological sex of what is being referred to, as in *the man — he, the woman — she, the house — it*. A sentimental attachment to an inanimate object may result in its being referred to with the feminine pronoun, as in *She's a good ship.*

In German the distinction between masculine, feminine, and neuter applies not only to pronouns, but also to nouns. The gender of a German noun is a grammatical feature and has no essential connection, either biological or psychological, with the sex of the person or thing referred to. It is true that most nouns that refer to male beings belong to the masculine gender: **der Mann, der Junge, der Bruder**. It is also true that most nouns that refer to females are feminine in gender: **die Frau, die Tante, die Mutter**. But there are also neuter nouns that refer to females (**das Mädchen**), masculine nouns that refer to females (**der Sopran** *soprano*), feminine nouns referring to males (**die Schildwache** *sentry*), etc. Nouns that refer to inanimate objects or abstract concepts may be masculine, feminine, or neuter: **der Zug, die Angst, das Eis**.

There is no simple general rule by means of which the gender of a noun can be determined from its meaning. Some nouns exhibit certain formal properties that are associated with a particular gender, however (you have seen that nouns ending in the suffix **-in** are feminine, for example, in Grammar §8.1); these will be pointed out in subsequent units as the opportunity arises.

9.4 Cases of Nouns

English pronouns have different forms, their use being determined by the function of the pronoun in the sentence. The form *I* is used for the subject, *me* for the object of a verb or preposition, and *mine* in the possessive function. Other subject forms are *he, she, they, we*, with corresponding object forms *him, her, them, us*, and possessives *his, hers, theirs, ours*.

The function of a noun or pronoun in a sentence, together with the form of that noun or pronoun associated with that particular function, is called its *case*. German has four cases: nominative, accusative, dative, and genitive. These correspond roughly to the English subject, direct object, indirect object, and possessive.

9.5 Limiting Adjectives in the Nominative and Accusative Cases

There is a small group of words in German that are called *limiting adjectives*. They are grouped together because they share certain inflectional features, and they all function in much the same way.

Definite article

The nominative and accusative forms of the definite article are as follows:

	Masculine	*Feminine*	*Neuter*	*Plural*
Nom.	der Hut	die Tante	das Haus	die Unfälle
Acc.	den Hut	die Tante	das Haus	die Unfälle

Der-words

The following words are inflected like **der** and are therefore called **der**-words: **dieser** *this*, **jeder** *each, every*, **jener** *that*, **mancher** *many, many a*, **solcher** *such* (ordinarily used only in the plural), and **welcher** *which?* They all follow the pattern:

	Masculine	*Feminine*	*Neuter*	*Plural*
Nom.	dieser Hut	diese Tante	dieses Haus	diese Unfälle
Acc.	diesen Hut	diese Tante	dieses Haus	diese Unfälle

Indefinite article

Note how this differs from the **der**-words in the nominative singular masculine and in the nominative and accusative singular neuter. The word **ein** has no plural.

	Masculine	*Feminine*	*Neuter*
Nom.	ein Hut	eine Tante	ein Haus
Acc.	einen Hut	eine Tante	ein Haus

Possessive adjectives

The German possessive adjectives and their English equivalents are:

	Singular		*Plural*	
1st person	mein	my	unser	our
2nd person familiar	dein	your	euer	your
3rd person	sein	his, its	ihr	their
	ihr	her, its		
	sein	its		
2nd person standard (singular and plural)		Ihr	your	

Ein-words

Kein *no, not a, not any* and the possessive adjectives are inflected like **ein** and are called **ein**-words. Unlike **ein**, however, they do have plural forms.

	Masculine	*Feminine*	*Neuter*	*Plural*
Nom.	dein Hut	deine Tante	dein Haus	deine Unfälle
Acc.	deinen Hut	deine Tante	dein Haus	deine Unfälle

The stem **euer** is usually shortened to **eur-** when an ending is added: **euer Hut**, but **euren Hut**, **eure Tante**. Less frequently **unser** may be shortened to **unsr-** before an ending: **unser Bruder**, **unsren Bruder**, **unsre Tante**. Usually the full form **unser-** is used, however: **unseren Bruder**, **unsere Tante**.

Note that the **(e)r** is part of the stem of the possessive adjectives **unser** and **euer**; it is *not an ending*. Compare the following forms:

Stem	*Nominative*	*Accusative*
dies-	dies**er** Hut	dies**en** Hut
unser-	unser Hut	unser**en** Hut
eu(e)r-	euer Hut	eur**en** Hut
mein-	mein Hut	mein**en** Hut

Summary of limiting adjectives in the nominative and accusative cases

	Masculine	*Feminine*	*Neuter*	*Plural*
Nom.	der	die	das	die
Acc.	**den**	die	das	die
Nom.	dieser	diese	dieses	diese
Acc.	**diesen**	diese	dieses	diese
Nom.	ein	eine	ein	
Acc.	**einen**	eine	ein	
Nom.	mein	meine	mein	meine
Acc.	**meinen**	meine	mein	meine

Note the following points:

1. The forms of the definite article are very similar to the endings of the **der**-words.

2. Accusative case forms differ from nominative case forms only in the masculine singular. In the feminine, neuter, and plural the nominative and accusative forms are identical.

3. The three genders are not distinguished in the plural.

9.6 The Nominative Case

The nominative case is used for the subject, the predicate noun, or direct address.

1. The subject of a clause or sentence is in the nominative case:

Der Zug läuft ein.
Ist **der Milchmann** versichert?
Die Form is vollkommen unmodern.
Da sitzt **meine Freundin Lilo**.

Wann beginnen **die Vorlesungen?**
Die älteren Studenten haben alle viel Erfahrung.

2. A predicate noun is a noun that follows such verbs as **sein** *be* and refers to the same thing that the subject refers to. Predicate nouns are in the nominative case:

Hans ist **mein Bruder**.
Das ist nur **ein Sprichwort**.

Dann sind wir also **alte Bekannte**.

3. Expressions of direct address are in the nominative case:

Guten Tag, **Herr Hartmann**.
Es ist heiß heute, **Tante Inge**.

Mensch, da, kannst du sehen?

The nominative case answers the question **wer** *who?* or **was** *what?*:

Wer ist bestimmt versichert?
Der Milchmann ist bestimmt versichert.

Wer liegt auf der Straße?
Die alte Frau liegt auf der Straße.

Wer kommt um die Ecke herum?
Das Kind kommt um die Ecke herum.

Wer ist das?
Das ist **der Student**.
Das sind **die Studenten**.

Was läuft ein?
Der Zug läuft ein.

Was schwappt über die Straße?
Die ganze Milch schwappt über die Straße.

Was ist es?
Es ist **die Zeitung**.
Es sind **die Zeitungen**.

9.7 The Accusative Case

The accusative case may be used in a number of different functions.

1 The direct object of a verb refers to the recipient of the action of a verb. German direct objects are in the accusative case:

Christa kauft **einen Hut**.
Kennst du **meinen Mann**?
Ich habe **eine Zeitung**.

Siehst du **das Blaulicht**?
Ich bitte **dich**.

2 Many expressions of greeting and leave-taking are in the accusative case:
Guten Morgen! *Good morning!*
Guten Tag! *Good day! Hello!*

Guten Abend! *Good evening!*
Gute Nacht! *Good night!*

A verb of wishing is implied in such expressions: (*I wish you a*) *good morning*. They may thus be regarded as direct objects of the implied verbs.

3 Definite time or duration of time may be expressed by means of the accusative case:

Du kannst nicht **jeden Monat** einen Hut kaufen.   *every month*
Davon kannst du **jede Woche** einen Hut kaufen.   *every week*
Ich habe diesen Hut schon **ein Jahr**.   *for a year*

4 Certain prepositions take objects that are in the accusative case (to be treated more fully in Unit 10):

Er läuft **um die Ecke**.

The accusative case answers the question **wen?** or **was?**:

Wen lernt sie kennen?
Sie lernt **den Mann** kennen.

Was hat sie auf der Stirn?
Sie hat **den Angstschweiß** auf der Stirn.

Wen sieht Ilse?
Sie sieht **ihre Freundin Lilo**.

Was kauft Herr Hartmann?
Er kauft **eine Zeitung**.

Wen meinst du?
Ich meine **das Kind**.

Was sieht Peter?
Er sieht **einen Unfall**.

9.8 Identification Expressions

In English we may request and provide identifications in the following manner (subjects are in boldface):

What's that? ***It***'s a newspaper.
What is it? ***It***'s a newspaper.

What are these? ***These*** are newspapers.
Who's that? ***That***'s Mr. and Mrs. Hartmann.

The subject in each of the answers above is the "identifier" *that, it, these*. Whether the verb is singular *is* or plural *are* therefore depends on whether the identifier is singular or plural. In German the situation is quite different, however. The subject is not the identifier, but rather the thing(s) or person(s) being identified. Whether the verb is singular or plural is thus determined by what is being identified. The identifiers are **es**, **das**, and **dies**. They are always singular and neuter, regardless of the number and gender of what is being identified. Thus (subjects in boldface):

Was ist es? Es ist **eine Zeitung**.
        Es sind **Zeitungen**.

Was ist dies? Dies ist **eine Zeitung**.
        Dies sind **Zeitungen**.

Wer ist das? Das ist **Herr Hartmann**.
        Das sind **Herr und Frau Hartmann**.

WRITING

A. Present Tense Verb Forms

Copy the sentences and insert the correct present tense form of the verb in parentheses:

1 _____ du keinen Hut? (haben)
2 Wo _____ ihr denn? (sein)
3 Uwe _____ uns auch. (helfen)
4 Was _____ du denn plötzlich? (laufen)
5 Heike _____ häufig von uns. (sprechen)
6 Herr und Frau Hartmann _____ Eis. (essen)
7 Der Monat _____ zu Ende. (gehen)
8 _____ du ihn schön, Christa? (finden)

B. Imperative Verb Forms

Use each of the following expressions to write a **wir**-command, a **Sie**-command, an **ihr**-command, and a **du**-command:

1 mal schauen
2 mal abwarten
3 Fräulein Schneider helfen
4 das Eis essen
5 nett sein

C. Der-Words and ein-Words

Copy the sentences and insert the German forms that correspond to the English words in parentheses:

1 Wo ist _____ Wagen? (our)
2 _____ Straße ist schlimm. (this)
3 Kennst du _____ Tante? (his)
4 Ich kenne _____ Sprichwort. (many a)
5 _____ Sparbuch ist deine Sache. (your)
6 Wir sehen _____ Kind nicht. (her)
7 _____ Hut meinst du? (which)
8 Das ist _____ Zug. (a)
9 Seht ihr _____ Bruder? (your)
10 Das sind _____ Vorlesungen. (not any)
11 Kaufst du _____ Hut? (your)
12 _____ Zeitungen lese ich nicht. (such)
13 Wo ist denn _____ Milchmann? (the)
14 _____ Freundin heißt Lilo. (my)
15 Das sind _____ Erzählungen. (our)
16 Siehst du _____ Unfall? (the)
17 Ihr wohnt dort, und _____ Studenten wohnen hier. (your)

D. Identification Expressions

Write the corresponding German sentences:

1 Who's that?
2 That's Heinz.
3 This is my wife.
4 It's Heike and Uwe.
5 Is it our stories?
6 Are these the students?

E. Expressions in the Accusative Case

Write the corresponding German sentences:

1 I'm buying a hat.
2 Does she see the train?
3 We depart at seven.
4 We depart every day at seven.
5 Every month she buys a hat.
6 I've had this hat for a year. (*German present tense!*)
7 He's had the car for a month.
8 We've had her violin for a week.
9 Good morning, Miss Müller.

F. Spelling: Vowel Quantity

Determine whether the letters in boldface represent long vowels or short vowels, and identify the orthographic feature that indicates this:

Ihr, T**a**ge, **u**nd, w**o**, d**a**nn, M**o**nat, G**e**ld, **a**lle, m**a**cht, h**ie**r, **i**mmer, kn**a**pp, d**u**, m**u**ß, s**e**ht, **o**b, M**u**tter, V**a**ter, d**o**ch, W**o**che, m**ü**ssen, s**e**hr, k**o**mme, Erz**ä**hlung, St**ä**dte

READING PRACTICE

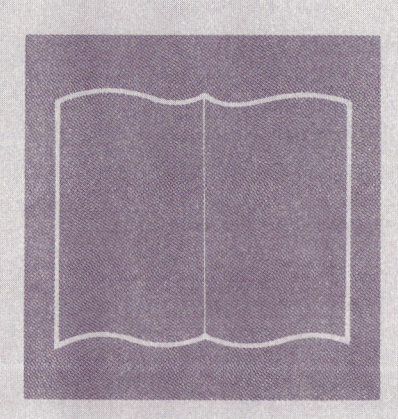

Haben Sie schon ein Sparbuch?

Die meisten Monate haben 30 oder 31 Tage. Haben Ihre Monate auch 30 oder 31 Tage? Wir meinen, haben Sie tatsächlich jeden Monat Geld genug für 30 oder 31 Tage, oder ist Ihr Geld schon um den 25. alle? Ja? Das ist eine schlimme Sache. Aber so geht es heute, Geld ist immer knapp.

Hier kann ein Sparbuch helfen. Viele Bücher sind gut, aber das gute, alte Sparbuch ist immer noch am besten. Jedenfalls wenn das Geld knapp ist. Sie brauchen nämlich kein Geld, ein Sparbuch zu kaufen. Im Gegenteil, Sie brauchen nur zu warten, und das Geld kommt zu Ihnen. Ihr Sparbuch „macht" Ihnen Geld: jedes Jahr 4% (Prozent)!

Ist das nicht eine hübsche Sache? Wenn der Monat zu Ende geht, Ihr Geld aber schon alle ist, und Sie—sagen wir—einen neuen Hut kaufen möchten, dann können Sie das tun,—wenn Sie ein Sparbuch haben. Oder vielleicht habe Sie mehr Interesse an einer alten Geige oder an einem neuen Wagen? Ihr Sparbuch kann Ihnen viel helfen!

Unit 10

DIALOG

Der neue Hut (Schluß)

1 **Frau Wegner:** Was kostet der Hut dort im Fenster, bitte?

2 **Verkäuferin:** Der Hut ist ein Gedicht, nicht wahr? Nur vierundachtzig Mark.

3 **Frau Wegner:** Wirklich? Sie haben kein Glück, das Gedicht ist zu teuer für mich.

4 **Verkäuferin:** Wie finden Sie das Hütchen dort?

5 **Frau Wegner:** Welches? Das kleine? Scheußlich!

6 **Verkäuferin:** Manche Kundin mag solche Hüte leiden. Sie sind billig.

The New Hat (Conclusion)

1 What does the hat in the window cost, please?

kosten (er kostet) · **das Fenster (im Fenster** *dat.***)**

2 The hat is a dream, isn't it? Only eighty-four marks.

das Gedicht poem, "dream" (*i.e. something very nice*) · **wahr** true **nicht wahr?** isn't it? doesn't it? · **die Mark,** *pl.* **die Mark**

3 Really? You're out of luck. The dream is too expensive for me.

das Glück (kein Glück *acc.***)** · **ich (mich** *acc.***)**

4 What do you think of the little hat over there?

das Hütchen *acc.* little hat *diminutive of* **der Hut**

5 Which one? The little one? Hideous!

klein (kleine) · **scheußlich** hideous, atrocious, abominable

6 Lots of customers like such hats. They're cheap.

die Kundin (female) customer **der Kunde** (male) customer · **leiden mögen** like **mögen (mag) leiden** suffer; tolerate · **billig** cheap, inexpensive

7 **Frau Wegner:** So sehen sie auch aus. Ohne mich!

8 **Verkäuferin:** Schauen Sie doch einmal durch diese große Auswahl hier.

9 **Frau Wegner:** Danke, ich möchte meinen Mann erst fragen. Wissen Sie, ich tue nichts ohne oder gegen ihn!

10 **Verkäuferin:** Natürlich, gnädige Frau, ich verstehe Sie vollkommen!

SUPPLEMENT

Direct object pronouns

1 Meinst du mich?

2 Ja, ich meine dich.

3 Meinst du uns?

4 Ja, ich meine euch.

5 Wen meinen Sie, Herr Professor?

6 Ich meine Sie, Herr Held.

Prices

7 Was kostet der Hut?

8 Er kostet vierundachtzig Mark.

9 Wieviel kostet die Zeitung?

10 Sie kostet dreißig Pfennig.

11 Wieviel kostet das Buch?

12 Es kostet zehn Mark fünfzig.

7	They look it, too. Not for me!	**ohne mich** *acc.* without me, leave me out
8	Won't you just look through this big selection here?	**groß (große)** · **die Auswahl (diese große Auswahl** *acc.***)**
9	Thanks, I'd like to ask my husband first. You know, I don't do anything without or against him.	**er (ihn** *acc.***)**
10	Of course, Madam, I understand you perfectly.	**gnädig (gnädige)** gracious · **verstehen (ich verstehe)**

---

1 Do you mean me?

2 Yes, I mean you.

3 Do you mean us?

4 Yes, I mean you.

5 Whom do you mean, Professor?

6 I mean you, Mr. Held.

7 What does the hat cost?

8 It costs eighty-four marks.

9 How much does the newspaper cost?

10 It costs thirty pfennigs.

11 How much does the book cost?

12 It costs ten marks fifty.

AUDIOLINGUAL DRILLS

A. Directed Dialog

Fragen Sie, was der Hut dort im Fenster kostet!
Was kostet der Hut dort im Fenster?

Antworten Sie, daß er nur vierundachtzig Mark kostet!
Er kostet nur vierundachtzig Mark.

Sagen Sie, daß die Verkäuferin kein Glück hat!
Die Verkäuferin hat kein Glück.

Sagen Sie, daß der Hut zu teuer für Frau Wegner ist!
Der Hut ist zu teuer für Frau Wegner.

Fragen Sie, wie Frau Wegner das Hütchen dort findet!
Wie findet Frau Wegner das Hütchen dort?

Antworten Sie, daß sie es scheußlich findet!
Sie findet es scheußlich.

Sagen Sie, daß manche Kundin solche Hüte leiden mag!
Manche Kundin mag solche Hüte leiden.

Sagen Sie, daß sie billig sind!
Sie sind billig.

Sagen Sie, daß sie auch so aussehen!
Sie sehen auch so aus.

Fragen Sie, ob Frau Wegner durch die große Auswahl schaut!
Schaut Frau Wegner durch die große Auswahl?

Antworten Sie, daß sie nicht durch die große Auswahl schaut!
Sie schaut nicht durch die große Auswahl.

Sagen Sie, daß Frau Wegner ihren Mann erst fragen möchte!
Frau Wegner möchte ihren Mann erst fragen.

Sagen Sie, daß sie nichts ohne oder gegen ihn tut!
Sie tut nichts ohne oder gegen ihn.

Fragen Sie, ob die Verkäuferin die Frau versteht!
Versteht die Verkäuferin die Frau?

Sagen Sie, daß sie sie vollkommen versteht!
Sie versteht sie vollkommen.

B. Direct Object Pronouns (*See Grammar* §10.3)

1 Substitute the provided accusative form of the pronoun:

Er kennt mich. **dich**
Er kennt dich. **ihn**
Er kennt ihn. **sie**
Er kennt sie. **es**
Er kennt es. **uns**

Er kennt uns. **euch**
Er kennt euch. **sie alle**
Er kennt sie alle. **Sie, Herr Hartmann**
Er kennt Sie, Herr Hartmann.

2 Replace the object pronoun with a new object pronoun that agrees with the cue.

Example:
Er sieht mich. **der Junge**
Er sieht ihn.

Er sieht mich. **du**
Er sieht dich. **er**
Er sieht ihn. **das Kind**
Er sieht es. **die Frau**
Er sieht sie. **wir**
Er sieht uns. **ich**
Er sieht mich. **das Mädchen**

Er sieht es. **ihr**
Er sieht euch. **der Professor**
Er sieht ihn. **Peter und Ilse**
Er sieht sie. **das Sparbuch**
Er sieht es. **der neue Hut**
Er sieht ihn.

C. Nominative and Accusative Pronouns

3 Answer the questions in the affirmative, using pronouns wherever possible.

Example:
Sehen Sie das Licht?
Ja, ich sehe es.

Sehen Sie den Hut?
Ja, ich sehe ihn.

Kaufen Sie die Geige?
Ja, ich kaufe sie.

Lesen Sie die Zeitung?
Ja, ich lese sie.

Sehen Sie die Studenten?
Ja, ich sehe sie.

Finden Sie das Podium?
Ja, ich finde es.

Haben Sie das Geld?
Ja, ich habe es.

Sehen Sie den Streifenwagen?
Ja, ich sehe ihn.

Meinen Sie dieses Buch?
Ja, ich meine es.

4 Continue as above, but in addition replace the noun subject with the corresponding pronoun.

Example:
Kauft Herr Held das Buch?
Ja, er kauft es.

Hat Frau Hartmann das Sparbuch?
Ja, sie hat es.

Sieht Herr Müller den Milchwagen?
Ja, er sieht ihn.

Kauft Tante Inge den Hut?
Ja, sie kauft ihn.

Sehen Heike und Uwe das Blaulicht?
Ja, sie sehen es.

Lesen Herr und Frau Hartmann die Zeitung?
Ja, sie lesen sie.

Kennt das Kind die Erzählungen?
Ja, es kennt sie.

D. Prepositions with the Accusative Case (*See Grammar* §10.4)

für for

5 Substitute the accusative form of the new noun or pronoun.

Example:
Der Hut ist zu teuer für ihn.   **wir**
Der Hut ist zu teuer für uns.   **mein Mann**
Der Hut ist zu teuer für meinen Mann.

Der Hut ist zu teuer für mich.   **du**
Der Hut ist zu teuer für dich.   **die Frau**
Der Hut ist zu teuer für die Frau.   **ihr**
Der Hut ist zu teuer für euch.   **die Studenten**

Der Hut ist zu teuer für die Studenten.   **er**
Der Hut ist zu teuer für ihn.   **diese Kundin**
Der Hut ist zu teuer für diese Kundin.   **wir**
Der Hut ist zu teuer für uns.

ohne without

6 Substitute the accusative form of the new noun or pronoun:

Ich tue nichts ohne ihn.   **ihr**
Ich tue nichts ohne euch.   **unser Bruder**
Ich tue nichts ohne unseren Bruder.   **du**

Ich tue nichts ohne dich.   **diese Studenten**
Ich tue nichts ohne diese Studenten.   **er**
Ich tue nichts ohne ihn.

gegen against

7 Substitute the accusative form of the new noun or pronoun:

Er hat nichts gegen dich.   **wir**
Er hat nichts gegen uns.   **solche Erzählungen**

Er hat nichts gegen solche Erzählungen.　**Sie, Frau Hartmann**
Er hat nichts gegen Sie, Frau Hartmann.　**Ihr Mann**
Er hat nichts gegen Ihren Mann.　**ihr**
Er hat nichts gegen euch.

durch through

8 Replace the noun object of the preposition, or the verb, as indicated.

Example:
Sie gehen durch den Zug.　**laufen**
Sie laufen durch den Zug.　**Straße**
Sie laufen durch die Straße.

Sie laufen durch die Straße.　**Zug**　　　　Sie schauen durch die Auswahl.　**sehen**
Sie laufen durch den Zug.　**gehen**　　　Sie sehen durch die Auswahl.　**Fenster**
Sie gehen durch den Zug.　**Stadtbahn**　　Sie sehen durch das Fenster.　**kommen**
Sie gehen durch die Stadtbahn.　**schauen**　Sie kommen durch das Fenster.　**Straße**
Sie schauen durch die Stadtbahn.　**Auswahl**　Sie kommen durch die Straße.

um around

9 Replace the object of the preposition, or the verb, as indicated.

Example:
Er kommt um den Platz herum.　**laufen**
Er läuft um den Platz herum.　**unser Haus**
Er läuft um unser Haus herum.

Er läuft um unser Haus herum.　**gehen**　　Er läuft um meinen Wagen herum.
Er geht um unser Haus herum.　**eine Ecke**　　　　　　　　　　　　　　　**jene Laterne**
Er geht um eine Ecke herum.　**kommen**　　Er läuft um jene Laterne herum.　**gehen**
Er kommt um eine Ecke herum.　　　　　　　Er geht um jene Laterne herum.　**er**
　　　　　　　　　　　　　　mein Wagen　Er geht um ihn herum.　**kommen**
Er kommt um meinen Wagen herum.　**laufen**　Er kommt um ihn herum.

E. The Question-Words Wer? Who?, Wen? Whom?, Was? What?
(*See Grammar* §§9.6, 9.7)

10 Change the following statements into questions by replacing the noun with **wer**, **wen**, or **was**, as may be required, at the beginning of the question.

Example:
Uwe ist hier.
Wer ist hier?

Er meint Hans.
Wen meint er?

Er hat die Laterne.
Was hat er?

Das ist ein Sparbuch.
Was ist das?

Er sieht den Milchmann.
Wen sieht er?

Er hat eine Wunde.
Was hat er?

Er meint seinen Bruder.
Wen meint er?

Das ist ihre Freundin.
Wer ist das?

Er sieht den Wagen.
Was sieht er?

Aller Anfang ist schwer.
Was ist schwer?

Er sieht die Studenten.
Wen sieht er?

Die Ecke ist dort.
Was ist dort?

Dort kommt seine Freundin.
Wer kommt dort?

Das ist unser Podium.
Was ist das?

Er sieht Frau Hartmann.
Wen sieht er?

Er findet Tante Inge.
Wen findet er?

Heike möchte mitkommen.
Wer möchte mitkommen?

F. Prices (*See Grammar* §10.5)

11 Change the price by adding five **Pfennig** each time until the price is **acht Mark zwanzig**:

Das Buch kostet sieben Mark fünfundachtzig.
Das Buch kostet sieben Mark neunzig.
Das Buch kostet seiben Mark fünfundneunzig.
Das Buch kostet acht Mark.
Das Buch kostet acht Mark fünf.
Das Buch kostet acht Mark zehn.
Das Buch kostet acht Mark fünfzehn.
Das Buch kostet acht Mark zwanzig.

G. Questions and Answers

Was kostet der Hut im Fenster?
Er kostet vierundachtzig Mark.

Was sagt die Verkäuferin über den Hut?
Sie sagt, er ist ein Gedicht.

Hat die Verkäuferin Glück?
Nein, sie hat kein Glück.

Für wen ist das Gedicht zu teuer?
Es ist zu teuer für Frau Wegner.

Wie findet Frau Wegner das Hütchen?
Sie findet es scheußlich.

Sind solche Hüte teuer?
Nein, sie sind billig.

Was sagt Frau Wegner?
Sie sagt, daß sie auch so aussehen.

Wie ist die Auswahl?
Die Auswahl ist groß.

Wen möchte Frau Wegner erst fragen?
Sie möchte ihren Mann erst fragen.

Versteht die Verkäuferin Frau Wegner?
Ja, sie versteht sie vollkommen.

GRAMMAR

10.1 Word-Formation

Neuter noun suffixes -*chen*, -*lein*

The suffixes **-chen** and **-lein** may be attached to many German nouns to form *diminutive* nouns, i.e. nouns that convey the meaning of "smallness," together with all that that implies: youth, endearment, lack of physical size, and in some contexts lack of significance. Diminutive nouns are neuter, and their plurals are identical to their singular forms (see Grammar §10.2). The stem vowel of most diminutive nouns is umlauted, if possible. Thus **der Hut** + **-chen** = **das Hütchen** *little hat, cute hat*. The suffix **-chen** tends to predominate in the northern area of Germany and in the standard literary language, while **-lein** is the more frequent form in the south. Here are some more examples:

das Fenster	das Fensterchen	*little window*
das Haus	das Häuschen	*little house*
der Kopf	das Köpfchen	*little (child's) head*
der Mann	das Männchen	*little (old) man*
die Stadt	das Städtchen	*small town*

Some diminutive nouns have become standardized and have acquired special meanings, such as **das Fräulein** *Miss, young lady* (**die Frau** *Mrs., woman* + **-lein**) and **das Mädchen** *girl* (**die Magd** *maid* + **-chen**).

10.2 Noun Plurals

The plural of most English nouns is formed by adding the sound [s], [z], or [ʌz], spelled *s* or *es*, to the singular stem. The sound [s] is used in *cats, books, cups*; [z] is used in *trees, bears, dogs*; and [ʌz] is added in *faces, roses, bushes*. There are also a few nouns whose plural is formed by changing the vowel of the stem, as *mouse — mice, man — men, foot — feet*. There are some that add [z] and undergo other changes as well, such as *wife — wives, loaf — loaves*. Some are identical in the singular and plural: *sheep — sheep, trout — trout, series — series*. A few nouns of foreign origin have retained their original plural forms: *alumnus — alumni, phenomenon — phenomena, lied — lieder, kibbutz — kibbutzim*.

The plural of German nouns is also formed in a variety of ways, although they are different from the English plural formations. Just as English plural forms are automatic for speakers of English, so are German plural forms automatic for German speakers. Just as you say *boxes* and *oxen* (but not *boxen* or *oxes*), the speaker of German selects the plural forms **Tage** *days* and **Bücher** *books* (but never **Täger** or **Buche**). Incorrect plural forms sound just as bad to speakers of German as "two mouses" or "three foots" do to speakers of English.

Some German nouns are unchanged in the plural. Others are made plural by the modification of the stem vowel, indicated by the umlaut symbol (¨) over the vowel letter. Still others are made plural by the addition of various endings, some with umlaut and some without. They may be grouped as follows:

Group I	Plural ending: none. Some umlaut.
Group II	Plural ending: **-e**. Some umlaut.
Group III	Plural ending: **-er**. Umlaut whenever possible.
Group IV	Plural ending: **-(e)n**. Never umlaut.
Group V	Plural ending: **-(e)n**, but this **-(e)n** also occurs in all singular cases except the nominative. Never umlaut.
Group VI	Plural ending: various. Never umlaut.

While it is helpful to understand these groupings, the best way to learn and remember the plural of a noun is to memorize it along with the nominative singular form. The plural forms of the nouns that have appeared in Units 1 to 10 are given below, arranged by group. Each group is further divided according to gender. If umlaut is possible within a group, there is one column for nouns that do not umlaut and another for nouns that do umlaut. (But if a noun with umlaut appears in the nonumlaut column, it is because the singular form also has umlaut.) Compound nouns are not included as separate items in the chart. A few nouns have been omitted because their plurals are rare or nonexistent, or because they will be given special treatment later.

List of Noun Plurals, Units 1 to 10

Group I Plural Ending: None

Masculine	Feminine	Neuter
Most masculines in **-el, -en, -er**	Only two: **die Mutter** *mother* **die Tochter** *daughter*	All neuters in **-el, -en, -er**; all nouns in **-chen, -lein**
Umlaut: some	*Umlaut:* both	*Umlaut:* none
- der Fahrer, die Fahrer; der Morgen, die Morgen; der Müller, die Müller; der Schneider, die Schneider; der Verkäufer, die Verkäufer; der Wagen, die Wagen **¨** der Bruder, die Brüder	**¨** die Mutter, die Mütter; die Tochter, die Töchter	**-** das Fräulein, die Fräulein; das Hütchen, die Hütchen; das Mädchen, die Mädchen; das Viertel, die Viertel

Group II Plural Ending: -e, ¨e

Masculine	Feminine	Neuter
Many monosyllabics; a few polysyllabics	About 20 common monosyllabics	Only a few
Umlaut: some	*Umlaut:* all	*Umlaut:* none
-e der Freund, die Freunde; der Monat, die Monate; der Pfennig, die Pfennige; der Tag, die Tage; der Teil, die Teile; der Unterschied, die Unterschiede **¨e** der Anfang, die Anfänge; der Hut, die Hüte; der Kopf, die Köpfe; der Platz, die Plätze; der Raum, die Räume; der Wolf, die Wölfe; der Zug, die Züge	**¨e** die Angst, die Ängste; die Nuß, die Nüsse; die Stadt, die Städte	**-e** das Gedicht, die Gedichte; das Gegenteil, die Gegenteile; das Jahr, die Jahre; das Wort, die Worte

Group III Plural Ending: -er, ⸚er

Masculine A few monosyllabics Umlaut: whenever possible			Neuter Most monosyllabic neuters and all neuters in **-tum** Umlaut: whenever possible	
-er (Rare. None in Units 1–10)	⸚er der Gott, die Götter der Mann, die Männer	-er das Kind, die Kinder das Licht, die Lichter	⸚er das Buch, die Bücher das Haus, die Häuser das Wort, die Wörter	

Group IV Plural Ending: -(e)n

Masculine Only a few Umlaut: none	Feminine Almost all feminines Umlaut: none	Neuter Only a few Umlaut: none
-(e)n der Professor, die Professoren	-(e)n die Bahn, die Bahnen die Ecke, die Ecken die Einführung, die Einführungen die Erfahrung, die Erfahrungen die Erzählung, die Erzählungen die Fahrerin, die Fahrerinnen die Form, die Formen die Frage, die Fragen die Frau, die Frauen die Freundin, die Freundinnen die Geige, die Geigen die Göttin, die Göttinnen die Heldin, die Heldinnen die Kiste, die Kisten die Kreuzung, die Kreuzungen die Kundin, die Kundinnen die Laterne, die Laternen die Professorin, die Professorinnen die Sache, die Sachen die Schneiderin, die Schneiderinnen die Stelle, die Stellen die Straße, die Straßen die Studentin, die Studentinnen die Tante, die Tanten die Verkäuferin, die Verkäuferinnen die Vorlesung, die Vorlesungen die Woche, die Wochen die Wölfin, die Wölfinnen die Wunde, die Wunden die Zeitung, die Zeitungen	-(e)n das Ende, die Enden

Group V Plural Ending: -(e)n

Masculine

All masculines that have **-(e)n** in all singular cases except the nominative. Included are all masculines in **-e** that refer to living beings.

Umlaut: none

-(e)n

der Held, die Helden
der Herr, die Herren
der Junge, die Jungen
der Kunde, die Kunden
der Mensch, die Menschen
der Student, die Studenten

Note the following:

Das Wort occurs twice in the charts: once in Group II and once in Group III. The two plural forms have different meanings. The plural **die Worte** refers to words in connected discourse, as in **die Worte Schillers** *the words of Schiller*. The plural **die Wörter**, however, refers to words that are not combined in a meaningful expression, such as words in a list.

When the plural suffix **-en** is added to **der Professor**, the stress shifts one syllable toward the right, so that it falls on the second-to-last syllable of the word: **der Pro'fessor, die Profes'soren**. This is true of all words whose stem ends in weakly stressed **-or**: **der 'Doktor** *man with a doctorate*, **die Dok'toren**; **der 'Traktor** *tractor*, **die Trak'toren**.

The final **n** of feminine nouns ending in the weakly stressed suffix **-in** (Group IV) is always doubled before the plural ending **-en** is added.

Singular and plural of nouns

Change the noun subject to the plural:

Der Fahrer ist rücksichtslos.
Die Fahrer sind rücksichtslos.

Der Bruder ist nett.
Die Brüder sind nett.

Der Schneider ist gut.
Die Schneider sind gut.

Der Verkäufer ist da hinten.
Die Verkäufer sind da hinten.

Das Mädchen ist tüchtig.
Die Mädchen sind tüchtig.

Das Hütchen ist teuer.
Die Hütchen sind teuer.

Der Wagen ist neu.
Die Wagen sind neu.

Der Tag geht zu Ende.
Die Tage gehen zu Ende.

Das Jahr geht zu Ende.
Die Jahre gehen zu Ende.

Der Freund kommt mit.
Die Freunde kommen mit.

Der Teil ist klein.
Die Teile sind klein.

Der Monat geht zu Ende.
Die Monate gehen zu Ende.

Das Gedicht ist scheußlich.
Die Gedichte sind scheußlich.

Der Unterschied ist groß.
Die Unterschiede sind groß.

Der Hut ist billig.
Die Hüte sind billig.

Es ist der Wolf.
Es sind die Wölfe.

Der Kopf ist klein.
Die Köpfe sind klein.

Die Stadt ist schön.
Die Städte sind schön.

Der Platz ist frei.
Die Plätze sind frei.

Der Zug ist schnell.
Die Züge sind schnell.

Der Anfang ist schwer.
Die Anfänge sind schwer.

Der Unfall ist schlimm.
Die Unfälle sind schlimm.

Der Raum ist schön.
Die Räume sind schön.

Der Pfennig ist neu.
Die Pfennige sind neu.

Das Kind ist nett.
Die Kinder sind nett.

Das Haus ist teuer.
Die Häuser sind teuer.

Der Mann ist tüchtig.
Die Männer sind tüchtig.

Das Wort ist schwer.
Die Wörter sind schwer.

Das Buch ist ganz neu.
Die Bücher sind ganz neu.

Der Professor ist alt.
Die Professoren sind alt.

Die Form ist unmodern.
Die Formen sind unmodern.

Die Frau ist klein.
Die Frauen sind klein.

Die Bahn ist schnell.
Die Bahnen sind schnell.

Die Woche geht zu Ende.
Die Wochen gehen zu Ende.

Die Stelle ist rutschig.
Die Stellen sind rutschig.

Die Straße ist schlecht.
Die Straßen sind schlecht.

Die Geige ist teuer.
Die Geigen sind teuer.

Die Laterne ist gut.
Die Laternen sind gut.

Die Ecke ist rutschig.
Die Ecken sind rutschig.

Die Wunde ist schlimm.
Die Wunden sind schlimm.

Die Tante ist alt.
Die Tanten sind alt.

Die Kiste ist leicht.
Die Kisten sind leicht.

Die Zeitung ist gut.
Die Zeitungen sind gut.

Die Vorlesung ist unmöglich.
Die Vorlesungen sind unmöglich.

Die Erzählung ist gut.
Die Erzählungen sind gut.

Die Einführung ist langweilig.
Die Einführungen sind langweilig.

Die Kreuzung ist rutschig.
Die Kreuzungen sind rutschig.

Die Frage ist leicht.
Die Fragen sind leicht.

Die Freundin ist hübsch.
Die Freundinnen sind hübsch.

Die Kundin ist nett.
Die Kundinnen sind nett.

Die Verkäuferin ist schlecht.
Die Verkäuferinnen sind schlecht.

Die Studentin wartet.
Die Studentinnen warten.

Der Mensch ist gut.
Die Menschen sind gut.

Der Student ist neu.
Die Studenten sind neu.

Der Junge ist groß.
Die Jungen sind groß.

Der Held ist tüchtig.
Die Helden sind tüchtig.

Der Kunde kauft nichts.
Die Kunden kaufen nichts.

Der Herr ist unmöglich.
Die Herren sind unmöglich.

10.3 Personal Pronouns, Nominative and Accusative Cases

| | *Singular* | | | | | *Plural* | | | *Standard* |
	1	*2*	*3 M*	*3 F*	*3 N*	*1*	*2*	*3 M, F, N*	*2*
Nom.	ich	du	er	sie	es	wir	ihr	sie	Sie
Acc.	mich	dich	ihn	sie	es	uns	euch	sie	Sie

10.4 Prepositions with the Accusative Case

Both English and German have small classes of words called *prepositions*. Prepositions characteristically occur with nouns or pronouns, called *objects* of the prepositions, and together they form *prepositional phrases*:

to the city
from my older brother
under the car
in a few minutes

The object of a German preposition must be in one of three cases: accusative, dative, or genitive. Some German prepositions always take accusative objects, others take only dative objects, and a few occur only with the genitive case. Some take either the accusative case or the dative case, depending on what they mean.

The most important German prepositions that govern the accusative case are:

durch through

Schauen Sie **durch** diese Auswahl!
Look *through* this selection.

für for

Der Hut ist zu teuer **für** mich.
The hat is too expensive *for* me.

gegen against; around, toward (*with time expressions*)

Ich tue nichts **gegen** ihn.
I don't do anything *against* him.

Uwe kommt **gegen** fünf Uhr.
Uwe is coming *around* five o'clock.

ohne without

Ich tue nichts **ohne** ihn.
I don't do anything *without* him.

um around; at (*with time expressions*)

Der Streifenwagen kommt **um** den Platz herum.
The patrol car is coming *around* the square.

Der Zug kommt **um** fünf Uhr an.
The train arrives *at* five o'clock.

10.5 Prices

German prices are expressed in terms of **Deutsche Mark** and **Pfennige**. There are one hundred **Pfennige** in a **Mark**. Although the noun **Pfennig** has a plural form **Pfennige**, only the singular is used in expressing prices. Thus:

zehn Pfennig
sechzig Pfennig
hundert Pfennig (= eine Mark)

In German writing, the decimal point is indicated by a comma. The phrase **Deutsche Mark** is symbolized by **DM**, which may either precede or follow the numbers:

DM 8,20 *or* 8,20 DM   acht Mark zwanzig
DM 5,32 *or* 5,32 DM   fünf Mark zweiunddreißig

WRITING

A. Word Copying

Copy the words in boldface.

1. Both the sounds [ç] and [x] are represented by **ch**. [ç] is also represented by **g** in the suffix **-ig** if it is not followed by a vowel or by the suffix **-lich**:

   Ich sehe **dich doch noch nicht**.
   Eigentlich kann es **endlich** losgehen.
   Dein **Sparbuch** ist deine **Sache**.
   Er liest **langweilig**.
   Ist das so **eilig**?
   Der **dreißigste** August.

2. The sound [f] is represented by **v**, **f**, **ff** and by **ph** in words of foreign origin:

   Im **Vorlesungsraum**.
   Ist Eis denn **Gift**?
   Das ist **fein**.
   So gegen **fünf**.
   Er kann **viel helfen**.
   Die **Einführung** in die **Philosophie**.

3. The sound [p] is represented by **p** (not **ph**), **pp** and by **b** when it is final in a word or syllable or final but inflected with a voiceless consonant:

   Der **Platz** hier ist noch frei.
   Das Geld ist **knapp**.
   Fragen Sie, **ob** . . .
   Abgemacht.
   Eine **hübsche** Sache.
   Sie **glaubt** daran.

4. The sound [k] is represented chiefly by **ck** and **k**, and by **g** when it is final in a syllable or final and inflected with a voiceless consonant. This does not apply to the suffix **-ig** [ıç] as in **häufig** or **ng** [ŋ] as in **Vorlesung**:

   Das **schmeckt** am besten.
   Guten **Tag**, Heike.
   Unser **Zug** läuft ein.
   Hans **sagt**, das ist fein.
   Üben **sagst** du?
   Aber natürlich auch **tagsüber**.

5. The combination sound [ts] is represented chiefly by **z**, **ts**, and **tz**:

   Ich gehe **zum** Baden.
   Ich kaufe eine **Zeitung**.
   Da hinten an der **Kreuzung**.
   Seit dem **zweiundzwanzigsten** August.
   Nichts wie hin.
   Jetzt kippt er sogar noch um.

6. The umlaut symbol is a part of German spelling. The umlaut vowels are represented by the unmodified spelling of the vowel plus the umlaut symbol over it. If the umlaut symbol is ignored, the word is misspelled and it could even be a different word (**schon** *already*; **schön** *beautiful*):

Die Sonne scheint so **schön**.
Ich muß Geige **üben**.
Tüchtig, tüchtig, Mädchen.

Was **läufst** du denn so **plötzlich**?
Hier **läuft nämlich** unser Zug ein.
Natürlich, gnädige Frau.

B. Verb Forms

Copy the sentences and insert the correct verb form; some sentences require an imperative form:

1 _____ mal durch das Fenster, Heinz! (schauen)
2 Christa _____ ihren Hut unmodern. (finden)
3 _____ Sie mal an seine Erzählungen, Frau Hartmann! (denken)
4 Du _____ heute keinen Hut. (kaufen)
5 Das Hütchen _____ nur fünfundzwanzig Mark. (kosten)
6 _____ nicht so schnell, mein Junge! (essen)
7 Warum _____ du so viel von uns? (sprechen)
8 Der Hut _____ billig _____. (aussehen)
9 Frau Wegner _____ nichts ohne ihren Mann. (tun)
10 _____ die Verkäuferin durch die Auswahl? (schauen)
11 Um wieviel Uhr _____ unser Zug _____? (einlaufen)
12 Jedenfalls _____ das Geld knapp. (sein)
13 _____ du denn kein Sparbuch? (haben)
14 Die Kundin _____ nicht, wieviel es kostet. (raten)
15 Wann _____ du die Zeitung, Peter? (lesen)

C. Prepositions

Copy the sentences and insert the German prepositions that correspond to the English words in parentheses:

1 Ich möchte _____ den Zug schauen. (through)
2 Herr Hartmann tut nichts _____ seine Frau. (without)
3 Der Zug fährt _____ sieben Uhr ab. (at)
4 Die Studenten laufen _____ die Straßen. (through)
5 Wir kommen _____ zwei Uhr an. (around)
6 Dieses Hütchen ist zu billig _____ mich. (for)
7 Wir gehen nicht _____ Uwe und Heike. (without)
8 Der Junge läuft _____ die Ecke. (around)
9 Sie hat nichts _____ dich, Günther. (against)
10 Dieser Platz ist _____ meinen Mann. (for)

D. Accusative Case Forms

Copy the sentences and insert the accusative case form of the given pronoun or limiting adjective:

1 Ich tue nichts gegen _____. (er)
2 Wie finden Sie _____ Hut? (dieser)
3 Ich kaufe nichts ohne _____ Frau. (mein)
4 Siehst du _____ Kreuzung? (der)
5 Der Junge läuft gegen _____ Mutter. (sein)
6 Sie geht _____ Woche zum Baden. (jeder)
7 _____ siehst du, Heinz? (wer)
8 Das Buch ist zu teuer für _____. (wir)
9 Das Mädchen schaut durch _____ Auswahl. (jener)
10 Wir fahren _____ Monat von Wien nach Hamburg. (jeder)
11 Hans läuft um _____ Wagen herum. (unser)
12 Die Verkäuferin hat _____ Glück. (kein)
13 Wir tun nichts ohne _____. (ihr)
14 Sie hat nichts gegen _____, Herr Müller. (Sie)
15 Ohne _____! (wir)
16 Rat mal, _____ ich sehe, Christa! (wer)

E. Prices

Write the corresponding German sentences, using Arabic numerals and the abbreviation **DM** for the prices:

1 How much does the hat cost?
2 It (*gender!*) costs seventy marks twenty.
3 What do the newspapers cost?
4 They cost two marks ten.
5 These books cost fifty marks.
6 Her book costs only ten marks fifteen.

LISTENING PRACTICE

Listen to the recorded conversation; then answer the following questions.

Lilo und Peter

1 Wo ist der Hut?
2 Warum mag Lilo nicht sagen, wieviel der Hut kostet?
3 Wieviel kostet er?
4 Warum ist das nicht so schlimm?

Unit 11

LEBKUCHEN

DIALOG

Der Schrank aus der Kiste (Anfang)

1 **Margrit:** Du, Gerhard, da kommt eine Kiste mit der Post. Von wem mag sie wohl sein?

2 **Gerhard:** Ich gehe dem Postboten mal entgegen. Schau, wieviel Mühe er mit dem Paket hat.

3 **Margrit:** Frag aber gleich, vielleicht gehört es uns gar nicht.

4 **Gerhard:** Wahrscheinlich ist es der Schrank vom Versandgeschäft.

The Cabinet out of the Box (Beginning)

der Schrank, *pl.* die Schränke · die Kiste, *pl.* die Kisten (der Kiste *dat.*)

1 Hey, Gerhard, there comes a box in the mail. I wonder who it can be from?

die Post (der Post *dat.*) · wer (wem *dat.*) · wohl I wonder, do you suppose; probably; well

2 I'll just go meet the mailman. Look how much trouble he's having with the package.

entgegengehen go to, toward   entgegen toward + gehen · der Postbote (dem Postboten *dat.*) die Post + der Bote, *pl.* die Boten (Group V) messenger · die Mühe   wieviel Mühe *used as a subordinating conjunction* · das Paket, *pl.* die Pakete (dem Paket *dat.*)

3 But ask right away. Maybe it doesn't even belong to us.

wir (uns *dat.*) · gar nicht not at all, not even

4 It's probably the cabinet from the mail-order house.

vom = von dem · das Versandgeschäft   der Versand shipment + das Geschäft, *pl.* die Geschäfte business

5 **Margrit:** Was, ein Schrank aus dieser Kiste? Das glaube ich nicht!

6 **Gerhard:** Warum nicht? Es sind ja nur die Einzelteile.

7 **Margrit:** Und wir sollen sie zu einem Schrank zusammenbauen?

8 **Gerhard:** Mit dem richtigen Werkzeug, denke ich, gelingt es mir.

9 **Margrit:** Na, hoffentlich gefällt er uns, wenn er fertig ist.

10 **Gerhard:** Wenn nicht, schicken wir ihn den Leuten einfach wieder zurück.

(Fortsetzung folgt)

SUPPLEMENT

Days of the week

1 Die Tage heißen: (der) Sonntag, (der) Montag, (der) Dienstag, (der) Mittwoch, (der) Donnerstag, (der) Freitag, (der) Samstag oder (der) Sonnabend.

2 Er kommt am Montag von Köln.

3 Er fährt am Mittwoch nach Freiburg.

5	What, a cabinet out of this box? That I don't believe!	**dieser Kiste** *dat.*
6	Why not? Of course, it's only the separate pieces.	**das Einzelteil einzeln** separate *adj.* + **der (das) Teil,** *pl.* **die Teile**
7	And we're supposed to put them together into a cabinet?	**zu** into, to · **einem Schrank** *dat.* · **zusammenbauen zusammen** together + **bauen** build
8	With the right tools, I think I'll be able to do it.	**das Werkzeug (dem richtigen Werkzeug** *dat.*) tool *or* tools *collective* · *The introductory prepositional phrase governs the word order of the parenthetical* **denke ich** *as well as of the main clause* · **gelingen (es gelingt mir** *lit.* it succeeds to me) succeed · **ich (mir** *dat.*)
9	Well, I hope we'll like it when it's finished.	**gefallen: du gefällst, er gefällt (er gefällt uns** we like it *lit.* it is pleasing to us) please · **fertig** finished, ready
10	If not, we'll simply send it back to the people.	**die Leute** people *no singular form* (**den Leuten** *dat.*) · **zurückschicken zurück** back, in the opposite direction + **schicken** send

(To be continued)

1	The days are called: Sunday, Monday, Tuesday, Wednesday, Thursday, Friday, Saturday.	**heißen** be called **ich heiße Gerhard** my name is Gerhard · *There are two names for Saturday.* **Samstag** *is used mainly in the south and* **Sonnabend** *in the north.*
2	He's coming from Cologne on Monday.	**am Montag** *dat.*
3	He's going to Freiburg on Wednesday.	

4   Er kommt am Sonntag an.

Times of day

5   Die Tageszeiten heißen: (der) Morgen, (der) Vormittag, (der) Mittag, (der) Nachmittag, (der) Abend, (die) Nacht, (die) Mitternacht.

6   Er kommt am Morgen an.

7   Er kommt am Vormittag an.

8   Er kommt am Mittag an.

9   Er kommt am Nachmittag an.

10   Er kommt am Abend an.

11   Er kommt in der Nacht an.

12   Er kommt um Mitternacht an.

Months of the year

13   Die Monate heißen: (der) Januar, (der) Februar, (der) März, (der) April, (der) Mai, (der) Juni, (der) Juli, (der) August, (der) September, (der) Oktober, (der) November, (der) Dezember.

14   Mein Bruder kommt im Januar an.

15   Mein Vater fährt im April ab.

16   Wir fahren am zehnten Juni nach Hamburg.

17   Es geht am siebten November los.

Seasons of the year

18   Die Jahreszeiten heißen: (der) Frühling, (der) Sommer, (der) Herbst, (der) Winter.

19   Er kommt im Herbst von Berlin.

20   Wir fahren im Frühling nach Deutschland.

4	He's arriving on Sunday.	
5	The times of day are called: morning, forenoon, noon, afternoon, evening, night, midnight.	die Tageszeit, *pl.* die Tageszeiten der Tag + die Zeit time
6	He's arriving in the morning.	der Morgen, *pl.* die Morgen
7	He's arriving in the forenoon.	der Vormittag, *pl.* die Vormittage
8	He's arriving at noon.	der Mittag, *pl.* die Mittage
9	He's arriving in the afternoon.	der Nachmittag, *pl.* die Nachmittage
10	He's arriving in the evening.	der Abend, *pl.* die Abende
11	He's arriving at (in the) night.	die Nacht, *pl.* die Nächte (der Nacht *dat.*)
12	He's arriving at midnight.	die Mitternacht die Mitte middle + die Nacht
13	The months are called: January, February, March, April, May, June, July, August, September, October, November, December.	der Monat, *pl.* die Monate
14	My brother is arriving in January.	im Januar *dat.*
15	My father is leaving in April.	
16	We're going to Hamburg on the tenth of June.	am zehnten Juni *dat.*
17	It starts on the seventh of November.	
18	The seasons are called: spring, summer, autumn, winter.	die Jahreszeit, *pl.* die Jahreszeiten das Jahr year + die Zeit time
19	He's coming from Berlin in the autumn.	im Herbst *dat.*
20	We're going to Germany in the spring.	(das) Deutschland deutsch German + das Land, *pl.* die Länder country, land

Hohe Munte, Tirol/Österreich · Hohe Munte, Tyrol/Austria · Hohe Munte, le Tyrol/Autriche · Hohe Munte, Tirolo/Austria
Hohe Munte, Tirol/Oostenrijk

1969	Sonntag Sunday Dimanche	Montag Monday Lundi	Dienstag Tuesday Mardi	Mittwoch Wednesday Mercredi	Donnerstag Thursday Jeudi	Freitag Friday Vendredi	Samstag Saturday Samedi
Januar January Janvier Gennaio Januari	5 12 19 26	6 13 20 27	7 14 21 28	1 8 15 22 29	2 9 16 23 30	3 10 17 24 31	4 11 18 25
	Domenica Söndag Zondag	Lunedì Måndag Maandag	Martedì Tisdag Dinsdag	Mercoledì Onsdag Woensdag	Giovedì Torsdag Donderdag	Venerdì Fredag Vrijdag	Sabato Lördag Zaterdag

Foto: T. Schneiders · Michel Kunstverlag Nürnberg · 53 69 2

AUDIOLINGUAL DRILLS

A. Directed Dialog

Sagen Sie, daß da eine Kiste mit der Post kommt!
Da kommt eine Kiste mit der Post.

Fragen Sie, von wem sie wohl sein mag!
Von wem mag sie wohl sein?

Sagen Sie, daß Gerhard dem Postboten entgegengeht!
Gerhard geht dem Postboten entgegen.

Sagen Sie, daß der Mann viel Mühe mit dem Paket hat!
Der Mann hat viel Mühe mit dem Paket.

Fragen Sie, wem das Paket gehört!
Wem gehört das Paket?

Antworten Sie, daß es Margrits Schrank vom Versandgeschäft ist!
Es ist Margrits Schrank vom Versandgeschäft.

Fragen Sie, ob ein Schrank aus dieser Kiste kommen soll!
Soll ein Schrank aus dieser Kiste kommen?

Sagen Sie, daß Margrit das nicht glaubt!
Margrit glaubt das nicht.

Sagen Sie, daß es nur die Einzelteile sind!
Es sind nur die Einzelteile.

Fragen Sie, was Margrit und Gerhard mit den Einzelteilen tun sollen!
Was sollen Margrit und Gerhard mit den Einzelteilen tun?

Antworten Sie, daß sie sie zu einem Schrank zusammenbauen sollen!
Sie sollen sie zu einem Schrank zusammenbauen.

Sagen Sie, daß es Gerhard gelingt!
Es gelingt Gerhard.

Sagen Sie, daß der Schrank Margrit und Gerhard hoffentlich gefällt!
Der Schrank gefällt Margrit und Gerhard hoffentlich.

Fragen Sie, ob sie den Schrank zurückschicken!
Schicken sie den Schrank zurück?

Antworten Sie, daß sie ihn nicht zurückschicken!
Sie schicken ihn nicht zurück.

B. Dative Case: Indirect Object of Verbs (*See Grammar* §§11.3–11.5)

1 Repeat the following sentences. Note that nouns must end in **-n** in the dative plural:

Ich schicke dem Mann ein Paket.
Ich schicke der Frau ein Paket.
Ich schicke dem Kind ein Paket.
Ich schicke den Leuten ein Paket.

2 Substitute the new noun as the indirect object.

Example:
Er kauft dem Professor einen Hut.   **Frau**
Er kauft der Frau einen Hut.

Er kauft der Frau einen Hut.   **Bruder**
Er kauft dem Bruder einen Hut.   **Tante**
Er kauft der Tante einen Hut.   **Eismann**
Er kauft dem Eismann einen Hut.   **Freundin**
Er kauft der Freundin einen Hut.   **Kind**
Er kauft dem Kind einen Hut.   **Postbote**

Er kauft dem Postboten einen Hut.   **Leute**
Er kauft den Leuten einen Hut.   **Studentin**
Er kauft der Studentin einen Hut.   **Junge**
Er kauft dem Jungen einen Hut.   **Kundinnen**
Er kauft den Kundinnen einen Hut.

3 Substitute the new dative pronoun:

Peter schickt mir ein Paket.   **dir**
Peter schickt dir ein Paket.   **uns**
Peter schickt uns ein Paket.   **euch**
Peter schickt euch ein Paket.   **ihm**

Peter schickt ihm ein Paket.   **ihr**
Peter schickt ihr ein Paket.   **ihnen**
Peter schickt ihnen ein Paket.

4 Change the dative noun object to a pronoun.

Example:
Ich kaufe dem Mann eine Zeitung.
Ich kaufe ihm eine Zeitung.

Ich kaufe dem Kind ein Buch.
Ich kaufe ihm ein Buch.

Ich kaufe der Frau ein Buch.
Ich kaufe ihr ein Buch.

Ich kaufe den Leuten ein Buch.
Ich kaufe ihnen ein Buch.

Ich kaufe dem Professor ein Buch.
Ich kaufe ihm ein Buch.

Ich kaufe der Kundin ein Buch.
Ich kaufe ihr ein Buch.

Ich kaufe den Studenten ein Buch.
Ich kaufe ihnen ein Buch.

Ich kaufe dem Bruder ein Buch.
Ich kaufe ihm ein Buch.

Ich kaufe der Tante ein Buch.
Ich kaufe ihr ein Buch.

5 Change the accusative noun object to a pronoun and place it before the dative noun object.

Example:
Wir schicken dem Eismann einen Schrank.
Wir schicken ihn dem Eismann.

Wir schicken der Frau einen Schrank.
Wir schicken ihn der Frau.

Wir schicken unserem Bruder das Werkzeug.
Wir schicken es unserem Bruder.

Wir schicken der Frau eine Zeitung.
Wir schicken sie der Frau.

Wir schicken ihren Kindern das Werkzeug.
Wir schicken es ihren Kindern.

Wir schicken unserem Bruder eine Zeitung.
Wir schicken sie unserem Bruder.

Wir schicken ihren Kindern Bücher.
Wir schicken sie ihren Kindern.

6 Answer the questions in the affirmative, changing both noun objects to pronouns and placing the accusative pronoun object before the dative pronoun object.

Example:
Erklärt er dem Studenten die Erzählung?
Ja, er erklärt sie ihm.

Erklärt er dem Studenten das Gedicht?
Ja, er erklärt es ihm.

Kauft er den Studentinnen die Bücher?
Ja, er kauft sie ihnen.

Erklärt er der Kundin das Gedicht?
Ja, er erklärt es ihr.

Kauft er dem Jungen die Bücher?
Ja, er kauft sie ihm.

Schickt er der Kundin das Gedicht?
Ja, er schickt es ihr.

Schickt er dem Jungen die Bücher?
Ja, er schickt sie ihm.

Schickt er der Kundin den Hut?
Ja, er schickt ihn ihr.

Schickt er dem Jungen das Paket?
Ja, er schickt es ihm.

Schickt er den Studentinnen den Hut?
Ja, er schickt ihn ihnen.

Schickt er seiner Frau das Paket?
Ja, er schickt es ihr.

Kauft er den Studentinnen den Hut?
Ja, er kauft ihn ihnen.

C. Verbs That Govern the Dative Case (*See Grammar* §11.5)

7 Substitute the new noun phrase or pronoun as the dative object of the verb:

Der Schrank gefällt dem Mann.   **diese Kundin**
Der Schrank gefällt dieser Kundin.   **unser Bruder**

Der Schrank gefällt unserem Bruder. **wir**
Der Schrank gefällt uns. **ihre Kinder**
Der Schrank gefällt ihren Kindern.

Sie können mir helfen. **das Mädchen**
Sie können dem Mädchen helfen. **die Frauen**
Sie können den Frauen helfen. **er**
Sie können ihm helfen. **seine Freundin**
Sie können seiner Freundin helfen.

Warum glaubst du ihm nicht? **die Leute**
Warum glaubst du den Leuten nicht? **ich**
Warum glaubst du mir nicht? **wir**
Warum glaubst du uns nicht? **diese Studentin**
Warum glaubst du dieser Studentin nicht?

Diese Kiste gehört mir. **du**
Diese Kiste gehört dir. **meine Mutter**
Diese Kiste gehört meiner Mutter. **ihr**
Diese Kiste gehört euch. **das Kind**
Diese Kiste gehört dem Kind.

Es gelingt ihr nicht. **ich**
Es gelingt mir nicht. **der Postbote**
Es gelingt dem Postboten nicht. **er**
Es gelingt ihm nicht. **deine Tante**
Es gelingt deiner Tante nicht.

Kannst du mir nicht antworten? **der Junge**
Kannst du dem Jungen nicht antworten? **unsere Kundinnen**
Kannst du unseren Kundinnen nicht antworten? **das Fräulein**
Kannst du dem Fräulein nicht antworten? **wir**
Kannst du uns nicht antworten?

Ich danke dir. **ihr**
Ich danke euch. **der Professor**
Ich danke dem Professor. **die Verkäuferin**
Ich danke der Verkäuferin. **Sie, Herr Hartmann**
Ich danke Ihnen, Herr Hartmann.

Sie geht ihnen entgegen. **die Kundin**
Sie geht der Kundin entgegen. **der Student**
Sie geht dem Studenten entgegen. **er**
Sie geht ihm entgegen. **jene Kinder**
Sie geht jenen Kindern entgegen.

8 Answer in the affirmative, changing nouns to pronouns:

Gefällt dem Professor dieses Buch?
Ja, es gefällt ihm.

Kann Rolf den Frauen helfen?
Ja, er kann ihnen helfen.

Glaubt Fräulein Schneider dem Studenten?
Ja, sie glaubt ihm.

Gehören diese Sachen deiner Mutter?
Ja, sie gehören ihr.

Gelingt es Ihrem Mann?
Ja, es gelingt ihm.

Antwortet der Junge seiner Tante?
Ja, er antwortet ihr.

Danken die Kinder dem Eismann?
Ja, sie danken ihm.

Geht Herr Schneider den Kindern entgegen?
Ja, er geht ihnen entgegen.

D. Accusative and Dative Cases Mixed

9 Answer the questions using the new words:

Wen sehen Sie?   **ein Eismann**
Ich sehe einen Eismann.

Wem helfen Sie?   **eine Frau**
Ich helfe einer Frau.

Wen lernen Sie kennen?   **der Professor**
Ich lerne den Professor kennen.

Wem gefällt der Schrank?   **das Kind**
Der Schrank gefällt dem Kind.

Was kaufen Sie?   **das Werkzeug**
Ich kaufe das Werkzeug.

Wem kaufen Sie es?   **mein Bruder**
Ich kaufe es meinem Bruder.

Wen sehen Sie?   **das Mädchen**
Ich sehe das Mädchen.

Wem gelingt es?   **die Studenten**
Es gelingt den Studenten.

Was kaufen Sie?   **ein Hut**
Ich kaufe einen Hut.

Wem kaufen Sie ihn?   **meine Tante**
Ich kaufe ihn meiner Tante.

Was schicken Sie zurück?   **der Schrank**
Ich schicke den Schrank zurück.

Wem schicken Sie ihn zurück?
                          das Versandgeschäft
Ich schicke ihn dem Versandgeschäft zurück.

Wem gehört die Kiste?   **meine Freundin**
Die Kiste gehört meiner Freundin.

E. Time Expressions (*See Grammar* §11.6)

10 Substitute the new time expression with the appropriate prepositional element before it:

Er fährt im Frühling von Hamburg ab.   **Winter**
Er fährt im Winter von Hamburg ab.   **Januar**

Er fährt im Januar von Hamburg ab. **Mittwoch**
Er fährt am Mittwoch von Hamburg ab. **Mitternacht**
Er fährt um Mitternacht von Hamburg ab. **Sonntag**
Er fährt am Sonntag von Hamburg ab. **Nacht**
Er fährt in der Nacht von Hamburg ab. **Morgen**
Er fährt am Morgen von Hamburg ab. **März**
Er fährt im März von Hamburg ab. **Mittag**
Er fährt am Mittag von Hamburg ab. **Februar**
Er fährt im Februar von Hamburg ab. **Abend**
Er fährt am Abend von Hamburg ab. **Juli**
Er fährt im Juli von Hamburg ab. **Nachmittag**
Er fährt am Nachmittag von Hamburg ab. **August**
Er fährt im August von Hamburg ab.

F. Questions and Answers

Wie heißt der elfte Dialog?
Er heißt „Der Schrank aus der Kiste".

Wem geht Gerhard entgegen?
Er geht dem Postboten entgegen.

Von wem mag die Kiste wohl sein?
Sie ist wohl vom Versandgeschäft.

Wem gehört das Paket?
Es gehört Margrit und Gerhard.

Was ist in der Kiste?
Ein Schrank ist in der Kiste.

Was müssen Margrit und Gerhard tun?
Sie müssen die Einzelteile zu einem Schrank zusammenbauen.

Gelingt das Gerhard?
Ja, es gelingt ihm.

Was tun Margrit und Gerhard mit dem Schrank, wenn er ihnen nicht gefällt?
Sie schicken ihn den Leuten einfach zurück.

GRAMMAR

11.1 Word-Formation

Compound nouns

einzeln separate, single + **der (das) Teil** part, piece = **das Einzelteil** separate part
das Jahr year + **die Zeit** time = **die Jahreszeit** season
die Post mail; post office + **der Bote** messenger = **der Postbote** mailman

der Tag day + **die Zeit** time = **die Tageszeit** time of day
der Versand shipment + **das Geschäft** store, business = **das Versandgeschäft** mail-order house
das Werk work; factory + **das Zeug** thing = **das Werkzeug** tool(s)

1.2 Singular and Plural of Nouns

der Abend, die Abende
der Bote (*acc.* den Boten), die Boten
das Geschäft, die Geschäfte
die Kiste, die Kisten
der Monat, die Monate
der Morgen, die Morgen

die Nacht, die Nächte
das Paket, die Pakete
der Schrank, die Schränke
der (das) Teil, die Teile
die Zeit, die Zeiten

1.3 Limiting Adjectives and Personal Pronouns in the Nominative, Accusative, and Dative Cases

Limiting adjectives

	Masculine	*Feminine*	*Neuter*	*Plural*
Nom.	der	die	das	die
Acc.	den	die	das	die
Dat.	dem	der	dem	den
Nom.	dieser	diese	dieses	diese
Acc.	diesen	diese	dieses	diese
Dat.	diesem	dieser	diesem	diesen
Nom.	mein	meine	mein	meine
Acc.	meinen	meine	mein	meine
Dat.	meinem	meiner	meinem	meinen

Personal pronouns

	Singular					*Plural*			*Standard*
	1	*2*	*3 M*	*3 F*	*3 N*	*1*	*2*	*3*	*2*
Nom.	ich	du	er	sie	es	wir	ihr	sie	Sie
Acc.	mich	dich	ihn	sie	es	uns	euch	sie	Sie
Dat.	mir	dir	ihm	ihr	ihm	uns	euch	ihnen	Ihnen

11.4 Noun Endings in the Dative Case

An ending **-e** is sometimes added to masculine and neuter nouns of one syllable in the dative singular. This ending is somewhat archaic, however, and appears in modern spoken German only in a few standardized expressions like **nach Hause** (*toward*) *home* and **zu Hause** *at home*. In the plural the dative ending is **-n**; this is always attached to the plural form of a noun in the dative case, as long as that plural form does not already end in **-n** or in **-s**:

	Singular	*Plural*
Nom.	der Bruder	die Brüder
Dat.	dem Bruder	de**n** Brüder**n**
Nom.	die Straße	die Straßen
Dat.	der Straße	de**n** Straßen
Nom.	das Hotel	die Hotels
Dat.	dem Hotel	de**n** Hotels

Most masculine nouns whose plural is formed by adding **-n** or **-en** to the singular stem (Group V, Grammar §10.2) also have this ending in the accusative singular and dative singular:

	Singular	*Plural*
Nom.	der Student	die Student**en**
Acc.	den Student**en**	die Student**en**
Dat.	dem Student**en**	den Student**en**

Other nouns that follow the pattern of **der Student** are **der Held** and **der Mensch**. Taking the ending **-n** are **der Junge**, **der Kunde**, and **der Postbote**. **Der Herr** has **-n** in the accusative and dative singular, but **-en** in the plural: **der Herr, den Herrn, dem Herrn,** *pl.* **die Herren**.

11.5 Uses of the Dative Case

The dative case occurs in several functions in German, among which are those presented here.

1. The indirect object of a verb refers to the person to whom or for whom something is done. German indirect objects are in the dative case, while direct objects are in the accusative case (Grammar §9.7):

Mein Bruder hat es **mir** erzählt.
My brother told it to me.

Wir schicken ihn **den Leuten** zurück.
We'll send it back to the people.

Er kauft **seiner Frau** einen Hut.
He's buying his wife a hat.

Es macht **mir** Spaß.
It's fun for me.

Unlike English, German uses no preposition with the indirect object of a verb. The dative case form alone is sufficient to indicate that the word is an indirect object.

When a finite verb is followed by a dative (indirect) object and an accusative (direct) object, the order of those two objects is strictly regulated by the following two rules:

a. If the accusative object is a noun, then it follows the dative object.

b. If the accusative object is a personal pronoun, then it precedes the dative object.

Note how the position of the accusative object shifts in relation to the dative object, depending on whether the accusative object is a personal pronoun or a noun:

Ich schicke **ihm** ein Paket.
Ich schicke es **ihm**.

Er kauft **seiner Frau** den Schrank.
Er kauft ihn **seiner Frau**.

Wir erklären **den Studenten** die Erzählungen.
Wir erklären sie **den Studenten**.

2 Some verbs govern the dative case; that is, they automatically require a dative object, not an accusative object. Those that you have learned so far are: **danken** *thank*, **helfen** *help*, **entgegengehen** *go toward*, **gehören** *belong*, **antworten** *answer*, **gefallen** *like*, **gelingen** *succeed*, **glauben** *believe*.

Sie dankt **ihm**.
She is thanking him.

Wir müssen **ihr** helfen.
We have to help her.

Er geht **dem Postboten** entgegen.
He goes toward the mailman.

Es gehört **mir** nicht.
It doesn't belong to me.

Er antwortet **ihr** nicht.
He doesn't answer her.

Du gefällst **mir**.
I like you. (You please me.)

Es gelingt **mir**.
I succeed. (It is successful to me.)

Ich glaube **dir** nicht, Hans.
I don't believe you, Hans.

The verb **glauben** may also occur with an accusative object; the accusative object then refers to the thing believed (a story, report, rumor, etc.), while the dative object refers to the person:

Ich glaube es **ihm** nicht.
I don't believe what he says.

3 Certain prepositions occur with objects in the dative case; this will be treated more thoroughly in Unit 12.

Was ist mit **dem Üben**?
What about practice? (What's with the practice?)

The dative case answers the question **wem**?

Wem hat er es erzählt?
Er hat es **mir** erzählt.

Von wem mag die Kiste wohl sein?
Sie ist von **meinem Vater**.

11.6 Time Expressions

The names of the days, the months, the seasons, and the parts of the day are introduced in the Supplement of this unit. All the names are masculine except **die Nacht** and **die Mitternacht**. The month names are similar to those of English, but you must pay attention to the stress in

ˈJuli, Apˈril, Auˈgust.

These names are often used in prepositional phrases, similar to English *on Monday, in the winter, at midnight, in July*, etc.

On a day of the week = **am** (contraction of **an** + **dem**):

Wir fahren **am Montag** nach Berlin.
We're going to Berlin on Monday.

Kommt er **am Donnerstag** an?
Is he arriving on Thursday?

At or *in* a part of a day = **am (an + dem)**:

Er kommt **am Morgen**.
He's coming in the morning.

Am Mittag gehen wir zum Baden.
We go swimming at noon.

Two exceptions to this are **in der Nacht** *at night, in the night* and **um Mitternacht** *at midnight*:

Fahren Sie **in der Nacht** nach München?
Are you travelling to Munich at night?

Der Zug läuft **um Mitternacht** ein.
The train pulls in at midnight.

In a season or month = **im** (contraction of **in** + **dem**):

Er fährt **im Winter** ab.
He's leaving in the winter.

Im November kannst du dir einen Hut kaufen.
You can buy yourself a hat in November.

WRITING

A. Singular and Plural of Nouns

Copy the sentences and insert the forms that correspond to the English in parentheses:

1. Da kommen _____ _____. (the mailmen)
2. Mußt du _____ _____ zusammenbauen? (the separate parts)
3. Er schickt uns _____ _____. (a package)
4. Von wem mögen _____ _____ wohl sein? (these boxes)
5. _____ _____ sind in Berlin. (his stores)
6. Ist das nicht _____ _____? (our cabinet)
7. Wo sind denn _____ _____? (her children)
8. _____ _____ sieht schlimm aus. (every accident)
9. Sind _____ _____ langweilig? (his lectures)
10. Kennen Sie _____ _____? (my girl friend)
11. _____ _____ haben kein Interesse an Tagesfragen. (such persons)
12. Ist das _____ _____? (your husband)
13. _____ _____ sehen billig aus. (those little hats)
14. _____ _____ verstehen das nicht. (the salesladies)

B. Accusative and Dative Objects

Copy the sentences and insert the correct case form of the word in parentheses:

1. Kaufst du _____ _____ diesen Schrank? (deine Frau)
2. Diese Sachen gehören _____. (Sie)
3. Sehen Sie _____ _____ dort rechts? (unser Haus)
4. Geh _____ _____ entgegen! (die Leute)
5. Ich schicke es _____ _____. (mein Bruder)
6. Der Professor erklärt _____ uns. (sie *sg.*)
7. _____ _____ ist nichts passiert. (der Fahrer)
8. Die Leute schicken _____ _____ ein Buch. (jedes Mädchen)
9. Kennst du _____ denn? (sie *pl.*)
10. Von _____ ist die Kiste? (wer)
11. Ich kaufe _____ meiner Tante. (er)
12. Kann sie _____ nicht helfen? (wir)
13. Dieser Schrank gefällt _____. (ich)
14. Wir schicken _____ _____ ein Paket. (die Kinder)

15 Gelingt es _____ ? (ihr)
16 Bauen Sie _____ den Schrank zusammen? (sie *pl.*)
17 Ich glaube _____ nicht. (er)
18 Du mußt _____ _____ danken. (die Verkäuferin)

C. Order of Objects

Arrange the elements in the correct order:

1 Ich kaufe / einen Hut / meiner Frau .
2 Hoffentlich schickt er / das Paket / uns .
3 Herr Held baut / es / seiner Freundin / zusammen .
4 Heute erklärt sie / es / mir .
5 Ich erzähle / es / unseren Kindern .
6 Kannst du / das Gedicht / mir / erklären ?
7 Wann schicken Sie / die Kiste / den Leuten ?
8 Ich glaube / es / ihnen .
9 Glaubst du / seine Erzählung / dem Jungen ?
10 Schick / den Schrank / ihm / zurück !

D. Time Expressions

Write the corresponding German expressions:

1 We arrive in the afternoon.
2 Is Uwe leaving on Tuesday?
3 In the summer we eat ice cream.
4 What do you do at midnight?
5 The lecture begins in the evening.
6 In April most of it happens.
7 Why are you leaving at night?

READING PRACTICE

Im Buchgeschäft

Am Schillerplatz ist ein neues Buchgeschäft. Die Verkäufer da sind sehr nett. Nun, Verkäufer in Buchgeschäften sind wohl fast immer nett. Vielleicht hat das mit den Büchern zu tun?

Jedenfalls finde ich Verkäufer in Hutgeschäften lange nicht so nett wie die Verkäufer in Buchgeschäften.

„Mein" Buchgeschäft hat viele, viele Bücher. Man kann eigentlich alles haben. Und wenn ich ein bestimmtes Buch nicht finde, dann frage ich eben einen netten Verkäufer. Oder eine hübsche Verkäuferin. Ich glaube, heute nachmittag gehe ich wieder in mein Buchgeschäft. Vielleicht kann ich wieder ein bestimmtes Buch nicht finden. Dann muß ich natürlich die hübsche Verkäuferin fragen.

Unit 12

springerle

DIALOG

Der Schrank aus der Kiste (Schluß)

1 **Gerhard:** Er ist es also! Und schon seit dem dritten Juli ist er unterwegs!

2 **Margrit:** Du meinst: seine Einzelteile! Im Augenblick besteht er nur aus diesen Brettern und Schrauben hier.

3 **Gerhard:** Nicht mehr lange. Es macht mir Spaß, ihn dir zusammenzubauen.

4 **Margrit:** Hoffentlich klappt es auch. Ich kann dir dabei nicht helfen.

5 **Gerhard:** Das macht nichts. Holst du mir bitte den Schraubenzieher aus dem Werkzeugkasten?

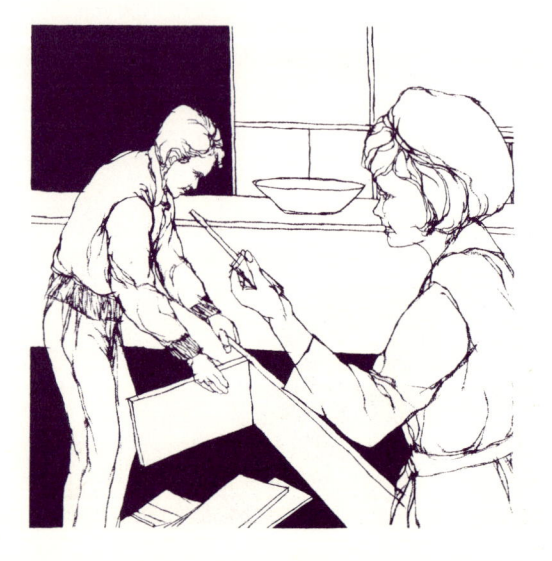

The Cabinet out of the Box (Conclusion)

1. Well, that's what it is! And it's been on the way since the third of July.

   der Juli (dem dritten Juli *dat.*) · **unterwegs** on the way **unter** under + **der Weg** way, road

2. You mean its separate pieces! At the moment it only consists of these boards and screws here.

   der Augenblick (im Augenblick *dat.*) **das Auge** eye + **der Blick** glance · **bestehen aus** consist of · **das Brett,** *pl.* **die Bretter · die Schraube,** *pl.* **die Schrauben**

3. Not for long. It'll be fun for me to put it together for you.

   viel much   **mehr** more

4. I hope it'll work too. I can't help you with it.

   klappen (es klappt) clap; work, fit · **dabei** = **da** + **bei**

5. That doesn't matter. Will you please get me the screwdriver out of the toolbox?

   der Schraubenzieher   die Schraube + **der Zieher** instrument for pulling · **der Werkzeugkasten   das Werkzeug** + **der Kasten,** *pl.* **die Kästen** box

6 **Margrit:** Was ist mit diesem Ding? Es liegt schon seit heute morgen hier im Zimmer.

7 **Gerhard:** Ja, der ist genau der richtige. Doch nun laß mich bitte mit meiner Arbeit allein.

8 **Margrit:** Gern. Ich gehe solange zu Mutter hinüber. Vater kommt bald nach Hause.

9 **Gerhard:** Gut. In einer Stunde steht hier ein Schrank wie aus unserem Katalog entsprungen.

10 **Margrit:** Ich wünsche dir viel Glück. Also, ich bin bald wieder zu Hause.

SUPPLEMENT

Directions

1 Die Himmelsrichtungen sind:

der Norden	nördlich
der Süden	südlich
der Osten	östlich
der Westen	westlich
der Nordosten	nordöstlich
der Südosten	südöstlich
der Nordwesten	nordwestlich
der Südwesten	südwestlich

2 Schleswig-Holstein liegt im Norden Deutschlands.

3 Der Bodensee liegt im Süden Deutschlands.

6	What about this thing? It's been lying here in the room since this morning.	**das Ding,** *pl.* **die Dinge** · **das Zimmer,** *pl.* **die Zimmer**
7	Yes, that's just the right one. But now please leave me alone with my work.	**genau** just, exactly, precisely · **lassen: du läßt, er läßt allein lassen** leave alone · **die Arbeit,** *pl.* **die Arbeiten**
8	Gladly. Meanwhile I'll go over to Mother's. Father is coming home soon.	**hinübergehen hinüber** over, across + **gehen** · **die Mutter,** *pl.* **die Mütter** · **der Vater,** *pl.* **die Väter** · **nach Hause kommen** come home
9	Fine. In an hour a cabinet will be standing here as if it had come out of our catalog.	**die Stunde,** *pl.* **die Stunden** · **der Katalog,** *pl.* **die Kataloge** · **entspringen (entsprungen** *past participle used as a predicate adjective*) escape, rise **springen** jump
10	I wish you lots of luck. So, I'll be back home soon.	**wieder** again · **zu Hause sein** be (at) home

---

1	The points of the compass are:	**die Himmelsrichtung der Himmel** sky, heaven + **die Richtung,** *pl.* **Richtungen** direction

the north	north, northern, northerly
the south	south, southern, southerly
the east	east, eastern, easterly
the west	west, western, westerly
the northeast	northeast, northeastern, northeasterly
the southeast	southeast, southeastern, southeasterly
the northwest	northwest, northwestern, northwesterly
the southwest	southwest, southwestern, southwesterly

2	Schleswig-Holstein is in the north of Germany.	**im Norden** *dat.* · **Deutschlands** *gen.*
3	Lake Constance is in the south of Germany.	

4 Bayern liegt im Süden Deutschlands.

5 Dresden liegt im Osten Deutschlands.

6 Der Schwarzwald liegt im Südwesten.

7 Österreich und die Schweiz liegen südlich von Deutschland.

8 Berlin liegt südöstlich von Hamburg.

9 Der Schwarzwald liegt nordöstlich vom Bodensee.

10 Im Süden grenzt Deutschland an Österreich und die Schweiz.

Germany's neighbors

11 Deutschlands Nachbarländer heißen: Frankreich, Luxemburg, Belgien, die Niederlande, Dänemark, Polen, die Tschechoslowakei, Österreich und die Schweiz.

4	Bavaria is in the south of Germany.	
5	Dresden is in the east of Germany.	
6	The Black Forest is in the southwest.	**der Schwarzwald** **schwarz** black + **der Wald**, *pl.* **Wälder** forest
7	Austria and Switzerland are south of Germany.	
8	Berlin is southeast of Hamburg.	
9	The Black Forest is northeast of Lake Constance.	
10	In the south, Germany borders on Austria and Switzerland.	**grenzen (es grenzt)** border
11	Germany's neighboring countries are called: France, Luxemburg, Belgium, the Netherlands, Denmark, Poland, Czechoslovakia, Austria, and Switzerland.	**das Nachbarland** **der Nachbar** neighbor + **das Land**, *pl.* **Länder** country, state

AUDIOLINGUAL DRILLS

A. Directed Dialog

Fragen Sie, wie lange der Schrank schon unterwegs ist!
Wie lange ist der Schrank schon unterwegs?

Antworten Sie, daß er schon seit dem dritten Juli unterwegs ist!
Er ist schon seit dem dritten Juli unterwegs.

Sagen Sie, daß er nur aus diesen Brettern und Schrauben besteht!
Er besteht nur aus diesen Brettern und Schrauben.

Fragen Sie, ob es Gerhard Spaß macht, den Schank zusammenzubauen!
Macht es Gerhard Spaß, den Schrank zusammenzubauen?

Antworten Sie, daß es ihm Spaß macht!
Es macht ihm Spaß.

Fragen Sie, ob es auch klappt!
Klappt es auch?

Antworten Sie, daß es hoffentlich klappt!
Es klappt hoffentlich.

Sagen Sie, daß Margrit ihm dabei nicht helfen kann!
Margrit kann ihm dabei nicht helfen.

Sagen Sie, daß das nichts macht!
Das macht nichts.

Fragen Sie, ob Margrit den Schraubenzieher holen soll!
Soll Margrit den Schraubenzieher holen?

Antworten Sie, daß der Schraubenzieher schon seit heute morgen im Zimmer liegt!
Der Schraubenzieher liegt schon seit heute morgen im Zimmer.

Sagen Sie, daß Margrit Gerhard mit seiner Arbeit allein lassen soll!
Margrit soll Gerhard mit seiner Arbeit allein lassen.

Sagen Sie, daß Margrit solange zu Mutter hinübergeht!
Margrit geht solange zu Mutter hinüber.

Sagen Sie, daß Margrits Vater bald nach Hause kommt!
Margrits Vater kommt bald nach Hause.

Sagen Sie, daß Margrit bald wieder zu Hause ist!
Margrit ist bald wieder zu Hause.

B. Prepositions with the Dative Case (*See Grammar* §12.3)

aus out of, of, from

1   Substitute the dative form of the new noun:

Sie holt es aus dem Zimmer.   **die Kiste**
Sie holt es aus der Kiste.   **dieses Paket**
Sie holt es aus diesem Paket.   **unsere Schränke**
Sie holt es aus unseren Schränken.   **mein Werkzeugkasten**
Sie holt es aus meinem Werkzeugkasten.   **jene Stadt**
Sie holt es aus jener Stadt.   **die Geschäfte**
Sie holt es aus den Geschäften.   **ihr Wagen**
Sie holt es aus ihrem Wagen.

2 Substitute the dative form of the new name:

Wir kommen aus Frankreich. **Deutschland**
Wir kommen aus Deutschland. **die Schweiz**
Wir kommen aus der Schweiz. **Österreich**
Wir kommen aus Österreich. **Schleswig-Holstein**
Wir kommen aus Schleswig-Holstein. **die Tschechoslowakei**
Wir kommen aus der Tschechoslowakei.

außer except (for)

3 Substitute the dative form of the new noun:

Er hat nichts außer diesem Buch. **jene Zeitung**
Er hat nichts außer jener Zeitung. **sein Wagen**
Er hat nichts außer seinem Wagen. **diese Bretter**
Er hat nichts außer diesen Brettern. **eine Kiste**
Er hat nichts außer einer Kiste. **der Hut**
Er hat nichts außer dem Hut. **unsere Schränke**
Er hat nichts außer unseren Schränken. **eure Geige**
Er hat nichts außer eurer Geige.

bei near, beside, with, at the house of

4 Substitute the dative form of the new noun:

Steht sie bei der Kiste? **der Professor**
Steht sie bei dem Professor? **das Haus**
Steht sie bei dem Haus? **ihre Pakete**
Steht sie bei ihren Paketen? **ein Student**
Steht sie bei einem Studenten? **jede Kundin**
Steht sie bei jeder Kundin? **unser Geschäft**
Steht sie bei unserem Geschäft? **die Kästen**
Steht sie bei den Kästen?

5 Substitute the dative form of the new pronoun:

Wann ist er bei uns? **ich**
Wann ist er bei mir? **ihr**
Wann ist er bei euch? **du**
Wann ist er bei dir? **er**
Wann ist er bei ihm? **Sie, Herr Held**
Wann ist er bei Ihnen, Herr Held?

mit with

6 Substitute the dative form of the new noun:

Da kommt er mit der Kiste. **unser Schrank**
Da kommt er mit unserem Schrank. **der Junge**
Da kommt er mit dem Jungen. **meine Bücher**

Da kommt er mit meinen Büchern. **das Geld**
Da kommt er mit dem Geld. **die Verkäuferin**
Da kommt er mit der Verkäuferin. **jene Kisten**
Da kommt er mit jenen Kisten. **sein Schraubenzieher**
Da kommt er mit seinem Schraubenzieher.

7 Substitute the dative form of the new pronoun:

Geht Heike mit dir zum Baden? **ihr**   Geht Heike mit dir zum Baden? **er**
Geht Heike mit euch zum Baden? **wir**   Geht Heike mit ihm zum Baden? **sie** *sg.*
Geht Heike mit uns zum Baden? **du**   Geht Heike mit ihr zum Baden?

nach after; about; toward, to

8 Substitute the dative form of the new noun:

Sie kommt nach einem Tag. **ein Monat**
Sie kommt nach einem Monat. **eine Woche**
Sie kommt nach einer Woche. **zwei Jahre**
Sie kommt nach zwei Jahren. **drei Monate**
Sie kommt nach drei Monaten. **die Arbeit**
Sie kommt nach der Arbeit. **ihre Vorlesung**
Sie kommt nach ihrer Vorlesung.

Fragen Sie nach dem Eismann! **diese Straße**
Fragen Sie nach dieser Straße! **unser Buch**
Fragen Sie nach unserem Buch! **die Verkäuferinnen**
Fragen Sie nach den Verkäuferinnen! **der Postbote**
Fragen Sie nach dem Postboten! **seine Mutter**
Fragen Sie nach seiner Mutter!

Wir fahren heute nach München. **Bayern**
Wir fahren heute nach Bayern. **Schleswig-Holstein**
Wir fahren heute nach Schleswig-Holstein. **Österreich**
Wir fahren heute nach Österreich. **Köln**
Wir fahren heute nach Köln. **Dänemark**
Wir fahren heute nach Dänemark.

seit since; for

9 Substitute the dative form of the new noun:

Ich kenne ihn seit dem Sommer. **der Winter**
Ich kenne ihn seit dem Winter. **sein Unfall**
Ich kenne ihn seit seinem Unfall. **jene Vorlesung**

Ich kenne ihn seit jener Vorlesung.   **August**
Ich kenne ihn seit August.   **jener Morgen**
Ich kenne ihn seit jenem Morgen.

Wir kennen ihn schon seit acht Tagen.   **vier Jahre**
Wir kennen ihn schon seit vier Jahren.   **zwei Wochen**
Wir kennen ihn schon seit zwei Wochen.   **ein Monat**
Wir kennen ihn schon seit einem Monat.   **drei Tage**
Wir kennen ihn schon seit drei Tagen.   **eine Woche**
Wir kennen ihn schon seit einer Woche.

von about; from; of; by

10   Substitute the dative form of the new noun or pronoun:

Spricht er häufig von mir?   **seine Freundin**
Spricht er häufig von seiner Freundin?   **der Junge**
Spricht er häufig von dem Jungen?   **ihr**
Spricht er häufig von euch?   **unsere Kinder**
Spricht er häufig von unseren Kindern?   **diese Frau**
Spricht er häufig von dieser Frau?   **wir**
Spricht er häufig von uns?

Da kommt er von der Arbeit.   **sein Bruder**
Da kommt er von seinem Bruder.   **die Vorlesungen**
Da kommt er von den Vorlesungen.   **die Post**
Da kommt er von der Post.   **Hamburg**
Da kommt er von Hamburg.   **Berlin**
Da kommt er von Berlin.   **das Geschäft**
Da kommt er von dem Geschäft.

Peter ist ein Freund von mir.   **wir**
Peter ist ein Freund von uns.   **ihr**
Peter ist ein Freund von euch.   **mein Bruder**
Peter ist ein Freund von meinem Bruder.   **diese Leute**
Peter ist ein Freund von diesen Leuten.   **er**
Peter ist ein Freund von ihm.   **sie** *pl.*
Peter ist ein Freund von ihnen.

Ist dieses Gedicht von Schiller?   **du**
Ist dieses Gedicht von dir?   **sein Vater**
Ist dieses Gedicht von seinem Vater?   **die Studentin**
Ist dieses Gedicht von der Studentin?   **Herr Held**
Ist dieses Gedicht von Herrn Held?   **ein Junge**
Ist dieses Gedicht von einem Jungen?

zu to

11 Substitute the dative form of the new noun or pronoun:

Heute geht er zu seinem Bruder. **seine Tante**
Heute geht er zu seiner Tante. **jene Vorlesung**
Heute geht er zu jener Vorlesung. **er**
Heute geht er zu ihm. **wir**
Heute geht er zu uns. **unser Milchmann**
Heute geht er zu unserem Milchmann. **die Kundinnen**
Heute geht er zu den Kundinnen. **sie** *pl.*
Heute geht er zu ihnen. **eine Vorlesung**
Heute geht er zu einer Vorlesung.

Contractions

The prepositions **bei**, **von**, and **zu** combine with **dem** to form the contractions **beim**, **vom**, and **zum**. **Zu** also combines with **der** to form **zur**.

12 Substitute the new dative object:

Da steht er beim Wagen. **Fenster**
Da steht er beim Fenster. **Geschäft**
Da steht er beim Geschäft. **Tisch**
Da steht er beim Tisch. **Haus**
Da steht er beim Haus.

Wir kommen vom Geschäft. **Baden**
Wir kommen vom Baden. **Versandgeschäft**
Wir kommen vom Versandgeschäft. **Zug**
Wir kommen vom Zug. **Bodensee**
Wir kommen vom Bodensee.

13 Substitute the new dative object and the correct contraction:

Jetzt geht er zur Bahn. **Vorlesung**
Jetzt geht er zur Vorlesung. **Geschäft**
Jetzt geht er zum Geschäft. **Post**
Jetzt geht er zur Post. **Wagen**

Jetzt geht er zum Wagen. **Professor**
Jetzt geht er zum Professor. **Arbeit**
Jetzt geht er zur Arbeit.

C. The Question-Word **wem**? (*See Grammar* §11.5)

14 Change the following statements into questions by replacing the dative object with **wem**:

Er kauft seiner Frau einen Hut.
Wem kauft er einen Hut?

Es gelingt mir.
Wem gelingt es?

Der Schrank gefällt den Kindern.
Wem gefällt der Schrank?

Der Junge hilft der Frau.
Wem hilft der Junge?

Es ist dem Fahrer passiert.
Wem ist es passiert?

Er spricht von seinen Freundinnen.
Von wem spricht er?

Der Junge wohnt bei uns.
Bei wem wohnt der Junge?

Sie geht zu ihrer Mutter.
Zu wem geht sie?

D. Accusative and Dative Prepositions Mixed

15 Substitute the new preposition or object:

Ich tue nichts gegen ihn. **mit**
Ich tue nichts mit ihm. **die Kiste**
Ich tue nichts mit der Kiste. **ohne**
Ich tue nichts ohne die Kiste. **mein Mann**
Ich tue nichts ohne meinen Mann.

Peter läuft durch die Stadt. **das Haus**
Peter läuft durch das Haus. **nach**
Peter läuft nach dem Haus. **die Stadtbahn**
Peter läuft nach der Stadtbahn. **um**
Peter läuft um die Stadtbahn. **der Platz**
Peter läuft um den Platz. **von**
Peter läuft vom Platz.

Warum fahren Sie zur Post? **er**
Warum fahren Sie zu ihm? **ohne**
Warum fahren Sie ohne ihn? **die Kinder**
Warum fahren Sie ohne die Kinder? **mit**
Warum fahren Sie mit den Kindern?
                                der Postbote
Warum fahren Sie mit dem Postboten? **für**
Warum fahren Sie für den Postboten?

E. Directions (*See Grammar* §12.4)

16 Answer the questions as indicated:

Wo liegt Hamburg? **Norden**
Hamburg liegt im Norden.

Wo liegt Dresden? **Osten**
Dresden liegt im Osten.

Wo liegt der Schwarzwald? **Südwesten**
Der Schwarzwald liegt im Südwesten.

Wo liegt Bayern? **Süden**
Bayern liegt im Süden.

Wo liegt Schleswig-Holstein? **Norden**
Schleswig-Holstein liegt im Norden.

17 Answer the questions by giving the geographical location relative to Germany.

Example:
Wo liegt Frankreich? **westlich**
Frankreich liegt westlich von Deutschland.

Wo liegt Dänemark? **nördlich**
Dänemark liegt nördlich von Deutschland.

Wo liegt Polen? **östlich**
Polen liegt östlich von Deutschland.

Wo liegt die Schweiz? **südlich**
Die Schweiz liegt südlich von Deutschland.

Wo liegt Belgien? **westlich**
Belgien liegt westlich von Deutschland.

Wo liegt die Tschechoslowakei? **östlich**
Die Tschechoslowakei liegt östlich von Deutschland.

Wo liegen die Niederlande? **westlich**
Die Niederlande liegen westlich von Deutschland.

18 Answer the questions, using the correct preposition:

Wohin fahren Sie? **Polen**
Ich fahre nach Polen.

Wohin geht er? **die Post**
Er geht zur Post.

Wohin geht Uwe? **Berlin**
Uwe geht nach Berlin.

Wohin fährst du? **Belgien**
Ich fahre nach Belgien.

Wohin läuft er? **die Arbeit**
Er läuft zur Arbeit.

Wohin fährt Frau Hartmann? **Österreich**
Sie fährt nach Österreich.

Wohin läuft Peter? **seine Mutter**
Er läuft zu seiner Mutter.

Wohin fährt Tante Inge? **Frankreich**
Sie fährt nach Frankreich.

F. *Nach Hause, zu Hause* (See Grammar §12.3)

19 Substitute the new verb.

Example:
Der Junge kommt nach Hause. **sitzen**
Der Junge sitzt zu Hause.

Der Junge kommt nach Hause. **sitzen**
Der Junge sitzt zu Hause. **laufen**
Der Junge läuft nach Hause. **warten**
Der Junge wartet zu Hause. **bleiben**

Der Junge bleibt zu Hause. **gehen**
Der Junge geht nach Hause. **sein**
Der Junge ist zu Hause. **kommen**
Der Junge kommt nach Hause.

G. Questions and Answers

Wie lange ist der Schrank schon unterwegs?
Er ist schon seit dem dritten Juli unterwegs.

Wo sind die Einzelteile?
Sie sind in einer Kiste.

Wer baut den Schrank zusammen?
Gerhard baut ihn zusammen.

Kann Margrit ihm dabei helfen?
Nein, sie kann ihm dabei nicht helfen.

Was soll Margrit Gerhard holen?
Sie soll ihm einen Schraubenzieher holen.

Liegt der Schraubenzieher im Werkzeugkasten?
Nein, er liegt im Zimmer.

Wohin geht Margrit?
Sie geht zu ihrer Mutter hinüber.

Ist ihr Vater zu Hause?
Nein, aber er kommt bald nach Hause.

Was wünscht Margrit ihrem Mann?
Sie wünscht ihm viel Glück.

GRAMMAR

12.1 Word-Formation

Compound nouns

das Auge eye + **der Blick** glance = **der Augenblick** moment
der Boden floor, bottom + **der See** lake = **der Bodensee** Lake Constance
der Himmel sky, heaven + **die Richtung** direction = **die Himmelsrichtung** point of the compass
der Nachbar neighbor + **das Land** country, state = **das Nachbarland** neighboring country
die Schraube screw + **der Zieher** instrument for pulling = **der Schraubenzieher** screwdriver
schwarz black + **der Wald** forest = **der Schwarzwald** Black Forest
das Werkzeug tool(s) + **der Kasten** box = **der Werkzeugkasten** toolbox

12.2 Singular and Plural of Nouns

die Arbeit, die Arbeiten
das Brett, die Bretter
der Himmel, die Himmel
der Kasten, die Kästen
der Katalog, die Kataloge
das Land, die Länder (*but* die Niederlande *pl.*)
die Mutter, die Mütter
der Nachbar, die Nachbarn

die Richtung, die Richtungen
die Schraube, die Schrauben
der Schraubenzieher, die Schraubenzieher
der See, die Seen (*but* die See *sg. sea*)
die Stunde, die Stunden
der Vater, die Väter
der Wald, die Wälder
das Zimmer, die Zimmer

12.3 Prepositions with the Dative Case

In Unit 10 you learned five prepositions that always take objects in the accusative case. Now we shall take up the prepositions that automatically require that their objects be in the dative case.

aus out of, of, from

Was, ein Schrank **aus** dieser Kiste?
What, a cabinet *out of* this box?

Er kommt **aus** Berlin.
He's *from* Berlin.

Holst du mir den Schraubenzieher **aus** dem Werkzeugkasten?
Will you get me the screwdriver *from* the toolbox?

außer except (for)

Er hat nichts **außer** diesem Buch.
He has nothing *except for* this book.

Ich kenne kein Mädchen **außer** dir.
I know no girl *except* you.

bei near, beside, with, at the house of

Wann bist du **bei** uns?
When will you be *at our house*?

Sie liegt **bei** der Laterne.
She's lying *near* (*beside*) the streetlight.

Ich bleibe **bei** dir.
I'll stay *with* you.

mit with

Er hat Mühe **mit** dem Paket.
He's having trouble *with* the package.

Kannst du **mit** mir zum Baden gehen?
Can you go swimming *with* me?

Was ist **mit** dem Üben?
What about practice? (What's *with* the practice?)

nach after; about; toward, to

Sie kommt **nach** der Vorlesung.
She's coming *after* the lecture.

Wir fragen **nach** ihm.
We're asking *about* him.

Im Frühling fährt er **nach** Deutschland.
In the spring he's going *to* Germany.

seit since; for (*used only with expressions of time*)

Seit dem dritten August ist er dort.
He has been there *since* the third of August.

Ich kenne ihn schon **seit** einer Woche.
I've known him *for* a week.

von about; from; of; by

Ilse spricht häufig **von** Ihnen.
Ilse speaks *about* you often.

Uwe ist ein Freund **von** mir.
Uwe is a friend *of* mine.

Es ist der Schrank **von** dem Versandgeschäft.
It's the cabinet *from* the mail-order house.

Kennst du diese Gedichte **von** Schiller?
Do you know these poems *by* Schiller?

zu to; at

Er geht **zu** der Post.
He's going *to* the post office.

Der Junge bleibt **zu** Hause.
The boy stays *at* home.

Ich gehe solange **zu** meiner Mutter.
Meanwhile I'll go *to* my mother's.

Contractions

Some of these prepositions may be combined with a following definite article to form contractions. Those that normally occur are:

bei + dem = beim   Er steht dort **beim** Fenster.
von + dem = vom   Die Kiste kommt **vom** Versandgeschäft.
zu + dem = zum   Wir gehen **zum** Baden.
zu + der = zur   Er muß **zur** Post gehen.

Some problems of meaning

One of the most striking things about the German prepositions is that they seem to have so many different meanings. **Nach**, for example, means *after* if the object is somehow related to time, *about* if it is associated with the verb **fragen**, but *to* or *toward* if the object is a city, country, direction, etc. As your knowledge of German increases, you will learn several additional meanings of these prepositions. Most English prepositions have several meanings, too, as the following sentences illustrate:

I'm going *to* the store.
The final score was fifteen *to* seven.
Shall we leave it up *to* him?

The book is over there *by* the lamp.
It was written *by* Dr. Smith.
The door had been opened *by* force.
We met him only *by* chance.

He's *from* New York.
We play cards *from* time to time.
He dropped *from* exhaustion.

German prepositions and English prepositions have broad ranges of meaning. Furthermore, these ranges of meaning almost *never* coincide completely. The meaning of a German preposition may overlap with the meaning of an English preposition, but they do not correspond one hundred percent. This results in two facts: (1) a given German preposition is defined as being partially equivalent to several English prepositions, and (2) some German prepositions appear to have identical meanings (both **nach** and **zu** are translated with *to*, **von** and **aus** both mean *from*, etc.). You should pay particular attention to the following prepositions:

nach : zu to

Both of these prepositions may indicate motion toward a goal. **Nach** is used when that goal is a geographical location such as a town, state, country, or continent. Otherwise **zu** is used.

Wir fahren heute **nach** Deutschland.
Mußt du **zu** deinem Vater gehen?

These prepositions also occur in the expressions **nach Hause** and **zu Hause**. **Nach Hause** implies motion *toward home*, while **zu Hause** means specifically *at home*:

Gehst du **nach Hause**?
Ist er **zu Hause**?

aus : von from

These two prepositions may indicate a point of origin and are thus partially equivalent to English *from*. **Aus** refers to one's ultimate origin, e.g. his hometown or native country, while **von** refers to an immediate origin, e.g. where one got on the train:

Ich komme **aus** Berlin.   Da ist der Zug **von** München.
I'm *from* Berlin. (Berlin is my native city.)   There's the train *from* Munich.

bei : mit with

When the meaning is "in the vicinity of" or "in proximity to," then **bei** is the appropriate preposition. **Mit**, however, means "accompanied by." All three of these meanings are embraced by English *with*, but German makes a definite distinction between "proximity" and "accompaniment."

Er wohnt **bei** uns.   Ich gehe **mit** dir.
He lives *at our place*. (He lives *with* us.)   I'm going *with* you.

bei : von by

German **bei** should not be equated with English *by*, except when closeness or nearness is implied. When *by* refers to the author of a book, poem, etc., then its German equivalent is **von**:

Das Buch ist **bei** mir.
The book is *near* me (*next to* me, *at my house*).

Das Buch ist **von** Hemingway.
The book is *by* Hemingway. (Hemingway wrote the book.)

seit since; for

The preposition **seit** is used only with expressions that refer to time. It never means *since* in the causal sense, as in *Since it's raining, we'll stay home*. When the object is a point in time, **seit** is best rendered by English *since*; when the object is an extent of time, then it means *for*:

Ich kenne ihn **seit** Montag.	Ich kenne ihn **seit** vier Jahren.
I've known him *since* Monday.	I've known him *for* four years.

Notice that the German present tense verb form **kenne** corresponds to the English present perfect *I have known* in both of these sentences. The meaning here is this: my knowing of this person began at some time in the past and continues at the present time.

When **seit** plus an object refers to a duration of time, then the expression is equivalent to the use of the accusative case to indicate duration of time (Grammar §9.7). Thus:

Ich habe diesen Hut **seit zwei Jahren**.	Er wohnt **seit einer Woche** hier.
Ich habe diesen Hut **zwei Jahre**.	Er wohnt **eine Woche** hier.
Both mean: I've had this hat *for two years*.	*Both mean:* He's been living here *for a week*.

Wir kennen sie **seit vier Monaten**.
Wir kennen sie **vier Monate**.
Both mean: We've known her *for four months*.

The adverb **schon** is frequently used with **seit**-phrases and accusative time phrases:

Ich habe diesen Hut **schon seit zwei Jahren**.   Er wohnt **schon eine Woche** hier.
Wir kennen sie **schon seit vier Monaten**.

12.4 Directions

The German names of the points of the compass are presented in the Supplement of this unit. Notice that all the nouns are masculine (**der Norden**). The corresponding adjectives are formed by adding the suffix **-lich** to the stem and umlauting the stem vowel if possible (**nördlich**). The nouns typically occur with the following prepositions:

im (in dem) Norden   in the north   **nach** Norden   to (toward) the north
von Norden   from (out of) the north

The adjectives are followed by a **von**-phrase to indicate direction relative to a geographical location:

nördlich von Berlin   north of Berlin

12.5 Names of Countries

The names of the countries that border on Germany are listed in the Supplement. Notice that only *feminine* and *plural* country names are preceded by a definite article:

die Schweiz *fem.*
die Tschechoslowakei *fem.*
die Niederlande *pl.*

If the country name is neither feminine nor plural, then the definite article is not used:

Deutschland
in Österreich
von Dänemark
nach Belgien

Note: Do not use the preposition **nach** with feminine country names. To express motion toward a country whose name is feminine, use **in** plus the accusative case:

Wir fahren **nach** Deutschland.
But: Wir fahren **in die** Schweiz.
　　　Wir fahren **in die** Tschechoslowakei.

WRITING

A. Word Copying

1. Concentrate on the proper pronunciation of the sounds for **l** and **r** as you copy the words in boldface:

   Aller Anfang ist **leicht**.
   Eigentlich kann es nun **endlich losgehen**.
   Alle Vorlesungen beginnen **erst** um **viertel** nach **voll**.
   Mein **Bruder** hat es **mir erzählt**.
   Die **älteren** Studenten haben **alle viel Erfahrung**.
   Hoffentlich liest er nicht so **langweilig** wie **der alte Professor Wolf**.

2. Generally speaking, a vowel is long if it is final in a word or syllable, if it is followed by the letter **h**, if it is doubled, or if it is followed by only one consonant. Grammatical endings, such as the verb endings **-t** and **-st**, do not cause a vowel that is long in the infinitive to become short. Short vowels followed by only one consonant occur in a number of short words of high frequency, such as: **an, am, in, im, von, vom, um, mit, das, was, es, hat**. Copy the words that contain the long vowels in boldface:

Ist dies **I** hre erste V **o** rl **e** sung?
Mein Br **u** der hat es m **i** r erz **ä** hlt.
Und nicht n **u** r im St **u** dieren.

D **a** kann er **I** hnen als **o** nicht viel helfen.
Als **o**, es g **e** ht endlich l **o** s.
Ü ben sagst d **u** ?

B. Singular and Plural of Nouns

Copy the sentences. Insert the forms that correspond to the English in parentheses:

1. Wo ist denn _____ _____ ? (my screwdriver)
2. _____ _____ sind dort rechts. (the screws)
3. Was kosten _____ _____ ? (such catalogs)
4. Das sind _____ _____ . (our boards)
5. Ist das nicht _____ _____ ? (her mother)
6. _____ _____ sehen schön aus. (those rooms)
7. Wem gehören _____ _____ ? (these toolboxes)
8. Viele _____ grenzen an Deutschland. (countries)
9. Ist _____ _____ zu Hause? (his father)
10. Die Stadt liegt südlich von _____ _____ . (the forests)

C. Verb Forms

Arrange the elements to form meaningful German sentences. Verbs are given in their infinitive form, so you must change them to the form required by the sentence:

1. der Kasten / bestehen / nur aus Brettern und Schrauben .
2. gelingen / es Ihnen ?
3. ich / können / zusammenbauen / Ihnen / einen Schrank .
4. hoffentlich / klappen / es .
5. die Schraube / liegen / dort .
6. hinübergehen / du / zu deiner Mutter ?
7. wir / zurückschicken / den Leuten / es .
8. lassen / mich / mit meiner Arbeit allein !
9. im Augenblick / stehen / hier kein Schrank .
10. holen / ihr / mir / es ?
11. er / wünschen / mir / viel Glück .
12. warum / entgegengehen / Sie / dem Postboten ?

Read your sentences aloud, paying close attention to correct pronunciation and intonation. Be able to provide English equivalents for the German sentences you have written.

D. Prepositions

Copy the sentences and insert the German preposition that corresponds to the English word in parentheses:

1 Er kommt um viertel _____ fünf. (after)
2 Gehst du jetzt _____ der Post? (to the)
3 Ich habe nichts _____ meinem Wagen. (except)
4 Soll er _____ uns gehen? (with)
5 Wir können diese Bretter _____ einem Schrank zusammenbauen. (to)
6 Der Hut ist _____ meinem Mann. (from)
7 Die Kundin sitzt _____ dem Fenster. (near)
8 Fragt sie _____ mir? (about)
9 Wir wohnen _____ drei Jahren hier. (for)
10 Ist dieser Schrank _____ mich? (for)
11 Wir möchten _____ zehn Uhr gehen. (at)
12 Wann bist du _____ ihm? (at the house of)
13 Er soll bald _____ Belgien fahren. (to)
14 Was ist denn _____ diesem Ding? (with)
15 Kannst du mir die Zeitung _____ jenem Zimmer holen? (from)

E. Accusative and Dative Cases

Copy the sentences and insert the correct case forms of the words in parentheses:

1 Wir kommen aus _____ Schweiz. (die)
2 Wohnst du noch bei _____ Mutter? (dein)
3 Ich tue nichts ohne _____. (er)
4 Was ist _____ passiert? (Sie)
5 Er schickt _____ einen Kasten. (wir)
6 Es ist seit _____ sechzehnten August unterwegs. (der)
7 Ist das der Hut von _____ Geschäft? (sein)
8 Dieser Schrank gefällt _____ nicht. (ich)
9 Ich hole _____ _____ ein Buch. (der Junge)
10 Kommst du nach _____ Arbeit nach Hause? (die)
11 Da kommt er um _____ Platz herum. (der)
12 Kannst du mit _____ fahren? (er)
13 Hilf _____ _____! (diese Kinder)
14 Kennen Sie _____ Freund? (mein)
15 Dieses Hütchen gehört _____ Tante. (unser)
16 Ich wünsche _____ viel Glück. (sie *pl.*)
17 Glaubst du _____ Erzählungen? (ihr)

18 Ich glaube _____ nicht, Hans.   (du)
19 Die Kiste ist doch nicht für _____ Bruder.   (mein)
20 Jetzt geht sie zu _____ Freundin.   (unser)
21 Ich baue _____ zusammen.   (es)
22 Er baut _____ den Schrank zusammen.   (sie *sg.*)

F. Directions and Countries

Write the corresponding German sentences:

1 Germany lies south of Denmark.
2 Munich lies in the south of Germany.
3 Switzerland lies west of Austria.
4 Lake Constance lies southeast of the Black Forest.
5 Bremen lies in the north of Germany.
6 The Netherlands lie north of France.
7 Luxemburg borders on Belgium.
8 Czechoslovakia borders on Poland, Austria, and Germany.

LISTENING PRACTICE

Listen to the recorded passage, and then answer the questions below.

Deutschland und seine Nachbarländer

1 Wie heißen Deutschlands Nachbarländer?
2 Seit wann besteht Deutschland aus zwei Teilen?
3 An welche See grenzt Ostdeutschland im Norden?

Unit 13

DIALOG

Susi deckt den Mittagstisch (Anfang)

1 **Susi:** Kann ich dir etwas helfen, Mutti?

2 **Mutter:** Gern, mein Kind, magst du den Tisch decken?

3 **Susi:** Den Mittagstisch? Oh ja!

4 **Mutter:** Aber wirst du auch aufpassen? Es darf nichts kaputtgehen.

Susi Sets the Dinner Table (Beginning)

decken set (the table) · **der Mittagstisch der Mittag + der Tisch,** *pl.* **die Tische** table *The noon meal is the big meal of the day in a German family.*

1 Can I help you a little, Mommy?

können: ich kann, du kannst, er kann can · **etwas** some; something; somewhat, a little

2 Why yes, my child. Do you want to set the table?

gern gladly, with pleasure · **mögen: ich mag, du magst, er mag** like; want

3 The dinner table? Oh, yes!

4 But are you also going to be careful? Nothing must get broken.

werden *auxiliary for future tense:* **du wirst, er wird** · **aufpassen: du paßt auf, er paßt auf** be careful · **dürfen: ich darf, du darfst, er darf** may; must *with negative* · **kaputtgehen (es geht kaputt** it gets broken) **kaputt** broken, spoiled, out of order + **gehen**

5 **Susi:** Ich werde schon vorsichtig sein.

6 **Mutter:** Also, zuerst die Decke auf den Tisch und dann die Teller.

7 **Susi:** Soll ich den Löffel neben den Teller legen, Mutti?

8 **Mutter:** Der Löffel kommt hinter den Teller, das Messer und die Gabel kommen neben den Teller.

9 **Susi:** Dann kann ich die Teller ebensogut zwischen die Messer und die Gabeln stellen?

10 **Mutter:** Meinetwegen, du Schlaukopf! Aber ich werde die Suppe in die Schüssel füllen.

(Fortsetzung folgt)

SUPPLEMENT

1	Ich werde aufpassen.	1	I will be careful.
2	Er wird vorsichtig sein.	2	He will be careful.
3	Er braucht nicht zu spotten.	3	He doesn't have to be sarcastic.
4	Er bittet mich, es zu kaufen.	4	He asks me to buy it.
5	Ich darf zum Baden gehen.	5	I can (may, am permitted to) go swimming.
6	Ich kann Nuß-Eis kaufen.	6	I can (am able to) buy walnut ice cream.
7	Magst du solche Hüte leiden?	7	Do you like such hats?

5   I'll be careful, all right.

6   Well then, first the tablecloth on the table and then the plates.

zuerst first, first of all *adv.* · **die Decke,** *pl.* **die Decken** tablecloth; blanket; ceiling · **der Teller,** *pl.* **die Teller**

7   Am I supposed to put the spoon beside the plate, Mommy?

sollen: ich soll, du sollst, er soll · **der Löffel,** *pl.* **die Löffel** · **legen** put, lay, place

8   The spoon goes behind the plate, the knife and fork go beside the plate.

kommen come; *but here:* go, belong (in a place) · **das Messer,** *pl.* **die Messer** · **die Gabel,** *pl.* **die Gabeln**

9   Then can I just put the plates between the knives and forks?

ebensogut just as well

10 That's all right with me, you little fox. But I'll put the soup in the tureen.

meinetwegen as far as I'm concerned, for all I care · **der Schlaukopf   schlau** sly, cunning + **der Kopf,** *pl.* **die Köpfe** head · **die Schüssel,** *pl.* **die Schüsseln** bowl; tureen · **füllen** put, fill

(To be continued)

8	Mußt du Geige üben?	8	Must you practice the violin?
9	Sie soll den Tisch decken.	9	She is supposed to set the table.
10	Sie will nach Hause gehen.	10	She wants to go home.
11	Ich sehe dich auf dem Podium stehen.	11	I see you standing on the stage.
12	Sie hilft mir den Tisch decken.	12	She's helping me set the table.
13	Er läßt seine Bücher herumliegen.	13	He leaves his books lying around.

AUDIOLINGUAL DRILLS

A. Directed Dialog

Sagen Sie, daß Susi Mutti helfen kann!
Susi kann Mutti helfen.

Sagen Sie, daß sie den Mittagstisch deckt!
Sie deckt den Mittagstisch.

Sagen Sie, daß sie aber aufpassen muß!
Sie muß aber aufpassen.

Fragen Sie, ob Susi vorsichtig sein wird!
Wird Susi vorsichtig sein?

Antworten Sie, daß sie vorsichtig sein wird!
Sie wird vorsichtig sein.

Fragen Sie, was zuerst auf den Tisch kommt!
Was kommt zuerst auf den Tisch?

Antworten Sie, daß die Decke zuerst auf den Tisch kommt!
Die Decke kommt zuerst auf den Tisch.

Fragen Sie, was dann auf den Tisch kommt!
Was kommt dann auf den Tisch?

Antworten Sie, daß dann die Teller auf den Tisch kommen!
Dann kommen die Teller auf den Tisch.

Fragen Sie, ob Susi den Löffel neben den Teller legen soll!
Soll Susi den Löffel neben den Teller legen?

Sagen Sie, daß der Löffel hinter den Teller kommt!
Der Löffel kommt hinter den Teller.

Sagen Sie, daß das Messer und die Gabel neben den Teller kommen!
Das Messer und die Gabel kommen neben den Teller.

Sagen Sie, daß Susi die Teller auch zwischen die Messer und die Gabeln stellen kann!
Susi kann die Teller auch zwischen die Messer und die Gabeln stellen.

Fragen Sie, ob die Mutter die Suppe in die Schüssel füllen wird!
Wird die Mutter die Suppe in die Schüssel füllen?

Antworten Sie, daß sie die Suppe in die Schüssel füllen wird!
Sie wird die Suppe in die Schüssel füllen.

B. Dependent Infinitives with *zu* (*See Grammar* §13.3)

1 Substitute the new infinitive:

Er braucht nicht zu spotten. **lachen**
Er braucht nicht zu lachen. **übertreiben**
Er braucht nicht zu übertreiben. **aufpassen**
Er braucht nicht aufzupassen. **einsteigen**
Er braucht nicht einzusteigen. **mitkommen**
Er braucht nicht mitzukommen. **antworten**
Er braucht nicht zu antworten.

Die Leute beginnen zu kommen. **warten**
Die Leute beginnen zu warten. **abfahren**
Die Leute beginnen abzufahren. **spotten**
Die Leute beginnen zu spotten. **übertreiben**
Die Leute beginnen zu übertreiben. **ankommen**
Die Leute beginnen anzukommen. **essen**
Die Leute beginnen zu essen.

Ich bitte dich, es zu kaufen. **tun**
Ich bitte dich, es zu tun. **machen**
Ich bitte dich, es zu machen. **erklären**
Ich bitte dich, es zu erklären. **versichern**
Ich bitte dich, es zu versichern. **zusammenbauen**
Ich bitte dich, es zusammenzubauen. **zurückschicken**
Ich bitte dich, es zurückzuschicken.

C. The Future Tense (*See Grammar* §13.4)

2 Substitute the new phrase:

Ich werde vorsichtig sein. **einen Hut kaufen**
Ich werde einen Hut kaufen. **dem Jungen helfen**
Ich werde dem Jungen helfen. **nach Hause gehen**
Ich werde nach Hause gehen. **schon aufpassen**
Ich werde schon aufpassen.

Du wirst nett sein. **bei uns bleiben**
Du wirst bei uns bleiben. **ihn kennenlernen**
Du wirst ihn kennenlernen. **ihm nicht glauben**
Du wirst ihm nicht glauben. **heute abfahren**
Du wirst heute abfahren.

Wird er zu Hause bleiben? **vorsichtig sein**
Wird er vorsichtig sein? **dort aussteigen**
Wird er dort aussteigen? **es zurückschicken**
Wird er es zurückschicken? **mich verstehen**
Wird er mich verstehen?

3 Substitute the new subject:

   Er wird einen Wagen kaufen. **wir**
   Wir werden einen Wagen kaufen. **Inge**
   Inge wird einen Wagen kaufen. **Vater und Mutter**
   Vater und Mutter werden einen Wagen kaufen. **du**
   Du wirst einen Wagen kaufen. **das Mädchen**
   Das Mädchen wird einen Wagen kaufen. **ich**
   Ich werde einen Wagen kaufen. **ihr**
   Ihr werdet einen Wagen kaufen.

D. The Modal Auxiliaries (*See Grammar* §13.5)

dürfen may, can, be permitted to; must *with negative*

4 Substitute the new subject:

   Wir dürfen heute zum Baden gehen. **er**
   Er darf heute zum Baden gehen. **ihr**
   Ihr dürft heute zum Baden gehen. **die Kinder**
   Die Kinder dürfen heute zum Baden gehen. **du**
   Du darfst heute zum Baden gehen. **ich**
   Ich darf heute zum Baden gehen.

können can, be able to

5 Substitute the new subject:

   Kann er einen Wagen kaufen? **wir**
   Können wir einen Wagen kaufen? **die Kinder**
   Können die Kinder einen Wagen kaufen? **ich**
   Kann ich einen Wagen kaufen? **ihr**
   Könnt ihr einen Wagen kaufen? **du**
   Kannst du einen Wagen kaufen?

mögen want to, like to; would like to *in subjunctive*

6 Substitute the new subject:

   Wir mögen solche Hüte nicht leiden. **er**
   Er mag solche Hüte nicht leiden. **ihr**
   Ihr mögt solche Hüte nicht leiden. **ich**
   Ich mag solche Hüte nicht leiden. **du**

Du magst solche Hüte nicht leiden. **die Männer**
Die Männer mögen solche Hüte nicht leiden.

7 Substitute the new phrase:

Ich möchte mitkommen. **Geige üben**
Ich möchte Geige üben. **den Tisch decken**
Ich möchte den Tisch decken. **meinen Mann fragen**
Ich möchte meinen Mann fragen. **durch diese Auswahl schauen**
Ich möchte durch diese Auswahl schauen. **die Verkäuferin kennenlernen**
Ich möchte die Verkäuferin kennenlernen.

müssen must, have to

8 Substitute the new subject:

Ich muß wahrscheinlich Geige üben. **Heike**
Heike muß wahrscheinlich Geige üben. **wir**
Wir müssen wahrscheinlich Geige üben. **ihr**
Ihr müßt wahrscheinlich Geige üben. **du**
Du mußt wahrscheinlich Geige üben. **die Kinder**
Die Kinder müssen wahrscheinlich Geige üben.

sollen be supposed to, be said to

9 Substitute the new subject:

Wann soll ich den Tisch decken? **ihr**
Wann sollt ihr den Tisch decken? **du**
Wann sollst du den Tisch decken? **wir**
Wann sollen wir den Tisch decken? **Susi**
Wann soll Susi den Tisch decken? **die Kinder**
Wann sollen die Kinder den Tisch decken?

wollen want to; intend to

10 Substitute the new subject:

Susi will etwas helfen. **die Kinder**
Die Kinder wollen etwas helfen. **du**
Du willst etwas helfen. **ihr**
Ihr wollt etwas helfen. **ich**
Ich will etwas helfen. **wir**
Wir wollen etwas helfen.

Modal auxiliaries mixed

11 Answer the question in the negative; then form a new question with the new modal auxiliary.

Example:
Darfst du heute mitkommen?
Nein, ich darf heute nicht mitkommen. **wollen**

Willst du heute mitkommen?
Nein, ich will heute nicht mitkommen.

Magst du heute mitkommen?
Nein, ich mag heute nicht mitkommen. **müssen**

Mußt du heute mitkommen?
Nein, ich muß heute nicht mitkommen. **wollen**

Willst du heute mitkommen?
Nein, ich will heute nicht mitkommen. **können**

Kannst du heute mitkommen?
Nein, ich kann heute nicht mitkommen. **dürfen**

Darfst du heute mitkommen?
Nein, ich darf heute nicht mitkommen. **sollen**

Sollst du heute mitkommen?
Nein, ich soll heute nicht mitkommen. **mögen**

Magst du heute mitkommen?
Nein, ich mag heute nicht mitkommen.

12 Answer in the affirmative, and form a new question with the new modal auxiliary.

Example:
Kann er das?
Ja, das kann er. **wollen**

Will er das?
Ja, das will er.

Mag er das?
Ja, das mag er. **müssen**

Muß er das?
Ja, das muß er. **dürfen**

Darf er das?
Ja, das darf er. **sollen**

Soll er das?
Ja, das soll er. **wollen**

Will er das?
Ja, das will er. **können**

Kann er das?
Ja, das kann er. **mögen**

Mag er das?
Ja, das mag er.

E. The Verbs *sehen, helfen, lassen* with Dependent Infinitives
(*See Grammar* § 13.6)

13 Substitute the new subject:

Sehen Sie mich auf dem Podium stehen? **du**
Siehst du mich auf dem Podium stehen? **ihr**
Seht ihr mich auf dem Podium stehen? **er**
Sieht er mich auf dem Podium stehen?

Ich lasse ihn zum Baden gehen. **du**
Du läßt ihn zum Baden gehen. **er**
Er läßt ihn zum Baden gehen. **ihr**
Ihr laßt ihn zum Baden gehen.

Wir helfen ihr den Tisch decken. **er**
Er hilft ihr den Tisch decken. **ich**
Ich helfe ihr den Tisch decken. **du**
Du hilfst ihr den Tisch decken.

14 Answer the question by using the given phrase:

Was siehst du ihn tun? **zum Baden gehen**
Ich sehe ihn zum Baden gehen.

Was siehst du sie tun? **um die Ecke laufen**
Ich sehe sie um die Ecke laufen.

Was hilfst du ihm tun? **einsteigen**
Ich helfe ihm einsteigen.

Was hilfst du ihnen tun? **die Zeitung lesen**
Ich helfe ihnen die Zeitung lesen.

Was läßt du mich tun? **Eis kaufen**
Ich lasse dich Eis kaufen.

Was läßt du ihn tun? **nach Hause fahren**
Ich lasse ihn nach Hause fahren.

F. Questions and Answers

Wie kann Susi ihrer Mutter helfen?
Sie kann den Mittagstisch decken.

Und was kommt dann auf den Tisch?
Die Teller kommen dann auf den Tisch.

Wird Susi aufpassen?
Ja, sie wird aufpassen.

Wohin kommen die Löffel?
Sie kommen hinter den Teller.

Was sagt sie?
Sie sagt, sie wird schon vorsichtig sein.

Was kommt neben den Teller?
Das Messer und die Gabel kommen neben den Teller.

Was kommt zuerst auf den Tisch?
Die Decke kommt zuerst auf den Tisch.

Was wird Susis Mutter gleich tun?
Sie wird gleich die Suppe in die Schüssel füllen.

GRAMMAR

13.1 Word-Formation

Compound nouns

der Mittag noon + **der Tisch** table = **der Mittagstisch** dinner table
schlau sly, cunning + **der Kopf** head = **der Schlaukopf** sly person, cunning person, "fox"

13.2 Singular and Plural of Nouns

die Decke, die Decken
die Gabel, die Gabeln
der Kopf, die Köpfe
der Löffel, die Löffel

das Messer, die Messer
die Schüssel, die Schüsseln
der Teller, die Teller
der Tisch, die Tische

13.3 The Dependent Infinitive

A common kind of verb phrase in English is one that contains a finite verb plus an infinitive:

I [begin] [to study].

We [have] [to hurry].

I [can] [go].

We [see] him [run].

Such infinitives are called *dependent* infinitives; they are dependent on the finite verbs with which they occur. Sometimes a dependent infinitive is accompanied by *to*, as in the first two examples above; sometimes there is no *to*, as in the third and fourth examples. The presence or absence of this *to* is determined by the finite verb, i.e. *begin* and *have* require *to* but *can* and *see* do not. A similar situation exists in German; some dependent infinitives have **zu** and some do not, and this is determined by the finite verb with which the infinitive occurs.

A dependent infinitive in German is an associated element; as such it stands in last position in its own clause (Grammar §2.2), unless the clause is a dependent one, in which case the finite verb is in last position and thus follows the dependent infinitive (Grammar §§3.2, 3.3, 7.4):

Ich [möchte] heute mit Uwe zum Baden [gehen].

Ich |bitte| dich, mir den Schrank |zu kaufen|.

Sie fragt, ob wir zum Baden |gehen||können|.

Verbs that take a dependent infinitive with *zu*

Most verbs that can be used with a dependent infinitive require **zu**. So far you have learned **brauchen**, **beginnen**, and **bitten**:

Du brauchst gar nicht zu spotten.
You really don't have to be sarcastic.

Man braucht nur zu fragen.
One only has to ask.

Sie beginnt zu studieren.
She begins to study.

Ich bitte dich zu bleiben.
I ask you to stay. (Please stay.)

If the infinitive has a separable prefix, then the **zu** goes between the prefix and verb stem:

Er braucht nicht mitzukommen.
He doesn't have to come along.

Ich bitte dich abzuwarten.
I ask you to wait and see. (Please wait and see.)

Verbs that take a dependent infinitive without *zu*

A dependent infinitive is used without **zu** as follows:

With the present tense of **werden** to form the *future tense*
With the *modal auxiliaries*
With a few *other verbs* such as **sehen**, **helfen**, and **lassen**

3.4 The Future Tense

In English the future tense is formed by combining *shall* or *will* with an infinitive:

We *shall leave* for Berlin tomorrow.
I *will be* careful.

The words *shall* and *will*, in these constructions, are called *future auxiliaries*; they are auxiliary verbs used to form the future tense. German too forms its future tense by means of a future auxiliary plus a dependent infinitive. The German future auxiliary is **werden**:

Wirst du aufpassen?
Will you be careful?

Susi sagt, daß sie vorsichtig sein wird.
Susi says that she'll be careful.

Ich werde die Suppe in die Schüssel füllen.
I'll put the soup in the tureen.

The future tense is used less commonly in German than in English. In German the present tense verb forms are frequently used instead, particularly if an adverb of time points clearly to the future:

Was tust du denn heute nachmittag?
Tell me, what are you going to do (what will you do) this afternoon?

The verb **werden** has other functions in addition to that of future auxiliary; these will be pointed out as the need arises.

The forms of *werden*

ich werde	wir werden
du wirst	ihr werdet
er, sie, es wird	sie, Sie werden

13.5 The Modal Auxiliaries

Such verbs as *can, could, may, might, must, should, would* are modal auxiliaries; they indicate whether the action or condition expressed by the accompanying infinitive is possible, permissible, necessary, obligatory, etc.

The modals in English do not have a complete set of forms; they have no infinitive forms, no past participles, and in some instances no past tense forms. The missing forms have to be paraphrased. The past tense form of *go* is *went*, but *must* has no past tense; we use *had to* instead. The German modals, however, have a complete set of forms: infinitives, past participles, and past tense forms, just like other verbs.

dürfen may, can, be permitted to (expresses the idea of *permission*; in the negative it expresses *prohibition*, e.g. must not)

Darf ich gehen?   Du darfst nicht lachen.
May I go?   You must not laugh.

können can, be able to (*ability* or *possibility*; also *permission*)

Heike kann Geige spielen.   Du kannst Eis kaufen.
Heike can (is able to) play the violin.   You can (may) buy some ice cream.

Er kann viel helfen.
He can help a lot.

mögen want to, like to (idea of *inclination* or *possibility*; generally used in the negative, and also in the subjunctive)

Magst du den Tisch decken?
Do you want to set the table?

Ich mag das nicht.
I don't like that.

Vom wem mag das sein?
Who can it be from?

Ich möchte auch gehen.
I'd like to go, too.

müssen must, have to (idea of *necessity*; in the negative it expresses *lack of necessity*, not prohibition)

Ich muß Geige üben.
I must (have to) practice the violin.

Du mußt nicht nach Hause gehen.
You don't have to go home. (*Not*: You mustn't go home.)

sollen be supposed to, be said to (idea of *obligation* or *reputation*)

Er soll es heute tun.
He's supposed to do it today.

Er soll langweilig sein.
He is said to be boring.

Soll ich mitgehen?
Am I supposed to (should I) go along?

wollen want to, intend to (idea of *desire* or *intent*)

Sie will einen Hut kaufen.
She wants to buy a hat.

Ich will es den Leuten zurückschicken.
I intend to send it back to the people.

Some problems of meaning

müssen : dürfen

In English, when we negate *must*, we change the meaning from necessity to prohibition: *You must do that* becomes *You must not do that*. In German, however, the addition of **nicht** to **müssen** simply results in the removal of necessity, changing necessity to lack of necessity:

Du mußt nach Hause gehen.
You must go home. (It is necessary that you go home.)

Du mußt nicht nach Hause gehen.
You don't have to go home. (It is not necessary that you go home.)

The idea of prohibition is expressed in German through a different modal, **dürfen**:

Du darfst nicht nach Hause gehen.
You mustn't go home.

können : dürfen

Strictly speaking, the verb **können** is used to express ability and **dürfen** to express permission. Just as Americans are not very careful about differentiating between *can* and *may* (except in formal situations such as public speeches and term papers), so do many Germans use **können** and **dürfen** interchangeably when the idea of permission is implied. Both of the following sentences request permission:

Darf ich dir etwas helfen, Mutti?
Kann ich dir etwas helfen, Mutti?

wollen : werden

Remember that **wollen** (**er will**) is a modal meaning *want to*, and that English *will* is equivalent to German **werden**.

The modal auxiliaries without infinitives

As in English, the German modal auxiliaries may occur without a dependent infinitive at all:

Kann er es tun? — Ja, er kann.
Can he do it?   Yes, he can.

Unlike English, however, German permits the use of a direct object in such infinitiveless constructions. In order for a direct object to occur in English, the modal must be accompanied by a dependent infinitive:

Kannst du das tun? — Ja, ich kann das.
Can you do that?   Yes, I can (do that).

Present tense forms of the modal auxiliaries

	dürfen	können	mögen	müssen	sollen	wollen
ich	darf	kann	mag	muß	soll	will
du	darfst	kannst	magst	mußt	sollst	willst
er, sie, es	darf	kann	mag	muß	soll	will
wir	dürfen	können	mögen	müssen	sollen	wollen
ihr	dürft	könnt	mögt	müßt	sollt	wollt
sie, Sie	dürfen	können	mögen	müssen	sollen	wollen

13.6 The Verbs *sehen, helfen,* and *lassen*

The verbs **sehen**, **helfen**, and **lassen** — plus a few others — may occur with dependent infinitives. When they do, **zu** is not used:

Ich sehe dich auf dem Podium stehen.
I see you standing on the stage.

Er läßt seine Bücher herumliegen.
He leaves his books lying around.

Susi hilft Mutti den Tisch decken.
Susi helps Mommy set the table.

In addition to the meaning *leave*, the verb **lassen** may also mean *let, allow to, permit to*:

Er läßt mich zum Baden gehen.
He lets me go swimming.

Notice that **sehen**, **helfen**, and **lassen** take objects in the above sentences (**dich**, **Mutti**, **seine Bücher**, and **mich**). These objects in turn are the agents of the action expressed by the infinitives. In the first example the person doing the seeing is **ich**, while the one standing is **dich**. In the second example **Susi** does the helping, but **Mutti** is setting the table. **Er** in the third sentence is the one who does the leaving, but it is the **Bücher** that lie around. In the fourth sentence **er** grants permission, but **mich** goes swimming.

The German modal auxiliaries, however, may not take a direct object. When an object occurs with a modal construction, it is the object of the infinitive, not of the modal. Compare:

Susi hilft Mutti den Tisch decken.
Susi will Mutti helfen.

In the first sentence **Mutti** is the object of **hilft** and the agent of **decken**. In the second sentence **Mutti** is the object of the infinitive **helfen**; **will** takes no object. In a sentence like:

Ich kann das.
I can (do) that.

the word **das** is the object of an implied infinitive **tun**, not of the modal **kann**.

WRITING

A. Singular and Plural of Nouns

Copy the sentences and insert the forms that correspond to the English words in parentheses:

1 Willst du _____ _____ auf den Tisch legen?   (this tablecloth)
2 _____ _____ kommen auch auf den Tisch.   (the forks)
3 Ich kenne _____ _____.   (his stories)
4 Er hat _____ _____ mit dem Paket.   (no trouble)
5 Kannst du _____ _____ sehen?   (my spoon)

6 _____ _____ sind teuer. (such toolboxes)
7 _____ _____ sind billig. (these knives)
8 Warten _____ _____ noch? (the boys)
9 _____ _____ sieht schön aus. (our tureen)
10 _____ _____ steht dort. (the dinner table)
11 Aber _____ _____ darf nicht kaputtgehen. (my table)
12 Sind das nicht _____ _____? (her plates)

B. Future Tense

Rewrite the sentences in the future tense:

1 Ich kaufe dieses Hütchen.
2 Kommen Sie denn mit?
3 Wir erklären es Ihnen mal.
4 Warum paßt du nie auf?
5 Die Vorlesung beginnt um fünf.
6 Wir sind alte Bekannte.
7 Heike glaubt an das Sprichwort.
8 Steigt ihr in Bonn aus?

Rewrite the dependent clause in the future tense; leave the main clause in the present tense:

9 Sie sagt, daß sie den Tisch deckt.
10 Ich möchte wissen, ob du zu Hause bist.
11 Sagen Sie mir, wann die Leute ankommen!
12 Er sagt, daß es ihm gelingt.
13 Sie fragt, ob die Schränke ihr gefallen.
14 Ich sage, daß wir den Hut einfach zurückschicken.

C. Modal Auxiliaries

Arrange the elements to form meaningful German sentences. The modals are given in their infinitive form, so you must change them to the appropriate finite form:

1 ihr / wollen / helfen / der Frau .
2 sollen / decken / ich / den Tisch ?
3 Peter / können / zusammenbauen / den Schrank .
4 wann / dürfen / essen / wir ?
5 mögen / leiden / Sie / solche Hüte nicht ?
6 du / müssen / sein / vorsichtig .
7 dürfen / erklären / ich / das ?
8 sollen / zurückschicken / ihr / den Schrank ?
9 Hans und Inge / können / hinübergehen / zu Mutter .
10 wollen / kennenlernen / du / Herrn Hartmann ?

11 die Kinder / müssen / aufpassen / auch .
12 ich / mögen / glauben / ihm nicht .
13 Er sagt, daß Susi / können / helfen / Mutti .
14 Fragen Sie, ob wir / sollen / aufpassen / auch heute !
15 Wissen Sie, warum ich / müssen / sein / vorsichtig ?
16 Mutti sagt, daß die Schüssel / dürfen / kaputtgehen / nicht .

Read your sentences aloud with correct pronunciation and intonation. Be able to give English equivalents.

D. Dependent Infinitives with and without *zu*

Copy the sentences and insert the correct form of the infinitive:

1 Hilfst du mir den Schrank _____? (put together)
2 Ich bitte dich _____! (pay attention)
3 Siehst du den Jungen _____? (running)
4 Ihr könnt uns _____. (help)
5 Es beginnt _____. (rain)
6 Kannst du es ihm nicht _____? (believe)
7 Wir lassen ihn zu Hause _____. (stay)
8 Sie brauchen doch nicht _____. (come along)
9 Sie sieht ihn die Einzelteile zu einem Schrank _____. (put together)
10 Jetzt beginnt er schon _____. (overdo it)

E. Word Copying

1 Watch the consonant clusters carefully as you copy the words in boldface:

Der **Milchwagen rutscht**.
Sie hat noch den **Angstschweiß** auf der **Stirn**.
Dies ist eine ganz **schlechte, rutschige Straße**.
Quatsch, rücksichtslos!
Täuschst du dich auch nicht?
Seit dem **zweiundzwanzigsten** August **zwölf** Unfälle . . .

2 Generally speaking, a vowel is short if it is followed by two or more consonants other than **h**. Remember that **ch** is unpredictable, and **ss** between vowels is assurance that the foregoing vowel is short. Copy the words in which the short vowels are in boldface:

Klar, das m **a** cht d **o** ch n **i** chts.
Der M **i** lchmann **i** st best **i** mmt vers **i** chert.
Es **i** st n **i** cht **a** llzu schl **i** mm.

Die Frau hat eine Pl **a** tzwunde am K **o** pf.
Dies **i** st eine g **a** nz schl **e** chte, r **u** tschige Straße.
Wir m **ü** ssen ihr h **e** lfen.

READING PRACTICE

Gegen Mittag

Es ist 12.30 Uhr. Bald muß Vater nach Hause kommen. Er kommt jeden Mittag gegen 12.30 Uhr. Der Mittagstisch ist dann schon fertig, Vater kann nämlich nicht lange bleiben. Um 1.30 Uhr muß er wieder im Geschäft sein.

Heute will die kleine Inge den Mittagstisch decken. Sie wird bald sechs Jahre alt und kann ihrer Mutti schon viel helfen. Zuerst legt sie die Decke auf den Tisch, dann kommen Teller, Löffel, Messer und Gabeln. Aber die Suppe kann Inge noch nicht in die Schüssel füllen, das muß Mutti tun.

Da kommt Vater. ,,Ist der Mittagstisch von dir gedeckt?'' fragt er Inge. ,,Ja'', antwortet sie, ,,ich mag Mutti gern helfen.''

Unit 14

BACH

DIALOG

Susi deckt den Mittagstisch (Schluß)

1 **Vater:** Was ist denn heute mit dem Tisch los?

2 **Susi:** Außer der Suppenschüssel ist alles von mir gedeckt. Prima, was?

3 **Vater:** Du bist mir eine schöne Wirtin! Aber es wird wohl bald besser.

4 **Susi:** Wieso besser? Der Teller steht zwischen dem Messer und der Gabel.

5 **Vater:** Gut, aber das Messer muß rechts vom Teller liegen, und die Gabel links.

Susi Sets the Dinner Table (Conclusion)

1. What's the matter with the table today, anyway?

2. Except for the tureen everything was set by me. Pretty good, isn't it?

    alles all, everything · **decken (gedeckt** *past participle used as an adjective*) · **prima** *great, first-class*

3. You're some hostess! But I'm sure things will improve soon.

    du bist mir *lit.* you are for me · **die Wirtin,** *pl.* **die Wirtinnen   der Wirt,** *pl.* **die Wirte** innkeeper · **werden** (*here not the future auxiliary*) become   **besser werden** get better · **wohl** *indeed, to be sure*

4. What do you mean better? The plate is between the knife and the fork.

    wieso? how so?

5. Good, but the knife has to be to the right of the plate, and the fork to the left.

    links to the left

6 **Susi:** Liegen denn wenigstens die Löffel richtig?

7 **Vater:** Ja, hinter dem Teller, das stimmt.

8 **Susi:** Und wir sitzen hungrig vor unseren Tellern!

9 **Vater:** Dann wollen wir also essen. Guten Appetit!

10 **Susi:** Danke, Vati. Das nächste Mal will ich es besser machen.

SUPPLEMENT

1 Die Mutter stellt das gebratene Fleisch auf den Tisch.

2 Sie stellt den Kuchen auf den Tisch.

3 Sie stellt den Kaffee auch darauf.

4 Der Vater stellt das kalte Bier auf den Tisch.

5 Er stellt den Wein darauf.

6 Er stellt den Saft auch darauf.

7 Susi stellt das frische Brot auf den Tisch.

8 Sie stellt die Butter darauf.

9 Sie stellt die Marmelade auch darauf.

6	Well, are the spoons in the right place at least?	**wenigstens** at least · **richtig** right, correct(ly)
7	Yes, behind the plate; that's right.	
8	And we're sitting in front of our plates hungry.	
9	Well then, let's eat. I hope you enjoy it.	**der Appetit** appetite **guten Appetit** *lit. good appetite Germans customarily wish each other "good appetite" before starting to eat.*
10	Thanks, Daddy. Next time I intend to do it better.	**nah (das nächste** next; nearest *superl.*) near · **das Mal** one time, occurrence

---

1	The mother puts the roast meat on the table.	**braten: du brätst, er brät (gebratene** *past participle used as an adjective*) roast; bake; fry · **das Fleisch**
2	She puts the cake on the table.	**der Kuchen,** *pl.* **die Kuchen**
3	She puts the coffee on it, too.	**der Kaffee**
4	The father puts the cold beer on the table.	**das Bier,** *pl.* **die Biere** (*the plural means kinds of beer*)
5	He puts the wine on it.	**der Wein,** *pl.* **die Weine** (*the plural means kinds of wine*)
6	He puts the juice on it, too.	**der Saft,** *pl.* **die Säfte**
7	Susi puts the fresh bread on the table.	**das Brot**
8	She puts the butter on it.	**die Butter**
9	She puts the jam on it, too.	**die Marmelade**

10 Woraus kommt der Schrank?

11 Er kommt aus der Kiste.

12 Er kommt daraus.

13 Womit baut Gerhard ihn zusammen?

14 Er baut ihn mit dem Schraubenzieher zusammen.

15 Er baut ihn damit zusammen.

16 Wonach fragt der Mann?

17 Er fragt nach der Zeitung.

18 Er fragt danach.

19 Worüber sprechen die Kinder?

20 Sie sprechen über den Unfall.

21 Sie sprechen darüber.

22 Woran glaubt die Studentin?

23 Sie glaubt an das Sprichwort.

24 Sie glaubt daran.

25 Worauf warten die Studenten?

26 Sie warten auf die Vorlesung.

27 Sie warten darauf.

10   What does the cabinet come out of?

11   It comes out of the box.

12   It comes out of it.

13   What does Gerhard put it together with?

14   He puts it together with the screwdriver.

15   He puts it together with it.

16   What is the man asking about?

17   He's asking about the newspaper.

18   He's asking about it.

19   What are the children talking about?

20   They are talking about the accident.

21   They are talking about it.

22   What does the (girl) student believe in?

23   She believes in the proverb.

24   She believes in it.

25   What are the students waiting for?

26   They are waiting for the lecture.

27   They are waiting for it.

AUDIOLINGUAL DRILLS

A. Directed Dialog

Fragen Sie, was denn heute mit dem Tisch los ist!
Was ist denn heute mit dem Tisch los?

Antworten Sie, daß er von Susi gedeckt ist!
Er ist von Susi gedeckt.

Fragen Sie, ob es bald besser wird!
Wird es bald besser?

Sagen Sie, daß es bald besser wird!
Es wird bald besser.

Fragen Sie, wo der Teller steht!
Wo steht der Teller?

Sagen Sie, daß er zwischen dem Messer und der Gabel steht!
Er steht zwischen dem Messer und der Gabel.

Fragen Sie, ob das Messer rechts vom Teller liegen muß!
Muß das Messer rechts vom Teller liegen?

Antworten Sie, daß es rechts vom Teller liegen muß!
Es muß rechts vom Teller liegen.

Fragen Sie, ob die Gabel links vom Teller liegen muß!
Muß die Gabel links vom Teller liegen?

Sagen Sie, daß sie links vom Teller liegen muß!
Sie muß links vom Teller liegen.

Sagen Sie, daß die Löffel hinter dem Teller liegen!
Die Löffel liegen hinter dem Teller.

Sagen Sie, daß Mutter, Vater und Susi hungrig vor ihren Tellern sitzen!
Mutter, Vater und Susi sitzen hungrig vor ihren Tellern.

Sagen Sie, daß sie nun essen wollen!
Sie wollen nun essen.

Sagen Sie, daß Susi es das nächste Mal besser machen will!
Susi will es das nächste Mal besser machen.

B. The Verb *wissen* (See Grammar §14.3)

1 Substitute the new subject:

Ich weiß es nicht.   **wir**
Wir wissen es nicht.   **ihr**
Ihr wißt es nicht.   **du**

Du weißt es nicht.   **Lilo**
Lilo weiß es nicht.   **die Kinder**
Die Kinder wissen es nicht.

2 Substitute the new subject in the first clause:

Wir wissen nicht, wo Peter wohnt.   **Heike**
Heike weiß nicht, wo Peter wohnt.   **die Leute**
Die Leute wissen nicht, wo Peter wohnt.   **ich**

Ich weiß nicht, wo Peter wohnt.   **du**
Du weißt nicht, wo Peter wohnt.   **ihr**
Ihr wißt nicht, wo Peter wohnt.

C. Accusative/Dative Prepositions (See Grammar §14.4)

an to, toward; at (*location*); in, on (*time*)

3 Repeat the sentences. Note that **an** and **das** are contracted to **ans**, and **an** and **dem** are contracted to **am**:

Er geht ans Fenster.
Er steht am Fenster.

Er geht an den Tisch.
Er sitzt am Tisch.

Er geht an die Laterne.
Er steht an der Laterne.

4 Substitute the new object of the preposition:

Susi geht an den Tisch.   **das Fenster**
Susi geht ans Fenster.   **die Arbeit**
Susi geht an die Arbeit.   **das Podium**
Susi geht ans Podium.   **der Platz**
Susi geht an den Platz.

Der Junge steht am Fenster.   **die Kiste**
Der Junge steht an der Kiste.   **der Tisch**
Der Junge steht am Tisch.   **das Podium**
Der Junge steht am Podium.   **die Kreuzung**
Der Junge steht an der Kreuzung.

Wir fahren am Montag nach Hause.   **der Abend**
Wir fahren am Abend nach Hause.   **Donnerstag**
Wir fahren am Donnerstag nach Hause.   **der Morgen**
Wir fahren am Morgen nach Hause.   **Sonntag**
Wir fahren am Sonntag nach Hause.

auf on, onto; upon, on top of

5 Repeat the following sentences:

Er läuft auf das Podium. Er geht auf die Straße.
Er steht auf dem Podium. Er steht auf der Straße.

Die Decke kommt auf den Tisch.
Die Decke liegt auf dem Tisch.

6 Substitute the new object of the preposition:

Sie legt das Buch auf den Tisch. **die Kiste**
Sie legt das Buch auf die Kiste. **ihr Schrank**
Sie legt das Buch auf ihren Schrank. **die Pakete**
Sie legt das Buch auf die Pakete. **jener Kasten**
Sie legt das Buch auf jenen Kasten.

Warten Sie auf den Professor? **Ihre Freundin**
Warten Sie auf Ihre Freundin? **ich**
Warten Sie auf mich? **der Junge**
Warten Sie auf den Jungen? **das Mädchen**
Warten Sie auf das Mädchen?

Die Schrauben liegen auf der Kiste. **unser Schrank**
Die Schrauben liegen auf unserem Schrank. **die Bücher**
Die Schrauben liegen auf den Büchern. **der Teller**
Die Schrauben liegen auf dem Teller. **dieser Katalog**
Die Schrauben liegen auf diesem Katalog.

hinter behind

7 Repeat the following sentences:

Der Löffel kommt hinter den Teller. Ich fahre hinter das Haus.
Der Löffel liegt hinter dem Teller. Ich bleibe hinter dem Haus.

Er geht hinter die Kiste.
Er sitzt hinter der Kiste.

8 Substitute the new object of the preposition:

Das Kind läuft hinter die Post. **der Wagen**
Das Kind läuft hinter den Wagen. **diese Häuser**
Das Kind läuft hinter diese Häuser. **das Podium**
Das Kind läuft hinter das Podium. **der Mittagstisch**
Das Kind läuft hinter den Mittagstisch.

Steht er noch hinter dem Wagen? **unser Haus**
Steht er noch hinter unserem Haus? **ich**
Steht er noch hinter mir? **seine Tante**
Steht er noch hinter seiner Tante? **der Student**
Steht er noch hinter dem Studenten?

in into; in (*location*); at, in, during (*time*)

9 Repeat the following sentences. **In** and **das** are contracted to **ins**, and **in** and **dem** are contracted to **im**:

Wir gehen ins Geschäft.
Wir sind im Geschäft.

Sie geht in die Stadt.
Sie wohnt in der Stadt.

Er geht in den Vorlesungsraum.
Er sitzt im Vorlesungsraum.

10 Substitute the new object of the preposition:

Gehst du in die Stadt? **dieses Haus**
Gehst du in dieses Haus? **die Post**
Gehst du in die Post? **das Zimmer**
Gehst du ins Zimmer? **dein Zug**
Gehst du in deinen Zug?

Kommen Sie im Januar? **die Nacht**
Kommen Sie in der Nacht? **dieser Monat**
Kommen Sie in diesem Monat? **der Winter**
Kommen Sie im Winter? **diese Woche**
Kommen Sie in dieser Woche?

Die Bücher liegen in der Kiste. **unser Zimmer**
Die Bücher liegen in unserem Zimmer. **der Kasten**
Die Bücher liegen im Kasten. **die Schränke**
Die Bücher liegen in den Schränken. **ihr Paket**
Die Bücher liegen in ihrem Paket.

neben beside, at the side of

11 Repeat the following sentences:

Es kommt neben den Tisch.
Es liegt neben dem Tisch.

Es kommt neben das Messer.
Es liegt neben dem Messer.

Es kommt neben die Schüssel.
Es liegt neben der Schüssel.

12 Substitute the new object of the preposition:

Stellen Sie es neben die Kiste! **dieses Buch**
Stellen Sie es neben dieses Buch! **Ihr Teller**
Stellen Sie es neben Ihren Teller! **ich**
Stellen Sie es neben mich! **die Laterne**
Stellen Sie es neben die Laterne!

Er sitzt neben der Kiste. **du**
Er sitzt neben dir. **seine Freundin**
Er sitzt neben seiner Freundin. **das Podium**
Er sitzt neben dem Podium. **die Einzelteile**
Er sitzt neben den Einzelteilen.

über over, across; by way of; about; above

13 Repeat the following sentences:

Er legt die Decke über die Kiste.   Die Decke kommt über den Tisch.
Die Decke liegt über der Kiste.   Die Decke liegt über dem Tisch.

14 Substitute the new object of the preposition:

Der Junge läuft über die Straße. **der Platz**
Der Junge läuft über den Platz. **jene Kreuzung**
Der Junge läuft über jene Kreuzung. **der Schillerplatz**
Der Junge läuft über den Schillerplatz.

Lilo spricht über ihren Mann. **du**
Lilo spricht über dich. **das Gedicht**
Lilo spricht über das Gedicht. **die Tagesfragen**
Lilo spricht über die Tagesfragen.

Fahren Sie über München? **Hamburg**
Fahren Sie über Hamburg? **Stuttgart**
Fahren Sie über Stuttgart? **Bremen**
Fahren Sie über Bremen?

Ich sitze über meiner Arbeit. **diese Bücher**
Ich sitze über diesen Büchern. **das Gedicht**
Ich sitze über dem Gedicht. **seine Erzählung**
Ich sitze über seiner Erzählung. **das Buch**
Ich sitze über dem Buch.

unter under

15 Repeat the sentences:

Er läuft unter die Laterne.   Die Kiste kommt unter den Tisch.
Er steht unter der Laterne.   Die Kiste steht unter dem Tisch.

16 Substitute the new object of the preposition:

Er stellt die Kiste unter den Tisch. **das Podium**
Er stellt die Kiste unter das Podium. **die Bretter**
Er stellt die Kiste unter die Bretter. **der Wagen**
Er stellt die Kiste unter den Wagen.

Das Buch ist unter dem Tisch. **die Decke**
Das Buch ist unter der Decke. **dein Werkzeugkasten**
Das Buch ist unter deinem Werkzeugkasten. **diese Pakete**
Das Buch ist unter diesen Paketen.

vor in front of

17 Repeat the sentences:

Er läuft vor den Wagen.   Er geht vor die Post.
Er steht vor dem Wagen.   Er steht vor der Post.

18 Substitute the new object of the preposition:

Gehst du vor den Wagen? **unser Haus**   Er sitzt vor dem Wagen. **unser Haus**
Gehst du vor unser Haus? **das Fenster**   Er sitzt vor unserem Haus. **die Fenster**
Gehst du vor das Fenster? **das Geschäft**   Er sitzt vor den Fenstern. **das Geschäft**
Gehst du vor das Geschäft?   Er sitzt vor dem Geschäft.

zwischen between

19 Repeat the sentences:

Wir laufen zwischen die Häuser.
Wir stehen zwischen den Häusern.

Der Teller kommt zwischen das Messer und die Gabel.
Der Teller liegt zwischen dem Messer und der Gabel.

20 Substitute the new object of the preposition:

Der Junge geht zwischen die Häuser. **die Wagen**
Der Junge geht zwischen die Wagen. **der Tisch und die Kiste**
Der Junge geht zwischen den Tisch und die Kiste. **die Plätze**
Der Junge geht zwischen die Plätze.

Steht er zwischen den Häusern? **die Tische**
Steht er zwischen den Tischen? **ich und du**
Steht er zwischen mir und dir? **unsere Kinder**
Steht er zwischen unseren Kindern?

Dative and accusative cases mixed

21 Substitute the new verbal phrase:

Der Junge kommt an unser Haus. **stehen neben**
Der Junge steht neben unserem Haus. **kommen in**
Der Junge kommt in unser Haus. **sitzen in**
Der Junge sitzt in unserem Haus. **sitzen vor**

Der Junge sitzt vor unserem Haus. **gehen hinter**
Der Junge geht hinter unser Haus. **stehen hinter**
Der Junge steht hinter unserem Haus.

22 Substitute the new verbal phrase, or object of the preposition:

Er geht an den Tisch. **das Podium**
Er geht an das Podium. **sitzen auf**
Er sitzt auf dem Podium. **jene Straße**
Er sitzt auf jener Straße. **laufen über**
Er läuft über jene Straße. **der Schillerplatz**
Er läuft über den Schillerplatz. **stehen vor**
Er steht vor dem Schillerplatz. **die Geschäfte**
Er steht vor den Geschäften. **gehen in**
Er geht in die Geschäfte. **dieser Vorlesungsraum**
Er geht in diesen Vorlesungsraum. **sitzen neben**
Er sitzt neben diesem Vorlesungsraum.

23 Substitute the new verb, or objects of the preposition:

Der Teller steht zwischen dem Messer und der Gabel. **kommen**
Der Teller kommt zwischen das Messer und die Gabel. **der Löffel und die Gabel**
Der Teller kommt zwischen den Löffel und die Gabel. **stehen**
Der Teller steht zwischen dem Löffel und der Gabel. **die Messer und die Löffel**
Der Teller steht zwischen den Messern und den Löffeln. **kommen**
Der Teller kommt zwischen die Messer und die Löffel.

D. Wo- and *da*-Compounds (*See Grammar* §14.5)

24 Form questions with **wo**-compounds. A connecting **-r-** is used if the preposition begins with a vowel.

Example:
Er fragt nach der Zeitung.
Wonach fragt er?

Er denkt an den Unfall.
Woran denkt er?

Er macht es mit dem Schraubenzieher.   Sie warten auf den Milchwagen.
Womit macht er es?   Worauf warten sie?

Er spricht über das Gedicht.   Sie glaubt an das Sprichwort.
Worüber spricht er?   Woran glaubt sie?

Es kommt aus dem Kasten.
Woraus kommt es?

Es besteht aus Brettern und Schrauben.
Woraus besteht es?

Er sitzt auf der Kiste.
Worauf sitzt er?

25 Replace the prepositional phrase with the corresponding **da**-compound. A connecting **-r-** is used if the preposition begins with a vowel.

Example:
Er fragt nach dem Schillerplatz.
Er fragt danach.

Ich denke an seine Erzählungen.
Ich denke daran.

Er steht neben der Laterne.
Er steht daneben.

Warten Sie auf die Vorlesung?
Warten Sie darauf?

Er ist bei der Arbeit.
Er ist dabei.

Er glaubt nicht an das Sprichwort.
Er glaubt nicht daran.

Sie sitzt vor ihrem Haus.
Sie sitzt davor.

Es besteht nur aus den Einzelteilen.
Es besteht nur daraus.

Es liegt im Werkzeugkasten.
Es liegt darin.

Das Buch liegt unter dem Tisch.
Das Buch liegt darunter.

Wir laufen über den Schillerplatz.
Wir laufen darüber.

Sie sitzt zwischen dem Tisch und dem Podium.
Sie sitzt dazwischen.

Machst du es mit dem Werkzeug?
Machst du es damit?

E. **Wo** at what place?, *wohin* to what place?, *woher* from what place? *(See Grammar §14.6)*

26 Form questions with **woher?** and **wohin?**

Example:
Er kommt aus der Vorlesung.
Woher kommt er?

Er geht in die Stadt.
Wohin geht er?

Sie laufen nach Hause.
Wohin laufen sie?

Sie kommen vom Schillerplatz.
Woher kommen sie?

Er fährt nach München.
Wohin fährt er?

Er schickt das Paket nach Berlin.
Wohin schickt er das Paket?

Er kommt von der Bahn.
Woher kommt er?

27 Form questions with **wo?, wohin?,** or **woher?**:

Die Leute warten an der Ecke.
Wo warten die Leute?

Mutti schickt Susi zum Milchmann.
Wohin schickt Mutti Susi?

Der Kuchen steht auf dem Tisch.
Wo steht der Kuchen?

Peter holt das Paket aus dem Wagen.
Woher holt Peter das Paket?

Er legt das Buch in den Schrank.
Wohin legt er das Buch?

Fräulein Schneider wohnt am Schillerplatz.
Wo wohnt Fräulein Schneider?

Professor Wolf geht in den Vorlesungsraum.
Wohin geht Professor Wolf?

Mutter nimmt die Teller aus dem Schrank.
Woher nimmt Mutter die Teller?

Die Kinder sind auf der Straße.
Wo sind die Kinder?

Vater und Mutter bleiben zu Hause.
Wo bleiben Vater und Mutter?

Die Leute fahren in den Schwarzwald.
Wohin fahren die Leute?

F. Questions and Answers

Was fragt Susis Vater?
Er fragt, was mit dem Tisch los ist.

Was antwortet Susi?
Sie antwortet, daß alles außer der
   Suppenschüssel von ihr gedeckt ist.

Wird es bald besser?
Ja, es wird bald besser.

Wo stehen die Teller?
Sie stehen zwischen dem Messer und der Gabel.

Wo muß das Messer liegen?
Es muß rechts vom Teller liegen.

Und wo muß die Gabel liegen?
Sie muß links vom Teller liegen.

Wo liegen die Löffel?
Sie liegen hinter den Tellern.

Wie will Susi es das nächste Mal machen?
Sie will es das nächste Mal besser machen.

GRAMMAR

14.1 Word-Formation

Compound nouns

die Suppe soup + **die Schüssel** bowl = **die Suppenschüssel** tureen, soup bowl

The suffix *-lich*

The suffix **-lich** is added to nouns to make adjectives/adverbs. These often correspond to English words ending in *-al*, *-ly*, *-like*, *-ous*. Sometimes the meaning is *typical of*. The stem vowel of the noun is usually umlauted. Some words of this type you have had are: **endlich**, **nämlich**, **natürlich**, **tatsächlich**.

das Ende end + **-lich** = **endlich** final(ly)
der Name name + **-lich** = **nämlich** namely; you see
die Natur nature + **-lich** = **natürlich** natural(ly)
die Tatsache fact + **-lich** = **tatsächlich** factual(ly); actual(ly)

You will encounter a great many more adjectives/adverbs of this type and you will be expected to recognize their meanings. With the nouns you already know, for example, you should be able to recognize the following without difficulty:

der Abend	abendlich	evening; of *or* in the evening
die Angst	ängstlich	anxious; uneasy; timid
die Form	förmlich	formal; ceremonial
der Freund	freundlich	friendly
das Geschäft	geschäftlich	commercial; on business
das Glück	glücklich	lucky; happy
der Gott	göttlich	divine, godlike
das Haus	häuslich	domestic
das Jahr	jährlich	yearly, annual
das Kind	kindlich	childlike
der Mann	männlich	male, manly
der Mensch	menschlich	human, humane
der Monat	monatlich	monthly
die Mutter	mütterlich	motherly
die Nacht	nächtlich	nightly; at night
die Stunde	stündlich	hourly; every hour
der Tag	täglich	daily; every day

der Unterschied	unterschiedlich	different
der Vater	väterlich	fatherly
die Woche	wöchentlich*	weekly; every week
das Wort	wörtlich	literal, verbal

* Note the addition of an internal **-nt-**.

14.2 Singular and Plural of Nouns

das Bier, die Biere
der Kuchen, die Kuchen
der Saft, die Säfte

der Wein, die Weine
der Wirt, die Wirte
die Wirtin, die Wirtinnen

14.3 The Verb *wissen*

The English verb *know* may mean "have knowledge of" or "be acquainted with." In German, these two meanings are associated with two separate verbs: **wissen** and **kennen**.

know ⎧ have knowledge of   **wissen**
     ⎩ be acquainted with   **kennen**

Ich weiß es nicht.
I don't know.

Ich weiß, daß aller Anfang schwer ist.
I know that the first step is difficult.

Wissen Sie, wann der Zug nach München abfährt?
Do you know when the train to Munich leaves?

Ich kenne den Professor sehr gut.
I know the professor very well.

Ich kenne diese Stadt nicht.
I don't know this city. (I'm not acquainted with this city.)

Kennen Sie diese Gedichte?
Are you acquainted with these poems?

Present tense forms of *wissen*

The forms of **wissen**, like the forms of the modal auxiliaries, are irregular in the present tense:

ich weiß	wir wissen
du weißt	ihr wißt
er, sie, es weiß	sie, Sie wissen

4.4 Accusative/Dative Prepositions

The following prepositions may govern either the accusative or the dative case, depending on whether *direction* or *location* is being expressed. The accusative case, together with one of these prepositions, expresses the meaning of *motion toward a place*. It thus answers the question **wohin?** *to what place?*

When one of these prepositions occurs with an object in the dative case, it expresses the *location* of the action or condition. The dative thus answers the question **wo?** *at what place?* When used in expressions of time after the prepositions **an** and **in**, the dative answers the question **wann?** *at what time?*

The English meanings of the prepositions listed below are not exhaustive, but include only the contexts in which you have encountered them so far. You will learn additional meanings and functions of these prepositions as your knowledge of German increases.

an to, toward; at (*location*); in, on (*time*)

Wohin geht sie?	Sie geht **an den** Tisch.
	She is going *to the* table.
Wo ist sie?	Sie ist **am (an dem)** Tisch.
	She is *at the* table.
Wann kommt sie?	Sie kommt **am (an dem)** Nachmittag.
	She is coming *in the* afternoon.
	Sie kommt **am (an dem)** Mittwoch.
	She is coming *on* Wednesday.

auf on, onto; upon, on top of

Wohin kommt es?	Es kommt **auf den** Tisch.
	It goes *on the* table.
Wo liegt es?	Es liegt **auf dem** Tisch.
	It is lying *on top of the* table.

hinter behind

Wohin kommt der Löffel?	Er kommt **hinter den** Teller. It goes *behind the* plate.
Wo liegt der Löffel?	Er liegt **hinter dem** Teller. It lies *behind the* plate.

in into; in (*location*); at, in, during (*time*)

Wohin geht er?	Er geht **in die** Stadt. He is going *into the* city.
Wo ist er?	Er ist **im (in dem)** Vorlesungsraum. He is *in the* lecture hall.
Wann kommt er?	Er kommt **in der** Nacht. He is coming *at (during the, in the)* night.
	Er kommt **im (in dem)** Herbst. He is coming *in the* autumn.

neben beside, at the side of

Wohin legt sie das Messer?	Sie legt es **neben die** Schüssel. She is putting it *beside the* bowl.
Wo liegt das Messer?	Es liegt **neben der** Schüssel. It is lying *beside the* bowl.

über over, across; by way of; about; above

Wohin kommt die Decke?	Sie kommt **über den** Tisch. It goes *over (above) the* table.
Wo ist die Decke?	Sie ist **über dem** Tisch. It is *above the* table.
Wohin läuft er?	Er läuft **über die** Straße. He is running *across the* street.
Wo wohnt er?	Er wohnt **über dem** Geschäft. He lives *above the* store.
Wohin fahren sie?	Sie fahren **über Bremen** nach Hamburg. They are going to Hamburg *by way of* Bremen.
Worüber spricht er?	Er spricht **über das** Gedicht. He is talking *about the* poem.

unter under

Wohin stellen sie die Kiste?	Sie stellen sie **unter den** Tisch. They are putting it *under the* table.
Wo ist die Kiste?	Sie ist **unter dem** Tisch. It is *under the* table.

vor in front of

Wohin legt er die Gabel?	Er legt sie **vor den** Teller. He is putting it *in front of the* plate.
Wo liegt die Gabel?	Sie liegt **vor dem** Teller. It lies *in front of the* plate.

zwischen between

Wohin stellt sie den Teller?	Sie stellt ihn **zwischen das** Messer und **die** Gabel. She is putting it *between the* knife and *the* fork.
Wo steht der Teller?	Er steht **zwischen dem** Messer und **der** Gabel. It is *between the* knife and *the* fork.

The following contractions are commonly made in both speech and writing:

an + dem = **am**   an + das = **ans**
in + dem = **im**   in + das = **ins**

Some special uses of the accusative/dative prepositions

These prepositions often occur in combination with verbs or nouns to express neither direction nor location nor time. When this is so, the preposition usually takes an accusative object:

denken an think about	Ich denke **an deine** Erzählungen. I'm thinking *about your* stories.
glauben an believe in	Glaubst du **an das** Sprichwort? Do you believe *in the* proverb?
Interesse haben an be interested in (+ *dat*.)	Ich habe kein Interesse **an** Sprichwörtern. I'm not interested *in* proverbs.
antworten auf answer	Antworten Sie **auf meine** Frage! Answer *my* question.
warten auf wait for	Er wartet **auf die** Vorlesung. He is waiting *for the* lecture.

Erzählungen über stories about

lachen über laugh about

sprechen über talk about

Er kennt viele Erzählungen **über sie**.
He knows a lot of stories *about her*.

Er lacht **über den** Unfall.
He laughs *about the* accident.

Wir sprechen **über das** Buch.
We are talking *about the* book.

14.5 *Wo-* and *da-* Compounds

The pronoun substitute *wo*

The interrogative pronoun **was?** normally occurs at the beginning of a sentence and has the effect of making that sentence into a word question:

Was nimmst du?
Was ist da rechts bei der Laterne?
Was kostet der Hut dort im Fenster?
Was ist denn heute mit dem Tisch los?

If this interrogative pronoun should be governed by a preposition, however, then the preposition and the **was** are usually replaced by a compound consisting of **wo-** plus the preposition. If the preposition begins with a vowel, then **-r-** is inserted after the **wo-**. Thus:

nach was? becomes **wonach?**
auf was? becomes **worauf?**
an was? becomes **woran?**

Wonach fragt sie? *What is she asking about?*
Sie fragt **nach dem Wagen**. *She is asking about the car.*

Worauf wartet er? *What is he waiting for?*
Er wartet **auf die Vorlesung**. *He's waiting for the lecture.*

Woran denkst du? *What are you thinking about?*
Ich denke **an das Sprichwort**. *I'm thinking about the proverb.*

Note: These **wo**-compounds are never used to refer to persons. Thus:

Worauf warten Sie? *What are you waiting for?*
Auf wen warten Sie? *Whom are you waiting for?*

The pronoun substitute *da*

A prepositional phrase whose object does not refer to a person may often be replaced by a **da-**

compound, consisting of **da-** plus the preposition (with **-r-**, if the preposition begins with a vowel):

auf der Kiste   becomes   **darauf**
bei der Arbeit   becomes   **dabei**
nach dem Wagen   becomes   **danach**

Wir sitzen **auf der Kiste**.   We are sitting *on the box*.
Wir sitzen **darauf**.   We are sitting *on it*.

Er ist jetzt **bei der Arbeit**.   He is *at work* now.
Er ist jetzt **dabei**.   He is *at it* (i.e. *there*) now.

Sie fragt **nach dem Wagen**.   She is asking *about the car*.
Sie fragt **danach**.   She is asking *about it*.

Note: These **da**-compounds are never used to refer to persons. Thus:

Ich warte **darauf**.   I am waiting *for it*.
Ich warte **auf ihn**.   I am waiting *for him*.

4.6 *Wo, wohin,* and *woher*

In asking the question *where?* in German, it is necessary to differentiate between three distinct meanings: *at* what place, *to* what place, and *from* what place:

where ┬ at what place   **wo**
      ├ to what place   **wohin**
      └ from what place **woher**

Wo wohnst du, Hans?
Where (at what place) do you live, Hans?

Woher kommst du, Inge?
Where are you coming from, Inge?

Wohin gehst du, Peter?
Where (to what place) are you going, Peter?

It makes no sense to ask questions like **Wo gehst du?** or **Wohin bist du?** because the meanings of the question-words are not compatible with the meanings of the verbs. **Wo** implies a single location, whereas **gehst** implies motion toward some goal. In the second sentence **wohin** implies motion toward a goal, but the verb **bist** implies a single location.

WRITING

A. Singular and Plural of Nouns

Copy the sentences and insert the forms that correspond to the English words in parentheses:

1. Ich mag _____ _____ nicht leiden. (such wines)
2. Sind das denn _____ _____? (the hostesses)
3. Ißt du _____ _____? (your cake)
4. Wo sind _____ _____? (our spoons)
5. _____ _____ liegen links vom Teller. (these forks)
6. Susi füllt _____ _____ in die Schüssel. (the juice)
7. _____ _____ ist nicht gut. (this soup)
8. _____ _____ mache ich es besser. (this time)
9. Wohin soll ich _____ _____ stellen? (our plates)
10. Wir haben aber _____ _____. (no tablecloth)

B. Verbs

Arrange the elements to form German sentences. Where necessary change infinitives to finite verb forms. Use the future tense where indicated:

1. ich / wollen / entgegengehen / ihm .
2. du / brauchen / zusammenbauen / den Schrank / nicht .
3. er / bestehen / nur aus Brettern und Schrauben .
4. holen / den Schraubenzieher / mir !
5. wer / liegen / dort bei der Laterne ?
6. hinübergehen / du / zu deiner Mutter ?
7. hoffentlich / der Schrank / gefallen / uns . (*fut.*)
8. die Kisten / stehen / im Zimmer .
9. wünschen / du / Glück / mir ?
10. das / dürfen / sagen / du / nicht .
11. aber / ich / mögen / helfen / dir .
12. müssen / machen / er / es / besser ?
13. mit dem richtigen Werkzeug / gelingen / es / mir . (*fut.*)
14. die Schüssel / kaputtgehen .
15. aufpassen / gut !
16. du / wissen / es / auch nicht .
17. das Messer / sollen / kommen / neben den Teller .
18. der Tisch / sein / gedeckt / von mir .

19 wissen / ihr /,/ wo / sein / er ?
20 Susi / wollen / decken / den Tisch .
21 ich / wissen /,/ daß / du / können / helfen.
22 wir / zurückschicken / es / heute nachmittag . (*fut.*)

C. Accusative/Dative Prepositions

Insert the correct case form of the definite article:

1 Mein Buch ist auf _____ Tisch.
2 Stellen Sie die Kiste neben _____ Schrank!
3 Er spricht über _____ Unfall.
4 Was ist das dort unter _____ Laterne?
5 Er läuft schnell an _____ Podium.
6 Wollen wir in _____ Stadt gehen?
7 Was liegt hinter _____ Häusern?
8 Ich denke an _____ Gedicht.
9 Warten Sie auf _____ Professor?
10 Der Junge wartet vor _____ Post.
11 Die Schüssel soll auf _____ Decke kommen.
12 Steht der Teller zwischen _____ Löffeln?

D. *Wo*- and *da*-Compounds

For each of the following sentences, do two things: (1) change the prepositional phrase to the corresponding **da**-compound, and (2) change this to a question beginning with the corresponding **wo**-compound.

Example:
Er fragt nach dem Hut.
  1. Er fragt danach.
  2. Wonach fragt er?

1 Sie denkt immer an Tagesfragen.
2 Peter wartet auf seinen Zug.
3 Der Schrank besteht aus Einzelteilen.
4 Er glaubt nicht an diese Sprichwörter.
5 Es soll auf der Kiste liegen.
6 Die Leute sprechen über seine Erzählungen.
7 Er will nach der Stadtbahn fragen.

E. *Wo, wohin,* and *woher*

Insert **wo**, **wohin**, or **woher** in the blanks:

1 _____ bist du, Peter?
2 _____ kommen Sie?
3 _____ läufst du denn?
4 _____ steht mein Teller?
5 _____ stellst du meinen Teller?
6 _____ ist der Schraubenzieher?
7 _____ soll ich diese Kiste stellen?
8 _____ kennst du ihn?
9 Wissen Sie, _____ Herr Hartmann wohnt?
10 Kannst du mir sagen, _____ dieser Zug fährt?

LISTENING PRACTICE

Listen to the recorded conversations; then answer the following questions.

A. Susi und Vater

1 Was ist in der Kiste?
2 Was will Susi tun?
3 Warum soll Susi zu ihrer Mutter gehen?
4 Wer findet den Schraubenzieher?

B. Herr und Frau Schneider

1 Was will Herr Schneider tun?
2 Was muß er zuerst tun?
3 Mag Herr Schneider die Teller leiden?
4 Wie lange haben sie die Teller schon?

Unit 15

HANDEL

DIALOG

Ein Krankenbesuch (Anfang)

1 **Jürgen:** Tag, Onkel Richard, du machst ja schöne Geschichten!

2 **Onkel Richard:** Ja, mein Junge, so etwas hast du noch nicht gekonnt!

3 **Jürgen:** Wie geht es dir denn jetzt?

4 **Onkel Richard:** Oh, ganz gut, wie du siehst.

5 **Jürgen:** Wie ist der Herzanfall eigentlich gekommen?

Visiting a Patient (Beginning)

der Krankenbesuch   **der Kranke,** *pl.* **die Kranken** patient, sick person + **der Besuch,** *pl.* **die Besuche** visit   **besuchen** visit

1 Hello, Uncle Richard. You're really up to great things! (This is a fine story!)

der Onkel, *pl.* **die Onkel** · **die Geschichte,** *pl.* **die Geschichten** story; history; event, affair

2 Yes, my boy, you haven't been able to do anything like this yet.

können (du hast gekonnt)

3 How are you now, anyway?

4 Oh, pretty good, as you see.

ganz quite, entirely, very *weaker than* **sehr**

5 How did the heart attack actually come?

der Herzanfall   **das Herz,** *pl.* **die Herzen** heart + **der Anfall,** *pl.* **die Anfälle** attack · **kommen (er ist gekommen)**

6 **Onkel Richard:** Vermutlich habe ich ein bißchen zu flott gelebt. Du kennst mich ja.

7 **Jürgen:** Also, Onkel, sei jetzt schön brav und halte Ruhe!

8 **Onkel Richard:** Was bleibt mir hier anderes übrig?

9 **Jürgen:** Dann bist du sicher bald wieder auf den Beinen.

10 **Onkel Richard:** Natürlich, ich liege ja den ganzen Tag im Bett, schlafe ordentlich und bekomme laufend Medizin!

(Fortsetzung folgt)

SUPPLEMENT

1 Er ist heute hier gewesen.

2 Er ist heute früh gekommen.

3 Er ist heute morgen angekommen.

4 Er ist heute vormittag mitgekommen.

5 Er ist eben gegangen.

6 Er ist gestern mittag gegangen.

7 Er ist gestern nachmittag weggegangen.

6	Presumably I was living a little too high. After all, you know me.	**vermutlich** presumable (-ably) · **bißchen** *from the diminutive noun* **das Bißchen** little bite (bit) · **leben (ich habe gelebt)**
7	Well, Uncle, be good now and stay quiet.	**brav** good, well-behaved **schön brav** very good · **Ruhe halten** keep quiet **die Ruhe** rest, peace and quiet **halten: du hältst, er hält; er hat gehalten**
8	What else is there left for me here?	**übrigbleiben** be left, remain **übrig** left over + **bleiben: er ist geblieben**
9	Then you'll surely be back on your feet again soon.	**das Bein**, *pl.* **die Beine** leg
10	Of course. After all, I lie in bed all day, sleep a lot, and get medicine continually.	**das Bett**, *pl.* **die Betten** · **schlafen: du schläfst, er schläft; er hat geschlafen** · **ordentlich** proper(ly), orderly · **die Medizin**

(To be continued)

1	He was here today.	**sein (er ist gewesen)**
2	He came this morning.	**heute früh** this morning **früh** early
3	He arrived this morning.	**ankommen (er ist angekommen)**
4	He came along this morning.	**mitkommen (er ist mitgekommen)**
5	He just left.	**gehen (er ist gegangen)**
6	He left yesterday at noon.	
7	He went away yesterday afternoon.	

8 Er ist gestern abend losgegangen.

9 Er ist gestern nacht abgefahren.

10 Rolf bleibt bis morgen hier.

11 Rolf bleibt bis übermorgen hier.

12 Rolf ist vorgestern hier geblieben.

13 Mein Bruder ist morgens nie zu Hause.

14 Mein Bruder ist vormittags nie zu Hause.

15 Mein Bruder ist mittags nie zu Hause.

16 Mein Bruder kommt nachts nie nach Hause.

17 Mein Bruder kommt nachmittags immer nach Hause.

18 Mein Bruder kommt abends immer nach Hause.

19 Mein Bruder kommt sonntags immer nach Hause.

20 Sie ist vor einer Stunde hinübergegangen.

21 Sie bleibt bis vier Uhr dort.

22 Mein Onkel ist vor einem Monat nach Deutschland gefahren.

23 Mein Onkel will bis April dort bleiben.

24 Er ist vor einem Jahr hier gewesen.

25 Er wird in einem Jahr zurückkommen.

8	He started out last evening.	**losgehen (er ist losgegangen)**
9	He left last night.	**abfahren (er ist abgefahren)**
10	Rolf is staying here until tomorrow.	
11	Rolf is staying here until the day after tomorrow.	
12	Rolf stayed here the day before yesterday.	**bleiben (er ist geblieben)**
13	My brother is never at home mornings.	
14	My brother is never at home mornings.	
15	My brother is never at home at noon.	
16	My brother never comes home at night.	
17	My brother always comes home in the afternoon.	
18	My brother always comes home in the evening.	
19	My brother always comes home on Sundays.	
20	She went over there an hour ago.	**hinübergehen (sie ist hinübergegangen)**
21	She is staying there until four o'clock.	
22	My uncle went to Germany a month ago.	**fahren (er ist gefahren)**
23	My uncle wants to stay there until April.	
24	He was here a year ago.	
25	He'll come back in a year.	

AUDIOLINGUAL DRILLS

A. Directed Dialog

Sagen Sie, daß Onkel Richard schöne Geschichten macht!
Onkel Richard macht schöne Geschichten.

Sagen Sie, daß Jürgen so etwas noch nicht gekonnt hat!
Jürgen hat so etwas noch nicht gekonnt.

Fragen Sie, wie es dem Onkel jetzt geht!
Wie geht es dem Onkel jetzt?

Antworten Sie, daß es ihm ganz gut geht!
Es geht ihm ganz gut.

Fragen Sie, wie der Herzanfall eigentlich gekommen ist!
Wie ist der Herzanfall eigentlich gekommen?

Antworten Sie, daß der Onkel ein bißchen zu flott gelebt hat!
Der Onkel hat ein bißchen zu flott gelebt.

Sagen Sie, daß Jürgen ihn ja kennt!
Jürgen kennt ihn ja.

Sagen Sie, daß der Onkel jetzt schön brav sein soll!
Der Onkel soll jetzt schön brav sein.

Sagen Sie, daß er Ruhe halten soll!
Er soll Ruhe halten.

Fragen Sie, was ihm hier anderes übrigbleibt!
Was bleibt ihm hier anderes übrig?

Antworten Sie, daß ihm hier nichts anderes übrigbleibt!
Ihm bleibt hier nichts anderes übrig.

Sagen Sie, daß er dann sicher bald wieder auf den Beinen ist!
Dann ist er sicher bald wieder auf den Beinen.

Sagen Sie, daß er ja den ganzen Tag im Bett liegt!
Er liegt ja den ganzen Tag im Bett.

Sagen Sie, daß er ordentlich schläft!
Er schläft ordentlich.

Sagen Sie, daß er laufend Medizin bekommt!
Er bekommt laufend Medizin.

B. Present Perfect Tense: Regular Weak Verbs (*See Grammar* §§15.4–15.8)

Past participles of regular weak verbs like **leben** have **ge-** prefixed to the stem and **-t** suffixed to it: **gelebt**.

1 Substitute the new subject:

Onkel Richard hat zu flott gelebt.	**die Leute**	Wir haben zu flott gelebt.	**ihr**
Die Leute haben zu flott gelebt.	**du**	Ihr habt zu flott gelebt.	**ich**
Du hast zu flott gelebt.	**wir**	Ich habe zu flott gelebt.	

2 The verbs in this drill follow the pattern of **leben**. Substitute the new verb.

Example:
Er hat dieses Buch gehabt.   **kaufen**
Er hat dieses Buch gekauft.

Er hat es heute gesagt.	**kaufen**	Er hat es heute gelernt.	**bauen**
Er hat es heute gekauft.	**üben**	Er hat es heute gebaut.	**schicken**
Er hat es heute geübt.	**machen**	Er hat es heute geschickt.	**holen**
Er hat es heute gemacht.	**fragen**	Er hat es heute geholt.	**haben**
Er hat es heute gefragt.	**brauchen**	Er hat es heute gehabt.	
Er hat es heute gebraucht.	**lernen**		

3 Verbs that require a connecting **-e-** in the present tense also require it in the past participle. Substitute the new verb:

Er hat gestern nicht gewartet.	**antworten**	Er hat gestern nicht gespottet.	**warten**
Er hat gestern nicht geantwortet.	**spotten**	Er hat gestern nicht gewartet.	

4 Do not add the prefix **ge-** if the verb already begins with an unstressed, inseparable prefix, like **erzählen**, or if the verb ends in **-ieren**, like **studieren** and **passieren**. Repeat:

Mein Bruder hat es mir erzählt.   Das Paket hat der Frau gehört.
Mein Bruder hat es mir erklärt.   Fräulein Schneider hat Philosophie studiert.
Der Mann hat mich entschuldigt.   Dem Fahrer ist nichts passiert.
Ich habe den Wagen versichert.

5 The verbs in this drill are all regular weak verbs. Change the tense from present to present perfect:

Ich wohne in Köln.   Regnet es heute nachmittag?
Ich habe in Köln gewohnt.   Hat es heute nachmittag geregnet?

Das macht mir Spaß.   Hoffentlich klappt es auch.
Das hat mir Spaß gemacht.   Hoffentlich hat es auch geklappt.

Studierst du Medizin? Wir erklären es euch.
Hast du Medizin studiert? Wir haben es euch erklärt.

Wieviel kostet der Hut dort?
Wieviel hat der Hut dort gekostet?

C. Present Perfect Tense: Irregular Weak Verbs (See Grammar §§15.4–15.8)

The modal auxiliaries and **wissen** *know*

6 Substitute the new subject:

Jürgen hat es noch nicht gekonnt. **ich**
Ich habe es noch nicht gekonnt. **Rolf und Günther**
Rolf und Günther haben es noch nicht gekonnt. **ihr**
Ihr habt es noch nicht gekonnt. **du**
Du hast es noch nicht gekonnt.

Haben Sie es gewußt? **du** 　　　Haben wir es gewußt? **ihr**
Hast du es gewußt? **Inge** 　　　Habt ihr es gewußt?
Hat Inge es gewußt? **wir**

7 Substitute the new verb:

Hast du es eigentlich gekonnt? **dürfen** 　　　Hast du es eigentlich gewußt? **wollen**
Hast du es eigentlich gedurft? **sollen** 　　　Hast du es eigentlich gewollt? **müssen**
Hast du es eigentlich gesollt? **mögen** 　　　Hast du es eigentlich gemußt?
Hast du es eigentlich gemocht? **wissen**

denken think, **kennen** know

8 Substitute the new subject:

Wir haben daran gedacht. **du** 　　　Peter und Lilo haben daran gedacht. **er**
Du hast daran gedacht. **ihr** 　　　Er hat daran gedacht.
Ihr habt daran gedacht. **Peter und Lilo**

Haben Sie Herrn Held gekannt? **er** 　　　Hast du Herrn Held gekannt? **ich**
Hat er Herrn Held gekannt? **ihr** 　　　Habe ich Herrn Held gekannt?
Habt ihr Herrn Held gekannt? **du**

D. Present Perfect Tense: Strong Verbs (*See Grammar* §§15.4–15.8)

sein be, **werden** become

9 Substitute the new subject:

Ich bin bei ihm gewesen. **wir**
Wir sind bei ihm gewesen. **er**
Er ist bei ihm gewesen. **Heike und Uwe**

Heike und Uwe sind bei ihm gewesen. **du**
Du bist bei ihm gewesen. **ihr**
Ihr seid bei ihm gewesen.

Sie ist gestern krank geworden. **du**
Du bist gestern krank geworden. **wir**
Wir sind gestern krank geworden. **die Kinder**

Die Kinder sind gestern krank geworden. **ihr**
Ihr seid gestern krank geworden. **ich**
Ich bin gestern krank geworden.

10 Substitute the new subject or verb:

Uwe ist krank geworden. **sein**
Uwe ist krank gewesen. **wir**
Wir sind krank gewesen. **werden**
Wir sind krank geworden. **du**

Du bist krank geworden. **sein**
Du bist krank gewesen. **ich**
Ich bin krank gewesen. **werden**
Ich bin krank geworden.

lesen read, **sehen** see; **aussehen** appear; **essen** eat, **liegen** lie, **sitzen** sit; **bitten** ask

11 Substitute the new subject or verb:

Wir haben die Zeitung gelesen. **sehen**
Wir haben die Zeitung gesehen. **mein Vater**
Mein Vater hat die Zeitung gesehen. **lesen**

Mein Vater hat die Zeitung gelesen. **du**
Du hast die Zeitung gelesen. **sehen**
Du hast die Zeitung gesehen.

12 Substitute the new subject or predicate adjective:

Der Junge hat krank ausgesehen. **nett**
Der Junge hat nett ausgesehen. **Inge und Heike**
Inge und Heike haben nett ausgesehen. **schön**
Inge und Heike haben schön ausgesehen. **du**
Du hast schön ausgesehen. **besser**
Du hast besser ausgesehen.

13 Substitute the new subject or verb:

Haben Sie dort gesessen? **er**
Hat er dort gesessen? **liegen**
Hat er dort gelegen? **du**
Hast du dort gelegen? **essen**

Hast du dort gegessen? **ihr**
Habt ihr dort gegessen? **sitzen**
Habt ihr dort gesessen?

14 Substitute the new subject:

Ich habe ihn gebeten, Geige zu üben. **wir** Ihr habt ihn gebeten, Geige zu üben. **du**
Wir haben ihn gebeten, Geige zu üben. **Heike** Du hast ihn gebeten, Geige zu üben.
Heike hat ihn gebeten, Geige zu üben. **ihr**

helfen help, **nehmen** take, **sprechen** speak

15 Substitute the new subject:

Wir haben ihr geholfen. **ich**
Ich habe ihr geholfen. **du**
Du hast ihr geholfen. **Rolf und Günther**
Rolf und Günther haben ihr geholfen. **der Mann**
Der Mann hat ihr geholfen.

Hast du es aus der Kiste genommen? **ihr**
Habt ihr es aus der Kiste genommen? **die Mädchen**
Haben die Mädchen es aus der Kiste genommen? **er**
Hat er es aus der Kiste genommen? **ich**
Habe ich es aus der Kiste genommen?

Von wem hast du denn gesprochen? **Lilo**
Von wem hat Lilo denn gesprochen? **wir**
Von wem haben wir denn gesprochen? **ihr**
Von wem habt ihr denn gesprochen? **diese Leute**
Von wem haben diese Leute denn gesprochen?

finden find, **empfinden** feel, **beginnen** begin, **gelingen** succeed

16 Substitute the new direct (accusative) object:

Uwe hat die Kiste gefunden. **Geld** Uwe hat den Löffel gefunden. **Geige**
Uwe hat das Geld gefunden. **Suppe** Uwe hat die Geige gefunden.
Uwe hat die Suppe gefunden. **Löffel**

17 Substitute the new subject:

Ich habe es so empfunden. **meine Frau** Wir haben es so empfunden. **du**
Meine Frau hat es so empfunden. **Lilo** Du hast es so empfunden.
Lilo hat es so empfunden. **wir**

18 Substitute the new adverb of time:

Gestern haben wir mit der Arbeit begonnen. **vorgestern**
Vorgestern haben wir mit der Arbeit begonnen. **heute früh**

Heute früh haben wir mit der Arbeit begonnen. **gestern abend**
Gestern abend haben wir mit der Arbeit begonnen. **vor vier Wochen**
Vor vier Wochen haben wir mit der Arbeit begonnen.

Gestern ist es uns endlich gelungen. **heute**
Heute ist es uns endlich gelungen. **heute morgen**
Heute morgen ist es uns endlich gelungen. **gestern mittag**
Gestern mittag ist es uns endlich gelungen. **vorgestern**
Vorgestern ist es uns endlich gelungen.

bleiben stay, **aussteigen** get out, **einsteigen** get in; **scheinen** shine; **übertreiben** exaggerate

19 Substitute the new adverbial expression of place, or verb:

Sie ist in Hamburg geblieben. **aussteigen**   Sie ist dort eingestiegen. **in Bremen**
Sie ist in Hamburg ausgestiegen. **dort**   Sie ist in Bremen eingestiegen. **bleiben**
Sie ist dort ausgestiegen. **einsteigen**   Sie ist in Bremen geblieben.

20 Substitute the new adverb of time:

Die Sonne hat heute nicht geschienen. **gestern**
Die Sonne hat gestern nicht geschienen. **heute morgen**
Die Sonne hat heute morgen nicht geschienen. **vor drei Tagen**
Die Sonne hat vor drei Tagen nicht geschienen. **gestern vormittag**
Die Sonne hat gestern vormittag nicht geschienen.

21 Substitute the new subject:

Hast du wieder übertrieben? **wir**   Habe ich wieder übertrieben? **Peter**
Haben wir wieder übertrieben? **ihr**   Hat Peter wieder übertrieben?
Habt ihr wieder übertrieben? **ich**

braten roast, bake, fry, **schlafen** sleep, **halten** hold, **gefallen** please, **lassen** leave, **heißen** be called, **laufen** run

22 Substitute the new subject:

Mutter hat das Fleisch schon gebraten. **ich**   Ihr habt das Fleisch schon gebraten. **wir**
Ich habe das Fleisch schon gebraten. **du**   Wir haben das Fleisch schon gebraten.
Du hast das Fleisch schon gebraten. **ihr**

23 Substitute the new adverb of time:

Ich habe bis zehn Uhr geschlafen. **bis heute vormittag**
Ich habe bis heute vormittag geschlafen. **bis sechs Uhr**
Ich habe bis sechs Uhr geschlafen. **bis halb neun**

Ich habe bis halb neun geschlafen. **bis fünf**
Ich habe bis fünf geschlafen.

24 Substitute the new subject:

Onkel Richard hat Ruhe gehalten. **ich**
Ich habe Ruhe gehalten. **wir**
Wir haben Ruhe gehalten. **du**
Du hast Ruhe gehalten. **ihr**
Ihr habt Ruhe gehalten.

Der Hut hat mir gefallen. **die Bücher**
Die Bücher haben mir gefallen. **dein Wagen**
Dein Wagen hat mir gefallen. **das Mädchen**
Das Mädchen hat mir gefallen. **du**
Du hast mir gefallen.

Haben sie ihn allein gelassen? **ihr**
Habt ihr ihn allein gelassen? **seine Mutter**
Hat seine Mutter ihn allein gelassen? **du**
Hast du ihn allein gelassen? **wir**
Haben wir ihn allein gelassen?

Wie hat er eigentlich geheißen? **die Leute**
Wie haben die Leute eigentlich geheißen?
das Kind
Wie hat das Kind eigentlich geheißen? **du**
Wie hast du eigentlich geheißen? **er**
Wie hat er eigentlich geheißen?

Der Junge ist über die Straße gelaufen. **ich**
Ich bin über die Straße gelaufen. **du**
Du bist über die Straße gelaufen. **die Kinder**
Die Kinder sind über die Straße gelaufen. **ihr**
Ihr seid über die Straße gelaufen.

fahren drive, **abfahren** depart

25 Substitute the new adverbial expression or verb:

Hans ist heute abgefahren. **gestern**
Hans ist gestern abgefahren. **fahren**
Hans ist gestern gefahren. **von München**

Hans ist von München gefahren. **abfahren**
Hans ist von München abgefahren.

26 Substitute the new subject:

Wir haben den Wagen gefahren. **Peter**
Peter hat den Wagen gefahren. **du**
Du hast den Wagen gefahren. **ich**

Ich habe den Wagen gefahren. **Ilse und Lilo**
Ilse und Lilo haben den Wagen gefahren.

kommen come, **herumkommen** come around, **ankommen** arrive, **mitkommen** come along, **zurückkommen** come back, **bekommen** get

27 Substitute the new verb:

Die Leute sind heute früh gekommen. **ankommen**
Die Leute sind heute früh angekommen. **mitkommen**
Die Leute sind heute früh mitgekommen. **zurückkommen**
Die Leute sind heute früh zurückgekommen. **kommen**
Die Leute sind heute früh gekommen.

28 Substitute the new direct object:

   Haben sie den Wagen bekommen? **Geld**   Haben sie den Schrank bekommen? **Paket**
   Haben sie das Geld bekommen? **Medizin**   Haben sie das Paket bekommen?
   Haben sie die Medizin bekommen? **Schrank**

   gehen go, **losgehen** start out, **kaputtgehen** get broken, **entgegengehen** go toward

29 Substitute the new verb or subject:

   Ich bin schon gegangen. **die Leute**   Es ist schon losgegangen. **kaputtgehen**
   Die Leute sind schon gegangen. **losgehen**   Es ist schon kaputtgegangen. **die Teller**
   Die Leute sind schon losgegangen. **es**   Die Teller sind schon kaputtgegangen.

30 Substitute the new subject:

   Wir sind dem Jungen entgegengegangen. **ich**
   Ich bin dem Jungen entgegengegangen. **Tante Inge**
   Tante Inge ist dem Jungen entgegengegangen. **ihr**
   Ihr seid dem Jungen entgegengegangen. **Ilse und Peter**
   Ilse und Peter sind dem Jungen entgegengegangen. **du**
   Du bist dem Jungen entgegengegangen.

   stehen stand, **herumstehen** stand around, **verstehen** understand

31 Substitute the new subject:

   Der Tisch hat da hinten gestanden. **die Kinder**
   Die Kinder haben da hinten gestanden. **du**
   Du hast da hinten gestanden. **ich**
   Ich habe da hinten gestanden.

   Sie haben um den Wagen herumgestanden. **ihr**
   Ihr habt um den Wagen herumgestanden. **wir**
   Wir haben um den Wagen herumgestanden. **die Leute**
   Die Leute haben um den Wagen herumgestanden.

   Hast du ihn verstanden? **die Verkäuferin**
   Hat die Verkäuferin ihn verstanden? **ihr**
   Habt ihr ihn verstanden? **die Frauen**
   Haben die Frauen ihn verstanden?

   tun do

32 Substitute the new adverb of time:

   Was hast du heute nachmittag getan? **gestern**
   Was hast du gestern getan? **gestern abend**

Was hast du gestern abend getan? **vor zwei Jahren**
Was hast du vor zwei Jahren getan? **heute morgen**
Was hast du heute morgen getan? **am dritten Juni**
Was hast du am dritten Juni getan?

E. Transformation Drills, Weak and Strong Verbs

33 Change from the present to the present perfect tense. All verbs are weak and require the auxiliary **haben**.

Example:
Er lebt zu flott.
Er hat zu flott gelebt.

Er wohnt in diesem Haus.
Er hat in diesem Haus gewohnt.

Er arbeitet nur morgens.
Er hat nur morgens gearbeitet.

Das stimmt nicht ganz.
Das hat nicht ganz gestimmt.

Der Kuchen schmeckt gut.
Der Kuchen hat gut geschmeckt.

Die Kinder mögen die Milch nicht.
Die Kinder haben die Milch nicht gemocht.

Susi paßt gut auf.
Susi hat gut aufgepaßt.

Das Buch kostet zehn Mark.
Das Buch hat zehn Mark gekostet.

Wie meinst du das?
Wie hast du das gemeint?

Glaubst du nicht daran?
Hast du nicht daran geglaubt?

Wir legen das Buch auf den Tisch.
Wir haben das Buch auf den Tisch gelegt.

Stellt ihr den Tisch ins Zimmer?
Habt ihr den Tisch ins Zimmer gestellt?

Er weiß es einfach nicht.
Er hat es einfach nicht gewußt.

Ich erkläre die Geschichten.
Ich habe die Geschichten erklärt.

Denkst du häufig daran?
Hast du häufig daran gedacht?

Was antwortest du?
Was hast du geantwortet?

Du schaust unter den Wagen.
Du hast unter den Wagen geschaut.

Die Jungen warten ab.
Die Jungen haben abgewartet.

Hoffentlich klappt es auch.
Hoffentlich hat es auch geklappt.

Ich kann es heute nicht.
Ich habe es heute nicht gekonnt.

Tagsüber regnet es viel.
Tagsüber hat es viel geregnet.

Sie hat kein Interesse an Tagesfragen.
Sie hat kein Interesse an Tagesfragen gehabt.

Ich kenne ihn sehr gut.
Ich habe ihn sehr gut gekannt.

Das wünscht Margrit auch.
Das hat Margrit auch gewünscht.

Susi deckt den Mittagstisch.
Susi hat den Mittagstisch gedeckt.

Mutter füllt die Suppe in die Schüssel.
Mutter hat die Suppe in die Schüssel gefüllt.

Ihr lernt ihn heute kennen.
Ihr habt ihn heute kennengelernt.

Die Frauen lachen über die Geschichte.
Die Frauen haben über die Geschichte gelacht.

34 Change from the present to the present perfect. All verbs are strong and require the auxiliary **haben**:

Die Sonne scheint so schön.
Die Sonne hat so schön geschienen.

Der Onkel liegt im Bett.
Der Onkel hat im Bett gelegen.

Der Onkel schläft ordentlich.
Der Onkel hat ordentlich geschlafen.

Er bekommt laufend Medizin.
Er hat laufend Medizin bekommen.

Wir lassen ihn bald wieder allein.
Wir haben ihn bald wieder allein gelassen.

Wir beginnen heute morgen.
Wir haben heute morgen begonnen.

Ich tue es gern für dich.
Ich habe es gern für dich getan.

Der Wagen sieht neu aus.
Der Wagen hat neu ausgesehen.

Die Männer fahren den Wagen.
Die Männer haben den Wagen gefahren.

Die Leute übertreiben ein bißchen.
Die Leute haben ein bißchen übertrieben.

Sie findet den Hut im Schrank.
Sie hat den Hut im Schrank gefunden.

Die Leute sitzen am Tisch.
Die Leute haben am Tisch gesessen.

Sprichst du über die Geschichte?
Hast du über die Geschichte gesprochen?

Die Geschichten gefallen mir sehr gut.
Die Geschichten haben mir sehr gut gefallen.

Versteht ihr die Erzählung?
Habt ihr die Erzählung verstanden?

35 Change from the present to the present perfect. All verbs require the auxiliary **sein**:

Ich gehe heute mittag in die Stadt.
Ich bin heute mittag in die Stadt gegangen.

Dem Fahrer passiert nichts.
Dem Fahrer ist nichts passiert.

Der Fahrer ist ziemlich rücksichtslos.
Der Fahrer ist ziemlich rücksichtslos gewesen.

Der Wagen rutscht gegen die Laterne.
Der Wagen ist gegen die Laterne gerutscht.

Es gelingt ihm nicht.
Es ist ihm nicht gelungen.

Der Wagen kippt plötzlich um.
Der Wagen ist plötzlich umgekippt.

Es bleibt ihm nichts anderes übrig.
Es ist ihm nichts anderes übriggeblieben.

Die Milch schwappt über die Straße.
Die Milch ist über die Straße geschwappt.

Die Plätze hier sind noch frei.
Die Plätze hier sind noch frei gewesen.

Ich komme um dreiviertel zehn an.
Ich bin um dreiviertel zehn angekommen.

Wann fährst du eigentlich ab?
Wann bist du eigentlich abgefahren?

Gehst du gleich wieder hinüber?
Bist du gleich wieder hinübergegangen?

36 Change from the present to the present perfect:

Sie nimmt nie Brot.
Sie hat nie Brot genommen.

Er steigt in Bonn aus.
Er ist in Bonn ausgestiegen.

Wir wünschen dir viel Glück.
Wir haben dir viel Glück gewünscht.

Sie helfen mir häufig.
Sie haben mir häufig geholfen.

Du weißt es bestimmt.
Du hast es bestimmt gewußt.

Ich esse zuerst die Suppe.
Ich habe zuerst die Suppe gegessen.

Sie empfindet es wahrscheinlich so.
Sie hat es wahrscheinlich so empfunden.

Das Geld ist sehr knapp.
Das Geld ist sehr knapp gewesen.

Er will heute keine Milch.
Er hat heute keine Milch gewollt.

Man spottet über den Unfall.
Man hat über den Unfall gespottet.

Wir fahren schnell in die Stadt.
Wir sind schnell in die Stadt gefahren.

Gehst du gleich in die Vorlesung?
Bist du gleich in die Vorlesung gegangen?

Die Kiste steht unter dem Tisch.
Die Kiste hat unter dem Tisch gestanden.

Der Postbote kommt mit einem Paket.
Der Postbote ist mit einem Paket gekommen.

Der Mann wird alt.
Der Mann ist alt geworden.

Der Wagen rutscht über die Kreuzung.
Der Wagen ist über die Kreuzung gerutscht.

Die Bücher gehören ihm nicht.
Die Bücher haben ihm nicht gehört.

Er studiert immer tüchtig.
Er hat immer tüchtig studiert.

Wartest du auf mich?
Hast du auf mich gewartet?

Ich sehe ihn heute nachmittag.
Ich habe ihn heute nachmittag gesehen.

Der Milchwagen kippt tatsächlich um.
Der Milchwagen ist tatsächlich umgekippt.

Er bleibt bis Mittwoch in Köln.
Er ist bis Mittwoch in Köln geblieben.

Mein Vater arbeitet nachts.
Mein Vater hat nachts gearbeitet.

Sie mag dieses Nuß-Eis nicht.
Sie hat dieses Nuß-Eis nicht gemocht.

Die Kinder dürfen es nicht.
Die Kinder haben es nicht gedurft.

Ich gehe dem Mann entgegen.
Ich bin dem Mann entgegengegangen.

Das wissen wir nicht.
Das haben wir nicht gewußt.

Muß er es wirklich?
Hat er es wirklich gemußt?

Unser Zug läuft ein.
Unser Zug ist eingelaufen.

Verstehst du die Vorlesung?
Hast du die Vorlesung verstanden?

Der Mann hat eine Million Mark.
Der Mann hat eine Million Mark gehabt.

Mein Geld wird knapp.
Mein Geld ist knapp geworden.

Die Sachen sind sehr hübsch.
Die Sachen sind sehr hübsch gewesen.

Er sagt genau das Gegenteil.
Er hat genau das Gegenteil gesagt.

Der Unfall ist nicht allzu schlimm.
Der Unfall ist nicht allzu schlimm gewesen.

Die Frau hat eine Wunde.
Die Frau hat eine Wunde gehabt.

Tante Inge ist sehr nett.
Tante Inge ist sehr nett gewesen.

Er lacht darüber.
Er hat darüber gelacht.

Sie geht zu Mutter hinüber.
Sie ist zu Mutter hinübergegangen.

Wie heißt der Junge?
Wie hat der Junge geheißen?

F. Questions and Answers

Wie heißt der fünfzehnte Dialog?
Er heißt „Ein Krankenbesuch".

Wer ist krank?
Onkel Richard ist krank.

Was ist dem Onkel passiert?
Er hat einen Herzanfall gehabt.

Wie ist der Herzanfall gekommen?
Onkel Richard sagt, er hat wahrscheinlich ein bißchen zu flott gelebt.

Was sagt Jürgen seinem Onkel?
Er soll schön brav sein und Ruhe halten.

Geht es dem Onkel bald besser?
Ja, er ist sicher bald wieder auf den Beinen.

Was macht er den ganzen Tag?
Er liegt den ganzen Tag im Bett und schläft ordentlich.

Was bekommt er laufend?
Er bekommt laufend Medizin.

GRAMMAR

15.1 Word-Formation

Compound nouns

das Herz heart + **der Anfall** attack = **der Herzanfall** heart attack
der Kranke patient + **der Besuch** visit = **der Krankenbesuch** visit with a patient

15.2 Singular and Plural of Nouns

der Anfall, die Anfälle
das Bein, die Beine
der Besuch, die Besuche

das Bett, die Betten
die Geschichte, die Geschichten
der Onkel, die Onkel

15.3 Some More Time Expressions

1. The words **gestern**, **heute**, and **morgen** may be combined with the terms that refer to parts of the day to form adverbs of time:

   Was tust du **heute nachmittag**?
   What are you doing *this afternoon*?

   Ich gehe **morgen nachmittag** zu Mutter hinüber.
   I'm going over to Mother's *tomorrow afternoon*.

   Er ist **gestern abend** weggegangen.
   He went away *yesterday evening*.

   The word **früh** (literally *early*) is often used in such expressions, replacing **morgen** *morning*:

   heute morgen *or* **heute früh**   this morning
   morgen früh (*never* **morgen morgen**)   tomorrow morning

   When the words for morning, evening, etc. are used in these combinations, they are adverbs, not nouns, and are therefore not capitalized:

   der Vormittag
   but: heute vormittag

2. A suffix **-s** is attached to a word referring to a day, or to a part of a day, to form an adverb of time indicating *repeated occurrence* of the action or condition expressed by the verb:

   der Montag + -s = montags   Mondays
   der Morgen + -s = morgens   mornings, in the morning
   der Mittag + -s = mittags   at noon

| der Abend | + -s = **abends** | evenings, in the evening |
| die Nacht | + -s = **nachts** | nights, at night |

Note the difference in meaning between the two adverbial expressions:

Er kommt **am Abend** nach Hause.　　Er kommt **abends** nach Hause.
He'll come home in the evening.　　　He comes home evenings.

3　You have encountered several examples of the prepositions **in**, **an**, and **seit** in time expressions. Two more prepositions that frequently occur in time expressions are **bis** *until* and **vor** *ago*:

Mein Onkel wird **bis April** in Berlin bleiben.　　Er ist **vor einem Monat** hier gewesen.
My uncle will stay in Berlin *until April*.　　　　He was here *a month ago*.

Bis belongs to that group of prepositions that govern the accusative case (Grammar §10.4). **Vor**, like **in** and **an**, governs the dative case when used in time expressions.

Position of time adverbs

In German an adverbial expression of time precedes any other adverb that happens to be present in the predicate. This often results in a sequence of adverbs that is just the reverse of what occurs in English. Compare the German and English sentences:

Ich gehe **heute nachmittag** zum Baden.　　Sind wir **bald** zu Hause?
I'm going swimming *this afternoon*.　　　　Will we be home *soon*?

Wir fahren **morgen** nach Köln.
We're going to Cologne *tomorrow*.

The verb phrases in these sentences are:

　gehe . . . zum Baden
fahren . . . nach Köln
　sind . . . zu Hause

consisting of a *finite verb* and an *associated element*. As you learned in Unit 2, the associated element stands in last position in a main clause. Adverbs of time are not associated elements; accordingly, they *precede* those elements that make up the second part of the verb phrase.

15.4　Weak and Strong Verbs

German verbs, like English verbs, fall roughly into two categories:

1. Weak verbs, which form their past tense and past participle by means of a suffix (English *work, worked, worked*). The German past participle ends in **-(e)t**: **gelebt**, **geregnet**.

2. Strong verbs, which form their past tense and past participle by means of a vowel change (English *sing, sang, sung; eat, ate, eaten; fly, flew, flown*). The German past participle ends in **-(e)n**: **gesehen, getan**.

A number of strong verbs also have a vowel change in the **du** and **er** forms of the present tense, as was shown in Grammar §§7.3 and 8.4. The full list of principal parts of strong verbs will be given in Unit 20.

15.5 The Past Participle

Weak verbs

The past participle of a weak verb is formed by adding the weakly stressed prefix **ge-** and the suffix **-(e)t**. Those verbs that require the connecting **-e-** in the present tense also have it in the past participle:

Infinitive	*Past participle*
leb en	ge leb t
sag en	ge sag t
mach en	ge mach t
wart en	ge wart et
regn en	ge regn et

Strong verbs

The past participle of a strong verb is formed by adding the weakly stressed prefix **ge-** and the suffix **-(e)n** to the stem. Most strong verbs also have a vowel change in the stem of the past participle; the vowel change is generally not predictable and must therefore be memorized. A few have a consonant change as well.

These verbs have the same vowel in the past participle as in the infinitive:

Infinitive	*Past participle*
les en	ge les en
seh en	ge seh en
ess en	ge gess en
brat en	ge brat en
schlaf en	ge schlaf en
halt en	ge halt en
lass en	ge lass en
komm en	ge komm en
lauf en	ge lauf en
heiß en	ge heiß en

These verbs have a change from an **i**-sound in the infinitive to an **e**-sound in the past participle:

Infinitive	*Past participle*
lieg en	ge leg en
bitt en	ge bet en
sitz en	ge sess en

The verbs in this group have the diphthong **ei** [aɪ] in the infinitive, and the monophthong **ie** [i:] in the past participle:

bleib en	ge blieb en
schein en	ge schien en
steig en	ge stieg en

Some strong verbs have an **e**-sound in the infinitive and an **o**-sound in the past participle:

helf en	ge holf en
nehm en	ge nomm en
sprech en	ge sproch en
werd en	ge word en

Two verbs showing a vowel change from **eh** [e:] to short **a** [a], plus a consonant change, are:

steh en	ge stand en
geh en	ge gang en

A number of strong verbs have short **i** [ɪ] in the infinitive and short **u** [ʊ] in the past participle; so far you have had:

find en	ge fund en
spring en	ge sprung en

Two verbs that do not conform to any of the above patterns of vowel alternation are:

sei n	ge wes en
tu n	ge ta n

Irregular weak verbs

A few verbs form their past participle by suffixing **-t**, and also have changes in the stem itself. This group includes four of the modal auxiliaries, **wissen**, **denken**, **kennen**, and a few others that you have not encountered yet:

Infinitive	*Past participle*
dürf en	ge durf t
könn en	ge konn t
mög en	ge moch t

Infinitive	Past participle
müss en	ge muß t
wiss en	ge wuß t
denk en	ge dach t
kenn en	ge kann t

Separable prefixes

If a verb has a stressed (separable) prefix, the **ge-** of the past participle goes between the separable prefix and the stem:

Infinitive	Past participle
aussteigen	ausgestiegen
losgehen	losgegangen
umkippen	umgekippt
aufpassen	aufgepaßt

Inseparable prefixes

If a verb has a weakly stressed (inseparable) prefix, the **ge-** of the past participle *is not added*:

Infinitive	Past participle
erzählen	erzählt
versichern	versichert
gehören	gehört
empfinden	empfunden
entspringen	entsprungen
beginnen	begonnen
übertreiben	übertrieben

Verbs ending in *-ieren*

Verbs whose infinitives end in the suffix **-ieren** are weak. The prefix **ge-** is not added to their past participles:

Infinitive	Past participle
studieren	studiert
passieren	passiert

15.6 The Present Perfect Tense

The German present perfect tense is made up of the present form of the tense auxiliary **haben** or **sein** plus the past participle of the verb:

Mein Bruder **hat** es mir **erzählt**.
My brother told it to me.

Ich **habe** ein bißchen zu flott **gelebt**.
I lived a little too high.

Dem Fahrer **ist** nichts **passiert**.
Nothing happened to the driver.

The auxiliary **haben** is used to form the present perfect tense of all transitive verbs (verbs that take an accusative object) and of most intransitive verbs (verbs that do not take an accusative object):

Er **hat** den Unfall **gesehen**.
He saw the accident.

Er **hat** das Buch **gelesen**.
He read the book.

Er **hat** hier **gewohnt**.
He lived here.

Sein is used to form the present perfect tense of those intransitive verbs that denote a change of position or condition. Some of the most common ones are **gehen**, **kommen**, **laufen**, **fahren**, **steigen**, **gelingen**, **passieren**, and **werden**. The auxiliary **sein** is also used with the past participles of **sein** and **bleiben**, although these verbs do not show a change of position or condition:

Das Paket **ist** mit der Post **gekommen**.
The package came with the mail.

Ich **bin** gleich nach Hause **gegangen**.
I went home right away.

Dem Fahrer **ist** nichts **passiert**.
Nothing happened to the driver.

Jürgen **ist** bei Onkel Richard **gewesen**.
Jürgen was with Uncle Richard.

Er **ist** nicht lange bei ihm **geblieben**.
He didn't stay with him long.

Es **ist** mir endlich **gelungen**.
I finally succeeded.

A few verbs may be used either transitively or intransitively. An example is **fahren**. When it has a direct object, the auxiliary is **haben**; when it does not have an object, it is **sein**:

Günther **hat** den Wagen in die Stadt **gefahren**.
Günther drove the car into the city.

Günther **ist** in die Stadt **gefahren**.
Günther drove (rode) into the city.

15.7 Word Order with the Present Perfect Tense

In the present perfect tense the *auxiliary* is the finite verb and stands in either first position (yes-no questions), second position (independent statements and word questions), or last position (dependent clauses). The *past participle* is at the end of the clause, except in dependent clauses, where it precedes the finite verb:

Er [hat] das Buch [gelesen].

Er [ist] bei ihm [gewesen].

Wie [ist] der Herzanfall eigentlich [gekommen]?

[Hast] du ihn heute [gesehen]?

Sagen Sie, daß er ein bißchen zu flott [gelebt hat]!

Weißt du, ob er hier [gewohnt hat]?

Just as infinitives generally function as associated elements (Grammar §13.3), so do past participles function as associated elements when they occur in a present perfect verb construction.

15.8 Use of the Present Perfect Tense

In outward appearance, the German present perfect tense resembles the English present perfect tense closely; they both have an auxiliary and a past participle. The *meaning* of the present perfect tense is quite different in the two languages, however.

The English present perfect tense indicates that an action or condition, or the result thereof, began in the past but is continuing at the present time:

He *has lived* a little too high. (Implication: Now he has to pay for it.)
He *has started* the car. (Implication: The motor is running now.)
He *has gone* into the store. (Implication: He is still inside.)

The German present perfect tense simply places the action or condition in past time and indicates nothing at all about what might or might not be going on at the present. It is not equivalent to any one English verb tense but overlaps with several. It is normally used in conversation and in speaking or writing of a single past event:

Er hat zehn Jahre hier gewohnt.
He lived here for ten years.

Das habe ich auch gedacht.
That's what I thought (have thought, was thinking), too.

Ich habe ein bißchen zu flott gelebt.
I lived (have lived, was living) a little too high.

Mein Bruder hat es mir erzählt.
My brother told (has told, was telling) it to me.

In order to indicate that an action or condition began in the past and is continuing at the present time, German uses the *present tense* together with an adverbial expression that points back in time (Grammar §§9.7, 12.3):

Er wohnt einen Monat hier.
Er wohnt schon einen Monat hier.
Er wohnt seit einem Monat hier.
Er wohnt schon seit einem Monat hier.
All mean: He has been living here for a month.

WRITING

A. Singular and Plural of Nouns

Copy the sentences and insert the forms that correspond to the English words in parentheses:

1 Wie sind _____ _____ gekommen?   (the attacks)
2 Mit _____ _____ gelingt es mir nicht.   (this tool)
3 Du bist bald wieder auf _____ _____.   (the legs)

4 Kennst du eigentlich _____ _____ ?   (my girl friend)
5 _____ _____ sehen besser aus.   (those beds)
6 Die Gabel muß links _____ _____ liegen.   (from the plate)
7 Kannst du mir _____ _____ erzählen?   (a story)
8 Hast du denn _____ _____ ?   (no spoon)
9 _____ _____ hat vermutlich zu flott gelebt.   (our uncle)
10 Zuerst kommen _____ _____ auf den Tisch.   (these tablecloths)

B. Time Expressions

Copy the sentences and insert the German phrases that correspond to the English in parentheses:

1 Was hast du _____ _____ getan?   (yesterday morning)
2 Ich habe ihn _____ _____ _____ gesehen.   (five days ago)
3 Wir bleiben _____ _____ bei euch.   (until Wednesday)
4 Er fährt _____ _____ ab.   (tomorrow evening)
5 _____ lese ich meine Zeitung.   (mornings)
6 Er soll _____ _____ ankommen.   (this evening)
7 Onkel Richard schläft _____ .   (in the afternoon)

Arrange the adverbs in the correct order:

8 Wir fahren / nach Bonn / am dritten März .
9 Kannst du / morgen nachmittag / zu mir / kommen ?
10 Er ist / zu Hause / heute abend .
11 Du sollst / um zwei Uhr / am Schillerplatz / einsteigen .
12 Vater geht / in die Stadt / jeden Tag um halb neun .

C. The Present Perfect Tense

Arrange the elements to form German sentences. Use the present perfect tense:

1 wie / gehen / es / Ihnen ?
2 ich / leben / zu flott .
3 wollen / er / so etwas ?
4 warum / wissen / du / das / nicht ?
5 ich / haben / ein Sparbuch .
6 was / studieren / dein Bruder ?
7 das meiste / passieren / nachts .

8   wo / liegen / Onkel Richard ?
9   er / sitzen / auf dem Bett .
10 wie / aussehen / eure Tante ?
11 der Schrank / gefallen / uns .
12 aber / wo / finden / Sie / den Schraubenzieher ?
13 gestern / ich / bekommen / ein Paket .
14 wem / helfen / du ?
15 entgegengehen / ihr / dem Studenten ?
16 hoffentlich / klappen / es .
17 wieviel / kosten / dieser Hut ?
18 was / übrigbleiben / mir ?
19 wie / heißen / der Junge ?
20 natürlich / mitkommen / die Kinder .
21 und / ihr / übertreiben / es / gleich .
22 scheinen / die Sonne / gestern mittag ?
23 die Vorlesung / beginnen / gegen vier Uhr .
24 er / lassen / mich / allein .
25 wir / fahren / unseren Wagen / nach Berlin .
26 verstehen / du /,/ was / sagen / ich ?
27 Fragen Sie, wo / er / sein !
28 Antworten Sie, daß / Sie / kennenlernen / ihn !
29 Fragen Sie, ob / er / warten / darauf !
30 Sagen Sie, daß / Onkel Richard / werden / krank !

Read your sentences aloud with correct pronunciation and intonation. Be able to provide English equivalents.

D. Contrastive Tense Exercises

Write the corresponding German sentence:

1 Uncle Richard lived too high.
2 Did Uncle Richard live too high?
3 Hans was buying a newspaper.
4 Was Hans buying a newspaper?
5 I have seen Professor Müller.
6 Have you seen Professor Müller?
7 I have known him for five years.
8 I have known you for a long time.
9 She has been living here since November.
10 She has been living a little too high.

READING PRACTICE

Mein Onkel Richard

Mein Onkel Richard ist schon 43 Jahre alt. Ich bin erst acht. Er ist der große Bruder meiner Mutti. Und groß ist er wirklich. Mein Vati ist auch groß, aber doch nicht so groß wie mein Onkel Richard. Onkel Richard ist genau so nett wie meine Mutti. Aber er ist ein Mann, und das ist natürlich viel besser.

Sonntags kommt Onkel Richard fast immer zu uns. Er ist dann auch bei uns, und ich darf neben ihm sitzen. Das ist eine gute Sache. Wenn ich nicht mehr essen mag, sagt er immer: „Du brauchst nicht mehr essen, als du magst, mein Junge." Mutti sagt immer: „Du mußt mehr essen, Peter, dann wirst du schön groß." Aber wenn Onkel Richard da ist, sagt sie das nicht. Gestern ist Sonntag gewesen, aber Onkel Richard ist nicht gekommen. Vati sagt, daß Onkel Richard ins Krankenhaus gegangen ist. Hoffentlich kann Onkel Richard uns bald wieder besuchen. Ohne ihn ist der Sonntag richtig langweilig. Und ich muß dann auch immer so viel essen.

Unit 16

Friedrich der Grosse

DIALOG

Ein Krankenbesuch (Schluß)

1 **Christine:** Bist du bei Onkel Richard gewesen, Jürgen?

2 **Jürgen:** Ja, aber er sieht noch recht leidend aus, finde ich.

3 **Christine:** Wieso? Erzähl mal, wie es gewesen ist!

4 **Jürgen:** Also: Ich komme lachend ins Zimmer und treffe ihn lesend an.

5 **Christine:** Aber das ist doch mehr ein Zeichen dafür, daß er nicht sehr krank ist.

6 **Jürgen:** Das habe ich zuerst auch gedacht. Aber er hat gar nicht gelesen.

7 **Christine:** Wie kannst du das wissen?

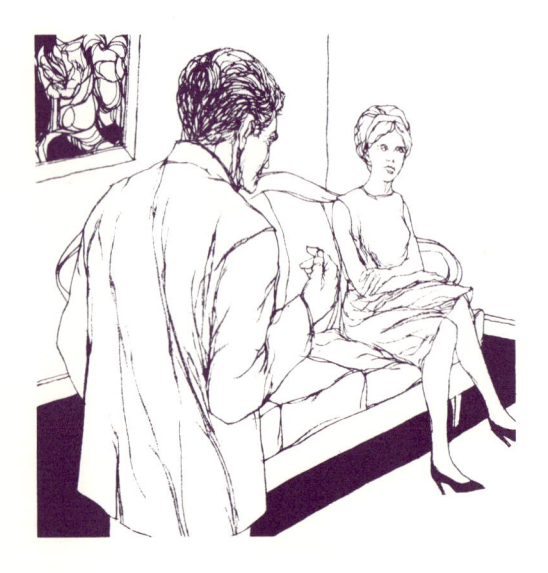

Visiting a Patient (Conclusion)

1. Were you with Uncle Richard, Jürgen?

2. Yes, but he still looks rather bad, I think.

    recht rather, very; right; just · **leiden: er hat gelitten (leidend** *pres. p.***)** suffer

3. What do you mean? Tell me how it was.

4. Well, I come into the room laughing and find him reading.

    lachen (lachend *pres. p.***)** · **antreffen** find, come across **treffen: du triffst, er trifft; er hat getroffen** meet; hit · **lesen (lesend** *pres. p.***)**

5. But that is really more of a sign that he isn't very sick.

    das Zeichen, *pl.* **die Zeichen** · **dafür = da + für** for it, for that

6. That's what I thought at first, too. But he wasn't reading at all.

7. How can you know that?

8 **Jürgen:**   Er hat die Zeitschrift falsch herum gehalten und ziemlich blaß ausgesehen.

9 **Christine:** Du meinst, er hat nur so getan, um dich zu beruhigen?

10 **Jürgen:**   Ganz gewiß. Jedenfalls bin ich sehr bald wieder weggegangen, damit der Besuch nicht zu anstrengend für ihn wird.

SUPPLEMENT

1 Er tut es nur, um Jürgen zu beruhigen.

2 Er hält die Zeitschrift, ohne zu lesen.

3 Er hat gearbeitet, statt Ruhe zu halten.

4 Das ist ein Zeichen dafür, daß er nicht krank ist.

5 Er wartet darauf, daß du ihm hilfst.

6 Sie hat nichts dagegen, daß wir weggehen.

7 Es kommt davon, daß er zu flott gelebt hat.

8 Er denkt nicht daran, so etwas zu sagen.

9 Er hat nicht daran gedacht, so etwas zu sagen.

8   He was holding the magazine upside down, and he looked quite pale.   **die Zeitschrift   die Zeit,** *pl.* **die Zeiten** time + **die Schrift,** *pl.* **die Schriften** writing · **falsch herum   falsch** false, wrong **herum** about, around

9   You mean he only did that to reassure you?

10 Sure. At any rate, I left again very soon so that the visit wouldn't become too strenuous for him.   **gewiß** sure(ly), certain(ly) · **weggehen** go away, leave   **weg** away, off + **gehen** · **werden** become *not the future auxiliary here*

---

1   He only does it to reassure Jürgen.

2   He holds the magazine without reading.

3   He worked instead of keeping quiet.   **arbeiten (er hat gearbeitet)** work

4   That is a sign that he's not sick.

5   He is waiting for you to help him.

6   She has nothing against our leaving.

7   It's because he lived too high. (It comes from it, that he lived too high.)   **kommen von (es kommt davon)** be due to, arise from, be caused by

8   He isn't thinking of saying such a thing. (He isn't thinking of it, to say such a thing.)

9   He didn't think of saying such a thing.

AUDIOLINGUAL DRILLS

A. Directed Dialog

Fragen Sie, ob Jürgen bei Onkel Richard gewesen ist!
Ist Jürgen bei Onkel Richard gewesen?

Antworten Sie, daß er bei ihm gewesen ist!
Er ist bei ihm gewesen.

Sagen Sie, daß Onkel Richard noch recht leidend aussieht!
Onkel Richard sieht noch recht leidend aus.

Sagen Sie, daß Jürgen Christine erzählen soll, wie es gewesen ist!
Jürgen soll Christine erzählen, wie es gewesen ist.

Sagen Sie, daß Jürgen lachend ins Zimmer kommt!
Jürgen kommt lachend ins Zimmer.

Sagen Sie, daß er Onkel Richard lesend antrifft!
Er trifft Onkel Richard lesend an.

Sagen Sie, daß das doch ein Zeichen dafür ist, daß er nicht sehr krank ist!
Das ist doch ein Zeichen dafür, daß er nicht sehr krank ist.

Sagen Sie, daß Jürgen das zuerst auch gedacht hat!
Jürgen hat das zuerst auch gedacht.

Sagen Sie, daß Onkel Richard gar nicht gelesen hat!
Onkel Richard hat gar nicht gelesen.

Fragen Sie, wie Jürgen das wissen kann!
Wie kann Jürgen das wissen?

Antworten Sie, daß der Onkel die Zeitschrift falsch herum gehalten hat!
Der Onkel hat die Zeitschrift falsch herum gehalten.

Sagen Sie, daß er ziemlich blaß ausgesehen hat!
Er hat ziemlich blaß ausgesehen.

Sagen Sie, daß er nur so getan hat, um Jürgen zu beruhigen!
Er hat nur so getan, um Jürgen zu beruhigen.

Sagen Sie, daß Jürgen jedenfalls sehr bald wieder weggegangen ist!
Jürgen ist jedenfalls sehr bald wieder weggegangen.

Sagen Sie, daß der Besuch für Onkel Richard anstrengend ist!
Der Besuch ist für Onkel Richard anstrengend.

B. New Verbs (*See Grammar* §16.3)

1 Substitute the new subject:

Wir haben ihn lesend angetroffen.　**Jürgen**
Jürgen hat ihn lesend angetroffen.　**ihr**
Ihr habt ihn lesend angetroffen.　**du**
Du hast ihn lesend angetroffen.

Onkel Richard hat viel gelitten.　**ich**
Ich habe viel gelitten.　**Peter und Lilo**
Peter und Lilo haben viel gelitten.　**der Vater**
Der Vater hat viel gelitten.

Bist du bald wieder weggegangen?　**ihr**
Seid ihr bald wieder weggegangen?　**Onkel Richard**
Ist Onkel Richard bald wieder weggegangen?　**die Leute**
Sind die Leute bald wieder weggegangen?

Er hat allein gearbeitet.　**du**
Du hast allein gearbeitet.　**ich**
Ich habe allein gearbeitet.　**wir**
Wir haben allein gearbeitet.

2 Change from the present tense to the present perfect:

Tante Inge leidet sehr viel.
Tante Inge hat sehr viel gelitten.

Arbeitest du zu Hause?
Hast du zu Hause gearbeitet?

Trifft er sie zu Hause an?
Hat er sie zu Hause angetroffen?

Sie gehen heute weg.
Sie sind heute weggegangen.

C. Idiomatic Use of the Present Tense (*See Grammar* §16.4)

3 Substitute the new time phrase:

Er arbeitet seit einem Monat in Bonn.　**schon einen Monat**
Er arbeitet schon einen Monat in Bonn.　**seit Freitag**
Er arbeitet seit Freitag in Bonn.　**seit zwei Jahren**
Er arbeitet seit zwei Jahren in Bonn.　**schon zwei Jahre**
Er arbeitet schon zwei Jahre in Bonn.　**schon seit April**
Er arbeitet schon seit April in Bonn.　**schon lange**
Er arbeitet schon lange in Bonn.　**seit vier Tagen**

Er arbeitet seit vier Tagen in Bonn.   **vier Tage**
Er arbeitet vier Tage in Bonn.   **seit dem siebten August**
Er arbeitet seit dem siebten August in Bonn.

4   Transform each statement using the present tense, **schon**, and an accusative expression of time to indicate how long the subject has been in the place mentioned.

Example:
Ich bin vor einem Monat nach München gekommen.
Ich bin schon einen Monat in München.

Er ist vor einer Woche nach Hamburg gegangen.
Er ist schon eine Woche in Hamburg.

Wir sind vor acht Tagen nach Köln gekommen.
Wir sind schon acht Tage in Köln.

Sie ist vor sechs Monaten nach Freiburg gefahren.
Sie ist schon sechs Monate in Freiburg.

Ich bin vor drei Jahren nach Berlin gekommen.
Ich bin schon drei Jahre in Berlin.

Du bist vor vier Wochen nach München gekommen.
Du bist schon vier Wochen in München.

D. The Present Participle (*See Grammar* §16.5)

5   Substitute the present participle of the verb whose 3rd singular form is given.

Example:
Ich treffe ihn lesend an.   **er lacht**
Ich treffe ihn lachend an.

Ich treffe ihn lachend an.   **er läuft**
Ich treffe ihn laufend an.   **er arbeitet**
Ich treffe ihn arbeitend an.   **er schläft**
Ich treffe ihn schlafend an.   **er sitzt**

Ich treffe ihn sitzend an.   **er steht**
Ich treffe ihn stehend an.   **er denkt**
Ich treffe ihn denkend an.   **er übt**
Ich treffe ihn übend an.

E. Um zu, ohne zu, (an)statt zu with an Infinitive (*See Grammar* §16.6)

6   Substitute the new infinitive with **zu**:

Er hat es getan, um uns zu beruhigen.   **sehen**
Er hat es getan, um uns zu sehen.   **helfen**

Er hat es getan, um uns zu helfen. **täuschen**
Er hat es getan, um uns zu täuschen. **antreffen**
Er hat es getan, um uns anzutreffen. **kennenlernen**
Er hat es getan, um uns kennenzulernen. **verstehen**
Er hat es getan, um uns zu verstehen.

Du hältst die Zeitschrift, ohne sie zu lesen. **sehen**
Du hältst die Zeitschrift, ohne sie zu sehen. **kaufen**
Du hältst die Zeitschrift, ohne sie zu kaufen. **verstehen**
Du hältst die Zeitschrift, ohne sie zu verstehen.

7 Substitute the new verb or verb phrase with *zu*:

Er hat gearbeitet, statt Ruhe zu halten. **zu Hause bleiben**
Er hat gearbeitet, statt zu Hause zu bleiben. **abfahren**
Er hat gearbeitet, statt abzufahren. **zum Baden gehen**
Er hat gearbeitet, statt zum Baden zu gehen. **hinübergehen**
Er hat gearbeitet, statt hinüberzugehen.

F. Anticipatory *da*-Compounds (*See Grammar* §16.7)

8 Substitute the new verb phrase:

Ich denke nicht daran, so etwas zu sagen. **vorsichtig sein**
Ich denke nicht daran, vorsichtig zu sein. **ihm entgegengehen**
Ich denke nicht daran, ihm entgegenzugehen. **zu flott leben**
Ich denke nicht daran, zu flott zu leben. **den Hut kaufen**
Ich denke nicht daran, den Hut zu kaufen. **ihm glauben**
Ich denke nicht daran, ihm zu glauben.

9 Substitute the new predicate adjective:

Das ist ein Zeichen dafür, daß er nicht krank ist. **alt**
Das ist ein Zeichen dafür, daß er nicht alt ist. **brav**
Das ist ein Zeichen dafür, daß er nicht brav ist. **hungrig**
Das ist ein Zeichen dafür, daß er nicht hungrig ist. **fertig**
Das ist ein Zeichen dafür, daß er nicht fertig ist. **tüchtig**
Das ist ein Zeichen dafür, daß er nicht tüchtig ist.

10 Substitute the new clause as a dependent *daß*-clause:

Er wartet darauf, daß du ihm hilfst. **du gehst weg**
Er wartet darauf, daß du weggehst. **wir passen auf**
Er wartet darauf, daß wir aufpassen. **es wird besser**

Er wartet darauf, daß es besser wird.   **sie kommt nach Hause**
Er wartet darauf, daß sie nach Hause kommt.   **es wird kalt**
Er wartet darauf, daß es kalt wird.   **wir machen es besser**
Er wartet darauf, daß wir es besser machen.

G. Questions and Answers

Was fragt Christine ihren Mann?
Sie fragt, ob er bei Onkel Richard gewesen ist.

Was soll Jürgen mal erzählen?
Er soll mal erzählen, wie es gewesen ist.

Wie ist Jürgen ins Zimmer gegangen?
Er ist lachend ins Zimmer gegangen.

Wie hat er den Onkel angetroffen?
Er hat ihn lesend angetroffen.

Was sagt Christine darauf?
Sie sagt, das ist mehr ein Zeichen dafür, daß er nicht sehr krank ist.

Warum stimmt das aber nicht?
Der Onkel hat gar nicht gelesen.

Wie kann Jürgen das wissen?
Onkel Richard hat die Zeitschrift falsch herum gehalten.

Warum ist Jürgen sehr bald wieder weggegangen?
Er ist sehr bald wieder weggegangen, damit der Besuch nicht zu anstrengend wird.

GRAMMAR

16.1 Word-Formation

Compound noun

die Zeit time + **die Schrift** writing = **die Zeitschrift** magazine

The suffix -*los*

The suffix **-los** is added to many nouns to form adjectives/adverbs denoting the meaning *without*.

The English equivalent is usually *-less*. **Die Rücksicht** *respect, consideration* thus yields **rücksichtslos** *inconsiderate; careless*. As in this instance, a connective **-s-** is sometimes used. Other minor spelling changes can also occur: see **endlos** and **namenlos** below. Words ending in **-los** based on nouns you know follow:

die Arbeit	arbeitslos	out of work, unemployed
das Ende	endlos	endless, interminable
der Gott	gottlos	godless
das Kind	kinderlos	childless
der Kopf	kopflos	headless; confused
die Mühe	mühelos	effortless, easy
der Name	namenlos	nameless
die Ruhe	ruhelos	restless
das Wort	wortlos	wordless, without saying a word

The prefix *un-*

The prefix **un-** is affixed to adjectives/adverbs and past participles used as adjectives to reverse the meaning. Thus **un-** + **möglich** *possible* = **unmöglich** *impossible* and **un-** + **modern** *modern* = **unmodern** *unfashionable, outmoded*. Some words you know whose meanings can be reversed in this manner are:

bestimmt	unbestimmt	indefinite; uncertain, undecided
endlich	unendlich	endless, infinite
frei	unfrei	unfree, not free
freundlich	unfreundlich	unfriendly
genau	ungenau	inaccurate, inexact
gern	ungern	unwillingly; reluctantly
gewiß	ungewiß	uncertain
kindlich	unkindlich	unchildlike, precocious
klar	unklar	vague; not clear; muddy; misty
natürlich	unnatürlich	unnatural
sicher	unsicher	insecure; unsteady; unsafe; uncertain
versichert	unversichert	uninsured
vollkommen	unvollkommen	imperfect
vorsichtig	unvorsichtig	not cautious; inconsiderate; imprudent
wahr	unwahr	untrue
wichtig	unwichtig	unimportant

The prefix **un-** is also affixed to nouns to reverse the meaning:

der Dank	der Undank	ingratitude
der Fall (fall, case, event)	der Unfall	accident
das Glück	das Unglück	misfortune; bad luck; disaster; accident; misery

der Mensch	der Unmensch	monster, brute
die Ruhe	die Unruhe	uneasiness; trouble; anxiety

16.2 Singular and Plural of Nouns

das Zeichen, die Zeichen die Zeitschrift, die Zeitschriften

16.3 Strong Verbs

Infinitive	3rd singular present	Past participle
antreffen	er trifft . . . an	hat angetroffen
leiden	er leidet	hat gelitten
weggehen	er geht . . . weg	ist weggegangen

16.4 Idiomatic Use of the Present Tense

It was pointed out in Grammar §§9.7, 12.3, and 15.8 that German and English have different ways of expressing an action or condition that began in the past and is still going on at the present time. In English this meaning is linked to the present perfect or present perfect progressive tense:

He *has lived* here.   He *has been living* here.

German conveys the same meaning through the use of the present tense, together with an adverb or adverbial phrase that points backward in time. This time phrase may be an accusative expression:

Ich **habe** diesen Hut **schon ein Jahr**.   I have had this hat for a year.

The time phrase may be a **seit**-phrase, with the object specifying a particular point in time or a duration of time:

Ich **kenne** ihn **seit Montag**.   Ich **kenne** ihn **seit vier Jahren**.
I have known him since Monday.   I have known him for four years.

The time phrase need not include a noun, but it may contain an adverb:

Wir **wohnen schon lange** in diesem Haus.   Ich **arbeite schon seit gestern**.
We have lived in this house for a long time.   I have been working since yesterday.

The adverb **schon**, as has already been explained, occurs very frequently in these expressions.

16.5 The Present Participle

The present participle of both weak and strong verbs is formed by adding the suffix **-end** to the stem of the verb:

Infinitive	*Present participle*
lach en	lach end
lauf en	lauf end
leid en	leid end
les en	les end
sei n	sei end

The German present participle functions as an adjective or an adverb:

Er sieht **leidend** aus.
He looks as if he's *suffering*. (He appears *suffering*.)

Ich komme **lachend** ins Zimmer und treffe ihn **lesend** an.
I come into the room *laughing* and find him *reading*.

Der Besuch ist zu **anstrengend** für ihn.
The visit is too *strenuous* for him.

The German present participle is similar in function and in meaning to the English *-ing* form of the verb (*suffering*, *laughing*, *reading* in the examples above). A major difference, however, lies in the fact that the English *-ing* verb may also be used in the formation of the progressive tenses, while the German present participle is not used in the formation of any tense. The English present progressive tense corresponds to the German present tense:

The sun *is shining*.
Die Sonne **scheint**.
Not: Die Sonne ist scheinend.

The milk truck *is skidding*.
Der Milchwagen **rutscht**.
Not: Der Milchwagen ist rutschend.

16.6 *Um zu, ohne zu, (an)statt zu* with an Infinitive

The three prepositions **um**, **ohne**, and **statt** (or its variant **anstatt**) form phrases with **zu** and an infinitive, with the following meanings:

um zu gehen	in order to go
ohne zu gehen	without going
(an)statt zu gehen	instead of going

Er hat es nur getan, **um** Jürgen **zu** beruhigen.
He did it only (in order) to calm Jürgen.

Er hält die Zeitschrift, **ohne** sie **zu** lesen.
He holds the magazine without reading it.

Er hat gearbeitet, **statt** Ruhe **zu** halten.
He worked instead of resting.

16.7 Anticipatory *da*-Compounds

In Grammar §14.5 you learned that **da**-compounds may replace certain prepositional phrases:

Er wartet **auf den Zug**.
Er wartet **darauf**.

Sie glaubt **an das Sprichwort**.
Sie glaubt **daran**.

It often happens, however, that the object of a preposition is not a noun or a pronoun, but rather an expression containing a verb. The following examples show how this works in English.

He is waiting for *the train to arrive*.
She believes in *practicing the violin every day*.
I'm thinking about *going to Denmark next summer*.

In German such expressions are either infinitive phrases with **zu**, or **daß**-clauses. They are anticipated by **da**-compounds:

Er denkt nicht **daran**, so etwas **zu sagen**.
He isn't thinking *of saying* such a thing. (He isn't thinking *of it*, *to say* such a thing.)

Er wartet **darauf**, **daß** du ihm **hilfst**.
He is waiting *for* you *to help* him. (He is waiting *for it*, *that* you *help* him.)

Das ist ein Zeichen **dafür**, **daß** er nicht sehr krank **ist**.
That is a sign *that* he *is*n't very sick. (That is a sign *for it*, *that* he *is*n't very sick.)

If there is no change in subject, then the **da**-compound anticipates an infinitive phrase, as in the first example above. If there is a change in subject, then the **da**-compound anticipates a **daß**-clause, as in the second and third examples.

WRITING

A. The Present Perfect Tense

Arrange the elements to form German sentences; use the present perfect tense:

1 ich / antreffen / Tante Inge / zu Hause / gestern .

2 ob / es / regnen / heute morgen ?
3 Onkel Richard / leiden / nicht sehr viel .
4 auch wenn / die Sonne / scheinen / so schön ?
5 um wieviel Uhr / weggehen / Sie ?
6 füllen / du / die Suppe / in die Schüssel ?
7 ihr / arbeiten / zu viel .
8 so etwas / mögen / ich nie .
9 er / bleiben / zu Hause / und / halten / Ruhe .
10 der Milchwagen / umkippen / an der Kreuzung .

B. Idiomatic Use of the Present Tense

Write the corresponding German sentences:

1 We have been working here since Monday.
2 I have known him for one week.
3 They have been living in this house for a long time.
4 He has been lying in bed for months.
5 I have been sitting here since two o'clock.
6 She has been studying for three years.
7 It has been raining since yesterday.
8 We have been waiting for two hours.

C. The Present Participle

Copy the sentences and insert the German word that corresponds to the English given in parentheses:

1 Diese Arbeit ist viel zu _____ für mich.   (strenuous)
2 Er ist _____ ins Zimmer gekommen.   (laughing)
3 Onkel Richard liegt _____ im Bett.   (sleeping)
4 Ich habe sie _____ angetroffen.   (reading)
5 Dann ist er _____ weggegangen.   (thinking)

D. *Um zu, ohne zu, (an)statt zu* with an Infinitive

Rewrite each pair of sentences as a single sentence containing a main clause and an infinitive phrase introduced by **um**, **ohne**, or **(an)statt**. In some cases a choice between the latter two is possible.

Example:
Onkel Richard tut es. Er will mich beruhigen.
Onkel Richard tut es, um mich zu beruhigen.

Wir sitzen vor unseren Tellern. Wir essen nicht.
Wir sitzen vor unseren Tellern, ohne zu essen.

Er arbeitet. Er soll Ruhe halten.
Er arbeitet, anstatt Ruhe zu halten.

1 Ich habe es getan. Ich will Sie kennenlernen.
2 Er liest das Buch. Er versteht es nicht.
3 Heike geht zum Baden. Sie soll Geige üben.
4 Der Milchwagen rutscht. Er kippt nicht um.
5 Er läuft über die Straße. Er will ihr helfen.
6 Er hat die Zeitung gehalten. Er hat sie nicht gelesen.
7 Der Mann wartet auf den Zug. Er soll nach Hause gehen.
8 Sie geht ins Geschäft. Sie will einen Hut kaufen.
9 Ich gehe zu Mutter hinüber. Ich soll hier bleiben.

E. Anticipatory *da*-Compounds

Combine each pair of sentences into a single sentence. If the two subjects are the same, use an infinitive phrase; if they are different, use a **daß**-clause.

Example:
Ich denke daran. Ich gehe nach Hause.
Ich denke daran, nach Hause zu gehen.

Ich warte darauf. Du hilfst mir.
Ich warte darauf, daß du mir hilfst.

1 Er denkt daran. Er geht bald wieder weg.
2 Das kommt davon. Du hast zu flott gelebt.
3 Wir warten darauf. Man hilft uns.
4 Sie hat daran gedacht. Sie hat den Hut gekauft.
5 Es ist ein Zeichen dafür. Es wird morgen regnen.
6 Es ist davon gekommen. Die Teller haben falsch gelegen.
7 Wir haben daran gedacht. Wir fahren nächste Woche ab.
8 Ich will darauf warten. Du baust mir den Schrank zusammen.

F. Sentence Completion

Complete the following sentences with any suitable sentence segments you know. Watch the word order.

Example:
Hans sagt, daß . . .
You could write: Hans sagt, daß es heute heiß ist.
or: Hans sagt, daß Tante Inge nett ist.
or: Hans sagt, daß Nuß-Eis am besten schmeckt.

1. Hans fragt, ob . . .
2. Uwe fragt Heike, was . . .
3. Fräulein Schneider meint, daß . . .
4. Herr Held antwortet, daß . . .
5. Der Unfall ist schlimm, aber . . .
6. Der Streifenwagen . . .
7. Ilse und Peter sind in der Stadtbahn und . . .
8. Peter denkt an . . .
9. Heinz sagt, daß Christa . . .
10. Christa sagt der Verkäuferin, daß . . .
11. Margrit sagt, daß der Postbote . . .
12. Gerhard will . . .
13. Der Schraubenzieher . . .
14. Susi legt . . .
15. Susi sagt ihrem Vater, daß . . .
16. Das Messer muß rechts . . .
17. Onkel Richard ist krank, und . . .
18. Ich bin weggegangen, damit . . .
19. Christine will wissen, . . .
20. Jürgen erzählt Christine, daß . . .

G. Prepositions

Copy the sentences and supply appropriate prepositions. Sometimes two or more prepositions may be equally suitable for a particular blank:

1. Hans ist _____ seiner Tante in die Stadt gegangen; sie bleiben den ganzen Tag _____ der Stadt.
2. Heike und Uwe sind nicht _____ Hause; sie sind _____ einer Stunde zum Baden gegangen.
3. Fräulein Schneider und Herr Held warten _____ eine Vorlesung; Fräulein Schneider sitzt _____ Herrn Held.
4. Herr Held glaubt nicht _____ das alte Sprichwort; er erzählt dem Mädchen _____ seiner Erfahrung damit.
5. Der Unfall ist _____ der Kreuzung passiert; Rolf und Günther laufen _____ die Kreuzung.
6. Eine alte Frau liegt _____ der Laterne; sie hat eine Wunde _____ der Stirn.
7. Peter will _____ eine Zeitung nicht abfahren; er kauft schnell eine Zeitung _____ 30 Pfennig.
8. Peter spottet _____ die Freundin von Ilse; er denkt _____ Ilses Geschichten über sie.
9. Christa will schon _____ einem Monat einen Hut kaufen; sie schaut _____ eine große Auswahl von Hüten.
10. Heinz gibt Christa kein Geld _____ einen Hut, und Christa kauft keinen Hut; sie tut nichts _____ ihren Mann.

LISTENING PRACTICE

Listen to the recorded conversation, and then answer the questions below.

Heinz und Rolf

1 Wo liegt Hans?
2 Was hat er?
3 Wer hat Rolf davon erzählt?
4 Warum glaubt Heinz nicht an den Herzanfall?
5 Was hofft Heinz?

Unit 17

IMMANUEL KANT

DIALOG

Am Verkaufsstand (Anfang)

1 **Verkäufer:** Sie wünschen, bitte?

2 **Käufer:** Ich möchte einige Ansichtskarten haben.

3 **Verkäufer:** Gern. Sehen Sie hier ruhig alles an. Diese kosten nur 15 Pfennig pro Stück.

4 **Käufer:** Haben Sie keine besseren Schwarzweißbilder, oder gute Farbfotos vielleicht?

At the Sales Booth (Beginning)

der Verkaufsstand der Verkauf, die Verkäufe sale + der Stand, die Stände booth, stand

1 May I help you?

2 I'd like a few picture postcards.

die Ansichtskarte die Ansicht, die Ansichten view + die Karte, die Karten card, ticket, map

3 Fine. Take your time and look through everything here. These cost only fifteen pfennigs apiece.

ruhig peaceful(ly), without hurrying · **ansehen (sehen . . . an)** look at · **pro** per · **das Stück, die Stücke** piece

4 Don't you have any better black-and-white pictures, or perhaps good color photographs?

gut, besser, am besten (besseren) · **das Schwarzweißbild** schwarz black + weiß white + das Bild, die Bilder picture · **das Farbfoto** die Farbe, die Farben color + das Foto, die Fotos

5   **Verkäufer:**   Natürlich. Sie sind wegen der höheren Herstellungskosten aber wesentlich teurer im Preis.

6   **Käufer:**   Das ist selbstverständlich. Wie teuer sind sie denn?

7   **Verkäufer:**   Die kleineren 30, die größeren 50 und 60 Pfennig.

8   **Käufer:**   Ist auch ein Bild des Domes dabei?

9   **Verkäufer:**   Ja, hier. Aufgenommen während des Festzugs anläßlich der 800-Jahr-Feier.

10 **Käufer:**   Die Aufnahme gefällt mir am besten. Ich nehme sie.

(Fortsetzung folgt)

SUPPLEMENT

1   Er kommt wegen der Feier nach Hause.

2   Ich fahre wegen der Feste nach München.

3   Er wird während des Besuches zu Hause sein.

4   Er hat während der Vorlesung geschlafen.

5	Of course. But because of the higher production costs they're considerably higher in price.	**hoch, höher, am höchsten (höheren)** · **die Herstellungskosten** *pl.* **die Herstellung** production + **die Kosten** *pl.* cost(s) **(wegen der höheren Herstellungskosten** *gen.*) · **teuer, teurer, am teuersten (teurer)** · **der Preis, die Preise**
6	That's obvious. How expensive are they, anyway?	**selbstverständlich** **selbst** self + **verständlich** understandable
7	The smaller ones thirty, the larger ones fifty and sixty pfennigs.	**klein, kleiner, am kleinsten (die kleineren)** · **groß, größer, am größten (die größeren)**
8	Is there also a picture of the cathedral among them?	**der Dom, die Dome (des Domes** *gen.*)
9	Yes, here. Taken during the festival procession on the occasion of the 800-year celebration.	**aufnehmen** take a photograph *or* recording; take up, receive · **der Festzug** **das Fest, die Feste** festival, feast + **der Zug, die Züge** procession, train **(während des Festzugs** *gen.*) · **die Feier, die Feiern** celebration, holiday **(anläßlich der 800-Jahr-Feier** *gen.*)
10	I like this photograph best. I'll take it.	**die Aufnahme, die Aufnahmen**

(To be continued)

1	He's coming home because of the celebration.	**wegen der Feier** *gen.*
2	I'm going to Munich because of the festivals.	**wegen der Feste** *gen. pl.*
3	He'll be at home during the visit.	**während des Besuches** *gen.*
4	He was sleeping during the lecture.	**während der Vorlesung** *gen.*

5 Trotz des Osterfestes will er arbeiten.

6 Trotz der Festtage will er wegfahren.

7 Trotz des Weihnachtsfestes muß er arbeiten.

8 Statt des Kuchens haben wir Brot gegessen.

9 Statt der Aufnahmen haben wir eine Zeitschrift gekauft.

10 Die Kirche steht jenseits des Flusses.

11 Das Kaufhaus steht diesseits des Domes.

12 Die Kirchen stehen innerhalb des Dorfes.

13 Die Kirchen stehen außerhalb des Waldes.

14 Die Kirchen stehen unterhalb der Stadt.

15 Die Kirchen stehen oberhalb der Stadt.

5	In spite of the Easter holiday he wants to work.	**das Osterfest** (das) **Ostern** Easter + **das Fest** (**trotz des Osterfestes** *gen*.)
6	In spite of the holidays he wants to leave.	**der Festtag** **das Fest** + **der Tag** (**trotz der Festtage** *gen. pl.*)
7	In spite of the Christmas festivity he has to work.	**das Weihnachtsfest** (die) **Weihnachten** *pl*. Christmas + **das Fest** (**trotz des Weihnachtsfestes** *gen*.)
8	Instead of cake we ate bread.	**statt des Kuchens** *gen*.
9	Instead of the photographs we bought a magazine.	**statt der Aufnahmen** *gen. pl*.
10	The church is beyond the river.	**die Kirche, die Kirchen · der Fluß, die Flüsse** (**jenseits des Flusses** *gen*.)
11	The department store is this side of the cathedral.	**das Kaufhaus** **der Kauf, die Käufe** purchase + **das Haus · diesseits des Domes** *gen*.
12	The churches are inside the village.	**das Dorf, die Dörfer** (**innerhalb des Dorfes** *gen*.)
13	The churches are outside of the forest.	**außerhalb des Waldes** *gen*.
14	The churches are below (at the lower end of) the city.	**unterhalb der Stadt** *gen*.
15	The churches are above (at the upper end of) the city.	**oberhalb der Stadt** *gen*.

AUDIOLINGUAL DRILLS

A. Directed Dialog

Fragen Sie, wie Dialog siebzehn heißt!
Wie heißt Dialog siebzehn?

Sagen Sie, daß er „Am Verkaufsstand" heißt!
Er heißt „Am Verkaufsstand".

Fragen Sie, was der Käufer haben möchte!
Was möchte der Käufer haben?

Antworten Sie, daß er einige Ansichtskarten haben möchte!
Er möchte einige Ansichtskarten haben.

Fragen Sie, wieviel die Karten kosten!
Wieviel kosten die Karten?

Sagen Sie, daß sie nur 15 Pfennig pro Stück kosten!
Sie kosten nur 15 Pfennig pro Stück.

Fragen Sie, ob der Verkäufer keine besseren Schwarzweißbilder oder gute Farbfotos hat!
Hat der Verkäufer keine besseren Schwarzweißbilder oder gute Farbfotos?

Antworten Sie, daß sie wegen der höheren Herstellungskosten aber wesentlich teurer im Preis sind!
Sie sind wegen der höheren Herstellungskosten aber wesentlich teurer im Preis.

Fragen Sie, wie teuer sie denn sind!
Wie teuer sind sie denn?

Sagen Sie, daß die kleineren 30, die größeren 50 und 60 Pfennig kosten!
Die kleineren kosten 30, die größeren 50 und 60 Pfennig.

Fragen Sie, ob auch ein Bild des Domes dabei ist!
Ist auch ein Bild des Domes dabei?

Sagen Sie, daß das Bild des Domes während des Festzugs aufgenommen ist!
Das Bild des Domes ist während des Festzugs aufgenommen.

Sagen Sie, daß es anläßlich der 800-Jahr-Feier aufgenommen ist!
Es ist anläßlich der 800-Jahr-Feier aufgenommen.

Fragen Sie, ob die Aufnahme dem Käufer gefällt!
Gefällt die Aufnahme dem Käufer?

Antworten Sie, daß sie ihm am besten gefällt!
Sie gefällt ihm am besten.

B. Genitive Case Forms (*See Grammar* §§17.3–17.5)

Feminine nouns do not have a genitive singular ending. The **der-** or **ein**-word ends in **-er**.

1 Repeat:

Die Vorlesungen der Professorin sind langweilig.
Hier ist ein Foto einer Kirche.
Wie findest du den Hut dieser Frau?
Wo ist das Haus eurer Tante?

2 Substitute the new feminine noun phrase:

Wie findest du den Hut der Frau? **seine Tante**
Wie findest du den Hut seiner Tante? **deine Kundin**
Wie findest du den Hut deiner Kundin? **unsere Freundin**
Wie findest du den Hut unserer Freundin? **jene Professorin**
Wie findest du den Hut jener Professorin?

Die Erzählungen der Frau sind langweilig. **diese Studentin**
Die Erzählungen dieser Studentin sind langweilig. **deine Tante**
Die Erzählungen deiner Tante sind langweilig. **jene Frau**
Die Erzählungen jener Frau sind langweilig. **die Kundin**
Die Erzählungen der Kundin sind langweilig.

Masculine nouns of Group V have the ending **-n** or **-en** in the genitive singular. The **der-** or **ein-**word ends in **-es**.

3 Repeat:

Es ist die Geschichte eines Helden.
Hier ist das Buch des Jungen.
Da ist der Wagen des Postboten.
Wo ist das Geld dieses Kunden?

4 Substitute the new noun phrase:

Wo ist der Wagen des Postboten? **unser Kunde**
Wo ist der Wagen unseres Kunden? **dieser Student**
Wo ist der Wagen dieses Studenten? **der Junge**
Wo ist der Wagen des Jungen? **jener Mensch**
Wo ist der Wagen jenes Menschen?

Neuter nouns and masculine nouns (not of Group V) whose stem ends in [s], [ʃ], or [st] have the genitive singular ending **-es**.

5 Repeat:

Hier ist ein Foto des Hauses.
Die Form des Tisches ist unmodern.
Er wohnt jenseits des Schillerplatzes.
Während des Herbstes bin ich in München.

6 Substitute the new noun phrase:

Hier ist eine Aufnahme unseres Hauses. **das Kaufhaus**

Hier ist eine Aufnahme des Kaufhauses.   **ihr Weihnachtsfest**
Hier ist eine Aufnahme ihres Weihnachtsfestes.   **der Schillerplatz**
Hier ist eine Aufnahme des Schillerplatzes.

Most neuter nouns and masculines (not of Group V) that contain one syllable, or more than one syllable with the stress falling on the last, have the genitive singular ending **-es**.

7 Repeat:

Die Form des Hutes ist unmodern.   Der Katalog dieses Geschäftes ist alt.
Februar ist der zweite Monat des Jahres.   Der Anfang des Gedichtes ist schön.

8 Substitute the new noun phrase:

Er kommt wegen des Buches.   **der Besuch**   Er kommt wegen des Paketes.   **ein Bild**
Er kommt wegen des Besuches.   **sein Freund**   Er kommt wegen eines Bildes.   **ihr Gedicht**
Er kommt wegen seines Freundes.   **das Paket**   Er kommt wegen ihres Gedichtes.

Most other neuter and masculine nouns—that is, polysyllabic ones that do not end in [s], [ʃ], or [st]—have the ending **-s** in the genitive singular.

9 Repeat:

Das ist der Onkel des Mädchens.   Wo liegt das Haus eures Bruders?
Siehst du den Freund des Fahrers?   Hier ist ein Bild jenes Fräuleins.

10 Substitute the new noun phrase:

Der Wagen des Fräuleins gefällt mir.   **unser Eismann**
Der Wagen unseres Eismanns gefällt mir.   **dein Bruder**
Der Wagen deines Bruders gefällt mir.   **ihr Onkel**
Der Wagen ihres Onkels gefällt mir.   **jenes Mädchen**
Der Wagen jenes Mädchens gefällt mir.   **sein Vater**
Der Wagen seines Vaters gefällt mir.

Most monosyllabic nouns that end in **-es** in the genitive singular drop the **-e-** when they are weakly stressed final components of compound nouns, as long as they do not end in [s], [ʃ], or [st].

11 Repeat:

Hier ist der Hut des Mannes.   Er kommt wegen des Geschäftes.
Hier ist der Hut des Milchmanns.   Er kommt wegen des Versandgeschäfts.

12 Substitute the new noun phrase:

Ich bin wegen des Buches hier.   **das Sparbuch**
Ich bin wegen des Sparbuchs hier.   **dieses Zeug**
Ich bin wegen dieses Zeuges hier.   **dieses Werkzeug**

Ich bin wegen dieses Werkzeugs hier. **der Zug**
Ich bin wegen des Zuges hier. **der Festzug**
Ich bin wegen des Festzugs hier.

The genitive plural form of a noun is identical with its nominative and accusative plural form. The **der-** or **ein-**word ends in **-er**.

13 Repeat:

Die Einzelteile der Schränke liegen dort.   Die Mutter dieser Kinder ist zu Hause.
Die Fenster unserer Zimmer liegen nach Süden.   Bist du wegen meiner Freundinnen gekommen?

14 Substitute the new plural noun phrase:

Siehst du das Bild der Studenten? **meine Freunde**
Siehst du das Bild meiner Freunde? **deine Kunden**
Siehst du das Bild deiner Kunden? **seine Brüder**
Siehst du das Bild seiner Brüder? **die Professoren**
Siehst du das Bild der Professoren? **eure Jungen**
Siehst du das Bild eurer Jungen? **diese Frauen**
Siehst du das Bild dieser Frauen? **die Mädchen**
Siehst du das Bild der Mädchen? **die Postboten**
Siehst du das Bild der Postboten? **ihre Verkäufer**
Siehst du das Bild ihrer Verkäufer? **jene Männer**
Siehst du das Bild jener Männer? **meine Kundinnen**
Siehst du das Bild meiner Kundinnen?

15 Substitute the new element in the genitive case:

Es sind die Bücher meines Bruders. **Freundin**
Es sind die Bücher meiner Freundin. **dein**
Es sind die Bücher deiner Freundin. **Mann**
Es sind die Bücher deines Mannes. **ihr**
Es sind die Bücher ihres Mannes. **Junge**
Es sind die Bücher ihres Jungen.

Ich tue es wegen der Sonne. **Unfall**
Ich tue es wegen des Unfalls. **dieser**
Ich tue es wegen dieses Unfalls. **Herstellungskosten**
Ich tue es wegen dieser Herstellungskosten. **der**
Ich tue es wegen der Herstellungskosten. **Osterfest**
Ich tue es wegen des Osterfestes.

Die Erzählungen des Professors gefallen mir. **dieser**
Die Erzählungen dieses Professors gefallen mir. **Professorin**
Die Erzählungen dieser Professorin gefallen mir. **ein**

Die Erzählungen einer Professorin gefallen mir.   **Student**
Die Erzählungen eines Studenten gefallen mir.   **der**
Die Erzählungen des Studenten gefallen mir.

Die Stadt liegt jenseits der Straße.   **Fluß**
Die Stadt liegt jenseits des Flusses.   **jener**
Die Stadt liegt jenseits jenes Flusses.   **Wälder**
Die Stadt liegt jenseits jener Wälder.   **ihr**
Die Stadt liegt jenseits ihrer Wälder.   **Haus**
Die Stadt liegt jenseits ihres Hauses.

Wie teuer sind die Aufnahmen des Domes?   **dieser**
Wie teuer sind die Aufnahmen dieses Domes?   **Kirche**
Wie teuer sind die Aufnahmen dieser Kirche?   **euer**
Wie teuer sind die Aufnahmen eurer Kirche?   **Festzug**
Wie teuer sind die Aufnahmen eures Festzugs?   **ein**
Wie teuer sind die Aufnahmen eines Festzugs?

C. Prepositions with the Genitive Case (*See Grammar* §17.5)

außerhalb outside of, **innerhalb** inside of, **oberhalb** above, **unterhalb** below, **diesseits** this side of, **jenseits** beyond

16 Substitute the new prepositional object or the new preposition:

Die Kirche steht innerhalb des Waldes.   **diese Stadt**
Die Kirche steht innerhalb dieser Stadt.   **außerhalb**
Die Kirche steht außerhalb dieser Stadt.   **unser Städtchen**
Die Kirche steht außerhalb unseres Städtchens.   **oberhalb**
Die Kirche steht oberhalb unseres Städtchens.   **jene Wälder**
Die Kirche steht oberhalb jener Wälder.   **unterhalb**
Die Kirche steht unterhalb jener Wälder.   **ihr Dorf**
Die Kirche steht unterhalb ihres Dorfes.   **diesseits**
Die Kirche steht diesseits ihres Dorfes.   **der Fluß**
Die Kirche steht diesseits des Flusses.   **jenseits**
Die Kirche steht jenseits des Flusses.

anläßlich on the occasion of, **trotz** in spite of, **während** during, **wegen** because of

17 Substitute the new prepositional object or the new preposition:

Er ist wegen des Osterfestes gekommen.   **ihr Festzug**
Er ist wegen ihres Festzugs gekommen.   **trotz**
Er ist trotz ihres Festzugs gekommen.   **unsere Feier**

Er ist trotz unserer Feier gekommen.   **während**
Er ist während unserer Feier gekommen.   **der Feiertag**
Er ist während des Feiertags gekommen.   **anläßlich**
Er ist anläßlich des Feiertags gekommen.   **die Festzüge**
Er ist anläßlich der Festzüge gekommen.

18 Substitute the new element:

Er kann wegen der Arbeit nicht kommen.   **Vorlesung**
Er kann wegen der Vorlesung nicht kommen.   **dieser**
Er kann wegen dieser Vorlesung nicht kommen.   **während**
Er kann während dieser Vorlesung nicht kommen.   **Besuch**
Er kann während dieses Besuches nicht kommen.   **ihr**
Er kann während ihres Besuches nicht kommen.   **trotz**
Er kann trotz ihres Besuches nicht kommen.   **Fest**
Er kann trotz ihres Festes nicht kommen.   **euer**
Er kann trotz eures Festes nicht kommen.   **wegen**
Er kann wegen eures Festes nicht kommen.   **Brüder**
Er kann wegen eurer Brüder nicht kommen.

statt instead of

19 Substitute the new prepositional object:

Statt des Vaters ist Günther gekommen.   **die Mutter**
Statt der Mutter ist Günther gekommen.   **das Kind**
Statt des Kindes ist Günther gekommen.   **dein Bruder**
Statt deines Bruders ist Günther gekommen.   **sein Mädchen**
Statt seines Mädchens ist Günther gekommen.   **euer Freund**
Statt eures Freundes ist Günther gekommen.   **ihre Kinder**
Statt ihrer Kinder ist Günther gekommen.   **unsere Tante**
Statt unserer Tante ist Günther gekommen.

um . . . willen for the sake of

20 Substitute the new prepositional object.

Example:
Er hat es um des Kindes willen getan.   **Lilo**
Er hat es um Lilos willen getan.   **meine Mutter**
Er hat es um meiner Mutter willen getan.

Der Mann hat es um dieses Kindes willen getan.   **sein Vater**
Der Mann hat es um seines Vaters willen getan.   **eure Tante**
Der Mann hat es um eurer Tante willen getan.   **unsere Brüder**
Der Mann hat es um unserer Brüder willen getan.   **dein Freund**
Der Mann hat es um deines Freundes willen getan.   **ihre Kinder**

Der Mann hat es um ihrer Kinder willen getan.   **Margrit**
Der Mann hat es um Margrits willen getan.   **der Schneider**
Der Mann hat es um des Schneiders willen getan.

D. Genitive Case in Expressions of Indefinite Time
(*See Grammar* §17.5)

21 Expand the sentences by placing the genitive indefinite time expression after the finite verb.

Example:
Er hat einen Herzanfall bekommen.   **Tag**
Er hat eines Tages einen Herzanfall bekommen.

Sie ist zu uns gekommen.   **Abend**
Sie ist eines Abends zu uns gekommen.

Wir sind nach München gefahren.   **Sonntag**
Wir sind eines Sonntags nach München gefahren.

Die Jungen sind zum Baden gegangen.   **Nachmittag**
Die Jungen sind eines Nachmittags zum Baden gegangen.

Sie sind nach Österreich gefahren.   **Winter**
Sie sind eines Winters nach Österreich gefahren.

Onkel Richard ist krank geworden.   **Morgen**
Onkel Richard ist eines Morgens krank geworden.

Seine Freunde haben bei uns gegessen.   **Mittag**
Seine Freunde haben eines Mittags bei uns gegessen.

Hier ist ein Unfall passiert.   **Nacht**
Hier ist eines Nachts ein Unfall passiert.

E. Questions with *wer, wen, wem, wessen*

22 Repeat:

Onkel Richard ist hier gewesen.
Wer ist hier gewesen?

Man hat den Postboten gesehen.
Wen hat man gesehen?

Die Geige hat Margrit gefallen.
Wem hat die Geige gefallen?

Das ist das Geschäft meines Freundes.
Wessen Geschäft ist das?

23 Formulate questions with **wer**, **wen**, **wem**, or **wessen**:

Das ist das Haus meines Onkels.
Wessen Haus ist das?

Man hat dem Studenten ein Paket geschickt.
Wem hat man ein Paket geschickt?

Da steht der Wagen meiner Tante.
Wessen Wagen steht da?

Dieses Buch gehört den Kindern.
Wem gehört dieses Buch?

Der alte Professor Wolf ist hier gewesen.
Wer ist hier gewesen?

Er hat die Karte von einem Freund bekommen.
Von wem hat er die Karte bekommen?

Es sind die Bücher der Studentinnen.
Wessen Bücher sind es?

Die Jungen sind über den Platz gelaufen.
Wer ist über den Platz gelaufen?

Der Hut ist für meine Frau.
Für wen ist der Hut?

Dem Fahrer ist ein Unfall passiert.
Wem ist ein Unfall passiert?

Das ist die Zeitschrift meiner Wirtin.
Wessen Zeitschrift ist das?

F. Questions and Answers

Wo ist der Käufer im siebzehnten Dialog?
Er ist am Verkaufsstand.

Was möchte er haben?
Er möchte einige Ansichtskarten haben.

Wie gefallen ihm die billigsten Karten?
Sie gefallen ihm nicht sehr gut.

Wonach fragt er?
Er fragt nach besseren Schwarzweißbildern oder guten Farbfotos.

Warum sind die Farbfotos wesentlich teurer?
Sie sind wegen der höheren Herstellungskosten wesentlich teurer.

Wie teuer sind die Farbfotos?
Die kleineren kosten 30 Pfennig, die größeren 50 und 60.

Wovon will der Käufer ein Farbfoto haben?
Er will ein Farbfoto vom Dom haben.

Warum hat es hier einen Festzug gegeben?
Die Stadt hat ihre 800-Jahr-Feier gehabt.

GRAMMAR

17.1 Word-Formation*

The suffix -*ung*

Many feminine nouns in **-ung** (*pl.* **-en**) have been derived from verbs by adding the suffix **-ung** to the verb stem (compare English *feel, feeling*). Familiar verb-noun pairs of this type are:

erzählen   relate, tell   die Erzählung, die Erzählungen   story
erfahren   find out; experience   die Erfahrung, die Erfahrungen   experience

Additional nouns related to verbs you know are:

beruhigen   calm   die Beruhigung   calming
empfinden   feel; perceive   die Empfindung   feeling; sensation; perception
entschuldigen   excuse   die Entschuldigung excuse; apology
halten   hold; keep; stop   die Haltung   posture; attitude
meinen   think; mean; say   die Meinung   opinion
sitzen   sit   die Sitzung   sitting; meeting
stellen   place; put   die Stellung   position; job
stimmen   be true; tune   die Stimmung   mood; atmosphere
üben   practice   die Übung   exercise; practice
versichern   insure   die Versicherung   insurance
wohnen   live; dwell   die Wohnung   apartment; dwelling

Some verbs you will recognize because you know the nouns derived from them are:

die Einführung   introduction; importation   einführen   introduce (to a subject); import
die Herstellung production   herstellen produce
die Kreuzung   crossing   kreuzen   cross
die Richtung   direction; way; line (of policy)   richten   direct, turn; set right
die Vorlesung   lecture   vorlesen   lecture

* From now on, compound nouns will not be treated separately in the *Word-Formation* sections, but will be listed together with other nouns in *Singular and Plural of Nouns*.

17.2 Singular and Plural of Nouns

die Ansicht, die Ansichten   die Farbe, die Farben
die Ansichtskarte, die Ansichtskarten   das Farbfoto, die Farbfotos
die Aufnahme, die Aufnahmen   die Feier, die Feiern
das Bild, die Bilder   das Fest, die Feste
der Dom, die Dome   der Festtag, die Festtage
das Dorf, die Dörfer   der Festzug, die Festzüge

der Fluß, die Flüsse
das Foto, die Fotos
die Herstellung, die Herstellungen
die Herstellungskosten (*pl.*)
die Karte, die Karten
der Kauf, die Käufe
der Käufer, die Käufer
das Kaufhaus, die Kaufhäuser
die Kirche, die Kirchen

die Kosten (*pl.*)
das Osterfest, die Osterfeste
der Preis, die Preise
das Schwarzweißbild, die Schwarzweißbilder
das Stück, die Stücke
der Verkauf, die Verkäufe
der Verkäufer, die Verkäufer
die Weihnachten (*pl.*)
das Weihnachtsfest, die Weihnachtsfeste

17.3 Limiting Adjectives and Personal Pronouns in the Nominative, Accusative, Dative, and Genitive Cases

Limiting adjectives

	Masculine	*Feminine*	*Neuter*	*Plural*
Nom.	der	die	das	die
Acc.	den	die	das	die
Dat.	dem	der	dem	den
Gen.	des	der	des	der
Nom.	dieser	diese	dieses	diese
Acc.	diesen	diese	dieses	diese
Dat.	diesem	dieser	diesem	diesen
Gen.	dieses	dieser	dieses	dieser
Nom.	mein	meine	mein	meine
Acc.	meinen	meine	mein	meine
Dat.	meinem	meiner	meinem	meinen
Gen.	meines	meiner	meines	meiner

Personal pronouns

The genitive forms of the personal pronouns are given in parentheses because they are rarely used in modern German.

	Singular					*Plural*			*Standard*
	1	*2*	*3 M*	*3 F*	*3 N*	*1*	*2*	*3*	*2*
Nom.	ich	du	er	sie	es	wir	ihr	sie	Sie
Acc.	mich	dich	ihn	sie	es	uns	euch	sie	Sie
Dat.	mir	dir	ihm	ihr	ihm	uns	euch	ihnen	Ihnen
Gen.	(meiner)	(deiner)	(seiner)	(ihrer)	(seiner)	(unser)	(euer)	(ihrer)	(Ihrer)

17.4 Noun Endings in the Genitive Case

1. Feminine nouns do not have a genitive singular ending:

   Hier ist ein Foto einer **Kirche**.
   Here is a photograph of a church.

   Wie findest du den Hut dieser **Frau**?
   How do you like this woman's hat?

2. Masculine nouns of Group V have the ending **-n** or **-en** in the genitive singular. The genitive singular form of these nouns is thus identical to the accusative and dative singular and the plural. The ending is **-n** if the stem ends in weakly stressed **-e**:

	Singular	Plural
Nom.	Junge	Junge n
Acc., Dat., Gen.	Junge n	

   If the stem does not end in weakly stressed **-e**, then the ending is **-en**:

	Singular	Plural
Nom.	Mensch	Mensch en
Acc., Dat., Gen.	Mensch en	

   An exception to the above is the noun **der Herr**; the ending is **-en** in the plural, but **-n** in the accusative, dative, and genitive singular:

	Singular	Plural
Nom.	Herr	Herr en
Acc., Dat., Gen.	Herr n	

3. Neuter nouns, and masculine nouns that do not belong to Group V, have the ending **-es** or **-s** in the genitive singular. The ending is **-es** if

   a. the stem contains only one syllable, or

   b. the stem contains two or more syllables the last of which is stressed, or

   c. the stem ends in [s], [ʃ], or [st], regardless of the number of syllables:

Nom., Acc., Dat.	Buch	Gedicht	Weihnachtsfest
Gen.	Buch es	Gedicht es	Weihnachtsfest es

   Otherwise the genitive singular ending is **-s**. This includes neuter and masculine nouns of two or more syllables that do not end in [s], [ʃ], or [st], and whose last syllable is weakly stressed. It also includes final components of compound nouns, as long as they do not end in [s], [ʃ], or [st]:

Nom., Acc., Dat.	Vater	Mädchen	Milchmann	Sparbuch
Gen.	Vater s	Mädchen s	Milchmann s	Sparbuch s

4   The ending **-s** is added to proper names in the genitive singular:

Dies ist Fräulein **Schneiders** erste Vorlesung.   Kennst du **Lilos** Mann?
This is Miss Schneider's first lecture.   Do you know Lilo's husband?

Notice, however, that German orthography does not prescribe an apostrophe here.

17.5 Uses of the Genitive Case

1   The genitive may be used to show possession. It *follows* the noun that refers to the thing possessed:

Der Wagen **meines Freundes** ist neu.   Wie findest du den Hut **dieser Frau**?
My friend's car is new.   How do you like this woman's hat?

2   The genitive case may be used to show various other relationships between two nouns. Most of these correspond to the English possessive or to *of* plus an object:

Wo ist die Mutter **dieses Kindes**?   Das Bild **des Domes** kostet 50 Pfennig.
Where is this child's mother?   The picture of the cathedral costs fifty pfennigs.

Die Vorlesung **des Professors** ist langweilig.   Es ist die Geschichte **eines Helden**.
The professor's lecture is boring.   It's the story of a hero.

Die Form **jenes Hutes** ist scheußlich.   Februar ist der zweite Monat **des Jahres**.
The shape of that hat is horrible.   February is the second month of the year.

3   The genitive case is used to express indefinite time, corresponding to such English phrases as *someday, one afternoon,* etc. These genitive time expressions, like other expressions of time, precede adverbs of manner, place, etc.:

Wir werden **eines Tages** nach Österreich fahren.
Someday we'll go to Austria.

Hier ist **eines Nachmittags** ein Unfall passiert.
An accident took place here one afternoon.

Wir haben ihn **eines Sonntags** am Schillerplatz getroffen.
We met him one Sunday at Schiller Square.

The feminine noun **die Nacht** may also occur in genitive time expressions. When it does, it behaves like a masculine noun, taking the genitive ending **-s**:

Hier ist **eines Nachts** ein Unfall passiert.
An accident took place here one night.

These genitive time expressions are closely related to the time adverbs in **-s** introduced in Grammar §15.3; the meanings are quite different, however:

eines Abends *one evening*
abends *evenings, in the evening*

4 Several prepositions govern the genitive case. Some of the more common ones are:

außerhalb outside of, out of, beyond

Die Kirche steht **außerhalb** dieser Stadt.
The church is located *outside of* this city.

innerhalb inside of, inside, within

Die Kirche steht **innerhalb** des Waldes.
The church is located *within* the forest.

oberhalb at the upper end of, above

Die Kirche steht **oberhalb** der Stadt.
The church is located *at the upper end of* the city.

unterhalb at the lower end of, below

Die Kirche steht **unterhalb** des Platzes.
The church is located *at the lower end of* the square.

diesseits this side of

Die Kirche steht **diesseits** des Flusses.
The church is located *this side of* the river.

jenseits the other side of, beyond

Die Kirche steht **jenseits** des Dorfes.
The church is located *the other side of* the village.

(an)statt instead of

Statt eures Onkels ist Günther gekommen.
Günther came *instead of* your uncle.

trotz in spite of

Er ist **trotz** des Unfalls zum Baden gegangen.
He went swimming *in spite of* the accident.

während during

Er ist **während** der Feiertage hier gewesen.
He was here *during* the holidays.

wegen because of, on account of

Er ist **wegen** des Festzugs gekommen.
He came *because of* the festival procession.

anläßlich on the occasion of

Er ist **anläßlich** der Feiertage gekommen.
He came *on the occasion of* the holidays.

um . . . willen for the sake of

Er hat es **um** des Kindes **willen** getan.
He did it *for the sake of* the child.

5   Most of the genitive expressions listed above are more common in written German than in the spoken language. In the informal speech of many Germans, as a matter of fact, the genitive is rare indeed. The genitive prepositions, if they are used at all, may take a dative object rather than a genitive object (**wegen dem Unfall** instead of **wegen des Unfalls**). Although common enough, even among educated Germans, this practice is considered somewhat substandard. Even more common, and more acceptable, is the replacement of the possessive genitive by a **von**-phrase:

Hier ist ein Foto **von meiner Freundin**. (= meiner Freundin)
Here is a photograph of my girl friend.

Das ist der Wagen **von meinem Onkel**. (= meines Onkels)
That is my uncle's car.

Er ist ein Freund **von meinem Bruder**. (= meines Bruders)
He is a friend of my brother's.

WRITING

A. Verbs

Arrange the elements to form German sentences; use the tense indicated:

1   ich / ansehen / diese Bilder .   (*pres. perf.*)
2   möchten / haben / Sie / einige Ansichtskarten ?   (*pres.*)
3   er / aufnehmen / diese Fotos / in Hamburg / eines Tages .   (*pres. perf.*)
4   solche Bilder / sein / zu teuer .   (*fut.*)
5   ein Bild des Domes / sein / auch dabei.   (*pres. perf.*)
6   welche Aufnahme / gefallen / Ihnen / am besten ?   (*pres.*)

7 ich / wollen / beruhigen / Onkel Richard . (*pres.*)
8 er / weggehen / bald wieder /,/ ohne . . . zu / die Zeitschrift / lesen . (*pres. perf.*)

B. The Present Perfect Tense

Rewrite the following narrative in the present perfect tense:

Onkel Richard hat einen Herzanfall. Er liegt den ganzen Tag im Bett. Es bleibt ihm nichts anderes übrig. Er bekommt laufend Medizin, und er schläft ordentlich.

Jürgen kommt lachend in Onkel Richards Zimmer und trifft ihn lesend an. Aber der Onkel liest gar nicht. Er hält die Zeitschrift falsch herum. Er sieht auch ziemlich blaß aus. Der Besuch wird sehr anstrengend für Onkel Richard, und Jürgen geht bald wieder weg.

C. Singular and Plural of Nouns

Copy the sentences and insert the German words that correspond to the English in parentheses:

1 _____ _____ liegen jenseits des Waldes. (the villages)
2 _____ _____ wollen Sie denn? (how many picture postcards)
3 Wessen _____ sind das? (photographs)
4 _____ _____ sind mir zu hoch. (these prices)
5 Das kommt von _____ _____. (the production costs)
6 Haben Sie denn _____ _____? (no black-and-white pictures)
7 Gehen Sie doch mal zu _____ _____! (that sales booth)
8 Die Elbe und der Rhein sind _____. (rivers)
9 _____ _____ sitzen herum und warten. (their salesmen)
10 _____ _____ sind im Dezember. (our holidays)

D. Genitive Case Forms

Copy the sentences and insert the genitive form of the noun phrase in parentheses:

1 Das Bild _____ _____ ist hübsch. (deine Freundin)
2 Wo ist das Buch _____ _____? (euer Vater)
3 Ich bin während _____ _____ zu Hause gewesen. (der Herbst)
4 Die Leute stehen alle außerhalb _____ _____. (das Kaufhaus)
5 Wie heißt die Tante _____ ____ ? (dieser Junge)

6 Das Geld _____ _____ ist fast alle.   (unsere Kinder)
7 Wir wollen während _____ _____ in München sein.   (das Osterfest)
8 Das Hütchen _____ _____ findet er scheußlich.   (seine Frau)
9 Ich habe den Katalog _____ _____ zurückgeschickt.   (das Versandgeschäft)
10 Die Farbe _____ _____ gefällt mir sehr gut.   (dein Hut)

E. Prepositions with the Genitive Case

Copy the sentences; insert the appropriate preposition:

1 Wir wohnen _____ des Dorfes.   (inside of)
2 Wir haben es _____ der Kinder getan.   (on account of)
3 _____ der Festtage werden wir abfahren.   (in spite of)
4 Er hat _____ unseres Besuches geschlafen.   (during)
5 _____ eines Schrankes hat er einen Kasten gebaut.   (instead of)
6 Der Fluß liegt _____ der Wälder.   (the other side of)
7 Der Dom steht _____ unserer Stadt.   (at the upper end of)

F. Time Expressions

Rewrite the sentences by supplying the German time expression that corresponds to the English in parentheses. Place the time expression after the finite verb:

1 Du fährst nach Zürich.   (tomorrow)
2 Sie ist in die Stadt gegangen.   (on Monday)
3 Ich arbeite zu Hause.   (all day)
4 Die Leute sind zu uns gekommen.   (at midnight)
5 Er will nach Köln fahren.   (someday)
6 Ich habe einen Unfall gehabt.   (at eleven o'clock)
7 Ilse muß ihrem Mann helfen.   (tomorrow morning)
8 Susi hat den Tisch gedeckt.   (one forenoon)
9 Wir haben diese Bilder gekauft.   (this morning)
10 Ich lese meine Zeitung.   (evenings)

Continue as above, but place the time expression after the pronoun object or objects:

11 Du kannst mir mit meiner Arbeit helfen.   (on Wednesday)
12 Hast du es gelesen?   (in the summer)
13 Ich werde es dir erklären.   (this afternoon)
14 Er hat uns eine Geschichte erzählt.   (one evening)

15 Ich kaufe dir ein hübsches Hütchen.   (in July)
16 Er hat es mir zusammengebaut.   (one night)

READING PRACTICE

Köln am Rhein

Köln ist eine sehr alte deutsche Stadt. Sie ist über 2 000 (zwei tausend) Jahre alt. Vor 2 000 Jahren hat es Deutschland natürlich noch nicht gegeben. Die Stadt hat bis 400 n. Chr. (nach Christus) zu Rom gehört.

Köln ist aber nicht nur alt, es ist auch groß. Heute wohnen nämlich mehr als 1 000 000 (eine Million) Menschen in und um Köln. Der Rhein, ein großer Fluß, läuft nach Norden hin durch die Stadt. Man kann sagen, daß Köln diesseits und jenseits des Flusses liegt.

Köln hat auch einen Dom. Auch dieser Dom ist recht alt, aber natürlich lange nicht so alt wie die Stadt. Der Kölner Dom ist noch nicht einmal ganz 700 Jahre alt. Er ist groß und schön und liegt in der Stadt gleich neben der Bahn und fast am Rhein. Wegen des Domes kommen jedes Jahr viele Leute nach Köln.

Aber auch die Stadt ist schön. Es gibt in Köln nämlich immer noch viele alte Häuser und hübsche, kleine Straßen. Und wem gefällt so etwas nicht? Wenn Sie einmal nach Köln fahren, werden Sie nicht nur den alten Dom, den ruhig laufenden Rhein und die alten Häuser und Straßen sehen, Sie werden auch große Wohnhäuser und moderne Kaufhäuser und Geschäfte sehen, wo man fast alles kaufen kann. Köln mag wohl eine alte Stadt sein, aber sie sieht doch recht modern aus!

Unit 18

Johann von Goethe

DIALOG

Am Verkaufsstand (Schluß)

1 **Verkäufer:** Darf es sonst noch etwas sein?

2 **Käufer:** Wessen Bild ist denn das auf der Titelseite der Illustrierten da?

3 **Verkäufer:** Oh, Sie kennen das reizende Mädchen nicht, den Stern der Sterne am Filmhimmel?

4 **Käufer:** Nein, keine Ahnung. Aber sie sieht gut aus.

5 **Verkäufer:** Es gibt keine hübschere! Eines Tages wird sie einen Oscar bekommen.

6 **Käufer:** Meinetwegen. Wie teuer ist die Zeitschrift?

At the Sales Booth (Conclusion)

1 Will there be anything else?

sonst else, besides, otherwise

2 Whose picture is that on the cover of the illustrated magazine there?

die Titelseite   der Titel, die Titel title + **die Seite, die Seiten** page, side · **illustrieren** illustrate   **die Illustrierte** *adj. noun* (**der Illustrierten** *gen.*)

3 Oh, you don't know the charming girl, the star of stars in filmland?

reizen charm, excite; irritate · **der Stern, die Sterne** · **der Filmhimmel   der Film, die Filme** + **der Himmel**

4 No, I've no idea. But she looks good.

die Ahnung, die Ahnungen presentiment (**Ich habe**) **keine Ahnung** I've no idea

5 There's none more beautiful. Some day she'll receive an Oscar.

es gibt there is, there are · **hübsch, hübscher, am hübschesten**

6 That's all right with me. How expensive is the magazine?

7	**Verkäufer:**	70 Pfennig. Ich hab' noch mehr Bilder von unserer Schönen, wollen Sie ein paar davon?
8	**Käufer:**	Um Himmels willen, nein; ich bin glücklich verheiratet! Das hier genügt mir.
9	**Verkäufer:**	Dann macht es zusammen 1 Mark 30.
10	**Käufer:**	Das ist billiger, als ich gedacht habe.

SUPPLEMENT

Adjective endings

1 Roter Wein schmeckt gut.

2 Kalte Milch schmeckt gut.

3 Frisches Brot schmeckt gut.

4 Alte Weine schmecken gut.

5 Dein kleiner Junge ist hier gewesen.

6 Seine nette Tante ist hier gewesen.

7 Ein hübsches Mädchen ist hier gewesen.

8 Meine kleinen Kinder sind hier gewesen.

9 Dieser neue Hut genügt mir.

10 Diese neue Zeitschrift genügt mir.

11 Dieses neue Bild genügt mir.

12 Diese neuen Karten genügen mir.

7	Seventy pfennigs. I have still more pictures of our beauty. Do you want a couple of them?	**hab'** = **habe** · **die Schöne** *adj. noun*
8	For heaven's sake, no! I'm happily married. This is enough for me.	**genügen** suffice (*governs the dative*)
9	Then it comes to one mark thirty altogether.	
10	That's cheaper than I thought.	**billig, billiger, am billigsten** · **als** *here a subordinating conjunction*

1 Red wine tastes good.

2 Cold milk tastes good.

3 Fresh bread tastes good.

4 Old wines taste good.

5 Your little boy was here.

6 His nice aunt was here.

7 A pretty girl was here.

8 My little children were here.

9 This new hat is enough for me.

10 This new magazine is enough for me.

11 This new picture is enough for me.

12 These new cards are enough for me.

Appositives

13 Susi trinkt ein Glas warme Milch.

14 Onkel Richard bekommt eine Flasche roten Wein.

15 Mutter nimmt eine Tasse starken Kaffee.

16 Vater ißt eine Scheibe schwarzes Brot.

17 Ich esse eine Portion grünen Salat.

13	Susi is drinking a glass of warm milk.	**trinken: er trinkt, er hat getrunken · das Glas, die Gläser**
14	Uncle Richard is getting a bottle of red wine.	**die Flasche, die Flaschen**
15	Mother is having a cup of strong coffee.	**die Tasse, die Tassen**
16	Father is eating a slice of black bread.	**die Scheibe, die Scheiben**
17	I'm eating a serving of green salad.	**die Portion, die Portionen**

AUDIOLINGUAL DRILLS

A. Directed Dialog

Fragen Sie, ob es sonst noch etwas sein darf!
Darf es sonst noch etwas sein?

Fragen Sie, wessen Bild denn das auf der Titelseite der Illustrierten da ist!
Wessen Bild ist denn das auf der Titelseite der Illustrierten da?

Fragen Sie, ob der Käufer das reizende Mädchen nicht kennt!
Kennt der Käufer das reizende Mädchen nicht?

Sagen Sie, daß es der Stern der Sterne am Filmhimmel ist!
Es ist der Stern der Sterne am Filmhimmel.

Sagen Sie, daß sie eines Tages einen Oscar bekommen wird!
Sie wird eines Tages einen Oscar bekommen.

Fragen Sie, wie teuer die Zeitschrift ist!
Wie teuer ist die Zeitschrift?

Antworten Sie, daß sie 70 Pfennig kostet!
Sie kostet 70 Pfennig.

Fragen Sie, ob der Verkäufer noch mehr Bilder von der Schönen hat!
Hat der Verkäufer noch mehr Bilder von der Schönen?

Antworten Sie, daß er noch mehr Bilder von der Schönen hat!
Er hat noch mehr Bilder von der Schönen.

Fragen Sie, ob der Käufer ein paar davon will!
Will der Käufer ein paar davon?

Sagen Sie, daß er es nicht will!
Er will es nicht.

Fragen Sie, ob er glücklich verheiratet ist!
Ist er glücklich verheiratet?

Antworten Sie, daß er glücklich verheiratet ist!
Er ist glücklich verheiratet.

Fragen Sie, wieviel es dann zusammen macht!
Wieviel macht es dann zusammen?

Sagen Sie, daß es dann zusammen 1 Mark 30 macht!
Es macht dann zusammen 1 Mark 30.

Sagen Sie, daß das billiger ist, als der Käufer gedacht hat!
Das ist billiger, als der Käufer gedacht hat.

B. Descriptive Adjectives: Weak Endings (*See Grammar* §18.3)

The weak adjective endings **-e** and **-en** are attached to a descriptive adjective that follows an inflected limiting adjective.

All genders — nominative singular

A descriptive adjective that modifies a nominative singular noun, and is preceded by a **der**-word, ends in **-e**.

1 Substitute the new noun:

Dieser alte Tisch gehört uns.   **Flasche**
Diese alte Flasche gehört uns.   **Glas**
Dieses alte Glas gehört uns.   **Teller**
Dieser alte Teller gehört uns.   **Tasse**

Diese alte Tasse gehört uns.   **Kasten**
Dieser alte Kasten gehört uns.   **Karte**
Diese alte Karte gehört uns.   **Bild**
Dieses alte Bild gehört uns.

2 Substitute the new noun or adjective:

Die alte Kiste kippt um.   **Wagen**
Der alte Wagen kippt um.   **neu**
Der neue Wagen kippt um.   **Weinglas**
Das neue Weinglas kippt um.   **voll**

Das volle Weinglas kippt um.   **Tasse**
Die volle Tasse kippt um.   **schön**
Die schöne Tasse kippt um.

Feminine and neuter — accusative singular

A descriptive adjective that modifies a feminine or neuter noun in the accusative singular, and is preceded by a **der**-word, ends in **-e**.

3 Substitute the new element:

Ich habe die neue Verkäuferin getroffen. **Kundin**
Ich habe die neue Kundin getroffen. **nett**
Ich habe die nette Kundin getroffen. **jener**
Ich habe jene nette Kundin getroffen. **Mädchen**
Ich habe jenes nette Mädchen getroffen. **jung**
Ich habe jenes junge Mädchen getroffen. **mancher**
Ich habe manches junge Mädchen getroffen.

Feminine — nominative and accusative singular

A descriptive adjective that modifies a feminine noun in the nominative or accusative singular, and is preceded by an **ein**-word, ends in **-e**.

4 Substitute the new nominative element:

Seine alte Wirtin ist angekommen. **ein**
Eine alte Wirtin ist angekommen. **neu**
Eine neue Wirtin ist angekommen. **Professorin**
Eine neue Professorin ist angekommen. **unser**
Unsere neue Professorin ist angekommen. **freundlich**
Unsere freundliche Professorin ist angekommen. **Tante**
Unsere freundliche Tante ist angekommen. **ihr**
Ihre freundliche Tante ist angekommen.

5 Substitute the new accusative element:

Er hat eine alte Geige. **mein**
Er hat meine alte Geige. **gut**
Er hat meine gute Geige. **Decke**
Er hat meine gute Decke. **ihr**

Er hat ihre gute Decke. **neu**
Er hat ihre neue Decke. **Illustrierte**
Er hat ihre neue Illustrierte. **kein**
Er hat keine neue Illustrierte.

In all other instances where a descriptive adjective is preceded by an inflected limiting adjective, the descriptive adjective ends in **-en**.

Masculine — accusative singular

6 Substitute the new element:

Er hat den schönen Hut noch nicht gesehen. **Dom**
Er hat den schönen Dom noch nicht gesehen. **groß**

Er hat den großen Dom noch nicht gesehen.   **unser**
Er hat unseren großen Dom noch nicht gesehen.   **Wagen**
Er hat unseren großen Wagen noch nicht gesehen.   **neu**
Er hat unseren neuen Wagen noch nicht gesehen.   **dein**
Er hat deinen neuen Wagen noch nicht gesehen.   **Tisch**
Er hat deinen neuen Tisch noch nicht gesehen.   **klein**
Er hat deinen kleinen Tisch noch nicht gesehen.   **dieser**
Er hat diesen kleinen Tisch noch nicht gesehen.   **Raum**
Er hat diesen kleinen Raum noch nicht gesehen.   **hübsch**
Er hat diesen hübschen Raum noch nicht gesehen.

All genders — dative singular

7 Substitute the new element:

Wir schicken es dem guten Mann zurück.   **Frau**
Wir schicken es der guten Frau zurück.   **nett**
Wir schicken es der netten Frau zurück.   **dieser**
Wir schicken es dieser netten Frau zurück.   **Mädchen**
Wir schicken es diesem netten Mädchen zurück.   **brav**
Wir schicken es diesem braven Mädchen zurück.   **ihr**
Wir schicken es ihrem braven Mädchen zurück.   **Wirtin**
Wir schicken es ihrer braven Wirtin zurück.   **alt**
Wir schicken es ihrer alten Wirtin zurück.   **unser**
Wir schicken es unserer alten Wirtin zurück.   **Onkel**
Wir schicken es unserem alten Onkel zurück.   **freundlich**
Wir schicken es unserem freundlichen Onkel zurück.

All genders — genitive singular

8 Substitute the new element:

Der Preis der alten Geige ist mir zu hoch.   **Buch**
Der Preis des alten Buches ist mir zu hoch.   **groß**
Der Preis des großen Buches ist mir zu hoch.   **dieser**
Der Preis dieses großen Buches ist mir zu hoch.   **Schüssel**
Der Preis dieser großen Schüssel ist mir zu hoch.   **schön**
Der Preis dieser schönen Schüssel ist mir zu hoch.   **dein**
Der Preis deiner schönen Schüssel ist mir zu hoch.   **Hut**
Der Preis deines schönen Hutes ist mir zu hoch.   **neu**
Der Preis deines neuen Hutes ist mir zu hoch.

All genders — all cases — plural

9 Nominative plural. Substitute the new element:

Die neuen Bücher liegen dort hinten. **Hüte**
Die neuen Hüte liegen dort hinten. **klein**
Die kleinen Hüte liegen dort hinten. **sein**
Seine kleinen Hüte liegen dort hinten. **Bilder**
Seine kleinen Bilder liegen dort hinten. **scheußlich**
Seine scheußlichen Bilder liegen dort hinten. **jener**
Jene scheußlichen Bilder liegen dort hinten. **Aufnahmen**
Jene scheußlichen Aufnahmen liegen dort hinten.

10 Accusative plural. Substitute the new element:

Seht ihr denn die kleinen Kinder nicht? **Kästen**
Seht ihr denn die kleinen Kästen nicht? **alt**
Seht ihr denn die alten Kästen nicht? **dieser**
Seht ihr denn diese alten Kästen nicht? **Frauen**
Seht ihr denn diese alten Frauen nicht? **hübsch**
Seht ihr denn diese hübschen Frauen nicht? **jener**
Seht ihr denn jene hübschen Frauen nicht? **Mädchen**
Seht ihr denn jene hübschen Mädchen nicht?

11 Dative plural. Substitute the new element:

Das Fest hat den alten Leuten sehr gut gefallen. **Männer**
Das Fest hat den alten Männern sehr gut gefallen. **jung**
Das Fest hat den jungen Männern sehr gut gefallen. **jener**
Das Fest hat jenen jungen Männern sehr gut gefallen. **Mädchen**
Das Fest hat jenen jungen Mädchen sehr gut gefallen. **klein**
Das Fest hat jenen kleinen Mädchen sehr gut gefallen. **euer**
Das Fest hat euren kleinen Mädchen sehr gut gefallen. **Brüder**
Das Fest hat euren kleinen Brüdern sehr gut gefallen.

12 Genitive plural. Substitute the new element:

Er ist wegen der schweren Kisten gekommen. **Pakete**
Er ist wegen der schweren Pakete gekommen. **viel**
Er ist wegen der vielen Pakete gekommen. **sein**
Er ist wegen seiner vielen Pakete gekommen. **Bücher**
Er ist wegen seiner vielen Bücher gekommen. **alt**
Er ist wegen seiner alten Bücher gekommen. **dieser**
Er ist wegen dieser alten Bücher gekommen. **Kästen**
Er ist wegen dieser alten Kästen gekommen.

Review of weak adjective endings, all cases

13 Expand each sentence by putting the indicated modifier before the noun.

Examples:
Ich finde ihren Hut scheußlich.   **billig**
Ich finde ihren billigen Hut scheußlich.

Unsere Farbfotos sind noch nicht fertig.   **neu**
Unsere neuen Farbfotos sind noch nicht fertig.

Der Mann ist weggefahren.   **alt**
Der alte Mann ist weggefahren.

Die Kundin ist eben hier gewesen.   **nett**
Die nette Kundin ist eben hier gewesen.

Ich habe einen Wagen gekauft.   **ander**
Ich habe einen anderen Wagen gekauft.

Hast du unseren Verkaufsstand gesehen?   **hübsch**
Hast du unseren hübschen Verkaufsstand gesehen?

Eure Kinder sind wirklich reizend.   **beide**
Eure beiden Kinder sind wirklich reizend.

Sie ist wegen des Buches zu ihm gegangen.   **neu**
Sie ist wegen des neuen Buches zu ihm gegangen.

Die Frau kann nicht mit uns fahren.   **krank**
Die kranke Frau kann nicht mit uns fahren.

Das Fräulein will etwas kaufen.   **jung**
Das junge Fräulein will etwas kaufen.

Haben sie meine Geige schon geschickt?   **schön**
Haben sie meine schöne Geige schon geschickt?

Wir schicken den Schrank einfach zurück.   **scheußlich**
Wir schicken den scheußlichen Schrank einfach zurück.

Er muß wegen seines Herzanfalls viel schlafen.   **schlimm**
Er muß wegen seines schlimmen Herzanfalls viel schlafen.

Sie sind mit einem Freund angekommen.   **gut**
Sie sind mit einem guten Freund angekommen.

Trotz seiner Unfälle fährt er immer noch zu schnell.   **viel**
Trotz seiner vielen Unfälle fährt er immer noch zu schnell.

Du kannst es mit diesem Werkzeug zusammenbauen.   **richtig**
Du kannst es mit diesem richtigen Werkzeug zusammenbauen.

Es ist an einer Kreuzung passiert.   **rutschig**
Es ist an einer rutschigen Kreuzung passiert.

Es ist mit den Kisten angekommen.   **schwer**
Es ist mit den schweren Kisten angekommen.

C. Descriptive Adjectives: Strong Endings (*See Grammar §18.3*)

The strong adjective endings are the same as the **der**-word endings except for the masculine and neuter genitive singular, which is **-en**. They are attached to descriptive adjectives that are not preceded by a **der**-word or by an inflected **ein**-word.

Descriptive adjective following an uninflected *ein*-word

Neuter—nominative singular: -es

14 Substitute the new element:

Hat hier ein kleines Paket gelegen?   **Bild**
Hat hier ein kleines Bild gelegen?   **alt**
Hat hier ein altes Bild gelegen?   **ihr**
Hat hier ihr altes Bild gelegen?   **Buch**
Hat hier ihr altes Buch gelegen?   **neu**

Hat hier ihr neues Buch gelegen?   **mein**
Hat hier mein neues Buch gelegen?   **Messer**
Hat hier mein neues Messer gelegen?   **gut**
Hat hier mein gutes Messer gelegen?   **unser**
Hat hier unser gutes Messer gelegen?

Neuter—accusative singular: -es

15 Substitute the new element:

Hans hat ein schönes Foto verkauft.   **Bild**
Hans hat ein schönes Bild verkauft.   **groß**
Hans hat ein großes Bild verkauft.   **mein**
Hans hat mein großes Bild verkauft.   **Haus**
Hans hat mein großes Haus verkauft.   **neu**

Hans hat mein neues Haus verkauft.   **unser**
Hans hat unser neues Haus verkauft.   **Geschäft**
Hans hat unser neues Geschäft verkauft.   **alt**
Hans hat unser altes Geschäft verkauft.   **sein**
Hans hat sein altes Geschäft verkauft.

Masculine—nominative singular: -er

16 Substitute the new element:

Mein alter Onkel ist plötzlich krank geworden.   **Schneider**
Mein alter Schneider ist plötzlich krank geworden.   **neu**
Mein neuer Schneider ist plötzlich krank geworden.   **unser**

Unser neuer Schneider ist plötzlich krank geworden.   **Fahrer**
Unser neuer Fahrer ist plötzlich krank geworden.   **gut**
Unser guter Fahrer ist plötzlich krank geworden.   **ihr**
Ihr guter Fahrer ist plötzlich krank geworden.   **Freund**
Ihr guter Freund ist plötzlich krank geworden.   **klein**
Ihr kleiner Freund ist plötzlich krank geworden.   **sein**
Sein kleiner Freund ist plötzlich krank geworden.

Review of weak and strong adjective endings with ein-words

17   Substitute the new element:

Dort rechts steht ein neuer Wagen.   **Haus**
Dort rechts steht ein neues Haus.   **schön**
Dort rechts steht ein schönes Haus.   **dein**
Dort rechts steht dein schönes Haus.   **Schrank**
Dort rechts steht dein schöner Schrank.   **groß**
Dort rechts steht dein großer Schrank.   **unser**
Dort rechts steht unser großer Schrank.   **Kiste**
Dort rechts steht unsere große Kiste.   **alt**
Dort rechts steht unsere alte Kiste.   **mein**
Dort rechts steht meine alte Kiste.   **Bett**
Dort rechts steht mein altes Bett.   **klein**
Dort rechts steht mein kleines Bett.   **euer**
Dort rechts steht euer kleines Bett.   **Verkaufsstand**
Dort rechts steht euer kleiner Verkaufsstand.   **hübsch**
Dort rechts steht euer hübscher Verkaufsstand.   **ihr**
Dort rechts steht ihr hübscher Verkaufsstand.   **Freundin**
Dort rechts steht ihre hübsche Freundin.   **flott**
Dort rechts steht ihre flotte Freundin.   **sein**
Dort rechts steht seine flotte Freundin.

Review of weak and strong adjective endings with der- and ein-words

18   Expand each sentence by putting the indicated adjective before the noun:

Mein Onkel ist plötzlich krank geworden.   **alt**
Mein alter Onkel ist plötzlich krank geworden.

Er hat die Zeitschriften gar nicht gelesen.   **neu**
Er hat die neuen Zeitschriften gar nicht gelesen.

Euer Fahrer ist wieder zu schnell gefahren.   **rücksichtslos**
Euer rücksichtsloser Fahrer ist wieder zu schnell gefahren.

Ich habe heute eine Schneiderin kennengelernt.   **tüchtig**
Ich habe heute eine tüchtige Schneiderin kennengelernt.

Wir gehen ungern in sein Geschäft.   **alt**
Wir gehen ungern in sein altes Geschäft.

Er hat euren Festzug nicht mehr gesehen.   **schön**
Er hat euren schönen Festzug nicht mehr gesehen.

Sie hat heute ihre Geige abgeholt.   **teuer**
Sie hat heute ihre teure Geige abgeholt.

Ich habe mir heute morgen einen Hut gekauft.   **hübsch**
Ich habe mir heute morgen einen hübschen Hut gekauft.

Jene Bücher gefallen mir gar nicht.   **billig**
Jene billigen Bücher gefallen mir gar nicht.

Dein Zimmer sieht wirklich nett aus.   **klein**
Dein kleines Zimmer sieht wirklich nett aus.

Habt ihr seine Freundin schon kennengelernt?   **neu**
Habt ihr seine neue Freundin schon kennengelernt?

Wir sind mit einem Zug angekommen.   **spät**
Wir sind mit einem späten Zug angekommen.

Er ist eigentlich kein Schneider.   **gut**
Er ist eigentlich kein guter Schneider.

Wir haben natürlich eine Weile auf dich gewartet.   **klein**
Wir haben natürlich eine kleine Weile auf dich gewartet.

Sie hat eine Stunde dort gesessen.   **ganz**
Sie hat eine ganze Stunde dort gesessen.

Er will eben nicht an die Sprichwörter glauben.   **alt**
Er will eben nicht an die alten Sprichwörter glauben.

Sie haben über jenen Unfall erzählt.   **schlimm**
Sie haben über jenen schlimmen Unfall erzählt.

An adjective without a preceding *der-* or *ein-*word

Nominative singular

19 Substitute the new noun in the nominative case. Drop the article and make the adjective ending agree:

Guter Wein wird immer teurer.   **das Brot**
Gutes Brot wird immer teurer.   **die Milch**
Gute Milch wird immer teurer.   **das Fleisch**
Gutes Fleisch wird immer teurer.   **das Bier**

Gutes Bier wird immer teurer.   **die Marmelade**
Gute Marmelade wird immer teurer.   **der Kaffee**
Guter Kaffee wird immer teurer.   **die Butter**
Gute Butter wird immer teurer.   **der Kuchen**
Guter Kuchen wird immer teurer.   **der Wein**
Guter Wein wird immer teurer.

Accusative singular

20   Repeat:

Die Leute wollen kalten Saft haben.
Die Leute wollen heiße Suppe haben.
Die Leute wollen frisches Bier haben.

21   Substitute the new noun in the accusative singular:

Jeder möchte frischen Fisch haben.   **Kaffee**
Jeder möchte frischen Kaffee haben.   **Butter**
Jeder möchte frische Butter haben.   **Fleisch**
Jeder möchte frisches Fleisch haben.   **Salat**
Jeder möchte frischen Salat haben.   **Marmelade**
Jeder möchte frische Marmelade haben.   **Bier**
Jeder möchte frisches Bier haben.   **Milch**
Jeder möchte frische Milch haben.   **Brot**
Jeder möchte frisches Brot haben.   **Kuchen**
Jeder möchte frischen Kuchen haben.

Dative singular

22   Repeat:

Der Mann hat nach gutem Wein gefragt.
Der Mann hat nach heißer Suppe gefragt.
Der Mann hat nach frischem Brot gefragt.

23   Substitute the new noun in the dative singular:

Der Mann hat nach frischem Kuchen gefragt.   **Milch**
Der Mann hat nach frischer Milch gefragt.   **Fleisch**
Der Mann hat nach frischem Fleisch gefragt.   **Brot**
Der Mann hat nach frischem Brot gefragt.   **Salat**
Der Mann hat nach frischem Salat gefragt.   **Butter**
Der Mann hat nach frischer Butter gefragt.   **Marmelade**
Der Mann hat nach frischer Marmelade gefragt.   **Bier**
Der Mann hat nach frischem Bier gefragt.

All genders — all cases — plural

24 Repeat:

Gute Ansichtskarten sind hier billig.
Hier kann man schöne Bilder kaufen.
Da kommt er mit neuen Zeitschriften.
Trotz guter Kunden geht sein Geschäft schlecht.

25 Substitute the indicated adjective for the plural limiting word:

Die Ansichtskarten sind billig. **schön**
Schöne Ansichtskarten sind billig.

Trotz seiner Kunden geht sein Geschäft schlecht. **viel**
Trotz vieler Kunden geht sein Geschäft schlecht.

Da kommt er mit seinen Ansichtskarten. **neu**
Da kommt er mit neuen Ansichtskarten.

Hier kann man solche Ansichtskarten kaufen. **hübsch**
Hier kann man hübsche Ansichtskarten kaufen.

Die Unfälle passieren hier, wenn es regnet. **schlimm**
Schlimme Unfälle passieren hier, wenn es regnet.

Du kannst doch deine Freunde mitnehmen. **gut**
Du kannst doch gute Freunde mitnehmen.

Trotz dieser Straßen fährt er sehr schnell. **schlecht**
Trotz schlechter Straßen fährt er sehr schnell.

Unsere Antworten gefallen ihm natürlich nicht. **falsch**
Falsche Antworten gefallen ihm natürlich nicht.

Mit solchen Wagen muß man gut aufpassen. **schnell**
Mit schnellen Wagen muß man gut aufpassen.

Er glaubt nicht an diese Sprichwörter. **alt**
Er glaubt nicht an alte Sprichwörter.

Two or more descriptive adjectives

26 If there are two or more descriptive adjectives, all have the same ending. Expand the following sentences by putting the indicated additional adjective just before the noun.

Example:
Mein Bruder hat einen schönen Wagen. **rot**
Mein Bruder hat einen schönen, roten Wagen.

Ihr kleiner Hut ist schon ein Jahr alt. **grün**
Ihr kleiner, grüner Hut ist schon ein Jahr alt.

Guter Wein ist sehr teuer. **alt**
Guter, alter Wein ist sehr teuer.

Dies ist eine ganz schlechte Straße. **rutschig**
Dies ist eine ganz schlechte, rutschige Straße.

Der Hut hat eine scheußliche Form. **unmodern**
Der Hut hat eine scheußliche, unmoderne Form.

Ich bin bei einem guten Freund gewesen. **alt**
Ich bin bei einem guten, alten Freund gewesen.

Hans hat es den netten Leuten geschickt. **jung**
Hans hat es den netten, jungen Leuten geschickt.

D. Adjectival Nouns (*See Grammar* §18.4)

27 Reduce the following sentences by dropping the noun.

Example:
Wer ist das auf der illustrierten Zeitschrift da?
Wer ist das auf der Illustrierten da?

Hast du etwas von dieser schönen Frau gelesen?
Hast du etwas von dieser Schönen gelesen?

Heute ist der dreizehnte Februar.
Heute ist der Dreizehnte.

Ein kranker Mensch muß viel schlafen.
Ein Kranker muß viel schlafen.

Ihr kleines Kind sieht noch ziemlich blaß aus.
Ihr Kleines sieht noch ziemlich blaß aus.

Das ist genau der richtige Schraubenzieher.
Das ist genau der Richtige.

Ich sehe dort einen bekannten Studenten.
Ich sehe dort einen Bekannten.

E. Comparison of Adjectives and Adverbs (*See Grammar* §§18.5, 18.6)

Comparative degree

28 Repeat:

Deine Tante ist alt.
Dein Onkel ist noch älter.

Sein Bruder hat lange gearbeitet.
Sein Vater hat noch länger gearbeitet.

29 Substitute the new element, insert the word **noch** before the adjective or adverb, and change the latter to the comparative degree with an umlaut:

Günthers Zimmer ist groß. **Rolf**
Rolfs Zimmer ist noch größer.

Ilses Hut ist alt. **Lilo**
Lilos Hut ist noch älter.

Seine Tante ist krank. **Onkel**
Sein Onkel ist noch kränker.

Peter sieht jung aus. **Heinz**
Heinz sieht noch jünger aus.

Jürgen ist stark. **Gerhard**
Gerhard ist noch stärker.

Es wird nachts im Süden kalt. **Norden**
Es wird nachts im Norden noch kälter.

Die Frauen haben lange gewartet. **Männer**
Die Männer haben noch länger gewartet.

Es kann im Osten warm werden. **Westen**
Es kann im Westen noch wärmer werden.

Im Südosten wird der Himmel schwarz.
 Nordwesten
Im Nordwesten wird der Himmel noch schwärzer.

30 Substitute the new element, add **noch** before the adjective or adverb, and change the latter to the comparative degree without umlaut:

Mein Wagen fährt schnell. **dein**
Dein Wagen fährt noch schneller.

Diese Kuchen sind frisch. **jener**
Jene Kuchen sind noch frischer.

Margrits Hut ist scheußlich. **Inge**
Inges Hut ist noch scheußlicher.

Hans hat klar geantwortet. **Inge**
Inge hat noch klarer geantwortet.

Es ist heute heiß gewesen. **gestern**
Es ist gestern noch heißer gewesen.

Unser Wagen ist teuer gewesen. **euer**
Euer Wagen ist noch teurer gewesen.

Der Raum dort ist voll. **hier**
Der Raum hier ist noch voller.

Die Kirche dort rechts ist klein. **links**
Die Kirche dort links ist noch kleiner.

Susi sieht blaß aus. **Hans**
Hans sieht noch blasser aus.

31 Substitute the new adjective:

Richard ist älter als Heinz. **nett**
Richard ist netter als Heinz. **jung**
Richard ist jünger als Heinz. **freundlich**
Richard ist freundlicher als Heinz. **groß**
Richard ist größer als Heinz. **blaß**

Richard ist blasser als Heinz. **krank**
Richard ist kränker als Heinz. **schnell**
Richard ist schneller als Heinz. **stark**
Richard ist stärker als Heinz. **alt**
Richard ist älter als Heinz.

Superlative degree

32 Repeat:

Rolf läuft schnell.
Günther läuft noch schneller.
Hans läuft am schnellsten.

Heike ist hübsch.
Lilo ist noch hübscher.
Inge ist am hübschesten.

Christa ist reizend.
Ilse ist noch reizender.
Susi ist am reizendsten.

33 Substitute the new adjective in the superlative degree:

Dieser Junge ist am schnellsten. **brav**
Dieser Junge ist am bravsten. **glücklich**
Dieser Junge ist am glücklichsten. **vorsichtig**
Dieser Junge ist am vorsichtigsten. **klein**

Dieser Junge ist am kleinsten. **schwer**
Dieser Junge ist am schwersten. **tüchtig**
Dieser Junge ist am tüchtigsten.

34 A connecting -**e**- is used before the superlative ending if the adjective ends in [s], [ʃ], or [t], except for present participles used as adjectives like **reizend**. Substitute the new adjective in the superlative degree:

Du bist am flottesten. **nett**
Du bist am nettesten. **blaß**
Du bist am blassesten. **ernst**

Du bist am ernstesten. **schlecht**
Du bist am schlechtesten.

35 Adjectives that have umlaut in the comparative also have it in the superlative. Substitute the new adjective in the superlative degree:

Dieses Mädchen ist am jüngsten. **nett**
Dieses Mädchen ist am nettesten. **krank**
Dieses Mädchen ist am kränksten. **schön**
Dieses Mädchen ist am schönsten. **brav**
Dieses Mädchen ist am bravsten. **alt**

Dieses Mädchen ist am ältesten. **reizend**
Dieses Mädchen ist am reizendsten. **jung**
Dieses Mädchen ist am jüngsten. **hübsch**
Dieses Mädchen ist am hübschesten. **ruhig**
Dieses Mädchen ist am ruhigsten.

Irregular comparisons

36 Repeat:

Das Wohnhaus ist hoch.
Das Kaufhaus ist noch höher.
Die Kirche ist am höchsten.

Der Fluß ist nah.
Der Wald ist noch näher.
Das Dorf ist am nächsten.

Heinz ist groß.
Gerhard ist noch größer.
Richard ist am größten.

Ich arbeite gern.
Ich schlafe noch lieber.
Ich esse am liebsten.

Herr Held studiert viel.
Fräulein Schneider studiert noch mehr.
Herr Wolf studiert am meisten.

Seine Arbeit ist gut.
Ihre Arbeit ist noch besser.
Deine Arbeit ist am besten.

37 Change from the positive to the comparative degree.

Example:
Rolf ist so groß wie Günther.
Rolf ist größer als Günther.

Das Kaufhaus ist so hoch wie die Kirche.
Das Kaufhaus ist höher als die Kirche.

Der Dom ist so nah wie das Kaufhaus.
Der Dom ist näher als das Kaufhaus.

Ilse ist so alt wie Lilo.
Ilse ist älter als Lilo.

Der Junge arbeitet so gern wie sein Vater.
Der Junge arbeitet lieber als sein Vater.

Herr Held studiert so viel wie Fräulein Schneider.
Herr Held studiert mehr als Fräulein Schneider.

Seine Arbeit ist so gut wie Rolfs.
Seine Arbeit ist besser als Rolfs.

Heike ist so reizend wie Margrit.
Heike ist reizender als Margrit.

Unser Kind ist so groß wie Susi.
Unser Kind ist größer als Susi.

38 Change from the comparative to the superlative degree.

Example:
Ich möchte lieber schlafen.
Ich möchte am liebsten schlafen.

Sein anderer Wagen fährt schneller.
Sein anderer Wagen fährt am schnellsten.

Ich glaube, die Kirche ist näher.
Ich glaube, die Kirche ist am nächsten.

Dieses Wohnhaus ist bestimmt höher.
Dieses Wohnhaus ist bestimmt am höchsten.

Hans ist wahrscheinlich älter.
Hans ist wahrscheinlich am ältesten.

Ich finde jenes Kind reizender.
Ich finde jenes Kind am reizendsten.

Gerhard ist doch sicher größer.
Gerhard ist doch sicher am größten.

Dieses Foto ist wirklich hübscher.
Dieses Foto ist wirklich am hübschesten.

Ihre Geige ist tatsächlich besser.
Ihre Geige ist tatsächlich am besten.

Diese Aufnahme vom Dom kostet mehr.
Diese Aufnahme vom Dom kostet am meisten.

Dieser Kunde hat länger gewartet.
Dieser Kunde hat am längsten gewartet.

Die Kinder möchten lieber zum Baden gehen.
Die Kinder möchten am liebsten zum Baden gehen.

Endings of comparative and superlative adjectives

The comparative and superlative forms of descriptive adjectives require the same declensional endings as the positive form.

39 Change from the positive to the comparative:

Der Mann fragt nach frischem Brot.
Der Mann fragt nach frischerem Brot.

Die kleinen Karten kosten 15 Pfennig pro Stück.
Die kleineren Karten kosten 15 Pfennig pro Stück.

Hans will mir ein gutes Foto machen.
Hans will mir ein besseres Foto machen.

Schöne Aufnahmen kann man nicht finden.
Schönere Aufnahmen kann man nicht finden.

Wir sind mit einem jungen Mann in die Stadt gefahren.
Wir sind mit einem jüngeren Mann in die Stadt gefahren.

Gibt es auch noch einen späten Zug?
Gibt es auch noch einen späteren Zug?

40 Change from the positive to the superlative:

Ihr großer Junge ist eben hier gewesen.
Ihr größter Junge ist eben hier gewesen.

Die alte Frau arbeitet noch immer im Kaufhaus.
Die älteste Frau arbeitet noch immer im Kaufhaus.

Mein guter Freund ist nach Amerika gefahren.
Mein bester Freund ist nach Amerika gefahren.

Ist dies seine hübsche Verkäuferin?
Ist dies seine hübscheste Verkäuferin?

Hat der Kunde die billigen Karten nicht gewollt?
Hat der Kunde die billigsten Karten nicht gewollt?

Die Kinder wollen in den nahen Wald gehen.
Die Kinder wollen in den nächsten Wald gehen.

F. Appositives (*See Grammar* §18.7)

The noun of quantity and the noun that follows it are in apposition. A descriptive adjective modifying the second noun takes the strong ending.

41 Repeat:

Mutter nimmt eine Tasse Kaffee.
Mutter nimmt eine Tasse starken Kaffee.

Susi trinkt ein Glas Milch.
Susi trinkt ein Glas warme Milch.

Vater ißt eine Scheibe Brot.
Vater ißt eine Scheibe frisches Brot.

42 Add the adjective between the noun of quantity and the noun in apposition:

Onkel Richard nimmt eine Flasche Wein.   **gut**
Onkel Richard nimmt eine Flasche guten Wein.

Tante Inge möchte eine Portion Salat.   **grün**
Tante Inge möchte eine Portion grünen Salat.

Frau Hartmann nimmt einen Teller Suppe.   **heiß**
Frau Hartmann nimmt einen Teller heiße Suppe.

Jürgen will eine Scheibe Brot.   **schwarz**
Jürgen will eine Scheibe schwarzes Brot.

Lilo ißt ein Stück Kuchen.   **warm**
Lilo ißt ein Stück warmen Kuchen.

Gerhard wünscht ein Glas Bier.   **kalt**
Gerhard wünscht ein Glas kaltes Bier.

Das Kind will eine Flasche Saft haben.   **rot**
Das Kind will eine Flasche roten Saft haben.

G. Questions and Answers

Wo sieht der Käufer das Bild der Schönen?
Er sieht es auf der Titelseite einer Illustrierten.

Wer ist das reizende Mädchen?
Sie ist der Stern der Sterne am Filmhimmel.

Was wird sie eines Tages vielleicht bekommen?
Sie wird eines Tages vielleicht einen Oscar bekommen.

Was kostet die Zeitschrift?
Sie kostet 70 Pfennig.

Von wem hat der Verkäufer noch mehr Bilder?
Er hat noch mehr Bilder von der Schönen.

Will der Käufer noch ein paar davon?
Nein, das eine Bild genügt ihm.

Warum will er nicht noch mehr Bilder von der Schönen?
Er sagt, daß er glücklich verheiratet ist.

Wieviel kosten die Zeitschrift und das Bild des Domes zusammen?
Sie kosten zusammen 1 Mark 30.

GRAMMAR

18.1 Word-Formation

Verbs in *-ieren*

Many weak verbs ending in **-ieren** (like **studieren**, **passieren**, and **illustrieren**) can be recognized because their stems, which are usually of foreign origin, occur in both English and German. Remember that the past participle does not have a **ge-** prefix (**hat studiert**, **ist passiert**, **hat illustriert**), and that main stress is on the first syllable of the ending [ˈiːʀən].

abstrahieren abstract	kommandieren command
sich amüsieren have a good time	komplizieren complicate
analysieren analyze	komponieren compose
debattieren debate	kondensieren condense
definieren define	konferieren confer
deklamieren declaim	konfrontieren confront
deklinieren decline	konstruieren construct
dekorieren decorate	korrigieren correct
delegieren delegate	marschieren march
demolieren demolish	notieren take a note of
denunzieren denounce	numerieren number
desertieren desert	operieren operate
detonieren detonate	polieren polish
dezimieren decimate	präparieren prepare
diagnostizieren diagnose	probieren try
diktieren dictate	reservieren reserve
formulieren formulate	respektieren respect
fotografieren photograph	synchronisieren synchronize
funktionieren function	telefonieren telephone
sich interessieren (für) be interested (in)	telegrafieren telegraph
kombinieren combine	

18.2 Singular and Plural of Nouns

die Ahnung, die Ahnungen	die Seite, die Seiten
der Film, die Filme	der Stern, die Sterne
die Flasche, die Flaschen	die Tasse, die Tassen
das Glas, die Gläser	der Titel, die Titel
die Portion, die Portionen	die Titelseite, die Titelseiten
die Scheibe, die Scheiben	der Wein, die Weine

18.3 Descriptive Adjectives

A predicate adjective does not take a declensional ending:

Der Platz hier ist noch **frei**.
The seat here is still free.

Es wird heute **heiß**.
It's getting hot today.

A descriptive adjective that precedes the noun it modifies takes a declensional ending.

The declensional ending is *weak* if the descriptive adjective is preceded by an inflected limiting adjective (any **der**-word, or an **ein**-word with an ending).

The declensional ending is *strong* if the descriptive adjective is *not* preceded by an inflected limiting adjective (no limiting adjective at all, or an **ein**-word without an ending).

Weak adjective declension

The weak adjective endings are **-e** and **-en**. They are attached to a descriptive adjective if it is preceded by a **der**-word, or by an **ein**-word with an ending. The weak adjective endings occur in the following distribution:

	Masculine	*Feminine*	*Neuter*	*Plural*
Nom.	dieser gut**e** Kuchen	diese gut**e** Milch keine gut**e** Milch	dieses gut**e** Eis	diese gut**en** Bücher keine gut**en** Bücher
Acc.	diesen gut**en** Kuchen keinen gut**en** Kuchen	diese gut**e** Milch keine gut**e** Milch	dieses gut**e** Eis	diese gut**en** Bücher keine gut**en** Bücher
Dat.	diesem gut**en** Kuchen keinem gut**en** Kuchen	dieser gut**en** Milch keiner gut**en** Milch	diesem gut**en** Eis keinem gut**en** Eis	diesen gut**en** Büchern keinen gut**en** Büchern
Gen.	dieses gut**en** Kuchens keines gut**en** Kuchens	dieser gut**en** Milch keiner gut**en** Milch	dieses gut**en** Eises keines gut**en** Eises	dieser gut**en** Bücher keiner gut**en** Bücher

Note that the descriptive adjective endings inside the box are **-e**; those outside are **-en**.

Strong adjective declension

The strong adjective endings are identical to the **der**-word endings, except in the masculine and neuter genitive singular. They are attached to a descriptive adjective if it is preceded by no limiting adjective at all or if it is preceded by an **ein**-word without an ending. They have the following distribution:

	Masculine	*Feminine*	*Neuter*	*Plural*
Nom.	gut**er** Kuchen kein gut**er** Kuchen	gut**e** Milch	gut**es** Eis kein gut**es** Eis	gut**e** Bücher
Acc.	gut**en** Kuchen	gut**e** Milch	gut**es** Eis kein gut**es** Eis	gut**e** Bücher
Dat.	gut**em** Kuchen	gut**er** Milch	gut**em** Eis	gut**en** Büchern
Gen.	gut**en** Kuchens	gut**er** Milch	gut**en** Eises	gut**er** Bücher

Note that the **ein**-word without an ending occurs only in the masculine nominative singular and in the neuter nominative and accusative singular. In all other instances the **ein**-word has an ending, and the following descriptive adjective must take the weak ending.

In the genitive singular masculine and neuter, the strong ending **-es** has been replaced by the weak ending **-en**.

If two or more descriptive adjectives occur in succession, they all have the same ending. A comma usually separates the adjectives:

Hans hat den nett**en**, jung**en** Leuten ein Bild geschickt.
Hans sent the nice young people a picture.

Ihr klein**er**, grün**er** Hut ist schon ein Jahr alt.
Her small green hat is already a year old.

Gut**er**, alt**er** Wein ist dieses Jahr sehr teuer.
Good, old wine is very expensive this year.

18.4 Adjectival Nouns

The noun of a German noun phrase may be omitted (compare English *young and old, the rich and the poor, the uneducated*). An adjective modifying that noun keeps its declensional ending, however:

Das ist der richtige Schraubenzieher.   That's the right screwdriver.
Das ist der richtig**e**.   That's the right one.

Sometimes the adjective is written with a small letter. This is the case when the omitted noun has just been stated in the immediately preceding context:

Willst du diesen Schraubenzieher haben?
Ja, bitte, der ist genau der richtige.

If the omitted noun is not stated in the immediate context, however, the adjective is capitalized. This is often the case with very familiar people, things, and concepts:

Kennst du denn die Schöne?
Tell me, do you know the beautiful woman?

Der Alte ist gerade hier gewesen.
The Old Man was just here.

Was kostet die Illustrierte da?
How much does the illustrated magazine here cost?

18.5 Comparison of Adjectives and Adverbs

The basic form of almost any German adjective can be used as an adverb:

Seine Arbeit ist **gut**. His work is *good*.
Er arbeitet **gut**. He works *well*.

Das Mädchen ist **schön**. The girl is *beautiful*.
Die Sonne scheint **schön**. The sun is shining *beautifully*.

Adjectives and adverbs in German, as in English, have three degrees of comparison: positive, comparative, and superlative. To form the comparative and superlative in English, the suffixes -(e)r and -(e)st are added to the positive stem of some adjectives and adverbs, and *more*, *most* are used with the positive of others: *fast, faster, (the) fastest*; *beautiful, more beautiful, (the) most beautiful*. To form the comparative and superlative in German, **-er** and **-(e)st** are added to the stem of the positive of all but a few irregular adjectives and adverbs.

schnell, schneller, der (die, das) schnellste; am schnellsten	fast, faster, the fastest; fastest
reizend, reizender, der (die, das) reizendste; am reizendsten	charming, more charming, the most charming; most charming

If the positive stem ends in [s], [ʃ], or [t] (spelled **s, ß, z, sch, d, t**), then a connecting **e** [ə] is inserted before the superlative suffix **-st** (except for present participles):

blaß	blasser	der blass**e**ste	am blass**e**sten
hübsch	hübscher	die hübsch**e**ste	am hübsch**e**sten
flott	flotter	der flott**e**ste	am flott**e**sten

If the positive stem ends in weakly stressed **-er**, then the **e** of this syllable is often dropped before the comparative suffix **-er**: **teuer, teurer, der teuerste; am teuersten**.

The stem vowel of the following common monosyllabic adjectives and adverbs is umlauted in the comparative and superlative. Some of these have not yet been used. Note that adverbs have only the **am** form of the superlative.

alt	old	älter	der älteste	am ältesten
arm	poor	ärmer	der ärmste	am ärmsten
hart	hard	härter	der härteste	am härtesten
jung	young	jünger	der jüngste	am jüngsten
kalt	cold	kälter	der kälteste	am kältesten
klug	clever	klüger	der klügste	am klügsten
krank	sick	kränker	der kränkste	am kränksten
kurz	short	kürzer	der kürzeste	am kürzesten
lang	long	länger	der längste	am längsten
oft	often	öfter		
scharf	sharp	schärfer	der schärfste	am schärfsten
schwach	weak	schwächer	der schwächste	am schwächsten
schwarz	black	schwärzer	der schwärzeste	am schwärzesten
stark	strong	stärker	der stärkste	am stärksten
warm	warm	wärmer	der wärmste	am wärmsten

The following adjectives and adverbs are irregular in their comparison:

bald	soon	eher		am ehesten
gern	willingly, gladly	lieber		am liebsten
groß	tall	größer	der größte	am größten
gut	good, well	besser	der beste	am besten
hoch	high, tall	höher	der höchste	am höchsten
nah	near	näher	der nächste	am nächsten
viel	much	mehr	der meiste	am meisten

The strong and weak adjective endings are added to the comparative and superlative forms when they are used attributively:

Es gibt keine hübschere Frau.
There is no more beautiful woman.

Der Onkel fragt nach frischerem Brot.
The uncle is asking about fresher bread.

Die schönsten Farbfotos sind selbstverständlich die teuersten.
The most beautiful color photographs are naturally the most expensive.

An exception is the comparative form **mehr** *more*, which does not take a declensional ending when used as an adjective:

Ich habe mehr Bilder von der Schönen.
I have more pictures of the beautiful woman.

8.6 Uses of the Positive, Comparative, and Superlative Degrees of Adjectives and Adverbs

The positive degree

The connective construction **so ... wie** *as ... as* is used with the positive degree of adjectives and adverbs, to assert or deny equality:

Günther ist so groß wie Richard.
Günther is as tall as Richard.

Hans läuft nicht so schnell wie Peter.
Hans doesn't run as fast as Peter.

The comparative degree

The comparative degree is used to assert or deny inequality with respect to something. The relationship *-er ... than* is expressed in German by means of the comparative plus **als**:

Ilse ist jung, aber Lilo ist jünger.
Ilse is young, but Lilo is younger.

Peter läuft schneller als Hans.
Peter runs faster than Hans.

Lilo ist jünger als Ilse.
Lilo is younger than Ilse.

Es ist billiger, als ich gedacht habe.
It's cheaper than I thought.

The comparative degree may be used to express the idea of "rather ..." without implying a comparison with anything else:

Ein älterer Herr ist hier gewesen.
A rather old (elderly) gentleman was here.

The superlative degree

The superlative degree of an adjective may be used to modify a noun:

Der größte Junge ist nicht immer der stärkste.
The tallest boy is not always the strongest (one).

Mein ältester Bruder heißt Richard.
My oldest brother's name is Richard.

When used in the predicate, the superlative form of an adjective must be preceded by **der**, **die**, or **das**, or by **am**, and take the appropriate declensional ending (either **-e** or **-en**). The superlative degree of an adverb is preceded by **am** and takes the ending **-en**:

Inge ist schön, Lilo ist noch schöner, aber Ilse ist **die schönste**.
Inge is beautiful, Lilo is even more beautiful, but Ilse is the most beautiful.

Hans ist stark, Uwe ist noch stärker, aber Heinz ist **der stärkste**.
Hans is strong, Uwe is even stronger, but Heinz is the strongest.

Morgens ist es warm, vormittags ist es noch wärmer, aber nachmittags ist es **am wärmsten**.
In the morning it's warm, in the forenoon it's even warmer, but in the afternoon it's warmest.

Du läufst schnell, er läuft noch schneller, aber ich laufe **am schnellsten**.
You run fast, he runs even faster, but I run fastest.

Idiomatic uses of *gern*

The adverb **gern** often accompanies a verb to express the idea of *liking* whatever is expressed by the verb:

Er arbeitet gern.
He likes to work. (He works gladly.)

Er schläft am liebsten.
Most of all he likes to sleep.

Er ißt lieber.
He prefers to eat.

Gern used with a form of **haben** and a direct object is expressed in English by the verb *like*:

Ich habe Brot gern.
I like bread.

Ich habe Nuß-Eis am liebsten.
I like walnut ice cream best.

Ich habe Kuchen lieber.
I like cake better.

18.7 Apposition

To express an amount of a substance, English uses two nouns (the first for the amount, the second for the substance) connected by the preposition *of*: *a cup of flour, a pound of sugar, a glass of water*. The same thing is expressed in German by means of two nouns in apposition; both are in the same case, and they are not connected by a preposition:

Sie stellt eine **Schüssel Suppe** auf den Tisch.
She is putting a *bowl of soup* on the table.

Sie trinkt eine **Tasse starken Kaffee**.
She's drinking a *cup of strong coffee*.

Ich nehme ein **Glas Bier**.
I'll have a *glass of beer*.

Susi bekommt ein **Glas frische Milch**.
Susi gets a *glass of fresh milk*.

Similarly, with proper names:

Er wohnt in der **Stadt Kiel**.
He lives in the *city of Kiel*.

Er kommt im **Monat Januar** an.
He is arriving in the *month of January*.

WRITING

A. Verbs

Arrange the elements to form German sentences; use the tense indicated:

1. diese Zeitschrift / genügen / mir . (*pres. perf.*)
2. es / geben / keine schönere . (*pres.*)
3. Susi / wollen / trinken / ein Glas Milch . (*pres.*)
4. meine Frau und ich / sein / verheiratet / glücklich . (*pres.*)
5. ansehen / diese Bilder /,/ Heinz !
6. können / aufnehmen / du / noch mehr Fotos ? (*pres.*)
7. wo / antreffen / ihr / den Verkäufer ? (*pres. perf.*)
8. sie (*sg.*) / aussehen / besser /,/ als / ich / denken / zuerst . (*pres. perf., both clauses*)
9. es / kommen / davon /,/ daß / er / leben / zu flott . (*first clause pres., second clause pres. perf.*)
10. Onkel Richard / kaufen / einige Aufnahmen /,/ ohne . . . zu / sie / ansehen . (*pres.*)
11. wissen / du /,/ wie lange / ich / haben / diesen alten Hut ? (*pres.*)
12. kennenlernen / Sie / die Schöne ? (*pres. perf.*)
13. es / geben / viele bessere Festzüge . (*fut.*)
14. trinken / Mutter / eine Tasse Kaffee ? (*pres. perf.*)
15. hoffentlich / gefallen / ihnen / dieser Bücherschrank . (*pres.*)

B. Nouns

Copy the sentences and insert the appropriate German word or phrase:

1. Diese _____ sehen ganz gut aus. (pages)
2. Hast du ihren neuen _____ gesehen? (film)
3. Sie ist wirklich der _____ _____ _____ . (star of stars)
4. Was kostet jene _____ ? (illustrated magazine)
5. Dort bekommt man immer die besten _____ . (wines)
6. Hol mir bitte zwei _____ aus dem Schrank! (bottles)
7. Unsere neuen _____ sind kaputtgegangen. (cups)
8. Das kleine Kind hat drei _____ gegessen. (servings)
9. Durch die Stadt laufen zwei _____ . (rivers)
10. Das ist ein _____ dafür, daß er kein Interesse an _____ hat. (sign; current events)
11. Die _____ dieser _____ sind mir viel zu hoch. (prices; bowls)
12. Susi hat ein _____ _____ getrunken. (glass of juice)
13. Vater ißt eine _____ _____ . (serving of meat)

14 Geben Sie mir bitte eine _____ _____ _____. (bottle of cold beer)
15 Ich möchte gern eine _____ _____ _____ haben. (cup of strong coffee)

C. Limiting Adjectives

Copy the sentences and supply the correct endings:

1 D____ Postbote kommt mit ein____ Kiste; Margrit weiß nicht, von w____ d____ Kiste kommt.
2 D____ Postbote stellt d____ Paket zwischen d____ Tisch und d____ Fenster, und Margrit wartet auf ihr____ Mann.
3 Gerhard kommt nach ein____ Stunde aus d____ Stadt; er meint, daß ein Schrank aus jen____ Paket kommen muß.
4 D____ Schrank ist nichts außer einig____ Einzelteilen; aus dies____ Einzelteilen will Gerhard ein____ Schrank bauen.
5 Gerhard kann d____ Schraubenzieher nicht in sein____ Werkzeugkasten finden, denn er liegt schon seit ein____ Tag unter d____ Tisch.
6 Margrit geht um ihr____ Tisch herum, findet d____ Werkzeug und gibt es ihr____ Mann.
7 Nun beginnt Gerhard, mit dies____ Brettern und Schrauben zu arbeiten; er will d____ Schrank in ein____ Stunde zusammenbauen.
8 Margrit geht solange zu ihr____ Mutter; sie wohnt in ein____ Wohnhaus hinter d____ Haus von Gerhard und Margrit.
9 Margrits Vater ist noch bei sein____ Arbeit, aber er fährt nach ein____ Stunde in sein____ Volkswagen um d____ Hausecke herum.
10 Er parkt sein____ Wagen hinter d____ Haus und kommt dann ins Haus zu sein____ Frau und Margrit.

D. Descriptive Adjectives

Copy the sentences and insert the adjectives with the correct endings:

1 Wir haben keine _____ Bilder. (besser)
2 _____ Wein schmeckt am besten. (rot)
3 Dieser _____ Junge heißt Fritz. (klein)
4 Bitte, geben Sie mir ein Stück _____ Kuchen! (frisch)
5 Wir sprechen gerade von _____ Bier. (deutsch)
6 Heute ist es ziemlich _____. (heiß)
7 Trotz der _____ Marmelade darf ich nichts essen. (gut)
8 Dort hinten steht ein _____ Wohnhaus. (modern)
9 Ist heute nicht der _____? (zehnt-)
10 Wir denken an _____, _____ Tage. (schön; ruhig)

11 Der Preis _____ Hüte kann recht hoch sein.   (neu)
12 Die Kinder haben der _____ Frau geholfen.   (alt)
13 Seine Besuche sind _____ geworden.   (langweilig)
14 Trotz _____ Mühe ist es ihm nicht gelungen.   (groß)
15 Es ist dem _____ nichts übriggeblieben.   (krank)
16 Die Farbe _____ Kaffees ist schwarz.   (stark)
17 Ich habe ein _____ Mädchen kennengelernt.   (reizend)
18 Hast du das Bild ihres _____ Kindes gesehen?   (klein)
19 Im Januar soll es _____ werden.   (kalt)
20 Nein, das ist doch nicht der _____.   (richtig)
21 Wir haben nichts außer _____ Zeitungen gefunden.   (alt)
22 Wo ist denn unser _____ Wein?   (teuer)
23 Eines _____ Tages wird sie einen Oscar bekommen.   (schön)
24 _____ Leute haben ein Sparbuch.   (viel)

E. Comparison of Adjectives and Adverbs

Copy the sentences and supply the appropriate German words or phrases:

1 Uwe ist _____ _____ Susi.   (smaller than)
2 Du mußt aber _____ sein.   (more careful)
3 Susi ist _____ _____ Inge.   (older than)
4 Inge ist _____ _____.   (the younger one)
5 Du bist das _____ Mädchen im ganzen Dorf.   (most charming)
6 Morgen wird es noch _____.   (warmer)
7 Der _____ Junge ist nicht immer der _____.   (tallest; happiest)
8 Abends ist es _____ _____.   (coldest)
9 Heute sind die Preise viel _____ _____ gestern.   (higher than)
10 Wir sind in die _____ Stadt gefahren.   (next)
11 Ich bin nicht _____ _____ _____ du.   (as small as)
12 Frischer Kuchen schmeckt _____ _____.   (best)
13 Richard läuft immer _____.   (faster)
14 Dieser Hut sieht _____ aus _____ der andere dort.   (more horrible than)
15 Jene Wälder liegen _____ _____.   (highest)
16 Diese Arbeit ist _____, _____ ich gedacht habe.   (more strenuous than)
17 Von allen Mädchen ist Lilo das _____.   (prettiest)
18 Nachts passiert das _____.   (most)
19 Er wohnt _____, _____ du denkst.   (closer than)
20 Unsere _____ Teller sind alle kaputtgegangen.   (best)
21 Der Mann will noch _____ Geld haben.   (more)
22 Die Ansichtskarten sind _____ schön _____ die Aufnahmen.   (less than)

LISTENING PRACTICE

Listen to the recorded passage, and then answer the questions below.

Der Festzug kommt

1. Wie heißt der Platz?
2. Wer steht auf dem Platz?
3. Wieviel Uhr ist es?
4. Warum sind die vielen Leute da?
5. Was kommt um die Ecke?

Unit 19

RECOMBINATION READING

Ein Student hat es gut

Ein Student hat es gut, sagt man. Aber was sagt man nicht alles?

Unser Student heißt Michael Winkler. Er ist zweiundzwanzig Jahre alt und studiert Philosophie auf der Universität^g* in Hamburg.

In Hamburg wohnen fast zwei Millionen Menschen. Hamburg ist also eine recht große Stadt. Aber es gibt wenig Platz, und Zimmer für Studenten sind knapp und teuer. Michael Winkler hat lange kein Zimmer gefunden. Schließlich hat er doch Glück gehabt. Aber sein Zimmer kostet 180,— Mark im Monat, ist ziemlich klein und ganz unmodern. Bett, Schrank, Tisch, das ist schon fast alles. Ist das nun Glück? Es ist tatsächlich Glück, denn bessere und größere Zimmer sind natürlich noch teurer. Und Michael hat nicht viel Geld. Aber er hat jetzt ein Zimmer und kann endlich studieren.

Frau Schmidt ist sehr nett. Frau Schmidt ist Michael Winklers Wirtin. Eine gute Wirtin ist fast wie eine Mutter für einen Studenten—oder wie eine Tante. Frau Schmidt ist so eine gute Wirtin. Sie macht jeden Tag Michaels Zimmer und sein Bett. Sie deckt ihm auch jeden Morgen den Tisch und kauft sogar mal für ihn ein, wenn er schnell in die Vorlesungen gehen muß.

* The superscript ^{g} means "guess!" It suggests that you can and should guess the meaning of the word from its appearance and from clues in the context. If the word could cause pronunciation problems, it is transcribed phonetically among the glosses. If the word is a noun, it is listed among the glosses so that its gender and plural form can be given.

UNIT 19 · RECOMBINATION READING

Michael [ˈmɪçaɛl]
die Universität [univɛrziˈtɛːt], **die Universitäten**

denn for *coord. conj.*

einkaufen (sie kauft ... ein)
go shopping

1. Was sagt man?
2. Wie heißt unser Student?
3. Wie alt ist er?
4. Was studiert er?
5. Wo studiert er?
6. Ist Hamburg eine kleine Stadt?
7. Wie viele Leute wohnen in Hamburg?
8. Gibt es viel Platz in Hamburg?
9. Sind Zimmer für Studenten billig?
10. Was hat Michael lange nicht gefunden?
11. Wieviel kostet sein Zimmer?
12. Ist sein Zimmer groß und modern?
13. Was steht in seinem Zimmer?
14. Sind bessere Zimmer noch teurer?
15. Hat Michael viel Geld?
16. Was kann er endlich tun?
17. Wie heißt Michaels Wirtin?
18. Ist sie eine gute Wirtin?
19. Wie oft macht sie sein Zimmer und sein Bett?
20. Wann kauft sie für ihn ein?

Aber jeden Monat 180,— Mark auf den Tisch des Hauses zu legen, ist nicht so leicht für einen Studenten. Das ist viel Geld. Man muß ja daran denken, daß Michael seiner Wirtin auch häufig genug hilft.

Michael hat drei Brüder. Sie gehen alle noch zur Schule.^g Dieter ist noch ein kleiner Junge, er geht erst in die Volksschule. Andreas und Christoph aber gehen schon auf die Oberschule oder aufs Gymnasium, wie man auch sagt. Sie wollen studieren, aber Vater Winkler hat nicht viel Geld. Er ist Postbote in München. Da muß Mutter Winkler als Verkäuferin in einem großen Kaufhaus mithelfen. Es ist ja nicht schwer, heute in Deutschland eine Stelle zu finden, wenn man etwas kann. Es gibt viele freie Stellen. Es geht den Winklers also nicht schlecht. Im Gegenteil, sie haben sogar ein kleines Haus und auch ein Sparbuch — wenn auch nicht allzu viel darauf ist.

Aber heute ist alles sehr teuer in Deutschland, und es wird noch laufend teurer. Michael kann jedenfalls nicht viel Geld von Vater und Mutter bekommen. Natürlich hat er ein Stipendium,^g wie sehr viele Studenten in Deutschland. Aber das ist nicht genug. Wenn er Geld braucht — und natürlich braucht er eigentlich immer Geld — muß er Halbtagsarbeit oder sogar Nachtarbeit^g finden. Das tun viele Stundenten, und in einer großen Stadt ist es auch leicht, solche Arbeit zu finden. Doch das ist Gift für das Studium.^g Wenn man studieren will, braucht man Geld. Aber wenn man arbeitet, kann man nicht studieren — oder doch lange nicht so gut studieren. Da liegt das Problem^g für Michael Winkler — und nicht nur für ihn!

Natürlich hat Michael Winkler viele Freunde. Die Freunde kommen mal hier, mal dort zusammen, dann und wann auch auf Michaels Zimmer. Man erzählt dann, lacht und liest, oder man geht mal zum Baden, in einen Film, ins Theater^g oder in ein Konzert.^g Und natürlich trinkt man auch mal ein Bier — oder zwei. Das ist alles kein Problem.

Aber Michael hat auch eine Freundin. Und mit Monika hat er es nicht immer so leicht. Sie ist eigentlich sehr nett, aber ihr Vater hat viel Geld. Das macht natürlich nichts. Aber Monika denkt zu wenig daran, daß das Geld bei Michael knapp ist. Sie sind schon seit August gute Freunde, aber nichts genügt ihr. Was ihr gefällt, möchte sie haben. Sie hat nur drei Interessen, so sieht es aus: kaufen, kaufen, kaufen. Und sie nimmt nur gute, teure Sachen. Natürlich muß ihr Vater das Geld geben, aber für Michael bleiben doch noch viele „kleine" Sachen. Michael hat es nicht leicht mit Monika. Wenn sie ein Rendezvous^g haben, muß Michael fast immer warten. Schließlich kommt sie lachend an, ohne ein Wort der Entschuldigung. Michael findet auch, daß sie zu viele — und zu gute! — Bekannte hat. Sie ist also bestimmt nicht langweilig, die gute Monika, sie ist im Gegenteil ein bißchen zu flott. Für Michael jedenfalls. Aber was soll man denn machen? Monika ist eigentlich ein nettes Mädchen, Michael hat sie wirklich gern. Außerdem sieht sie nicht nur gut aus, sie sieht sogar sehr gut aus. Aber das finden Michaels Freunde auch.

Ein Student hat viel zu tun. Dreizehn lange Jahre ist er zur Schule gegangen, und das Endexamen,^g das Abitur, war keine leichte Sache. Jetzt hat er vielleicht drei oder vier Stunden Vorle-

die Schule, die Schulen
All children enter **die Volksschule** *at age six. After four years about thirty percent transfer to a secondary school of which* **das Gymnasium** [gymˈnɑːzium], *or* **die Oberschule**, *is the main broad type.* **das Volk**, *pl.* **die Völker** people, peoples + **die Schule** · **Andreas** [anˈdʀeːas] · **Christoph** [ˈkʀɪstɔf]
das Gymnasium, die Gymnasien

das Stipendium [ʃtiˈpɛndium], **die Stipendien**
die Halbtagsarbeit part-time work
halb half + **der Tag** + **die Arbeit**
das Studium [ʃtuːdium], **die Studien**

das Problem [pʀoˈbleːm], **die Probleme**

das Theater [teˈɑːtəʀ], **die Theater** · **das Konzert** [kɔnˈtsɛʀt], **die Konzerte**

Monika [ˈmoːnikɑ]
das macht nichts that doesn't matter

was whatever *rel. pron.*

das Rendezvous [ʀɑ̃deˈvuː], **die Rendezvous** [ʀɑ̃deˈvuːs]

außerdem moreover, besides *adv.*
das Endexamen [ˈɛntɛksɑːmən], **die Endexamen**
das Abitur [abiˈtuːʀ], **die Abiture** *the final examination in the* **Gymnasium** *which a student must pass in order to enter a university* · **sein (war** *past tense*)

21 Ist es leicht für Michael, jeden Monat so viel Geld auf den Tisch zu legen?
22 Woran muß man auch denken?
23 Wie viele Brüder hat Michael?
24 Gehen sie alle zur Schule?
25 Wie heißt der jüngste?
26 Geht er auf die Oberschule?
27 Wie heißen die zwei älteren?
28 Gehen sie auf die Universität?
29 Hat Vater Winkler viel Geld?
30 In welcher Stadt wohnt Michaels Familie?
31 Wo arbeitet Mutter Winkler?
32 Ist es schwer, heute in Deutschland eine Stelle zu finden?
33 Gibt es viele freie Stellen?
34 Geht es den Winklers schlecht?
35 Haben die Winklers ein großes Haus?
36 Kann Michael viel Geld von Vater und Mutter bekommen?
37 Woher kommt sein Geld?
38 Genügt ihm das Stipendium?
39 Was muß ein Student finden, wenn er Geld braucht?
40 Wie geht das Studium, wenn ein Student arbeitet?
41 Was ist Michaels Problem?
42 Hat Michael viele Freunde?
43 Wo kommen sie zusammen?
44 Was tun sie, wenn sie zusammen sind?
45 Wie heißt Michaels Freundin?
46 Was hat ihr Vater?
47 Woran denkt sie zu wenig?
48 Seit wann sind Michael und Monika gute Freunde?
49 Woran hat Monika Interesse?
50 Wer gibt ihr das Geld?
51 Was bleibt für Michael?
52 Was muß Michael fast immer tun, wenn er und Monika ein Rendezvous haben?
53 Hat Monika viele gute Bekannte?
54 Ist die gute Monika langweilig?

sungen und Übungen^g am Tag. Und fast alle Vorlesungen sind voll. Es kann sogar sein, daß man gar keinen Platz findet, und es ist kein Spaß, im Stehen zu studieren. Dann muß ein guter Student auch lesen und ausarbeiten, was er notiert^g hat. Das sind sicher wieder drei oder vier Stunden am Tag. Wenn er das zehn Semester^g lang schön brav getan hat, dann kann er schon mal an das Staats^g- oder sogar an das Doktorexamen denken, ohne Angst zu haben. Viele Menschen haben keine Ahnung, was ein Student alles zu tun hat. Er hat es bestimmt nicht immer gut!

Aber natürlich studiert ein Student nicht immer. So ernst ist die Sache denn doch nicht. Da ist bestimmt auch sehr viel Spaß. Junge Menschen haben immer Spaß. Das Geld ist knapp— aber was macht das eigentlich? Sind die teuren Stunden die besten? Doch ganz bestimmt nicht. Es ist ein Glück, daß Glück fast nichts mit Geld zu tun hat. Man lernt während des Studiums viele interessante Menschen und Sachen kennen. Da sind die Freunde, da ist die Freundin, und man ist jung! Was will man eigentlich noch mehr? Außerdem macht eine jede Arbeit Spaß, es muß nur die richtige sein. Es ist schon so: Ein Student hat es gut!

was what *rel. pron.*
das Semester [zeˈmɛstəʀ], die Semester
der Staat, die Staaten · der Doktor
[ˈdɔktɔʀ], die Doktoren [dɔkˈtoːʀən]
was what *rel. pron.*

55 Wie sieht sie aus?
56 Wie lange ist ein Student zur Schule gegangen?
57 Was war keine leichte Sache?
58 Hat ein Student viele Vorlesungen und Übungen?
59 Was ist kein Spaß?
60 Was muß ein guter Student dann auch noch tun?
61 Wann kann ein Student an das Staatsexamen denken?
62 Hat ein Student viel zu tun?
63 Studiert ein Student immer?
64 Sind die teuersten Stunden die besten?
65 Was und wen lernt man während des Studiums kennen?
66 Wann macht eine Arbeit Spaß?

PHONOLOGY

Practice pronouncing the following words:

1 Make the [ɑ:] especially long:

s a gt, sog a r, a ber, j a, d a, t a tsächlich, T a g, m a l, h a ben, Sp a rbuch, b a den, V a ter, Ex a men, Sp a ß, br a v, get a n, St aa tsex a men, A hnung

2 Make the [a] especially short:

m a n, a lt, k a nn, H a mburg, a lso, kn a pp, l a nge, M a rk, g a nz, Schr a nk, d a s, a lles, f a st, T a nte, m a cht, d a nn, w a nn, Geldm a nn, w a s, h a t, S a chen, w a rten, l a chend, jedenf a lls, geg a ngen, Pl a tz, a n, d a ß

3 Make the [e:] especially long and be sure not to diphthongize it:

e r, e rste, e ben, w e nig, s e hr, j e den, l e gen, g e hen, e rst, schw e r, Probl e m, g e ben, j e denfalls, außerd e m, dreiz e hn, st e hen, w e nigstens, m e hr

4   Make the [ɛ] especially short:

Stud**e**nt, b**e**sten, M**e**nschen, B**e**tt, **e**s, d**e**nn, b**e**ssere, G**e**ld, j**e**tzt, **e**ndlich, n**e**tt, d**e**ckt, w**e**nn, schn**e**ll, mith**e**lfen, St**e**lle, **e**twas, schl**e**cht, Stip**e**ndium, Konz**e**rt, E**e**ntschuldigung, g**e**rn, d**e**nken, **e**rnst, l**e**rnt, k**e**nnen

5   Make the [i:] especially long and be sure not to diphthongize it:

w**i**r, Philosoph**i**e, stud**i**eren, Mediz**i**n, h**i**er, v**i**el, g**i**bt, z**i**emlich, **i**hm, **i**hn, D**i**eter, w**i**e, s**i**e, l**i**egt, l**i**est, B**i**er, **i**hr, s**i**eht, not**i**ert, schl**i**eßlich

6   Make the [ɪ] especially short:

n**i**cht, M**i**chael, W**i**nkler, **i**st, Gesch**i**chte, **i**n, Z**i**mmer, T**i**sch, s**i**nd, Schm**i**dt, W**i**rtin, h**i**lft, Chr**i**stoph, m**i**thelfen, f**i**nden, w**i**rd, G**i**ft, r**i**chtig, natürl**i**ch, F**i**lm, tr**i**nkt, m**i**t, n**i**chts, n**i**mmt, w**i**rkl**i**ch, best**i**mmt, **i**mmer, w**i**ll

7   Make the [o:] especially long and be sure not to diphthongize it:

gr**o**ß, s**o**gar, s**o**, w**o**hnen, Milli**o**nen, M**o**nat, V**o**rlesung, **O**berschule, Postb**o**te, als**o**, Pr**o**blem, sch**o**n, M**o**nika, **o**hne, n**o**tiert, **o**der

8   Make the [ɔ] especially short:

n**o**ch, d**o**ch, k**o**stet, M**o**rgen, V**o**lksschule, Christ**o**ph, w**o**llen, P**o**stbote, bek**o**mmen, K**o**nzert, k**o**mmt, fl**o**tt, v**o**ll, D**o**kt**o**r

9   Make the [u:] especially long and be sure not to diphthongize it:

g**u**t, n**u**n, n**u**r, st**u**dieren, t**u**t, z**u**, gen**u**g, Sch**u**le, Volkssch**u**le, Obersch**u**le, Sparb**u**ch, Abit**u**r, daz**u**, t**u**n

10   Make the [ʊ] especially short:

war**u**m, **u**nsere, Hamb**u**rg, gef**u**nden, **u**nmodern, M**u**tter, m**u**ß, J**u**nge, **u**nd, Aug**u**st, Entsch**u**ldigung, St**u**nden

11   Practice pronouncing the following words, making the long stressed vowels especially long and the short ones especially short:

g**u**t, m**a**n, w**a**s, s**a**gt, **a**lt, n**u**n, n**o**ch, gr**o**ß, k**a**nn, stud**i**eren, B**u**ch, n**i**cht, d**a**s, g**i**bt, Z**i**mmer, l**a**nge, St**ü**ck, M**o**nat, natürl**i**ch, v**i**el, n**e**tt, f**a**st, T**a**nte, T**a**g, B**e**tt, T**i**sch, w**e**nn, **e**r, m**u**ß, f**ü**r, gen**u**g, Sch**u**le, J**u**nge, sch**o**n, **a**ber, P**o**st, B**o**te, schl**e**cht, **u**nd, bek**o**mmen, **i**mmer, d**o**ch, g**i**bt, d**a**, Probl**e**m, m**a**l, d**o**rt, zus**a**mmen, Konz**e**rt, M**o**nika, s**e**hr, Aug**u**st, Inter**e**sse, S**a**che, w**a**rten, W**o**rt, best**i**mmt, G**e**genteil, fl**o**tt, m**a**chen, M**ä**dchen, g**e**rn, sog**a**r, Abit**u**r, St**u**nden, v**o**ll, f**i**nden, Sp**a**ß, not**i**ert, d**a**nn, z**e**hn, Sem**e**ster, br**a**v, St**aa**tsexamen, d**e**r, d**e**n, d**e**m, d**e**s, St**u**dium, j**u**ng, **A**rbeit, h**a**t

VOCABULARY

A. Singular and Plural of Nouns

das Abitur, die Abiture
der Doktor, die Doktoren
das Endexamen, die Endexamen
das Gymnasium, die Gymnasien
die Halbtagsarbeit, die Halbtagsarbeiten
das Konzert, die Konzerte
die Nachtarbeit, die Nachtarbeiten
die Oberschule, die Oberschulen
das Problem, die Probleme
das Rendezvous [-vuː], die Rendezvous [-vuːs]

die Schule, die Schulen
das Semester, die Semester
der Staat, die Staaten
das Stipendium, die Stipendien
das Studium, die Studien
das Theater, die Theater
die Übung, die Übungen
die Universität, die Universitäten
das Volk, die Völker
die Volksschule, die Volksschulen

B. Inference

There are many words that look very much alike in English and German, and it is important to get into the habit of guessing their meanings. It is true that you can sometimes be misled by graphic similarity when the meanings are actually quite different. However, if the meaning you guess fits the context, you can be quite sure that your guess is valid. Meanings guessed are remembered far better than those looked up in a glossary or dictionary. After you have had some practice in guessing the meanings of German words that resemble English words, such as the ones below, you will be ready for the next step, that is, guessing with the help of context the meanings of new words that do not resemble their English equivalents.

Read the following sentences and guess the meanings of the words in boldface:

1 Er hat sein ganzes Geld auf der Deutschen **Bank**.   **die Bank, die Banken**
2 Hamburg hat auch viel **Metallindustrie** [meˈtalɪnduˌstriː].   **die Industrie, die Industrien**
3 Mußt du denn zu dieser **Konferenz** [kɔnfeˈʀɛnts] nach Hannover fahren?   **die Konferenz, die Konferenzen**
4 Wenn Sie einen **Moment** [moˈmɛnt] warten wollen, kann ich Ihnen helfen.   **der Moment, die Momente**
5 Seit seinem Herzanfall muß er täglich **Tabletten** [taˈblɛtən] nehmen.   **die Tablette, die Tabletten**
6 Freitags ißt man in Deutschland viel **Fisch**.   **der Fisch, die Fische**
7 Der **Hammer** liegt im Werkzeugkasten.   **der Hammer, die Hämmer**
8 Die **Hand** hat fünf **Finger**.   **die Hand, die Hände · der Finger, die Finger**
9 A.   Ich war gestern in der **Oper** [ˈoːpəʀ].   **die Oper, die Opern**

B. Was gab es denn?
A. „Der Rosenkavalier" von Richard Strauß, das ist meine liebste **Oper**.
10 Michael hat seiner Freundin Monika sechs rote **Rosen** geschickt.   **die Rose, die Rosen**
11 Monikas Vater hat ein neues Haus mit einem schönen **Garten** gekauft.   **der Garten, die Gärten**
12 A. Ist sie nicht eine kopflose **Person** [pɛrˈzoːn]?   **die Person, die Personen**
B. Ja, manchmal kann man denken, sie ist nicht ganz **normal** [nɔrˈmaːl].
13 A. Kommst du heute mit ins Theater?
B. Nein, **Dramen** von Schiller sind mir nicht interessant genug.   **das Drama, die Dramen**
A. Du mußt dich wirklich mehr für **Kultur** [kʊlˈtuːʀ] interessieren.   **die Kultur**
B. Aber ich habe nun mal kein Interesse für **Tragödien** [traˈgøːdiən].   **die Tragödie, die Tragödien**
14 A. Hast du **Musik** [muˈziːk] gern?   **die Musik**
B. Ja sehr, aber ich habe kein **Instrument** [ɪnstruˈmɛnt].   **das Instrument, die Instrumente**

There are a number of German words which a speaker of English can understand more readily if he knows that German **pf** frequently corresponds to English *p*. We have already had **Pfennig**, which is the equivalent of English *penny*. Additional words of this kind are in the sentences below. With the help of the context provided, try to guess what the meaning is:

1 Ich möchte nur ein halbes **Pfund** Fleisch kaufen.   **das Pfund**
2 Die Mutter brät das Fleisch in der **Pfanne**.   **die Pfanne, die Pfannen**
3 Mögen Sie gern **Pfannkuchen**?
4 Es muß noch etwas **Pfeffer** ans Essen!   **der Pfeffer**
5 Nach dem Essen raucht Vater gern eine **Pfeife**.   **die Pfeife, die Pfeifen**
6 Möchten Sie einen **Apfel**?   **der Apfel, die Äpfel**
7 Meine Tante hat viele grüne **Pflanzen**.   **die Pflanze, die Pflanzen**
8 Im Winter kann man natürlich keine Rosen **pflanzen**.
9 Mögen Sie lieber Äpfel oder **Pflaumen**?   **die Pflaume, die Pflaumen**
10 Er ist gegen einen **Laternenpfahl** gelaufen.   **der Pfahl, die Pfähle**
11 Ein Pfahl und ein **Pfosten** sind fast dasselbe.   **der Pfosten, die Pfosten**
12 Wollen Sie eine Pfanne aus **Kupfer** oder aus einem anderen Metall?   **das Kupfer**

WRITING

A. Completion

Copy the sentences and supply the missing endings:

1 Susi ist ein klein____ Mädchen, aber sie will d____ Tisch decken.
2 Susi legt d____ neu____ Decke auf d____ groß____ Tisch.

3 Dann stellt sie d____ schön____ Teller (*pl.*) auf d____ neu____, weiß____ Decke.
4 Sie legt ein____ klein____ Löffel hinter jed____ Suppenteller und ein____ größer____ Löffel neben jed____ Teller.
5 Sie fragt ihr____ Mutter, ob sie die neu____ oder die alt____ Gabeln aus d____ klein____ Schrank holen soll.
6 Susi schaut durch ein groß____ Fenster und sieht ihr____ Vater schon diesseits d____ Platz____.
7 Sie geht ihr____ Vater entgegen und erzählt ihm von ihr____ viel____ Arbeit für ihr____ Mutter.
8 In wenig____ Minuten sind beide innerhalb d____ Haus____ und sitzen an ihr____ Mittagstisch.
9 Der Vater spricht über d____ gut____ Arbeit d____ tüchtig____ Mädchen____, bis d____ Mutter d____ heiß____ Suppe in d____ schön____ Suppenteller (*pl.*) füllt.
10 Nach d____ Essen geht Susi zu ihr____ nett____ Onkel hinüber und erzählt ihm von ihr____ schwer____ Arbeit für ihr____ Mutter und ihr____ Vater.

B. Structure Retention

Substitute the new words for those directly above them and make all the necessary changes.

Example:
Model sentence:
Die Mutter des kleinen Mädchens bleibt am Morgen zu Hause.

Substitutions:
    Vater   nett   Junge   kommt   Abend

New sentence:
Der Vater des netten Jungen kommt am Abend nach Hause.

1 Seine alte Tante hat einen schlimmen Unfall gehabt.
    nett Onkel   schlecht   Erfahrung   machen

2 Susi stellt das frische Brot, die Butter und die Marmelade auf den Tisch.
  Mutter   warm Kuchen   Wein   Kaffee

3 Ihr großer Junge ist gestern bei mir gewesen.
  Euer klein Mädchen   zu wir kommen

4 Ilse hat ihre alte Freundin Lilo im Zug gesehen.
  Rolf   Freund Hans   Vorlesung treffen

5 Der schnelle Zug nach Berlin fährt am Mittag von Hamburg ab.
  Ein   aus   ankommen Mitternacht München

6 Seine junge Frau möchte jeden Monat einen neuen Hut kaufen.
  Ihr nett Mann   Jahr   Wagen

7 Dein Bruder hat gefragt, ob er mitkommen darf.
   Sein Frau   sagen   daß   wollen

8 Diese freundliche Kundin meint, daß der Hut zu teuer für sie ist.
                Kunde antworten   Geige

9 Der junge Student hat sein Buch im Vorlesungsraum gelassen.
        Studentinnen   Bücher   Wagen   legen

10 Wenn der neue Schrank uns nicht gefällt, schicken wir ihn den Leuten zurück.
         Hüte   ihr   geben   ihr   Verkäufer

Unit 20

DIALOG

Ein unverhofftes Wiedersehen (Anfang)

1 Heinrich: Hallo, Werner, wir haben einander schon ewig nicht gesehen!

2 Werner: Mensch, Heinrich, wo kommst du denn her?

3 Heinrich: Ich wohne jetzt hier. Man muß ja auch mal umziehen.

4 Werner: Ich hatte schon von Helmut erfahren, daß du wieder irgendwo in Kiel lebst.

An Unexpected Reunion (Beginning)

unverhofft hoffen hope · **wiedersehen***: **er sieht wieder, er sah wieder, er hat wiedergesehen** see again   **wieder** again + **sehen**   **das Wiedersehen** reunion

1 Hello, Werner! We haven't seen each other for ages.

ewig eternal(ly), for ages

2 Man alive, Heinrich! Where did you come from?

wo . . . her from where?

3 I live here now. After all, one has to move once in a while.

umziehen: er zieht um, er zog um, er ist umgezogen move, change residences

4 I had already found out from Helmut that you're living someplace in Kiel again.

erfahren: er erfährt, er erfuhr, er hat erfahren find out, experience · **irgendwo** someplace

---

* Beginning with Unit 20, the 3rd singular forms of the present, past, and present perfect tenses will be given for new strong verbs.

5 **Heinrich:** Und ich hab' noch heute morgen zu meiner Frau gesagt: „Hier wohnte früher ein Schulfreund von mir".

6 **Werner:** Was, eine Frau hast du auch? Damals warst du noch nicht einmal verlobt!

7 **Heinrich:** Das hat sich kurz darauf geändert. Ich habe jetzt sogar einen Sohn und zwei Töchter.

8 **Werner:** Donnerwetter, Heinrich, wie das klingt!

9 **Heinrich:** Da kommt mein Bus um die Ecke. Fährst du auch mit in die Stadt?

10 **Werner:** Ja, jeden Morgen um diese Zeit.

(Fortsetzung folgt)

SUPPLEMENT

1 Er hat kein Glück.   1 He is out of luck.

2 Er hatte kein Glück.   2 He was out of luck.

3 Er hat kein Glück gehabt.   3 He was out of luck.

4 Er hatte kein Glück gehabt. 4 He had been out of luck.

5 Ich wohne jetzt in Kiel.   5 I live in Kiel now.

6 Ich wohnte früher in Kiel.   6 I lived in Kiel formerly.

5	And only this morning I said to my wife, "A school friend of mine used to live here."	**früher** formerly · **der Schulfreund** **die Schule** + **der Freund**
6	What, you have a wife, too? At that time you weren't even engaged!	**damals** at that time · **nicht einmal** not even · **verlobt** engaged
7	That changed shortly afterwards. Now I even have a son and two daughters.	**ändern** change **sich** *reflexive pronoun, here accusative* **sich ändern** be changed, undergo a change · **der Sohn, die Söhne** · **die Tochter, die Töchter**
8	I'll be darned, Heinrich! That sounds great!	**das Donnerwetter** *lit.* thunderstorm; *also a rather mild expletive used to express anger, surprise, delight, etc.* **der Donner** thunder + **das Wetter** weather · **klingen: er klingt, er klang, er hat geklungen**
9	There comes my bus around the corner. Are you going along to the city, too?	**der Bus, die Busse**
10	Yes, every morning at this time.	

(To be continued)

7	Ich habe früher in Kiel gewohnt.	7	I lived in Kiel formerly.
8	Ich hatte früher in Kiel gewohnt.	8	I had lived in Kiel formerly.
9	Er weiß es nicht.	9	He doesn't know it.
10	Er wußte es nicht.	10	He didn't know it.
11	Er hat es nicht gewußt.	11	He didn't know it.
12	Er hatte es nicht gewußt.	12	He hadn't known it.

13	Wir sind jetzt gute Freunde.	13	We are good friends now.
14	Wir waren damals gute Freunde.	14	We were good friends at that time.
15	Wir sind immer gute Freunde gewesen.	15	We were always good friends.
16	Wir waren immer gute Freunde gewesen.	16	We had always been good friends.
17	Ich fahre heute in die Stadt.	17	I am going into the city today.
18	Ich fuhr gestern in die Stadt.	18	I went into the city yesterday.
19	Ich bin oft in die Stadt gefahren.	19	I went into the city often.
20	Ich war nie in die Stadt gefahren.	20	I had never gone into the city.

AUDIOLINGUAL DRILLS

A. Directed Dialog

Sagen Sie, daß Heinrich und Werner einander schon ewig nicht gesehen haben!
Heinrich und Werner haben einander schon ewig nicht gesehen.

Fragen Sie, wo Heinrich denn her kommt!
Wo kommt Heinrich denn her?

Antworten Sie, daß man ja auch mal umziehen muß!
Man muß ja auch mal umziehen.

Sagen Sie, daß Werner schon von Helmut erfahren hatte, daß Heinrich in Kiel lebt!
Werner hatte schon von Helmut erfahren, daß Heinrich in Kiel lebt.

Fragen Sie, was Heinrich noch heute morgen zu seiner Frau gesagt hat!
Was hat Heinrich noch heute morgen zu seiner Frau gesagt?

Antworten Sie, er hat gesagt, daß ein Schulfreund von ihm früher hier wohnte!
Er hat gesagt, daß ein Schulfreund von ihm früher hier wohnte.

Sagen Sie, daß Heinrich damals noch nicht einmal verlobt war!
Heinrich war damals noch nicht einmal verlobt.

Sagen Sie, daß das sich kurz darauf geändert hat!
Das hat sich kurz darauf geändert.

Sagen Sie, daß Heinrich jetzt sogar einen Sohn und zwei Töchter hat!
Heinrich hat jetzt sogar einen Sohn und zwei Töchter.

Sagen Sie, daß da Heinrichs Bus um die Ecke kommt!
Da kommt Heinrichs Bus um die Ecke.

Fragen Sie, ob Werner auch mit in die Stadt fährt!
Fährt Werner auch mit in die Stadt?

Sagen Sie, daß er jeden Morgen um diese Zeit in die Stadt fährt!
Er fährt jeden Morgen um diese Zeit in die Stadt.

B. Past Tense: Weak Verbs (*See Grammar* §§20.2, 20.3)

1 Repeat:

Ich sagte es ihm gestern.   Wir sagten es ihm gestern.
Du sagtest es ihm gestern.   Ihr sagtet es ihm gestern.
Er sagte es ihm gestern.   Sie sagten es ihm gestern.

2 All the verbs in this drill follow the past tense pattern of **sagen**. Substitute the new subject or the new verb in the past:

Er sagte es gestern morgen.   **du**
Du sagtest es gestern morgen.   **kaufen**
Du kauftest es gestern morgen.   **wir**
Wir kauften es gestern morgen.   **brauchen**
Wir brauchten es gestern morgen.   **ich**
Ich brauchte es gestern morgen.   **machen**
Ich machte es gestern morgen.   **ihr**
Ihr machtet es gestern morgen.   **erklären**
Ihr erklärtet es gestern morgen.   **Rolf und Günther**
Rolf und Günther erklärten es gestern morgen.   **studieren**
Rolf und Günther studierten es gestern morgen.   **Fräulein Schneider**
Fräulein Schneider studierte es gestern morgen.

3 The verbs that require a connecting **-e-** in some forms of the present tense and in the past participle also require this **-e-** between the stem and the past tense sign **-te-**. Substitute the new subject or the new verb in the past:

Er wartete gar nicht.   **du**   Du arbeitetest gar nicht.   **wir**
Du wartetest gar nicht.   **arbeiten**   Wir arbeiteten gar nicht.   **spotten**

UNIT 20 · AUDIOLINGUAL DRILLS

Wir spotteten gar nicht. **ich**
Ich spottete gar nicht. **antworten**
Ich antwortete gar nicht. **ihr**

Ihr antwortetet gar nicht. **warten**
Ihr wartetet gar nicht. **die Kinder**
Die Kinder warteten gar nicht.

4 The irregular weak verb **wissen** *know*. The past tense has the same vowel as the past participle. Substitute the new subject of the main clause:

Sie wußten nicht, was er wollte. **Hans**
Hans wußte nicht, was er wollte. **wir**
Wir wußten nicht, was er wollte. **du**
Du wußtest nicht, was er wollte. **die Männer**

Die Männer wußten nicht, was er wollte. **Ilse**
Ilse wußte nicht, was er wollte. **ihr**
Ihr wußtet nicht, was er wollte. **ich**
Ich wußte nicht, was er wollte.

5 The modal auxiliaries. The past tense shows the same irregularities as the past participle. Substitute the new subject or the new modal auxiliary in the past tense:

Ich mochte es nicht tun. **du**
Du mochtest es nicht tun. **können**
Du konntest es nicht tun. **wir**
Wir konnten es nicht tun. **wollen**
Wir wollten es nicht tun. **ihr**
Ihr wolltet es nicht tun. **dürfen**

Ihr durftet es nicht tun. **er**
Er durfte es nicht tun. **sollen**
Er sollte es nicht tun. **das Mädchen**
Das Mädchen sollte es nicht tun. **müssen**
Das Mädchen mußte es nicht tun. **ich**
Ich mußte es nicht tun.

6 The irregular weak verbs **bringen** *bring* and **denken** *think*. The past tense shows the same irregularities as the past participle. Substitute the new subject:

Sie brachten ihr eine Tasse Kaffee. **du**
Du brachtest ihr eine Tasse Kaffee. **ihr**
Ihr brachtet ihr eine Tasse Kaffee. **wir**
Wir brachten ihr eine Tasse Kaffee. **ich**
Ich brachte ihr eine Tasse Kaffee. **ihr Mann**
Ihr Mann brachte ihr eine Tasse Kaffee.

Dachten Sie daran, nach Hause zu gehen? **er**
Dachte er daran, nach Hause zu gehen? **wir**
Dachten wir daran, nach Hause zu gehen? **du**
Dachtest du daran, nach Hause zu gehen? **ihr**
Dachtet ihr daran, nach Hause zu gehen?
   deine Tochter
Dachte deine Tochter daran, nach Hause zu gehen?

7 The irregular weak verb **kennen** *know*. The past tense has the same vowel as the past participle. Substitute the new subject:

Sie kannten die Stadt gar nicht. **ich**
Ich kannte die Stadt gar nicht. **mein Sohn**
Mein Sohn kannte die Stadt gar nicht. **du**

Du kanntest die Stadt gar nicht. **wir**
Wir kannten die Stadt gar nicht. **ihr**
Ihr kanntet die Stadt gar nicht.

8 The irregular weak verb **haben** *have*. Substitute the new subject:

Er hatte damals kein Geld. **du**
Du hattest damals kein Geld. **wir**
Wir hatten damals kein Geld. **ihr**

Ihr hattet damals kein Geld. **ich**
Ich hatte damals kein Geld. **unsere Freunde**
Unsere Freunde hatten damals kein Geld.

C. Past Tense: Strong Verbs (*See Grammar* §§20.2, 20.3)

9 Second person ending variants. Use a connecting **-e-** in the **du** form if the verb stem ends in [t], [d], [s], or [z] (spellings: **-t**, **-d**, **-ss**, **-ß**, **-s**), and in the **ihr** form if the stem ends in [t] or [d]. Substitute the new subject or past tense verb form with the correct ending:

Ich nahm die Zeitung.	**du**	Er saß am Tisch.	**du**
Du nahmst die Zeitung.	**las**	Du saßest am Tisch.	**schlief**
Du lasest die Zeitung.	**ihr**	Du schliefst am Tisch.	**ihr**
Ihr last die Zeitung.	**fand**	Ihr schlieft am Tisch.	**stand**
Ihr fandet die Zeitung.	**du**	Ihr standet am Tisch.	**du**
Du fandest die Zeitung.	**ließ**	Du standest am Tisch.	**blieb**
Du ließest die Zeitung.	**ich**	Du bliebst am Tisch.	**ich**
Ich ließ die Zeitung.	**bekam**	Ich blieb am Tisch.	**aß**
Ich bekam die Zeitung.	**ihr**	Ich aß am Tisch.	**du**
Ihr bekamt die Zeitung.		Du aßest am Tisch.	

10 **Sein** *be*. The past tense stem is **war**. Change from the present to the past tense:

Ich bin mit diesem Buch fertig.
Ich war mit diesem Buch fertig.

Dieses Semester ist anstrengend.
Dieses Semester war anstrengend.

Die Kinder sind heute bei uns.
Die Kinder waren heute bei uns.

Wann seid ihr wieder in Belgien?
Wann wart ihr wieder in Belgien?

Bist du Weihnachten zu Hause?
Warst du Weihnachten zu Hause?

Wir sind ja versichert.
Wir waren ja versichert.

11 **Werden** *become*. The past tense stem is **wurde**. Change from the present to the past tense:

Im April werde ich zwanzig Jahre alt.
Im April wurde ich zwanzig Jahre alt.

Warum wirst du so ernst?
Warum wurdest du so ernst?

Bei solchem Wetter werden die Straßen rutschig.
Bei solchem Wetter wurden die Straßen rutschig.

Wann werdet ihr damit fertig?
Wann wurdet ihr damit fertig?

12 **Geben** *give*, **essen** *eat*, **sehen** *see*, **liegen** *lie*, **lesen** *read*, **sitzen** *sit*, **bitten** *ask*. The vowel of the past tense stem of these verbs is [ɑ:], as in **gab**. The final consonants of **sitz-** change to [s] **ß**. Change to the past tense:

Ich gebe ihm ein Glas Wein.
Ich gab ihm ein Glas Wein.

Wir essen oft bei ihm.
Wir aßen oft bei ihm.

Du siehst blaß aus.
Du sahst blaß aus.

Der Onkel liegt im Bett.
Der Onkel lag im Bett.

Ihr lest die Zeitschrift nicht.
Ihr last die Zeitschrift nicht.

Sie bittet mich, es zu kaufen.
Sie bat mich, es zu kaufen.

Du sitzt auf der Kiste.
Du saßest auf der Kiste.

13 **Schlafen** *sleep*, **laufen** *run*, **lassen** *leave, allow*, **halten** *hold*, **heißen** *be called*, **raten** *guess*, **braten** *roast, bake, fry*, **gefallen** *please*. The past tense stem vowel of these verbs is [i:], as in **schlief**. Change to the past tense:

Ich schlafe immer sehr gut.
Ich schlief immer sehr gut.

Sein Freund heißt Michael.
Sein Freund hieß Michael.

Warum läufst du denn?
Warum liefst du denn?

Monika rät die Antwort nicht.
Monika riet die Antwort nicht.

Läßt du sie den Film sehen?
Ließest du sie den Film sehen?

Mutter brät das Fleisch.
Mutter briet das Fleisch.

Ich halte die Zeitschrift.
Ich hielt die Zeitschrift.

Die Arbeiten gefallen mir nicht.
Die Arbeiten gefielen mir nicht.

14 **Bleiben** *stay*, **scheinen** *shine*, **steigen** *climb*, **leiden** *suffer*, **übertreiben** *exaggerate*. The past stem of **leiden** is **litt**; the others have the vowel [i:], as in **blieb**. Change to the past tense:

Wir bleiben nur einen Tag dort.
Wir blieben nur einen Tag dort.

Hoffentlich leidest du nicht zu viel.
Hoffentlich littest du nicht zu viel.

Die Sonne scheint so schön.
Die Sonne schien so schön.

Ihr übertreibt die Sache ein bißchen.
Ihr übertriebt die Sache ein bißchen.

Steigst du in München aus?
Stiegst du in München aus?

15 **Umziehen** *move*. The past is **zog ... um**. Substitute the new subject:

Ich zog vor sechs Wochen um.   **wir**
Wir zogen vor sechs Wochen um.   **du**
Du zogst vor sechs Wochen um.   **der Mann**

Der Mann zog vor sechs Wochen um.   **ihr**
Ihr zogt vor sechs Wochen um.

16 **Kommen** *come*, **sprechen** *speak*, **treffen** *meet*, **nehmen** *take*, **bekommen** *receive*. The past stem vowel of these verbs is [ɑ:], as in **kam**. Change to the past tense:

Ich komme mit dem Bus.
Ich kam mit dem Bus.

Warum nehmt ihr denn kein Eis?
Warum nahmt ihr denn kein Eis?

Die beiden sprechen über den Besuch.
Die beiden sprachen über den Besuch.

Sie bekommen eine Kiste mit der Post.
Sie bekamen eine Kiste mit der Post.

Er trifft seinen Onkel lesend an.
Er traf seinen Onkel lesend an.

17 **Helfen** *help*, **springen** *jump*, **finden** *find*, **empfinden** *feel*, **beginnen** *begin*, **klingen** *sound*, **gelingen** *succeed*. The past stem vowel of these verbs is [a], as in **fand**. Change to the past tense:

Warum hilfst du ihm nicht?
Warum halfst du ihm nicht?

Springt er über die Kiste?
Sprang er über die Kiste?

Ich finde meinen Hut nicht.
Ich fand meinen Hut nicht.

Empfinden Sie es auch so?
Empfanden Sie es auch so?

Die Vorlesung beginnt um zehn.
Die Vorlesung begann um zehn.

Ihre Geige klingt gut.
Ihre Geige klang gut.

Es gelingt ihm, sein Abitur zu machen.
Es gelang ihm, sein Abitur zu machen.

18 **Tun** *do*. The past stem is **tat**. Substitute the new subject:

Er tat es, um mich zu beruhigen.   **die Leute**
Die Leute taten es, um mich zu beruhigen.   **du**
Du tatest es, um mich zu beruhigen.   **Ilse**
Ilse tat es, um mich zu beruhigen.   **ihr**
Ihr tatet es, um mich zu beruhigen.

19 **Gehen** *go*. The past stem is **ging**. Substitute the new subject:

Ich ging gestern abend ins Theater.   **die Studenten**
Die Studenten gingen gestern abend ins Theater.   **du**
Du gingst gestern abend ins Theater.   **er**
Er ging gestern abend ins Theater.   **ihr**
Ihr gingt gestern abend ins Theater.

20 **Stehen** *stand*, **verstehen** *understand*. The past stem is **(ver)stand**. Change to the past tense:

Ich stehe vor dem Fenster.
Ich stand vor dem Fenster.

Verstehst du seine Gedichte?
Verstandest du seine Gedichte?

Warum steht ihr alle zusammen?
Warum standet ihr alle zusammen?

Sie versteht mich einfach nicht.
Sie verstand mich einfach nicht.

D. Past Perfect Tense (*See Grammar* §20.5)

21 Repeat:

Ich hatte einige Karten gekauft.
Du hattest einige Karten gekauft.
Er hatte einige Karten gekauft.

Wir hatten einige Karten gekauft.
Ihr hattet einige Karten gekauft.
Sie hatten einige Karten gekauft.

22 Change from the present perfect to the past perfect tense:

Hast du Herrn Schneider gekannt?
Hattest du Herrn Schneider gekannt?

Er hat in der Vorlesung geschlafen.
Er hatte in der Vorlesung geschlafen.

Haben Sie die Post mitgebracht?
Hatten Sie die Post mitgebracht?

So etwas habt ihr nicht gekonnt.
So etwas hattet ihr nicht gekonnt.

Fräulein Schneider hat Philosophie studiert.
Fräulein Schneider hatte Philosophie studiert.

Ich habe eine Stunde auf dich gewartet.
Ich hatte eine Stunde auf dich gewartet.

Was hast du von Helmut erfahren?
Was hattest du von Helmut erfahren?

23 Repeat:

Ich war nach München gefahren.
Du warst nach München gefahren.
Er war nach München gefahren.

Wir waren nach München gefahren.
Ihr wart nach München gefahren.
Sie waren nach München gefahren.

24 Change from the present perfect to the past perfect tense:

Ich bin damals in Rom gewesen.
Ich war damals in Rom gewesen.

Wir sind zu ihm gegangen.
Wir waren zu ihm gegangen.

Der Mann ist plötzlich krank geworden.
Der Mann war plötzlich krank geworden.

Sie sind einen Monat dort geblieben.
Sie waren einen Monat dort geblieben.

Ist es dir gelungen?
War es dir gelungen?

Um wieviel Uhr seid ihr abgefahren?
Um wieviel Uhr wart ihr abgefahren?

25 Change from the past tense to the past perfect tense:

Das dachte ich auch.
Das hatte ich auch gedacht.

Unser Zug lief später ein.
Unser Zug war später eingelaufen.

Mein Sohn wollte die Fotos nicht.
Mein Sohn hatte die Fotos nicht gewollt.

Trafst du ihn dort?
Hattest du ihn dort getroffen?

Der Staat hatte kein Geld mehr.
Der Staat hatte kein Geld mehr gehabt.

Das Konzert begann um acht.
Das Konzert hatte um acht begonnen.

Wir zogen dann um.
Wir waren dann umgezogen.

Sie gab mir ein Glas Milch.
Sie hatte mir ein Glas Milch gegeben.

Vermutlich rutschte er.
Vermutlich war er gerutscht.

Onkel Richard bekam laufend Medizin.
Onkel Richard hatte laufend Medizin bekommen.

Damals hielt er auch Ruhe.
Damals hatte er auch Ruhe gehalten.

Ich stieg in Kiel aus.
Ich war in Kiel ausgestiegen.

Empfanden Sie es auch so?
Hatten Sie es auch so empfunden?

Er arbeitete den ganzen Tag.
Er hatte den ganzen Tag gearbeitet.

E. Questions and Answers

Wie heißt der neue Dialog?
Er heißt „Ein unverhofftes Wiedersehen".

Wie lange haben Heinrich und Werner einander nicht gesehen?
Sie haben einander schon ewig nicht gesehen.

Was hatte Werner von Helmut gehört?
Er hatte gehört, daß Heinrich wieder in Kiel wohnt.

Was sagte Heinrich zu seiner Frau?
Er sagte, daß früher ein Schulfreund von ihm hier wohnte.

Was hatte Werner von Heinrich nicht gewußt?
Er hatte nicht gewußt, daß Heinrich verheiratet ist.

Hat Heinrich auch Kinder?
Ja, er hat einen Sohn und zwei Töchter.

Was wollen die zwei Freunde jetzt tun?
Sie wollen mit dem Bus in die Stadt fahren.

Fährt Werner oft mit dem Bus in die Stadt?
Ja, er tut es jeden Morgen um diese Zeit.

GRAMMAR

0.1 Singular and Plural of Nouns

der Bus, die Busse
der Schulfreund, die Schulfreunde

der Sohn, die Söhne
die Tochter, die Töchter

20.2 Past Tense

The present perfect form of a German verb (Grammar §15.6) is a phrase consisting of an auxiliary verb (a form of **haben** or **sein**) plus a past participle:

Mein Bruder hat es mir erzählt.

Ist Onkel Richard schon wieder dort gewesen?

The past tense form, however, is a one-word verb form, not a phrase. It consists simply of a stem together with the appropriate personal ending. As is the case with past participles, we must distinguish between three kinds of verbs: regular weak verbs, strong verbs, and irregular weak verbs.

Weak verbs

The past tense form of a weak verb is derived from the present stem by adding to it a past tense suffix **-(e)te**, plus the personal ending. Those verbs that require a connecting **-e-** in the present tense (Grammar §7.3) and the past participle (Grammar §15.4) also have it in the past suffix:

Endings	sagen	arbeiten
-	sag te	arbeit ete
-st	sag te st	arbeit ete st
-	sag te	arbeit ete
-n	sag te n	arbeit ete n
-t	sag te t	arbeit ete t
-n	sag te n	arbeit ete n

Strong verbs

The past tense of a strong verb is formed by changing the stem vowel, and in some cases also by changing the stem-final consonant. To this past stem is added the appropriate personal ending. The various vowel changes and consonant changes will be discussed in more detail in Grammar §20.4. A connecting **-e-** sometimes appears between the past stem and the 2nd person endings; this is governed by the following rules:

1. If the stem ends in [t], [d], [s], or [z] (spelled **-t**, **-d**, **-ss**, **-ß**, **-s**), then the connecting **-e-** appears before the 2nd person singular ending **-st**. (In informal speech, this **-e-** may drop out.)

2. If the stem ends in [t] or [d], then the connecting **-e-** appears before the 2nd person plural ending **-t**.

Endings	sprechen	heißen	finden	bitten
-	sprach	hieß	fand	bat
-(e)st	sprach st	hieß est	fand est	bat est
-	sprach	hieß	fand	bat
-en	sprach en	hieß en	fand en	bat en
-(e)t	sprach t	hieß t	fand et	bat et
-en	sprach en	hieß en	fand en	bat en

Informal variants of the 2nd singular of **heißen**, **finden**, and **bitten** are: **hießt, fandst, batst**. Note that the **-s-** of the ending is dropped if the stem ends in [s], similar to the 2nd singular present (**du liest, du heißt**).

Irregular weak verbs

Some verbs form their past tense by changing the stem vowel (and some also by changing the final consonant) and adding the past suffix **-te**. The ones you have learned so far are:

Infinitive	*Past stem*
dürfen	durf te
können	konn te
mögen	moch te
müssen	muß te
wissen	wuß te
kennen	kann te
denken	dach te
bringen	brach te
haben	hat te

The modals **sollen** and **wollen** follow the pattern of the regular weak verbs in the formation of their past tense stems: **sollte, wollte**. A few additional verbs belong to this irregular weak group, but they involve no new patterns and will be introduced in later units.

20.3 Use of the Past Tenses

The modern uses of the various verb forms that refer to past time in English and German differ sharply in some respects. There are no forms in German which correspond to the English past progressive or past emphatic or to *used to* plus an infinitive. *I saw, I was seeing, I did see,* and *I used to see* are expressed by **ich habe gesehen** (present perfect) or **ich sah** (past), which are interchangeable under many conditions. Both are used in speaking of past events, actions, or conditions:

Das habe ich noch heute morgen zu meiner Frau gesagt.
Das sagte ich noch heute morgen zu meiner Frau.
Only this morning I was telling (told) my wife that.

Ja, wir haben ihn wirklich in Hamburg gesehen.
Ja, wir sahen ihn wirklich in Hamburg.
Yes, we really did see him in Hamburg.

Das hat mein Onkel auch immer getan.
Das tat mein Onkel auch immer.
My uncle always used to do that, too.

Present perfect tense

The present perfect is the usual past tense of conversation, although its use is not limited to conversation. It may be employed wherever the present perfect is used in English, except in speaking of an action that began in the past and is still going on in the present: *He has lived here for a month* — **Er wohnt schon seit einem Monat hier.**

Past tense

The past is used in speaking of an act being performed or a condition existing at the same time as, or in connection with, some other act or condition. For this reason it is the usual past tense of the narrative, of history, and of newspaper reporting. It is also often used in conversation to report a chain of events or the simultaneous occurrence of two or more past acts or conditions, although the present perfect may also be used. Much depends on the speaker and the situation.

The following examples illustrate some of the situations in which the past is preferred to the present perfect in German:

1. A chain of past events:

   Der Milchwagen kam um die Ecke, rutschte plötzlich an dieser Stelle und kippte dann sogar um.

   A speaker may begin by telling about an event in the present perfect, but after the first sentence or two he is almost certain to change over to the past:

   Heute Morgen sind Rolf und ich zum Schillerplatz gegangen, und dort haben wir einen schlimmen Unfall gesehen. Der Milchwagen kam um die Ecke und rutschte an der Kreuzung. Dann kippte er plötzlich sogar noch um. Als wir an der Stelle ankamen, lag eine alte Frau bei der Laterne. Sie hatte eine Platzwunde am Kopf und . . .

2. Simultaneous past events:

   Er schlief, während ich arbeitete.
   He slept (was sleeping) while I worked (was working).

Uwe las die Zeitung, Heike übte Geige, und ich deckte den Mittagstisch.
Uwe was reading the newspaper, Heike was practicing the violin, and I was setting the dinner table.

3   One past event begun after another:

Ich las gerade eine Erzählung, als er plötzlich ins Zimmer kam.
I was just reading a story when he suddenly came into the room.

Günther ging noch aufs Gymnasium, als Rolf mit seinem Studium begann.
Günther was still going to the *Gymnasium* when Rolf began his studies.

4   One past event begun after another which had lasted for a specified time and was still continuing at the time mentioned:

Ich wohnte schon zehn Jahre in Berlin, als er nach Freiburg fuhr.
I had lived (had been living) in Berlin for ten years when he went to Freiburg.

5   One past event completed before the beginning of another. As in English, the past perfect is used for the earlier event:

Als Heinrich nach Kiel zurückkam, war Werner schon weggegangen.
When Heinrich returned to Kiel, Werner had already left.

Although the present perfect is the preferred tense for dialog, there is a tendency to use the past of certain verbs even when speaking of single past events. This is true especially of **sein**, **haben**, **werden**, **wissen**, and all the modals:

Warum hast du denn gestern nicht gearbeitet?   Hat Helmut dir nicht alles erzählt?
Na, ich war doch noch in München.   Nein, denn er wußte Näheres selber nicht.

Rolf hat die Arbeit noch nicht gemacht.   Warum ist Heike nicht mitgekommen?
Das stimmt, er hatte leider keine Zeit.   Sie mußte Geige üben.

Weißt du, warum Lilo nach Hause gegangen ist?
Ja, sie wurde doch plötzlich krank.

0.4 Principal Parts of Strong and Irregular Verbs

The principal parts of a German verb are: *infinitive, past tense, past participle*. As in English, there are a number of vowel changes that occur in strong verbs; these changes, although not predictable from the form of the infinitive, do follow regular patterns, with minor variations.

It is impossible to determine from the form of the infinitive whether a given verb is weak or strong. For this reason it is important to *memorize* the principal parts of strong verbs. Begin now by learning the principal parts of the strong verbs in the drills of Unit 20. Then learn the principal parts of new strong verbs as you encounter them.

The verbs in the following list are grouped according to the vowel changes that occur in the past tense and the past participle. The present tense **er** form is included for those verbs that have a vowel change in the present tense; this you must learn along with the principal parts. Learn the auxiliary along with the past participle, too; remember that some verbs take either **haben** or **sein** in the present perfect, depending on whether there is a direct object **(ich bin gefahren, ich habe den Wagen gefahren)**.

Strong verbs

Infinitive	Present	Past	Present perfect	English
ei [aɪ]		**i** [ɪ]	**i** [ɪ]	
leiden		litt	hat gelitten	suffer
ei [aɪ]		**ie** [iː]	**ie** [iː]	
bleiben		blieb	ist geblieben	remain
scheinen		schien	hat geschienen	shine
steigen		stieg	ist gestiegen	climb
treiben		trieb	hat getrieben	drive
ie [iː]		**o** [oː]	**o** [oː]	
ziehen		zog	ist (hat) gezogen	move; pull
i [ɪ]		**a** [a]	**u** [ʊ]	
finden		fand	hat gefunden	find
gelingen		gelang	ist gelungen	succeed
klingen		klang	hat geklungen	sound
springen		sprang	ist gesprungen	jump
trinken		trank	hat getrunken	drink
i [ɪ]		**a** [a]	**o** [ɔ]	
beginnen		begann	hat begonnen	begin
e [ɛ]	**i** [ɪ]	**a** [a]	**o** [ɔ]	
helfen	hilft	half	hat geholfen	help
e [ɛ] or [eː] **o** [ɔ]	**i** [ɪ]	**a** [ɑː]	**o** [ɔ]	
kommen		kam	ist gekommen	come
nehmen	nimmt	nahm	hat genommen	take
sprechen	spricht	sprach	hat gesprochen	speak
treffen	trifft	traf	hat getroffen	meet
e [ɛ] **i** [ɪ]	**i** [ɪ]	**a** [ɑː]	**e** [ɛ]	
essen	ißt	aß	hat gegessen	eat
sitzen	sitzt	saß	hat gesessen	sit

Infinitive	Present	Past	Present perfect	English
e [eː]	**i, ie** [iː]	**a** [ɑː]	**e** [eː]	
i [ɪ]	**i** [ɪ]			
ie [iː]				
bitten		bat	hat gebeten	ask
geben	gibt	gab	hat gegeben	give
lesen	liest	las	hat gelesen	read
liegen		lag	hat gelegen	lie
sehen	sieht	sah	hat gesehen	see
treten	tritt	trat	ist (hat) getreten	step, kick
a [ɑː]	**ä** [ɛː]	**u** [uː]	**a** [ɑː]	
fahren	fährt	fuhr	ist (hat) gefahren	travel, drive
a [ɑː]	**ä** [ɛː]	**ie** [iː]	**a** [ɑː]	
[a]	[ɛ]		[a]	
braten	brät	briet	hat gebraten	roast
gefallen	gefällt	gefiel	hat gefallen	please
halten	hält	hielt	hat gehalten	hold
lassen	läßt	ließ	hat gelassen	leave, allow
raten	rät	riet	hat geraten	guess
schlafen	schläft	schlief	hat geschlafen	sleep
ei [aɪ]		**ie** [iː]	**ei** [aɪ]	
heißen		hieß	hat geheißen	be called
au [aʊ]	**äu** [ɔɪ]	**ie** [iː]	**au** [aʊ]	
laufen	läuft	lief	ist gelaufen	run

Other vowel changes

sein	ist	war	ist gewesen	be
gehen		ging	ist gegangen	go
stehen		stand	hat gestanden	stand
tun		tat	hat getan	do
werden	wird	wurde	ist geworden	become

Irregular weak verbs

Infinitive	Present	Past	Present perfect	English
dürfen	darf	durfte	hat gedurft	be allowed to
können	kann	konnte	hat gekonnt	be able to
mögen	mag	mochte	hat gemocht	like to
müssen	muß	mußte	hat gemußt	have to
wissen	weiß	wußte	hat gewußt	know
kennen		kannte	hat gekannt	know
denken		dachte	hat gedacht	think
bringen		brachte	hat gebracht	bring
haben	hat	hatte	hat gehabt	have

20.5 Past Perfect Tense

The past perfect tense is made up of the past tense of the auxiliary **haben** or **sein** and the past participle of the verb. Rules that you have already learned regarding position of the finite verb and past participle apply here as well. In fact, the past perfect tense is completely parallel to the present perfect, except that the auxiliaries are in the past tense form.

The use of the past perfect tense is very similar in German and English. It is used to tell of a past event that took place *at or before some point in past time,* even though this point in time may not be overtly expressed:

Ich hatte es von Helmut erfahren.
I had found out from Helmut.

Ich war zu Ilse hinübergegangen.
I had gone over to Ilse's.

Es war billiger, als ich gedacht hatte.
It was cheaper than I had thought.

Er war früher bei Onkel Richard gewesen.
He had been at Uncle Richard's earlier.

WRITING

A. Verbs

Arrange the elements to form German sentences; use the tense indicated:

1. Susi / decken / den Mittagstisch .   (*past perf.*)
2. wann / sein / du / bei uns ?   (*past*)
3. das / wollen / ich auch .   (*pres. perf.*)

4 dürfen / gehen / du / ins Theater ? (*pres.*)
5 was / erfahren / er / gestern ? (*pres. perf.*)
6 wir / umziehen / schon vor zwei Wochen . (*past perf.*)
7 aufpassen / du ? (*fut.*)
8 dann und wann / einkaufen / Frau Schmidt / für uns . (*past*)
9 das / machen / doch / nichts . (*pres. perf.*)
10 bekommen / du / ein gutes Stipendium ? (*past*)
11 warum / bitten / du / ihn / nicht /,/ uns zu helfen ? (*past*)
12 man / müssen / denken / an das Endexamen /,/ nicht wahr ? (*pres.*)
13 wann / gehen / ihr / in die Schule ? (*pres. perf.*)
14 warum / lesen / du / diese Zeitschrift ? (*past*)
15 wir / können / kaufen / keine besseren Bilder . (*past*)
16 sagen / deiner Frau /,/ daß / ich / wohnen / in Kiel / damals ! (*second clause past perf.*)
17 raten / ihr /,/ wer / sitzen / dort ? (*first clause past, second clause past perf.*)
18 Onkel Richard / werden / wieder krank / vorgestern . (*past perf.*)
19 wo / antreffen / Sie / ihn ? (*pres. perf.*)
20 Lilo / lassen / herumliegen / die Ansichtskarten . (*past*)
21 er / sitzen / allein am Tisch / und / essen . (*past, both clauses*)
22 bringen / er / eine Tasse Kaffee / Ihnen ? (*pres. perf.*)
23 ob / abfahren / er / schon ? (*past perf.*)
24 es / werden / viel kälter / morgen abend . (*fut.*)
25 diese Bilder / gefallen / am besten / mir . (*past perf.*)

B. Nouns and Adjectives

Copy the sentences and insert the correct German word or phrase:

1 Es war ein _____ Wiedersehen. (unexpected)
2 Wie viele _____ hat er jetzt? (sons)
3 Seid ihr denn wirklich _____? (engaged)
4 Wir haben ihn kurz vor _____ gesehen. (Christmas)
5 Der Hut sieht _____ aus, _____ ich dachte. (better than)
6 In _____ _____ gehst du denn? (which school)
7 Außerdem muß man an das _____ denken. (state exam)
8 In Deutschland gibt es viele _____ . (universities)
9 _____ Zimmer sind natürlich auch _____ . (larger; more expensive)
10 Unsere beiden _____ gehen aufs Gymnasium. (daughters)
11 Fährst du immer mit dem _____ ? (bus)
12 Das sind _____ von mir. (school friends)
13 Hast du wieder _____ gefunden? (part-time work)
14 Hans und Inge hatten gestern abend ein _____ . (date)
15 _____ Weine sind oft die _____ . (cheap; best ones)

C. Completion

Copy the sentences and supply the missing endings:

Ein jung____ Mann steht an ein____ klein____ Verkaufsstand und will einig____ Ansichtskarten haben. D____ billig____ Schwarzweißbilder gefallen ihm nicht. Er fragt nach besser____ Schwarzweißbilder____ und gut____ Farbfotos. D____ nett____, alt____ Verkäufer sagt, daß d____ Farbfotos wegen d____ höher____ Herstellungskosten wesentlich teur____ als die Schwarzweißbilder sind. D____ kleiner____ kosten 30, d____ größer____ 50 und 60 Pfennig. D____ jung____ Mann will ein groß____ Farbfoto d____ Dom____ kaufen. Unser gut____ Verkäufer hat auch ein schön____ Bild d____ Dom____. Es ist während d____ Festzug____ anläßlich d____ 800-Jahr-Feier aufgenommen. Dies____ Aufnahme gefällt unser____ jung____ Mann am best____, und er nimmt sie.

Dann fragt d____ tüchtig____, alt____ Verkäufer, ob es sonst noch etwas sein darf. Unser jung____ Mann will wissen, wessen Bild das auf d____ Titelseite ein____ illustriert____ Zeitschrift ist. Es ist ein groß____ Stern am Filmhimmel, aber d____ jung____ Mann kennt d____ reizend____ Mädchen nicht. Doch er sagt, daß sie gut aussieht. D____ Verkäufer meint, daß es kein hübscher____ Mädchen gibt. Er sagt, daß sie ein____ Tag____ ein____ Oscar bekommen wird. Er hat noch mehr Bilder von d____ Schön____, aber er kann sie d____ jung____ Mann nicht verkaufen, denn er ist glücklich verheiratet. D____ neu____ Zeitschrift und d____ groß____ Farbfoto d____ hoh____, alt____ Dom____ kosten zusammen ein____ Mark dreißig, und unser jung____, verheiratet____ Mann sagt: „Das ist billig____, als ich gedacht habe."

LISTENING PRACTICE

Listen to the recorded telephone conversation; then answer the following questions:

Käthe und Renate

1 Von wo spricht Käthe?
2 Was tut Käthe in Kiel?
3 Wie viele Menschen leben in Kiel?
4 Liegt Kiel an der Nordsee?
5 Wie alt ist die Universität in Kiel?
6 Wie heißt Käthes Freund, der Student?

Unit 21

Heinrich Heine

DIALOG

Ein unverhofftes Wiedersehen (Schluß)

1 **Heinrich:** Setz dich ans Fenster dort, da ist noch Platz für uns beide!

2 **Werner:** Gut, aber darf ich erst mal um eine Zigarette bitten? Ich habe meine vergessen.

3 **Heinrich:** Tut mir leid, aber sieh dorthin! Auf dem Schild steht: NICHT RAUCHEN.

4 **Werner:** Wieso, gibt es hier denn kein Raucherabteil mehr? Na, vielleicht ist das gar kein schlechter Gedanke.

5 **Heinrich:** Nun mußt du aber berichten! Hattest du nicht bereits dein Examen bestanden, als ich nach München zog?

An Unexpected Reunion (Conclusion)

1 Sit down at the window there. There's still room for both of us.

setzen set   **sich setzen** *acc. refl.*

2 O.K. But can I ask for a cigarette first? I forgot mine.

die Zigarette, die Zigaretten · **vergessen: er vergißt, er vergaß, er hat vergessen**

3 Sorry, but look over there. On the sign it says: NO SMOKING.

leid painful, disagreeable   **es tut mir leid** I'm sorry

4 How come? Isn't there a smoking section here any more? Well, maybe that's not such a bad idea.

das Raucherabteil   **der Raucher, die Raucher** smoker + **das Abteil, die Abteile** section, compartment · **der Gedanke,** *acc. dat. sg.* **Gedanken,** *gen. sg.* **Gedankens,** *pl.* **die Gedanken** idea

5 But now let's hear from you. Hadn't you already passed your exam when I moved to Munich?

berichten report · **bestehen: er besteht, er bestand, er hat bestanden** pass (an exam); consist · **als** *subord. conj.* when

6 Werner: Allerdings! Und danach hatte mich mein Vater in eine seiner Fabriken im Ausland gesteckt.

7 Heinrich: Ja, richtig, davon hatte ich noch gehört. Du warst ja zu deinem Vater ins Geschäft gegangen.

8 Werner: Oh, ich muß schon gleich aussteigen. Treffen wir uns heute noch irgendwo?

9 Heinrich: Natürlich, ruf mich doch im Büro an. Ich schreibe dir meine Telefonnummer auf.

10 Werner: Gut, hier sind Papier und Bleistift. Du weißt, ich war schon immer vergeßlich.

SUPPLEMENT

1 Meine Eltern sind nach Bayern gezogen.

2 Meine Großeltern sind umgezogen.

3 Meine Großmutter hat sich umgezogen.

4 Das Kind zieht sich aus.

5 Es zieht sich das Hemd aus.

6	Right. And after that my father had stuck me in one of his factories abroad.	**allerdings** to be sure · **die Fabrik, die Fabriken** · **das Ausland** foreign countries (in general)
7	Yes, right. I had heard about that, too. You had gone into your father's business, hadn't you?	
8	Oh, I have to get off right away now. Can we meet someplace later on today?	**treffen**: er trifft, er traf, er hat getroffen **sich treffen** *acc. refl.* meet each other
9	Of course. Why don't you just call me at the office? I'll write down my telephone number.	**anrufen**: er ruft an, er rief an, er hat angerufen call up **rufen** call, shout · **das Büro, die Büros** · **aufschreiben**: er schreibt auf, er schrieb auf, er hat aufgeschrieben **schreiben** write · **die Telefonnummer das Telefon, die Telefone + die Nummer, die Nummern**
10	Good. Here's paper and pencil. You know, I always was forgetful.	**das Papier, die Papiere** · **der Bleistift das Blei** lead + **der Stift, die Stifte** pencil, crayon; spike, peg · **vergeßlich vergessen** forget

---

1	My parents moved to Bavaria.	**die Eltern** *pl. only*
2	My grandparents moved.	**die Großeltern groß + die Eltern**
3	My grandmother changed clothes.	**die Großmutter groß + die Mutter** · **sich umziehen** *acc. refl.* change clothes
4	The child is undressing.	**sich ausziehen** *acc. refl.* undress
5	He is taking off his shirt.	**sich ausziehen** *dat. refl.* take off (articles of clothing) · **das Hemd, die Hemden**

6 Großvater zieht sich an.

7 Er zieht sich den Anzug an.

8 Meine Schwester hat sich an den Tisch gesetzt.

9 Unsere Nichte hat sich nicht geändert.

10 Unser Neffe hat sich entschuldigt.

11 Was kaufen Sie sich?

12 Was wünschen Sie sich?

13 Was denken Sie sich?

6	Grandfather is dressing.	**der Großvater** groß + der Vater · **sich anziehen** *acc. refl.* dress
7	He is putting on the suit.	**sich anziehen** *dat. refl.* put on (articles of clothing) · **der Anzug, die Anzüge**
8	My sister sat down at the table.	**die Schwester, die Schwestern**
9	Our niece hasn't changed. (*I.e.* she is still the same as she used to be.)	**die Nichte, die Nichten**
10	Our nephew excused himself.	**der Neffe, die Neffen** (Group V) · **sich entschuldigen** *acc. refl.* excuse oneself
11	What are you buying for yourself?	**sich kaufen** *dat. refl.* buy for oneself
12	What would you like to have? (What do you wish for yourself?)	**sich wünschen** *dat. refl.*
13	What do you imagine?	**sich denken** *dat. refl.* imagine

AUDIOLINGUAL DRILLS

A. Directed Dialog

Sagen Sie, daß Werner sich ans Fenster dort setzen soll!
Werner soll sich ans Fenster dort setzen.

Sagen Sie, daß da noch Platz für sie beide ist!
Da ist noch Platz für sie beide.

Sagen Sie, daß Werner erst mal um eine Zigarette bittet!
Werner bittet erst mal um eine Zigarette.

Sagen Sie, daß Werner seine vergessen hat!
Werner hat seine vergessen.

Sagen Sie, daß auf dem Schild NICHT RAUCHEN steht!
Auf dem Schild steht NICHT RAUCHEN.

Fragen Sie, ob es hier kein Raucherabteil mehr gibt!
Gibt es hier kein Raucherabteil mehr?

Sagen Sie, daß das vielleicht gar kein schlechter Gedanke ist!
Das ist vielleicht gar kein schlechter Gedanke.

Sagen Sie, daß Werner nun berichten muß!
Werner muß nun berichten.

Sagen Sie, daß er bereits sein Examen bestanden hatte, als Heinrich nach München zog!
Er hatte bereits sein Examen bestanden, als Heinrich nach München zog.

Sagen Sie, daß sein Vater ihn danach in eine seiner Fabriken im Ausland gesteckt hatte!
Sein Vater hatte ihn danach in eine seiner Fabriken im Ausland gesteckt.

Sagen Sie, daß Heinrich davon noch gehört hatte!
Heinrich hatte davon noch gehört.

Sagen Sie, daß Werner zu seinem Vater ins Geschäft gegangen war!
Werner war zu seinem Vater ins Geschäft gegangen.

Fragen Sie, ob Heinrich und Werner sich heute noch irgendwo treffen!
Treffen Heinrich und Werner sich heute noch irgendwo?

Sagen Sie, daß Heinrich seine Telefonnummer aufschreibt!
Heinrich schreibt seine Telefonnummer auf.

B. Reflexive Verbs (*See Grammar* §21.3)

Accusative reflexives

1 Repeat:

Ich setze mich ans Fenster.   Wir setzen uns ans Fenster.
Du setzt dich ans Fenster.   Ihr setzt euch ans Fenster.
Er setzt sich ans Fenster.   Sie setzen sich ans Fenster.
Sie setzt sich ans Fenster.   Setzen Sie sich ans Fenster, Herr Winkler?
Es setzt sich ans Fenster.

2 Substitute the new subject, and make the accusative reflexive pronoun agree with it in person and number:

Ich täusche mich nicht. **er**
Er täuscht sich nicht. **wir**
Wir täuschen uns nicht. **meine Eltern**
Meine Eltern täuschen sich nicht. **ihr**
Ihr täuscht euch nicht.

Hast du dich schon entschuldigt? **Ilse**
Hat Ilse sich schon entschuldigt? **ihr**
Habt ihr euch schon entschuldigt? **ihr Bruder**
Hat ihr Bruder sich schon entschuldigt? **ich**
Habe ich mich schon entschuldigt?

Wir müssen uns bald umziehen. **das Kind**
Das Kind muß sich bald umziehen. **du**
Du mußt dich bald umziehen. **ihr**
Ihr müßt euch bald umziehen. **meine Schwestern**
Meine Schwestern müssen sich bald umziehen.

Dein Neffe hat sich wenig geändert. **seine Nichte**
Seine Nichte hat sich wenig geändert. **wir**
Wir haben uns wenig geändert. **ihre Großeltern**
Ihre Großeltern haben sich wenig geändert. **du**
Du hast dich wenig geändert.

Er zog sich schnell an. **ich**
Ich zog mich schnell an. **das Kind**
Das Kind zog sich schnell an. **wir**
Wir zogen uns schnell an. **du**
Du zogst dich schnell an.

Dative reflexives

3 Repeat:

Ich ziehe mir das Hemd an.   Es zieht sich das Hemd an.
Du ziehst dir das Hemd an.   Wir ziehen uns neue Hemden an.
Er zieht sich das Hemd an.   Ihr zieht euch neue Hemden an.
Sie zieht sich das Hemd an.   Sie ziehen sich neue Hemden an.

4 Substitute the new subject, and make the reflexive pronoun agree:

Kaufst du dir einen Hut? **er**
Kauft er sich einen Hut? **ihr**
Kauft ihr euch einen Hut? **deine Nichte**
Kauft deine Nichte sich einen Hut? **die Jungen**
Kaufen die Jungen sich einen Hut?

Muß ich mir diesen Anzug anziehen? **er**
Muß er sich diesen Anzug anziehen? **du**
Mußt du dir diesen Anzug anziehen? **das Kind**
Muß das Kind sich diesen Anzug anziehen? **Werner**
Muß Werner sich diesen Anzug anziehen?

Wir hatten uns einen Sohn gewünscht.   **ich**
Ich hatte mir einen Sohn gewünscht.   **Frau Schmidt**
Frau Schmidt hatte sich einen Sohn gewünscht.   **ihr**
Ihr hattet euch einen Sohn gewünscht.   **meine Eltern**
Meine Eltern hatten sich einen Sohn gewünscht.

Hans zog sich das Hemd aus.   **ich**
Ich zog mir das Hemd aus.   **das Kind**
Das Kind zog sich das Hemd aus.   **du**
Du zogst dir das Hemd aus.   **er**
Er zog sich das Hemd aus.

So etwas kann ich mir nicht denken.   **er**
So etwas kann er sich nicht denken.   **wir**
So etwas können wir uns nicht denken.   **du**
So etwas kannst du dir nicht denken.   **ihr**
So etwas könnt ihr euch nicht denken.

The reciprocal pronoun *einander*

5 Substitute **einander** for the reflexive pronoun:

Wir kennen uns schon zehn Jahre.
Wir kennen einander schon zehn Jahre.

Ihr könnt euch heute abend treffen.
Ihr könnt einander heute abend treffen.

Sie haben sich immer gern gehabt.
Sie haben einander immer gern gehabt.

Wir rufen uns jeden Tag an.
Wir rufen einander jeden Tag an.

6 Substitute the reflexive pronoun for **einander**:

Wir sehen einander morgen früh.
Wir sehen uns morgen früh.

Habt ihr einander in der Vorlesung getroffen?
Habt ihr euch in der Vorlesung getroffen?

Wann haben sie einander kennengelernt?
Wann haben sie sich kennengelernt?

Wir rufen einander häufig an.
Wir rufen uns häufig an.

C. Irregular Imperatives (*See Grammar* §21.4)

7 Change the **sollen**-phrases to direct commands.

Examples:
Du sollst ihm eine Zigarette geben.
Gib ihm eine Zigarette!

Ihr sollt ihm die Bücher geben.
Gebt ihm die Bücher!

Du sollst ihm das Geld geben.
Gib ihm das Geld!

Du sollst mich doch mitnehmen.
Nimm mich doch mit!

Ihr sollt uns den Wagen geben.
Gebt uns den Wagen!

Ihr sollt nicht immer sprechen.
Sprecht nicht immer!

Du sollst uns am Schillerplatz treffen.
Triff uns am Schillerplatz!

Du sollst diese Geschichte lesen.
Lies diese Geschichte!

Ihr sollt uns morgen treffen.
Trefft uns morgen!

Du sollst den Kuchen nicht vergessen.
Vergiß den Kuchen nicht!

Ihr sollt nicht so viel essen.
Eßt nicht so viel!

Du sollst doch mal dorthin sehen.
Sieh doch mal dorthin!

Du sollst mir heute helfen.
Hilf mir heute!

D. Conjunctions (*See Grammar* §21.5)

8 Substitute the new conjunction, and put the finite verb of the second clause in the correct position.

Example:
Er spricht langsam, und wir verstehen ihn.   **damit**
Er spricht langsam, damit wir ihn verstehen.

Ich ziehe mich um, und ich kann ins Theater gehen.   **damit**
Ich ziehe mich um, damit ich ins Theater gehen kann.   **denn**
Ich ziehe mich um, denn ich kann ins Theater gehen.   **wenn**
Ich ziehe mich um, wenn ich ins Theater gehen kann.   **oder**
Ich ziehe mich um, oder ich kann ins Theater gehen.

9 Substitute the new main clause, and put the finite verb of the main clause after the **als**-clause.

Example:
Als wir dort wohnten, regnete es häufig.   **die Sonne schien**
Als wir dort wohnten, schien die Sonne.

Als wir dort wohnten, schien die Sonne fast immer.   **es regnete oft**
Als wir dort wohnten, regnete es oft.   **ich ging in die Schule**
Als wir dort wohnten, ging ich in die Schule.   **wir waren gute Freunde**
Als wir dort wohnten, waren wir gute Freunde.   **du warst zehn Jahre alt**
Als wir dort wohnten, warst du zehn Jahre alt.   **er hielt Ruhe**
Als wir dort wohnten, hielt er Ruhe.   **ich hatte noch ein Sparbuch**
Als wir dort wohnten, hatte ich noch ein Sparbuch.

10 Substitute the new phrase in the **wenn**-clause, with the finite verb last.

Example:
Wenn du Ruhe hältst, bist du bald wieder auf den Beinen.   **du schläfst ordentlich**
Wenn du ordentlich schläfst, bist du bald wieder auf den Beinen.

Wenn du ordentlich schläfst, bist du bald wieder auf den Beinen.   **du ißt genug**
Wenn du genug ißt, bist du bald wieder auf den Beinen.   **du trinkst viel**
Wenn du viel trinkst, bist du bald wieder auf den Beinen.   **du bekommst laufend Medizin**
Wenn du laufend Medizin bekommst, bist du bald wieder auf den Beinen.   **du bist schön brav**
Wenn du schön brav bist, bist du bald wieder auf den Beinen.   **du bleibst zu Hause**
Wenn du zu Hause bleibst, bist du bald wieder auf den Beinen.

E. Questions and Answers

Wohin setzen sich die Freunde?
Sie setzen sich an ein Fenster im Bus.

Warum bittet Werner seinen Freund um eine Zigarette?
Werner hat seine Zigaretten vergessen.

Warum raucht Werner nicht?
Es steht auf einem Schild, daß man im Bus nicht rauchen soll.

Meint Werner, daß das so schlimm ist?
Nein, denn er sagt, daß das vielleicht gar kein schlechter Gedanke ist.

Was hatte Werner gerade gemacht, als Heinrich von Kiel nach München zog?
Werner hatte gerade sein Examen bestanden.

Wo war Werner danach gewesen?
Er hatte für seinen Vater in einer Fabrik im Ausland gearbeitet.

Was wollen die Freunde heute noch tun?
Sie wollen sich noch irgendwo treffen, so daß sie noch mehr sprechen können.

Wo soll Werner Heinrich anrufen?
Werner soll Heinrich im Büro anrufen.

GRAMMAR

21.1 Word-Formation

Verb-noun pairs

As in English, there are many verb-noun pairs in German. Many of these relationships are immediately obvious: **fragen** *ask*, **die Frage** *the question*; **verkaufen** *sell*, **der Verkauf** *the sale*. Sometimes the related noun looks like the stem of the past or the past participle of the verb: **tun** *do*, **die Tat** *the deed*; **gehen** *walk*, **der Gang** *the walk*; **springen** *jump*, **der Sprung** *the jump*; **stehen** *stand*, **der Stand** *the stand*. Occasionally the stem vowel of the noun is unlike any of the vowels in the principal parts: **sprechen** *speak*, **der Spruch** *saying*; **fließen** *flow*, **der Fluß** *the river*. Other differences will be apparent in the lists below, but the relationship is often still clear enough, so that guessing the meanings of new words from derivational clues, with the help of context, is relatively easy. The practice of guessing can result in an enormous increase in your vocabulary, and words that are guessed are remembered best. The following list presents a number of nouns, mostly new ones, that are related to verbs you already know:

antworten answer	die Antwort, -en* answer
bauen build	der Bau, die Bauten building
berichten report	der Bericht, -e report
bitten ask, beg	die Bitte, -n request
decken cover; set (table)	die Decke, -n cover; cloth; blanket; ceiling
fahren drive; ride	die Fahrt, -en drive; ride
gefallen please	der Gefallen, - favor
glauben believe	der Glaube belief
grenzen border	die Grenze, -n border
helfen help	die Hilfe help
kaufen buy	der Kauf, ⸚e purchase
klingen sound; ring	der Klang, ⸚e sound; ring
laufen run	der Lauf, ⸚e current; track; career
leiden suffer	das Leid harm; wrong; sorrow
liegen lie	die Lage, -n situation; position
raten guess	der Rat counsel, advice
rauchen smoke	der Rauch smoke
regnen rain	der Regen rain
rufen call; shout	der Ruf, -e call; reputation
sagen say	die Sage, -n legend; fable
scheinen shine	der Schein, -e shine; light

* From now on the regular plural endings of nouns will be indicated as follows: - (no ending), -e, -er, -n, -en. If the stem vowel umlauts, this will also be shown: ⸚, ⸚e, ⸚er.

schlafen sleep	der Schlaf sleep
schmecken taste	der Geschmack taste
sitzen sit	der Sitz, -e seat
spotten ridicule, mock	der Spott mockery, ridicule
sprechen speak	die Sprache, -n language
	der Spruch, ⸗e saying; verdict
	das Gespräch, -e conversation
studieren study	das Studium, -ien study
verstehen understand	der Verstand understanding; reason; intelligence
wünschen wish	der Wunsch, ⸗e wish

The following list presents new verbs that are related to nouns you already know:

das Abteil, -e section; compartment	abteilen separate
der Anfang, ⸗e beginning	anfangen begin
der Anzug, ⸗e suit (of clothes)	anziehen put on
die Bahn, -en road; course; railway	bahnen make passable; pave
der Besuch, -e visit	besuchen visit
das Buch, ⸗er book	buchen book; record
der Dank thanks; gratitude	danken thank
der Fall, ⸗e fall; case (grammar; law)	fallen fall
die Farbe, -n color	färben dye; paint
die Feier, -n celebration	feiern celebrate
der Film, -e film	filmen film
das Geld, -er money	gelten be worth
das Glück happiness; luck	glücken succeed; turn out well
das Haus, ⸗er house	hausen house
die Hitze heat	heizen heat
der Hut, ⸗e hat	hüten protect; watch over
der Klatsch splash	klatschen splash; clap (hands); gossip
der Preis, -e price; prize	preisen praise
der Quatsch nonsense	quatschen talk nonsense
die Ruhe rest	ruhen rest
die Schule, -n school	schulen teach, train
der Schweiß sweat	schwitzen sweat
die Sonne sun	sonnen expose to the sun
der Tag, -e day	tagen dawn; meet
der Teil, -e part	teilen share; divide
der Unterschied, -e difference	unterscheiden differentiate
der Zug, ⸗e train; procession; pull(ing)	ziehen pull; move

21.2 Singular and Plural of Nouns

das Abteil, -e
der Anzug, ⸚e
der Bleistift, -e
die Fabrik, -en
der Gedanke, -ns, -n*
die Großmutter, ⸚
der Großvater, ⸚
das Hemd, -en
der Neffe, -n, -n
die Nichte, -n

die Nummer, -n
das Papier, -e
der Raucher, -
das Raucherabteil, -e
das Schild, -er
die Schwester, -n
das Telefon, -e
die Telefonnummer, -n
die Zigarette, -n

21.3 Reflexive Verbs

A reflexive verb is one whose *subject* and *pronoun object* both refer to the same person or thing:

She sees *herself* in the mirror.
I bought *myself* a new hat.
Those people have caused *themselves* a lot of trouble.

If the subject and object do not refer to the same person or thing, the verb is not reflexive:

She sees *me* in the mirror.
I bought *you* a new hat.
Those people have caused *us* a lot of trouble.

Reflexive pronouns

The German reflexive pronouns are identical with the personal pronouns in all but the 3rd person and the standard form of address:

1st person	mich mir		uns
2nd person	dich dir		euch
3rd person	sich		sich
standard		sich	

Unlike the 3rd person singular personal pronoun, and unlike the 1st and 2nd persons singular, the reflexive **sich** does not show a distinction between the accusative and dative cases.

---

* Whenever two endings are given, the first refers to the genitive singular, the second to the plural and the accusative and dative singular.

Accusative reflexives

Ich setze **mich**.
I sit down. (I seat myself.)

Ich täusche **mich** nicht.
I am not mistaken. (I am not deceiving myself.)

Sie hat **sich** angezogen.
She got dressed.

Wir hatten **uns** bei ihnen entschuldigt.
We had apologized to them.

Wie das Wetter **sich** geändert hat!
How the weather has changed!

Dative reflexives

Ich wollte **mir** eine Zeitung kaufen.
I wanted to buy (for myself) a newspaper.

Er hat **sich** einen neuen Wagen gewünscht.
He wished for a new car.

Können Sie **sich** so etwas denken?
Can you imagine such a thing?

Warum hast du **dir** diesen Anzug angezogen?
Why did you put on this suit?

Er zieht **sich** das Hemd aus.
He is taking off his shirt.

Some differences in meaning

In some instances the use of the reflexive pronoun merely specifies the recipient of the action of the verb; the meaning of the verb itself is not changed by the presence of the reflexive:

Ich kaufe **mir** einen Hut.	Ich kaufe **meinem Mann** einen Hut.
I buy myself a hat.	I buy my husband a hat.
Er setzte **sich** ans Fenster.	Er setzte **die Leute** ans Fenster.
He sat down (seated himself) at the window.	He seated the people at the window.

Some verbs, however, mean one thing when used nonreflexively and something quite different when used reflexively; or the meaning may change depending on whether the reflexive is accusative or dative:

Reflexive	*Nonreflexive*
Er hat **sich** umgezogen. He *changed clothes*.	Er ist umgezogen. He *moved*.
Er kann **sich** so etwas nicht denken. He can't *imagine* such a thing.	Er will nicht mehr daran denken. He doesn't want to *think* about it any more.

Accusative reflexive	*Dative reflexive*
Ich ziehe **mich** an. I'm *getting dressed*.	Ich ziehe **mir** das Hemd an. I'm *putting on* the shirt.
Ich ziehe **mich** aus. I'm *getting undressed*.	Ich ziehe **mir** den Anzug aus. I'm *taking off* the suit.

Einander

The plural reflexive pronouns **uns**, **euch**, **sich** may be ambiguous; that is, they may convey the meaning *ourselves, yourselves, themselves*, but they may also mean *each other*:

Diese Leute täuschen **sich**.
1. These people are deceiving *themselves* (are mistaken).
2. These people are deceiving *each other*.

When the intended meaning is *each other*, then the reciprocal pronoun **einander** may be used instead of the plural reflexive, thus avoiding any possible ambiguity:

Treffen wir **uns** heute noch irgendwo?
Treffen wir **einander** heute noch irgendwo?
Shall we meet someplace later on today?

Warum helft ihr **euch** nicht?
Warum helft ihr **einander** nicht?
Why don't you help each other?

Sie haben **sich** schon ewig nicht gesehen.
Sie haben **einander** schon ewig nicht gesehen.
They haven't seen each other for ages.

21.4 Irregular Imperatives

Turn back to Grammar §8.5 and review the descriptions of the German imperative verb forms. Note particularly the vowel change that occurs in the 2nd singular (**du**) imperative of certain verbs. Some new verbs that show this change from an **e**-sound to an **i**-sound are:

Infinitive	Du-*indicative*	Du-*imperative*
geben	gibst	gib!
treffen	triffst	triff!
sprechen	sprichst	sprich!
vergessen	vergißt	vergiß!

21.5 Conjunctions

A conjunction is a word that joins two words, phrases, or clauses:

John *and* Jean live over there.
He reads a lot of books *but* doesn't learn much.
I don't know *if* I can go along.

In German there are two kinds of conjunctions: *coordinating* and *subordinating*.

Coordinating conjunctions

Coordinating conjunctions are used to join coordinate elements in a sentence, i.e. elements of equal grammatical rank. They may join two main clauses in a compound sentence; the position of the finite verb in a main clause is not affected by the presence of a coordinating conjunction at the beginning of that clause:

Er spricht langsam, **und** wir verstehen ihn.
He speaks slowly, *and* we understand him.

Er zieht sich um, **denn** er will ins Theater gehen.
He is changing his clothes *because* he wants to go to the theater.

The German coordinating conjunctions are:

aber but, however

Diese Bilder sind gut, **aber** sie sind auch teuer.
These pictures are good, *but* they are also expensive.

denn for, because

Werner kann nicht rauchen, **denn** er hat seine Zigaretten vergessen.
Werner can't smoke *because* he forgot his cigarettes.

oder or

Übst du Geige, **oder** gehst du zum Baden?
Are you going to practice the violin, *or* are you going swimming?

sondern but, on the contrary

Sie helfen uns nicht, **sondern** wir helfen ihnen.
They aren't helping us, *but* we are helping them.

und and

Ich gehe zum Baden, **und** du übst Geige.
I'll go swimming *and* you practice the violin.

Subordinating conjunctions

Subordinating conjunctions are used to join a main clause and a dependent clause in a complex sentence. Dependent clauses have their finite verbs in last position (see Grammar §§3.2, 3.3, and 7.4); a subordinating conjunction thus has the effect of moving the finite verb of the clause to last position:

Ich weiß, **daß** du hier wohnst.
I know *that* you live here.

Als wir dort waren, regnete es häufig.
When we lived there, it rained a lot.

When the dependent clause stands first in the sentence, it is followed directly by the finite verb of the main clause, as in the second example above.

A few of the more common subordinating conjunctions are:

als when

Er hatte sein Examen schon bestanden, **als** ich nach München zog.
He had passed his exam *when* I moved to Munich.

damit so that, in order that

Ich ziehe mich um, **damit** ich ins Theater gehen kann.
I'm changing clothes *so that* I can go to the theater.

ob if, whether

Weißt du, **ob** die Sonne heute nachmittag scheint?
Do you know *if* the sun will be shining this afternoon?

obwohl although

Wir sagen ,,Sie'' zu einander, **obwohl** wir uns schon seit Jahren kennen.
We say "Sie" to each other, *although* we've known each other for years.

weil because

Er kann nicht rauchen, **weil** er seine Zigaretten vergessen hat.
He can't smoke *because* he forgot his cigarettes.

wenn if, when, whenever

Wenn du Ruhe hältst, bist du bald wieder auf den Beinen.
If you stay quiet, you'll soon be on your feet again.

wenn auch even though, even if

Wir haben ein Sparbuch, **wenn auch** nicht viel darauf ist.
We have a savings account, *even though* there isn't much in it.

Some problems of meaning

aber: sondern

The two coordinating conjunctions **aber** and **sondern** have very similar meanings, but they are used in different ways. If the meaning is *on the contrary*, then you have to use **sondern** and not **aber**. It occurs most often in the pattern **nicht X, sondern Y** *not X but on the contrary Y*:

Er heißt nicht Hans, **sondern** Rolf.
His name isn't Hans *but (on the contrary) Rolf*.

Er hilft mir nicht, **sondern** ich helfe ihm.
He isn't helping me, *but (on the contrary) I'm helping him*.

Er sieht leidend aus, **aber** ich kann ihm nicht helfen.
He looks bad, *but* I can't help him.

Du gehst ins Theater, **aber** ich muß zu Hause bleiben.
You go to the theater, *but* I have to stay home.

als: wenn

The two subordinating conjunctions **als** and **wenn** have similar meanings. They are used differently, however, and must not be confused. With a present tense verb, **wenn** means *if* or *whenever*:

Wenn die Sonne scheint, gehen wir zum Baden.
1. *If* the sun shines, we'll go swimming.
2. *Whenever* the sun shines, we go swimming.

With a past tense verb it means *whenever*, and clearly implies that the action or condition expressed by that verb was recurrent:

Wenn Michael in die Vorlesungen gehen mußte, kaufte Frau Schmidt für ihn ein.
Whenever Michael had to go to his lectures, Mrs. Schmidt went shopping for him.

Als with a past tense verb, however, refers to a single point or period in past time; it does not imply recurrence:

Er hatte sein Examen schon bestanden, **als** ich nach München zog.
He had passed his exam *when* I moved to Munich.

Als ich ins Zimmer kam, hielt er die Zeitschrift falsch herum.
When I came into the room, he was holding the magazine upside down.

WRITING

A. Verbs

Arrange the elements to form German sentences; use the tense indicated:

1 dürfen / bitten / ich / um eine Tasse Kaffee ?   (*pres.*)
2 er / umziehen / vor sechs Wochen .   (*past*)
3 sehen / dahin /,/ Werner !
4 hier / es / geben / kein Schild mehr .   (*pres.*)
5 außerdem / ich / sein / verlobt / noch nicht einmal .   (*pres.*)
6 geben / eine Zigarette / mir /,/ Heinrich !
7 er / anziehen / sich .   (*pres. perf.*)
8 vergessen / er / seine Telefonnummer ?   (*past. perf.*)
9 treffen / wir / im Geschäft / uns !
10 warum / du / berichten / von deiner Nichte / uns ?   (*past*)
11 das / sein / kein guter Gedanke .   (*past perf.*)
12 kommen / Sie / nach Hause / um fünf Uhr ?   (*pres. perf.*)
13 geben / eurem Vater / es /,/ Kinder !
14 ich / bitten / sie / um einen Bleistift .   (*pres. perf.*)
15 wollen / setzen / du / dich / ans Fenster dort ?   (*pres.*)
16 wann / ziehen / ihr / nach Bayern ?   (*pres. perf.*)
17 bestehen / du / das Staatsexamen ?   (*past perf.*)
18 vergessen / die Bücher / nicht /,/ Lilo !
19 es / tun / mir / leid .   (*past*)
20 aufschreiben / die Nummer /,/ Heinrich !
21 stecken / er / seinen Sohn / in eine seiner Fabriken ?   (*past*)
22 wir / gehen / ins Geschäft / zu unserem Großvater .   (*past*)
23 setzen / dich / an den Tisch / und / essen !
24 wann / du / treffen / deinen Neffen ?   (*past*)
25 anziehen / dir / den neuen Anzug !
26 als / er / anrufen / uns /,/ wir / sein / zu Hause / nicht .   (*past, both clauses*)

B. Nouns and Adjectives

Copy the sentences and supply the correct German word or phrase:

1. Hast du _____ _____ für mich? (a cigarette)
2. Das war _____ _____ _____. (the worst idea)
3. Es gibt _____ _____ mehr. (no smoking sections)
4. Warum bist du immer so _____? (forgetful)
5. Hat er dich in _____ _____ gesteckt? (a factory)
6. Ich wollte es mit _____ _____ aufschreiben. (my pencil)
7. Er hatte ihnen von _____ _____ _____ berichtet. (his younger nephew)
8. _____ _____ sind im Ausland. (our parents)
9. Was haben Sie von _____ _____ erfahren? (his sons)
10. _____ _____ Kinder haben sich schnell verändert. (your four)
11. Ich habe den Titel _____ _____ vergessen. (of this illustrated magazine)
12. Was steht denn auf _____ _____? (this sign)
13. Es war nur _____ _____ _____. (a short visit)
14. In _____ _____ _____ _____ wohnten wir in Frankfurt. (the good old times)
15. _____ _____ _____ sind alle ins Ausland gefahren. (our married daughters)
16. Vielleicht gehört es _____ _____ _____. (the other people)
17. Bringen Sie mir bitte _____ _____ _____ _____! (a bottle of cold beer)
18. Was ist denn mit _____ _____ _____ hier? (this green suit)
19. Er ist der Sohn _____ _____ _____. (of my best friend)
20. _____ _____ _____ ist ein Feiertag. (the thirtieth of May)

C. Reflexive Verbs

Write the corresponding German sentences:

1. Can you think about it?
2. Can you imagine such a thing?
3. He's getting dressed.
4. He's putting on his shirt.
5. My nephew moved.
6. My nephew changed his clothes.
7. I had gotten undressed.
8. I had taken off the suit.
9. Do we have to sit down at this table?
10. We've been sitting here for ages.

D. Conjunctions

Combine the sentences by means of the correct German conjunction; be sure to insert a comma between clauses:

1 (when)   Ich setzte mich ans Fenster. Ich sah den Wagen umkippen.
2 Ich gehe zum Baden.   (and)   Du darfst auch mit.
3 Er wird die Nummer aufschreiben.   (if)   Er kann einen Bleistift finden.
4 Willst du ins Theater gehen?   (or)   Bleibst du lieber zu Hause?
5 Ich wollte ihn um eine Zigarette bitten.   (but)   Er hatte seine auch vergessen.
6 Er ist bald weggegangen.   (so that)   Er konnte sich umziehen.
7 (whenever)   Sie setzte sich. Man rief sie an.
8 Michael hat Monika gern.   (because)   Sie sieht gut aus.
9 Ich kann Ihnen nicht sagen.   (whether)   Er ist noch zu Hause.
10 Sie ist ein bißchen zu flott.   (but)   Was soll man machen?

E. Structure Retention

Substitute the new words for those directly above them, and make all the necessary changes:

1 Wir haben uns eine ganze Woche nicht gesehen.
   Ihr   Jahr   treffen

2 Ich hatte das schon von meinem Bruder   erfahren.
   Du   dein   Schwester hören.

3 Früher wohnte ein   guter Schulfreund von mir in dieser Stadt.
   Damals leben   zwei alt   Tante   er   Dorf

4 Der frühere Schulfreund war damals noch nicht verlobt.
   Mein   heute

5 Er hat jetzt einen kleinen Sohn   und zwei größere Töchter.
           damals   Tochter   Söhne

6 Ich fahre jeden Tag   um diese Zeit in das kleine Dorf.
   Er   Woche an   Tag   nah Stadt

7 Sie setzen sich ans große Fenster.
   Wir   in alt Wagen

8 Darf ich erst mal um eine Zigarette bitten?
        wir   Bleistift

9 Du hattest dein Examen bestanden, als ich nach München zog.
   Ich   wir   Schweiz

10 Mein Vater hat mich in eine seiner Fabriken im Ausland gesteckt.
       Tante   ihr   Schulen   Belgien

READING PRACTICE

Werner Bäckers Vater

Werner Bäckers Vater ist ein älterer Herr, so Anfang sechzig. Er hat fünf Fabriken und viel Geld. Zwei seiner Fabriken sind in Deutschland, drei im Ausland. Die deutschen Fabriken liegen in Kiel und Hamburg, die ausländischen in Dänemark, Holland und Belgien. Eine sechste Fabrik lag in Ostdeutschland, bei Berlin. Aber Herr Bäcker weiß nicht, was ihr passiert ist.

Werners Vater denkt oft an alte Zeiten. Früher war alles besser, sagt man. Aber Herr Bäcker glaubt nicht recht daran. Natürlich ist es besser, jung zu sein, aber leicht war es früher auch nicht. Seit Anfang 1900 gab es oft schlimme Zeiten in Europa. Jedenfalls mußte Werners Vater schwer arbeiten. Es ist nicht so leicht, in schweren Zeiten aus einer Fabrik fünf, eigentlich ja sogar sechs Fabriken zu machen.

Aber Herr Bäcker hat auch gute Zeiten gesehen. Als er seine Frau kennenlernte und die Kinder kamen — zwei Söhne und zwei Töchter — das waren gewiß glückliche Zeiten. Und Arbeit hat ihm immer Spaß gemacht. Auch ist eigentlich nie jemand richtig krank gewesen in der Familie. Keiner mußte jedenfalls ins Krankenhaus. Das ist gewiß ein Glück.

Beide Söhne sind im Geschäft des Vaters. Werner, der ältere von den beiden, hat wirklich Interesse an Fabriken, aber Ulrich, der jüngere Sohn, hat gar keinen Spaß daran. Er hat es lieber, flott zu leben, statt zu arbeiten. Werners Vater ist natürlich unglücklich darüber, aber machen kann er auch nichts dagegen. Die Freunde sagen, daß Ulrich viel zu früh viel zu viel Geld hatte.

Unit 22

READING

Kleine Einführung in das „Sie"-Problem

Jedes Land hat seine Sitten. Das weiß jeder. Einige solche Sitten kann man gleich verstehen, sie sind dem Ausländer[g] ganz natürlich. Andere aber kann man nur schwer verstehen. Sie sind dem Ausländer fremd, und sie bleiben es ihm vielleicht für immer.

Man kann viel tun, um fremde Sitten besser zu verstehen. Zuerst muß man sie richtig kennen. Eine Sache richtig kennen, bedeutet ja fast immer, sie bald zu verstehen. Wenn ein Ausländer eine fremde Sitte erst einmal wirklich kennt, wird er sie wahrscheinlich sehr bald nicht mehr fremd finden. Und das ist ein guter Anfang.

Natürlich sind auch viele deutsche Sitten dem Ausländer fremd. Eine bestimmte Sitte findet der Amerikaner besonders eigenartig, fremd eben. Über diese wollen wir hier sprechen. Das ist die Sitte, zu fast allen Menschen „Sie" zu sagen. Für viele Amerikaner sieht das unmodern aus, sogar unfreundlich.

Tatsächlich macht der Deutsche mit „Sie" und „du" Unterschiede zwischen den Menschen, aber das hat nichts mit Klassen- oder Rangunterschieden zu tun. Ein „Sie" bedeutet nicht, daß man diesen Menschen noch zu fremd findet, um „du" zu ihm zu sagen. Es bedeutet, daß man diesen Menschen voll achtet. Dabei macht es gar keinen Unterschied, ob man mit ihm schon bekannt ist oder nicht. Natürlich kann man einen Menschen auch voll achten, wenn man „du" zu ihm sagt, aber „du" ist mehr ein Zeichen dafür, daß man ihn schon gut kennt, daß man vertraut mit ihm ist.

die Sitte, -n custom, habit
der Ausländer, -
fremd strange, foreign

bedeuten mean

besonders especially · eigenartig peculiar

die Klasse, -n (social) class · der Rang, ⸚e rank
achten respect · dabei with regard to this

vertraut intimate

1 Was hat jedes Land?
2 Was weiß jeder?
3 Kann man einige solche Sitten gleich verstehen?
4 Sind andere Sitten schwer zu verstehen?
5 Was muß man zuerst tun, um eine fremde Sitte zu verstehen?
6 Sind alle deutschen Sitten dem Ausländer fremd?
7 Was sagen die Deutschen zu fast allen Menschen?
8 Wie sieht das für viele Amerikaner aus?
9 Macht der Deutsche mit „du" und „Sie" Unterschiede zwischen den Menschen?
10 Hat das etwas mit Klassenunterschieden zu tun?
11 Ist „Sie" ein Zeichen dafür, daß man einen Menschen fremd findet?
12 Was bedeutet „Sie"?
13 Muß man bekannt sein, um „Sie" zu sagen?
14 Ist „du" ein Zeichen dafür, daß man einen Menschen nicht voll achtet?
15 Was ist das Zeichen für vertraute Freundschaft?

Mit Kindern ist man immer vertraut, man duzt sie also. Und kleine Kinder sind noch mit allen Menschen vertraut, sie duzen also alle. Sie tun das sogar noch, wenn sie in die Schule kommen. Sie werden zu ihrem Lehrer oder zu ihrer Lehrerin „Herr Meyer" oder „Fräulein (oder Frau) Schmidt" sagen, aber sie werden sie duzen. Das mag so vielleicht ein ganzes Jahr lang gehen, aber nicht viel länger. Dann tun die Kinder, wie sie es von den Erwachsenen gehört haben, sie siezen^g die „Großen", also auch ihre Lehrer.

Mit vierzehn oder fünfzehn Jahren sind Kinder keine richtigen Kinder mehr, man fängt an, sie zu siezen. Jetzt kommen auch viele von ihnen aus der Schule und gehen in die Lehre, sie werden Lehrlinge. Man wird noch „Hans" und „Erika" zu ihnen sagen, aber eben: „Hans, tun Sie doch mal dies!" oder „Erika, tun Sie doch mal das!"

Viele gehen natürlich auch noch weiter zur Schule. Für sie ist die Konfirmation^g der Stichtag. Von nun an werden fast alle Erwachsenen sie ganz so wie die Lehrlinge siezen. Nur die Lehrer werden sie immer noch duzen. In der Oberschule müssen die Schüler^g nämlich noch zwei Jahre warten, bis zu guter Letzt auch ihre Lehrer „Sie" zu ihnen sagen. Das ist dann natürlich ein großer Tag für die Schüler! Jetzt heißt es nicht mehr: „Hans, du mußt besser aufpassen," sondern: „Schulze, Sie müssen besser aufpassen!" Wenn das kein Ereignis ist! Die Schüler sind nun auch für die Schule keine Kinder mehr, sie sind offiziell^g erwachsen geworden, und ihre Lehrer müssen darauf Rücksicht nehmen.

Die normale^g Form des „Sie" ist nicht so kompliziert^g. Man sagt zu jedem fremden Erwachsenen „Sie", ganz gleich, ob es der Milchmann ist oder ein Professor. Und man muß natürlich gleichzeitig „Herr" Schulze oder „Frau" Hartmann dabei sagen. „Du" ist immer nur dann richtig, wenn man mit der Person^g wirklich gut vertraut ist. Dann, und nur dann, ist auch der Vorname^g am Platze. Nur zu fast erwachsenen Kindern kann man „Sie" zusammen mit dem Vornamen sagen.

Aber man muß noch etwas wissen, wenn man alles gut verstehen und richtig machen will, das Wichtigste vielleicht. Natürlich gibt es auch in Deutschland viele vertraute Freunde, alte und junge. Häufig kennen sie sich schon lange, vielleicht noch aus der Schulzeit^g. Vielleicht haben sie sich aber auch erst neu kennengelernt. Jedenfalls duzen sich vertraute Freunde, und sie nennen sich gleichzeitig bei ihren Vornamen. Aber in Amerika nennt man sich sehr viel häufiger beim Vornamen als in Deutschland. Und es geht auch sehr viel schneller. In Deutschland sagen sogar einige gute, alte Freunde „Sie" zu einander, obwohl sie sich vielleicht seit vielen Jahren kennen. Vielleicht nennen sie sich dabei noch nicht einmal bei ihren Vornamen. Sicher, das ist auch in Deutschland eine Ausnahme, aber es gibt doch so etwas. Jedenfalls werden sich deutsche Erwachsene keinesfalls bei ihren Vornamen nennen, wenn sie sich erst seit ein paar Tagen kennen. So schnell geht das in Deutschland nun einmal nicht.

Und es geht auch nicht so leicht. Fast immer bietet der Ältere dem Jüngeren Duz-Freundschaft an. Häufig genug trinkt man ein Glas Wein bei dieser Zeremonie^g. „Du" sagen und einander

duzen address with **du**

der Lehrer, - teacher **die Lehrerin, -nen**
lehren teach
der Ewachsene *adj. noun* grown-up, adult
wachsen; er wächst, er wuchs, er ist gewachsen grow
anfangen: er fängt an, er fing an, er hat angefangen begin
die Lehre, -n apprenticeship, instruction
der Lehrling, -e apprentice
die Konfirmation [kɔnfɪʀmatsiˈoːn] · **der Stichtag, -e** fixed day, deadline
der Schüler, -
zu guter Letzt finally, last of all

das Ereignis, -se event
Rücksicht nehmen auf etwas take something into consideration

ganz gleich no matter · **gleichzeitig** at the same time
die Person, -en · **der Vorname, -ns, -n** first name **vor** before + **der Name** name, *gen. sg.* **Namens**, *acc. dat. sg. and pl. all cases* **Namen**

das Wichtigste *adj. noun* the most important thing

nennen: er nennt, er nannte, er hat genannt name

die Ausnahme, -n exception
keinesfalls by no means

die Duz-Freundschaft friendship in which **du** is used · **anbieten: er bietet an, er bot an, er hat angeboten** offer
die Zeremonie, -n [tseʀemoˈniː]

16 Mit wem ist man immer vertraut?
17 Duzt man Kinder?
18 Mit wem sind kleine Kinder vertraut?
19 Was sagen die Kinder zu allen?
20 Duzen die Kinder zuerst auch ihre Lehrer?
21 Wie lange mag das so gehen?
22 Wann fängt man an, ein Kind zu siezen?
23 Wann kommen viele Kinder aus der Schule?
24 Gehen viele noch weiter zur Schule?
25 Wohin gehen sie dann?
26 Warum ist die Konfirmation ein wichtiger Tag?
27 Sagen die Lehrer immer noch „du" zu den Schülern?
28 Wie lange müssen die Schüler auf das „Sie" warten?
29 Sagt man „du" zu einem fremden Erwachsenen?
30 Was sagt man zu einem Milchmann?
31 Wann ist „du" richtig?
32 Wann ist der Vorname am Platze?
33 Gibt es viele vertraute Freunde in Deutschland?
34 Duzen sich vertraute Freunde?
35 Nennen sich vertraute Freunde bei ihren Vornamen?
36 Gibt es auch Ausnahmen?
37 Bietet der Jüngere dem Älteren Duz-Freundschaft an?
38 Was trinkt man bei dieser Zeremonie?

bei den Vornamen nennen, ist—bis auf Ausnahmen wenigstens—für Deutsche e i n e Sache und zusammen ein Zeichen für vertraute Freundschaft. Andererseits bedeutet ,,Sie'' sagen aber keinesfalls das Gegenteil! Und gerade das ist für Amerikaner nicht einfach zu verstehen.

Die Frau eines meiner guten Bekannten ist Amerikanerin[g]. Sie spricht schon recht gut Deutsch, aber sie hat noch immer Schwierigkeiten mit ,,du'' und ,,Sie'', wie sie lachend erzählt. Vor einigen Wochen ist es ihr wieder passiert, daß sie an einem Tage einen fremden Postboten geduzt hat, ihren Mann aber, als er später nach Hause kam, hat sie mit ,,Sie'' begrüßt. So ist es mit den fremden Sitten!

bis auf up to, except for · **e i n e** *Letters are spaced apart to indicate emphasis; the function is similar to that of italics or underlining in English.*
andererseits on the other hand
gerade das just that, precisely that
die Schwierigkeit, -en difficulty
begrüßen greet

39 Wen hat die Amerikanerin geduzt?
40 Wie hat sie ihren Mann begrüßt?

PHONOLOGY

A. Umlaut Sounds

Practice pronouncing the following words.

Make the [ø:] especially long and do not diphthongize it:

h ö ren, m ö gen, sch ö n, gr ö ßere, geh ö rt

Make the [œ] especially short:

m ö chte, k ö nnen, zw ö lf, pl ö tzlich

Make the [y:] especially long and do not diphthongize it:

nat ü rlich, ü ben, Sch ü ler, f ü r, Br ü der, gen ü gt, Einf ü hrung, Ü bungen, M ü he

Make the [ʏ] especially short:

Gl ü ck, zur ü ck, h ü bsch, d ü rfen, w ü nschen, m ü ssen, J ü ngeren, ber ü cksichtigen, M ü nchen, f ü nfzehn

B. Long and Short Vowels

Make the long stressed vowels especially long and the short ones especially short:

S i tten, g a nz, nat ü rlich, verst e hen, i mmer, l e rnen, zu e rst, S a che, f a st, b a ld, n o ch, g e rn, w e r, f i nden, A nfang, fr e md, gem a cht, u m, bek a nnt, bes o nders, m i t, g u t, a lle, Sch u le, o der, l ä nger, geh ö rt, L e hrer, H a ns, d o ch, d a s, St i chtag, n ä mlich, w a rten, d a nn, T a g, offizi e ll, norm a l, H e rr, Pers o n, m a n, m a chen, a lte, g i bt, Erw a chsene, d e r, d e m, Gl a s, b i s, zus a mmen, a ndererseits, G e genteil, l a chend, W o chen

C. Diphthongs

Pronounce all the diphthongs shorter and more crisply than in English. Remember that the second vowel elements should sound softer and even shorter than the first.

The first vowel element is [a]:

zw **ei** undzwanzig, k **ei** n, s **ei** n, l **ei** cht, kl **ei** ner, fr **ei** e, **ei** gentlich, **ei** ner, zw **ei**, **ei** n, s **ei** t, dr **ei**, bl **ei** ben, n **ei** n, dr **ei** zehn, viell **ei** cht, schr **ei** ben, **Ei** nführung, w **ei** ß, **ei** nige, gl **ei** ch, **ei** genartig, m **ei** nt, Z **ei** chen, M **ey** er, w **ei** ter, h **ei** ßt, Er **ei** gnis, dab **ei**, k **ei** nesfalls, W **ei** n, **ei** nfach, **ei** nigen

The first vowel element is [a]:

au ch, k **au** ft, **au** f, H **au** ses, K **au** fh **au** s, l **au** fend, dar **au** f, br **au** cht, **Au** sländer, vertr **au** t, **au** s, **au** fpassen, **au** ssieht, **Au** snahme, Fr **au**

The first vowel element is [ɔ]:

t **eu** er, h **äu** fig, h **eu** te, Verk **äu** ferin, D **eu** tschland, Fr **eu** nde, bed **eu** tet, Fr **äu** lein, n **eu**, Fr **eu** ndschaft

---

VOCABULARY

A. Singular and Plural of Nouns

die Amerikanerin, -nen
der Ausländer, -
die Ausnahme, -n
das Ereignis, -se
der Erwachsene, -n *adj. noun*
die Freundschaft, -en
die Klasse, -n
die Lehre, -n
der Lehrer, -
die Lehrerin, -nen

der Lehrling, -e
die Person, -en
der Rang, ⸚e
der Schüler, -
die Schulzeit, -en
die Schwierigkeit, -en
die Sitte, -n
der Stichtag, -e
der Vorname, -ns, -n
die Zeremonie, -n

B. Inference

With the help of the clues provided, guess the meanings of the words in boldface.

Words similar to English:

1. Sind Sie der **Kapitän** [kapiˈtɛːn] dieses Schiffes?   **der Kapitän, -e**
2. Ich brauche eine neue **Maschine** [maˈʃiːnə] für meine Fabrik.   **die Maschine, -n**
3. Tausend Meter sind ein **Kilometer** [kiloˈmeːtəʀ].   **das Kilometer, -**
4. A. In Deutschland gibt es **praktisch** nur drei **Parteien** [paʀˈtaɪ̯ən].   **die Partei, -en**
   B. Wieso **praktisch**?
   A. Nun, die anderen **Parteien** haben keine große **politische** [poˈliːtɪʃə] Bedeutung.
   B. Welche **Partei** hast du denn am liebsten?
   A. Ach, ich interessiere mich nicht sehr für **Politik** [poliˈtiːk], ich bin ein **unpolitischer** [ˈʊnpoˌliːtɪʃəʀ] Mensch.   **die Politik**
5. Ein amerikanisches Pfund hat 454 **Gramm**, aber ein deutsches Pfund hat 500 **Gramm**.   **das Gramm, -e**
6. Tausend Gramm (oder zwei Pfund) sind ein **Kilogramm** [ˈkiːlogʀam].
7. A. Die Mutter kauft ein Viertelpfund **Schokolade** [ʃokoˈlaːdə].   **die Schokolade**
      Wieviel Gramm kauft sie also?
   B. Sie kauft 125 Gramm **Schokolade**.
8. A. Sie kauft die Schokolade nicht im Geschäft, sondern auf dem **Markt**.   **der Markt, ⸚e**
   B. Kann man denn Schokolade auf dem **Markt** kaufen?
   A. Auf einem deutschen **Markt** kann man fast alles kaufen.
9. A. Peter muß jetzt erst einmal zwei Jahre zum **Militär** [miliˈtɛːʀ].   **das Militär**
   B. Er wird bestimmt ein guter **Soldat** [zɔlˈdaːt] sein.   **der Soldat, -en, -en**
   A. Ja, und später will er zur **Polizei** [poliˈtsaɪ] gehen und **Polizist** [poliˈtsɪst] werden.   **die Polizei · der Polizist, -en, -en**
10. Möchten Sie noch eine Tasse **Tee** zu Ihrem Kuchen?   **der Tee**
11. A. Ist dieser **Ring** aus **Gold**?   **der Ring, -e · das Gold**
    B. Ja. Ich habe **Gold** viel lieber als **Silber**.   **das Silber**
12. Mein Haus ist mein **Heim**.   **das Heim, -e**
13. Mach doch bitte die **Lampe** im Nebenzimmer aus!   **die Lampe, -n**
14. Susi, hier ist noch kein Pfeffer und noch kein **Zucker** auf dem Tisch!   **der Zucker**

A number of words of foreign origin which are spelled with z, pronounced [ts], in German, are spelled with c in English. Known examples are: **die Medizin** *medicine*, **die Zeremonie** *ceremony*, **die Konferenz** *conference*. Below are some new ones:

1. Zwischen Kultur und **Zivilisation** [tsiviliza̯tsiˈoːn] soll kein Unterschied sein?   **die Zivilisation**
2. Ich möchte mal wieder in einen **Zirkus** [ˈtsɪʀkʊs] gehen.   **der Zirkus, -se**
3. Rauchen Sie auch **Zigarren** [tsiˈgaʀən]?   **die Zigarre, -n**

4 Die Bahn fuhr bis ins **Zentrum** [ˈtsɛntʀʊm]. **das Zentrum, -tren**
5 Schon der kleinste Organismus [ɔʀɡaˈnɪsmʊs] hat sehr viele **Zellen**. **die Zelle, -n**

The sound [k] is usually written **k** or **ck** in German and not *c* as in English. Known examples are: **die Konfirmation** *confirmation*, **der Onkel** *uncle*, **die Musik** *music*. Below are some new ones:

1 Hast du schon einen **Kalender** [kaˈlɛndəʀ] für das neue Jahr? **der Kalender, -**
2 Später kam er sogar mit seinem Vater in **Konflikt** [kɔnˈflɪkt]. **der Konflikt, -e**
3 Wie lange hatte er **Kontakt** [kɔnˈtakt] mit diesen Menschen? **der Kontakt, -e**
4 Sei doch nicht immer so **konservativ** [kɔnzɛʀvaˈtiːf]!
5 Teller haben natürlich **konkave** [kɔnˈkaːvə] Form.
6 Ist dieses Bild tatsächlich eine **Kopie** [koˈpiː]? **die Kopie, -n**
7 Früher war er nicht so **kritisch** [ˈkʀiːtɪʃ].
8 Professor Müller ist ein guter **Kollege** [kɔˈleːɡə] von mir. **der Kollege, -n, -n**
9 Über die Politik von heute habe ich keinen **Kommentar** [kɔmɛnˈtaːʀ]. **der Kommentar, -e**
10 Wieviel **Kalorien** [kaloˈʀiːən] darf deine Frau täglich essen? **die Kalorie, -n**
11 Susi kann noch kein Mittagessen **kochen**. **der Koch, ⸚e**
12 Kochen Sie mit **Kohle** oder mit Gas? **die Kohle, -n**

Many German words which are spelled with **z** or **tz**, pronounced [ts], are spelled with *t* in English. Known examples are: **zwanzig** *twenty*, **erzählen** *tell*, **zu** *to, too*, **sitzen** *sit*, **das Herz** *heart*. Below are some new ones:

1 Wie hoch war der **Zoll** für die Zigaretten? **der Zoll, ⸚e**
2 Unsere **Angorakatze** trinkt gern Milch. **die Katze, -n**
3 Diese Katze ist ganz **zahm**.
4 Dieser Busch hat schon einen grünen **Zweig**. **der Zweig, -e**
5 Die **Zunge** ist das wichtigste Artikulationsorgan [ˌaʀtikulatsiˈoːnsɔʀɡaːn]. **die Zunge, -n**
6 Über diesen **Witz** kann ich nicht lachen. **der Witz, -e**
7 Heute ist es sehr warm. Bei dieser **Hitze** brauchen wir nicht zu **heizen**. **die Hitze**
8 Der Fischer reparierte sein **Netz**. **das Netz, -e**
9 Ich möchte gern das **Salz** und den Pfeffer. **das Salz**

WRITING

A. Structure Retention and Variation

Substitute the new words for those directly above them and make all the necessary changes. A line indicates that the word above it is to be omitted. Such omissions and some of the substitutions will require changes in structure.

Example:
Model sentence: Er sagt, daß sein Vater ihn in ein fremdes Geschäft gesteckt hat.
───── Eltern ───── Fabrik schicken

New sentence: Er sagt, seine Eltern haben ihn in eine fremde Fabrik geschickt.

1 Werner blieb in Kiel, und Heinrich zog nach München um.
                          als

2 Auf dem Schild steht, daß du in diesem Abteil nicht rauchen darfst.
               wir   Bus   sollen

3 Er erzählt   gerade, wo er die ganze Zeit   gewesen ist.
   berichten gestern, was   Jahr tun

4 Er hat   ein halbes Jahr   in einer Fabrik   gearbeitet.
   werden   ganz Monat   Ausland

5 Ich glaube nun, daß mein alter Freund sein Examen bestanden hat.
  Wir wissen gestern ───── unser klein Freundin

6 Sie sind gestern wegen des schlechten Wetters nicht angekommen.
  Ich   trotz   schön   mitgehen

7 Hast du   gestern gesagt, daß ich dich im Büro anrufen soll?
      ihr   nun   ───── wir   Stadt   können

8 Mein Bruder   kommt   heute   nicht mit, weil er krank ist.
     Schwester mitfahren gestern   denn

9 Ich sehe   mir die Nummer an, denn ich bin so vergeßlich.
  Er aufschreiben   weil

10 Werner wohnt jetzt   mit seiner Frau   und seinen Kindern in Kiel.
              damals   Großeltern   Brüder

B. The Past Perfect Tense

Rewrite the following sentences in the past perfect tense:

1 Rolf und Günther gingen zum Schillerplatz.
2 Dort sahen sie einen schlimmen Unfall.
3 Der Milchwagen kam zu schnell um die Ecke.
4 Er rutschte plötzlich an der Kreuzung.
5 Dann kippte er sogar noch um.
6 Die ganze Milch schwappte über die Straße.
7 Die Jungen liefen schnell zu der Stelle.
8 Dort lag eine alte Frau bei der Laterne.
9 Sie hatte eine Platzwunde am Kopf.
10 Bald kam der Streifenwagen um die Ecke.

C. Dehydrated Sentences

This exercise is similar to those of previous units in which you were instructed to "arrange the elements to form German sentences." Here, however, you are given only the basic forms of the words, so you have to modify them according to the grammatical requirements of the sentences. Furthermore, most of the **der**-words and **ein**-words are missing, and you will have to supply them. Often several choices are possible. Write all sentences in the *past tense*.

Example:
Dehydrated sentence: Heike / sollen / Geige / üben / aber / sie / gehen / mit / Freund / zu / Baden

Complete sentence: Heike sollte Geige üben, aber sie ging mit einem Freund zum Baden.

1 Hans / und / Tante Inge / gehen / Tag / in / Stadt
2 Sonne / scheinen / und / es / sein / heiß / Tag
3 Hans / wollen / Eis / kaufen / aber / er / haben / kein / Geld
4 nett / Tante / geben / er / ein / Mark
5 er / sehen / Eismann / und / laufen / zu / er
6 Hans / bitten / um / Nuß-Eis / und / bekommen / Portion / für / fünfundzwanzig / Pfennig
7 klein / Freund / von / er / stehen / an / Eiswagen
8 gut / klein / Freund / haben / kein / Pfennig / aber / er / wollen / auch / Eis
9 dann / kaufen / Hans / Portion / Eis / für / Freund
10 Tante Inge / nehmen / kein / Eis / und / Hans / zurückgeben / sie / halb / Mark

Unit 23

MENDELSSOHN

DIALOG

Das Treffen bei Familie Kellner (Anfang)

1 **Heinrich:** Stell dir vor, Renate, ich habe den Klassenkameraden getroffen, von dem ich dir erzählte!

2 **Renate:** Meinst du den Werner Bäcker, der früher in dieser Gegend wohnte?

3 **Heinrich:** Ja, er stand einfach an der Bushaltestelle.

4 **Renate:** Na, das ist wirklich ein Zufall! Hast du ihn gleich wiedererkannt?

5 **Heinrich:** Sofort! Er ist noch derselbe feine Kerl, der er immer war.

The Meeting at Kellners' (Beginning)

das Treffen *infinitive used as noun* · **die Familie, -n** · **der Kellner, -** waiter

1 Imagine, Renate, I met the classmate I was telling you about.

sich vorstellen *dat. refl.* · **der Klassenkamerad   die Klasse, -n** class + **der Kamerad, -en, -en** companion, comrade, pal

2 Do you mean Werner Bäcker, who used to live in this neighborhood?

der Bäcker, - baker · **die Gegend, -en** area, region

3 Yes. He was simply standing at the bus stop.

die Bushaltestelle   der Bus, -se bus + **halt** *from* **halten** stop + **die Stelle, -n** place

4 Well, that is really a coincidence. Did you recognize him right away?

der Zufall, ⸗e coincidence, chance · **wiedererkennen   wieder** + **erkennen** recognize

5 Immediately. He's still the same fine fellow that he always was.

sofort immediately, right away

6 **Renate:**   Warum hast du ihn nicht gleich mitgebracht?

7 **Heinrich:** Das habe ich tun wollen, aber er hat erst heute abend Zeit.

8 **Renate:**   Aber für eine Abendgesellschaft habe ich überhaupt nichts anzuziehen!

9 **Heinrich:** In dem Kleid, das du jetzt trägst, kannst du dich überall sehen lassen.

10 **Renate:**   Das habe ich mir denken können. Es sieht dir ähnlich, Sparsamkeit in die Form eines Kompliments zu kleiden.

(Fortsetzung folgt)

SUPPLEMENT

1 Bring mir den Mantel, der dort über dem Stuhl hängt.

2 Bring mir die Mütze, die dort an der Tür hängt.

3 Bring mir das Buch, das dort auf dem Fußboden liegt.

4 Bring mir die Schuhe, die dort auf dem Fußboden liegen.

5 Ist das der Rock, den du gekauft hast?

6 Ist das die Hose, die du getragen hast?

6	Why didn't you bring him along right away?	
7	That's what I wanted to do, but he doesn't have time until this evening.	**erst** *with time expression* not until
8	But I don't have a thing to put on for an evening party.	**die Abendgesellschaft** **der Abend** + **die Gesellschaft, -en** party; society; company · **überhaupt** generally, altogether **überhaupt nichts** nothing at all
9	In the dress you have on now you can let yourself be seen anywhere.	**das Kleid, -er** dress **die Kleider** dresses; clothes · **tragen: er trägt, trug, hat getragen** wear; carry · **überall** anywhere, everywhere · **sehen lassen** let be seen
10	I could have guessed that. It's just like you to disguise frugality in the form of a compliment.	**ähnlich** like, similar **es sieht dir ähnlich** it's just like you · **die Sparsamkeit** · **das Kompliment, -e**

(To be continued)

1	Bring me the coat that's hanging there on the chair.	**der Mantel, ⸚** · **der Stuhl, ⸚e** · **hängen: er hängt, hing, hat gehangen**
2	Bring me the cap that's hanging there on the door.	**die Mütze, -n** · **die Tür, -en**
3	Bring me the book that's lying there on the floor.	**der Fußboden** **der Fuß, ⸚e** foot + **der Boden, ⸚** floor, ground
4	Bring me the shoes that are lying there on the floor.	**der Schuh, -e**
5	Is that the skirt that you bought?	**der Rock, ⸚e**
6	Are those the trousers that you wore?	**die Hose, -n** trousers, pair of pants

7 Wo ist das Hemd, das du gewaschen hast?

8 Wo sind die Kleider, die du angesehen hast?

9 Das ist der Freund, von dem ich dir erzählte.

10 Das ist die Frau, von der ich dir erzählte.

11 Kennst du das Mädchen, von dem ich dir erzählte?

12 Kennst du die Leute, von denen ich dir erzählte?

13 Wie heißt der Mann, dessen Mantel an der Tür hängt?

14 Wie heißt die Frau, deren Mantel an der Tür hängt?

15 Wie heißt das Kind, dessen Schuhe auf dem Fußboden liegen?

16 Wie heißen die Leute, deren Schuhe auf dem Fußboden liegen?

7   Where is the shirt that you washed?   waschen: er wäscht, wusch, hat gewaschen

8   Where are the clothes that you looked at?

9   That is the friend about whom I told you.

10   That is the woman about whom I told you.

11   Do you know the girl about whom I told you?

12   Do you know the people about whom I told you?

13   What is the name of the man whose coat is hanging on the door?

14   What is the name of the woman whose coat is hanging on the door?

15   What is the name of the child whose shoes are lying on the floor?

16   What are the names of the people whose shoes are lying on the floor?

AUDIOLINGUAL DRILLS

A. Directed Dialog

Fragen Sie, was Renate sich vorstellen soll!
Was soll Renate sich vorstellen?

Antworten Sie, daß Heinrich den Klassenkameraden getroffen hat, von dem er Renate erzählte!
Heinrich hat den Klassenkameraden getroffen, von dem er Renate erzählte.

Sagen Sie, daß er den Werner Bäcker meint, der früher in dieser Gegend wohnte!
Er meint den Werner Bäcker, der früher in dieser Gegend wohnte.

Sagen Sie, daß er einfach an der Bushaltestelle stand!
Er stand einfach an der Bushaltestelle.

Sagen Sie, daß das wirklich ein Zufall ist!
Das ist wirklich ein Zufall.

Fragen Sie, ob Heinrich ihn gleich wiedererkannt hat!
Hat Heinrich ihn gleich wiedererkannt?

Antworten Sie, daß er ihn sofort wiedererkannt hat!
Er hat ihn sofort wiedererkannt.

Sagen Sie, daß er noch derselbe feine Kerl ist, der er immer war!
Er ist noch derselbe feine Kerl, der er immer war.

Fragen Sie, warum er ihn jetzt nicht gleich mitgebracht hat!
Warum hat er ihn jetzt nicht gleich mitgebracht?

Antworten Sie, daß Heinrich das tun wollte!
Heinrich wollte das tun.

Sagen Sie, daß Werner aber erst heute abend Zeit hat!
Werner hat aber erst heute abend Zeit.

Sagen Sie, daß Renate für eine Abendgesellschaft überhaupt nichts anzuziehen hat!
Renate hat für eine Abendgesellschaft überhaupt nichts anzuziehen.

Sagen Sie, daß sie sich in dem Kleid, das sie jetzt trägt, überall sehen lassen kann!
Sie kann sich in dem Kleid, das sie jetzt trägt, überall sehen lassen.

Sagen Sie, daß Renate sich das denken konnte!
Renate konnte sich das denken.

Sagen Sie, daß es ihrem Mann ähnlich sieht, Sparsamkeit in die Form eines Kompliments zu kleiden!
Es sieht ihrem Mann ähnlich, Sparsamkeit in die Form eines Kompliments zu kleiden.

B. New Strong and Irregular Weak Verbs

1 **Tragen** *wear, carry* follows the pattern of **fahren**—**er trägt, trug, hat getragen**. Change the tense as indicated:

Er trägt seine neuen Schuhe.   *past*
Er trug seine neuen Schuhe.   *pres. perf.*
Er hat seine neuen Schuhe getragen.   *fut.*
Er wird seine neuen Schuhe tragen.   *pres.*
Er trägt seine neuen Schuhe.

2 **Waschen** *wash* follows the pattern of **fahren**, except that the stem vowel of the present tense and the past participle is short — **er wäscht, wusch, hat gewaschen**. Change the tense as indicated:

Wäschst du meine Hemden? *past*
Wuschest du meine Hemden? *past perf.*
Hattest du meine Hemden gewaschen? *fut.*

Wirst du meine Hemden waschen? *pres.*
Wäschst du meine Hemden?

3 **Hängen** *hang* has the principal parts **er hängt, hing, hat gehangen**. Change the tense as indicated:

Die Mäntel hängen an der Tür. *pres. perf.*
Die Mäntel haben an der Tür gehangen. *fut.*
Die Mäntel werden an der Tür hängen. *past*

Die Mäntel hingen an der Tür. *pres.*
Die Mäntel hängen an der Tür.

4 **Anfangen** *begin* is similar to **hängen** — **er fängt an, fing an, hat angefangen**. Change the tense as indicated:

Sie fängt an, davon zu erzählen. *past*
Sie fing an, davon zu erzählen. *pres. perf.*
Sie hat angefangen, davon zu erzählen. *fut.*

Sie wird anfangen, davon zu erzählen. *pres.*
Sie fängt an, davon zu erzählen.

5 **Anbieten** *offer* follows the pattern of **ziehen**, but without the consonant changes — **er bietet an, bot an, hat angeboten**. Change the tense as indicated:

Ich biete ihm ein Glas Wein an. *past*
Ich bot ihm ein Glas Wein an. *fut.*
Ich werde ihm ein Glas Wein anbieten. *pres. perf.*
Ich habe ihm ein Glas Wein angeboten. *pres.*
Ich biete ihm ein Glas Wein an.

6 **Nennen** *name* and **erkennen** *recognize* both follow the pattern of **kennen** — **er nennt, nannte, hat genannt; er erkennt, erkannte, hat erkannt**. Change the tense as indicated:

Sie nennen sich beim Vornamen. *past*
Sie nannten sich beim Vornamen. *pres. perf.*
Sie haben sich beim Vornamen genannt. *pres.*
Sie nennen sich beim Vornamen.

Erkennst du ihn denn nicht? *pres. perf.*
Hast du ihn denn nicht erkannt? *past*
Erkanntest du ihn denn nicht? *pres.*
Erkennst du ihn denn nicht?

C. Demonstrative Adjectives and Pronouns
(*See Grammar* §§23.3, 23.4)

Forms of **der**, **die**, and **das** may be used as demonstrative adjectives or demonstrative pronouns. As such they are stressed and have the meanings *this*, *that*, *this one*, *that one*, *these*, or *those*.

7 Nominative case. Repeat:

Der Schraubenzieher ist genau der richtige.
Der ist genau der richtige.

Die Aufnahme gefällt mir am besten.
Die gefällt mir am besten.

Das Hemd ist aber besonders schön.
Das ist aber besonders schön.

Die Schuhe sind mir zu teuer.
Die sind mir zu teuer.

8 Accusative case. Repeat:

Den Wagen möchte ich kaufen.
Den möchte ich kaufen.

Die Mütze nehme ich mit.
Die nehme ich mit.

Das Kleid finde ich scheußlich.
Das finde ich scheußlich.

Die Anzüge brauche ich nicht.
Die brauche ich nicht.

9 Dative case. The demonstrative pronoun is **denen** in the dative plural. Repeat:

Dem Schlaukopf helfe ich nicht.
Dem helfe ich nicht.

Bei der Wirtin wohne ich lieber nicht.
Bei der wohne ich lieber nicht.

In dem Kleid kannst du dich überall sehen lassen.
In dem kannst du dich überall sehen lassen.

Den Leuten gebe ich keinen Pfennig.
Denen gebe ich keinen Pfennig.

10 Genitive case. The demonstrative pronoun has an extra syllable in all genitive forms. The masculine and neuter are **dessen**; the feminine and the plural are **deren**. Repeat:

Die Fotos des Verkäufers sind nicht gut genug.
Dessen Fotos sind nicht gut genug.

Den Hut der Studentin mag ich nicht leiden.
Deren Hut mag ich nicht leiden.

Die Mütze des Kindes gefällt mir nicht.
Dessen Mütze gefällt mir nicht.

Die Preise der Geschäfte steigen immer höher.
Deren Preise steigen immer höher.

11 Substitute the demonstrative pronoun for the demonstrative adjective plus noun.

Examples:
Der Mantel gefällt mir am besten.
Der gefällt mir am besten.

Das Kind der Frau ist aber schlau.
Deren Kind ist aber schlau.

Bei den Leuten kaufe ich nichts.
Bei denen kaufe ich nichts.

Der Rock ist genau der richtige.
Der ist genau der richtige.

Das Kleid da ist das beste.
Das da ist das beste.

Die Männer da hinten sind arbeitslos.
Die da hinten sind arbeitslos.

Die Sitte kann er nicht verstehen.
Die kann er nicht verstehen.

Ich habe bei den Leuten da gewohnt.
Ich habe bei denen da gewohnt.

Den Rock möchte ich gern haben.
Den möchte ich gern haben.

Das Kleid des Kindes ist hübsch.
Dessen Kleid ist hübsch.

Mit dem Fahrer fahre ich lieber nicht.
Mit dem fahre ich lieber nicht.

Der Studentin da wird die Sache nie gelingen.
Der da wird die Sache nie gelingen.

Das Brot des Bäckers dort ist immer frisch.
Dessen Brot dort ist immer frisch.

Die Medizin nehme ich doch lieber nicht.
Die nehme ich doch lieber nicht.

Die Preise der Schuhe hier sind viel zu hoch.
Deren Preise hier sind viel zu hoch.

Ich möchte dem Kind ein neues Hemd kaufen.
Ich möchte dem ein neues Hemd kaufen.

Für den Jungen tue ich es gern.
Für den tue ich es gern.

Ich meine die Schuhe da auf dem Stuhl.
Ich meine die da auf dem Stuhl.

Die Gläser der Wirtin sind immer sauber.
Deren Gläser sind immer sauber.

D. Relative Pronouns (*See Grammar* §23.5)

12 Nominative case. Substitute the new noun and make all appropriate changes:

   Er ist derselbe feine Kerl, der er immer war.   **Frau**
   Sie ist dieselbe feine Frau, die sie immer war.   **Kind**
   Es ist dasselbe feine Kind, das es immer war.   **Menschen**
   Sie sind dieselben feinen Menschen, die sie immer waren.

13 Accusative case. Substitute the new noun and make all appropriate changes:

   In dem Anzug, den du jetzt trägst, siehst du nett aus.   **Mütze**
   In der Mütze, die du jetzt trägst, siehst du nett aus.   **Hemd**
   In dem Hemd, das du jetzt trägst, siehst du nett aus.   **Schuhen**
   In den Schuhen, die du jetzt trägst, siehst du nett aus.

14 Dative case. Substitute the new noun and make all appropriate changes:

   Ich habe den Freund getroffen, von dem ich dir erzählte.   **Freundin**
   Ich habe die Freundin getroffen, von der ich dir erzählte.   **Kind**
   Ich habe das Kind getroffen, von dem ich dir erzählte.   **Leute**
   Ich habe die Leute getroffen, von denen ich dir erzählte.

15 Genitive case. Replace the first noun and make all appropriate changes:

   Der Junge, dessen Vater wir angerufen haben, ist krank.   **Studentin**
   Die Studentin, deren Vater wir angerufen haben, ist krank.   **Kind**
   Das Kind, dessen Vater wir angerufen haben, ist krank.   **Kinder**
   Die Kinder, deren Vater wir angerufen haben, sind krank.

16 Combine the following pairs of sentences by making the second one a relative clause.

Example:
Ich meine den Mann. Er war gerade hier.
Ich meine den Mann, der gerade hier war.

Ich meine den Kameraden. Er wohnte hier.
Ich meine den Kameraden, der hier wohnte.

Meinst du die Freundin? Sie steht da.
Meinst du die Freundin, die da steht?

Er meint das Kind. Es läuft über die Straße.
Er meint das Kind, das über die Straße läuft.

Wollt ihr die Bücher? Sie liegen auf dem Tisch.
Wollt ihr die Bücher, die auf dem Tisch liegen?

Wir haben den Wagen gesehen. Du wolltest ihn kaufen.
Wir haben den Wagen gesehen, den du kaufen wolltest.

Heute kommt die Kundin. Ich erzählte dir von ihr.
Heute kommt die Kundin, von der ich dir erzählte.

Da steht der Freund. Ich bin mit ihm in die Schule gegangen.
Da steht der Freund, mit dem ich in die Schule gegangen bin.

Dort ist der Lehrer. Sein Sohn arbeitet im Ausland.
Dort ist der Lehrer, dessen Sohn im Ausland arbeitet.

Hier sind die Gabeln. Ich habe sie dir gekauft.
Hier sind die Gabeln, die ich dir gekauft habe.

Heute kam die Frau. Ihr Mann unterrichtet an der Oberschule.
Heute kam die Frau, deren Mann an der Oberschule unterrichtet.

Das Kleid ist hübsch. Sie trägt es jetzt.
Das Kleid, das sie jetzt trägt, ist hübsch.

Die Leute stehen da hinten. Ich habe ihnen geholfen.
Die Leute, denen ich geholfen habe, stehen da hinten.

Das Kind ißt Nuß-Eis. Seine Mutter hat uns angerufen.
Das Kind, dessen Mutter uns angerufen hat, ißt Nuß-Eis.

Die Professorin ist sehr gut. Ich habe sie jetzt.
Die Professorin, die ich jetzt habe, ist sehr gut.

Der Junge geht zum Baden. Du hast ihm den Kuchen gegeben.
Der Junge, dem du den Kuchen gegeben hast, geht zum Baden.

Die Eltern haben eben angerufen. Ihre Kinder sind hier.
Die Eltern, deren Kinder hier sind, haben eben angerufen.

The forms of **welcher** are also used as relative pronouns, but less frequently than the forms of **der**. In its function as a relative pronoun, **welcher** has no genitive form.

17 Nominative case. Substitute the new noun and make all other necessary changes:

Der Student, welcher hier war, heißt Schneider. **Studentin**
Die Studentin, welche hier war, heißt Schneider. **Mädchen**
Das Mädchen, welches hier war, heißt Schneider. **Leute**
Die Leute, welche hier waren, heißen Schneider.

18 Accusative case. Substitute the new noun and make all other necessary changes:

Wo ist der Schrank, welchen wir bekommen haben? **Tasse**
Wo ist die Tasse, welche wir bekommen haben? **Bild**
Wo ist das Bild, welches wir bekommen haben? **Ansichtskarten**
Wo sind die Ansichtskarten, welche wir bekommen haben?

19 Dative case. Substitute the new noun and make all other necessary changes:

Kennst du den Jungen, welchem wir geholfen haben? **Frau**
Kennst du die Frau, welcher wir geholfen haben? **Kind**
Kennst du das Kind, welchem wir geholfen haben? **Leute**
Kennst du die Leute, welchen wir geholfen haben?

20 Change the preposition and its relative pronoun object to a **wo**-compound.

Example:
Hier liegt das Buch, über welches er sprach.
Hier liegt das Buch, worüber er sprach.

Kennst du das Geschäft, für welches er arbeitet?
Kennst du das Geschäft, wofür er arbeitet?

Der Tisch, auf dem die Zeitung liegt, steht in der Ecke.
Der Tisch, worauf die Zeitung liegt, steht in der Ecke.

Das Buch, an das ich gedacht habe, liegt dort.
Das Buch, woran ich gedacht habe, liegt dort.

Die Züge, mit denen wir fahren, sind ziemlich alt.
Die Züge, womit wir fahren, sind ziemlich alt.

Das sind die Sachen, aus welchen ein Schrank besteht.
Das sind die Sachen, woraus ein Schrank besteht.

Die Vorlesung, auf die wir warten, soll gut sein.
Die Vorlesung, worauf wir warten, soll gut sein.

Das ist eine Ausnahme, auf die man Rücksicht nehmen muß.
Das ist eine Ausnahme, worauf man Rücksicht nehmen muß.

21 Substitute the new antecedent of the relative pronoun:

Ich gebe dir etwas, was dir gefällt.   **alles**
Ich gebe dir alles, was dir gefällt.   **nichts**
Ich gebe dir nichts, was dir gefällt.   **manches**
Ich gebe dir manches, was dir gefällt.   **vieles**
Ich gebe dir vieles, was dir gefällt.

Er kauft immer das Beste, was er finden kann.   **alles**
Er kauft immer alles, was er finden kann.   **das Billigste**
Er kauft immer das Billigste, was er finden kann.   **das Schönste**
Er kauft immer das Schönste, was er finden kann.   **das Teuerste**
Er kauft immer das Teuerste, was er finden kann.

22 Substitute the new main clause:

Er kommt nach Hause, was uns natürlich gefällt.   **er bleibt hier**
Er bleibt hier, was uns natürlich gefällt.   **es geht ihm besser**
Es geht ihm besser, was uns natürlich gefällt.   **er kommt morgen**
Er kommt morgen, was uns natürlich gefällt.   **sie ist sehr nett**
Sie ist sehr nett, was uns natürlich gefällt.

23 Combine the pairs of sentences by making the second one a relative clause. Use a form of the relative pronoun **der** or **was**, as may be required:

Ich habe den Klassenkameraden gesehen. Er wohnte hier.
Ich habe den Klassenkameraden gesehen, der hier wohnte.

Ich habe etwas gesehen. Es wird euch gefallen.
Ich habe etwas gesehen, was euch gefallen wird.

Es war ein Abend. Ich werde ihn nie vergessen.
Es war ein Abend, den ich nie vergessen werde.

Erzähl mir alles! Du weißt es.
Erzähl mir alles, was du weißt!

Wie heißt die Frau? Sie hat uns angerufen.
Wie heißt die Frau, die uns angerufen hat?

Mein Onkel ist wieder krank. Das tut mir sehr leid.
Mein Onkel ist wieder krank, was mir sehr leid tut.

Wo sind die Leute? Wir haben ihnen geholfen.
Wo sind die Leute, denen wir geholfen haben?

Kennst du die Schöne? Ihr Bild ist in der Zeitung.
Kennst du die Schöne, deren Bild in der Zeitung ist?

Er tut alles. Er kann es.
Er tut alles, was er kann.

Ich kaufe nichts. Es gefällt mir nicht.
Ich kaufe nichts, was mir nicht gefällt.

24 Substitute the new **wer**-clause:

Wer viel Geld hat, kann so etwas kaufen.   **wer arbeiten will**
Wer arbeiten will, kann so etwas kaufen.   **wer vorsichtig ist**
Wer vorsichtig ist, kann so etwas kaufen.   **wer gut aufpaßt**
Wer gut aufpaßt, kann so etwas kaufen.   **wer genug Geld hat**
Wer genug Geld hat, kann so etwas kaufen.

25 Substitute the new **was**-clause:

Was er gesagt hat, stimmt einfach nicht.   **was du geschrieben hast**
Was du geschrieben hast, stimmt einfach nicht.   **was wir gelesen haben**
Was wir gelesen haben, stimmt einfach nicht.   **was ihr erzählt**
Was ihr erzählt, stimmt einfach nicht.   **was ich notierte**
Was ich notierte, stimmt einfach nicht.

E. Questions and Answers

Wen hat Heinrich getroffen?
Er hat den Klassenkameraden getroffen, von dem er Renate erzählte.

Wer ist dieser Klassenkamerad?
Er ist der Werner Bäcker, der früher in dieser Gegend wohnte.

Wo hat Heinrich ihn getroffen?
Es war an der Bushaltestelle.

Wie kam es, daß Heinrich seinen alten Freund sofort wiedererkennen konnte?
Es war nicht schwer, weil Werner noch derselbe ist, der er immer war.

Warum hat Heinrich seinen Freund nicht gleich mitgebracht?
Das wollte er tun, aber Werner hatte erst am Abend Zeit.

Was sagt Renate über die kommende Abendgesellschaft?
Sie sagt, sie hat dafür überhaupt nichts anzuziehen.

Und was sagt Heinrich?
Er sagt, daß sie sich in dem Kleid, das sie jetzt trägt, überall sehen lassen kann.

Konnte Renate sich so etwas denken?
Ja, denn sie sagt, daß es ihm ähnlich sieht.

GRAMMAR

23.1 Word-Formation

Infinitive as noun

Many German infinitives are frequently used as singular neuter nouns. Some known examples are: **das Baden** *swimming, bathing*; **das Studieren** *studying*; **das Stehen** *standing*; **das Wiedersehen** *seeing again, reunion*; **das Treffen** *meeting*. The best English equivalent of an infinitive-noun is usually in the form of the gerund, but sometimes other forms equate just as well with the German. Thus, **das Essen** may mean *eating* in one context, *food* in another, and *meal* in still another. Some additional infinitives you know which frequently occur as nouns are:

denken	think	das Denken	thinking
einsteigen	get on, in	das Einsteigen	getting on, boarding
erzählen	relate	das Erzählen	relating
fahren	drive; ride	das Fahren	driving; riding
gehen	go	das Gehen	walking
helfen	help	das Helfen	helping
kennen	know	das Kennen	knowing
können	be able	das Können	being able; ability
lachen	laugh	das Lachen	laughing; laughter
laufen	run; walk	das Laufen	running; walking
rauchen	smoke	das Rauchen	smoking
sitzen	sit	das Sitzen	sitting
sprechen	speak	das Sprechen	speaking
verstehen	understand	das Verstehen	understanding
wissen	know	das Wissen	knowing; knowledge
wohnen	live, reside	das Wohnen	living, residing

3.2 Singular and Plural of Nouns

die Abendgesellschaft, -en	der Kellner, -
der Bäcker, -	der Klassenkamerad, -en, -en
der Boden, ⸚	das Kleid, -er
die Familie, -n	das Kompliment, -e
der Fuß, ⸚e	der Mantel, ⸚
der Fußboden, ⸚	die Mütze, -n
die Gegend, -en	der Rock, ⸚e
die Gesellschaft, -en	der Schuh, -e
die Haltestelle, -n	der Stuhl, ⸚e
die Hose, -n	die Tür, -en
der Kamerad, -en, -en	der Zufall, ⸚e

3.3 The Demonstrative Adjective *der*

The forms of the definite article may be used as demonstrative adjectives with the meanings *this*, *that*, *these*, or *those*. As such they are stressed:

Der Wagen dort ist der bessere.
That car there is the better one.

In **dem** Kleid kannst du dich überall sehen lassen.
In *that (this)* dress you can be seen anywhere.

Die Medizin nehme ich doch lieber nicht.
I'd rather not take *this (that)* medicine.

Die Schuhe sind zu teuer.
Those (these) shoes are too expensive.

3.4 The Demonstrative Pronoun *der*

The demonstrative pronoun **der** expresses the meanings *this one*, *that one*, *these*, *those*. It differs from the demonstrative adjective in two respects: (1) it is not followed by a noun, and (2) the genitive forms, and the form of the dative plural, have an extra syllable **-en**.

	Singular			*Plural*
Nom.	der	die	das	die
Acc.	den	die	das	die
Dat.	dem	der	dem	**denen**
Gen.	**dessen**	**deren**	**dessen**	**deren**

Der ist genau der richtige.
That one is just the right one.

Den möchte ich kaufen.
I'd like to buy *that one*.

Dem helfe ich am liebsten.
I'd like best to help *that one*.

Dessen Fotos sind nicht gut genug.
That one's photos aren't good enough.

Deren Hut mag ich nicht leiden.
I don't like *that one's* hat.

Denen gebe ich keinen Pfennig.
To those I'll not give a pfennig.

23.5 Relative Pronouns

The following sentence contains two clauses:

That is the man / whom we met yesterday.

The first is a main clause, the second a *relative* clause. The relative clause is related to, or modifies, the word *man* in the main clause. We call *whom* a relative pronoun, and *man* its antecedent. Similarly, the two clauses *The hat is pretty* and *that you bought* may be combined in one sentence:

The hat that you bought is pretty.

The word *that* is the relative pronoun, and *hat* its antecedent.

Forms of the German relative pronouns

The German relative pronouns, like the definite article and the demonstrative pronoun, have several forms reflecting case, gender, and number. They are identical to the forms of the demonstrative pronoun, differing from the definite article only in the genitive, and in the dative plural.

The *gender* and *number* of the relative pronoun are determined by the gender and number of the antecedent:

Der alte **Mann, der** gestern hier war, heißt Bäcker.
Die **Frau, die** dort an der Haltestelle steht, ist meine Tante.
Das **Kind, das** da über die Straße läuft, ist unser Sohn.
Viele **Leute, die** hier wohnen, sind alt.

The *case* of the relative pronoun is determined by its function within the relative clause; it has nothing to do with the case of the antecedent:

Nom. Der alte Mann, **der** gestern hier war, heißt Bäcker.
Acc. Der alte Mann, **den** wir getroffen haben, heißt Bäcker.
Dat. Der alte Mann, von **dem** ich dir erzählte, heißt Bäcker.
Gen. Der alte Mann, **dessen** Tochter Philosophie studiert, heißt Bäcker.

The forms of **welcher** are sometimes used as relative pronouns, but less frequently than the forms of **der**. The relative pronoun **welcher** has no genitive forms, however.

Er ist derselbe, **welcher** der alten Frau geholfen hatte.
He is the same one who had helped the old woman.

Position and structure of the relative clause

The relative clause follows as soon as possible after its antecedent. It may thus follow the main clause, or be embedded within the main clause:

Wie heißt der kleine Junge, der eben hier war?
Der Junge, der eben hier war, heißt Hans.

Relative clauses are dependent clauses; like all dependent clauses they are set off from the main clause by commas. The finite verb of a relative clause stands in last position in the clause. Compare:

Wo ⎡ist⎤ der Postbote? Er ⎡hat⎤ uns dieses Paket gebracht.

Wo ⎡ist⎤ der Postbote, der uns dieses Paket gebracht ⎡hat⎤?

If the relative pronoun is the object of a preposition, then that preposition is the first word in the relative clause. Otherwise the relative pronoun stands first. Compare:

Wo ist die Studentin, **auf die** wir gewartet haben?
Wo ist die Studentin, **die** früher hier wohnte?

Wo-compounds as relative pronoun substitutes

A **wo**-compound sometimes replaces a relative pronoun *if* (1) the relative pronoun is the object of a preposition *and* (2) the relative pronoun does not refer to a person. The preposition becomes the second element of the **wo**-compound, and the relative pronoun is replaced by **wo(r)-**:

Da kommt der Zug, **auf den** du wartest.
Da kommt der Zug, **worauf** du wartest.
Here comes the train *that* you are waiting *for*.

Die Sprichwörter, **an die** er glaubt, sind alt.
Die Sprichwörter, **woran** er glaubt, sind alt.
The proverbs *that* he believes *in* are old.

Although these **wo**-compounds certainly occur frequently as substitutes for prepositions plus relative pronouns, the latter are always correct and often even preferable.

The indefinite relative pronoun *was*

The relative pronoun is **was** if the antecedent is one of the following:

1 One of the indefinite neuter elements **alles, etwas, manches, nichts,** or **vieles**:

Ich gebe dir **alles, was** dir gefällt.
I'll give you *everything that* pleases you.

2 A superlative adjective used as a neuter noun:

Er kauft **das Beste,** was er finden kann.
He buys *the best that* he can find.

3 An entire clause:

Er kommt nach Hause, was uns natürlich gefällt.
He's coming home, which of course pleases us.

The general relative pronouns *wer* and *was*

Wer and **was** may function as question words, occurring either in direct questions or in indirect questions:

Wer ist das?	**Was** hat er gekauft?
Who is that?	*What* did he buy?
Weißt du, **wen** ich getroffen habe?	Ich sage dir, **was** er gekauft hat.
Do you know *whom* I met?	I'll tell you *what* he bought.

They may also function as relative pronouns without antecedents, however, with the meanings *whoever, what, that which, whatever*:

Wer viel Geld hat, kann so etwas kaufen.
Whoever has a lot of money can buy such a thing.

Was er gesagt hat, stimmt einfach nicht.
What he said is simply not true.

23.6 Some Notes on Nouns

Group I

A few masculine nouns of Group I ending in **-en** lack the ending **-n** in the nominative singular: **der Name, der Gedanke**. Except for this they are regular in Group I: **der Name, den Namen, dem Namen, des Namens,** *pl.* **die Namen,** etc.

The neuter noun **das Hertz** is inflected like Group I nouns except that it lacks the ending **-en** in the nominative and accusative singular: **das Herz, das Herz, dem Herzen, des Herzens,** *pl.* **die Herzen**, etc.

Group II

The **-s** of Group II nouns ending in **-nis** is doubled when the noun is inflected: **das Ereignis, des Ereignisses,** *pl.* **die Ereignisse**. *Note also*: **der Bus, des Busses, die Busse**.

Group IV

The **-n** of Group IV feminine nouns in **-in** is doubled in the plural: **die Freundin, die Freundinnen**.

Masculine and neuter nouns of Group IV must not be confused with the nouns of Group V. The **-(e)n** ending in Group IV is added only for the plural. The genitive singular ending is **-(e)s**, just as it is for masculine and neuter nouns of Groups I, II, and III:

	Singular	*Plural*
Nom.	der Staat	die Staaten
Acc.	den Staat	die Staaten
Dat.	dem Staat	den Staaten
Gen.	des Staates	der Staaten

Other nouns which follow this pattern are: **das Auge, das Bett, der Doktor, das Ende, das Hemd, der Nachbar, der Professor**.

Group V

All nouns of Group V are masculine. The ending **-(e)n** is added in the accusative, dative, and genitive singular as well as in the plural:

	Singular	*Plural*
Nom.	der Kunde	die Kunden
Acc.	den Kunden	die Kunden
Dat.	dem Kunden	den Kunden
Gen.	des Kunden	der Kunden

Other nouns which follow this pattern are: **der Bote, der Held, der Junge, der Kamerad, der Kollege, der Kunde, der Mensch, der Neffe, der Polizist, der Präsident, der Soldat**.

New nouns that follow this pattern will hereafter be indicated as follows: **der Kunde, -en, -en**.

Group VI (irregulars)

A number of nouns of recent foreign origin have **-s** in all plural cases. Some are: **das Auto, die Autos; das Büro, die Büros; das Foto, die Fotos; das Hotel, die Hotels.**

A few nouns of classical origin ending in **-ium** have plurals in **-ien**. Those you know are **das Gymnasium, die Gymnasien; das Podium, die Podien; das Stipendium, die Stipendien; das Studium, die Studien.**

Other types of irregularities occur occasionally: **das Drama, die Dramen; das Zentrum, die Zentren.**

WRITING

A. Dehydrated Sentences

Arrange the elements to form German sentences. Modify the basic forms of the words as required, and use the tense indicated:

1. man / sollen / achten / jed- / Mensch / voll   (*pres.*)
2. was / bedeuten / das?   (*pres. perf.*)
3. er / anfangen / schon   (*past*)
4. wir / sich nennen / bei / Vorname   (*past*)
5. tragen / doch / dein / grün / Rock / Christa!
6. man / duzen / Kinder / weil / man / sein / vertraut / mit / sie   (*pres., both clauses*)
7. warum / du / waschen / der Rock?   (*pres.*)
8. unser- / Mützen / hängen / hinter / die Tür   (*pres. perf.*)
9. er / anbieten / eine Zigarette / ich   (*past*)
10. waschen / dein / Hemd / und / lassen / hängen / es / auf / der Stuhl!
11. die Amerikanerin / begrüßen / ihr- / Mann / mit „Sie"   (*past perf.*)
12. können / sich vorstellen / du / so etwas?   (*pres.*)
13. hoffentlich / du / wiedererkennen / dein- / alt- / Klassenkamerad   (*pres. perf.*)
14. heute abend / tragen / ich / mein- / neu- / Kleid   (*fut.*)
15. es / sehen / du / ähnlich / Heinrich   (*pres.*)
16. in / der Hut / ich / können / sich sehen lassen / überhaupt nicht   (*pres.*)

B. Infinitive as Noun

Copy the sentences and supply the correct German noun:

1. Das _____ ist schwer.   (running)

2 Ich habe ihn beim _____ gesehen. (eating)
3 Beim _____ muß man aufpassen. (getting in)
4 Nachts ist das _____ am schlimmsten. (driving)
5 Das _____ macht ihm Spaß. (laughing)
6 Er wollte ihr beim _____ helfen. (shopping)
7 In dieser Stadt ist das _____ sehr teuer. (living)
8 Sie findet das _____ recht schwer. (reading)

C. Nouns and Adjectives

Copy the sentences and supply the correct German forms:

1 Dieser Film ist nur für _____. (adults)
2 _____ _____ sind oft schwer zu verstehen. (foreign customs)
3 Hast du _____ _____ _____ gefunden? (my good shoes)
4 Auf der Oberschule hatte er _____ _____. (many difficulties)
5 Man soll _____ _____ helfen. (the foreigners)
6 Damit machen wir aber _____ _____. (no class distinctions)
7 Die Zeitung liegt auf _____ _____. (the floor)
8 Bis auf _____ stimmt das. (exceptions)
9 Gehen _____ _____ noch zur Schule? (these apprentices)
10 Die _____ _____ gehen jeden Tag zur Schule. (smaller pupils)
11 Von _____ _____ _____ habe ich nichts gehört. (my old classmate)
12 Hast du schon wieder _____ _____ gekauft? (new clothes)
13 Der Lehrer hat _____ _____ darauf genommen. (no consideration)
14 Haben Sie früher in _____ _____ gewohnt? (this neighborhood)
15 Wir wollten über _____ _____ sprechen. (many events)

D. Relative Clauses

Combine the sentences by making the second one a relative clause:

1 Wo sind die Zeitungen? Ich habe sie gestern gehabt.
2 Er sprach mit dem Schüler. Du sahst ihn gestern.
3 Dort ist die Kiste. Mit ihr hat er Mühe gehabt.
4 Ich kenne den Mann. Er fährt so schnell.
5 Er spricht von dem Dorf. Es liegt nördlich von hier.
6 Die Geschichte ist endlos. Ich lese sie jetzt.
7 Hier kommen die Leute. Mit ihnen muß ich zum Baden gehen.
8 Der Junge heißt Peter. Du hast ihm den Kuchen gegeben.

9 Da kommt der Professor. Seine Vorlesungen sind so langweilig.
10 Wo wohnt die Frau? Ihr Sohn studiert Medizin.

Replace the preposition and its object with the correct **wo**-compound:

11 Wer hat das Buch geschrieben, über das wir gesprochen haben?
12 Der Bus, auf den wir gewartet haben, kam nicht.
13 Die Erzählungen, an die ich denke, sind ziemlich lang.
14 Das ist eine Sache, auf die ich keine Rücksicht genommen habe.
15 Kennst du die Städte, durch die wir gefahren sind?
16 Die Bretter und Schrauben, aus denen der Schrank eigentlich bestehen soll, hat er vergessen.

Copy the sentences and supply the correct relative pronoun:

17 Sagen Sie mir alles, _____ passiert ist!
18 _____ so etwas kaufen kann, muß viel Geld haben.
19 Ilse ist noch dieselbe nette Freundin, _____ sie immer war.
20 Hier ist nichts, _____ mir gefällt.
21 Das war das Schönste, _____ ich gesehen habe.
22 Der Junge, _____ Vater in diesem Geschäft arbeitet, heißt Heinz.
23 Er will bis Montag bei uns bleiben, _____ mich glücklich macht.
24 _____ tüchtig arbeitet, wird das Examen bestehen.
25 Das ist die Wirtin, in _____ Haus ich wohnte.
26 _____ du mir gegeben hast, will ich nicht haben.
27 Man hört manches, _____ man nicht glauben kann.
28 Wenn es regnet, werden die Straßen rutschig, _____ schlimm sein kann.

LISTENING PRACTICE

Listen to the recorded description; then answer the questions.

Heinrich Kellner, Kiel, Poststraße 34

1 Wohnen Kellners direkt in der Stadt?
2 Wie lange muß man von der Stadt aus dorthin fahren?
3 Ist Kellners Haus groß und neu?
4 Wie sehen die Häuser in der Poststraße aus?
5 Warum wohnen Kellners nicht in einem großen Haus?

Unit 24

GEORG HEGEL

DIALOG

Das Treffen bei Familie Kellner (Schluß)

1 **Heinrich:** Schön, Werner, daß du da bist. Dies hier ist meine Frau.

2 **Werner:** Guten Abend, Frau Kellner, ich freue mich, Sie kennenzulernen.

3 **Renate:** Ich auch, Heinrich hat mir schon viel von Ihnen erzählt.

4 **Werner:** Na, das wird wohl nicht so toll gewesen sein. Ich war nicht gerade ein Musterschüler.

5 **Renate:** Seine Berichte waren sogar ausgesprochen nett. Wann haben Sie Heinrich denn aus den Augen verloren?

6 **Werner:** Nun, ich denke, es wird wohl bald sechs Jahre her sein.

The Meeting at Kellners' (Conclusion)

1 Nice that you're here, Werner. This is my wife.

2 Good evening, Mrs. Kellner. I'm happy to meet you.

sich freuen *acc. refl.* be glad, happy

3 Me too. Heinrich has already told me a lot about you.

4 Well, that probably wasn't so great. I wasn't exactly a model student.

toll great; funny; furious · **der Musterschüler das Muster**, - model, pattern + **der Schüler**, - pupil

5 His reports were even very nice. When did you lose sight of Heinrich, anyway?

ausgesprochen very, distinct(ly) *pp. of* **aussprechen** pronounce · **verlieren: er verliert, verlor, hat verloren** lose

6 Well, I think it must be almost six years ago.

her ago; here, to this place

7 **Renate:**   Sechs Jahre! Warum hast du nie etwas von dir hören lassen, Heinrich?

8 **Werner:**   Ja, darauf hab' ich leider vergeblich warten müssen. Ich habe ja nicht wissen können, wo er steckt!

9 **Renate:**   Aber nun kommen Sie herein! Wir wollen uns einen gemütlichen Abend machen.

10 **Werner:**   Darauf freue ich mich schon! Es wird eine Menge zu erzählen geben.

SUPPLEMENT

1 Ich werde die Handtücher waschen müssen.

2 Ich habe die Strümpfe waschen müssen.

3 Er wird die Mütze finden können.

4 Er hat die Taschentücher finden können.

5 Hast du deine Schuhe suchen wollen?

6 Warum haben wir nicht mitgehen dürfen?

7 Sie hat die Kinder spielen lassen.

8 Ich weiß, daß sie die Kinder hat spielen lassen.

9 Er hat den Mantel dort liegen lassen.

10 Er sagt, daß er den Mantel dort hat liegen lassen.

7	Six years! Why didn't you ever let yourself be heard from, Heinrich?	**hören lassen** allow to be heard (*cf.* **sehen lassen**)
8	Yes, unfortunately I had to wait in vain for that. After all, I couldn't know where he was.	**stecken** *intrans.* be; *trans.* put, stick
9	But now come on in! Let's have a nice evening.	**hereinkommen herein** *separable prefix* in (**her** to this place + **ein** in) + **kommen** · **gemütlich** comfortable, cozy · **sich machen** *dat. refl.* make for oneself
10	I'm already looking forward to it. There'll be a lot to tell.	**sich freuen auf** + *acc.* look forward to · **die Menge, -n** quantity, crowd **eine Menge** a lot

---

1	I will have to wash the towels.	**das Handtuch die Hand, ⸚e** hand + **das Tuch, ⸚er** cloth
2	I had to wash the stockings.	**der Strumpf, ⸚e**
3	He will be able to find the cap.	
4	He was able to find the handkerchiefs.	**das Taschentuch die Tasche, -n** pocket + **das Tuch, ⸚er** cloth
5	Did you want to look for your shoes?	**suchen** look for, seek
6	Why weren't we permitted to go along?	
7	She let the children play.	**spielen** play
8	I know that she let the children play.	
9	He left the coat lying there.	
10	He says that he left the coat lying there.	

11 Sie hat sich überall sehen lassen.

12 Jeder weiß, daß sie sich überall hat sehen lassen.

13 Hast du etwas von dir hören lassen?

14 Meinst du, daß du etwas von dir hast hören lassen?

11 She let herself be seen everywhere.

12 Everyone knows that she let herself be seen everywhere.

13 Did you let yourself be heard from?

14 Do you mean that you let yourself be heard from?

AUDIOLINGUAL DRILLS

A. Directed Dialog

Sagen Sie, es ist schön, daß Werner da ist!
Es ist schön, daß Werner da ist.

Sagen Sie, daß Werner sich freut, Frau Kellner kennenzulernen!
Werner freut sich, Frau Kellner kennenzulernen.

Sagen Sie, daß Heinrich Renate schon viel von Werner erzählt hat!
Heinrich hat Renate schon viel von Werner erzählt.

Sagen Sie, daß das wohl nicht so toll gewesen sein wird!
Das wird wohl nicht so toll gewesen sein.

Sagen Sie, daß Werner nicht gerade ein Musterschüler war!
Werner war nicht gerade ein Musterschüler.

Sagen Sie, daß Heinrichs Berichte sogar ausgesprochen nett waren!
Heinrichs Berichte waren sogar ausgesprochen nett.

Fragen Sie, wann Werner Heinrich denn aus den Augen verloren hat!
Wann hat Werner Heinrich denn aus den Augen verloren?

Antworten Sie, daß es wohl bald sechs Jahre her sein wird!
Es wird wohl bald sechs Jahre her sein.

Fragen Sie, warum Heinrich nie etwas von sich hat hören lassen!
Warum hat Heinrich nie etwas von sich hören lassen?

Antworten Sie, daß Werner darauf leider vergeblich hat warten müssen!
Werner hat darauf leider vergeblich warten müssen.

Sagen Sie, daß er ja nicht hat wissen können, wo Heinrich steckt!
Er hat ja nicht wissen können, wo Heinrich steckt.

Sagen Sie, daß Werner aber nun hereinkommen soll!
Werner soll aber nun hereinkommen.

Sagen Sie, daß sie sich einen gemütlichen Abend machen wollen!
Sie wollen sich einen gemütlichen Abend machen.

Sagen Sie, daß Werner sich schon darauf freut!
Werner freut sich schon darauf.

Sagen Sie, daß es eine Menge zu erzählen geben wird!
Es wird eine Menge zu erzählen geben.

B. A New Strong Verb

1 **Verlieren** *lose* follows the pattern of **ziehen**, but without the consonant changes — **er verliert, verlor, hat verloren**. Substitute the new accusative object:

Wir haben ihn aus den Augen verloren.   **unseren Freund**
Wir haben unseren Freund aus den Augen verloren.   **sie**
Wir haben sie aus den Augen verloren.   **den Studenten**
Wir haben den Studenten aus den Augen verloren.   **einander**
Wir haben einander aus den Augen verloren.   **uns**
Wir haben uns aus den Augen verloren.

2 Change the tense as indicated:

Wer hat seine Schuhe verloren? *past perf.*   Wer wird seine Schuhe verlieren? *pres. perf.*
Wer hatte seine Schuhe verloren? *pres.*   Wer hat seine Schuhe verloren?
Wer verliert seine Schuhe? *fut.*

C. The Dependent Infinitive with *zu* (*See Grammar* §§13.3, 24.3)

3 Substitute the new infinitive and supply **zu**:

Ich habe nichts anzuziehen.   **erzählen**   Ich habe nichts zu verlieren.   **anbieten**
Ich habe nichts zu erzählen.   **tun**   Ich habe nichts anzubieten.
Ich habe nichts zu tun.   **verlieren**

4 Substitute the new infinitive phrase, with **zu**:

Wir haben uns gefreut, ihn kennenzulernen. **sie wiedersehen**
Wir haben uns gefreut, sie wiederzusehen. **mit ihnen gehen**
Wir haben uns gefreut, mit ihnen zu gehen. **ihr helfen**
Wir haben uns gefreut, ihr zu helfen. **die Stadt ansehen**
Wir haben uns gefreut, die Stadt anzusehen. **wieder bei dir sein**
Wir haben uns gefreut, wieder bei dir zu sein.

5 Substitute the new main clause:

Er hat vergessen, das zu tun. **es sieht dir ähnlich**
Es sieht dir ähnlich, das zu tun. **ich freue mich**
Ich freue mich, das zu tun. **wir fangen an**
Wir fangen an, das zu tun. **ich bitte dich**
Ich bitte dich, das zu tun.

D. Double Infinitives (*See Grammar* §24.4)

6 Substitute the new subject:

Darauf hast du leider warten müssen. **ich**
Darauf habe ich leider warten müssen. **er**
Darauf hat er leider warten müssen. **wir**
Darauf haben wir leider warten müssen. **die Leute**
Darauf haben die Leute leider warten müssen. **ihr**
Darauf habt ihr leider warten müssen.

Das hat er nicht wissen können. **wir**
Das haben wir nicht wissen können. **du**
Das hast du nicht wissen können. **ich**

Das habe ich nicht wissen können. **ihr**
Das habt ihr nicht wissen können. **die anderen**
Das haben die anderen nicht wissen können.

7 Substitute the new subject or modal auxiliary:

Ich habe das nicht tun wollen. **ihr**
Ihr habt das nicht tun wollen. **müssen**
Ihr habt das nicht tun müssen. **er**
Er hat das nicht tun müssen. **können**
Er hat das nicht tun können. **wir**
Wir haben das nicht tun können. **mögen**

Wir haben das nicht tun mögen. **du**
Du hast das nicht tun mögen. **dürfen**
Du hast das nicht tun dürfen. **die Schüler**
Die Schüler haben das nicht tun dürfen. **sollen**
Die Schüler haben das nicht tun sollen. **ich**
Ich habe das nicht tun sollen.

8 Substitute the new subject:

Ich hatte mir einen Wagen kaufen wollen.   **meine Eltern**
Meine Eltern hatten sich einen Wagen kaufen wollen.   **du**
Du hattest dir einen Wagen kaufen wollen.   **sein Großvater**
Sein Großvater hatte sich einen Wagen kaufen wollen.   **ihr**
Ihr hattet euch einen Wagen kaufen wollen.   **wir**
Wir hatten uns einen Wagen kaufen wollen.

9 Substitute the new subject or modal auxiliary:

Ich hatte mich umziehen müssen.   **du**
Du hattest dich umziehen müssen.   **wollen**
Du hattest dich umziehen wollen.   **ihr**
Ihr hattet euch umziehen wollen.   **dürfen**
Ihr hattet euch umziehen dürfen.   **wir**
Wir hatten uns umziehen dürfen.   **müssen**
Wir hatten uns umziehen müssen.   **meine Großmutter**
Meine Großmutter hatte sich umziehen müssen.   **können**
Meine Großmutter hatte sich umziehen können.   **seine Großeltern**
Seine Großeltern hatten sich umziehen können.

10 Expand by adding the indicated modal auxiliary.

Examples:
Er hat so etwas nie getan.   **können**
Er hat so etwas nie tun können.

Wir sind zu Hause geblieben.   **müssen**
Wir haben zu Hause bleiben müssen.

Ich habe es nicht gewußt.   **können**
Ich habe es nicht wissen können.

Die Kinder sind zu Hause geblieben.   **müssen**
Die Kinder haben zu Hause bleiben müssen.

Wir haben eine Uhr gekauft.   **wollen**
Wir haben eine Uhr kaufen wollen.

Hast du deine Arbeit nicht getan?   **mögen**
Hast du deine Arbeit nicht tun mögen?

Ihr seid in die Stadt gegangen.   **sollen**
Ihr habt in die Stadt gehen sollen.

Er hat den Wagen nicht gefahren.   **dürfen**
Er hat den Wagen nicht fahren dürfen.

11 Expand and transform the following sentences by adding the indicated dependent infinitive.

Example:
So etwas hat der Schlaukopf noch nie gekonnt.   **tun**
So etwas hat der Schlaukopf noch nie tun können.

Der Schlaukopf hat es nicht gekonnt.   **tun**
Der Schlaukopf hat es nicht tun können.

Warum hattest du es gewollt?   **kaufen**
Warum hattest du es kaufen wollen?

Ich habe diesen Mantel nie gemocht.   **leiden**
Ich habe diesen Mantel nie leiden mögen.

Ihr habt in die Stadt gesollt.   **fahren**
Ihr habt in die Stadt fahren sollen.

Wir hatten nicht ins Theater gedurft.   **gehen**
Wir hatten nicht ins Theater gehen dürfen.

Ich habe damals kein Deutsch gekonnt.   **sprechen**
Ich habe damals kein Deutsch sprechen können.

Haben die Schüler es gemußt?   **schreiben**
Haben die Schüler es schreiben müssen?

Hören, **helfen**, **lassen**, and **sehen** follow the pattern of the modals in the perfect tenses.

12 Substitute the new subject:

Ich habe ihn wieder weggehen hören.   **wir**
Wir haben ihn wieder weggehen hören.   **er**
Er hat ihn wieder weggehen hören.   **die Freunde**
Die Freunde haben ihn wieder weggehen hören.   **ihr**
Ihr habt ihn wieder weggehen hören.   **du**
Du hast ihn wieder weggehen hören.

13 Expand and transform the following sentences by adding the indicated dependent infinitive.

Example:
Mein Klassenkamerad hatte mich nicht gesehen.   **kommen**
Mein Klassenkamerad hatte mich nicht kommen sehen.

Ich hatte Werner dort gesehen.   **stehen**
Ich hatte Werner dort stehen sehen.

Sie hatte die Kinder im Haus gelassen.   **spielen**
Sie hatte die Kinder im Haus spielen lassen.

Wir hatten euch gehört.   **sprechen**
Wir hatten euch sprechen hören.

Ich habe dich leider nicht gehört.   **abfahren**
Ich habe dich leider nicht abfahren hören.

Warum habt ihr das da gelassen?   **liegen**
Warum habt ihr das da liegen lassen?

Habt ihr den Milchwagen gesehen?   **rutschen**
Habt ihr den Milchwagen rutschen sehen?

Hattest du deinen Freund nicht gehört?   **kommen**
Hattest du deinen Freund nicht kommen hören?

14 Change the following sentences to the present perfect tense. Note that the "double infinitive" construction does not occur when the dependent infinitive is preceded by **zu**.

Examples:
Ich höre ihn sprechen.
Ich habe ihn sprechen hören.

Die Mutter hat viel zu kaufen.
Die Mutter hat viel zu kaufen gehabt.

Der Klassenkamerad kann erst heute abend kommen.
Der Klassenkamerad hat erst heute abend kommen können.

Wir sehen Heike auf dem Podium stehen.
Wir haben Heike auf dem Podium stehen sehen.

Ihr habt noch viel zu üben.
Ihr habt noch viel zu üben gehabt.

Mußt du das ganze Buch lesen?
Hast du das ganze Buch lesen müssen?

Ich habe leider viel zu tun.
Ich habe leider viel zu tun gehabt.

Mein Neffe will in einer Fabrik arbeiten.
Mein Neffe hat in einer Fabrik arbeiten wollen.

Warum lassen sie ihn nicht kommen?
Warum haben sie ihn nicht kommen lassen?

15 Substitute the new dependent infinitive:

Er sagt, daß er hat warten müssen.   **stehen**
Er sagt, daß er hat stehen müssen.   **lachen**
Er sagt, daß er hat lachen müssen.   **aussteigen**
Er sagt, daß er hat aussteigen müssen.   **weggehen**
Er sagt, daß er hat weggehen müssen.   **zurückkommen**
Er sagt, daß er hat zurückkommen müssen.

16 Begin the following sentences with **Er sagt, daß** . . . :

Er hat vergeblich warten müssen.
Er sagt, daß er vergeblich hat warten müssen.

Sie haben ihn kommen lassen.
Er sagt, daß sie ihn haben kommen lassen.

Sie hatte sich das denken können.
Er sagt, daß sie sich das hatte denken können.

Ihr hattet ihn nicht weggehen hören.
Er sagt, daß ihr ihn nicht hattet weggehen hören.

Du hast in die Stadt gehen wollen.
Er sagt, daß du in die Stadt hast gehen wollen.

Du hattest den Wagen ankommen sehen.
Er sagt, daß du den Wagen hattest ankommen sehen.

17 Change the following sentences to the future.

Example:
Ich muß nächsten Monat in die Schweiz fahren.
Ich werde nächsten Monat in die Schweiz fahren müssen.

Sie wollen sich einen Wagen kaufen.
Sie werden sich einen Wagen kaufen wollen.

Er darf nicht zum Baden gehen.
Er wird nicht zum Baden gehen dürfen.

Wir sehen ihn im Garten arbeiten.
Wir werden ihn im Garten arbeiten sehen.

Warum kannst du denn nicht mitfahren?
Warum wirst du denn nicht mitfahren können?

Laßt ihr die Kinder in einen Film gehen?
Werdet ihr die Kinder in einen Film gehen lassen?

Die Kundin mag dieses Kleid nicht leiden.
Die Kundin wird dieses Kleid nicht leiden mögen.

Ich höre ihn Geige spielen.
Ich werde ihn Geige spielen hören.

Er soll in ein Geschäft gehen.
Er wird in ein Geschäft gehen sollen.

E. Future of Probability (*See Grammar* §24.5)

18 The future tense with the adverb **wohl** is used to indicate present probability. Substitute the new prepositional phrase:

Er wird wohl zu Hause sein.   **im Geschäft**
Er wird wohl im Geschäft sein.   **in Berlin**
Er wird wohl in Berlin sein.   **an der Haltestelle**
Er wird wohl an der Haltestelle sein.   **bei seinen Eltern**
Er wird wohl bei seinen Eltern sein.   **in seinem Zimmer**
Er wird wohl in seinem Zimmer sein.

19 The future perfect tense with **wohl** is used to indicate past probability. Substitute the new subject:

Er wird wohl viel Mühe damit gehabt haben.   **du**
Du wirst wohl viel Mühe damit gehabt haben.   **die Kinder**
Die Kinder werden wohl viel Mühe damit gehabt haben.   **ihr**
Ihr werdet wohl viel Mühe damit gehabt haben.   **der Junge**
Der Junge wird wohl viel Mühe damit gehabt haben.   **die Studenten**
Die Studenten werden wohl viel Mühe damit gehabt haben.   **er**
Er wird wohl viel Mühe damit gehabt haben.

F. Questions and Answers

Worüber freut Werner sich?
Er freut sich, Frau Kellner kennenzulernen.

Woher weiß Renate so viel über Werner?
Heinrich hatte ihr viel von ihm erzählt.

Was sagt Werner dazu?
Er sagt, daß es wohl nicht so toll gewesen sein wird.

Warum sagt er so etwas?
Er meint, daß er nicht gerade ein Musterschüler war.

Wie waren Heinrichs Berichte?
Renate sagt, daß sie ausgesprochen nett waren.

Wann hatte Werner Heinrich aus den Augen verloren?
Werner meint, daß es wohl bald sechs Jahre her sein wird.

Warum hatte Werner nicht an Heinrich geschrieben?
Er hatte nicht wissen können, wo Heinrich steckt.

Was wollen die Freunde tun?
Sie wollen sich einen gemütlichen Abend machen.

GRAMMAR

24.1 Word-Formation

Separable prefixes of verbs

The separable prefixes of verbs usually have rather concrete, specific meanings which can be recognized without too much difficulty. Many of them are prepositions which, when used with basic infinitives, have the force of adverbs: **ausgehen** *go out*; **aufstehen** *get up*; **mitkommen** *come along*. The meaning of the prefix is not necessarily literal: **aufschreiben** *write down*; **aufmachen** *open (a door)*. The preposition **in** becomes **ein** as a verbal prefix: **einlaufen** *run in; arrive at the station (train)*; **einkaufen** *shop (buy in)*; **einschlafen** *fall asleep*. Some of the separable prefixes are adverbs in their own right and can readily be understood when they are used as prefixes: **los** *loose* → **loslassen** *release*; **heim** *home* → **heimkommen** *come home*; **zusammen** *together* → **zusammenbauen** *build together (assemble)*; **her** *hither* → **herkommen** *come (toward the speaker)*; **hin** *thither* → **hingehen** *go there (away from the speaker)*; **herauskommen** *come out (toward the speaker)*; **hinaufsteigen** *climb up (away from the speaker)*; **herunterrutschen** *slide down (toward the speaker)*.

In order to illustrate how only one prefix can affect the meaning of many basic verbs, let us examine the effect of the preposition **an** as a prefix of some basic verbs you know. **An** has the English equivalents *at, on, onto, in, into, to*, depending on the context. In other words, the notion of approaching or being nearby is suggested. As a verbal prefix **an-** usually has this meaning, but it may also have the meaning of *begin to*.

Some examples of the prefix **an-** expressing the notion of approaching or being nearby are:

bauen	build	anbauen	build onto (a building)
grenzen	border	angrenzen	be adjacent to
haben	have	anhaben	have on (a coat)
hören	hear	anhören	listen to
kommen	come	ankommen	arrive
laufen	run	anlaufen	come running along; run toward
nehmen	take	annehmen	accept; take on (a job)
rufen	call	anrufen	call to; call up (phone)
schauen	look	anschauen	look at
sehen	see	ansehen	look at
sprechen	speak	ansprechen	address (a person)
ziehen	pull	anziehen	put (pull) on (clothes)

Some examples of **an-** expressing the notion of *begin to* are:

braten	roast	anbraten	(begin to) roast
fangen	catch	anfangen	begin
heizen	heat	anheizen	(begin to) heat
kochen	cook	ankochen	boil partially, parboil
lernen	learn	anlernen	give initial training to (a person)
rauchen	smoke	anrauchen	begin to smoke (a cigar)

4.2 Singular and Plural of Nouns

der Bericht, -e   die Menge, -n
die Hand, ⸚e   der Strumpf, ⸚e
der Handschuh, -e   die Tasche, -n
das Handtuch, ⸚er   das Taschentuch, ⸚er

4.3 The Dependent Infinitive with *zu*

Review the material on dependent infinitives in Grammar §13.3. The dependent infinitive usually stands at the end of a main clause:

Er beginnt zu sprechen.   Er hat begonnen zu sprechen.
He's beginning to speak.   He began to speak.

Er begann zu sprechen.
He began to speak.

The dependent infinitive with **zu** may occur either *after* the verb phrase (as in the last example above) or *inside* the verb phrase; that is, it may either follow or precede the final element in a verb phrase (past participle, or infinitive without **zu**). It is preferable to have it follow this last element, however. The following examples show this variation; in each pair of German sentences the first one has the preferred word order:

Er hat begonnen zu sprechen.
Er hat zu sprechen begonnen.
He began to speak.

Er hat vergessen zu kommen.
Er hat zu kommen vergessen.
He forgot to come.

Die Kinder hatten angefangen zu spielen.
Die Kinder hatten zu spielen angefangen.
The children had begun to play.

Hoffentlich werden sie nicht vergessen zu kommen.
Hoffentlich werden sie nicht zu kommen vergessen.
I hope they won't forget to come.

The dependent **zu**-infinitive may be expanded to include more than just **zu** and the verb, by adding elements such as objects or adverbs. These additional elements must precede the infinitive:

Er hat vergessen, nach Hause **zu gehen**.	Ich hatte gehofft, das Examen **zu bestehen**.
He forgot *to go* home.	I had hoped *to pass* the examination.

Note that these expanded infinitive phrases are set off by commas.

24.4 The Double Infinitive

The modal auxiliaries may occur with dependent infinitives, without **zu**. Compare the infinitives in the two sentences:

Du brauchst nicht **zu spotten**.	Du darfst nicht **spotten**.

The future tense of a modal auxiliary is formed with **werden** plus the infinitive of the modal:

Er **muß** in die Stadt gehen.	Er **wird** in die Stadt gehen **müssen**.
He *has to* go to the city.	He *will have to* go to the city.

The two infinitives at the end of the sentence **gehen müssen** constitute what we call a *double infinitive*. The first one, **gehen**, is dependent on the second one, and **müssen** in turn is dependent on the future auxiliary **wird**.

The present perfect or past perfect tense of a modal is formed with the tense auxiliary **haben** plus the past participle of the modal:

Er **muß** in die Stadt.
He *has to* go to the city.

Er **hatte** in die Stadt **gemußt**.
He *had had to* go to the city.

Er **hat** in die Stadt **gemußt**.
He *had to* go to the city.

If the modal auxiliary has a dependent infinitive, however, then the present perfect and past perfect tenses are formed with **haben** plus the *double infinitive*:

Er **hat** in die Stadt **gehen müssen**.
He *had to go* to the city.

Er **hatte** in die Stadt **gehen müssen**.
He *had had to go* to the city.

The form that the modal auxiliary assumes in the perfect tenses thus depends on whether or not it occurs with a dependent infinitive in that sentence. Note that the auxiliary is **haben**, not **sein**:

Without dependent infinitive	*With dependent infinitive*
hat gedurft	hat gehen dürfen
hat gekonnt	hat gehen können
hat gemocht	hat gehen mögen
hat gemußt	hat gehen müssen
hat gesollt	hat gehen sollen
hat gewollt	hat gehen wollen

Word order

In a double infinitive construction, the modal auxiliary follows its dependent infinitive. Furthermore, the double infinitive is always the *very last element in its clause*. In a dependent clause in which there is a double infinitive, then, the tense auxiliary stands not at the end, but before the double infinitive. This is the one exception to the rule that places the finite verb last in a dependent clause. Compare:

Er sagt, daß er in die Stadt gegangen ⌐ist⌐.   Er sagt, daß er in die Stadt ⌐muß⌐.

Er sagt, daß er in die Stadt ⌐hat⌐ gehen müssen.

hören, helfen, lassen, and *sehen*

The verbs **hören, helfen, lassen,** and **sehen**—and a few others—behave in a manner similar to modal auxiliaries, in that they may take dependent infinitives without **zu** and they form double infinitives:

Ich höre ihn **wegfahren**.
I hear him driving away.

Ich habe ihn **wegfahren hören**.
I heard him driving away.

Siehst du die Kinder **spielen**?
Do you see the children playing?

Hast du die Kinder **spielen sehen**?
Did you see the children playing?

Ich weiß, daß sie sich überall **sehen** läßt.
I know that she lets herself be seen everywhere.

Ich weiß, daß sie sich überall hat **sehen lassen**.
I know that she let herself be seen everywhere.

24.5 Future of Probability

The future tense may be used to refer to future time (see Grammar §13.4):

Er **wird** bald zu Hause **sein**.   He *will be* home soon.

It may also be used to express probability in the present time; in this function the adverb **wohl** *probably* usually accompanies it:

Er **wird wohl** zu Hause **sein**.   He *is probably* at home. (He *must be* at home.)

The future perfect tense is composed of a finite form of **werden** plus the perfect infinitive (that is, a past participle together with the infinitive form of its tense auxiliary). With the adverb **wohl** the future perfect tense is used to express probability in past time:

Er **wird wohl** zu Hause **gewesen sein**.
He *was probably* at home.

Sie **werden wohl** viel Mühe damit **gehabt haben**.
They *probably had* a lot of trouble with it.

WRITING

A. Completion

Copy and complete the following with appropriate verbs in the past tense. Choose all verbs from the list provided:

aufstehen, aufstellen, (sich) legen, liegen, (sich) setzen, sitzen, stecken, stehen, (sich) stellen

Herr Held _____ auf einem Stuhl im Vorlesungsraum. Neben ihm _____ noch ein Stuhl, der frei war. Plötzlich _____ Fräulein Schneider vor ihm und fragte etwas. Herr Held _____ schnell auf und bot ihr den freien Stuhl an. Fräulein Schneider zog ihren Mantel aus und

_____ ihn über den Stuhl. Dann _____ sie ihr Halstuch in die Tasche des Mantels. Sie _____ sich auf den Stuhl neben Herrn Held. Ein Mann holte das Podium aus der Ecke und _____ es auf. Dann _____ er eine Lampe auf das Podium. Nun kam der Professor in den Raum. Er _____ seinen Mantel auf den Tisch in der Ecke. Neben dem Podium _____ ein Stuhl für ihn, aber er _____ sich nicht darauf. Er _____ sich vor das Podium und _____ das Manuskript darauf. Nun _____ es also vor ihm, und die Vorlesung konnte beginnen.

B. Dehydrated Clauses

Complete and combine as directed.

Combine into one sentence, making the dehydrated clause the subordinate clause in the past tense. Some words will have to be supplied.

Example:
Ich hatte schon fertig studiert.   als / er / kommen / Stuttgart
Complete sentence: Ich hatte schon fertig studiert, als er nach Stuttgart kam.

1 Wir waren schon ins Ausland gegangen.   als / du / ziehen / Hannover
2 Sie hatten uns nichts darüber gesagt.   daß / Lilo / sein / so / krank
3 Wart ihr schon abgefahren?   als / Ilse / ankommen
4 Er hatte nicht schreiben können.   weil / er / wissen / Nummer / nicht
5 Hattest du es nicht erfahren?   daß / er / sein / verlobt

Combine into one sentence, making the dehydrated clause the main clause in the past perfect.

Example:
Als ich auf das Gymnasium kam,   machen / er / Abitur / schon
Complete sentence: Als ich auf das Gymnasium kam, hatte er das Abitur schon gemacht.

6 Als ich das Geschäft in Worms kaufte,   umziehen / er / schon
7 Daß ihr in Belgien wart,   erzählen / Hans / wir / nicht
8 Weil er Amerika mal sehen wollte,   leben / Jahr / dort
9 Damit der Besuch nicht anstrengend wurde,   weggehen / Jürgen / bald / wieder
10 In welcher Stadt er damals war,   können / ich / doch / nicht / wissen

C. Dehydrated Sentences

Modify the basic forms of the words as needed and construct sentences using the past tense in one clause and the past perfect in the other.

Example:
als / du / München / ziehen / bestehen / ich / Examen / schon
Als du nach München zogst, hatte ich mein Examen schon bestanden.

1. als / Werner / Freund / Bus / treffen / sehen / er / schon / ewig / nicht
2. Werner / wollen / wissen / woher / Heinrich / kommen
3. Werner / erfahren / schon / Helmut / daß / Heinrich / wieder / Kiel / leben
4. als / Werner / Kiel / wohnen / kennenlernen / er / Heinrichs Frau / nicht
5. ich / bestehen / mein / Examen / schon / als / ihr / Hamburg / umziehen
6. als / er / Amerika / fahren / ich / kaufen / ein / neu / Fabrik / schon
7. wir / wohnen / zehn / Jahr / Berlin / als / wir / Bonn / ziehen / müssen
8. wie / ich / damals / wissen / können / in / welch- / Geschäft / er / arbeiten ?
9. als / wir / dort / ankommen / wegfahren / du / schon / wieder
10. Heinrich / sagen / sein / Frau / schon / daß / Werner / früher / hier / wohnen

D. Future of Probability

Use the future tense with **wohl** to express the following in German. Place **wohl** immediately after the finite verb or the pronoun object:

1. He is probably eating walnut ice cream.
2. She is probably going swimming.
3. He must be waiting for it.
4. She probably knows him.
5. They probably live in this neighborhood.
6. His reports are probably very nice.

Use the future perfect with **wohl** to express the following in German:

7. They probably reassured him.
8. She must have received the package.
9. You must have had a lot of work.
10. They probably came in the evening.
11. He probably heard about it.
12. It probably happened at night.

READING PRACTICE

Heinrich und Renate

Werner und Heinrich hatten sich vor Jahren aus den Augen verloren, denn Werner ging zu seinem Vater ins Geschäft, und Heinrich zog nach München. Bald darauf lernte Heinrich Renate kennen, seine jetzige Frau. Das war in Innsbruck, und es kam so:

Heinrich war damals Student an der Universität München gewesen. Er hatte im Wintersemester viel gearbeitet, weil er im nächsten Semester sein Staatsexamen machen wollte.

Eines Tages sagte sein Professor zu ihm: ,,Kellner, Sie sehen ziemlich angestrengt aus. Lassen Sie die Bücher mal ein bißchen allein und machen Sie sich ein paar schöne Tage''.

Genau dasselbe hatte Heinrich sich auch schon gedacht. Das ewige Studieren war wirklich ein wenig zu viel gewesen. Schon drei Tage später saß er im Zug nach Innsbruck.

Das war Anfang April. Was macht man Anfang April in Innsbruck? Zum Schilaufen[g] ist es schon ziemlich spät, und für den schönen Tiroler Sommer ist es noch zu früh.

Heinrich ging also zuerst einfach einmal zur Universität in Innsbruck. Nur so zum Spaß. Und da sah er plötzlich Renate. Sie wollte einige Bücher für ihre Semesterarbeit holen. Nun, was soll ein junger Mann tun, wenn er eine hübsche Studentin sieht, die mit ihren Büchern so viel Mühe hat und so hilflos aussieht?

Heinrich hat ihr einfach geholfen, hat ein bißchen mit ihr gesprochen, hat ihre Telefonnummer aufgeschrieben . . . und danach ging alles sehr schnell. Heinrich und Renate hatten nicht nur ,,ein paar schöne Tage'', sie hatten die schönsten Tage, die man sich denken kann.

Heinrich und Renate fahren noch heute gern und oft nach Innsbruck. Nicht im Winter und auch nicht im Sommer, sondern im Frühling. Sie finden es im April am schönsten in Innsbruck.

Unit 25

BRAHMS

READING

Von deutschen Schulen

Schulen haben in Deutschland eine Tradition^g von fast zwölfhundert Jahren. Das muß man wissen, wenn man das eigenartige und komplizierte^g deutsche Schulwesen verstehen will. Zwölfhundert Jahre sind eine lange Zeit. Menschen kommen und gehen, Neues wird alt, und Altes kann wieder neu werden. Jedenfalls steckt in diesen zwölfhundert Jahren eine Menge Erfahrung.

Seit zweihundertfünfzig Jahren besteht eine allgemeine Schulpflicht in Deutschland (in Weimar sogar schon seit 1619). Heute müssen alle Kinder von ihrem 6. bis zum 18. Lebensjahr zur Schule gehen, davon neun Jahre auf eine „Ganzzeitschule", das heißt auf eine Schule, in der man sechs Tage in der Woche Unterricht hat. Danach genügt es, wenn man sechs bis acht Stunden in der Woche eine Spezialschule^g besucht. Viele Kinder — eigentlich sind sie nun ja gar keine Kinder mehr — sind dann nämlich schon als Lehrlinge in einer dreijährigen^g Berufsausbildung, und in dieser Zeit brauchen sie dann eben nur noch sechs bis acht Stunden in der Woche zur Schule zu gehen.

Der Schulbesuch ist heute bis auf Ausnahmen frei. Man braucht für seine Kinder kein Schulgeld zu bezahlen, auch nicht, wenn man sie auf eine Höhere Schule schicken will.

Mit sechs Jahren beginnt also für die deutschen Kinder der Ernst des Lebens. Vielleicht sind

UNIT 25 · READING 541

die Tradition, -en [tʀaditsiˈoːn]
das Schulwesen educational system
Neues *adj. noun* that which is new, new things
Altes *adj. noun* that which is old, old things

bestehen exist; consist · **allgemein** general, common · **die Schulpflicht** compulsory education **die Pflicht, -en** duty
der Unterricht instruction
spezial [ʃpetsiˈaːl]
die Berufsausbildung professional training
der Beruf, -e profession **die Ausbildung** education, training **die Bildung, -en** education

bezahlen pay

1 Seit wann gibt es Schulen in Deutschland?
2 Müssen alle Kinder heute zur Schule gehen?
3 Seit wann besteht eine allgemeine Schulpflicht in Deutschland?
4 Wer muß heute zur Schule gehen?
5 Wie viele Jahre gehen die Kinder auf eine Ganzzeitschule?
6 Wie viele Tage hat man dort Unterricht?
7 Ist es sehr teuer, die Kinder in die Schule zu schicken?
8 Was fängt an, wenn man sechs Jahre alt ist?

sie früher schon im Kindergarten gewesen, doch das war ja freiwillig[g] und hauptsächlich Spiel. Jetzt aber wird es ernst, sie m ü s s e n nämlich, wenn sie nicht krank sind, in die Schule. Viele Kinder freuen sich natürlich darüber, aber doch nicht alle.

Die Volksschule

Zuerst müssen sie eine bestimmte, allgemeine Schule besuchen, die Volksschule. Der Name „Volksschule" ist ungefähr zweihundert Jahre alt und bedeutet: Schule für alle, Schule für das ganze Volk und nicht nur für die Kinder von Leuten, die Geld genug haben, um ihre Kinder auf teuren Privatschulen[g] erziehen zu lassen.

Aber eben auch für diese Kinder. Wenigstens vier Jahre nämlich müssen auch sie auf der Volksschule bleiben. Erst dann kann man, nach einem Examen, auf die Mittelschule oder auf die Oberschule überwechseln. Dorthin geht man dann noch einmal sechs (Mittelschule) oder neun Jahre (Oberschule). Natürlich kann man auch noch später überwechseln, aber das gibt meistens einige Schwierigkeiten, denn das Programm[g] der einzelnen Schulen ist sehr verschieden.

Die meisten Kinder (tatsächlich sind es ungefähr 70%) bleiben auf der Volksschule. Und warum auch nicht? Sie haben hier einen guten allgemeinen Unterricht und können, wenn sie wollen, auch eine fremde Sprache lernen, zumeist Englisch[g]. Und es gibt nach einer solchen Schulausbildung auch genug Berufe für sie. Am häufigsten werden sie Spezialarbeiter und -arbeiterinnen (in Deutschland ist ja sehr viel Industrie), oder sie gehen in einen der vielen Handwerkerberufe, in denen sie heute häufig mehr Geld bekommen als manche Akademiker[g].

Die Mittelschule

Die Mittelschule ist schwerer. Sie ist in ihrem Plan wohl immer noch recht allgemein, aber doch nicht mehr so sehr wie die Volksschule. Ihre Ziele liegen höher. So werden in der Mittelschule auch schon zwei Fremdsprachen unterrichtet. Das sind meistens Englisch und Französisch[g], vielleicht auch einmal Spanisch[g].

Wenn die Kinder diese Schule durchlaufen haben, bekommen sie, was man in Deutschland „Mittlere Reife" nennt. Das ist, nach vollkommener Berufsausbildung natürlich, eine Qualifikation[g] für gute Stellungen in vielen Berufen, vor allem in der Industrie und in der Technik[g], aber auch bei der Post, bei der Bahn und in der freien Wirtschaft. Manche Berufe kann man ohne Mittlere Reife überhaupt nicht erlernen, Ingenieur[g] etwa. Für andere genügt auch die Mittlere Reife noch nicht. Man muß auf eine Oberschule gehen, sie ganz durchlaufen und unbedingt sein Abitur machen.

Die Oberschule

Oberschulen heißen auch Höhere Schulen oder Gymnasien. Hier sollen nur die wirklich intelligenten[g] Kinder neun Jahre lang speziell[g] geschult werden. Aber Kinder sind ja nicht nur mehr

der Kindergarten, ⸚ · hauptsächlich principally **die Hauptsache, -n** main point · **das Spiel, -e** game, play **sich freuen über etwas** *acc. refl.* be happy about something

ungefähr approximately, about

privat [pʀiˈvaːt] · **erziehen** bring up, educate **erziehen lassen** have educated, cause to be educated

überwechseln change over

das Programm, -e [pʀoˈgʀam] · **einzeln** individual, separate **verschieden** *adj.* different % = **Prozent** [pʀoˈtsɛnt] **pro** per

zumeist mostly, for the most part

der Handwerker, - artisan, workman · **der Akademiker, -** [akaˈdeːmikəʀ]

der Plan, ⸚e plan, schedule **das Ziel, -e** goal **unterrichten** instruct **der Unterricht** instruction

durchlaufen run through, pass through **die Mittlere Reife** examination after ten years of school **die Reife** maturity · **die Qualifikation, -en** [kvalifikatsiˈoːn] **die Technik** [ˈtɛçnɪk] **die Wirtschaft, -en** domestic economy, economic system **erlernen** learn · **der Ingenieur, -e** [ɪnʒeniˈøːʀ] ([ʒ] = sound of **s** in *pleasure*) **unbedingt** absolute(ly) **intelligent** [ɪntɛliˈgɛnt] **speziell** [ʃpetsiˈɛl] · **geschult werden** *pass. voice* be taught, be schooled

9 Freuen sich die Kinder darüber, in die Schule zu gehen?

10 Wie heißt die erste, allgemeine Schule?
11 Muß man viel Geld haben, um die Kinder in die Volksschule zu schicken?
12 Was bedeutet der Name „Volksschule"?
13 Wie lange müssen die Kinder auf der Volksschule bleiben?
14 Wann kann man auf die Mittelschule oder die Oberschule überwechseln?
15 Was muß man zuerst tun?
16 Wie lange geht man auf die Mittelschule?
17 Wie lange geht man auf die Oberschule?
18 Haben alle Schulen dasselbe Programm?
19 Wo bleiben die meisten Kinder?
20 Kann man dort eine Fremdsprache lernen?

21 Ist die Volksschule schwerer als die Mittelschule?
22 Welche Fremdsprachen kann man auf einer Mittelschule lernen?
23 Wann bekommt man die Mittlere Reife?
24 Wo kann man mit der Mittleren Reife eine gute Stellung finden?
25 Kann man ohne die Mittlere Reife Ingenieur werden?

26 Wie heißen Oberschulen auch?
27 Müssen die Kinder auf der Oberschule intelligent sein?

oder weniger intelligent, sie sind auch ganz verschieden begabt. So gibt es denn verschiedene Oberschultypen^g.

Natürlich kann es nun nicht so viele Schultypen wie Begabungen geben, aber es existieren^g doch wenigstens vier. Auf der einen Oberschule hat man etwa mehr Fremdsprachen, auf einer anderen dafür mehr mathematisch-naturwissenschaftlichen Unterricht, wie Mathematik, Physik, Chemie und Biologie. In dem einen fremdsprachlichen Gymnasium kann man mehr moderne (Englisch, Französisch), in einem anderen mehr alte Fremdsprachen (Latein^g, Griechisch^g) lernen. Fremdsprachen und Naturwissenschaften werden auf jeder Höheren Schule täglich von der ersten bis zur letzten Klasse gegeben. Und sie sind auch immer alle Hauptfächer, sogar in jenen (wenigen) Oberschulen, in denen daneben auch musische Fächer Hauptfächer sind.

So haben wir jetzt diese Oberschultypen:

1. Altsprachliches (humanistisches) Gymnasium (18%)
2. Neusprachliches Gymnasium (50% aller Oberschulen)
3. Mathematisch-naturwissenschaftliches Gymnasium (30%)
4. Musisches Gymnasium (2%)

Das Schuljahr beginnt auch in Deutschland im Herbst. Das ist für alle Schüler die wichtigste Zeit des Jahres. Da bleibt man nämlich „sitzen", oder man wird in die neue, höhere Klasse „versetzt". Es kommt darauf an, ob man zu schlecht oder noch gut genug für das Klassenziel war. Wenn man zu schlecht war, so muß man das ganze Schuljahr noch einmal machen. Wer aber zum dritten Mal „sitzenbleibt", muß das Gymnasium verlassen. Jüngere Schüler wechseln dann fast immer auf die Mittelschule über, ältere aber gehen in einen Beruf.

Man kann, wenn man will, auch auf der Oberschule seine Mittlere Reife machen. So spart man sich die Oberstufe des Gymnasiums, aber man muß natürlich genau so lange zur Schule gehen wie die Mittelschüler.

Besonders die Oberstufe der Höheren Schule ist wirklich schwer. Die Statistik^g sagt, daß nur ungefähr 20 % der Oberschüler das Abitur erreichen. Das ist schon für die, die es nicht erreichen, schlimm, denn die meisten Oberschüler wollen natürlich gern studieren.

Studieren kann aber nur, wer sein Abitur bestanden hat. Das Abitur (oder die Reifeprüfung, wie man auch häufig sagt) ist nun einmal Bedingung für jeden, der auf die Universität (Hochschule) will.

Natürlich kann man seine Reifeprüfung auch nachholen. Es gibt Extraschulen dafür, auf die auch frühere Volks- oder Mittelschüler gehen können. Aber das ist wirklich anstrengend und nur für sehr gut begabte Leute mit viel Energie^g.

Zu den wichtigsten Unterschieden zwischen amerikanischen und deutschen Schulen gehört es, daß in Deutschland jedes einmal begonnene Fach im Lehrplan^g bleibt. Das ist ein Grundsatz, von dem es fast keine Ausnahme gibt. Wer also auf einem Gymnasium etwa Englisch als

verschieden *adv.* differently, to various degrees · **begabt** talented, gifted
der Typ, -en [ty:p]
die Begabung, -en talent, gift
dafür instead · **mathematisch** [matemaˈtiːʃ] · **wissenschaftlich** scientific **die Wissenschaft, -en** science · **die Natur** [naˈtuːʀ] · **die Mathematik** [matemaˈtiːk]
die Physik [fyˈziːk] · **die Chemie** [çeˈmiː] · **die Biologie** [bioloˈgiː]
Latein [laˈtaɪn]
werden gegeben *pass. voice* are given
das Hauptfach, ⸚er main subject, major
das Fach, ⸚er subject · **musisch** artistic

sitzenbleiben fail, not pass on to the next grade
man wird versetzt *pass. voice* one is advanced · **ankommen auf etwas** depend on something   **es kommt darauf an, ob** it depends on whether
verlassen leave, leave behind
sich sparen *dat. refl.* spare
die Oberstufe, -n *last three years in a German* **Gymnasium   die Stufe, -n** stage, level
die Statistik [ʃtaˈtɪstɪk]
erreichen reach, attain · **die, die** the ones who
die Reifeprüfung, -en *final examination in the* **Gymnasium = das Abitur**
die Bedingung, -en condition
nachholen make up (an examination)

die Energie [enɛʀˈgiː]
jedes einmal begonnene Fach = jedes Fach, das man einmal begonnen hat · **der Grundsatz, ⸚e** principle

28 Müssen ihre Eltern viel Geld haben?
29 Sind diese Kinder alle gleich begabt?
30 Kann man Fremdsprachen auf jeder Höheren Schule lernen?
31 Wann beginnt das Schuljahr?
32 Was passiert, wenn man zu schlecht war?
33 Was muß ein Schüler tun, wenn er zum dritten Mal sitzenbleibt?
34 Wohin gehen die Schüler, wenn sie das Gymnasium verlassen müssen?
35 Erreichen alle Oberschüler das Abitur?
36 Was muß man tun, wenn man auf die Universität will?
37 Gibt es Unterschiede zwischen amerikanischen und deutschen Schulen?
38 Was ist einer der wichtigsten Unterschiede?

erste, Latein als zweite, Französisch als dritte und Griechisch als vierte Fremdsprache lernt, der wird die frühere Fremdsprache immer behalten, wenn die neue beginnt, und eines Tages also vier Fremdsprachen in seinem Stundenplan*g* haben,—neben all den anderen Fächern natürlich.

Genug Information*g* für den Anfang? Es läßt sich noch eine Menge von deutschen Schulen sagen, aber für einen ersten Überblick mag dies hier genügen.

behalten keep
die Information [ɪnfɔʀmatsiˈoːn] · **es läßt
sich sagen** it can be said

der Überblick, -e overall view, survey

PHONOLOGY

A. Long Vowels, Short Vowels, Diphthongs

Make the long stressed vowels especially long, the short ones especially short, and the diphthongs crisp:

Sch u le, Tradit i o n, m a n, kompliz ie rt, l a nge, k o mmen, g e hen, a lt, M e nge, W e sen, Pfl i cht, m ü ssen, a lle, T a g, U nterricht, a cht, St u nden, W o che, bes u chen, K i nder, sch o n, n u r, n o ch, Au snahme, fr ei, br au chen, au f, h eu te, au ch, D eu tschland, L a nd, L e ben, Sp ie l, l ei cht, sich fr eu en, g a nz, L eu te, h a ben, priv a t, Ex a men, Progr a mm, s e hr, war u m, Spr a che, Ber u f, Industr ie, H a ndwerker, h äu fig, k ö nnen, Akad e miker, Pl a n, Z ie l, M i ttelschule, Franz ö sisch, Sp a nisch, d a s, n a ch, Qualifikati o n, Positi o n, P o st, Ingeni eu r, m u ß, Abit u r, m a chen, Gymn a sium, nat u rwissenschaftlich, U nterricht, E nglisch, schw e r, i hr, Kl a ssen, h ö here, O berschule, M i schung, g i bt, v ie rte, V ie rtel, zu e rst, O stern, a ber, verl a ssen, w i ll, m i ttlere, Sch ü ler, stud ie ren, gem a cht, n a chmachen, fr ü here, k ö nnen, b ö se, Pr ü fung, amerik a nisch, F a ch, Pl a n, h a t, beh a lten, h a ben, a nderen, A nfang, s a gen, m a g, Ü berblick, gen ü gen

B. Fricatives

Make the [j] with more friction than in English *yes*:

j eder, j a, J ahr, j etzt, j edenfalls, Lebens j ahr, drei j ährig, j enen, j üngere, Schul j ahr

In pronouncing [ç] be careful not to approach [ʃ]. The German [ç] is a whispered [j]:

Unterri ch t, eigentli ch, nämli ch, ni ch t, vielleich t, freiwilli g, si ch, weni g stens, natürli ch, tatsä ch lich, am häufi g sten, man ch e, re ch t, unterri ch tet, dur ch laufen, Te ch nik, wirkli ch, naturwissenschaftli ch, fremdsprachli ch, rücksi ch tslos, Fä ch er, tägli ch, altsprachli ch, neusprachli ch, Grie ch isch, mögli ch, schle ch t, errei ch en, häufi g

Make the [ʃ] with exaggerated lip rounding:

deut**sch**, **Sch**ule, Deut**sch**land, Men**sch**en, **s**teckt, be**s**teht, **S**tunden, **S**pezialschule, **sch**on, **S**piel, be**s**timmte, Volks**sch**ule, Mittel**sch**ule, Ober**sch**ule, **s**päter, **Sch**wierigkeiten, ver**sch**ieden, **S**prache, **sch**werer, Engli**sch**, Französi**sch**, **S**pani**sch**, Wirt**sch**aft, naturwissen**sch**aftlich, Angst**sch**weiß, musi**sch**, alt**s**prachlich, neu**s**prachlich, Mi**sch**ung, Griechi**sch**, **sch**lecht, Volks**sch**üler, **s**tudieren, Ge**sch**äft, Unter**sch**ied, amerikani**sch**

Be sure to pronounce [x] with friction and not as [k]:

dana**ch**, a**ch**t, Wo**ch**e, besu**ch**t, brau**ch**en, no**ch**, au**ch**, do**ch**, Spra**ch**e, na**ch**, ma**ch**en, altspra**ch**lich, neuspra**ch**lich, Fa**ch**, Ho**ch**schule

---

VOCABULARY

A. Singular and Plural of Nouns

der Akademiker, -
die Bedingung, -en
die Begabung, -en
der Beruf, -e
das Fach, ⸚er
der Garten, ⸚
der Grundsatz, ⸚e
der Handwerker, -
das Hauptfach, ⸚er
die Industrie, -n
der Ingenieur, -e

die Oberstufe, -n
die Pflicht, -en
der Plan, ⸚e
das Programm, -e
die Qualifikation, -en
die Reifeprüfung, -en
das Spiel, -e
die Tradition, -en
der Typ, -en
der Überblick, -e
das Ziel, -e

B. Inference

With the help of the clues provided, guess the meanings of the words in boldface.

Words similar to English:

1 Ich habe mir einen besseren **Fotoapparat** [ˈfoːtoapaʀɑːt] für Farbfotos gekauft.   **der Apparat, -e**
2 Möchten Sie eine **Banane** [baˈnɑːnə] oder einen Apfel?   **die Banane, -n**
3 Willst du mit dem großen **Ball** spielen, Susi?   **der Ball, ⸚e**

4 Der Apfel schmeckt noch **bitter**, er ist noch nicht **reif**.
5 Mein Großvater kann sehr schlecht sehen, er ist fast **blind**.
6 Kochen Sie **elektrisch** [eˈlɛktrɪʃ] oder mit Gas?
7 Oh, es regnet. Das ist gut für das junge **Gras**.   **das Gras**
8 Das Brot ist schon alt und **hart**. Ich kann es nicht essen.
9 Haben Sie eine **Landkarte** von Europa?   **die Karte, -n**
10 Heizen Sie mit **Öl** oder mit Gas?   **das Öl**
11 Wenn Susi „Gute Nacht" sagt, **küßt** sie ihre Mutter immer.
12 Darf ich Ihnen **Likör** [liˈkøːʀ] oder Wein anbieten?   **der Likör, -e**
13 Ist dieses **Material** [mateʀiˈɑːl] aus Metall?   **das Material, -ien**
14 Er ist ein guter **Mechaniker** [meˈçɑːnɪkəʀ], besonders für Volkswagen.   **der Mechaniker, -**
15 Sein Wagen hat einen starken **Motor** [moˈtoːʀ].   **der Motor, -en**

Many words spelled with *th* in English are spelled with **d** in German. Some known examples are *thank* **Dank**, *thing* **Ding**, *thunder* **donnern**. An awareness of this principle makes it possible to recognize many new words:

1 Diese Scheibe Brot ist ziemlich **dick**.
2 Du bist aber **dünn** geworden, warst du krank?
3 Er hatte einen langen **Dorn** im Finger.   **der Dorn, -en**
4 Wo ist mein Geld? Hier ist doch wohl kein **Dieb** im Haus.   **der Dieb, -e**
5 A. Es war heiß heute, bist du auch so **durstig**?
  B. Jetzt nicht mehr, aber ich hatte auch großen **Durst**.   **der Durst**
6 Unser Garten ist voller **Disteln**.   **die Distel, -n**
7 Auch der **Daumen** ist ein Finger.   **der Daumen, -**
8 Plato war ein großer **Denker**.   **der Denker, -**
9 Geh jetzt, Susi, und nimm dein **Bad**.   **das Bad, ⸚er**
10 Zwischen den Häusern war nur ein kleiner **Pfad**.   **der Pfad, -e**
11 Er war zu lange und zu schwer krank, der **Tod** war für ihn kein Unglück.   **der Tod**
12 Diese Schuhe sind nicht aus **Leder**.   **das Leder**
13 Es ist so leicht wie eine **Feder**.   **die Feder, -n**

In English and German there are numerous words of foreign origin which are spelled with *th*. A known example is **das Theater** *the theater*. These are pronounced with [t] in German:

1 Ich glaube, er studiert **Theologie** [teoloˈgiː].   **die Theologie**
2 Wie heißt doch das **Thema** [ˈteːmɑ] seiner Doktorarbeit?   **das Thema, die Themen**
3 Seine Vorlesungen sind mir zu **theoretisch** [teoˈʀeːtɪʃ].
4 Kennst du schon seine neueste **Theorie** [teoˈʀiː]?   **die Theorie, -n**
5 Seine **These** [ˈteːzə] ist sicher falsch.   **die These, -n**
6 Man sagt, er ist ein guter **Therapeut** [teʀɑˈpɔɪt], seine **Therapie** [teʀɑˈpiː] hat mir jedenfalls gut geholfen.   **der Therapeut, -en · die Therapie**
7 Das **Thermometer** [tɛʀmoˈmeːtəʀ] ist heute nacht stark gefallen.   **das Thermometer, -**
8 Ich glaube, der **Thermostat** [tɛʀmoˈstɑːt] ist kaputt.   **der Thermostat, -en**

WRITING

A. Dehydrated Sentences

Modify the basic forms of the words as required and construct sentences, making relative clauses with the words between the double diagonal lines.

Example:
Wo / sein / Strümpfe // ich / waschen / gestern // ?
Wo sind die Strümpfe, die ich gestern gewaschen habe?

1. Wer / gehören / Hemd // heute morgen / liegen / auf / Boden // ?
2. Hier / sitzen / klein / Kind // Mütze / sein / verloren //
3. Mantel // mein / Schwester / vorgestern / kaufen // hängen / hinter / Tür
4. Dort / stehen / Schuhe // du / sollen / tragen //
5. Wo / kaufen / du / gestern / Bretter // aus / du / wollen / zusammenbauen / Schrank // ?
6. Da / liegen / Sachen // mit / spielen / Susi / gestern //
7. Handtücher // ich / kaufen / letzt / Woche // können / ich / nicht / finden
8. Rock // du / wollen / tragen // liegen / vor / Stunde / auf / Stuhl
9. Das / sein / Kleid // in / du / sich / können / überall / sehen / lassen //
10. Hose // er / gestern / tragen // aussehen / gut

B. Completion

Write the following sentences and complete them by choosing for each blank a single appropriate word from the list provided:

aber, als, aus, damit, dann, daß, denn, nach, ob, obwohl, oder, um, wann, warum, weil, wenn, wie, wohin, zu

1. Hans läuft schneller _____ Susi.
2. Vater kommt heute genau _____ vier Uhr _____ Hause.
3. Weißt du, _____ ich morgen _____ Amerika fahre?
4. Die Schuhe sind teuer, _____ sie sehen gut _____.
5. Können Sie mir sagen, _____ der Bus hier hält?
6. Weißt du nicht, _____ der Zug ankommen soll?
7. Ich glaube, _____ der Zug _____ zehn Uhr einlaufen soll.
8. Günther läuft so schnell _____ Rolf.
9. Er kann nicht mitkommen, _____ er ist krank.
10. Er mußte _____ Hause bleiben, _____ er krank ist.
11. _____ er krank ist, will er doch mitfahren.

12 Hoffentlich gefällt mir der Rock, _____ er fertig ist.
13 Ich ging gleich wieder weg, _____ er schlafen konnte.
14 Zuerst kommt die Decke auf den Tisch, und _____ das Essen.
15 Ich möchte wissen, _____ er nicht gekommen ist.
16 Er tat nur so, _____ dich _____ beruhigen.
17 Jetzt fährt er los, _____ ich weiß nicht, _____ er fahren will.
18 Der eine Junge kommt bestimmt, _____ ich bin nicht sicher, _____ es Rolf _____ Günther sein wird.

Unit 26

DIALOG

Die Klassenreise (Anfang)

1 **Walter:** Du, Michael, weißt du schon, daß nachher noch so ein altes Schloß besichtigt werden soll?

2 **Michael:** Was, noch eins? Ich hatte keine Ahnung, daß überhaupt so viele Schlösser gebaut worden sind.

3 **Walter:** Ja, man hat tatsächlich das Gefühl, daß wir alle Schlösser gesehen haben müssen.

4 **Michael:** Ich bin für einen Besichtigungsstreik. Es muß ein gemeinsamer Klassenbeschluß herbeigeführt werden.

The Class Trip (Beginning)

1 Hey, Michael! Do you know that afterwards another old castle like this one is to be visited?

die Klassenreise die Klasse, -n class + die Reise, -n trip

so ein such a one, one like it · **das Schloß, ⸗sser** castle · **besichtigen** inspect, visit, view · **besichtigt werden** *passive infinitive dependent on* **soll**

2 What, another one? I had no idea that so many castles were built.

gebaut worden sind *pres. perf. pass.*

3 Yes. You actually have the feeling that we must have seen all the old castles.

das Gefühl, -e feeling, sense

4 I'm in favor of a visitation strike. A joint class resolution will have to be passed.

die Besichtigungsstreik die Besichtigung, -en inspection, visitation, viewing + der Streik, -s *or* -e strike · **der Klassenbeschluß** die Klasse, -n + der Beschluß, ⸗sse resolution, decision · **herbeiführen** pass (a rule, etc.) **herbeigeführt werden** *passive infinitive dependent on* **muß**

5 Walter: Nicht schlecht, das muß ich sagen. Ich trommle den ganzen Verein zusammen.

6 Michael: Wart mal, ich glaube, das kann noch besser gemacht werden.

7 Walter: Noch besser? Wieso? Was meinst du damit?

8 Michael: Glaubst du, daß ein richtiger Fremdenführer aus dem Konzept gebracht werden kann?

9 Walter: Ein Fremdenführer? Na, klar! Fremdenführer sind doch wie Papageien.

10 Michael: Ich will's versuchen. Wenn es klappt, werden wir in einer Stunde unseren Spaß gehabt haben.

(Fortsetzung folgt)

SUPPLEMENT

1 Die Tür wird langsam geschlossen.

2 Die Kiste wurde dorthin geschoben.

3 Die schönsten Tage sind hier genossen worden.

4 Das Geld war vorhin verborgen worden.

5 Das Ziel wird bald erreicht werden.

5	Not bad, I must say. I'll call the whole group together.	**zusammentrommeln** (*coll.*) **zusammen** together + **trommeln** drum · **der Verein, -e** association, club
6	Wait a minute. I believe that it can be done even better.	**gemacht werden** *passive infinitive dependent on* **kann**
7	Even better? How? What do you mean by that?	
8	Do you think that a real tourist guide can be sidetracked?	**der Fremdenführer** **der Fremde, -n** stranger + **der Führer, -** guide · **das Konzept, -e** rough copy **aus dem Konzept bringen** sidetrack, disconcert · **gebracht werden** *passive infinitive dependent on* **kann**
9	A tourist guide? Well, you bet! After all, tourist guides are like parrots.	**der Papagei, -en** parrot
10	I'll try it. If it works, we'll have had our fun in an hour.	**will's = will es**

(To be continued)

1	The door is being closed slowly.	**schließen: er schließt, schloß, hat geschlossen** close **wird geschlossen** *pres. pass.*
2	The box was (being) shoved there.	**schieben: er schiebt, schob, hat geschoben** shove **wurde geschoben** *past pass.*
3	The loveliest days were enjoyed here.	**genießen: er genießt, genoß, hat genossen** enjoy **sind genossen worden** *pres. perf. pass.*
4	The money had been hidden before.	**verbergen: er verbirgt, verbarg, hat verborgen** hide **war verborgen worden** *past perf. pass.*
5	The goal will be reached soon.	**wird erreicht werden** *fut. pass.*

6 Alles muß besser gemacht werden.

7 Kann es heute noch gewaschen werden?

8 Er sagt, daß die Schüler nicht erzogen werden wollten.

9 Nachdem er das Examen bestand, zog er nach München.

10 Nach seinem Examen machte er eine Reise nach Innsbruck.

11 Nachher genoß er die Ferien.

12 Bevor ich nach Freiburg fuhr, kannte ich sie nicht.

13 Vor der Reise nach München kannte ich sie nicht.

14 Vorher kannten wir uns nicht.

6	Everything must be done better.	**gemacht werden** *pass. inf.*
7	Can it be washed today?	**gewaschen werden** *pass. inf.*
8	He says that the pupils did not want to be educated.	**erzogen werden** *pass. inf.*
9	After he passed the exam, he moved to Munich.	**nachdem** *subord. conj.* after
10	After his exam he took a trip to Innsbruck.	**nach** *prep.* after
11	Afterward he enjoyed the vacation.	**nachher** *adv.* afterward
12	Before I went to Freiburg, I didn't know her.	**bevor** *subord. conj.* before
13	Before the trip to Munich I didn't know her.	**vor** *prep.* before
14	Earlier (before) we didn't know each other.	**voher** before, earlier = **vorhin**

AUDIOLINGUAL DRILLS

A. Directed Dialog

Fragen Sie, wie der neue Dialog heißt!
Wie heißt der neue Dialog?

Antworten Sie, daß er „Die Klassenreise" heißt!
Er heißt „Die Klassenreise".

Fragen Sie, ob nachher noch so ein altes Schloß besichtigt werden soll!
Soll nachher noch so ein altes Schloß besichtigt werden?

Antworten Sie, daß nachher noch so ein altes Schloß besichtigt werden soll!
Nachher soll noch so ein altes Schloß besichtigt werden.

Sagen Sie, daß Michael keine Ahnung hatte, daß so viele Schlösser gebaut worden sind!
Michael hatte keine Ahnung, daß so viele Schlösser gebaut worden sind.

Sagen Sie, man hat das Gefühl, daß man alle Schlösser gesehen haben muß!
Man hat das Gefühl, daß man alle Schlösser gesehen haben muß.

Sagen Sie, daß Michael für einen Besichtigungsstreik ist!
Michael ist für einen Besichtigungsstreik.

Sagen Sie, daß ein gemeinsamer Klassenbeschluß herbeigeführt werden muß!
Ein gemeinsamer Klassenbeschluß muß herbeigeführt werden.

Sagen Sie, daß Walter den ganzen Verein zusammentrommelt!
Walter trommelt den ganzen Verein zusammen.

Sagen Sie, daß Michael glaubt, das kann noch besser gemacht werden!
Michael glaubt, das kann noch besser gemacht werden.

Fragen Sie, was er damit meint!
Was meint er damit?

Fragen Sie, ob ein richtiger Fremdenführer aus dem Konzept gebracht werden kann!
Kann ein richtiger Fremdenführer aus dem Konzept gebracht werden?

Antworten Sie, daß das klar ist!
Das ist klar.

Sagen Sie, daß Fremdenführer doch wie Papageien sind!
Fremdenführer sind doch wie Papageien.

Sagen Sie, daß Michael es versuchen will!
Michael will es versuchen.

Sagen Sie, daß sie in einer Stunde ihren Spaß gehabt haben werden!
Sie werden in einer Stunde ihren Spaß gehabt haben.

B. New Strong Verbs

1 **Genießen** *enjoy* and **schließen** *close* follow the pattern of **bieten**, except that the past tense and past participle have short [ɔ]— **er genießt, genoß, hat genossen; er schließt, schloß, hat geschlossen**. Change the tense as indicated:

Er genießt die Reise. *pres. perf.*
Er hat die Reise genossen. *fut.*
Er wird die Reise genießen. *past perf.*
Er hatte die Reise genossen. *past*
Er genoß die Reise.

Ich schließe die Tür. *past*
Ich schloß die Tür. *pres. perf.*
Ich habe die Tür geschlossen. *past perf.*
Ich hatte die Tür geschlossen. *fut.*
Ich werde die Tür schließen.

2 **Schieben** *shove* follows the pattern of **bieten** — **er schiebt, schob, hat geschoben**. Change the tense as indicated:

Wir schieben die Kiste unter den Tisch. *pres. perf.*
Wir haben die Kiste unter den Tisch geschoben. *past*

Wir schoben die Kiste unter den Tisch. *past perf.*
Wir hatten die Kiste unter den Tisch geschoben. *fut.*
Wir werden die Kiste unter den Tisch schieben.

3 **Verbergen** *hide* follows the pattern of **helfen**—**er verbirgt, verbarg, hat verborgen.** Change the tense as indicated:

Hast du das Geld verborgen? *fut.*
Wirst du das Geld verbergen? *pres.*
Verbirgst du das Geld? *past*

Verbargst du das Geld? *past perf.*
Hattest du das Geld verborgen?

C. The Passive Voice (*See Grammar* §26.3)

Present tense

4 Substitute the new subject:

Du wirst getäuscht. **wir**
Wir werden getäuscht. **der Fremdenführer**
Der Fremdenführer wird getäuscht. **ihr**
Ihr werdet getäuscht. **ich**
Ich werde getäuscht. **die Lehrerinnen**
Die Lehrerinnen werden getäuscht.

5 Substitute the new subject or the past participle of the new verb:

Die Pakete werden schon geschickt. **du**
Du wirst schon geschickt. **holen**
Du wirst schon geholt. **der Kellner**
Der Kellner wird schon geholt. **fahren**
Der Kellner wird schon gefahren. **ihr**
Ihr werdet schon gefahren. **achten**

Ihr werdet schon geachtet. **ich**
Ich werde schon geachtet. **erkennen**
Ich werde schon erkannt. **die Herren**
Die Herren werden schon erkannt. **sehen**
Die Herren werden schon gesehen.

Past tense

6 Substitute the new subject:

Der Neffe wurde immer mitgenommen. **die Eltern**
Die Eltern wurden immer mitgenommen. **ich**
Ich wurde immer mitgenommen. **du**
Du wurdest immer mitgenommen. **ihr**
Ihr wurdet immer mitgenommen. **wir**
Wir wurden immer mitgenommen.

7 Substitute the new subject or the past participle of the new verb:

Ich wurde vorhin gesehen. **ihr**
Ihr wurdet vorhin gesehen. **aufnehmen**
Ihr wurdet vorhin aufgenommen. **wir**
Wir wurden vorhin aufgenommen. **anrufen**
Wir wurden vorhin angerufen. **der Lehrling**
Der Lehrling wurde vorhin angerufen. **beruhigen**
Der Lehrling wurde vorhin beruhigt. **du**
Du wurdest vorhin beruhigt. **entschuldigen**
Du wurdest vorhin entschuldigt. **die Schüler**
Die Schüler wurden vorhin entschuldigt. **erziehen**
Die Schüler wurden vorhin erzogen.

Present perfect tense

8 Substitute the new subject:

Ich bin bezahlt worden. **wir**
Wir sind bezahlt worden. **die Handwerker**
Die Handwerker sind bezahlt worden. **du**
Du bist bezahlt worden. **ihr**
Ihr seid bezahlt worden. **der Lehrer**
Der Lehrer ist bezahlt worden.

9 Substitute the new subject or the past participle of the new verb:

Der Lehrer ist nicht verstanden worden. **du**
Du bist nicht verstanden worden. **anrufen**
Du bist nicht angerufen worden. **die Freunde**
Die Freunde sind nicht angerufen worden. **besuchen**
Die Freunde sind nicht besucht worden. **ihr**
Ihr seid nicht besucht worden. **bezahlen**
Ihr seid nicht bezahlt worden. **wir**
Wir sind nicht bezahlt worden. **schieben**
Wir sind nicht geschoben worden. **ich**
Ich bin nicht geschoben worden. **begrüßen**
Ich bin nicht begrüßt worden.

Past perfect tense

10 Substitute the new subject:

Der Junge war zu Hause erzogen worden. **wir**
Wir waren zu Hause erzogen worden. **ich**
Ich war zu Hause erzogen worden. **du**
Du warst zu Hause erzogen worden. **Hans und Susi**
Hans und Susi waren zu Hause erzogen worden. **ihr**
Ihr wart zu Hause erzogen worden.

11 Substitute the new subject or the past participle of the new verb:

Das Schloß war nachher besichtigt worden. **die Kirchen**
Die Kirchen waren nachher besichtigt worden. **besuchen**
Die Kirchen waren nachher besucht worden. **wir**
Wir waren nachher besucht worden. **verstehen**
Wir waren nachher verstanden worden. **ihr**
Ihr wart nachher verstanden worden. **erkennen**
Ihr wart nachher erkannt worden. **du**
Du warst nachher erkannt worden. **sehen**
Du warst nachher gesehen worden. **der Dom**
Der Dom war nachher gesehen worden.

Future tense

12 Substitute the new subject:

Der Schüler wird unterrichtet werden. **ihr**
Ihr werdet unterrichtet werden. **du**
Du wirst unterrichtet werden. **ich**
Ich werde unterrichtet werden. **die Lehrlinge**
Die Lehrlinge werden unterrichtet werden. **wir**
Wir werden unterrichtet werden.

13 Substitute the new subject or the past participle of the new verb:

Die Tür wird bald geschlossen werden. **die Fenster**
Die Fenster werden bald geschlossen werden. **bringen**
Die Fenster werden bald gebracht werden. **der Kuchen**
Der Kuchen wird bald gebracht werden. **genießen**
Der Kuchen wird bald genossen werden. **die Feiertage**
Die Feiertage werden bald genossen werden. **vergessen**
Die Feiertage werden bald vergessen werden. **du**
Du wirst bald vergessen werden. **besuchen**
Du wirst bald besucht werden. **ihr**
Ihr werdet bald besucht werden. **fahren**
Ihr werdet bald gefahren werden.

Modals with the passive voice

14 Substitute the new modal or the past participle of the new main verb:

Das kann morgen gemacht werden. **sollen**
Das soll morgen gemacht werden. **versuchen**
Das soll morgen versucht werden. **müssen**
Das muß morgen versucht werden. **waschen**

Das muß morgen gewaschen werden.   **können**
Das kann morgen gewaschen werden.   **aufschreiben**
Das kann morgen aufgeschrieben werden.

Transformations

15 Transform the active sentences into passive sentences, keeping the same tense. Change the accusative object of the active verb to the subject of the passive verb. Omit the subject of the active verb.

Example:
Er besucht seinen Onkel.
Sein Onkel wird besucht.

Wir besichtigen das Schloß.
Das Schloß wird besichtigt.

Ich bezahle die Handwerker.
Die Handwerker werden bezahlt.

Er hat dich erkannt.
Du bist erkannt worden.

Wir haben euch angerufen.
Ihr seid angerufen worden.

Hatte man uns begrüßt?
Waren wir begrüßt worden?

Wo hatten sie die Kinder erzogen?
Wo waren die Kinder erzogen worden?

Sie beruhigte ihren Vater.
Ihr Vater wurde beruhigt.

Ich hole den neuen Schraubenzieher.
Der neue Schraubenzieher wurde geholt.

Sie wird einen neuen Hut kaufen.
Ein neuer Hut wird gekauft.

Wir werden Susi mitbringen.
Susi wird mitgebracht werden.

D. *Ein*-Words as Pronouns (*See Grammar* §26.4)

16 Supply the **ein**-word pronoun that corresponds to the given noun phrase.

Example:
Wo ist seine?   **sein Werkzeug**
Wo ist seines?

Das ist meines.   **ihr Buch**
Das ist ihres.   **ihre Mütze**
Das ist ihre.   **deine Mütze**
Das ist deine.   **dein Kleid**
Das ist deines.   **ihr Kleid**

Das ist ihres.   **ihr Hut**
Das ist ihrer.   **mein Hut**
Das ist meiner.   **meine Mäntel**
Das sind meine.   **keine Mäntel**
Das sind keine.

Hast du meinen gesehen?	**seinen Anzug**	Hast du keines gesehen?	**keinen Film**
Hast du seinen gesehen?	**seine Schuhe**	Hast du keinen gesehen?	**unseren Film**
Hast du seine gesehen?	**ihre Schuhe**	Hast du unseren gesehen?	**unsere Fabrik**
Hast du ihre gesehen?	**ihr Kleid**	Hast du unsere gesehen?	**meine Fabrik**
Hast du ihres gesehen?	**kein Kleid**	Hast du meine gesehen?	

E. Questions and Answers

Wie heißt der neue Dialog?
Er heißt „Die Klassenreise".

Was müssen die Schüler noch tun?
Sie müssen noch ein altes Schloß besichtigen.

Was hatte Michael nicht gewußt?
Er hatte nicht gewußt, daß so viele Schlösser gebaut wurden.

Gefallen die alten Schlösser den Jungen?
Nein, sie wollen keine Schlösser mehr besichtigen.

Was muß herbeigeführt werden?
Ein gemeinsamer Klassenbeschluß muß herbeigeführt werden.

Trommelt Walter die anderen Schüler zusammen?
Nein, denn Michael glaubt, daß das besser gemacht werden kann.

Was will Michael tun?
Er will den Fremdenführer aus dem Konzept bringen.

Glaubt Walter, daß es ihnen gelingen wird?
Ja, denn er meint, daß die Fremdenführer nicht besonders intelligent sind.

GRAMMAR

26.1 Word-Formation

Inseparable prefixes of verbs

The meanings of most of the inseparable prefixes are not always as concrete or specific as those of the separable ones. However, the general meaning can be detected in many verbs with these prefixes:

zer- idea of disintegration, destruction

beißen	bite	zerbeißen	bite to pieces
brechen	break	zerbrechen	break to pieces; smash
legen	lay	zerlegen	take apart
stören	disturb	zerstören	destroy

ent- idea of escape, away from, off

decken	cover	entdecken	discover; expose
gehen	go	entgehen	escape
kleiden	dress	(sich) entkleiden	undress
kommen	come	entkommen	escape, get away
lassen	let	entlassen	dismiss, discharge
laufen	run	entlaufen	run away
springen	jump	entspringen	run away, escape; rise (river)
ziehen	pull	entziehen	take away from; deprive of

er- idea of completion of the activity indicated by the basic verb or transition into the state indicated by the noun or adjective from which the verb with **er-** is derived

a. Idea of completion of an activity:

arbeiten	work	erarbeiten	attain by hard work
bitten (um)	beg, ask (for)	erbitten	beg, ask (for); obtain by begging
blicken	look	erblicken	catch sight of
fahren	drive	erfahren	experience; find out
finden	find	erfinden	invent
freuen	make glad	erfreuen	bring joy to
füllen	fill	erfüllen	fulfill
geben	give	ergeben	yield; produce
halten	hold	erhalten	maintain; receive
hoffen	hope	erhoffen	expect
holen	get, fetch	(sich) erholen	recuperate; rest
kennen	know	erkennen	recognize
leben	live	erleben	experience
lernen	learn	erlernen	acquire through learning
liegen	lie	erliegen	succumb
nennen	name, call	ernennen	nominate, appoint
raten	guess; advise	erraten	guess correctly
scheinen	shine; seem	erscheinen	make an appearance
setzen	place	ersetzen	replace
sparen	save	(sich) ersparen	save up; save (effort)
tragen	carry; wear	ertragen	endure
trinken	drink	ertrinken	drown

warten wait	erwarten expect
ziehen pull	erziehen raise; educate

b. Idea of transition into a state:

frisch fresh	sich erfrischen refresh oneself
ganz whole	ergänzen supplement, complete
die Hitze heat	erhitzen heat
hoch high	erhöhen raise
kalt cold	sich erkälten catch cold
klar clear	erklären explain, clarify
krank ill	erkranken become ill
leicht easy	erleichtern make easy, facilitate
möglich possible	ermöglichen make possible
neu new	erneue(r)n renew
schwer heavy; difficult	erschweren make more difficult
warm warm	erwärmen warm up
das Ziel goal	erzielen accomplish

ver- idea of intensification or bringing forward to completion the action of the simple verb; transition into the state indicated by the noun or adjective from which the verb with **ver-** is derived; reversal of the meaning of the basic verb, often with the idea of error, injury or disadvantage

a. Idea of intensification or completion:

arbeiten work	verarbeiten work up into; manufacture
brennen burn	verbrennen burn up
decken cover	verdecken cover (tracks); hide
fallen fall	verfallen decay
geben give	vergeben give away; forgive
hören hear	verhören interrogate
lachen laugh	verlachen laugh at, ridicule
lassen let, leave	verlassen abandon
leben live	verleben spend, pass (time)
nehmen take	vernehmen find out; cross-examine
rauchen smoke	verrauchen go off in smoke; spend on tobacco
schicken send	verschicken send off
sichern secure	versichern insure; assure
sinken sink	versinken sink (out of sight)
spotten mock, scoff	verspotten mock, scoff at
sprechen speak	versprechen promise
stecken stick; put	(sich) verstecken hide; conceal
suchen look for	versuchen try
tragen carry	vertragen tolerate, endure

b. Idea of transition into a state:

alt old	veralten become obsolete
ander other	verändern change, alter
arm poor	verarmen become poor
besser better	verbessern improve
billig cheap	verbilligen lower the price of; cheapen
blaß pale	verblassen fade
dunkel dark	verdunkeln make dark
ein one	vereinen unite
das Eis ice	vereisen ice up; freeze (meat)
der Film film	verfilmen film
das Gift poison	vergiften poison
das Glas glass	verglasen glaze
größer larger	vergrößern enlarge
der Hunger hunger	verhungern starve
jung young	verjüngen rejuvenate
kleiner smaller	verkleinern make smaller
kurz short	verkürzen shorten
länger longer	verlängern lengthen
mehr more	vermehren increase
nein no	verneinen decry; answer in negative
schön beautiful	verschöne(r)n embellish, beautify
spät late	sich verspäten be late; be delayed
stark strong	verstärken strengthen
süß sweet	versüßen sweeten
wirklich real	verwirklichen realize, make real
die Wunde wound	verwunden wound

c. Reversal of meaning; idea of error:

achten respect	verachten despise
bieten offer, bid	verbieten forbid, prohibit
brauchen need; use	verbrauchen use up, consume
bringen bring	verbringen spend (one's time)
fahren drive	sich verfahren get lost (while driving somewhere)
hören hear	sich verhören misunderstand
kaufen buy	verkaufen sell
legen lay, place	verlegen misplace; remove
lernen learn	verlernen forget
raten advise	verraten betray
spielen play	verspielen gamble away
wünschen wish	verwünschen curse; bewitch

be- idea of providing with something — as such the chief effect is often to make an intransitive verb transitive rather than to change its essential meaning

arbeiten	work	bearbeiten	work up, over
danken	thank	sich bedanken	thank; decline
decken	cover	bedecken	cover up
fragen	ask	befragen	interrogate; consult
grenzen	border	begrenzen	border
grüßen	greet	begrüßen	greet
halten	hold	behalten	keep
kommen	come	bekommen	get, receive
lachen	laugh	belachen	laugh at (a joke)
leben	live	beleben	enliven; resuscitate
lehren	teach	belehren	teach, inform
raten	advise; guess	beraten	give advice to
schauen	look	beschauen	look over
schließen	close	beschließen	conclude; decide
schreiben	write	beschreiben	describe
sehen	see	besehen	look over
setzen	set, place	besetzen	occupy
sitzen	sit	besitzen	sit upon; possess
sprechen	speak	besprechen	discuss
stehen	stand	bestehen	exist; undergo; pass (exam)
suchen	look for, hunt	besuchen	visit
tragen	carry; wear	betragen	amount to
tragen	carry; wear	sich betragen	behave
treffen	hit; meet	betreffen	concern
treten	step	betreten	step on; enter

26.2 Singular and Plural of Nouns

der Beschluß, ⸚sse
die Besichtigung, -en
der Fremdenführer, -
das Gefühl, -e
das Konzept, -e
der Papagei, -en
die Reise, -n
das Schloß, ⸚sser
der Streik, -s *or* -e
der Verein, -e

26.3 The Passive Voice

Meaning of the passive voice

In the sentence

Viele Leute besichtigen das alte Schloß.　　　A lot of people visit the old castle.

the subject is **viele Leute** *a lot of people*; it is carrying out the action expressed by **besichtigen** *visit*. The direct object is **das alte Schloß** *the old castle*; it is receiving the action expressed by the verb:

Subject ⟶ **Verb** ⟶ **Object**

Viele Leute besichtigen das alte Schloß.

This sentence is in the *active voice*; the subject is the agent, the object the receiver.

But in the sentence

Das alte Schloß wird besichtigt.　　　The old castle is being visited.

the subject is **das alte Schloß** *the old castle*; here it is the receiver, not the agent. The agent is not even mentioned (although it may be; this will be taken up in Grammar §27.3). The sentence is in the *passive voice*:

Subject ⟵ **Verb**

Das alte Schloß wird besichtigt.

Every passive sentence is related structurally to an underlying active sentence. It is convenient, and instructional, to regard the passive sentence **Das alte Schloß wird besichtigt** as being derived from an active sentence like **Viele Leute besichtigen das alte Schloß**. This is a purely structural relationship, however, and does not imply that the active and passive sentences are equivalent in meaning. Their meanings are in fact quite different. The active sentence focuses attention on *the agent and its activity* (the people and what they are doing), while the passive focuses attention on *the state of the receiver* (the castle).

Tense formation

The passive voice in German is formed by the auxiliary **werden** plus the past participle of the main verb. In forming the various tenses, it is the auxiliary **werden** that changes.

1　*Present tense*　　Das Schloß **wird** besichtigt.　　　The castle *is being* visited.

　　The passive auxiliary is a present tense form of **werden**.

2　*Past tense*　　Das Schloß **wurde** besichtigt.　　　The castle *was being* visited.

The passive auxiliary is a past tense form of **werden**.

3   *Present perfect tense*   Das Schloß **ist** besichtigt **worden**.
                                     The castle *has been* (*was being*) visited.

The passive auxiliary is a present perfect form of **werden**; the tense auxiliary is a present form of **sein**, and the past participle is **worden**.

4   *Past perfect tense*   Das Schloß **war** besichtigt **worden**.
                                   The castle *had been* visited.

The passive auxiliary is a past perfect form of **werden**; the tense auxiliary is a past form of **sein**, and the past participle is **worden**.

5   *Future tense*   Das Schloß **wird** besichtigt **werden**.
                           The castle *will be* visited.

The passive auxiliary is in the infinitive form; it is dependent on the future auxiliary **wird**.

Summary and comparison

wird	... **besichtigt**	*is being visited*
wurde	... **besichtigt**	*was being visited*
ist	... **besichtigt worden**	*has been visited*
war	... **besichtigt worden**	*had been visited*
wird	... **besichtigt werden**	*will be visited*

Modals with the passive voice

The passive infinitive is made up of the past participle of the main verb followed by the infinitive of the passive auxiliary **werden**. It is used in the formation of the future tense of the passive voice, as has been pointed out above. It may also occur with modal auxiliaries:

Es **soll** nachher besichtigt werden.   Das **kann** besser gemacht werden.
It *is supposed to* be visited afterward.   That *can* be done better.

Ein Beschluß **muß** herbeigeführt werden.
A resolution *has to* be passed.

Such sentences may be put into other tenses, of course; the verb phrase then becomes rather involved, but actually follows the patterns of tense formation that you have already learned:

Present	Das **kann** besser gemacht werden.
Past	Das **konnte** besser gemacht werden.
Present perfect	Das **hat** besser gemacht werden **können**.
Past perfect	Das **hatte** besser gemacht werden **können**.
Future	Das **wird** besser gemacht werden **können**.

Notice the "double infinitive" in the last three sentences. Also notice that the basic passive construction — **gemacht werden** — does not change.

Summary of functions of *werden*

The verb **werden** occurs in three different functions:

1 Independent verb meaning *become, get*

Es wird kalt.
It's getting cold.

2 Future auxiliary, together with an infinitive

Ich werde meinen Onkel besuchen.
I will visit my uncle.

3 Passive auxiliary, together with a past participle

Die Schüler werden unterrichtet.
The pupils are being instructed.

26.4 *Ein*-Words as Pronouns

The **ein**-words may function as pronouns, similar to English *mine, yours, his,* etc. When used as pronouns, the **ein**-words take the appropriate strong adjective ending. The neuter **-es** is usually shortened to **-s**.

Ist das dein Mantel? — Ja, das ist **meiner**.
Wessen Buch ist das? — Das ist **meins**.
Sehen wir noch ein Schloß? — Ja, wir sehen noch **eins**.
Hast du einen Hut? — Nein, ich habe **keinen**.
Von wessen Mann haben wir gesprochen? — Ich glaube, wir haben von **ihrem** gesprochen.

26.5 Before and After

The word *before* can be used in all of these sentences:

1. He called us up before he left.
2. He called us up before midnight.
3. He called us up before.

Although the same word is used, it has a different function in each sentence. In 1 it is a conjunction, in 2 a preposition, and in 3 an adverb. German uses different words for these different functions:

Conjunction: **bevor** *before*
Preposition: **vor** *before; ago*
Adverb: **vorher, vorhin** *before, formerly, earlier*

Bevor er nach München zog, bestand er das Examen.
Before he moved to Munich, he passed the exam.

Vor zwei Uhr hat er uns angerufen.
Before two o'clock he called us up.

Ich hatte das schon **vorher** gewußt.
I had known that *before*.

A similar situation exists with regard to the German words that mean *after*, although here English has a separate form for the adverb:

Conjunction: **nachdem** *after*
Preposition: **nach** *after*
Adverb: **nachher** *afterward*

Nachdem er nach München zog, lernte er Renate kennen.
After he moved to Munich, he met Renate.

Nach seinem Examen machte er eine Reise.
After his exam he took a trip.

Wir gehen **nachher** ins Theater.
We'll go to the theater *afterward*.

WRITING

A. Nouns and Adjectives

Copy the sentences and supply the correct words or phrases:

1 Diese _____ _____ gefallen mir nicht.   (old castles)
2 Die Schüler haben _____ _____ herbeigeführt.   (their resolutions)
3 Hast du _____ _____ gesehen?   (many parrots)
4 Er hat _____ _____ schon gegeben.   (such reports)
5 Bist du für oder gegen _____ _____ _____ ?   (these eternal inspections)
6 Ich mag _____ _____ nicht leiden.   (such tourist guides)
7 Der _____ _____ ist auch mitgekommen.   (entire club)
8 Er hat eine _____ _____ genossen.   (good professional training)
9 Wie _____ _____ hat er studiert?   (many subjects)
10 Hast du auch _____ _____ gekauft?   (new clothes)

B. Double Infinitives

Rewrite the following sentences in the present perfect tense:

1. Ich höre ihn im nächsten Zimmer spielen.
2. Der Professor will die Nachbarländer besuchen.
3. Läßt du die Schuhe auf dem Tisch liegen?
4. Die Lehrlinge müssen sofort bezahlt werden.
5. Das kann leider nicht besser gemacht werden.

Rewrite the subordinate clauses in the present perfect tense:

6. Er sagt, daß er ihn nie spielen hörte.
7. Der Fahrer sagte, daß er uns zum Schloß fahren will.
8. Ich habe gelesen, daß man hier viel bauen muß.
9. Sie erklärte, daß sie nicht mitgehen darf.
10. Weißt du, ob wir das Schloß besichtigen sollen?

C. Dehydrated Sentences

Modify the forms as required and construct passive sentences, using the tense indicated. The verb that you should write in the passive voice is in boldface.

alt / Kirchen / **bauen** / damals   (*past*)
Die alten Kirchen wurden damals gebaut.

1. Tür / **schließen** / vorhin   (*pres. perf.*)
2. alles / **machen** / viel besser   (*fut.*)
3. Lehrlinge / **bezahlen** / schon?   (*past perf.*)
4. Dom / **besichtigen** / nachher   (*pres.*)
5. es / müssen / **versuchen**   (*pres.*)
6. Fremdenführer / können / **bringen** / aus / Konzept   (*past*)
7. viel / Sachen / sollen / **verbergen** / vermutlich   (*pres. perf.*)
8. sein / Gedichte / **verstehen** / leider / nie   (*pres.*)
9. Stern / Sterne / können / **erkennen** / immer   (*pres.*)
10. unser / Kinder / **erziehen** / in / Schweiz   (*fut.*)

D. *Ein*-Words as Pronouns

Write short answers to the following questions using an **ein**-word pronoun.

Example:
Haben Sie einen neuen Wagen gekauft?
Ja, ich habe einen gekauft.

1. Haben Sie eine Kirche gesehen?
2. Sind das Ihre Taschentücher?
3. Trinken Sie noch ein Glas Milch?
4. Rauchen Sie ihre Zigaretten?

5   Kommt da ein Junge?
6   Ist das sein Bleistift?

7   Haben Sie kein neues Kleid gekauft?
8   Holen Sie einen Schraubenzieher?

E. Before and After

Copy the sentences and supply **bevor**, **vor**, or **vorher** (or **vorhin**), as required:

1 ____ sind wir zum Baden gegangen.
2 Sie werden ____ der Vorlesung zu uns kommen.
3 Das Paket wurde ____ zurückgeschickt.
4 ____ er den Herzanfall hatte, hatte er zu flott gelebt.
5 ____ dem Konzert hat er nach Hause gehen müssen.
6 Sie hatte durch die ganze Auswahl geschaut, ____ sie den Hut kaufte.

Copy the sentences and supply **nachdem**, **nach**, or **nachher**:

7   Sie hat den Hut gekauft, ____ sie durch die Auswahl geschaut hatte.
8   Wir gehen ____ dem Essen ins Theater.
9   Die Schüler wollten ____ einen gemeinsamen Klassenbeschluß herbeiführen.
10 ____ der Besichtigung sind sie alle wieder weggegangen.
11 Kommen Sie doch ____ zu uns!
12 ____ wir den Dom besichtigten, kauften wir einige Bilder davon.

LISTENING PRACTICE

Listen to the recorded conversation; then answer the following questions.

Anja und Sabine

1 Warum muß Anja ins nächste Schloß getragen werden?
2 Wie heißt die Klassenlehrerin?
3 Wie alt sind die Mädchen?
4 Was soll Frau Walker lieber tun?
5 Warum interessiert Ruth sich auch nicht für Jungen?
6 Wie heißt ihr Freund?
7 Wer soll Frau Walker fragen?

Unit 27

DIALOG

Die Klassenreise (Schluß)

1 **Fremdenführer:** Meine Damen und Herren! Dieses Schloß wurde im Jahre 1782 erbaut.

2 **Michael:** Ist nicht im Kriege ein Teil durch Brand zerstört worden?

3 **Fremdenführer:** Ja, aber es wurde alles wieder im alten Stile errichtet.

4 **Michael:** Auch dieser große Empfangssaal hier?

5 **Fremdenführer:** Auch er. — Hier wurde damals getanzt, gelacht und gesungen.

6 **Michael:** Nicht empfangen? — Wann ist der letzte König eigentlich gestorben?

The Class Trip (Conclusion)

1. Ladies and Gentlemen! This castle was built in the year 1782.

2. Wasn't a part destroyed by fire during the war?

3. Yes, but everything was built up again in the old style.

4. This big reception hall, too?

5. It too. Here they used to dance, laugh, and sing.

6. Didn't they "receive"? Just when did the last king die?

die Dame, -n · **erbauen** build (up), construct

der Krieg, -e im Kriege *dative singular with the optional dative singular ending* **-e** · **der Brand, ⸚e** · **zerstören** destroy **stören** disturb

der Stil, -e · **errichten** build up, erect, establish **richten** set right, adjust

der Empfangssaal **der Empfang, ⸚e** reception + **der Saal, die Säle** hall, large room

tanzen dance · **singen: er singt, sang, hat gesungen** sing

empfangen: er empfängt, empfing, hat empfangen receive · **der König, -e** · **sterben: er stirbt, starb, ist gestorben** die

7 **Fremdenführer:** Nun, richtig genommen ist er „gestorben worden".

8 **Michael:** „Gestorben worden"? Er wurde also ermordet?

9 **Fremdenführer:** Ich fahre in meinen Ausführungen fort. Wo war ich doch unterbrochen worden?

10 **Walter:** Im Jahre 1782, denke ich, Herr Fremdenführer.

SUPPLEMENT

1 Das Schloß wurde durch Brand zerstört.

2 Das Schloß wurde von den Schülern besichtigt.

3 Sie ist gar nicht gesehen worden.

4 Man hat sie gar nicht gesehen.

5 Sie hat sich gar nicht sehen lassen.

6 Sie war gar nicht zu sehen.

7 Der Professor kann nicht erreicht werden.

8 Man kann den Professor nicht erreichen.

9 Der Professor läßt sich nicht erreichen.

10 Der Professor ist nicht zu erreichen.

7   Now, strictly speaking, he "was made to die." ist „gestorben worden" *A deliberately ungrammatical expression, for humorous effect; the guide means "murdered."*

8   "Made to die"? So he was murdered? **ermorden** murder

9   I'll continue with my comments. Now where had I been interrupted? **fortfahren: er fährt fort, fuhr fort, ist fortgefahren** continue **fort** away, further + **fahren** go, drive · **die Ausführung, -en** · **unter'brechen: er unterbricht, unterbrach, hat unterbrochen** interrupt **unter** *is weakly stressed and inseparable* **brechen** break

10 In the year 1782, I think, Mr. Tourist Guide. **Herr Fremdenführer** *Titles are normally preceded by* **Herr** *or* **Frau** *in direct address.*

---

1   The castle was destroyed by fire.

2   The castle was visited by the pupils.

3   She hasn't been seen at all.

4   One hasn't seen her at all.

5   She hasn't let herself (couldn't) be seen at all.

6   She wasn't to (couldn't) be seen at all.

7   The professor can't be reached.

8   One can't reach the professor.

9   The professor doesn't let himself (can't) be reached.

10 The professor is not to (can't) be reached.

11 Du mußt ihn gesehen haben.

12 Wer kann so etwas gesagt haben?

13 Er soll die Zeitung gelesen haben.

14 Wir werden unseren Spaß gehabt haben.

11 You must have seen him.

12 Who can have said such a thing?

13 He is supposed to have read the newspaper.

14 We will have had our fun.

AUDIOLINGUAL DRILLS

A. Directed Dialog

Sagen Sie, daß dieses Schloß im Jahre 1782 erbaut wurde!
Dieses Schloß wurde im Jahre 1782 erbaut.

Fragen Sie, ob im Kriege nicht ein Teil durch Brand zerstört worden ist!
Ist im Kriege nicht ein Teil durch Brand zerstört worden?

Antworten Sie, daß ein Teil durch Brand zerstört worden ist!
Ein Teil ist durch Brand zerstört worden.

Sagen Sie, daß aber alles wieder im alten Stile errichtet wurde!
Aber alles wurde wieder im alten Stile errichtet.

Fragen Sie, ob auch dieser große Empfangssaal wieder im alten Stile errichtet wurde!
Wurde auch dieser große Empfangssaal wieder im alten Stile errichtet?

Antworten Sie, daß auch er im alten Stile neu errichtet wurde!
Auch er wurde im alten Stile neu errichtet.

Sagen Sie, daß hier damals getanzt, gelacht und gesungen wurde!
Hier wurde damals getanzt, gelacht und gesungen.

Fragen Sie, ob hier damals nicht empfangen wurde!
Wurde hier damals nicht empfangen?

Antworten Sie, daß hier damals auch empfangen wurde!
Hier wurde damals auch empfangen.

Fragen Sie, wann der König eigentlich gestorben ist!
Wann ist der König eigentlich gestorben?

Sagen Sie, daß er ermordet wurde!
Er wurde ermordet.

Sagen Sie, daß der Fremdenführer in seinen Ausführungen fortfährt!
Der Fremdenführer fährt in seinen Ausführungen fort.

Fragen Sie, wo er doch unterbrochen worden war!
Wo war er doch unterbrochen worden?

Antworten Sie, daß er im Jahre 1782 unterbrochen worden war!
Er war im Jahre 1782 unterbrochen worden.

B. New Strong Verbs

1 **Singen** *sing* follows the pattern of **finden — er singt, sang, hat gesungen**. Change the tense as indicated:

Man singt jeden Abend.   *pres. perf.*
Man hat jeden Abend gesungen.   *past perf.*
Man hatte jeden Abend gesungen.   *fut.*

Man wird jeden Abend singen.   *past*
Man sang jeden Abend.

2 **Empfangen** *receive* follows the pattern of **fangen — er empfängt, empfing, hat empfangen**. Change the tense as indicated:

Der König empfängt den Boten.   *past*
Der König empfing den Boten.   *past perf.*
Der König hatte den Boten empfangen.   *fut.*

Der König wird den Boten empfangen.   *pres. perf.*
Der König hat den Boten empfangen.

3 **Sterben** *die* follows the pattern of **helfen — er stirbt, starb, ist gestorben**. Change the tense as indicated:

Wann stirbt der König?   *fut.*
Wann wird der König sterben?   *pres. perf.*
Wann ist der König gestorben?   *past*

Wann starb der König?   *past perf.*
Wann war der König gestorben?

4 **Brechen** *break* and **unterbrechen** *interrupt* follow the pattern of **sprechen — er bricht, brach, hat gebrochen; er unterbricht, unterbrach, hat unterbrochen**. Change the tense as indicated:

Susi wird den Teller in Stücke brechen.   *pres.*
Susi bricht den Teller in Stücke.   *pres. perf.*
Susi hat den Teller in Stücke gebrochen.   *past perf.*
Susi hatte den Teller in Stücke gebrochen.   *past*
Susi brach den Teller in Stücke.

Der Junge hat den Fremdenführer unterbrochen.   *fut.*
Der Junge wird den Fremdenführer unterbrechen.   *past perf.*
Der Junge hatte den Fremdenführer unterbrochen.   *pres.*

Der Junge unterbricht den Fremdenführer. *pres. perf.*
Der Junge hat den Fremdenführer unterbrochen.

C. Agents of Passive Verbs *(See Grammar §27.2)*

5   Substitute the new object of the preposition:

Die Kirche wird von vielen Leuten besichtigt.   **die Schüler**
Die Kirche wird von den Schülern besichtigt.   **unser Verein**
Die Kirche wird von unserem Verein besichtigt.   **der alte König**
Die Kirche wird von dem alten König besichtigt.   **eine schöne Dame**
Die Kirche wird von einer schönen Dame besichtigt.   **alle Ausländer**
Die Kirche wird von allen Ausländern besichtigt.   **meine Eltern**
Die Kirche wird von meinen Eltern besichtigt.

6   Substitute the new subject:

Die Kirche ist durch Brand zerstört worden.   **die Geschäfte**
Die Geschäfte sind durch Brand zerstört worden.   **der Dom**
Der Dom ist durch Brand zerstört worden.   **die Schlösser**
Die Schlösser sind durch Brand zerstört worden.   **das Haus**
Das Haus ist durch Brand zerstört worden.   **der Saal**
Der Saal ist durch Brand zerstört worden.   **die Fabriken**
Die Fabriken sind durch Brand zerstört worden.

D. Subjectless Passives *(See Grammar §27.3)*

7   Substitute the past participle of the new verb:

Hier wurde damals gelacht.   **singen**
Hier wurde damals gesungen.   **tanzen**
Hier wurde damals getanzt.   **spielen**
Hier wurde damals gespielt.   **unterrichten**
Hier wurde damals unterrichtet.   **bauen**

Hier wurde damals gebaut.   **schlafen**
Hier wurde damals geschlafen.   **schreiben**
Hier wurde damals geschrieben.   **arbeiten**
Hier wurde damals gearbeitet.

8   Transform the active sentences into subjectless passives and delete the agent. Do not change the tense.

Example:
Man tanzt jeden Abend.
Jeden Abend wird getanzt.

Man ißt um zwei Uhr.
Um zwei Uhr wird gegessen.

Man hat hier gebaut.
Hier ist gebaut worden.

Man sang im großen Saal.
Im großen Saal wurde gesungen.

Man spielt im Kindergarten.
Im Kindergarten wird gespielt.

Man arbeitet überall.
Überall wird gearbeitet.

Man hat damals geschrieben.
Damals ist geschrieben worden.

Man schläft nachts.
Nachts wird geschlafen.

9   Begin each sentence with the false subject **es**; put the time adverb after the finite verb.

Example:
Jeden Abend wird getanzt.
Es wird jeden Abend getanzt.

Gegen halb acht wird gegessen.
Es wird gegen halb acht gegessen.

Damals ist viel gesungen worden.
Es ist damals viel gesungen worden.

Gestern abend wurde hier gespielt.
Es wurde gestern abend hier gespielt.

Morgen wird viel getrunken werden.
Es wird morgen viel getrunken werden.

Im Sommer wurde tüchtig gearbeitet.
Es wurde im Sommer tüchtig gearbeitet.

E. Substitutes for the Passive Voice (*See Grammar* §27.4)

man

10   Change the following sentences from the passive to the active, and supply **man** as the subject. Keep the same tense. The new direct object goes right after the finite verb.

Example:
Die Tür wird geschlossen.
Man schließt die Tür.

Unser Onkel wird oft besucht.
Man besucht unseren Onkel oft.

Der König ist dort ermordet worden.
Man hat den König dort ermordet.

Der Dom war einmal zerstört worden.
Man hatte den Dom einmal zerstört.

Das Schloß wird wieder errichtet werden.
Man wird das Schloß wieder errichten.

Die Vorlesung ist unterbrochen worden.
Man hat die Vorlesung unterbrochen.

Die Geschäfte wurden um sieben Uhr geschlossen.
Man schloß die Geschäfte um sieben Uhr.

Ein neuer Schrank ist zusammengebaut worden.
Man hat einen neuen Schrank zusammengebaut.

sich *with an active verb*

11 Change the sentences from the passive to the active; keep the same subject, but add the reflexive pronoun **sich**.

Example:
Die Tür wird geschlossen.
Die Tür schließt sich.

Die Fenster wurden geschlossen. Mein Mantel wird gefunden werden.
Die Fenster schlossen sich. Mein Mantel wird sich finden.

Das Buch ist gefunden worden. Es wird verstanden.
Das Buch hat sich gefunden. Es versteht sich.

sich lassen *plus a dependent infinitive*

12 Substitute the new subject or infinitive:

Der Lehrer läßt sich nicht erreichen. **meine Tante**
Meine Tante läßt sich nicht erreichen. **unterbrechen**
Meine Tante läßt sich nicht unterbrechen. **die Kinder**
Die Kinder lassen sich nicht unterbrechen. **unterrichten**
Die Kinder lassen sich nicht unterrichten. **der Schüler**
Der Schüler läßt sich nicht unterrichten. **sehen**
Der Schüler läßt sich nicht sehen. **ihr**
Ihr laßt euch nicht sehen. **besuchen**
Ihr laßt euch nicht besuchen. **ich**
Ich lasse mich nicht besuchen.

13 Change the following sentences from the passive voice to **sich lassen** plus infinitive:

Er kann nicht erreicht werden. Die große Kiste kann nicht verborgen werden.
Er läßt sich nicht erreichen. Die große Kiste läßt sich nicht verbergen.

Sie können überall gesehen werden. Kann er nicht bezahlt werden?
Sie lassen sich überall sehen. Läßt er sich nicht bezahlen?

Du kannst nicht unterbrochen werden.
Du läßt dich nicht unterbrechen.

sein + zu + *infinitive*

14 Substitute the new subject or infinitive:

Mein alter Mantel ist nicht zu tragen.   **diese Schuhe**
Diese Schuhe sind nicht zu tragen.   **kaufen**
Diese Schuhe sind nicht zu kaufen.   **sein Buch**
Sein Buch ist nicht zu kaufen.   **finden**
Sein Buch ist nicht zu finden.   **die Lehrlinge**
Die Lehrlinge sind nicht zu finden.   **anrufen**
Die Lehrlinge sind nicht anzurufen.

15 Change the following sentences from the passive voice to constructions containing a form of **sein** plus **zu** plus an infinitive:

Die Studentin kann dort erreicht werden.
Die Studentin ist dort zu erreichen.

Der Fremdenführer konnte nicht unterbrochen werden.
Der Fremdenführer war nicht zu unterbrechen.

Alles kann hier gelesen werden.
Alles ist hier zu lesen.

Das Schloß kann nachher besichtigt werden.
Das Schloß ist nachher zu besichtigen.

Der Freund soll gleich mitgebracht werden.
Der Freund ist gleich mitzubringen.

Die Schrauben dürfen nicht vergessen werden.
Die Schrauben sind nicht zu vergessen.

Alle Türen müssen vorher geschlossen werden.
Alle Türen sind vorher zu schließen.

F. The Passive with Dative Objects (*See Grammar* §27.5)

16 Substitute the new noun or pronoun in the dative case:

Dem Mann wird geholfen.   **er**
Ihm wird geholfen.   **die Dame**
Der Dame wird geholfen.   **ein Junge**
Einem Jungen wird geholfen.   **ihr**

Euch wird geholfen.   **die Leute**
Den Leuten wird geholfen.   **ich**
Mir wird geholfen.

17 Substitute the new noun in the dative case, or the past participle of the new verb:

Ist dem Mann geholfen worden?   **die Dame**
Ist der Dame geholfen worden?   **danken**
Ist der Dame gedankt worden?   **das Mädchen**
Ist dem Mädchen gedankt worden?   **antworten**
Ist dem Mädchen geantwortet worden?   **die Eltern**
Ist den Eltern geantwortet worden?   **glauben**
Ist den Eltern geglaubt worden?

18 Transform the following sentences from the active to the passive. Keep the same tense. Delete the agent in the passive sentence.

Example:
Man hilft dem Fahrer.
Dem Fahrer wird geholfen.

Man antwortet der jungen Frau.
Der jungen Frau wird geantwortet.

Man hat dem Fremdenführer gedankt.
Dem Fremdenführer ist gedankt worden.

Man glaubte ihm nicht.
Ihm wurde nicht geglaubt.

Hatte man den Leuten geholfen?
War den Leuten geholfen worden?

Man wird ihnen bald antworten.
Ihnen wird bald geantwortet werden.

G. The Perfect Infinitive (See Grammar §27.6)

19 Substitute the past participle of the new verb:

Der Junge muß geschlafen haben. **laufen**
Der Junge muß gelaufen sein. **tanzen**
Der Junge muß getanzt haben. **weggehen**
Der Junge muß weggegangen sein. **singen**

Der Junge muß gesungen haben. **aussteigen**
Der Junge muß ausgestiegen sein. **schreiben**
Der Junge muß geschrieben haben.

20 Expand the following sentences by inserting the modal or future auxiliary as the finite verb:

Er hat es gesehen. **müssen**
Er muß es gesehen haben.

Wen hast du gemeint? **können**
Wen kannst du gemeint haben?

Wir haben unseren Spaß gehabt. **werden**
Wir werden unseren Spaß gehabt haben.

Er ist dort ausgestiegen. **können**
Er kann dort ausgestiegen sein.

Sie haben einen Beschluß herbeigeführt. **sollen**
Sie sollen einen Beschluß herbeigeführt haben.

Ist der König gestorben? **können**
Kann der König gestorben sein?

Er ist eigentlich ermordet worden. **sollen**
Er soll eigentlich ermordet worden sein.

H. Questions and Answers

Wann wurde das Schloß erbaut?
Es wurde im Jahre 1782 erbaut.

Wie ist es durch den Krieg gekommen?
Ein Teil ist durch Brand zerstört worden.

Was hat man nachher getan?
Man hat alles wieder im alten Stile errichtet.

Was wurde damals im großen Empfangssaal gemacht?
Dort wurde getanzt, gelacht, gesungen und empfangen.

Was fragt Michael über den König?
Er fragt, wann er eigentlich gestorben ist.

Wie antwortet der Fremdenführer?
Er sagt, richtig genommen ist der König „gestorben worden".

Was will der Fremdenführer tun?
Er will in seinen Ausführungen fortfahren.

Warum tut er das nicht gleich?
Er hat vergessen, wo er unterbrochen worden war.

GRAMMAR

27.1 Singular and Plural of Nouns

die Ausführung, -en
der Brand, ⸚e
die Dame, -n
der Empfang, ⸚e

der König, -e
der Krieg, -e
der Saal, Säle
der Stil, -e

27.2 The Passive Voice: Agents

In the active voice the subject does the acting; it is the agent of the active verb. In the passive voice, however, the subject is *acted upon*. The agent of a passive verb is expressed by means of a prepositional phrase:

Subject: Agent ⟶ **Object: Receiver**
Active   A lot of people   visit   the old castle.

Subject: Receiver ⟵ **Object: Agent**
Passive   The old castle   is visited   by a lot of people.

In English the preposition that introduces the agent of a passive verb is *by*. In German it is **von** (the person performing the action) or **durch** (the cause or instrument by which the action is carried out):

Die Kirche wird **von** vielen Leuten besichtigt.
The church is visited *by* a lot of people.

Der Dom ist **durch** Brand zerstört worden.
The cathedral has been destroyed *by* fire.

7.3 Subjectless Passives

In German it is possible to construct sentences in the passive voice which indicate neither the the agent nor the receiver of the action; attention is focused only on the action itself, while the instigator and the goal of the action are simply disregarded. These passive sentences have no subject; the finite verb is always singular. Since such constructions are not possible in English, we supply a subject for the English equivalents:

Jeden Abend wird getanzt.
People dance every evening.
Or: There is dancing every evening.

Wird schon wieder gearbeitet?
Are people working again?
Or: Is work going on again?

Hier wurde damals gesungen.
People sang here then.
Or: There was singing here then.

Wann wird gegessen?
When do we (they, people) eat?

Note that first position is occupied by an adverb, by the finite verb, or by a question-word. The pronoun **es** may be used in first position:

Es wurde damals viel gearbeitet.   There was a lot of work going on then.

We call this a "false subject." It occupies first position, but really has no other function at all; it doesn't even have a meaning, that is, it does not refer to anything that might have been named earlier. Indeed, if an adverb is moved into first position, then this **es** disappears altogether:

Damals wurde viel gearbeitet. (*Not:* Damals wurde **es** viel gearbeitet.)
There was a lot of work going on then.

7.4 Substitutes for the Passive Voice

There are several active constructions in German which, although differing considerably from the passive in structure, are closely related to it in meaning.

The impersonal pronoun **man** *one, someone, we, you, they, people*

Man schließt die Tür um sechs.
They close the door at six.
Or: The door is closed at six.

Man hat den König ermordet.
Someone murdered the king.
Or: The king was murdered.

Das sagt **man** einfach nicht!
You just don't say that!
Or: That just isn't said!

The reflexive pronoun **sich** *with an active verb*

Die Tür **schließt sich**.
The door *is (being) closed.*

Es **versteht sich**.
It *is understood* (self-evident).

Das Buch **hat sich gefunden**.
The book *has been found.*

Obviously, doors don't close themselves, books don't find themselves, and things can't understand themselves; the real agents are implied but not specified.

sich lassen *plus a dependent infinitive*

Der Fremdenführer **läßt sich** nicht **unterbrechen**.
The tourist guide *will* not *let himself* (*can*not) *be interrupted*.

Du kannst **dich** überall **sehen lassen**.
You can *let yourself be seen* (you can *show up*) anywhere.

Note that the German infinitives (**unterbrechen, sehen**) are rendered with English passives.

sein + **zu** + *infinitive*

Der Professor **ist** nicht **zu erreichen**.
The professor *can*not *be reached.*

Was er gesagt hat, **ist** einfach nicht **zu verstehen**.
What he said just *can*not *be understood.*

Der Fremdenführer **war** nicht **zu unterbrechen**.
The tourist guide *could*n't *be interrupted.*

27.5 The Passive with Dative Objects

If we regard a passive sentence as being derived from an active sentence, then we observe the following:

1. The active verb is replaced by the corresponding passive verb construction;

2. The subject of the active sentence becomes the object of a preposition in the passive sentence; and

3. The direct (accusative) object of the active verb becomes the subject of the passive verb.

This latter adjustment—changing the object of the active verb to the subject of the passive verb—is possible only with *accusative* objects. If the active verb has a *dative* object, then it remains in the dative case in the passive voice, that is, it is not changed to a subject. Note the following transformations:

Active voice			*Passive voice*			
Agent —		→ **Receiver**	**Receiver** ←	—	**Agent**	
Das Kind	besucht	den Onkel.	Der Onkel	wird	von dem Kind	besucht.
Das Kind	hilft	dem Onkel.	**Dem Onkel**	wird	von dem Kind	geholfen.

7.6 The Perfect Infinitive

The perfect infinitive is a construction composed of the past participle of the main verb plus the infinitive of its tense auxiliary:

Infinitive	*Perfect infinitive*
gehen	gegangen sein
aussteigen	ausgestiegen sein
tanzen	getanzt haben
empfinden	empfunden haben

As you have already learned, the perfect infinitive occurs in the future perfect construction (Grammar §24.5):

Er wird **gegangen sein**.
He will *have gone*.

Er wird wohl viel Mühe damit **gehabt haben**.
He probably *had* a lot of trouble with it.

The perfect infinitive may also occur with modal auxiliaries. The modal is the finite verb; the perfect infinitive is dependent on the modal and stands in last position (unless the clause is dependent, in which case the finite verb follows the perfect infinitive):

Er muß **geschlafen haben**.
He must *have slept* (*been sleeping*).

Er soll im Jahre 1654 **gestorben sein**.
He is said to *have died* in 1654.

Sie kann es nicht **gesehen haben**.
She can't *have seen* it.

Such constructions may be changed to the future tense simply by adding the future auxiliary and shifting the modal, as an infinitive, to the end of the clause:

Er wird **geschlafen haben müssen**.   He will *have to have slept*.

Passive verb phrases may also undergo these expansions:

Present perfect passive	Er ist gesehen worden. He has been seen.
Modal + perfect passive infinitive	Er muß gesehen worden sein. He must have been seen.
Future tense	Er wird gesehen worden sein müssen. He will have to have been seen.

When the modal auxiliary **muß** is added, the tense auxiliary goes to the end of the clause as an infinitive **sein**. When this is put into the future tense, the future auxiliary **wird** is added, and the modal goes to the end of the clause as an infinitive **müssen**. Such constructions are admittedly rare; we present them here only to illustrate how consistently German verb phrases are expanded.

WRITING

A. Nouns and Adjectives

Copy the sentences and supply the correct words or phrases:

1. Er wollte in _____ _____ fortfahren. (his comments)
2. Man hatte keine _____ _____ herbeigeführt. (joint resolutions)
3. Wann wurden diese _____ _____ errichtet? (various castles)
4. Ich wollte eigentlich _____ _____ machen. (longer trips)
5. Damals waren seine _____ noch nicht zu Ende. (wars)
6. Meine _____ und _____! (ladies, gentlemen)
7. Die _____ _____ finde ich scheußlich. (separate styles)
8. Er war doch kein _____ _____. (talented king)
9. Das Wohnhaus wurde durch _____ zerstört. (fire)
10. In diesen _____ wurde oft getanzt. (halls)
11. Die _____ der Kinder wurden unterbrochen. (games)
12. _____ _____ _____ sind dort zu sehen. (many beautiful gardens)
13. _____ _____ sind klar. (our goals)
14. Die _____ _____ sind alle vorher gestorben. (various kings)

B. Dehydrated Sentences

Modify the forms as required and construct sentences using the tense and voice indicated. The double diagonal lines represent clause boundaries:

1. Dame / unterbrechen / klein / Junge   (*pres. perf. pass.*)
2. während / Krieg / Kirche / zerstören / Brand   (*past pass.*)
3. groß / Empfangssaal / tanzen / singen   (*past perf. pass.*)
4. sterben / König / Jahr / 1750?   (*pres. perf. act.*)
5. fortfahren / in / dein / Ausführungen!
6. König / empfangen / Dame / in / Empfangssaal   (*past act.*)
7. unterbrechen / ich / nicht / Hans!
8. er / wollen / versuchen // Lehrer / Konzept / bringen   (*past act.*)
9. nachdem / ich / ziehen / Schweiz // wir / verlieren / aus / Augen   (*first clause past perf. act., second clause past act.*)
10. bevor / Schloß / zerstören / Brand // viel / Leute / besichtigen / es   (*first clause past pass., second clause past perf. act.*)

C. Relative Clauses

Combine the following pairs of sentences, making the appropriate one a relative clause with **was** or **wer**.

Examples:
Er kommt bald nach Kiel zurück. Das freut mich sehr.
Er kommt bald nach Kiel zurück, was mich sehr freut.

Er hat genug Geld. Er kann sich einen Wagen kaufen.
Wer genug Geld hat, kann sich einen Wagen kaufen.

1. Man hat es nicht im Kopf. Man muß es in den Beinen haben.
2. Er studiert tüchtig. Er wird das Examen bestehen.
3. Seine Vorlesungen sind sehr klar. Das macht das Studium leichter.
4. Er will nicht mehr laufen. Er kann einen Bus nehmen.
5. Die Geschäfte schließen um sechs. Es gefällt mir gar nicht.
6. Es gehört ihm nicht. Er darf es nicht mitnehmen.
7. Er hält die Zeitschrift falsch herum. Es muß schon etwas bedeuten.
8. Er möchte das Schloß sehen. Er kann gleich mitfahren.
9. Das Wetter ist heute sehr schön. Das freut mich sehr.
10. Man tut es nicht gern. Man kann es bleiben lassen.

D. Passive Voice and Its Equivalents

Write corresponding German sentences using a subjectless passive construction. Begin the sentence with an adverb or with the "false subject" **es**.

Example:
There was playing and singing going on here.
Es wurde hier gespielt und gesungen.
Or: Hier wurde gespielt und gesungen.

1 People are studying diligently there.
2 They danced a lot at that time.
3 There was building in the city.
4 People are searching everywhere.
5 They did their washing on Monday.
6 There was little writing and note-taking.

Rewrite each of the following sentences twice: once using **sich lassen** with an infinitive, and once using **sein + zu** with an infinitive.

Example:
Man kann das Fenster schließen.
a. Das Fenster läßt sich schließen.
b. Das Fenster ist zu schließen.

7 Man konnte ihn nicht unterbrechen.
8 Wo kann man euch erreichen?
9 Man kann die Kirche auch montags besichtigen.
10 Man konnte jene Schüler gar nicht erziehen.
11 Wo soll man ihn denn treffen?
12 Kann man den Fremdenführer aus dem Konzept bringen?

Rewrite the following sentences in the passive voice. Do not change the tense:

13 Wir besuchten unseren alten Onkel oft.
14 Der Junge hat der Frau geholfen.
15 Viele Leute genießen die Reise nach Dänemark.
16 Susi hat den Tisch gedeckt.
17 Die Studenten werden dem Professor keinesfalls glauben.
18 Das Kind begrüßte mich.
19 Die Schüler hatten den Lehrer aus dem Konzept gebracht.
20 Die Handwerker verbargen das Geld in der Fabrik.

E. Controlled Composition

Write a report of about 150 words on „Ein unverhofftes Wiedersehen" of Units 20 and 21. Do not use dialog but rather report the incident as an outside observer. You might begin as follows:

Eines Morgens kam Heinrich zu seiner Bushaltestelle. Da sah er plötzlich seinen alten Schulkameraden Werner stehen. Sie hatten einander schon ewig nicht gesehen. Natürlich freuten sie sich sehr. Heinrich erklärte seinem Freund, daß er jetzt wieder in Kiel wohnt. Noch am selben Morgen hatte er seiner Frau gesagt, daß . . .

READING PRACTICE

Schloß Augustusburg bei Köln

Zwischen Köln und Bonn liegt, nicht weit von Köln, die Stadt Brühl. In Brühl leben ungefähr 40 000 Menschen, und Brühl hat natürlich alles, was zu einer Stadt dieser Größe[g] gehört. Man kann also wegen sehr vieler verschiedener Sachen nach Brühl fahren.

Die meisten Leute kommen allerdings nur wegen einer einzigen Sache nach Brühl: wegen des Schlosses Augustusburg. Das Schloß wurde in den Jahren 1725–1770 im Stil des Spätbarock[g] errichtet, ist wirklich schön und wird heute jährlich von vielen tausend Menschen besichtigt.

Man kann lange in Schloß und Schloßgarten umhergehen, so viel gibt es dort zu sehen. Natürlich wohnt heute keiner mehr im Schloß Augustusburg. Schloß Augustusburg ist schon lange ein Museum[g].

Es ist klar, daß das Schloß Augustusburg nicht von einem, sondern von vielen Baumeistern[g] gebaut wurde. Man arbeitete 45 Jahre daran, bevor das Schloß endlich fertig war. Der beste von allen Baumeistern war Balthasar Neumann (1687–1753), ein sehr guter Architekt[g], der eigentlich in Würzburg lebte und dort die bekannte „Würzburger Residenz" mitgebaut hatte.

Das Schloß Augustusburg wurde erst vor 200 Jahren fertig. Es ist also nicht besonders alt. Aber es steht genau an der gleichen Stelle, wo früher zwei andere Schlösser gestanden hatten. Zuerst wurde an dieser Stelle im Jahre 1284 ein Schloß errichtet. Das wurde bald zerstört, im 14. Jahrhundert[g] aber wieder neu errichtet. 1689 zerstörten die Franzosen[g] auch dieses Schloß. Auf den Resten[g] dieser beiden alten Schlösser steht heute das Schloß Augustusburg.

Unit 28

WAGNER

THE NIBELUNGENLIED

READING

Der Lehrerberuf in Deutschland

Der Lehrer hat ohne Frage einen der wichtigsten Berufe überhaupt. Von seiner Arbeit hängt es wesentlich ab, welchen Grad[g] des Wissens die nächste Generation[g] erreichen wird. Und das heißt heute auch, wie gut oder schlecht sie leben wird.

Viel wichtiger als dieses Wissen ist aber noch sein direkter und indirekter Einfluß auf die jungen Menschen. Nach den Eltern ist der Lehrer oft die wichtigste Person im Leben der Kinder. Seine Erziehung formt[g] sie häufig für ihr ganzes späteres Leben.

Es ist daher immer interessant zu wissen, wieviel Bedeutung eine Gesellschaft dem Lehrberuf zuspricht, wie sie ihre Lehrer achtet, wie gut sie sie ausbildet und auch, wie sie sie bezahlt. Schauen wir uns das mal kurz in Deutschland an.

Der Volksschullehrer

Wer in Deutschland Lehrer werden will, muß Abitur haben. Zukünftige Volksschullehrer müssen dann sechs Semester auf einer Universität oder auf einer Pädagogischen Hochschule

abhängen von depend on
der Grad, -e · die Generation, -en [generatsiˈoːn]

der Einfluß, ⸗sse influence

die Bedeutung, -en meaning, significance
· **die Gesellschaft, -en** *here* society
zusprechen award, grant
sich anschauen *dat. refl.* sich ansehen*

zukünftig future
pädagogisch [pɛdaˈgoːgɪʃ]

1. Wer hat einen der wichtigsten Berufe überhaupt?
2. Was hängt von der Arbeit des Lehrers ab?
3. Hat der Lehrer einen Einfluß auf die jungen Menschen?
4. Ist dieser Einfluß wichtig?
5. Wer sind die wichtigsten Personen im Leben eines Kindes?
6. Was muß man haben, wenn man Lehrer werden will?
7. Wo muß der zukünftige Volksschullehrer studieren?
8. Wie viele Semester muß er dort studieren?

* Whenever a familiar German equivalent is available, it will be used instead of an English translation in the notes to the readings.

studieren. Danach gibt es ein Examen, die sogenannte Erste Lehrerprüfung. Wenn sie bestanden ist, sind die Kandidaten[g] Junglehrer.

Ihre Berufsausbildung ist nun aber noch nicht beendet. Die Junglehrer müssen nämlich noch ein zweijähriges Schulpraktikum[g] und eine ganze Menge Studienseminare[g] machen. Am Ende dieser Zeit steht dann die Zweite Lehrerprüfung. Ist auch sie bestanden, so ist aus dem Junglehrer endlich ein echter Lehrer geworden.

Es gibt heute lange nicht genug Volksschullehrer in Deutschland. Das ist schon jetzt schlimm genug, aber es sieht so aus, als ob das Problem in einigen Jahren noch sehr viel ernster sein wird. Bedenklich ist auch die Tatsache, daß fast alle zukünftigen Volksschullehrer Frauen, also Volksschullehrerinnen sein werden. Was früher ein echter Männerberuf war, wird bald ein typischer Frauenberuf sein.

Der Mittelschullehrer

Mittelschullehrer sind durchweg Volksschullehrer, die noch ein bestimmtes Fach dazu studiert haben; eine Fremdsprache oder Mathematik vielleicht, denn in der Mittelschule ist der Unterricht ja schon spezialisierter[g]. In der Volksschule haben die Kinder, die kleineren jedenfalls, keine Fachlehrer, sondern sie haben alle Unterrichtsfächer meistens nur bei einem einzigen Lehrer. In der Mittelschule werden sie wenigstens drei Fachlehrer haben. Gymnasiasten[g] aber werden in fast jedem Fach von einem anderen Lehrer unterrichtet. Spezialisten[g] bekommen überall auf der Welt mehr Geld, natürlich auch in Deutschland. Es geht dem Mittelschullehrer also finanziell[g] besser als dem Volksschullehrer.

Der Oberschullehrer

Und dem Oberschullehrer geht es noch besser. Er muß aber auch länger studieren, und sein Studium wird in der Regel schwerer sein als das seiner zukünftigen Volks- und Mittelschulkollegen. Er muß nämlich auf die Universität gehen, ein Studium an einer Pädagogischen Hochschule genügt für seine Berufsausbildung nicht mehr. Sein Universitätsstudium soll wenigstens acht Semester dauern. Doch das ist Theorie. In der Regel werden es zehn Semester und in manchen Fächern auch noch mehr.

Jeder zukünftige Gymnasiallehrer hat wenigstens zwei Spezialfächer zu studieren, aber daneben muß er natürlich auch noch viele andere, allgemeinere Vorlesungen besuchen und darin sein Wissen nachweisen.

Am Ende seines Studiums steht dann ein großes Examen, die sogenannte Erste Staatsprüfung. Danach kommt der Kandidat für zwei Jahre an eine Höhere Schule. Er ist jetzt Studienreferendar und darf auch schon unterrichten. Aber ältere Kollegen passen auf ihn auf, denn diese zwei Jahre gehören noch zur Berufsausbildung des Gymnasiallehrers. Er bekommt auch noch nicht viel Geld für seine Arbeit und muß noch regelmäßig Studienseminare besuchen.

sogenannt so-called · **bestanden** *past participle as predicate adjective*
der Kandidat, -en, -en [kandiˈdaːt] · **der Junglehrer, -** junior teacher
beenden finish
das Praktikum [ˈpraktikum] · **das Seminar, -e** [zemiˈnaːʀ]
Ist auch sie bestanden = wenn auch sie bestanden ist
echt genuine
bedenklich doubtful; critical

durchweg fast immer, meistens · **dazu** in addition
spezialisieren [ʃpetsialiˈziːʀən]
einzig single, only
der Gymnasiast, -en, -en [gymnaziˈast]
der Spezialist, -en, -en [ʃpetsiaˈlɪst]

finanziell [finantsiˈɛl]

die Regel, -n rule   **in der Regel** durchweg, fast immer, meistens

dauern last

nachweisen: er weist nach, wies nach, hat nachgewiesen point out, indicate, prove
der Studienreferendar, -e [ʀefeʀɛnˈdaːʀ] Lehrerkandidat an der Oberschule nach der Ersten Staatsprüfung
regelmäßig regular(ly)

9 Was gibt es danach?
10 Ist die Berufsausbildung nach der Ersten Lehrerprüfung beendet?
11 Was muß der Junglehrer dann noch machen?
12 Was muß er dann tun, um ein echter Lehrer zu werden?
13 Gibt es genug Volksschullehrer in Deutschland?
14 Wird die Sache besser?
15 Ist der Lehrerberuf in Deutschland nur für Männer?

16 Haben die kleineren Kinder in der Volksschule viele verschiedene Lehrer?
17 Wie viele Fachlehrer haben die Kinder in der Mittelschule?
18 Haben die Gymnasiasten noch mehr Lehrer?
19 Wer bekommt mehr Geld: der Volksschullehrer oder der Mittelschullehrer?

20 Wie geht es dem Oberschullehrer?
21 Wer muß am längsten studieren: der Oberschullehrer, der Mittelschullehrer oder der Volksschullehrer?
22 Muß der Oberschullehrer auch auf die Universität gehen?
23 Wie lange soll sein Studium auf der Universität dauern?
24 Wie lange dauert es tatsächlich?
25 Wie viele Spezialfächer muß der zukünftige Gymnasiallehrer studieren?
26 Wann macht er die Erste Staatsprüfung?
27 Darf ein Studienreferendar schon unterrichten?
28 Bekommt ein Studienreferendar viel Geld für seine Arbeit?
29 Was muß er noch regelmäßig tun?

War er in diesen zwei Jahren gut genug, dann kann er seine Zweite Staatsprüfung machen, und erst wenn er auch sie besteht, ist dann schließlich aus einem alten Studienreferendar ein junger Studienassessor geworden. Ein richtiger Gymnasiallehrer ist er damit aber immer noch nicht. Er unterrichtet wohl und bekommt dafür jetzt auch gutes Geld, aber er muß meistens noch zwei oder drei Jahre warten, bis er endlich Studienrat wird. So heißen die Lehrer an Höheren Schulen in Deutschland.

Eigentlich ist die Ausbildung eines Lehrers nie wirklich beendet. Es gibt immer viele Kurse[g] für Lehrer aller Fächer. Hier hören sie Vorlesungen und diskutieren[g] und empfangen so immer neue Anregungen für ihre wichtige Arbeit.

Man kann natürlich mit dem Ziel studieren, Volks- oder Mittelschullehrer oder auch Studienrat zu werden, aber man kann eigentlich nicht mit dem Ziel studieren, Lehrer an einer Pädagogischen Hochschule oder womöglich sogar an einer Wissenschaftlichen Hochschule (Universität) zu werden.

Der Lehrer an einer Pädagogischen Hochschule

Lehrer an Pädagogischen Hochschulen sind meistens ausgebildete Lehrer. Aus ihren Schulen werden sie dann — in der Regel wegen sehr guter Lehrerqualitäten[g] und großer Erfahrung — an Pädagogische Hochschulen berufen. Sie sind hochqualifizierte[g] Spezialisten und viele von ihnen haben den Doktorgrad[g] in ihren Fächern.

Der Universitätsprofessor

Lehrer an Wissenschaftlichen Hochschulen (Universitäten) sind dagegen fast nie ausgebildete Lehrer. Sie haben sich meistens schon früh spezialisiert, sich dabei besonders ausgezeichnet

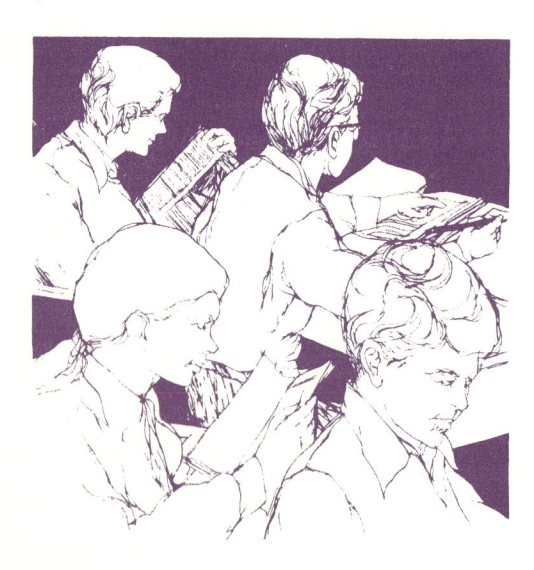

War er ... gut genug = wenn er ... gut genug war
der Studienassessor, -en [aˈsɛsɔʀ] Lehrerkandidat an der Oberschule nach der Zweiten Staatsprüfung
der Studienrat, ⸚e Lehrer an der Oberschule
der Rat, ⸚e counselor, adviser; advice
der Kurs, -e
diskutieren [dɪskuˈtiːʀən]
die Anregung, -en stimulus, impulse

womöglich vielleicht

ausgebildet trained **bilden** form, shape
die Qualität, -en [kvaliˈtɛːt]
berufen: er beruft, berief, hat berufen appoint · **qualifizieren** [kvalifiˈtsiːʀən]

sich auszeichnen *acc. refl.* distinguish oneself

30 Wie kann ein Studienreferendar zu einem Studienassessor werden?
31 Wie lange muß der Studienassessor warten, bevor er endlich Studienrat wird?

32 Wie wird man Lehrer an einer Pädagogischen Hochschule?
33 Was müssen diese Lehrer schon haben?
34 Müssen sie auch den Doktorgrad haben?

35 Wer darf bei einem Professor weiterstudieren?

und ihr Studium sicher mit einem besonders „guten" Doktorgrad beendet. Den besten unter ihnen fragt ein Professor dann vielleicht, ob er nicht bei ihm weiterstudieren will. Der junge Doktor muß dann kleinere wissenschaftliche Arbeiten machen und heißt offiziell: Wissenschaftliche Hilfskraft oder Wissenschaftlicher Hilfsarbeiter[g]. Eine Wissenschaftliche Hilfskraft bekommt nur sehr wenig Geld, muß aber noch sehr viel studieren.

Das mag so ein oder zwei Jahre gehen. Wenn dem Professor dann die Arbeiten und die Entwicklung seiner Hilfskraft gefallen, fragt er ihn womöglich, ob er sein Assistent[g] werden will. Als Wissenschaftlicher Assistent arbeitet unser Doktor nun mit seinem Professor zusammen, lernt die besonderen wissenschaftlichen Probleme seines Faches genau kennen und ist seines Professors „rechte Hand". Inzwischen wird er auch anfangen, eine spezielle Frage zu studieren und darüber eine große Arbeit zu schreiben. Nach vier bis sechs Jahren so spezieller Studien kann er sich dann endlich als Hochschullehrer qualifizieren, er kann sich „habilitieren". Die Habilitation ist ein Examen, das aus drei Teilen besteht: (1) Eine schriftliche[g], wissenschaftliche Arbeit (die natürlich größer und wichtiger sein muß als die Doktorarbeit), (2) eine Prüfung vor der ganzen Fakultät[g] (in der jeder Professor Fragen stellen kann) und (3) eine Probevorlesung.

Geht alles gut und hat der Kandidat schon vorher eine Reihe guter kleinerer wissenschaftlicher Arbeiten publiziert[g], so wird die Fakultät ihn habilitieren. Jetzt erst darf er Vorlesungen halten, denn jetzt erst ist er Hochschullehrer. Und wenn er recht fleißig bleibt, so wird eine andere Universität ihn schließlich auch einmal als Professor in seinem Fach in ihre Fakultät berufen.

Alle Lehrer werden, wenn sie erst einmal Lehrer sind, in Deutschland recht gut bezahlt. Natürlich verdienen manche Geschäftsleute mehr als sie (einige sogar sehr viel mehr), aber die Lehrer haben es gewiß nicht schlecht. Mit Ausnahme der (relativ[g] wenigen) Lehrer an privaten Schulen sind sie auch alle Beamte. Dadurch sind sie und ihre Familien sozial und finanziell so gut wie vollkommen gesichert. Und das ist schließlich nicht so unwichtig, wenn der Lehrberuf für gute junge Leute auch heute noch seine Anziehungskraft haben soll.

die Hilfskraft, ⸚e helper, assistant   **die Kraft, ⸚e** strength; worker

die Entwicklung, -en development
der Assistent, -en, -en [asɪsˈtɛnt]

besondere special
inzwischen in the meantime
habilitieren [habiliˈtiːʀən] die Qualifikation als Hochschullehrer bekommen
die Habilitation [habilitatsiˈoːn]
die Fakultät, -en [fakʊlˈtɛːt] · **die Probe, -n** test, trial
Geht alles gut = wenn alles gut geht
publizieren [publiˈtsiːʀən]   **hat der Kandidat ... publiziert** = wenn der Kandidat ... publiziert hat
fleißig industrious(ly), diligent(ly)
verdienen earn   **der Verdienst, -e** earnings, gain, profit
relativ [ʀelaˈtiːf]
der Beamte, -n *adj. noun* official; civil servant
die Anziehungskraft, ⸚e attraction

36 Wie heißt ein Doktor, der bei einem Professor studiert?
37 Wie lange dauert das?
38 Was kann passieren, wenn seine Arbeiten dem Professor gefallen?
39 Was tut der Assistent neben seiner Arbeit mit dem Professor?
40 Was kann er nach vier oder sechs Jahren tun?
41 Aus wieviel Teilen besteht die Habilitation?
42 Wann darf der junge Doktor Vorlesungen halten?
43 Was kann passieren, wenn der neue Hochschullehrer recht fleißig bleibt?
44 Werden deutsche Lehrer gut bezahlt?
45 Hat der Lehrerberuf für gute junge Leute noch Anziehungskraft?

PHONOLOGY

A. Fricatives

Practice pronouncing the following at a relatively brisk pace and distinguish clearly between [ç] and [ʃ], and between [j] and [x]:

wi **ch** ti g sten, wel **ch** er, nä **ch** ste, errei **ch** en, au **ch**, schle **ch** t, no **ch**, **sch** on, **j** ung, Men **sch**, na **ch**, vielei **ch** t, häufi **g**, **s** päteres, Gesell **sch** aft, zu **s** pricht, a **ch** tet, **sch** auen, Deut **sch** land, Volks **sch** ullehrer, Ho **ch** schule, **s** tudieren, dana **ch**, **J** unglehrer, nämli **ch**, zwei **j** ährig, ma **ch** en, **s** teht, be **s** tanden, endli **ch**, e **ch** t, ni **ch** t, **sch** limm, **j** etzt, bedenkli **ch**, Tatsa **ch** e, **j** edenfalls, typi **sch** er, be **s** timmtes, Fa **ch**, Fremd **s** prache, Unterri **ch** t, **j** a, **s** pezialisierter,

Unterri**ch**tsfä**ch**er, Fa**ch**lehrer, natürli**ch**, **sch**werer, a**ch**t, man**ch**en, **S**pezialfächer, besu**ch**en, **S**taatsprüfung, regelmäßi**g**, be**s**teht, **sch**ließli**ch**, eigentli**ch**, wissen**sch**aftli**ch**, womögli**ch**, Hoch**sch**ule, ho**ch**qualifiziert, **S**pezialisten, ausgezei**ch**net, re**ch**te, inzwi**sch**en, **sch**reiben, si**ch**, **sch**riftli**ch**e, fleißi**g**, man**ch**e, Ge**sch**äftsleute, gesi**ch**ert

B. Long Vowels, Short Vowels, Diphthongs

Practice pronouncing the following at a relatively brisk pace and watch especially all vowel qualities and quantities, and all diphthongs:

L e̲ hrer, o̲ hne, Fr a̲ ge, Ber u̲ f, ü̲ berh au pt, e s, w e̲ sentli ch, Gr a d, wi ssen, n ä̲ chste, e rr ei chen, h eu te, au ch, g u̲ t, schl e cht, l e̲ ben, sch o̲ n, Ei nfl u̲ ß, P e̲ rs o̲ n, f o rmt, h äu fig, ei̲ ne, Bed eu̲ tung, g a nzes, i mmer, i ntere ss ant, a chtet, u nd, bez a̲ hlt, u ns, d a s, m a̲ l, e̲ ben, a nsch au en, w e̲ r, z u̲ künftig, m ü ssen, d a nn, s e chs, g i bt, E x a̲ men, best a nden, K a ndid a̲ t, n ä̲ mlich, m a chen, zw ei j ä̲ hri ges, l a nge, gen u̲ g, schl i mm, s o̲, o b, Pr o̲ bl e̲ m, n o ch, T a̲ tsache, f a st, w e̲ rden, fr ü̲ her, e̲ chter, t y̲ pisch, M i ttelsch u̲ lehrer, best i mmtes, M a̲ thematik, vi ellei cht, U nterri cht, o ft, n u r, i n, v o n, a nderen, bek o mmen, ü̲ ber a ll, fin a nzi e ll, D eu̲ tschl a nd, d e sh a lb, m u ß, gen ü̲ gt, Th e o̲ rie, m a nchen, zw ei, Pr ü̲ fungen, a n, k o mmt, ä̲ ltere, geh ö̲ ren, A rb ei t, regelm ä̲ ßig, bes u̲ chen, gen u̲ g, St aa tsprüfung, e rst, w e nn, gew o rden, w a rten, b i s, St u̲ dienr a̲ t, K u rse, f ü̲ r, h ö̲ ren, empf a ngen, A n- r e̲ gung, m i t, Z ie̲ l, H o chsch u̲ le, U niv e rsit ä̲ t, m ei stens, d a nn, Erf a̲ hrung, D o kt o̲ r, Gr a d, fr ü̲ h, fr a gt, H i lfskraft, w e nn, d e m, zus a mmen, Pr o̲ bl e̲ me, k e nnen, H a nd, a nf a ngen, Fr a̲ ge, F a kult ä̲ t, Pr o̲ be, v o rher, r e cht, F a ch, verd ie̲ nen, m a nche, s e̲ hr, v ie̲ l, m e̲ hr, gew i ß, priv a̲ t, B ea mte, s o zi a̲ l, v o llk o mmen, ges i chert, s o ll

---

VOCABULARY

A. Singular and Plural of Nouns

die Anregung, -en
die Anziehungskraft, ⸚e
der Assistent, -en, -en
der Beamte, -n *adj. noun*
die Bedeutung, -en
der Einfluß, ⸚sse
die Entwicklung, -en
die Fakultät, -en

die Generation, -en
der Grad, -e
der Gymnasiast, -en, -en
die Hilfskraft, ⸚e
der Kandidat, -en, -en
der Kollege, -n, -n
der Kurs, -e
die Probe, -n

die Qualität, -en
die Regel, -n
der Spezialist, -en, -en
der Studienassessor, -en
der Studienrat, ⸚e
der Studienreferendar, -e
das Studienseminar, -e
die Theorie, -n

B. Inference

Words similar to English:

1 Das Konzert hatte nur eine kurze **Pause** von zehn Minuten.   **die Pause, -n**
2 Plötzlich war alles **still**, kein Mensch sagte ein Wort.
3 Ist das Messer auch **scharf** genug, um dieses Fleisch zu schneiden?
4 Hier ist ein **Scheck** über 500,— Mark.   **der Scheck, -s**
5 Hans, deine **Wollsocken** sind schon wieder kaputt!   **die Socke, -n**
6 Fällt hier im Winter viel **Schnee**?   **der Schnee**
7 Ich habe großen Durst. Bringen Sie mir doch bitte ein Glas **Wasser**!   **das Wasser**
8 Wenn man nicht **schwimmen** kann, bringt Baden keinen Spaß.   **schwimmen: er schwimmt, schwamm, ist (hat) geschwommen**
9 Für die Bedeutung eines Wortes ist der **Stamm** am wichtigsten.   **der Stamm, ⸚e**
10 Wie schmeckt dir dieser **Tabak** [ˈtɑːbak] in der Pfeife?   **der Tabak**
11 Wieviel **Benzin** [bɛnˈtsiːn] brauchst du pro 100 Kilometer mit deinem Auto?   **das Benzin**
12 Einige Straßen in dieser alten, kleinen Stadt sind nicht mehr als drei Meter **breit**. Das ist nicht **breit** genug für unseren Bus. Wir müssen aussteigen und ein Stück zu Fuß gehen.

Many words spelled with **t** in German have *d* in English. Known examples are: **tanzen** *dance*, **trinken** *drink*, **das Bett** *bed*, **kalt** *cold*. Below are some new ones:

1 Der Fluß hier ist nicht **tief** genug zum Baden.
2 Durch diesen kleinen Fluß kann man sogar **waten**.
3 Ich habe in der Nacht wieder einen **Traum** gehabt. **Träumst** du nachts auch so viel?   **der Traum, ⸚e**
4 Der Unfall war scheußlich, der Fahrer war sofort **tot**.
5 Der Fahrer war aber auch wie der **Teufel** gefahren.   **der Teufel, -**
6 Musik habe ich ja gern, Hans, aber mußt du so **laut** spielen?
7 Er wohnt an einem kleinen Fluß in einem hübschen, grünen **Tal** im Schwarzwald.   **das Tal, ⸚er**
8 Dieses Stück Papier ist viel zu groß. Du mußt es wenigstens zweimal **falten**.
9 Jeder Mensch hat ungefähr fünf Liter **Blut**.   **das Blut**
10 Seine Wunde ist schlimm, sie **blutet** immer noch.
11 Der Weihnachtsmann hat einen langen, weißen **Bart**.   **der Bart, ⸚e**
12 Nach dem Krieg gab es wenig zu essen. Es war eine große **Not**.   **die Not, ⸚e**
13 Das Wasser kommt schon. In einer halben Stunde ist die **Flut** da.   **die Flut, -en**

WRITING

A. Dehydrated Sentences

Write sentences in the passive voice in the tense indicated:

1. hier / damals / empfangen / tanzen (*pres. perf.*)
2. Professor / vergessen / im Zug / Mantel (*past*)
3. Lehrling / schließen / sechs Uhr / Geschäft (*pres. perf.*)
4. die Versandkompanie / bauen / nächstes Jahr / Kaufhaus (*fut.*)
5. Männer / zerstören / im Krieg / Schloß (*past perf.*)
6. hier / damals / viel / singen / lachen (*past*)
7. Dame / unterbrechen / oft / Fremdenführer (*pres.*)
8. in diesem Saal / ermorden / König (*past perf.*)
9. die ganze Schule / besichtigen / nächste Woche / Dom (*fut.*)
10. Brand / zerstören / zweimal / Kirche (*pres. perf.*)

B. Controlled Composition

Write a report of about 150 words on „Die Schloßbesichtigung". Do not use dialog and try a variety of passive constructions. You might begin as follows:

Nach langer Zeit wird von Meiers eine Stadt besucht, die sie von früher kennen. Sie war im Kriege fast vollkommen zerstört worden. Aber inzwischen ist sehr viel gebaut worden. Herr Meier sagt, daß noch sehr viel mehr gebaut werden wird. Manches wurde wieder im alten Stile errichtet. Ob auch das alte Schloß im Kriege zerstört worden war? . . .

Unit 29

DIALOG

Was wäre, wenn . . . (Anfang)

1 **Hartmut:** Du, Kurt, hast du schon mal daran gedacht, was wäre, wenn wir im Lotto gewännen?

2 **Kurt:** Du meinst, wenn wir beinahe alles kaufen könnten, was wir wollten?

3 **Hartmut:** Nicht beinahe alles, sondern alles! Und hätten noch immer Geld zuviel!

4 **Kurt:** Ich ginge erst einmal sehr gut und vornehm essen.

5 **Hartmut:** Immer essen, du alter Epikureer. Du solltest statt dessen lieber an deine Bildung denken!

6 **Kurt:** Gut, was hättest du also vorzuschlagen?

What Would It Be Like If . . .
(Beginning)

1. Say, Kurt, have you ever thought of what it would be like if we won in the lottery?

2. You mean, if we could buy almost everything that we wanted?

3. Not almost everything, but everything! And still had too much money!

4. First I'd go and have a good dinner in a fine restaurant.

5. Always eating, you old epicure. Instead of that you ought to be thinking of your education.

6. O.K. So what would you have to suggest?

wäre *subj. II*

das Lotto, -s lotto *short for* **die Lotterie, -n · gewinnen: er gewinnt, gewann, hat gewonnen** (**gewännen** *subj. II*)

könnten, wollten *subj. II*

hätten *subj. II*

ginge *subj. II* · **vornehm** of superior rank; distinguished, fashionable, high-class

der Epikureer, - · **solltest** *subj. II*

vorschlagen: er schlägt vor, schlug vor, hat vorgeschlagen

7 **Hartmut:** Ich denke, man müßte zuerst eine Bildungsreise machen.

8 **Kurt:** Die Venus von Milo und so? Ich fände junge, lebende Damen besser als alte von Stein!

9 **Hartmut:** Sei doch vernünftig, das gute Leben könnte danach ja immer noch kommen!

10 **Kurt:** Du meinst: Feste, Sportwagen, Reisen in den sonnigen Süden usw.?

(Fortsetzung folgt)

SUPPLEMENT

1 Wenn Susi nur zu Hause wäre!

2 Wenn ich nur eine Zigarette hätte!

3 Wenn er sich nur nicht aufregte!

4 Wenn du nur nicht so vergeßlich wärest!

5 Wenn ich nur einen besseren Mantel hätte!

6 Wenn er doch nicht immer so viel fluchte!

7 Würden Sie mir bitte die Butter bringen?

8 Dürfte ich das rote Kleid mal anprobieren?

9 Möchten Sie sonst noch etwas?

10 Ich hätte gern ein Glas Bier.

11 Du hättest weglaufen können.

7	I think first we'd have to take an educational trip.	**müßte** *subj. II* · **die Bildungsreise die Bildung + die Reise eine Reise machen** take a trip
8	Venus de Milo and all that? I'd find young, live ladies better than old ones made of stone.	**fände** *subj. II* · **der Stein, -e**
9	Oh, be sensible. After all, the "good life" could still come afterwards.	**vernünftig** sensible, reasonable · **das Leben, -**
10	You mean parties, sports cars, trips to the sunny south, etc.?	**der Sportwagen der Sport** sport, sports **+ der Wagen** · **usw.** *abbr. for* **und so weiter** and so forth **weit** far

(To be continued)

1	If only Susi were home!	
2	If only I had a cigarette!	
3	If only he wouldn't get excited!	**sich aufregen** get excited · **aufregte** *subj. II*
4	If only you weren't so forgetful!	
5	If only I had a better coat!	
6	If only he wouldn't swear so much!	**fluchen** swear, curse · **fluchte** *subj. II*
7	Would you please bring me the butter?	**würden** *subj. II*
8	Might I try on the red dress?	**dürfte** *subj. II* · **anprobieren** try on
9	Would you like anything else?	**möchte** *subj. II*
10	I would like a glass of beer.	
11	You could have run away.	

12 Ich hätte anrufen sollen.

13 Das hätten Sie nicht sagen sollen.

14 Sie hätten die Nummer doch aufschreiben können.

15 Er hätte sich für die Schule interessieren sollen.

12 I should have called up.

13 You shouldn't have said that.

14 You could have written the number down.

15 He should have been interested in the school.   **sich interessieren für** *acc. refl.* be interested in

---

AUDIOLINGUAL DRILLS

A. Directed Dialog

Fragen Sie, wie der neue Dialog heißt!
Wie heißt der neue Dialog?

Antworten Sie, daß er „Was wäre, wenn . . ." heißt!
Er heißt, „Was wäre, wenn . . ."

Fragen Sie, was wäre, wenn Hartmut und Kurt im Lotto gewännen!
Was wäre, wenn Hartmut und Kurt im Lotto gewännen?

Fragen Sie, ob Hartmut meint, daß sie dann beinahe alles kaufen könnten, was sie wollten?
Meint Hartmut, daß sie dann beinahe alles kaufen könnten, was sie wollten?

Antworten Sie, daß Hartmut nicht beinahe alles, sondern alles meint!
Hartmut meint nicht beinahe alles, sondern alles.

Sagen Sie, daß sie dann noch immer Geld zuviel hätten!
Sie hätten dann noch immer Geld zuviel.

Sagen Sie, daß Kurt erst einmal sehr gut und vornehm essen ginge!
Kurt ginge erst einmal sehr gut und vornehm essen.

Sagen Sie, daß Kurt statt dessen lieber an seine Bildung denken sollte!
Kurt sollte statt dessen lieber an seine Bildung denken.

Fragen Sie, was Hartmut also vorzuschlagen hätte!
Was hätte Hartmut also vorzuschlagen?

Antworten Sie, daß er denkt, man müßte zuerst eine Bildungsreise machen!
Er denkt, man müßte zuerst eine Bildungsreise machen.

Fragen Sie, ob Hartmut die Venus von Milo meint!
Meint Hartmut die Venus von Milo?

Antworten Sie, daß Kurt junge, lebende Damen besser als alte von Stein fände!
Kurt fände junge, lebende Damen besser als alte von Stein.

Sagen Sie, daß Kurt doch vernünftig sein sollte!
Kurt sollte doch vernünftig sein.

Sagen Sie, daß das gute Leben danach ja immer noch kommen könnte!
Das gute Leben könnte danach ja immer noch kommen.

Fragen Sie, ob Hartmut Feste, Sportwagen, Reisen in den sonnigen Süden usw. meint!
Meint Hartmut Feste, Sportwagen, Reisen in den sonnigen Süden usw.?

B. New Strong Verbs

1 **Gewinnen** win follows the pattern of **beginnen**—**er gewinnt, gewann, hat gewonnen.** Change the tense or the subject as indicated:

Er gewinnt im Lotto.   *past*
Er gewann im Lotto   *ich*
Ich gewann im Lotto.   *fut.*
Ich werde im Lotto gewinnen.   **ihr**

Ihr werdet im Lotto gewinnen.   *past perf.*
Ihr hattet im Lotto gewonnen.   **du**
Du hattest im Lotto gewonnen.

2 **Vorschlagen** suggest follows the pattern of **fahren**—**er schlägt vor, schlug vor, hat vorgeschlagen.** Change the tense or the subject as indicated:

Ich schlage eine Bildungsreise vor.   **er**
Er schlägt eine Bildungsreise vor.   *fut.*
Er wird eine Bildungsreise vorschlagen.   **wir**
Wir werden eine Bildungsreise vorschlagen.   *pres. perf.*
Wir haben eine Bildungsreise vorgeschlagen.   **ihr**
Ihr habt eine Bildungsreise vorgeschlagen.   *past*
Ihr schlugt eine Bildungsreise vor.

3 **Nachweisen** point out, prove follows the pattern of **schreiben**—**er weist nach, wies nach, hat nachgewiesen.** Change the tense or the subject as indicated:

Weist er die Theorie nach?   *past*
Wies er die Theorie nach?   **du**
Wiesest du die Theorie nach?   *fut.*
Wirst du die Theorie nachweisen?   **wir**
Werden wir die Theorie nachweisen?   *pres. perf.*
Haben wir die Theorie nachgewiesen?   **ihr**
Habt ihr die Theorie nachgewiesen?

C. Present Subjunctive II: Weak Verbs
(*See Grammar* §§29.3, 29.4, 29.8)

The present subjunctive II form of weak verbs is identical with the past indicative form.

4 Practice the following "if only" sentences, substituting the new subject or adverbial phrase:

Wenn er nur in Stuttgart wohnte!   **du**
Wenn du nur in Stuttgart wohntest!   **im Süden**
Wenn du nur im Süden wohntest!   **wir**
Wenn wir nur im Süden wohnten!   **in der Stadt**
Wenn wir nur in der Stadt wohnten!   **ich**
Wenn ich nur in der Stadt wohnte!   **in einem alten Schloß**
Wenn ich nur in einem alten Schloß wohnte!

5 Substitute the present subjunctive II form of the new weak verb:

Wenn du nur nicht so viel arbeitetest!   **studieren**
Wenn du nur nicht so viel studiertest!   **lachen**
Wenn du nur nicht so viel lachtest!   **spotten**
Wenn du nur nicht so viel spottetest!   **tanzen**
Wenn du nur nicht so viel tanztest!   **verdienen**
Wenn du nur nicht so viel verdientest!   **fluchen**
Wenn du nur nicht so viel fluchtest!

D. Present Subjunctive II: Strong Verbs (*See Grammar* §29.4)

The present subjunctive II form of strong verbs is derived from the past indicative form. Umlaut the stem vowel if possible, and add the subjunctive ending: singular **-e**, **-est**, **-e**, plural **-en**, **-et**, **-en**.

6 Practice the following "if only" sentences, substituting the new subject or adverbial phrase:

Wenn er nur hier wäre!   **Tante Inge**
Wenn Tante Inge nur hier wäre!   **zu Hause**
Wenn Tante Inge nur zu Hause wäre!   **du**
Wenn du nur zu Hause wärest!   **dort**
Wenn du nur dort wärest!   **wir**
Wenn wir nur dort wären!   **im Ausland**
Wenn wir nur im Ausland wären!

7 Substitute the present subjunctive II form of the new strong verb:

Wenn sie nur mitkäme!   **weggehen**
Wenn sie nur wegginge!   **gewinnen**
Wenn sie nur gewänne!   **fortfahren**
Wenn sie nur fortführe!   **einsteigen**
Wenn sie nur einstiege!   **anfangen**
Wenn sie nur anfinge!   **umziehen**
Wenn sie nur umzöge!   **anrufen**
Wenn sie nur anriefe!

E. Present Subjunctive II: Modals, Irregular Weak Verbs
(*See Grammar* §29.4)

The present subjunctive II form of these irregular verbs is derived from the past indicative form.

Modal auxiliaries

The present subjunctive II form of **sollen** and **wollen** is identical with their past indicative form. The present subjunctive II of the other modals is derived from the past indicative by umlauting the stem vowel.

8 Substitute the new subject or the present subjunctive II form of the new modal:

Ich könnte eine Reise machen. **du**
Du könntest eine Reise machen. **sollen**
Du solltest eine Reise machen. **er**
Er sollte eine Reise machen. **mögen**
Er möchte eine Reise machen. **wir**
Wir möchten eine Reise machen. **müssen**

Wir müßten eine Reise machen. **ihr**
Ihr müßtet eine Reise machen. **wollen**
Ihr wolltet eine Reise machen. **Käthe**
Käthe wollte eine Reise machen. **dürfen**
Käthe dürfte eine Reise machen. **du**
Du dürftest eine Reise machen.

Kennen and *nennen*

The present subjunctive II of **kennen** and **nennen** (and a few other verbs that you have not learned yet) is derived from the past indicative by replacing the vowel **a** [a] by **e** [ε].

9 Substitute the new subject:

Wenn du ihn nur kenntest! **ich**
Wenn ich ihn nur kennte! **meine Eltern**
Wenn meine Eltern ihn nur kennten! **Susi**
Wenn Susi ihn nur kennte! **ihr**
Wenn ihr ihn nur kenntet! **wir**
Wenn wir ihn nur kennten!

Wenn er mich nur beim Vornamen nennte! **Käthe**
Wenn Käthe mich nur beim Vornamen nennte! **du**
Wenn du mich nur beim Vornamen nenntest! **die Leute**
Wenn die Leute mich nur beim Vornamen nennten! **ihr**
Wenn ihr mich nur beim Vornamen nenntet! **er**
Wenn er mich nur beim Vornamen nennte!

Other irregular verbs

The present subjunctive II of the irregular verbs **haben**, **werden**, **bringen**, **denken**, and **wissen** is derived from the past indicative by umlauting the stem vowel.

10 Substitute the new subject:

Wenn ich nur mehr Zeit hätte! **wir**
Wenn wir nur mehr Zeit hätten! **du**
Wenn du nur mehr Zeit hättest! **ihr**
Wenn ihr nur mehr Zeit hättet! **die Studenten**
Wenn die Studenten nur mehr Zeit hätten!

Wenn er doch nicht immer so ernst würde! **du**
Wenn du doch nicht immer so ernst würdest! **Frau Hartmann**
Wenn Frau Hartmann doch nicht immer so ernst würde! **ihr**
Wenn ihr doch nicht immer so ernst würdet! **die Kinder**
Wenn die Kinder doch nicht immer so ernst würden!

Wenn du mich nur nicht immer aus dem Konzept brächtest! **er**
Wenn er mich nur nicht immer aus dem Konzept brächte! **die Schüler**
Wenn die Schüler mich nur nicht immer aus dem Konzept brächten! **ihr**
Wenn ihr mich nur nicht immer aus dem Konzept brächtet! **der Kerl**
Wenn der Kerl mich nur nicht immer aus dem Konzept brächte!

Wenn er doch nicht immer an Sportwagen dächte! **du**
Wenn du doch nicht immer an Sportwagen dächtest! **ihr**
Wenn ihr doch nicht immer an Sportwagen dächtet! **die Jungen**
Wenn die Jungen doch nicht immer an Sportwagen dächten! **Anja**
Wenn Anja doch nicht immer an Sportwagen dächte!

Wenn ich nur etwas davon wüßte! **wir**
Wenn wir nur etwas davon wüßten! **du**
Wenn du nur etwas davon wüßtest! **Kurt**
Wenn Kurt nur etwas davon wüßte! **meine Eltern**
Wenn meine Eltern nur etwas davon wüßten!

F. Subjunctive II: Past Tense (*See Grammar* §29.5)

The past subjunctive II is formed with **hätte** or **wäre** plus the past participle of the main verb.

11 Substitute the new subject or the past participle of the new verb:

Wenn du ihn nur gefragt hättest! **ich**
Wenn ich ihn nur gefragt hätte! **kennen**
Wenn ich ihn nur gekannt hätte! **wir**
Wenn wir ihn nur gekannt hätten! **besuchen**
Wenn wir ihn nur besucht hätten! **die Klassenkameraden**
Wenn die Klassenkameraden ihn nur besucht hätten! **sehen**

Wenn die Klassenkameraden ihn nur gesehen hätten! **der Junge**
Wenn der Junge ihn nur gesehen hätte! **verstehen**
Wenn der Junge ihn nur verstanden hätte! **du**
Wenn du ihn nur verstanden hättest!

12 Substitute the new subject or the past participle of the new verb:

Wenn sie nur nicht mitgekommen wäre! **du**
Wenn du nur nicht mitgekommen wärest! **aussteigen**
Wenn du nur nicht ausgestiegen wärest! **er**
Wenn er nur nicht ausgestiegen wäre! **sterben**
Wenn er nur nicht gestorben wäre! **die Leute**
Wenn die Leute nur nicht gestorben wären! **umziehen**
Wenn die Leute nur nicht umgezogen wären! **ihr**
Wenn ihr nur nicht umgezogen wäret! **weggehen**
Wenn ihr nur nicht weggegangen wäret! **Lilo**
Wenn Lilo nur nicht weggegangen wäre!

13 Change from the present subjunctive II to the past subjunctive II:

Wenn wir nur in Kiel wohnten!   Wenn du ihn nur kenntest!
Wenn wir nur in Kiel gewohnt hätten!   Wenn du ihn nur gekannt hättest!

Wenn du nur nicht so viel arbeitetest!   Wenn es doch nicht immer so kalt würde!
Wenn du nur nicht so viel gearbeitet hättest!   Wenn es doch nicht immer so kalt geworden wäre!

Wenn Tante Inge nur zu Hause wäre!
Wenn Tante Inge nur zu Hause gewesen wäre!   Wenn er das nur nicht wüßte!
    Wenn er das nur nicht gewußt hätte!

Wenn sie doch nur mitkäme!
Wenn sie doch nur mitgekommen wäre!   Wenn ich nur im Lotto gewänne!
    Wenn ich nur im Lotto gewonnen hätte!

Modal auxiliaries and **hören, helfen, lassen,** and **sehen,** plus a dependent infinitive, form the "double infinitive" construction in the past subjunctive II.

14 Substitute the new subject or modal auxiliary:

Er hätte eine Reise machen sollen. **du**   Ich hätte eine Reise machen dürfen. **ihr**
Du hättest eine Reise machen sollen. **können**   Ihr hättet eine Reise machen dürfen. **müssen**
Du hättest eine Reise machen können. **ich**   Ihr hättet eine Reise machen müssen. **wir**
Ich hätte eine Reise machen können. **dürfen**   Wir hätten eine Reise machen müssen.

15 Change from the present subjunctive II to the past subjunctive II:

Du könntest eine Bildungsreise machen.   Wenn er nur eine Reise machen dürfte!
Du hättest eine Bildungsreise machen können.   Wenn er nur eine Reise hätte machen dürfen!

Er müßte Ruhe halten.
Er hätte Ruhe halten müssen.

Wenn er nur Ruhe halten könnte!
Wenn er nur Ruhe hätte halten können!

Du müßtest an deine Bildung denken.
Du hättest an deine Bildung denken müssen.

Wenn du nur an deine Bildung denken möchtest!
Wenn du nur an deine Bildung hättest denken mögen!

Sie ließe sich überall sehen.
Sie hätte sich überall sehen lassen.

Wenn ich sie nur spielen sähe!
Wenn ich sie nur hätte spielen sehen!

Wir wollten gern mithelfen.
Wir hätten gern mithelfen wollen.

Er könnte beinahe alles kaufen.
Er hätte beinahe alles kaufen können.

Wenn wir ihn nur wegfahren hörten!
Wenn wir ihn nur hätten wegfahren hören!

G. Present Subjunctive II: *würde*-Alternative
(*See Grammar* §29.6)

The **würde**-alternative of the present subjunctive II is a phrase consisting of **würde** plus the infinitive of the main verb.

16 Substitute the new subject or the new infinitive:

Würden Sie heute nachmittag mitkommen?   **er**
Würde er heute nachmittag mitkommen?   **weggehen**
Würde er heute nachmittag weggehen?   **die Studentinnen**
Würden die Studentinnen heute nachmittag weggehen?   **anrufen**
Würden die Studentinnen heute nachmittag anrufen?   **ihr**
Würdet ihr heute nachmittag anrufen?   **beginnen**
Würdet ihr heute nachmittag beginnen?   **du**
Würdest du heute nachmittag beginnen?   **mithelfen**
Würdest du heute nachmittag mithelfen?

17 Change from the present indicative to the **würde**-alternative of the present subjunctive II:

Kommt sie denn nicht mit?
Würde sie denn nicht mitkommen?

Wir fahren morgen ab.
Wir würden morgen abfahren.

Ich denke gar nicht daran.
Ich würde gar nicht daran denken.

Ich freue mich auf die Reise.
Ich würde mich auf die Reise freuen.

Geben Sie mir die Butter?
Würden Sie mir die Butter geben?

Sie interessiert sich für alte Schlösser.
Sie würde sich für alte Schlösser interessieren.

Er regt sich nie auf.
Er würde sich nie aufregen.

Das Studium dauert acht Semester.
Das Studium würde acht Semester dauern.

Die Studenten unterbrechen seine Vorlesung nicht.
Die Studenten würden seine Vorlesung nicht unterbrechen.

Gehst du solange zu deiner Mutter hinüber?
Würdest du solange zu deiner Mutter hinübergehen?

H. Questions and Answers

Was täte Kurt zuerst, wenn er und Hartmut im Lotto gewännen?
Er ginge erst einmal sehr gut und vornehm essen.

Wie nennt Hartmut seinen Freund?
Er nennt ihn einen alten Epikureer.

Woran sollte Kurt statt dessen denken?
Er sollte lieber an seine Bildung denken.

Was hätte Hartmut vorzuschlagen?
Er meint, man müßte zuerst eine Bildungsreise machen.

Was möchte Hartmut gerne sehen?
Er möchte am liebsten die Venus von Milo sehen.

Was fände Kurt besser als alte Damen von Stein?
Er fände junge, lebende Damen eigentlich besser.

Wie antwortet Hartmut darauf?
Er sagt, das gute Leben könnte ja immer noch kommen.

Woran denkt Kurt dabei?
Er denkt an Feste, Sportwagen, Reisen in den sonnigen Süden usw.

GRAMMAR

29.1 Word-Formation

Ge-prefix nouns

A number of masculine and neuter nouns have been derived from verbs by attaching the prefix **Ge-** to the verb stem and (usually) modifying the stem itself. Some of these nouns have a "collective" meaning, that is, they refer to several individual things as if they were all one. Others refer to the instrument by means of which the action of the underlying verb is accomplished. Still others refer to the results of the action. Some **Ge-**nouns derived from verbs that you already know are given in the following list:

bauen	build	das Gebäude, - building, edifice
brauchen	need; use	der Gebrauch, ⸚e use
decken	cover	das Gedeck, -e cover; table setting
denken	think	der Gedanke, -ns, -n thought
fahren	drive, travel	das Gefährt, -e vehicle
fallen	fall	das Gefälle slope, grade
folgen	follow	das Gefolge, - retinue
fragen	ask	das Gefrage questioning
halten	hold, keep	das Gehalt, ⸚er salary
hängen	hang	das Gehänge, - garland, festoon
helfen	help	der Gehilfe, -n, -n assistant; clerk
hören	hear	das Gehör (sense of) hearing
klappen	clatter	das Geklapper clatter(ing)
lachen	laugh	das Gelächter laughter
laufen	run	das Gelaufe running around
rufen	call	das Gerufe calling, shouting
		das Gerücht, -e rumor
schmecken	taste	der Geschmack, ⸚e taste, flavor
sehen	see	das Gesicht, -er face
setzen	set, place	das Gesetz, -e law
sitzen	sit	das Gesäß, -e seat
spotten	mock	das Gespött mockery
sprechen	speak	das Gespräch, -e conversation
stellen	place, put	das Gestell, -e stand, rack

suchen   seek   das Gesuch, -e   application (for a job)
trinken   drink   das Getränk, -e   beverage
wissen   know   das Gewissen   conscience

29.2 Singular and Plural of Nouns

die Bildungsreise, -n   der Sport
der Epikureer, -   der Sportwagen, -
das Lotto, -s   der Stein, -e

29.3 The Subjunctive Mood

The grammatical term *mood* comes from Latin *modus*; it means "mode" or "manner." The German verb system has three moods: indicative, imperative, and subjunctive. Each mood has its own set of verb forms, and each one is used for a particular "manner of expression."

The indicative mood is used to represent something as a fact:

Hier scheint die Sonne jeden Tag.   Wenn die Sonne scheint, gehen wir zum Baden.
The sun shines here every day.   If the sun shines, we'll go swimming.

The imperative mood is used for commands (see Grammar §§8.5, 21.4):

Kurt, sei doch vernünftig!   Schauen Sie mal durch diese Auswahl hier!
Kurt, please be reasonable!   Just look through this selection here.

The subjunctive mood, however, is used in order to represent something as being *contrary to fact*. The specific situations in which the German subjunctive occurs are few and easily recognizable; they will be treated in detail in Grammar §29.8, in §30.3, and in §§32.1 and 32.2.

The subjunctive in English

Unlike German, English no longer has a set of verb forms that we can call "subjunctive." The subjunctive function is expressed through special uses of the indicative forms. The *present subjunctive* is expressed by means of *past indicative verb forms*:

Past indicative	*Present subjunctive*
They *lived* in Bonn.	If only they *lived* in Bonn!
Aunt Inge *was* at home.	If only Aunt Inge *were* at home!
Last year John *could* speak German.	If only John *could* speak German!

Notice two things about the present subjunctive sentences: (1) past indicative verb forms are used to express *present* time, and (2) the situations expressed in the subjunctive sentences *do not exist*, i.e. the implication is that they *do not* live in Bonn, that Aunt Inge *is not* at home, and that John *cannot* speak German.

The English *past subjunctive* is expressed by means of *past perfect indicative verb forms*:

Past perfect indicative	*Past subjunctive*
They *had lived* in Bonn.	If only they *had lived* in Bonn!
Aunt Inge *had been* at home.	If only Aunt Inge *had been* at home!
John *had been* able to speak German.	If only John *had been* able to speak German!

Notice that (1) the past perfect indicative forms are used to express *past* time in the subjunctive, and (2) the subjunctive situations *did not exist*, i.e. they *did not* live in Bonn, Aunt Inge *was not* at home, and John *was not* able to speak German.

In addition to these verbs whose indicative forms are used in subjunctive functions, English has a number of auxiliary verbs that may have subjunctive meaning, e.g. *would, could, might, ought, should,* etc.

The German subjunctive

German has a complete set of verb forms for the subjunctive mood. There are two subjunctive types: subjunctive I, whose forms are derived from the stem of the infinitive (to be taken up in Unit 32), and subjunctive II, whose forms are derived from the past tense stem. Subjunctive II has two tenses: present and past. (Recall that the indicative mood has six tenses: present, present perfect, past, past perfect, future, and future perfect.)

9.4 Present Subjunctive II Forms

Endings

The subjunctive endings differ somewhat from the endings of the indicative. They are the same for weak verbs and strong verbs:

-e	-en
-est	-et
-e	-en

Weak verbs

The present subjunctive II of regular weak verbs is identical with the past indicative:

Past indicative	Present subjunctive II
fragte	fragte
fragtest	fragtest
fragte	fragte
fragten	fragten
fragtet	fragtet
fragten	fragten

Strong verbs

The present subjunctive II is derived from the past indicative stem by umlauting the stem vowel (if possible) and adding the appropriate subjunctive ending:

Infinitive	Past stem	+ umlaut	+ ending →	Present subjunctive II
kommen	kam-	käm-	-e	käme, kämest, etc.
tun	tat-	tät-	-est	täte, tätest, etc.
fahren	fuhr-	führ-	-e	führe, führest, etc.
ziehen	zog-	zög-	-en	zöge, zögest, etc.
rufen	rief-	rief-	-et	riefe, riefest, etc.
steigen	stieg-	stieg-	-en	stiege, stiegest, etc.

A few strong verbs do not follow this pattern of derivation. The ones that you know are:

Infinitive	Past indicative	Present subjunctive II
helfen	half	hülfe
stehen	stand	stünde
sterben	starb	stürbe
beginnen	begann	begönne

Tense auxiliaries

Infinitive	Past indicative	Present subjunctive II
haben	hatte	hätte
sein	war	wäre
werden	wurde	würde

Irregular weak verbs

Infinitive	Past indicative	Present subjunctive II
bringen	brachte	brächte
denken	dachte	dächte
wissen	wußte	wüßte
kennen	kannte	kennte
nennen	nannte	nennte

Modal auxiliaries (with subjunctive meanings)

Infinitive	Past indicative	Present subjunctive II	
dürfen	durfte	dürfte	might
können	konnte	könnte	could
mögen	mochte	möchte	would like to
müssen	mußte	müßte	might, would have to
sollen	sollte	sollte	should, ought to
wollen	wollte	wollte	wish, would want to

Note that **sollen** and **wollen** are regular weak verbs and accordingly do not take umlaut in the present subjunctive II.

29.5 Past Subjunctive II

The past subjunctive II is a phrase consisting of the subjunctive II form of the tense auxiliary **(hätte, wäre)** plus the past participle of the main verb. Note that there is no "present perfect" or "past perfect" subjunctive; the subjunctive mood has *only one* tense referring to past time, compared to the indicative's three.

Infinitive	Present subjunctive II	Past subjunctive II
kommen	käme	wäre gekommen
bringen	brächte	hätte gebracht
schlagen	schlüge	hätte geschlagen
gehen	ginge	wäre gegangen

29.6 The *würde*-Alternatives

The present subjunctive II verb form may occur as the main verb of a clause:

Es **kostete** zuviel.
It *would cost* too much.

Wir **brächten** Ihnen eine Tasse Kaffee.
We *would bring* you a cup of coffee.

The following constructions may also occur, however:

Es **würde** zuviel **kosten**.
It *would cost* too much.

Wir **würden** Ihnen eine Tasse Kaffee **bringen**.
We *would bring* you a cup of coffee.

The present subjunctive II and the **würde** + *infinitive* construction are alternative expressions. Both **kostete** and **würde** . . . **kosten** correspond to English *would cost*. The **würde**-alternative is favored in spoken German, especially when the present subjunctive II form of the verb would be identical with the past indicative form, as is the case with **kostete**. The two expressions — the present subjunctive II and its **würde**-alternative — are *not* different tenses; both refer to present, future, or universal time.

A similar relationship exists between the past subjunctive II and its **würde**-alternative. This is made up of **würde** plus the perfect infinitive of the main verb:

Es **hätte** zuviel **gekostet**.
Es **würde** zuviel **gekostet haben**.
It *would have cost* too much.

Wir **hätten** Ihnen eine Tasse Kaffee **gebracht**.
Wir **würden** Ihnen eine Tasse Kaffee **gebracht haben**.
We *would have brought* you a cup of coffee.

Again, these are *not* two different tenses; both refer to past time. Whereas the present **würde**-alternative is preferred to the present subjunctive II, however, the past **würde**-alternative is seldom used, especially in spoken German. The less complicated past subjunctive II is generally chosen.

29.7 Subjunctive II: Summary of Tenses

	Indicative		*Subjunctive II*
Present	er zieht	*Present*	er zöge
Future	er wird ziehen		er würde ziehen
Past	er zog		
Present perfect	er hat gezogen	*Past*	er hätte gezogen
Past perfect	er hatte gezogen		er würde gezogen haben
Future perfect	er wird gezogen haben		

29.8 Some Uses of Subjunctive II

You may find it helpful to think of the German subjunctive II in terms of its English counterparts. This is useful only to a limited extent, because the verb systems of the two languages are so different—not only in their forms, but also in how they use their forms. The following observations are generally true:

1. The German present subjunctive II and its **würde**-alternative are appropriate where English uses *would, could, might, ought,* or *should* plus an infinitive, or where English uses a past indicative form to express present time:

   I *would suggest* a trip. { Ich **schlüge** eine Reise **vor**.
   Ich **würde** eine Reise **vorschlagen**.

   If he only *did*n't *smoke*! { Wenn er nur nicht **rauchte**!
   Wenn er nur nicht **rauchen würde**!

2. The German past subjunctive II and its **würde**-alternative are appropriate where English uses *would have, could have, might have, ought to have,* or *should have* plus a past participle, or where English uses a past perfect indicative construction to express simple past time:

   I *would have suggested* a trip. { Ich **hätte** eine Reise **vorgeschlagen**.
   Ich **würde** eine Reise **vorgeschlagen haben**.

Wishes contrary to fact ("if only")

These expressions are **wenn**-clauses in German, and therefore the finite verb must stand at the end (unless there is a double infinitive, in which case it stands third from the end). They normally include the adverb **nur** or **doch**, or both:

Wenn er nur in Stuttgart wohnte!
If only he lived in Stuttgart!

Wenn du ihn nur gekannt hättest!
If only you had known him!

Wenn du doch nur nicht so viel arbeitetest!
If only you wouldn't work so much!

Wenn Sie ihn nur hätten fragen dürfen!
If only you might have asked him!

Wenn ich nur diesen Hut kaufen könnte!
If only I could buy this hat!

Wenn du doch nicht immer fluchen würdest!
If only you wouldn't swear all the time!

Politeness

The use of a subjunctive II form in place of an otherwise entirely appropriate indicative form may convey a tone of special courtesy:

Würden Sie heute mitkommen?
Would you come along this afternoon?

Ich hätte lieber ein Glas Wein.
I would prefer a glass of wine.

Könnten Sie mir bitte helfen?
Could you please help me?

Dürfte ich eine Bildungsreise vorschlagen?
May (might) I suggest an educational trip?

Ich möchte diese Zeitung lesen.
I would like to read this newspaper.

Subjunctive statements with modals

The present subjunctive meanings of the modal auxiliaries are given above in Grammar §29.4. Additional examples of these are:

Du solltest an deine Bildung denken.
You ought to (should) think about your education.

Feste und Sportwagen könnten danach kommen.
Parties and sports cars could come later.

Man müßte zuerst den Dom besichtigen.
One would have to visit the cathedral first.

In the past subjunctive II, the modal and its dependent infinitive form a double infinitive. Note particularly the meaning of the verb phrases:

Er **hätte** eine Reise **machen sollen**.
He *should have taken* a trip.

Du **hättest** Ruhe **halten können**.
You *could have stayed* quiet.

Wenn er nur daran **hätte denken wollen**!
If only he *had wanted to think* about it!

Das **hätte** sie doch nicht **sagen dürfen**.
She *shouldn't have said (ought not to have been permitted to say)* that.

WRITING

A. Dehydrated Sentences

Write German sentences in the subjunctive II using the given elements and the tense indicated; be able to give English meanings:

1 Hans / können / gehen / zum Baden   (*pres.*)
2 das / sein / hübsch / Sache   (*past*)
3 was / sein / mit / Üben?   (*pres.*)
4 sehen / du / mich / stehen / Podium?   (*pres.*)
5 ich / glauben / daran / gerne   (*pres.* **würde**-*alt.*)
6 es / losgehen / endlich   (*pres.*)
7 du / täuschen / dich   (*pres.*)
8 Frau / haben / schlimm / Wunde / Kopf   (*past*)
9 ich / mögen / kaufen / Zeitung   (*pres.*)
10 wenn / dasselbe / darin / stehen / nur / nicht immer   (*pres.*)
11 Freundin / sitzen / dort   (*pres.*)
12 ich / kennenlernen / lieber / Student   (*past*)
13 wir / sein / alt / Bekannte   (*pres.*)
14 wenn / ihr / übertreiben / nur nicht   (*pres.*)
15 wir / finden / Hut / schön   (*pres.*)
16 Frau / können / kaufen / jed- / Monat / neu / Mantel   (*past*)
17 wenn / du / haben / Sparbuch / nur   (*past*)
18 wenn / Hütchen / kosten / nur nicht so viel   (*pres.*)
19 ich / schauen / gern / durch / Auswahl   (*past*)
20 wir / wissen / das / nicht   (*pres.*)
21 wenn / du / entgegengehen / ihm / nur   (*past*)
22 wenn / es / gelingen / mir / doch mal   (*pres.* **würde**-*alt.*)
23 Arbeit / machen / Spaß / mir   (*pres.* **würde**-*alt.*)
24 Werkzeug / liegen / ander / Zimmer   (*pres.*)
25 wenn / Susi / es / machen / besser / nur mal   (*pres.*)
26 du / sollen / stellen / Gabel / neben / Teller   (*past*)
27 Mutti / sollen / füllen / Suppe / Schüssel   (*past*)
28 Onkel Richard / können / leben / ruhiger   (*past*)
29 wenn / klein / Kerl / leiden / nur nicht   (*pres.*)
30 ich / tun / es // um / ihn / beruhigen   (*pres.* **würde**-*alt.*)
31 Besuch / werden / zu anstrengend   (*pres.*)
32 wenn / Sie / haben / billiger / Ansichtskarten / nur   (*past*)
33 dürfen / es / sein / sonst noch etwas?   (*pres.*)
34 wenn / es / geben / mehr / Kuchen / doch nur   (*pres.*)
35 wenn / ich / denken / das Fest / nur   (*past*)
36 er / umziehen / lieber / nach München   (*pres.*)
37 du / sollen / vergessen / Zigaretten / nicht   (*past*)
38 ihr / sollen / vorstellen / es / euch   (*pres.*)
39 ich / können / mitbringen / ihn   (*past*)
40 wir / müssen / warten / vergeblich / auf ihn   (*pres.*)

LISTENING PRACTICE

Listen to the recorded radio interview; then answer the following questions.

Der Wirtschaftskommentar

1 Wer ist Professor Schmüser?
2 Worüber sprechen Professor Schmüser und der Reporter?
3 Werden die Preise in Westdeutschland höher?
4 Werden die Verdienste auch höher?
5 Wieso ist die wirtschaftliche Situation in Westdeutschland besser als in vielen anderen Ländern?
6 Was ist mit dem Export?
7 Könnte die Lage schlimm werden?

Unit 30

PHILOSOPHIE

FRIEDRICH NIETZSCHE

DIALOG

Was wäre, wenn ... (Schluß)

1 **Kurt:** Du machst ja plötzlich ein Gesicht, als ob schon sieben Tage Regenwetter wäre.

2 **Hartmut:** Die Post ist eben gekommen, und ein Einschreibbrief von Herrn Jäger, unserem „treuen" Hauswirt, ist auch dabei.

3 **Kurt:** Na, und? Was könnte ein kleiner Hausbesitzer von stolzen Millionären schon wollen?

4 **Hartmut:** Ich wollte, du hörtest jetzt mit dem Unsinn auf. Hier, lies du!

5 **Kurt:** Oh, oh, da steht: Wenn wir nicht wenigstens die Miete des Vormonats bezahlen könnten, ...

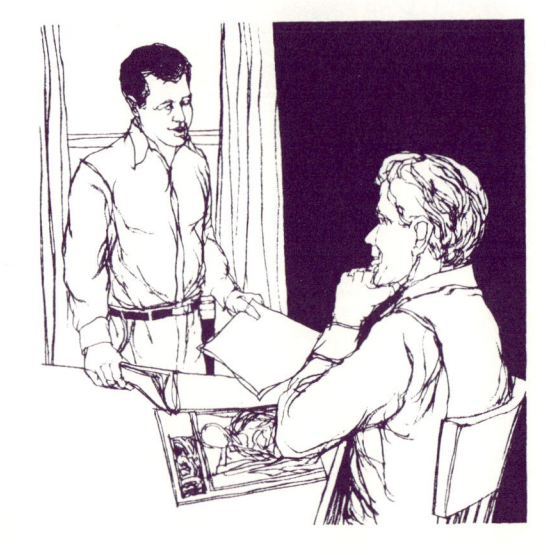

What Would It Be Like If . . . (Conclusion)

1 All at once you have a glum look on your face.

das Regenwetter der Regen, - rain + **das Wetter** weather

2 The mail just came and there's also a registered letter with it from Mr. Jäger, our "faithful" landlord.

der Einschreibbrief einschreiben register, enter (in a book) + **der Brief, -e** letter · **der Jäger,** - hunter **jagen** hunt, chase · **der Hauswirt das Haus + der Wirt** innkeeper, host

3 So what? What could a lowly house owner want of proud millionaires, anyway?

der Hausbesitzer das Haus + der Besitzer, - owner **besitzen** own, possess · **der Millionär, -e**

4 I wish you'd stop that nonsense now. Here, you read.

wollte *pres. subj. II* wish · **aufhören** stop · **der Unsinn der Sinn, -e** sense; mind

5 Oh, oh! It says here if we couldn't at least pay last month's rent, . . .

die Miete, -n rent **mieten** rent · **der Vormonat, -e vor + der Monat**

6 Hartmut: . . . sähe er sich leider gezwungen . . . usw. Den Rest kann ich mir denken.

7 Kurt: Da hätten wir die Geschichte! Es ist zum Heulen! Was ist nun mit deiner Bildungsreise?

8 Hartmut: Ach, meinst du wirklich, wir würden als Millionäre zufriedener gewesen sein?

9 Kurt: Na, unsere Lage wäre im Augenblick dann immerhin nicht so düster.

10 Hartmut: Da hast du recht! Aber nun sollten wir uns überlegen, wie wir unseren Hausherrn am besten beruhigen.

SUPPLEMENT

1 Ich wollte, daß das Mädchen nicht so schluchzen würde!

2 Ich wünschte, daß der Junge nicht so schmatzen würde!

3 Ich möchte, daß du nicht so wüst trampeln würdest!

4 Ich wünschte, daß sie nicht so geldsüchtig wäre!

5 Er sieht aus, als ob er einen Rahmbonbon lutschte.

6 Er tut, als ob er die Probleme nicht auseinanderhalten könnte.

7 Es sieht aus, als wenn es regnen würde.

6	... he would unfortunately find himself forced ... etc. The rest I can imagine.	**sich sehen** *acc. refl.* · **zwingen: er zwingt, zwang, hat gezwungen** compel, force, oblige · **der Rest, -e** rest, that which remains
7	Now we've had it! What a shame! Now what about your educational trip?	**heulen** howl, scream, weep **das Heulen** *infinitive used as noun*
8	Oh well, do you really think we'd have been happier as millionaires?	**zufrieden** happy, satisfied
9	Well, at least our situation wouldn't be so gloomy at the moment.	**die Lage, -n** situation, position · **düster** gloomy, somber, dark
10	You're right about that! But now we ought to give some thought to how we can best calm our landlord.	**recht haben** be right · **überlegen** consider, reflect **sich überlegen** *dat. refl.* think over · **der Hausherr** **das Haus** + **der Herr**

1	I wish the girl wouldn't sob so!	**wollte** *pres. subj. II* · **schluchzen** sob
2	I wish the boy wouldn't smack his lips so!	**wünschte** *pres. subj. II* · **schmatzen** smack with the lips
3	I wish you wouldn't stamp so violently!	**wüst** wild, riotous · **trampeln** stamp
4	I wish she weren't so greedy for money!	**geldsüchtig** **das Geld** + **süchtig** having a mania for something, addicted to
5	He looks as if he were sucking on a piece of candy.	**der Rahmbonbon** taffy **der Rahm** cream + **der Bonbon, -** *or* **-s** [bɔŋˈbɔŋ] candy · **lutschen** suck
6	He acts as if he couldn't keep the problems separate.	**auseinanderhalten** keep separate, tell apart **auseinander** separate, apart + **halten**
7	It looks as if it would rain.	

8   Wenn die Sonne scheint, geht Kurt zum Baden.

9   Wenn die Sonne schiene, ginge Kurt zum Baden.

10 Wenn die Sonne schiene, würde Kurt zum Baden gehen.

11 Wenn die Sonne geschienen hätte, wäre Kurt zum Baden gegangen.

8 If the sun shines, Kurt will go swimming. (*Or:* Whenever the sun shines, Kurt goes swimming.)

9 If the sun would shine, Kurt would go swimming.

10 If the sun would shine, Kurt would go swimming.

11 If the sun had shone, Kurt would have gone swimming.

AUDIOLINGUAL DRILLS

A. Directed Dialog

Sagen Sie, Hartmut macht ja plötzlich ein Gesicht, als ob schon sieben Tage Regenwetter wäre!
Hartmut macht ja plötzlich ein Gesicht, als ob schon sieben Tage Regenwetter wäre.

Sagen Sie, daß die Post eben gekommen ist!
Die Post ist eben gekommen.

Sagen Sie, daß ein Einschreibbrief von Herrn Jäger, ihrem „treuen" Hauswirt, auch dabei ist!
Ein Einschreibbrief von Herrn Jäger, ihrem „treuen" Hauswirt, ist auch dabei.

Fragen Sie, was ein kleiner Hausbesitzer von stolzen Millionären denn schon wollen könnte!
Was könnte ein kleiner Hausbesitzer von stolzen Millionären denn schon wollen?

Antworten Sie, Hartmut wollte, daß Kurt jetzt mit dem Unsinn aufhörte!
Hartmut wollte, daß Kurt jetzt mit dem Unsinn aufhörte.

Fragen Sie, ob Kurt und Hartmut nicht wenigstens die Miete des Vormonats bezahlen könnten!
Könnten Kurt und Hartmut nicht wenigstens die Miete des Vormonats bezahlen?

Fragen Sie, wozu Herr Jäger sich leider gezwungen sähe!
Wozu sähe Herr Jäger sich leider gezwungen?

Antworten Sie, daß Hartmut sich den Rest denken kann!
Hartmut kann sich den Rest denken.

Sagen Sie, daß die Geschichte zum Heulen ist!
Die Geschichte ist zum Heulen.

Fragen Sie, was nun mit Hartmuts Bildungsreise ist!
Was ist nun mit Hartmuts Bildungsreise?

Fragen Sie, ob die beiden als Millionäre zufriedener gewesen sein würden!
Würden die beiden als Millionäre zufriedener gewesen sein?

Sagen Sie, daß ihre Lage im Augenblick dann immerhin nicht so düster wäre!
Ihre Lage wäre im Augenblick dann immerhin nicht so düster.

Sagen Sie, daß da Kurt recht hat!
Da hat Kurt recht.

Sagen Sie, daß die beiden aber nun überlegen sollten!
Die beiden sollten aber nun überlegen.

Fragen Sie, wie die beiden ihren Hausherrn am besten beruhigen!
Wie beruhigen die beiden ihren Hausherrn am besten?

B. New Strong Verb

1 **Zwingen** *compel* follows the pattern of **singen** — **er zwingt, zwang, hat gezwungen.** Change the tense or the subject as indicated:

Ich zwinge ihn nicht zu bezahlen. *pres. perf.*
Ich habe ihn nicht gezwungen zu bezahlen. **du**
Du hast ihn nicht gezwungen zu bezahlen. *fut.*
Du wirst ihn nicht zwingen zu bezahlen. **wir**
Wir werden ihn nicht zwingen zu bezahlen. *past*
Wir zwangen ihn nicht zu bezahlen. **ihr**
Ihr zwangt ihn nicht zu bezahlen.

C. Subjunctive II: *als ob, als wenn* (See Grammar §30.3)

2 Practice the German "as if" construction, substituting the new verb or verb phrase in the main clause.

Example:
Er tut, als ob er krank wäre. **ein Gesicht machen**
Er macht ein Gesicht, als ob er krank wäre.

Er tut, als ob er nicht zufrieden wäre. **sprechen**
Er spricht, als ob er nicht zufrieden wäre. **aussehen**

Er sieht aus, als ob er nicht zufrieden wäre.   **ein Gesicht machen**
Er macht ein Gesicht, als ob er nicht zufrieden wäre.   **heulen**
Er heult, als ob er nicht zufrieden wäre.   **tun**
Er tut, als ob er nicht zufrieden wäre.

Du tust, als wenn du Angst hättest.   **aussehen**
Du siehst aus, als wenn du Angst hättest.   **ein Gesicht machen**
Du machst ein Gesicht, als wenn du Angst hättest.   **sprechen**
Du sprichst, als wenn du Angst hättest.   **schluchzen**
Du schluchzt, als wenn du Angst hättest.   **tun**
Du tust, als wenn du Angst hättest.

3 Change the verb of the dependent clause from the present subjunctive II to the past subjunctive II:

Er tut, als ob er krank wäre.
Er tut, als ob er krank gewesen wäre.

Du siehst aus, als ob du Angst hättest.
Du siehst aus, als ob du Angst gehabt hättest.

Sie macht ein Gesicht, als wenn etwas los wäre.
Sie macht ein Gesicht, als wenn etwas los gewesen wäre.

Er tut, als wenn er etwas wüßte.
Er tut, als wenn er etwas gewußt hätte.

Du siehst aus, als ob du mitgehen wolltest.
Du siehst aus, als ob du hättest mitgehen wollen.

Es sieht aus, als wenn es regnete.
Es sieht aus, als wenn es geregnet hätte.

Du sprichst, als ob du dich dafür interessiertest.
Du sprichst, als ob du dich dafür interessiert hättest.

Er tut, als ob er ausstiege.
Er tut, als ob er ausgestiegen wäre.

D. Subjunctive II: Wishes Introduced by Verbs of Wishing (*See Grammar* §30.3)

4 Substitute the new subject of the dependent clause:

Ich wollte, daß du mit dem Unsinn aufhörtest.   **er**
Ich wollte, daß er mit dem Unsinn aufhörte.   **wir**

Ich wollte, daß wir mit dem Unsinn aufhörten.   **ihr**
Ich wollte, daß ihr mit dem Unsinn aufhörtet.   **die Studenten**
Ich wollte, daß die Studenten mit dem Unsinn aufhörten.

Ich wünschte, ich hätte besser aufgepaßt.   **du**
Ich wünschte, du hättest besser aufgepaßt.   **wir**
Ich wünschte, wir hätten besser aufgepaßt.   **Kurt**
Ich wünschte, Kurt hätte besser aufgepaßt.   **ihr**
Ich wünschte, ihr hättet besser aufgepaßt.

Herr Jäger möchte, daß wir die Miete bezahlen würden.   **du**
Herr Jäger möchte, daß du die Miete bezahlen würdest.   **ich**
Herr Jäger möchte, daß ich die Miete bezahlen würde.   **ihr**
Herr Jäger möchte, daß ihr die Miete bezahlen würdet.   **die Leute**
Herr Jäger möchte, daß die Leute die Miete bezahlen würden.

Ich wollte, du wärest hier gewesen.   **Hartmut**
Ich wollte, Hartmut wäre hier gewesen.   **die Beamten**
Ich wollte, die Beamten wären hier gewesen.   **ihr**
Ich wollte, ihr wäret hier gewesen.   **die Studentinnen**
Ich wollte, die Studentinnen wären hier gewesen.

5 Change the verb of the dependent clause from the present subjunctive II to its **würde**-alternative:

Ich möchte, daß du damit aufhörtest.
Ich möchte, daß du damit aufhören würdest.

Wollte sie wirklich, daß ich mitkäme?
Wollte sie wirklich, daß ich mitkommen würde?

Wir wünschten, die Kinder lutschten nicht so viel.
Wir wünschten, die Kinder würden nicht so viel lutschen.

Ich wollte, ich hätte einmal recht.
Ich wollte, ich würde einmal recht haben.

Ich wollte, daß du es dir überlegtest.
Ich wollte, daß du es dir überlegen würdest.

Wir wollten, es gäbe nicht so viel Regen.
Wir wollten, es würde nicht so viel Regen geben.

Der Lehrer möchte, daß die Schüler besser aufpaßten.
Der Lehrer möchte, daß die Schüler besser aufpassen würden.

Ich wünschte, daß die Lage nicht so düster aussähe.
Ich wünschte, daß die Lage nicht so düster aussehen würde.

E. Subjunctive II: Conditional Sentences (*See Grammar* §30.3)

6 Real conditions and their results are expressed in the indicative mood. Substitute the new direct object in the second clause:

Wenn ich im Lotto gewinne, kaufe ich mir einen Sportwagen. **Haus**
Wenn ich im Lotto gewinne, kaufe ich mir ein Haus. **Schloß**
Wenn ich im Lotto gewinne, kaufe ich mir ein Schloß. **Fabrik**
Wenn ich im Lotto gewinne, kaufe ich mir eine Fabrik. **Anzug**
Wenn ich im Lotto gewinne, kaufe ich mir einen Anzug.

Unreal conditions and their hypothetical results are expressed with the subjunctive II. In English the result is frequently constructed with *would, could,* etc.

7 Substitute the new subject in the **wenn**-clause:

Wenn er hier wäre, freute ich mich. **du**
Wenn du hier wärest, freute ich mich. **deine Eltern**
Wenn deine Eltern hier wären, freute ich mich. **Tante Inge**
Wenn Tante Inge hier wäre, freute ich mich. **ihr**
Wenn ihr hier wäret, freute ich mich. **Günther**
Wenn Günther hier wäre, freute ich mich.

8 Substitute the new subject in both clauses:

Wenn ich im Lotto gewänne, machte ich eine Bildungsreise. **du**
Wenn du im Lotto gewännest, machtest du eine Bildungsreise. **wir**
Wenn wir im Lotto gewännen, machten wir eine Bildungsreise. **ihr**
Wenn ihr im Lotto gewännet, machtet ihr eine Bildungsreise. **er**
Wenn er im Lotto gewänne, machte er eine Bildungsreise. **ich**
Wenn ich im Lotto gewänne, machte ich eine Bildungsreise.

The verb of the result clause may be the present **würde**-alternative; the meaning is the same as that of the present subjunctive II.

9 Substitute the new subject in the result clause:

Wenn die Sonne schiene, würden wir zum Baden gehen. **du**
Wenn die Sonne schiene, würdest du zum Baden gehen. **ihr**
Wenn die Sonne schiene, würdet ihr zum Baden gehen. **Kurt und Anja**
Wenn die Sonne schiene, würden Kurt und Anja zum Baden gehen. **ich**
Wenn die Sonne schiene, würde ich zum Baden gehen. **Hans**
Wenn die Sonne schiene, würde Hans zum Baden gehen.

10 Substitute the new subject in both clauses:

Wenn du mehr arbeitetest, würdest du die Prüfung bestehen. **ich**
Wenn ich mehr arbeitete, würde ich die Prüfung bestehen. **wir**

Wenn wir mehr arbeiteten, würden wir die Prüfung bestehen. **er**
Wenn er mehr arbeitete, würde er die Prüfung bestehen. **ihr**
Wenn ihr mehr arbeitetet, würdet ihr die Prüfung bestehen. **du**
Wenn du mehr arbeitetest, würdest du die Prüfung bestehen.

11 Change the verb in the result clause from the present subjunctive II to its **würde**-alternative:

Wenn die Sonne schiene, ginge ich zum Baden.
Wenn die Sonne schiene, würde ich zum Baden gehen.

Wenn er mehr arbeitete, bestünde er die Prüfung.
Wenn er mehr arbeitete, würde er die Prüfung bestehen.

Wenn du hier wärest, freute ich mich.
Wenn du hier wärest, würde ich mich freuen.

Wenn wir im Lotto gewännen, kauften wir uns einen Sportwagen.
Wenn wir im Lotto gewännen, würden wir uns einen Sportwagen kaufen.

Wenn du mehr Geld hättest, schlüge ich eine Reise vor.
Wenn du mehr Geld hättest, würde ich eine Reise vorschlagen.

Wenn sie es wüßte, schriebe sie es auf.
Wenn sie es wüßte, würde sie es aufschreiben.

Wenn es regnete, blieben wir alle zu Hause.
Wenn es regnete, würden wir alle zu Hause bleiben.

Wenn wir mehr Zeit hätten, sähe die Lage nicht so düster aus.
Wenn wir mehr Zeit hätten, würde die Lage nicht so düster aussehen.

The verbs of both clauses may be in the past subjunctive II. In English the result is often expressed with *would have*, *could have*, etc.

12 Substitute the new subject in the **wenn**-clause:

Wenn du hier gewesen wärst, hätte ich mich gefreut. **er**
Wenn er hier gewesen wäre, hätte ich mich gefreut. **meine Freunde**
Wenn meine Freunde hier gewesen wären, hätte ich mich gefreut. **ihr**
Wenn ihr hier gewesen wäret, hätte ich mich gefreut. **Renate**
Wenn Renate hier gewesen wäre, hätte ich mich gefreut. **du**
Wenn du hier gewesen wärst, hätte ich mich gefreut.

13 Substitute the new subject in both clauses:

Wenn er nicht so vergeßlich gewesen wäre, hätte er sie besucht. **du**
Wenn du nicht so vergeßlich gewesen wärst, hättest du sie besucht. **ihr**
Wenn ihr nicht so vergeßlich gewesen wäret, hättet ihr sie besucht. **wir**
Wenn wir nicht so vergeßlich gewesen wären, hätten wir sie besucht. **ich**

Wenn ich nicht so vergeßlich gewesen wäre, hätte ich sie besucht.   **er**
Wenn er nicht so vergeßlich gewesen wäre, hätte er sie besucht.

14   Change the tense of the verbs in both clauses from present to past:

Wenn sie hier wäre, freute ich mich.
Wenn sie hier gewesen wäre, hätte ich mich gefreut.

Wenn du nicht so vergeßlich wärest, besuchtest du uns.
Wenn du nicht so vergeßlich gewesen wärest, hättest du uns besucht.

Wenn wir mehr arbeiteten, wäre unsere Lage besser.
Wenn wir mehr gearbeitet hätten, wäre unsere Lage besser gewesen.

Wenn die Sonne schiene, ginge er zum Baden.
Wenn die Sonne geschienen hätte, wäre er zum Baden gegangen.

Wenn ich im Lotto gewänne, kaufte ich mir ein Haus.
Wenn ich im Lotto gewonnen hätte, hätte ich mir ein Haus gekauft.

Wenn es regnete, blieben wir zu Hause.
Wenn es geregnet hätte, wären wir zu Hause geblieben.

Wenn ihr mehr Zeit hättet, gelänge es euch.
Wenn ihr mehr Zeit gehabt hättet, wäre es euch gelungen.

Wenn ich es wüßte, sagte ich es dir.
Wenn ich es gewußt hätte, hätte ich es dir gesagt.

The result clause may precede the **wenn**-clause in a conditional sentence.

15   Substitute the new subject in the **wenn**-clause:

Die Lage wäre nicht so schlimm, wenn du mehr gearbeitet hättest.   **ich**
Die Lage wäre nicht so schlimm, wenn ich mehr gearbeitet hätte.   **wir**
Die Lage wäre nicht so schlimm, wenn wir mehr gearbeitet hätten.   **er**
Die Lage wäre nicht so schlimm, wenn er mehr gearbeitet hätte.   **ihr**
Die Lage wäre nicht so schlimm, wenn ihr mehr gearbeitet hättet.   **die Jungen**
Die Lage wäre nicht so schlimm, wenn die Jungen mehr gearbeitet hätten.

16   Reverse the positions of the clauses:

Wenn du hier wärest, freute ich mich.
Ich freute mich, wenn du hier wärest.

Wenn ich mehr Zeit hätte, würde es mir gelingen.
Es würde mir gelingen, wenn ich mehr Zeit hätte.

Wenn es geregnet hätte, wäre er zu Hause geblieben.
Er wäre zu Hause geblieben, wenn es geregnet hätte.

Wenn du es gewußt hättest, wäre unsere Lage jetzt besser.
Unsere Lage wäre jetzt besser, wenn du es gewußt hättest.

Wenn wir im Lotto gewonnen hätten, würden wir eine Reise machen.
Wir würden eine Reise machen, wenn wir im Lotto gewonnen hätten.

Wenn du nicht immer fluchtest, würde ich mich freuen.
Ich würde mich freuen, wenn du nicht immer fluchtest.

Wenn er wollte, käme er mit.
Er käme mit, wenn er wollte.

Wenn ich es tun könnte, würde ich gerne spielen.
Ich würde gerne spielen, wenn ich es tun könnte.

Wenn wir ihn kennten, sprächen wir mit ihm.
Wir sprächen mit ihm, wenn wir ihn kennten.

Wenn die Straße nicht so rutschig wäre, könnten wir schneller fahren.
Wir könnten schneller fahren, wenn die Straße nicht so rutschig wäre.

The double infinitive construction with modals and with **hören**, **helfen**, **lassen**, and **sehen** is also used in the subjunctive.

17 Substitute the new subject in the result clause:

Wenn es nicht geregnet hätte, hätten wir zum Baden gehen können.   **du**
Wenn es nicht geregnet hätte, hättest du zum Baden gehen können.   **ich**
Wenn es nicht geregnet hätte, hätte ich zum Baden gehen können.   **ihr**
Wenn es nicht geregnet hätte, hättet ihr zum Baden gehen können.   **wir**
Wenn es nicht geregnet hätte, hätten wir zum Baden gehen können.

18 Change the tense of the verbs in both clauses from present to past:

Wenn die Sonne schiene, könnten wir zum Baden gehen.
Wenn die Sonne geschienen hätte, hätten wir zum Baden gehen können.

Wir freuten uns sehr, wenn du mitkommen wolltest.
Wir hätten uns sehr gefreut, wenn du hättest mitkommen wollen.

Ich könnte eine Reise machen, wenn ich mehr Geld hätte.
Ich hätte eine Reise machen können, wenn ich mehr Geld gehabt hätte.

Wenn er zu Hause wäre, hörten wir ihn spielen.
Wenn er zu Hause gewesen wäre, hätten wir ihn spielen hören.

Ich ließe dich sprechen, wenn du etwas davon wüßtest.
Ich hätte dich sprechen lassen, wenn du etwas davon gewußt hättest.

Er hülfe ihr den Tisch decken, wenn er es tun könnte.
Er hätte ihr den Tisch decken helfen, wenn er es hätte tun können.

Wenn er sich erreichen ließe, riefen wir ihn an.
Wenn er sich hätte erreichen lassen, hätten wir ihn angerufen.

Lilo dürfte mitgehen, wenn es nicht regnete.
Lilo hätte mitgehen dürfen, wenn es nicht geregnet hätte.

F. Omission of *wenn* and *ob* (*See Grammar* §30.4)

The subordinating conjunction **wenn** may be omitted; the finite verb is then shifted from last position, or from third-from-last position in the case of double infinitives, to fill the position vacated by **wenn**.

19 Remove **wenn** and put the finite verb in its place:

Wenn er nur in Stuttgart wohnte!
Wohnte er nur in Stuttgart!

Wenn du nur nicht so viel fluchtest!
Fluchtest du nur nicht so viel!

Wenn sie nur mitkäme!
Käme sie nur mit!

Wenn wir nur mitgehen dürften!
Dürften wir nur mitgehen!

Wenn er sich nur erreichen ließe!
Ließe er sich nur erreichen!

Wenn sie doch nicht immer so aufgeregt würde!
Würde sie doch nicht immer so aufgeregt!

Wenn der König nur nicht gestorben wäre!
Wäre der König nur nicht gestorben!

Wenn ich nur mehr gearbeitet hätte!
Hätte ich nur mehr gearbeitet!

Wenn wir nur im Lotto gewonnen hätten!
Hätten wir nur im Lotto gewonnen!

Wenn du nur an deine Bildung gedacht hättest!
Hättest du nur an deine Bildung gedacht!

Wenn du nur nicht immer an deine Bildung denken würdest!
Würdest du nur nicht immer an deine Bildung denken!

Wenn sie nur eine Reise hätte machen können!
Hätte sie nur eine Reise machen können!

Wenn wir ihn nur hätten wegfahren hören!
Hätten wir ihn nur wegfahren hören!

20 Remove **wenn** from the **wenn**-clause and put the finite verb in its place:

Wenn sie hier wären, so würden wir uns freuen.
Wären sie hier, so würden wir uns freuen.

Wenn ich im Lotto gewonnen hätte, so würde ich eine Reise machen.
Hätte ich im Lotto gewonnen, so würde ich eine Reise machen.

Wenn die Sonne geschienen hätte, so wären wir zum Baden gegangen.
Hätte die Sonne geschienen, so wären wir zum Baden gegangen.

Wenn du mehr gearbeitet hättest, dann könntest du die Prüfung bestehen.
Hättest du mehr gearbeitet, dann könntest du die Prüfung bestehen.

Wenn ich nicht so vergeßlich wäre, dann hätte ich ihn besucht.
Wäre ich nicht so vergeßlich, dann hätte ich ihn besucht.

Wenn du Ruhe gehalten hättest, dann wärest du jetzt wieder auf den Beinen.
Hättest du Ruhe gehalten, dann wärest du jetzt wieder auf den Beinen.

Wenn ich es wüßte, so würde ich es dir sofort sagen.
Wüßte ich es, so würde ich es dir sofort sagen.

The **wenn** or **ob** of the **als wenn**, **als ob** construction may be omitted; the finite verb then replaces it.

21 Remove **ob** from the **als ob**-clause and put the finite verb in its place:

Er tut, als ob er nicht zufrieden wäre.
Er tut, als wäre er nicht zufrieden.

Er hat getan, als ob er Angst gehabt hätte.
Er hat getan, als hätte er Angst gehabt.

Es sieht aus, als ob es regnen würde.
Es sieht aus, als würde es regnen.

Sie macht ein Gesicht, als ob etwas los wäre.
Sie macht ein Gesicht, als wäre etwas los.

Er spricht, als ob er sich dafür interessierte.
Er spricht, als interessierte er sich dafür.

Er sah aus, als ob er sehr viel gelitten hätte.
Er sah aus, als hätte er sehr viel gelitten.

22 Remove **wenn** from the **als wenn**-clause and put the finite verb in its place:

Er sieht aus, als wenn er einen Rahmbonbon lutschte.
Er sieht aus, als lutschte er einen Rahmbonbon.

Sie tun, als wenn Sie die Probleme nicht auseinanderhalten könnten.
Sie tun, als könnten Sie die Probleme nicht auseinanderhalten.

Du machst ein Gesicht, als wenn du etwas sagen wolltest.
Du machst ein Gesicht, als wolltest du etwas sagen.

Sie tut, als wenn sie hätte mitgehen wollen.
Sie tut, als hätte sie mitgehen wollen.

Es sieht aus, als wenn etwas passieren könnte.
Es sieht aus, als könnte etwas passieren.

Er hat so getan, als wenn die Lage besser geworden wäre.
Er hat so getan, als wäre die Lage besser geworden.

G. Questions and Answers

Wie sieht Hartmuts Gesicht plötzlich aus?
Er macht ein Gesicht, als ob schon sieben Tage Regenwetter wäre.

Warum macht er so ein Gesicht?
Der Postbote hat einen Einschreibbrief von ihrem Hauswirt gebracht.

Was will Herr Jäger denn?
Er möchte die Miete des Vormonats haben.

Warum braucht Hartmut den Rest des Briefes gar nicht erst zu hören?
Weil er sich den Rest schon denken kann.

Was ist an der Geschichte denn zum Heulen?
Es ist zum Heulen, daß sie kein Geld haben, um die Miete zu bezahlen.

Würden die beiden als Millionäre zufriedener gewesen sein?
Das kann wirklich kein Mensch wissen.

Was wäre in diesem Augenblick für Kurt und Hartmut so schön gewesen?
Es wäre schön gewesen, wenn sie Millionäre gewesen wären.

Was müssen sie sich nun überlegen?
Nun müssen sie sich überlegen, wie sie Herrn Jäger am besten beruhigen.

GRAMMAR

30.1 Word-Formation

Nouns in -e

Many feminine nouns denoting quality or condition have been derived from adjectives by attaching the suffix **-e**. Most of these nouns have no plural, and all have umlaut if possible. Some examples that you know are: **groß** *big*, **die Größe, -n** *size*; **heiß** *hot*, **die Hitze** *heat*. Below are some new nouns formed from familiar adjectives:

blaß	pale	die Blässe	paleness, pallor
breit	wide	die Breite, -n	breadth, width; latitude
dick	thick	die Dicke, -n	thickness; fatness; density
fremd	strange	die Fremde	foreign land
früh	early	die Frühe	early morning
grün	green	die Grüne	green(ness)
gut	good	die Güte	goodness; quality
hart	hard	die Härte, -n	hardness
hoch	high	die Höhe, -n	height
kalt	cold	die Kälte	cold, chilliness
kurz	short	die Kürze	shortness, brevity
lang	long	die Länge, -n	length; tallness; longitude
nah	near	die Nähe	nearness; vicinity
rot	red	die Röte	redness; blush (of shyness)
scharf	sharp	die Schärfe, -n	sharpness
schwach	weak	die Schwäche, -n	weakness
stark	strong	die Stärke, -n	strength
still	quiet	die Stille	stillness, silence
süß	sweet	die Süße	sweetness
tief	deep	die Tiefe, -n	depth
treu	faithful	die Treue	fidelity, loyalty
warm	warm	die Wärme	warmth

0.2 Singular and Plural of Nouns

der Bonbon, - *or* -s
der Brief, -e
der Einschreibbrief, -e
das Gesicht, -er
der Hausbesitzer, -
der Hausherr, -n, -en
der Hauswirt, -e
der Jäger, -
die Lage, -n
der Millionär, -e
der Rahmbonbon, - *or* -s
der Rest, -e
der Vormonat, -e

0.3 Other Uses of Subjunctive II

In Grammar §29.8 you saw that the subjunctive II is used in wishes contrary to fact ("if only" wishes), in expressions of politeness ("would you please," "I would prefer," etc.), and in expressing certain meanings with the modal auxiliaries (*would, could, should, might, ought to,* etc.). Now we turn our attention to three more functions of the subjunctive II: the German "as if" construction, wishes introduced by wishing-verbs, and conditional sentences.

als ob, als wenn as if

A clause beginning with **als ob** or **als wenn** *as if* ordinarily contains a subjunctive II verb. Since such clauses are dependent clauses, the finite verb stands last (or third from last if there is a double infinitive):

Er tut, als ob er krank wäre.
He acts as if he were sick.

Du siehst aus, als wenn du hättest mitgehen wollen.
You look as if you had wanted to go along.

Wishes introduced by verbs of wishing

German expressions equivalent to English "I wish that . . ." have subjunctive II verbs in both clauses. The most common wishing-verbs are **mögen**, **wollen**, and **wünschen**:

Ich wollte, daß du mit dem Unsinn aufhörtest.
I wish that you would stop (with) that nonsense.

Ich wünschte, ich hätte besser aufgepaßt.
I wish I had paid better attention.

Er möchte, daß wir die Miete bezahlen würden.
He wishes that we would pay the rent.

Notice that the finite verb is in second position if the dependent clause is not introduced by a subordinating conjunction (second example).

Conditional sentences

A *conditional sentence* is a two-clause sentence consisting of a **wenn**-clause (the condition) and a *result* clause (the result or conclusion of the fulfillment of the condition). The **wenn**-clause is a dependent clause, so its finite verb stands in last position (or third from last, if there is a double infinitive). The result clause is an independent clause, so its finite verb is in either first position (yes-no questions) or second position. This is the typical pattern:

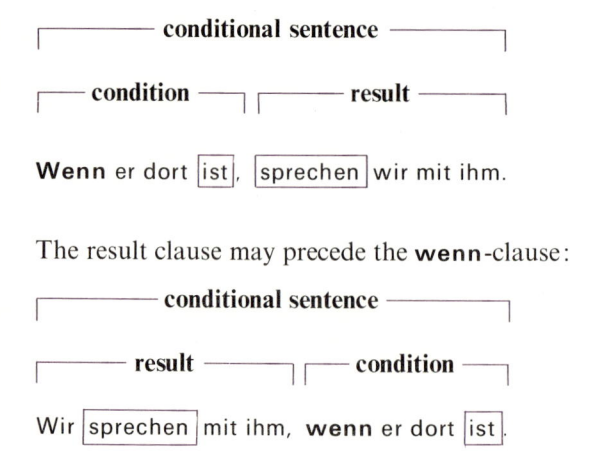

```
┌──── conditional sentence ────┐
┌── condition ──┐ ┌── result ──┐
```

Wenn er dort |ist|, |sprechen| wir mit ihm.

The result clause may precede the **wenn**-clause:

```
┌──── conditional sentence ────┐
┌──── result ────┐ ┌── condition ──┐
```

Wir |sprechen| mit ihm, **wenn** er dort |ist|.

In the examples given above, the finite verbs are in the present indicative. Notice how the meaning changes as we alter the verb forms from present indicative to present subjunctive II and then to past subjunctive II:

1. *Pres. ind.*   Wenn er dort ist, sprechen wir mit ihm.
                   If he is there, we'll speak with him.

2. *Pres. subj. II* Wenn er dort wäre, sprächen wir mit ihm.
                   If he were there, we would speak with him.

3. *Past subj. II*   Wenn er dort gewesen wäre, hätten wir mit ihm gesprochen.
If he had been there, we would have spoken with him.

The implications expressed by the different verb forms are as follows:

1. *Pres. ind.*   There is a real possibility that the condition exists, i.e. that he *is* there; if he *is*, then the result *will* really take place, i.e. we *will* speak with him.

2. *Pres. subj. II*   The condition *does not* exist, i.e. he *is not* there; the result is only hypothetical and *will not* take place, i.e. we *will not* speak with him.

3. *Past subj. II*   The condition *did not* exist; the result *did not* take place.

Examples 2 and 3 are called *conditions contrary to fact*. They state the circumstances under which something would take place (or would have taken place), but at the same time express the fact that those circumstances do not (or did not) exist. Here are some more examples:

Wenn ich im Lotto gewonnen hätte, hätten wir eine Reise gemacht.
If I had won in the lottery, we would have taken a trip.

Implication: I *did not* win, and we *did not* take a trip.

Wenn die Sonne schiene, ginge er zum Baden.
If the sun were shining, he would go swimming.

Implication: the sun *is not* shining, so he *is not* going swimming.

Ich hätte ihn besucht, wenn ich nicht so vergeßlich wäre.
I would have visited him if I were not so forgetful.

Implication: I *am* forgetful, and I *did not* visit him.

The *würde*-alternative in conditional sentences

The **würde** + *infinitive* construction is frequently used in place of the present subjunctive II in a conditional sentence, especially in the result clause:

Wenn ich Zeit hätte, **besuchte** ich ihn.
Wenn ich Zeit hätte, **würde** ich ihn **besuchen**.
If I had time I *would visit* him.

Du **bestündest** die Prüfung, wenn du mehr gearbeitet hättest.
Du **würdest** die Prüfung **bestehen**, wenn du mehr gearbeitet hättest.
You *would pass* the test if you had worked more.

There is a tendency to avoid the **würde** + *infinitive* construction in the **wenn**-clause, and use only the present or past subjunctive II. The **würde**-alternative does occur here, though, especially in conversational German:

Es wäre besser, wenn du mitkommen würdest.
It would be better if you came (would come) along.

30.4 Omission of *wenn* and *ob*

In English, the *if* of an *if*-clause may sometimes be omitted; the finite verb then goes to the beginning of the clause:

If only you *had* been there!
Had you only been there!

If you *had* paid attention, you would have learned something.
Had you paid attention, you would have learned something.

Similarly, the German conjunction **wenn** may be omitted from a **wenn**-clause; the finite verb then occupies the position vacated by **wenn**:

Wenn du nur nicht so vergeßlich ⎡wärest⎤ !

⎡Wärest⎤ du nur nicht so vergeßlich!

Wenn ich im Lotto gewonnen ⎡hätte⎤, so würde ich eine Reise machen.

⎡Hätte⎤ ich im Lotto gewonnen, so würde ich eine Reise machen.

When the result clause follows the **wenn**-clause, it is often introduced by **so** or **dann** *then*. This is particularly frequent after a **wenn**-clause from which the **wenn** has been omitted:

Wenn er hier wäre, (so) würden wir uns freuen.
If he were here, (then) we would be glad.

Hätte ich das gewußt, dann wäre unsere Lage besser.
Had I known that, then our situation would be better.

Wäre er nicht so vorsichtig, so hätte er einen Unfall gehabt.
Were he not so careful, then he would have had an accident.

The finite verb may also replace the **ob** or **wenn** of the **als ob**, **als wenn** construction:

Er tut, **als ob** er nicht zufrieden ⎡wäre⎤ .

Er tut, **als** ⎡wäre⎤ er nicht zufrieden.

He acts as if he weren't satisfied.

Du siehst aus, **als wenn** du Angst ⎡hättest⎤ .

Du siehst aus, **als** ⎡hättest⎤ du Angst.

You look as if you were afraid.

WRITING

A. Dehydrated Sentences

Write the following in the subjunctive II, using the tense that seems most appropriate to you:

1. Er tut, als ob / er / sein / krank
2. Sie sieht aus, als / schlafen / sie / ganz / Nacht / nicht
3. Er machte ein Gesicht, als / haben / er / Angst
4. Es war, als wenn / er / wiedererkennen / ich / nicht
5. Da / haben / wir / Geschichte
6. Dürfen / haben / ich / Flasche / Rotwein?
7. Wir / haben / gern / noch / Tasse / Kaffee
8. Ich / gehen / gern / einmal / mit / Sie / Theater
9. Werden / geben / Sie / ich / bitte / Salz?
10. Wenn / wir / nur / einmal / können / gewinnen / in / Lotto!
11. Wenn / Leute / werden / schicken / Schrank / doch / bald!
12. Müssen / fliegen / er / nur / nicht / so viel!
13. Ankommen / er / doch / bald!
14. Du / sollen / denken / an / dein / Bildung
15. Wir / können / besuchen / mal / Schloß
16. Er / mögen / machen / gern / Reise
17. Ihr / sollen / fahren / nicht / so rücksichtslos
18. Ich / wollen // ihr / aufhören / mit / Unsinn
19. Tante Inge / wünschen // Onkel Richard / leben / nicht / so flott
20. Er / mögen // daß / du / fahren / nicht / so rücksichtslos
21. Der Besitzer / wollen // daß / wir / bezahlen / sofort / Miete

Write the following as conditional sentences in the subjunctive II, referring to *present time*. Use the **würde**-alternative only where **werden** appears:

22. Wenn / Susi / schluchzen / nicht / so laut // ihre Mutter / sein / glücklicher
23. Wenn / Tante Inge / heulen / nicht // ihr Neffe / werden / haben / sie / lieber
24. Es / sein / schön // wenn / Günther / aufhören / endlich / mit / Unsinn
25. Ich / werden / freuen / mich // wenn / du / wollen / lutschen / nicht / laufend / Rahmbonbon
26. Wenn / Hans / trampeln / nicht / so wüst // er / werden / sein / nett / Junge

Write the following as conditional sentences in the subjunctive II, referring to *past time*. Use the **würde**-alternative only where **werden** appears:

27. Wenn / er / sein / nicht / so geldsüchtig // ich / können / leiden / er / besser
28. Er / interessieren / sich / dafür // wenn / er / wissen / etwas / davon
29. Die Klasse / werden / lernen / mehr // wenn / Lehrer / aufregen / sich / nicht immer

30 Es / gelingen / der Student // wenn / er / auseinanderhalten / die Probleme
31 Wenn / er / haben / nicht / recht // so / er / werden / arbeiten / nicht so viel

B. Controlled Composition

In about 150 words write what you would do if you were to win a large sum of money in a lottery. You might begin as indicated below and then develop your story with ideas suggested by some of the vocabulary listed. Make use of the patterns and words that you are familiar with; do not try to create new ones!

Wenn ich eine große Menge Geld im Lotto gewänne, würde ich mir erst einmal . . .

Reise, Stadt, Ausland, besuchen, besichtigen, Fest, Sportwagen, Anzug, Kleider, Schloß, Dom, Venus von Milo, Universität, studieren, Bildung

---

READING PRACTICE

Theater in Deutschland

Wer vom französischen Theater spricht, meint Paris. Das englische Theater wird in London gemacht, das amerikanische in New York. Natürlich gibt es auch in vielen anderen Städten dieser Länder ausgezeichnete Theater, aber wirklich bedeutend sind doch nur die Hauptstädte[g].

Das ist in Deutschland ganz anders. Wer vom deutschen Theater spricht, meint nicht nur Berlin oder Bonn. Er meint nicht einmal andere große Städte wie Hamburg, München, Frankfurt oder Köln. Er meint tatsächlich das ganze Land. In Deutschland wird nicht nur überall Theater gespielt, in Deutschland wird tatsächlich überall selbständiges Theater gespielt, und das hat wenig zu tun mit dem, was in der Hauptstadt gerade Mode[g] ist.

Diese Tatsache hat eine lange Geschichte. Ihr Anfang liegt wohl in dem extremen Föderalismus[g], den Deutschland vor 1871 erlebt hat. Jedes einzelne der vielen kleinen Länder und Ländchen innerhalb Deutschlands hatte sein eigenes Kulturleben[g] und war stolz darauf. Und das Theater war überall das Zentrum des Kulturlebens.

Heute gibt es in dem relativ kleinen Westdeutschland schon wieder rund 300 Theater. Das sind eine ganze Menge, wenn man bedenkt, daß nach dem 2. Weltkrieg so gut wie alles wieder neu aufgebaut werden mußte. Und alle diese 300 Theater sind Berufstheater, die neun oder

Spielplan der Hamburger Bühnen

Theater	Sa., 8. Nov.	So., 9. Nov.	Mo., 10. Nov.	Di., 11. Nov.
Hamburgische Staatsoper Dammtorstr. Ruf 35 15 55	19.30–22 Uhr Sbd. – Abo. 1 **Der Barbier von Sevilla**	19.30–22.30 U. fr. Kartenvk. In neuer Inszen. u. Einstudierg. **Julius Caesar**	19.30–22.15 U. geschl. Auff. **Zar und Zimmermann**	19.30–22 Uhr Di. – Abo 3 **Cinderella** Ballett
Deutsches Schauspielhs. Kirchenallee 24 08 53/54	15–17.15 Uhr Nachm.-Preise **Der Tartuffe** 20–22.15 Uhr **Gullivers Reisen**	15–18 Uhr Nachm.-Preise **Herr Puntila und sein Knecht Matti** 20–22.15 Uhr **Der Tartuffe**	20–21.30 Uhr für Volksbühne **Woyzeck**	20–22.15 Uhr **Der Tartuffe**
Thalia Theater Gerhart-Hauptm.-Pl. Ruf 33 04 44	16–18.30 Uhr **Das Haus der Temperamente** 20–22.45 Uhr **Viel Lärm um Nichts** (ausverkauft)	16–18.30 Uhr **Hadrian VII** 20–22.45 Uhr **Viel Lärm um Nichts** (ausverkauft)	20–22.20 Uhr **Amphitryon**	20–22.30 Uhr **Hadrian VII**

„Thalia um 11": „Der Architekt und der Kaiser von Assyrien" von Arrabal mit Martin Benrath und Peter Striebeck. Premiere heute, 8. Nov., **23** Uhr

Hamburger Kammerspiele Ruf 44 51 62 — 20 Uhr | 20 Uhr Volksb. | 20 Uhr Volksb. | 20 Uhr zum Jubiläum ihrer **50jährigen** Bühnentätigkeit **Ida Ehre** in „**Mutter Courage und ihre Kinder**" von Bertolt Brecht

Ohnsorg-Th. Ruf 34 75 74 — Tägl. 20 Uhr, heute **auch** 16.30 Uhr (heute ausvkft.) **Smuggelbröders**. Sonntag, 20 Uhr: **Een Mann mit Charakter**

Theat. i. Zim. 446539/450968 — Täglich 20 Uhr **Was ist an Tolen so sexy?** von Ann Jellicoe

Das Junge Th. Mundsburg Tel. 22 44 44 — Täglich 20 Uhr, ab Sonntag auch VB. **Davor** von Günter Grass Regie: Richard Münch

Altonaer Th. Ruf 77 46 46 — In Altona: **Der Fall Winslow**, heute, 16 u 20 U., f. Abo, VB u. f. Vk. **Gute Geschäfte**, 9. Nov., f. VB u. fr. Verk., 20 Uhr In Harburg: **Der Fall Winslow**, 10. bis 15. Nov. für Abo, 20 Uhr

Die kleine Komödie Ruf 34 05 61 u. 34 26 44 — Uraufführung — Nur noch **7** Vorstellungen Täglich 20.30 Uhr (außer sonntags) **Claus Wilcke, Christiane Nielsen** **Spiel mit Variationen** Komödie von Ernst Jacobsohn mit Gerda-Maria Jürgens, Ursula Mellin, Marina Ried

Ahrweilers „rendezvous" Ruf 34 26 44 — Täglich 21 Uhr außer sonntags **Früh-ling(k)s-Erwachen** mit Lia Pahl, Peter Ahrweiler u. a.

Theater für Kinder 382538 — **Der Floh ist weg** Nur noch 2 Wochen! Mo.–Fr. 16.30, sbds. u. stgs. 14.30 u. 17 Uhr

Operettenhaus Tel. 31 37 37 — Das erfolgreichste, herrlichste Musical der Welt tgl. 20 U. (auß. montags), sbds. u. stgs. auch 16 U. (ermäß. Pr.) **MY FAIR LADY** Heidi Brühl, Carlos Werner, Benno Hoffmann, Kurt Waitzmann und das große Ensemble, Inszenierung: Christian Wölffer

elf Monate im Jahr regelmäßig spielen, nicht Amateurgruppen*g*, die nur sechs- oder zehnmal im Jahr spielen. Mehr als 20 Millionen Menschen gehen jährlich in diese Theater.

Die Theaterspielpläne*g* zeigen ein sehr verschiedenartiges Bild. Mehr als ein Drittel aller Stücke sind z.B. von ausländischen Autoren*g*. Dauernd wechselt außerdem Modernes mit Altem. Am wichtigsten ist aber immer das kulturelle*g* Niveau*g* der Stücke. Theater nur so zum Spaß ist ziemlich selten in Deutschland, das ist für die meisten mehr die Domäne*g* des Kinos.

Wohl gibt es heute in Deutschland auch Ensuite-Theater*g*, Theater also, die ein bestimmtes Stück jeden Tag wochen- oder sogar monatelang spielen. Die meisten Theater sind aber Repertoire-Theater*g* mit täglich wechselndem Spielplan.

Das kostet natürlich viel Geld. Aber bis jetzt stecken die Deutschen dieses Geld gern in ihre Theater, denn für die meisten von ihnen nimmt das Theater einen sehr hohen Platz in der kulturellen Rangordnung des Lebens ein.

Unit 31

READING

Der Ehemann aus der Zeitung

Wie lernen sich die jungen Leute in Deutschland kennen? Nun, meistens natürlich wie überall sonst auf der Welt, aber da gibt es doch auch etwas, was viele Amerikaner recht fremd und eigenartig finden: Institute[g] für Ehevermittlung oder Eheanbahnung nämlich.

Ehevermittlungsinstitute sind nicht typisch[g] deutsch. In vielen Ländern gibt es davon viel mehr als in Deutschland, und manchmal haben sie eine so alte Tradition, daß man solche Vermittlung von Ehen deshalb tatsächlich eine Sitte des Landes nennen kann. Nicht so in Deutschland. Aber es gibt dort doch immerhin 260 private Institute für Ehevermittlung, die viel besucht werden. Die westdeutschen Eheanbahner haben in den ersten zwanzig Jahren nach dem Kriege ungefähr 650 000 Ehen vermittelt, das sind 7% aller Ehen in diesem Zeitraum.

Die Statistik sagt, daß 60% aller Kunden Frauen sind und nur 40% Männer. Und die Kunden

der Ehemann, ⸚er ein verheirateter Mann
die Ehe, -n marriage

die Welt, -en world
das Institut, -e [ɪnstiˈtuːt] · **die Ehevermittlung,** -en professional matchmaking ·
die Eheanbahnung, -en die Ehevermittlung
deshalb therefore, for that reason

der Eheanbahner, - professional matchmaker
vermitteln mediate, arrange · **der Zeitraum** period of time **der Raum,** ⸚e room, hall, space

1. Was finden viele Amerikaner fremd und eigenartig?
2. Findet man solche Institute nur in Deutschland?
3. Kann man diese Ehevermittlungsinstitute eine deutsche Sitte nennen?
4. Wie viele Institute für Ehevermittlung gibt es in Deutschland?
5. Sind die meisten Kunden Frauen oder Männer?

Heiraten · Bekanntschaften

80, arm aber nett, su. nerin, apart, häusl. nk. B 91729 Abend-

nerin bis 40 J., schlk., Beamter, lebensfroh, eschied. Heirat nicht Freundl. Zuschr. erb. unter PH 4135

f. einfache Freizeit- student, 29/1,78. ten unter K 42272

bspartnerin für Sep- von 27jährigem Bildzuschr. PZ 3328

e Freizeitgestaltung. schaften nach Ihren iche Unterlagen von lin 15, Fach 774 H. groß, humorvoll, mö. dchen kennenlernen. 1559 Abdbl. tstituiert, sucht Frei- nicht über 38 J., mit Bild unter PS

Bekanntschaft einer ame. Zuschr. m. Bild Tel.-Angabe erbeten bdbl.

e, 25 J., 1,76, wünscht ennenzulernen. Zus- mit Bild (zur.) PM

Gepflegte, jung aussehende Dame, Anfang 40, möchte Herrn mit Herz und Verstand, nicht unter 1,75 m groß, 40–50 Jahre alt kennenlernen. Nur ernstgemeinte Zuschriften (mit Bild), zurück. VF 3322 Tageblatt.
Kaufmann, 29 Jahre alt, 1,76 m, sucht nette, sportliche Lebenspartnerin ohne Kinder zwecks Heirat. Bildzuschriften erwünscht (zurück) unter VZ 1075 Tageblatt.
Bin 40 Jahre alt, 1,71 m groß, seit 5 Jahren geschieden. Suche gutaussehende, treue Frau. VE 2711 Tageblatt.
Welche junge Dame bis 25 Jahre möchte einen gutaussehenden Herrn kennenlernen zwecks späterer Heirat? Bin Beamter mit gutem Einkommen, 30 Jahre alt, 1,76 m groß. Habe eigene Wohnung und Wagen. Hobby: Musik, Tanzen, Tennis. Bildzuschriften erwünscht. VH 8335 Tageblatt.
Welcher nette, intelligente junge Mann sucht nette Partnerin für Freizeit (Theater, Tanz, Diskussion etc.)? Bin 26, 1,61m, dunkel, schlank. VE 5962 Tageblatt.
Ob es "sie" gibt? (Wirklich nett, schön und natürlich, von 20 bis 26 Jahre, 1,60–1,70 m groß) Bestimmt! Aber ob "sie" antwortet? Das erhofft ein junger Herr, 35 Jahre alt, 1,80 m, blond, sportlicher Typ. Zuschrift bitte mit Foto (zurück). PZ 2595 Tageblatt.

Langweiliger Geigenspieler (32, 1,85) mit Brille, Abitur, Lehrerprüfung, neuem Wagen und weiteren Vorteilen (Tanzfreude, Naturfreund, sportlich, humorvoll) sucht Partnerin. D 22350 Tageblatt.
Charmante Dame, 48 Jahre, 1,64 m, schlank, gute Figur, sportlich, elegant, musikliebend, mit großer schöner Wohnung möchte Lebenskameraden kennenlernen. Zuschriften erwünscht unter B 34 506 Tageblatt.
Wünsche Zweitehe mit netter, gutaussehender Dame, die so jung sein sollte wie möglich, ohne mich zu alt zu finden. HK 5766 Tageblatt.
Sind Sie die richtige Frau für mich? 38jährig, 1,82 m, dunkel, weitgereist, politisch konservativ, Beamter, möchte attraktive Dame bis 30 Jahre (ohne Kind) kennenlernen. TR 3745 Tageblatt.
Junger Mann, 39 Jahre, blond, sucht einfaches solides Mädel mit oder ohne Kind. R 29844 Tageblatt.
Attraktive junge Dame, 28/1,72, schlank und sportlich, mit guter Allgemeinbildung, wünscht die Bekanntschaft eines gebildeten Herrn zwecks gemeinsamer Freizeitgestaltung. Bildzuschrift (zurück) an FB 6524 Tageblatt.
Suche gutaussehenden jungen Herrn, 21–27 Jahre, guter Tänzer, zwecks Bekanntschaft. Bin Sekretärin, 21 Jahre, 1,65, blond, schlank. Zuschrift unter GV 7118 Tageblatt.

Erfolgreicher Ingenie Erscheinung, natu seriöse, gescheite, mante Ehegefährti 90271 Abdbl.
Angestellter, 54/175 häuslich, geistig int warmherzige, volls tin, evtl. Bildzusc (zurück). Angebot Abl.
Ingenieur, 30/1,80, m ten Teenager zw. F Bildzuschr. erb. (z Abl.
Junger Mann, 24/1,6 Mädel, Kind angene terer Heirat. Zusch Telefonangabe. PA
Kraftfahrer, 46, eig. Lande, Raum Neus einf. jüngere Dame zw. spät. Heirat. P.
Hamburger, 37/1,81, m schuldl. gesch., mit ter 10, Junge 9 J. s u. Frau. Zuschrifte (zur.) u. Telef.-Ang
Dipl.-Kfm. 48—Dipl.-I Kfm. 54—Jurist 55— Ehe. Inst. Lachmar
Geschäftsm., 60 J., 1 pension m. Reitpfe renhaus, möchte Dame, mgl. im Al Heirat kennenler angenehm. PD 3843

sind jung, das ist besonders eigenartig. Das Alter^g der Kunden soll bei den Frauen im Durchschnitt um 22, bei den Männern um 30 Jahre liegen.

Die Vermittler haben natürlich lange Listen^g für ihre Kunden, aber häufig setzen sie auch Annoncen^g in Zeitungen, um so den richtigen Partner^g für einen Kunden ausfindig zu machen. Die meisten deutschen Zeitungen und Zeitschriften bringen solche Annoncen, denn nicht nur Ehevermittler von Beruf, auch viele Privatleute suchen so ihr Glück. Und manche scheinen es wirklich gefunden zu haben!

Die Männer suchen heute angeblich meistens mütterliche, häusliche Frauentypen, die gut aussehen und gute Kameraden sind. Pin-up-Girls sind, für die Ehe wenigstens, nicht gefragt. Dafür möchte der Mann gutes Essen und ein gemütliches Zuhause^g. Aber auch in der Öffentlichkeit will der Mann heute auf die gesuchte Frau stolz sein können. Auch die deutschen Mädchen wollen, so heißt es, meistens einen väterlichen, häuslichen Mann, einen richtigen Familienvater. Dabei braucht er aber nicht gut auszusehen. Einen „schönen" Mann lehnen die meisten sogar ab. Und zu jung sollte er auch nicht sein. Die meisten deutschen Mädchen finden angeblich den lebenserfahrenen^g Mann von vierzig Jahren gerade richtig, weil er sie besser versteht als ein junger. Aber er muß gepflegt sein, sonst wird die moderne deutsche Durchschnittsfrau den modernen deutschen Durchschnittsmann nicht mögen. So sagen jedenfalls die Leute, die ihre Mitmenschen^g nach ihren Meinungen fragen. Und die sollten es doch eigentlich wissen, die Herren Meinungsforscher!

Mögen die Meinungsforscher viel wissen, die Statistiker^g wissen fast alles; natürlich auch über die Ehe! Sie sagen, daß die Ehen in Deutschland heute sogar noch etwas besser halten als vor dem Kriege. Jedenfalls gibt es heute viel weniger Scheidungen als bald nach dem Krieg. Von 10 000 Ehen werden jetzt im Durchschnitt nur noch 35 Ehen geschieden. Und das sind zum großen Teil junge oder kinderlose Ehen. Ein „Ehemann aus der Zeitung" jedenfalls scheint durchaus nicht schlechter zu sein als jeder andere.

das Alter, -
der Durchschnitt, -e average   **der Schnitt**, -e cut, slice
die Liste, -n · **die Annonce**, -n [aˈnõːsə]
der Partner, - · **ausfindig machen** finden
bringen *here* print
scheinen *here* seem, appear

angeblich alleged(ly), supposed(ly)

die Öffentlichkeit public, publicity

ablehnen refuse

gepflegt sein be well groomed

der Meinungsforscher, - pollster   **die Meinung**, -en opinion   **der Forscher** researcher   **forschen** investigate
halten *here* endure, hold up, last
die Scheidung, -en divorce
scheiden: er scheidet, schied, hat geschieden separate, divorce   **sie sind geschieden** they are divorced · **zum großen Teil** largely, in large part
durchaus nicht keinesfalls, bestimmt nicht

6   Wie alt sind die Kunden solcher Institute im Durchschnitt?
7   Wo sind die Annoncen zu finden?
8   Welchen Frauentyp suchen die Männer angeblich?
9   Welchen Typ suchen die Mädchen?
10 Warum soll der gesuchte Mann nicht zu jung sein?
11 Woher wissen wir all das?
12 Werden viele Ehen heutzutage geschieden?
13 Ist ein Ehemann aus der Zeitung schlechter als andere Ehemänner?

Deutschland – Reiseland

Das alte Vorkriegsdeutschland[g] war ein bekanntes Reiseland. Nicht nur die Deutschen reisten[g] viel, besonders natürlich im Sommer, es kamen auch immer viele Ausländer zu Besuch.

Die Bundesrepublik Deutschland ist heute nur noch ein kleines Land, kaum halb so groß wie das Deutschland von 1937. Und nicht nur Deutschlands Größe hat sich seit den zwanziger[g] und dreißiger[g] Jahren verändert, fast alles ist anders geworden. Aber ein Reiseland ist Deutschland ungeachtet all der Veränderungen immer noch. Die neuen Statistiken über Deutschland als Reiseland können sich neben den alten sehr wohl sehen lassen.

Heutzutage kommen neben Europäern[g] besonders viele Amerikaner nach Deutschland. Aber auch die Deutschen reisen wieder viel in ihrer Heimat. Häufig reisen sie natürlich auch ins europäische[g] Ausland, besonders gern nach Italien[g], aber die meisten bleiben doch in ihrer Heimat. Die Auswahl an schönen Plätzen ist dort durchaus groß genug.

Besonders wichtig für das Reisen ist das Verkehrsnetz. Und das ist nun wirklich gut. Nur gibt es leider viel zu viele Menschen und Autos auf kleinem Raum, aber das ist nicht nur ein Reiseproblem. Es ist eben alles recht eng im heutigen[g] Deutschland. Die Bevölkerungsdichte ist viel zu groß. Die Bundesrepublik gehört ja zu den Ländern, in denen auf der ganzen Welt durchschnittlich die meisten Menschen auf einem Quadratkilometer (km^2) leben.

Aber auch das Verkehrsnetz ist eng. Besonders eng und gut ist das Netz der Eisenbahnen. Mit der Eisenbahn kann man in Deutschland fast überallhin[g] relativ schnell und billig kommen.

Die deutschen Autobahnen sind meistens nicht ganz so gut wie ihr Ruf (der Verkehr ist eben zu groß geworden), aber zweifellos auch nicht schlecht. Man kann heute auf ihnen, wenn man will, ohne Aufenthalt von Flensburg bis Basel fahren. Natürlich werden noch laufend neue Autobahnen gebaut, aber im Augenblick wird der Verkehr schneller größer als das weitverzweigte Netz der Autobahnen.

Nun, so weit verzweigt ist das Autobahnnetz eigentlich noch gar nicht, aber das allgemeine Straßennetz ist tatsächlich sehr weit verzweigt. Und in der Regel sind die Straßen auch gut.

Es läßt sich immer noch bequem reisen in Deutschland, denn man fährt ja nicht nur, wenn man reist. Man schaut sich um oder man liegt in der Sonne, man besichtigt besondere Plätze oder besucht alte Bekannte, man macht neue Bekanntschaften[g] oder geht einfach spazieren. Und für all diese Dinge (und noch mehr) ist Deutschland gut. Man findet überall hübsche Hotels[g] und Gasthäuser[g], teure und billigere. Jeder Ausländer, der in der Bundesrepublik reist, sollte aber auch einige der vielen kleinen, gemütlichen Gaststätten besuchen, die es überall im Lande gibt.

die Bundesrepublik, -en federal republic
der Bund, ⸚e federation, union · **kaum** hardly
sich verändern *acc. refl.* change, become different
ungeachtet *prep. with gen.* trotz · **die Veränderung, -en** change
heutzutage nowadays · **der Europäer, -** [ɔɪroˈpɛːɐ̯]
die Heimat, *pl.* **die Heimatländer** native country, homeland
Italien [iˈtɑːliən]
das Verkehrsnetz, -e traffic system   **der Verkehr** traffic
eng narrow, small, crowded · **die Bevölkerungsdichte** population density   **die Bevölkerung, -en** population
das Quadratkilometer (*abbr.* **km²** *or* **qkm**) square kilometer   **das Quadrat, -e** square
die Eisenbahn, -en railroad   **das Eisen** iron
die Autobahn, -en superhighway
zweifellos without doubt, doubtless   **der Zweifel, -** doubt
der Aufenthalt, -e stop
weitverzweigt with many branches

bequem comfortable
sich umschauen *acc. refl.* look around
spazierengehen [ʃpaˈtsiːʀən-] take a walk
das Hotel, -s
das Gasthaus, ⸚er restaurant, inn   **der Gast, ⸚e** guest
die Gaststätte, -n restaurant   **die Stätte, -n** place

14 War Deutschland auch vor dem Krieg ein bekanntes Reiseland?
15 Waren es nur Deutsche, die in Deutschland reisten?
16 Wie groß ist die Bundesrepublik Deutschland heute?
17 Wer kommt heutzutage nach Deutschland?
18 Wohin reisen viele Deutsche besonders gern?
19 Wo bleiben die meisten?
20 Was ist für das Reisen besonders wichtig?
21 Was ist in Deutschland viel zu groß?
22 Wie kann man fast überallhin schnell und billig kommen?

23 Warum sind die meisten Autobahnen nicht so gut wie ihr Ruf?
24 Wie weit könnte man auf den Autobahnen fahren, wenn man wollte?
25 Kann man in Deutschland immer noch bequem reisen?

26 Was tut man auch, wenn man reist?
27 Was sollte jeder Ausländer besuchen, wenn er in Deutschland reist?

Das Klima^g ist mild^g in Deutschland. Es wird eigentlich nie richtig heiß im Sommer und selten^g wirklich kalt im Winter. Dafür gibt es aber viel Regen, in den deutschen Alpen^g etwa 2 000 mm im Jahresdurchschnitt. Darüber freuen sich natürlich die Wintersportler^g, besonders die Schiläufer, wenn der viele Regen im Winter als Schnee herunterkommt. Aber der Regen hat auch im Sommer seinen Vorteil: alles ist nämlich schön frisch und grün.

Der Reisende kann in Deutschland fast alles finden, was er sucht: große und kleine, moderne und alte Städte, gute Gaststätten und viel schöne, freie Natur, besonders Wald. Fast 30% der ganzen Bundesrepublik ist mit Wald bestanden, und wer nicht schon einmal stundenlang^g in deutschen Wäldern spazierenging, der kennt Deutschland noch nicht.

Am bekanntesten ist Deutschlands Süden. Hier liegen die Alpen, eine besonders reizvolle Gebirgslandschaft. Aber es gibt nach Norden zu auch sonst noch viel bergige Landschaft, wenn diese Mittelgebirge auch lange nicht so hoch sind wie die Alpen. Schließlich aber wird das Land weiter nach Norden zu ganz flach. Doch die großen, grünen Flächen^g, meistens Gras und Wald, haben auch ihren eigenartigen Reiz.

Wer gern im Freien^g badet, hat es überall in Deutschland gut, am besten aber doch wohl im Norden. Hier liegt das Meer, die Nordsee, mit vielen idealen^g Badeplätzen. Eigentlich ist auch die Ostsee ein kleines Meer. Viele Leute fahren lieber dorthin, weil das Klima da milder ist als an der Nordsee und der Sandstrand vielleicht noch besser: ein Feriengebiet, wie man es sich, besonders für Kinder, kaum schöner wünschen kann.

das Klima
mm *abbr. for* **das Millimeter,** -
der Wintersportler, - **der Sportler,** - ·
der Schiläufer, - skier   **der Schi** (*also* **Ski**), **-er** [ʃiː]
der Vorteil, -e advantage

bestanden covered
reizvoll attractive, charming
die Gebirgslandschaft, -en mountainous landscape   **das Gebirge,** - mountain range
der Berg, -e mountain   **die Landschaft, -en** landscape · **bergig** mountainous
das Mittelgebirge, - highlands, uplands
flach flat
der Reiz, -e charm, fascination   **reizvoll, reizend**
baden bathe
das Meer, -e ocean · **ideal** [ideˈɑːl]
der Sandstrand, ⸚e sandy beach   **der Sand**
der Strand, ⸚e shore · **das Feriengebiet, -e** vacation area   **die Ferien** *pl.* [ˈfeːʀiən] freie Tage   **das Gebiet, -e** die Gegend

28 Wie ist das Klima in Deutschland?
29 Regnet es viel in Deutschland?
30 Wer freut sich über den vielen Schnee?
31 Hat der Regen auch seinen Vorteil?
32 Gibt es viel Wald in Deutschland?
33 Wer kennt Deutschland noch nicht?
34 Wo liegen die Alpen?
35 Wie ist das Land weiter nach Norden zu?
36 Wo kann man besten baden?
37 Warum fahren viele Leute lieber an die Ostsee als an die Nordsee?

Der Rhein ist vielleicht noch bekannter als das Alpengebiet, hauptsächlich wegen seines guten Weines. Aber jeder Reisende wird bald herausfinden^g, daß man nicht nur am Rhein, Deutschlands berühmtestem Fluß, gute Weine trinkt!

Da wir nun beim Baden und Trinken sind, muß noch von den vielen Stellen in Deutschland erzählt werden, die tatsächlich nur für Baden und Trinken da sind, den vielen, vielen, meistens schon recht alten Kurorten. Man kann einen Kurort leicht von anderen Orten unterscheiden, vor seinem Ortsnamen wird nämlich „Bad" stehen. In solchen „Bädern" nun badet man nicht einfach in Wasser. Mit dem Trinken ist auch nicht etwa Bier und Wein gemeint. Vielmehr badet man in Heilquellen und trinkt auch daraus. Fast jede Heilquelle ist anders und hilft gegen besondere Krankheiten^g. Eine solche Kur ist anstrengend, und so gibt es in diesen Kurorten meistens gepflegte Parks^g, in denen die Kranken sich erholen können, und die Ruhe finden, die sie brauchen.

Denkt man nun noch an die Menschen, die sich überall im Lande (nicht nur des guten Geschäftes wegen!) über Fremde freuen, so kann man wohl zustimmen: Deutschland ist ein schönes Reiseland.

berühmt weit bekannt

da *subord. conj.* since, because

der Kurort, -e health resort, spa **die Kur, -en** cure **der Ort, -e** place, town
vielmehr rather, much more
die Heilquelle, -n mineral spring, spa
heilen cure **die Quelle, -n** spring, source
die Krankheit, -en
der Park, -s · **sich erholen** *acc. refl.* recover

zustimmen agree

38 Warum ist der Rhein vielleicht noch bekannter als das Alpengebiet?
39 Welche Orte existieren hauptsächlich für Baden und Trinken?
40 Wozu sind die Heilquellen gut?
41 Wo können die Kranken sich erholen?

42 Können Sie zustimmen: Deutschland ist ein schönes Reiseland?

PHONOLOGY

A. Review of [l]

Review the German sound l [l] in the Phonology of Unit 3 and then pronounce the following, concentrating especially on a perfect [l]:

lernen, Leute, Deutschland, natürlich, überall, Welt, viele, Vermittlung, nämlich, als, manchmal, alte, solche, tatsächlich, zählen, soll, liegen, lange, Listen, Glück, wirklich, angeblich, mütterlich, häuslich, gemütlich, Öffentlichkeit, wollen, väterlich, Familienvater, ablehnen, lebenserfahren, weil, gepflegt, jedenfalls, halten, bald, kinderlos, schlechter, klein, halb, Zahlen, wohl, lassen, Ausland, Italien, bleiben, Auswahl, Platz, leider, Problem, durchschnittlich, Bundesrepublik, Quadratkilometer, relativ, schnell, billig, zweifellos, will, Flensburg, Basel, laufend, Augenblick, allgemein, tatsächlich, Regel, läßt, liegt, Hotels, Klima, mild, selten, kalt, viel, Beispiel, Millimeter, Alpen, reizvoll, Sportler, Vorteil, Wald, einmal, stundenlang, Gebirgslandschaft, Mittelgebirge, schließlich, flach, ideal, Badeplatz, lieber, weil, milder, Fluß, stellen, erzählt, leicht, Heilquelle, hilft, deshalb, gepflegt, sich erholen

B. Review of [R]

Review the German sound r [R] in the Phonology of Unit 3 and then pronounce the following, concentrating especially on perfect [R]-sounds:

1 Amerikaner, recht, fremd, Freund, Tradition, privat, Krieg, Prozent, Frauen, ihre, richtigen, Jahren, Zeitschriften, bringen, Beruf, Kameraden, gefragt, braucht, gerade, fragen, Herren, groß, andere, Reise, Bundesrepublik, Größe, Raum, relativ, Ruf, fahren, Regel, Straßen, teure, billigere, Regen, darüber, frisch, grün, frei, reizvolle, Gras, Reiz, Sandstrand, Feriengebiet, Rhein, trinke, besondere, Krankheiten, anstrengend, Ruhe, brauchen, Freunde, freuen

2 kennenlernen, eigenartig, Ehevermittlung, wirklich, Partner, lebenserfahren, vierzig, versteht, modern, Durchschnitt, Meinungsforscher, wird, durchaus, gern, Flensburg, Verkehrsnetz, verzweigt, Sportler, wirklich, geworden, Gebirgslandschaft, bergig, Norden, dorthin, erzählt, Kurort, Parks

3 natürlich, mehr, für, nur, ihr, sogar, vor, der, er, sehr, Vorkriegsdeutschland, Verkehrsnetz, gehört, Uhr, fährt, umher, Natur, wer, hier, wir, werden, Kurort, Meer

4 aber, Ländern, Eheanbahner, immerhin, aller, Männer, besonders, Alter, mütterlich, väterlich, besser, jünger, über, weniger, kinderlos, jeder, Sommer, Ausländer, anders, Europäer, Amerikaner, ihrer, leider, Quadratkilometer, schneller, oder, Winter, besonders, Wäldern, lieber, milder, schöner, bekannter, unterscheiden, Bädern, Wasser, sondern

VOCABULARY

A. Singular and Plural of Nouns

das Alter, -
die Annonce, -n
der Aufenthalt, -e
das Auto, -s
die Autobahn, -en
die Bekanntschaft, -en
der Berg, -e
die Bevölkerung, -en
der Bund, ⸚e
der Durchschnitt, -e
die Ehe, -n
der Eheanbahner, -
die Eheanbahnung, -en
der Ehemann, ⸚er
die Ehevermittlung, -en
die Eisenbahn, -en
der Europäer, -
die Fläche, -n
der Forscher, -
der Gast, ⸚e
das Gasthaus, ⸚er
die Gaststätte, -n
das Gebiet, -e
das Gebirge, -
die Heilquelle, -n
das Hotel, -s

das Institut, -e
die Krankheit, -en
die Kur, -en
der Kurort, -e
die Landschaft, -en
die Liste, -n
das Meer, -e
die Meinung, -en
der Millimeter (mm), -
der Park, -s
der Partner, -
das Quadrat, -e
der Raum, ⸚e
der Reiz, -e
der Sandstrand, ⸚e
die Scheidung, -en
der Schi, -er
der Schiläufer, -
der Sportler, -
der Statistiker, -
die Veränderung, -en
das Verkehrsnetz, -e
der Vorteil, -e
die Welt, -en
der Zweifel, -

B. Inference

With the help of the clues provided, guess the meanings of the words in boldface:

1 Wer Medizin studiert und alle seine Prüfungen bestanden hat, ist Mediziner oder **Arzt**.   **der Arzt**, ⸚e
2 In der Stadt leben und arbeiten die **Städter** [ˈʃtɛːtɚ], auf dem Lande leben und arbeiten die **Bauern**.   **der Städter**, - · **der Bauer**, -n
3 Ein Wald besteht aus vielen **Bäumen**; ein **Baum** macht noch keinen Wald.   **der Baum**, ⸚e
4 Was, ihr habt zu Weihnachten keinen **Tannenbaum** gehabt?   **die Tanne**, -n

5 Die meisten Bäume haben **Blätter**, aber der Tannenbaum hat **Nadeln**. Die Blätter fallen im Herbst ab, die Nadeln aber nicht.   **das Blatt, ⸚er · die Nadel, -n**
6 Im Zimmer ist der Fußboden, das Zimmer hat auch vier **Wände** und eine **Decke**.   **die Wand, ⸚e · die Decke, -n**
7 Der Boden unter freiem Himmel heißt nicht mehr Fußboden, sondern **Erdboden**.   **die Erde, -n**
8 Wenn die Erde gut ist, kann man im Garten schöne **Blumen** pflanzen.   **die Blume, -n**
9 Im Sommer **blühen** die Blumen in allen Farben.
10 Meine Augen werden immer schlechter, jetzt kann ich die Zeitung nicht mehr ohne **Brille** lesen.   **die Brille, -n**
11 Gibt es hier denn keine **Brücke** über den Fluß? Ich muß auf die andere Seite.   **die Brücke, -n**
12 Wer im Haus ist, ist **drinnen**. Durch das Fenster kann man nach **draußen** sehen.
13 Kannst du sehen? Dort **drüben** auf der anderen Seite der Straße geht Hans mit seiner Tante Inge.
14 Wo Licht ist, ist es **hell**, wo kein Licht ist, ist es **dunkel**.
15 Wer viel weiß, ist klug, wer nur wenig weiß, ist **dumm**.
16 Das erste Essen am Morgen heißt **Frühstück**.   **das Frühstück**
17 Nicht alle Leute, die fleißig zur Kirche gehen, sind wirklich **fromm**.
18 Obwohl Susi heute **böse** war, ist sie doch ein wirklich nettes Mädchen.
19 Ich habe ihn nie gemocht, aber nachdem er so viel Schlechtes über mich gesagt hat, werde ich ihm **erst recht** nicht helfen.
20 A. Er hat seine Krankheit von einem Spezialarzt **behandeln** lassen.
   B. War er mit der **Behandlung** zufrieden?   **die Behandlung, -en**
21 A. Kommst du heute abend mit ins Kino?
   B. Ich weiß noch nicht. Eigentlich hatte ich die **Absicht** (= beabsichtigte ich), heute mal früh zu Bett zu gehen.   **die Absicht, -en · absichtlich**
22 Schon wenn die **Verkehrsampel** gelbes Licht zeigt, muß man stoppen, nicht erst bei rotem Licht.   **die Ampel, -n**
23 Bei diesem schlechten Wetter zu Fuß gehen zu müssen, ist gewiß nicht **angenehm**.
24 Sie **zündete** sich eine Zigarette nach der anderen an. Sie rauchte laufend.
25 Ich habe mir gleich die Medizin aus der **Apotheke** mitgebracht, die mein Arzt mir **verschrieben** hat.   **die Apotheke, -n**
26 Manche glauben, daß man im nächsten Krieg keine **Atomwaffen** gebrauchen wird.   **die Waffe, -n**
27 Machst du bitte mal das Fenster auf? In diesem verrauchten Zimmer kann man ja kaum noch **atmen**.   **der Atem**
28 Er ist so groß, daß man ihn einen **Riesen** nennen könnte.   **der Riese, -n, -n**
29 Hast du deine **Schulaufgaben** für morgen schon gemacht, Susi?   **die Aufgabe, -n**
30 Ihr neuer Regenmantel ist **außen** blau und **innen** rot.
31 Sollen wir bis morgen den ganzen Dialog **auswendig** lernen?
32 Fahren Sie mich schnell zum **Bahnhof**, mein Zug geht in vierzehn Minuten.   **der Bahnhof, ⸚e**
33 A. Du, Inge, meine Sommerhose ist zu klein, sie **paßt** mir nicht mehr!

B. Ich hab' es ja immer gesagt, Richard: du hast über Winter einen richtigen kleinen **Bauch** bekommen.   **der Bauch,** ⸚**e**
34 Der Kellner **bedient** seine Gäste.
35 Der **Leutnant befahl** seinen Soldaten, schneller zu **marschieren.**   **befehlen: er befiehlt, befahl, hat befohlen** (*dat.*)
36 Gestern ist mir ein alter Klassenkamerad auf der Straße **begegnet.**   **begegnen** (*dat.*)

WRITING

A. Real to Unreal Conditions

Change the following real conditions to unreal ones in the appropriate tense of the subjunctive II.

Example:
Wenn er in der Stadt gewesen ist, hat er bestimmt auch das neue Gebäude gesehen.
Wenn er in der Stadt gewesen wäre, hätte er bestimmt auch das neue Gebäude gesehen.

1 Wenn er genug Geld dafür gehabt hat, ist er sicher ins Theater gegangen.
2 Wenn das Wetter wärmer ist, pflanzen wir unsere Rosen.
3 Wenn er endlich den Arzt besucht, wird es ihm auch bald besser gehen.
4 War das Kind unruhig, so mußte es gleich ins Bett gehen.
5 Wenn du vorsichtig fährst, kann auch nichts passieren.
6 Ist der Junge in der Schule fleißig, so ist der Lehrer auch mit ihm zufrieden.

B. Semicontrolled Composition

Write a story of about 150 words relating what you would do if you had no money and the landlord wanted you to move out of your room unless you could pay last month's rent in a week.

Unit 32

Kriechspur

Parken verboten

Kreuzung

Engpass

Kreuzung verboten

Verbot für Motorfahrräder

Sackgasse

GRAMMAR

32.1 Indirect Discourse. Subjunctive I

In English and in German there are two ways of reporting what somebody else has said or written. One way is to quote him directly, reproducing his exact words and enclosing them in quotation marks. This is *direct discourse*:

Herr Hartmann sagt: ,,Ich bin immer sehr vorsichtig."
Mr. Hartmann said, "I am always very careful."

The introductory statement is followed by a colon in German, but by a comma in English.

The alternative to this is to report Mr. Hartmann's words indirectly, conveying the same information as with direct discourse but without reproducing his exact words. This is *indirect discourse*:

Mr. Hartmann said (that) he is always very careful.

In direct discourse the point of view shifts from that of the *reporter* in the introductory statement to that of the *person being quoted* in the quotation. In indirect discourse, however, the point of view remains the reporter's throughout.

Indirect discourse is treated in much the same way in German, except for one important difference: the reporter must choose between three different verb forms, depending on what his attitude is toward what he is reporting. He may use the indicative, the subjunctive I, or the subjunctive II. The attitudes implied by these in indirect discourse are as follows:

1. *Indicative.* The reporter agrees with or supports what he is reporting:

    Herr Hartmann sagte, daß er immer sehr vorsichtig **ist**.

    By using the indicative here, the reporter implies that he agrees with Mr. Hartmann's statement.

2. *Subjunctive I.* The reporter is taking as objective an attitude as possible, and wishes to imply neither agreement nor disagreement:

    Herr Hartmann sagte, daß er immer sehr vorsichtig **sei**.

    The subjunctive I form here implies that the reporter does not want to be held responsible for this statement; he is merely passing on information.

3. *Subjunctive II.* The reporter is definitely skeptical about what he is reporting:

    Herr Hartmann sagte, daß er immer sehr vorsichtig **wäre**.

    The use of the subjunctive II implies that the reporter has reason to believe that Mr. Hartmann's statement is not completely correct, i.e. he really is not always very careful.

These three distinctions are carefully preserved in formal speech and writing, but often tend to be replaced by a simple two-way distinction—indicative and subjunctive II—in everyday conversation.

Present subjunctive I forms

The endings for the subjunctive I are the same as those for the subjunctive II:

Subjunctive I	*Subjunctive II*
ich sprech -e	ich spräch -e
du sprech -est	du spräch -est
er sprech -e	er spräch -e
wir sprech -en	wir spräch -en
ihr sprech -et	ihr spräch -et
sie sprech -en	sie spräch -en

The only verb that does not follow this pattern is **sein**; it has no ending in the 1st and 3rd persons singular: **ich sei**, **er sei**.

The stem on which the subjunctive I is based is that of the infinitive. The vowel of the stem does not change in the 2nd and 3rd persons singular, as it does in some verbs in the indicative.

	sein	haben	werden	leben	müssen	wissen
ich, er	sei	habe	werde	lebe	müsse	wisse
du	seiest	habest	werdest	lebest	müssest	wissest
wir, sie	seien	haben	werden	leben	müssen	wissen
ihr	seiet	habet	werdet	lebet	müsset	wisset

Past subjunctive I forms

The past tense of the subjunctive I is analogous to the past tense of the subjunctive II. It is a phrase consisting of the present subjunctive I form of the tense auxiliary (**sei**, **habe**) plus the past participle of the main verb:

Present subjunctive I	*Past subjunctive I*	*Past subjunctive II*
Er komme.	Er **sei** gekommen.	Er wäre gekommen.
Sie esse.	Sie **habe** gegessen.	Sie hätte gegessen.
Er steige aus.	Er **sei** ausgestiegen.	Er wäre ausgestiegen.
Sie rufe uns an.	Sie **habe** uns angerufen.	Sie hätte uns angerufen.

Future subjunctive I forms

The future tense of the subjunctive I is a phrase consisting of the present subjunctive I of **werden** plus an infinitive. It is analogous to the future indicative and to the **würde**-alternative of the subjunctive II:

Future indicative	*Future subjunctive I*
Er wird kommen.	Er **werde** kommen.
Sie wird uns anrufen.	Sie **werde** uns anrufen.

Future perfect subjunctive I forms

The future perfect of the subjunctive I is a phrase consisting of the present subjunctive I of **werden** plus a perfect infinitive. The phrase is similar to that of the future perfect indicative and to that of the **würde**-alternative of the past subjunctive II:

Future perfect indicative	*Future perfect subjunctive I*
Er wird gekommen sein.	Er **werde** gekommen sein.
Sie wird uns angerufen haben.	Sie **werde** uns angerufen haben.

Tense usage in indirect discourse

The tense of the verb used in the indirect quotation corresponds to the tense of the indicative verb used in the original quotation. If the original verb was in the present tense, then the indirect discourse verb must also be in the present tense. If the original verb was in any of the three indicative tenses that refer to past time, then the indirect discourse verb must be in the past tense. If the original verb was in the future or future perfect tense, then the indirect discourse verb must be in the future or future perfect tense respectively.

Er sagt, Er sagte, Er hat gesagt, Er hatte gesagt,	„Ich gehe zum Baden."	er gehe zum Baden.
		er ginge zum Baden.
	„Ich ging zum Baden." „Ich bin zum Baden gegangen." „Ich war zum Baden gegangen."	er sei zum Baden gegangen.
		er wäre zum Baden gegangen.
	„Ich werde zum Baden gehen."	er werde zum Baden gehen.
		er würde zum Baden gehen.
	„Ich werde zum Baden gegangen sein."	er werde zum Baden gegangen sein.
		er würde zum Baden gegangen sein.

Subjunctive I in indirect discourse: an example

The finite verb forms in boldface in the following report are all in the subjunctive I. Notice that as long as the subjunctive is used for indirect discourse, it is not necessary to insert reminders such as *and then he said, he continued,* etc.

Onkel Richard lag im Krankenhaus. Sein Neffe Jürgen besuchte ihn. Er kam zur Tür herein und fragte ihn, wie es ihm denn **gehe**. Wie er sehen **könne**, nicht so schlecht, versuchte der Onkel seinen Neffen zu beruhigen. Wahrscheinlich **habe** er nur ein bißchen zu flott gelebt, Jürgen **kenne** ihn ja. In ein paar Tagen **sei** er sicher schon wieder auf den Beinen.

Jürgen blieb skeptisch. Jedenfalls erzählte er später seiner Frau, sein Onkel **habe** noch sehr blaß ausgesehen. Und weil der Onkel sein Buch falsch herum gehalten **habe**, **habe** er gewußt, daß er noch gar nicht wieder lesen **könne** und ihn nur **habe** beruhigen wollen. Jürgen **sei** darum bald wieder gegangen, damit der Besuch für seinen Onkel nicht zu anstrengend **werde**.

Subjunctive II in indirect discourse: an example

In this account of Jürgen's visit to his Uncle Richard, the finite verbs in indirect statements are in the subjunctive II:

Onkel Richard lag im Krankenhaus. Sein Neffe Jürgen besuchte ihn. Er kam zur Tür herein und fragte ihn, wie es ihm **ginge**. Wie er sehen **könnte**, nicht so schlecht, versuchte der Onkel seinen Neffen zu beruhigen. Wahrscheinlich **hätte** er nur ein bißchen zu flott **gelebt**, er **kennte** ihn ja. In ein paar Tagen **wäre** er sicher schon wieder auf den Beinen.

Jürgen blieb skeptisch. Jedenfalls erzählte er später seiner Frau, sein Onkel **hätte** noch sehr blaß **ausgesehen**. Und weil der Onkel sein Buch falsch herum **gehalten hätte**, **hätte** er gewußt, daß er noch gar nicht wieder **lesen könnte** und ihn nur **hätte beruhigen wollen**. Er **wäre** darum bald wieder **weggegangen**, damit der Besuch für seinen Onkel nicht zu anstrengend **würde**.

Preferred forms

Both the subjunctive I and the subjunctive II may appear in the same sentence or paragraph. In contemporary spoken German the subtle differences in attitude expressed by the two subjunctives are quite generally overlooked (but not in written or formal German!), and the choice depends on the speech habits of the individual. The tendency is to avoid subjunctive I forms, and to use subjunctive II forms instead. In fact, *the subjunctive II is mandatory* whenever the subjunctive I form would be identical with the indicative.

Der Student sagte: ,,Die Professoren haben nicht immer recht."
Der Student sagte, daß die Professoren nicht immer recht **hätten**.

The indirect discourse verb must be the subjunctive II form **hätten**, because the subjunctive I form **haben** is not distinguishable from the indicative.

Writing practice

Rewrite the following sentences in indirect discourse, putting the finite verb of the indirect statement into the subjunctive I. Logic often requires a change of subject and other elements which must agree with it.

Write the following without **daß**. There will be no change of word order.

Examples:
Er sagte: ,,Sie kommt um drei nach Hause."
Er sagte, sie komme um drei nach Hause.

Er sagte: ,,Günther hat einen Unfall gesehen."
Er sagte, Günther habe einen Unfall gesehen.

Er sagte: ,,Ich bin gestern mit meinem neuen Wagen nach Köln gefahren."
Er sagte, er sei gestern mit seinem neuen Wagen nach Köln gefahren.

1 Er sagte: ,,Helmut fährt mit uns nach Köln."
2 Er sagte: ,,Sie kann die Vorlesung nicht verstehen."
3 Er sagte: ,,Ich weiß die Antwort einfach nicht."
4 Er sagte: ,,Die Kinder sind heute bei ihrer Tante."
5 Er sagte: ,,Ich werde morgen nach München fahren."
6 Er sagte: ,,Das Schloß ist im Kriege zerstört worden."
7 Er sagte: ,,Der Professor hatte über Schiller gelesen."
8 Er sagte: ,,Ich schlief damals sehr wenig."

Introduce the indirect statement with **daß**. The word order will have to be changed to dependent word order.

Examples:
Er sagte: ,,Ich verkaufe mein Haus wieder."
Er sagte, daß er sein Haus wieder verkaufe.

Er antwortete: ,,Rolf ist heute in die Stadt gegangen."
Er antwortete, daß Rolf heute in die Stadt gegangen sei.

9 Er sagte zu mir: ,,Du bist leider zu spät gekommen."
10 Er sagte zu ihm: ,,Du hast deinen Wagen falsch geparkt."
11 Er meinte: ,,Onkel Richard hat zu flott gelebt."
12 Sie sagte: ,,Frau Wegner will einen neuen Hut."
13 Er sagte: ,,Er kommt um zehn Uhr mit dem Flugzeug an."
14 Er berichtete: ,,Man hatte das Institut schon geschlossen."
15 Sie schrieb: ,,Ich fand meinen Mann durch einen Ehevermittler."
16 Er versicherte uns: ,,Ich verdiente dort im Durchschnitt 1000,— Mark monatlich."

Rewrite the following sentences in indirect discourse, beginning each sentence as indicated. Use the subjunctive II wherever the subjunctive I would be like the indicative.

Examples:
Er sagte, daß . . .   „Ich habe meine Zigaretten vergessen."
Er sagte, daß er seine Zigaretten vergessen habe.

Sie fragten, ob . . .   „Schließen die Geschäfte schon vor sechs?"
Sie fragten, ob die Geschäfte schon vor sechs schlössen.

17 Er berichtete, daß . . .   „Meine Frau hat gestern einen Unfall gehabt."
18 Großmutter hat erzählt, daß . . .   „Die Kinder haben den ganzen Tag im Freien gespielt."
19 Mein Onkel hat angerufen, daß . . .   „Mein Partner und ich fahren nächste Woche nach Italien."
20 Mein Freund schrieb neulich, daß . . .   „Ich werde endlich heiraten."
21 Meine beiden Neffen fragten, ob . . .   „Können wir nächsten Sommer wieder zu Besuch kommen?"
22 Die Leute sagten, daß . . .   „Wir sind schon viermal in Frankreich gewesen."
23 Der Professor meint, . . .   „Diese Arbeiten sind ausgezeichnet."
24 Die Schüler sagten, . . .   „Wir wissen die Antwort darauf nicht."

Write the following passage as a report in indirect discourse. Use the subjunctive I when it is different from the indicative; otherwise use the subjunctive II. Begin as follows: Mein alter Freund Werner erzählte mir gestern, daß . . .

„Ich bin jetzt glücklich verheiratet. Du weißt ja, daß ich vorher nie das richtige Mädchen finden konnte. Einige waren zu dumm, andere zu flott oder nicht flott genug. Da habe ich denn schließlich an ein Ehevermittlungsinstitut geschrieben. Ich bekam sofort einen netten Brief zurück und Bilder von drei hübschen Mädchen im Alter von 22, 24 und 27 Jahren. Sie gefielen mir alle drei, und ich nahm zunächst mit der Jüngsten Kontakt auf. Aber sie interessierte mich schon bald nicht mehr, denn sie wollte immer nur etwas kaufen. Darauf brachte der Vermittler mich mit der Vierundzwanzigjährigen zusammen. Diese junge Dame war eigentlich sehr nett, aber sie wollte abends zu oft tanzen gehen, und sie war auch nicht gerade besonders intelligent. Die dritte aber war genau die Richtige, und sie ist jetzt meine Frau. Heute abend wirst du sie kennenlernen."

In about 150 words relate in indirect discourse what Heinrich told his wife after meeting his old friend Werner at the bus stop. Begin as follows and use either the subjunctive I or the subjunctive II, but avoid subjunctive I forms that are like the indicative:

Heinrich erzählte seiner Frau von dem unverhofften Wiedersehen an der Bushaltestelle. Er sei wie gewöhnlich im letzten Moment dort angekommen, und plötzlich habe er einen alten Schulkameraden gesehen. Er hätte Werner gleich wiedererkannt, denn . . .

32.2 Other Uses of Subjunctive I

First person imperative

The subjunctive I form may be used as an imperative in the 1st person plural (see the **wir**-imperative, Grammar §8.5):

Gehen wir zum Baden!
Let's go swimming!

Steigen wir ein!
Let's get on!

Fixed formulas

Gott sei Dank!
Thank goodness! (Thanks be to God!)

Lang lebe die Königin!
Long live the queen!

Grüß' Gott! (*from:* Grüße dich Gott!) *A common greeting in Southern Germany*
Hello! (May God greet you!)

32.3 The Indefinite Pronoun *man*

The English indefinite pronoun *one* is often replaced by the 3rd person singular masculine *he*:

When *one* has taken a trip, *he* has a lot to tell.

In German, however, the corresponding indefinite pronoun **man** is not interchangeable with **er**. If the subject of a clause is **man**, and the subject is repeated in following clauses, **man** must continue to be used:

Wenn **man** eine Reise gemacht hat, hat **man** viel zu erzählen.
When *one* has taken a trip, *he* has a lot to tell.

The accusative case form of **man** is **einen**, and the dative is **einem**. The genitive, **eines**, is rare.

Dieser Mann zwingt einen, sofort zu bezahlen.
This man forces *you* to pay immediately.

Man kann sagen, was man will, sie glaubt einem einfach nicht.
You can say whatever you want; she won't believe *you*.
Or: People can say whatever they want; she won't believe *them*.

Writing practice

Write the following sentences supplying the impersonal **man**, **einen**, or **einem** as may be required:

1. Muß _____ den Dialog auswendig lernen?
2. Warum will er _____ nie glauben?
3. Bei einer roten Verkehrsampel muß _____ stoppen.
4. Die Kur kann _____ wieder heilen.
5. In diesem verrauchten Zimmer kann _____ kaum atmen.
6. Er gibt _____ immer mehr, als _____ haben will.
7. Wenn _____ nicht genug zu Fuß geht, bekommt _____ einen Bauch.
8. So etwas gefällt _____ ja nicht!
9. Wenn _____ heiraten möchte und den richtigen Partner nicht finden kann, kann _____ zu einem Eheanbahnungsinstitut gehen.
10. _____ kann nicht immer sagen, was _____ denkt.
11. Wenn _____ alt wird, kann _____ meistens nicht mehr so gut laufen.
12. Was _____ sucht, wird _____ auch finden.
13. Was _____ nicht will, sollte _____ auch nicht tun.
14. Was _____ nicht im Kopfe hat, muß _____ in den Beinen haben.
15. Das viele Heulen kann _____ nervös machen.

2.4 Descriptive Adjectives after Expressions of Indefinite Quantity

Andere *other*, **einige** *a few*, **folgende** *the following*, **mehrere** *several*, **viele** *many*, and **wenige** *few* may stand at the beginning of a noun phrase. When they do, they have strong endings. They are descriptive adjectives, so another descriptive adjective following one of these will also have a strong ending:

Andere alte Bücher liegen dort hinten.
Other old books are lying back there.

Noch sind mehrere gute Plätze frei.
Several good seats are still free.

Wir haben viele alte Zeitschriften gelesen.
We read many old journals.

Wenige gute Hotels sind dort zu finden.
Few good hotels can be found there.

Sie ist die Tante einiger kleiner Kinder.
She is the aunt of a few small children.

Das hängt von folgenden wichtigen Tatsachen ab.
That depends on the following important facts.

Alle *all* and **beide** *both* are limiting adjectives, not descriptive adjectives. An adjective following one of these will have the weak ending, not the strong one:

Alle jungen Leute werden morgen kommen.
All young people will come tomorrow.

Kennen Sie alle großen Städte Europas?
Are you familiar with all the large cities of Europe?

Beide alten Freunde sind hier gewesen.
Both old friends were here.

Wir haben beiden kleinen Kindern ein Buch geschickt.
We sent a book to both little children.

Die Arbeit beider neuen Studenten gefällt mir.
The work of both new students pleases me.

Forms of **alle** may be used in the singular:

Fast aller alte Wein ist teuer.   Almost all old wine is expensive.

The uninflected form **all** is used when a **der**-word follows:

All die jungen Leute werden morgen kommen.   All diese alten Bücher sind zu verkaufen.
All the young people will come tomorrow.   All these old books are to be sold.

Writing practice

Copy and supply the missing endings:

1. Er hat noch ander____ schön____ Farbfotos vom Dom.
2. Die Preise mehrer____ groß____ Wagen sind viel zu hoch.
3. Wir kommen in einig____ wenig____ Minuten zurück.
4. Warum wollt ihr nicht all____ alt____ Eisen verkaufen?
5. Beid____ jung____ Freunde sind auch mitgekommen.
6. Viel____ jung____, intelligent____ Menschen sind gegen den Krieg.
7. Habt ihr beid____ klein____ Kindern ein____ Werkzeugkasten geschickt?
8. All____ jung____ Leute sollten dies____ interessant____ Buch lesen.
9. Er hat sein____ neuest____ Theorie mit folgend____ wichtig____ Statistiken nachgewiesen.
10. Wegen d____ schlecht____ Wetters sind nur wenig____ fleißig____ Studenten zur Vorlesung gekommen.

32.5 Word Order

Basic structure of the German sentence

German sentence structure was outlined in its essentials in Grammar §§2.1, 2.2, and 2.3 (the predicate); 3.2 and 3.3 (position of the finite verb); 6.4 (shifting elements to first position); 13.3 (infinitives); 15.3 (time adverbs); 15.7 (past participles); and 24.4 (double infinitives).

The typical German sentence consists of two parts, namely, a subject and a predicate:

Subject	Predicate
Hans	läuft.

Of these two parts the predicate is the more complex. It may consist of a single finite verb, as in **Hans läuft**, or it may be a phrase made up of two or more words:

	Subject	Predicate	
		I	II
1	Es	ist	heiß.
2	Eis	ist	kein Gift.
3	Heike	kommt	mit.
4	Rolf	geht	in die Stadt.
5	Ich	muß	arbeiten.
6	Er	hat	geschlafen.
7	Es	wurde	zerstört.
8	Ich	warte	auf die Vorlesung.
9	Sie	glaubt	an das Sprichwort.
10	Wir	bitten	um Hilfe.

In the examples above, the predicate consists of a single verb phrase. Part I of the verb phrase is reserved exclusively for the finite verb. Part II may be occupied by one or more associated elements. The examples above contain as associated elements (1) a predicate adjective; (2) a predicate noun; (3) a separable prefix; (4) an adverbial phrase of direction; (5) a dependent infinitive; (6) a past participle in a present perfect verb construction; (7) a past participle in a passive construction; and (8, 9, and 10) prepositional objects.

If part II is taken up by more than one associated element, then it in turn may be regarded as consisting of two subparts. The second of these is filled by a past participle or an infinitive, or both, while the first contains one of the other associated elements:

	Subject	Predicate		
		I	II	
			a	b
1	Es	ist	heiß	gewesen.
2	Eis	soll	Gift	sein.
3	Sie	will	mit-	kommen.
4	Er	ist	in die Stadt	gegangen.
5	Wir	mußten	auf den Zug	warten.

These sentences contain in position IIa (1) a predicate adjective; (2) a predicate noun; (3) a separable prefix; (4) an adverbial phrase of direction; and (5) a prepositional object. IIb is filled by an infinitive (2, 3, and 5) or a past participle (1 and 4).

A further degree of complexity arises when position IIb contains two elements:

	Subject	Predicate		
		I	IIa	IIb
1	Es	soll	heiß	gewesen sein.
2	Sie	müssen	auseinander-	gehalten werden.
3	Er	wird	auf den Zug	gewartet haben.
4	Wir	haben	aus-	steigen wollen.
5	Sie	sind	mit-	gebracht worden.

In sentences 1, 2, and 3, position IIb is filled by a past participle plus an infinitive, in that order. Sentence 4 has a double infinitive in this position, and in sentence 5 it is taken up by the two past participles of the perfect passive construction.

Predicate elements not in the verb phrase

All the sentences above contain a subject and a predicate. The predicate in each one contains only a verb or a verb phrase. The predicate may contain additional elements, however, that do not belong to the verb phrase. Such elements — objects, certain adverbs, and sentence negators such as **nicht** — go between part I and part II of the verb phrase:

	Subject	Verb phrase I		Verb phrase II
1	Hans	will	Eis	kaufen.
2	Wir	haben	Ihnen	helfen wollen.
3	Kurt	geht	heute	zum Baden.
4	Der Hut	ist	doch	unmöglich.
5	Das Schloß	wurde	durch Brand	zerstört.
6	Der Anzug	ist	nicht	der richtige.

In these sentences the predicate elements which do not belong to the verb phrase are (1) an accusative object; (2) a dative object; (3) an adverb of time; (4) an adverb expressing the speaker's attitude; (5) an adverbial phrase of manner; and (6) the negator **nicht**. If *two or more* such elements occur in the slot between parts I and II of the verb phrase, then their order relative to one another is subject to certain restrictions.

Order of adverbs and adverbial phrases

The normal sequence of adverbs is *time—manner—place*:

     Time   **Manner**   **Place**
Er ist gestern mit dem Zug nach München gefahren.

Order of objects

A sentence may contain both an accusative and a dative object. If the accusative object is a personal pronoun, then it precedes the dative object:

Wir geben **es** dem König.   Wir geben **es** ihm.

If the accusative object is not a personal pronoun, then it follows the dative object:

Wir schicken dem Jungen **ein Buch**.   Wir schicken ihm **etwas**.
Wir schicken ihm **ein Buch**.

Order of objects in relation to adverbs

Personal pronoun objects and reflexive pronouns precede adverbs; they come first in the slot between parts I and II of the verb phrase:

	Personal pronoun objects	Adverbs	
Mein Bruder hat	es	gestern	gekauft.
Mein Bruder hat	es mir	am 3. Juli	geschickt.
Mein Bruder hat	sich	auf deinen Besuch	gefreut.
Mein Bruder hat	ihnen	heute damit	geholfen.
Mein Bruder hat	es	doch auch	gewußt.

Objects that are not personal pronouns or reflexives generally follow adverbs:

	Personal pronouns	Adverbs	Non-personal pronoun objects	
Er hat	es ihm	gestern		gekauft.
Er hat	ihm	gestern	etwas	gekauft.
Er hat	ihm	gestern	ein Buch	gekauft.
Er hat		gestern	dem Jungen ein Buch	gekauft.

Variations in the order of objects and adverbs

The statements above describe only the *normal* sequence of adverbs, objects, or combinations thereof that occur between part I and part II of the verb phrase. These sequences may be altered in numerous ways, but always according to this principle: *the element that carries new information goes last, while elements with no new information go first.*

1. Er hat es dem Jungen **gestern** gegeben.
2. Sie hat das Buch **mir** geschickt.
3. Er ist nach München **mit dem Zug** gefahren.

In these sentences the sequence of objects and adverbs is *different* from those described above, yet each sentence is perfectly acceptable. The element that carries new information is (1) the time adverb **gestern**, which thus follows rather than precedes the object; (2) the indirect object **mir**, which thus follows rather than precedes the noun direct object; and (3) the adverbial phrase of manner **mit dem Zug**, which thus follows rather than precedes the adverb of place. The fact that **gestern**, **mir**, and **mit dem Zug** are indeed the carriers of new information in these sentences becomes clear if we regard each sentence as an answer to a particular question:

1 *answers the question* **Wann** hat er es dem Jungen gegeben?
2 *answers the question* **Wem** hat sie das Buch geschickt?
3 *answers the question* **Wie** ist er nach München gefahren?

Position of negatives

The word **nicht** may be used to negate a sentence. When it occurs in this function, it *immediately precedes part II of the verb phrase*. It will therefore precede (1) a predicate adjective, (2) a predicate nominative, (3) a separable prefix, (4) an adverb of place, (5) a dependent infinitive, (6 and 7) a past participle, or (8) a prepositional object:

1. Es ist **nicht** heiß.
2. Der Mann ist **nicht** mein Onkel.
3. Sie kommt **nicht** mit.
4. Er geht **nicht** in die Stadt.
5. Du sollst **nicht** arbeiten.
6. Er hat **nicht** geschlafen.
7. Es wurde **nicht** zerstört.
8. Ich warte **nicht** auf die Vorlesung.

The negator **nicht** will therefore *follow* an object (2 and 3) or an adverb of time (4 and 5); if there is no object or time adverb, it will follow the finite verb (1):

1. Er hat **nicht** gearbeitet.
2. Ich hatte meinen alten Freund **nicht** wiedererkannt.
3. Wir werden es ihnen **nicht** erzählen.
4. Du hast es ihm gestern **nicht** gegeben.
5. Er konnte mir letzte Woche **nicht** helfen.

Nicht may also serve to negate a single element within a sentence, rather than the entire sentence; it *precedes* the element that it negates:

Es wurde **nicht im 17. Jahrhundert** zerstört, sondern im 16.
It wasn't destroyed in the seventeenth century, but in the sixteenth.

Nicht Susi, sondern Hans hat Eis gekauft.
Not Susi, but Hans bought ice cream.

Er ist **nicht gestern** gekommen, sondern vorgestern.
He didn't come yesterday, but the day before yesterday.

The rules governing the position of **nicht** also apply to the negators **nie** *never*, **niemals** *never*, **noch nie** *never yet*, and **gar nicht** *not at all*:

Ich hatte meinen alten Freund **nie** wiedergesehen.
Wir werden es ihnen **niemals** erzählen.
Er hat **noch nie** gearbeitet.
Du hast es ihm gestern **gar nicht** gegeben.
Er hat **niemals** das Schloß, sondern immer nur den Dom gesehen.

The negatives **nichts, gar nichts, kein** *as direct objects*

The negative pronoun objects **nichts** *nothing* and **gar nichts** *nothing at all* follow the position patterns of noun objects, as do also the pronoun object forms of **kein** *none, not one, not any*:

Ich habe dem Mann **nichts** gesagt.
Sie hat mir **gar nichts** erzählt.
Er hatte viele Äpfel, aber er hat mir **keinen** davon gegeben.

Writing practice

Copy the sentences, putting the adverbs in the normal order:

1 Wir kommen (nach Hause / morgen).
2 Der Dom wurde (durch Brand / im 18. Jahrhundert) zerstört.
3 Sind Sie (nach Berlin / vor zwei Wochen / mit dem Bus) gefahren?
4 Peter wollte (in die Schweiz / nach seinem Examen) fahren.
5 Viele Menschen reisen (an die Ostsee / heutzutage).
6 Meinetwegen kannst du (ins Theater / jeden Abend) gehen.
7 Du bist (auf den Beinen / bald wieder).

Copy the sentences, putting the objects in the normal order:

8 Mein Bruder hat (einen neuen Schrank / seiner Frau) gekauft.
9 Der Professor schrieb (einen Brief / mir).
10 Kannst du (es / ihm) morgen schicken?
11 Erzähl (etwas / mir)!
12 Sie brauchen (gar nichts / ihnen) zu geben.

13 Ich wollte (etwas / dem kleinen Jungen) bringen.
14 Der Student hat (es / dem Professor) nachweisen müssen.

Copy the sentences, putting the objects and adverbs in normal order:

15 Er hatte (seine Prüfung / dann) bestanden.
16 Wir wollen (ihn / morgen gegen 3 Uhr) besuchen.
17 Kannst du (nachher / es / mir) geben?
18 Ich habe (in seinem Zimmer / ihn) getroffen.
19 Michael studierte (Medizin / damals).
20 Es ist (endlich / mir) gelungen.
21 Wir werden (das Schloß / heute) besichtigen.

Rewrite the sentences so that the words in boldface become the carriers of new information:

22 Wir werden **morgen** in die Stadt fahren.
23 Er hat **unserer Tochter** den Sportwagen gegeben.
24 Ich möchte **sofort** das Schloß besichtigen.
25 Wir haben **am Montag** den alten Leuten geholfen.
26 Er studiert **erst seit zwei Jahren** Philosophie.
27 Sie hat sich **vor zwei Wochen** den Hut gekauft.
28 Die Leute wollten **mir** das Paket schicken.

Change the affirmative sentences to negative sentences by inserting an appropriate negator:

29 Wir arbeiten heute abend.
30 Er hat ihn besucht.
31 Ich will es Ihnen erzählen.
32 Du hättest das tun sollen.
33 Das Institut ist heute geschlossen.
34 Wir können die Miete des Vormonats bezahlen.
35 Er kann die zwei Probleme auseinanderhalten.
36 Die Schüler sind zu ihrem Lehrer gegangen.
37 Sie ist an die Nordsee gereist.
38 Nur dieses alte Schloß war damals zerstört worden.
39 Herr Hartmann ist heute zu Hause.
40 Er überlegt es sich.
41 Ich schrieb ihre Telefonnummer auf.

VOCABULARY

A. Word-Formation

The suffix *-heit*

The suffix **-heit** forms abstract feminine nouns, chiefly from adjectives, but sometimes from other nouns or from verbal elements. Some known examples are: **schön** *beautiful*, **die Schönheit** *beauty*; **krank** *ill*, **die Krankheit** *illness*. Below are some new ones formed from words you know:

blind	blind	die Blindheit	blindness
dunkel	dark	die Dunkelheit	darkness
falsch	false	die Falschheit	falseness; treachery
fein	fine	die Feinheit	fineness; delicateness
frei	free	die Freiheit	freedom
fremd	foreign, strange	die Fremdheit	foreignness, strangeness
gewiß	certain	die Gewißheit	certainty
gleich	equal	die Gleichheit	equality
das Kind	child	die Kindheit	childhood
klar	clear	die Klarheit	clarity
mehr	more	die Mehrheit	majority
der Mensch	human being	die Menschheit	humanity
schlau	cunning	die Schlauheit	cunning
sicher	certain; secure	die Sicherheit	certainty; security
wahr	true	die Wahrheit	truth
wild	wild	die Wildheit	wildness; fury

The suffix *-keit*

The suffix **-keit** forms abstract feminine nouns, chiefly from adjectives in **-ig** and **-lich**. The expanded suffix **-igkeit** is added to adjectives that do not have a suffix. Some known examples are: **öffentlich** *public*, **die Öffentlichkeit** *public*; **schwierig** *difficult*, **die Schwierigkeit** *difficulty*. Below are some new ones formed from adjectives that you know:

ähnlich	similar, like	die Ähnlichkeit	similarity, likeness
ängstlich	anxious	die Ängstlichkeit	anxiety
feierlich	festive	die Feierlichkeit	festivity
festlich	festive	die Festlichkeit	festivity
fleißig	industrious	die Fleißigkeit	industriousness
genau	exact	die Genauigkeit	exactness, precision
häufig	frequent	die Häufigkeit	frequency
neu	new	die Neuigkeit	something new; piece of news
süß	sweet	die Süßigkeit	sweetness

tüchtig able; efficient	die Tüchtigkeit ability; excellence
unendlich infinite	die Unendlichkeit infinity
unwichtig unimportant	die Unwichtigkeit unimportance

The suffix -*schaft*

The suffix **-schaft** forms feminine nouns from adjectives, verbal elements, and singular or plural nouns to denote an activity, a relationship, or a collective idea. Some known examples are: **der Wirt** *innkeeper*, **die Wirtschaft** *inn; household; economy;* **das Land** *land*, **die Landschaft** *landscape;* **wissen** *know*, **die Wissenschaft** *scientific study;* **der Freund** *friend*, **die Freundschaft** *friendship*. Below are some new ones related to words you know:

der Arbeiter worker	die Arbeiterschaft working class
der Arzt physician	die Ärzteschaft medical society
bekannt acquainted	die Bekanntschaft acquaintanceship
der Bote messenger	die Botschaft message; embassy
der Bruder brother	die Brüderschaft brotherhood; fellowship
der Feind enemy	die Feindschaft hostility
gemein common	die Gemeinschaft community
der Herr master	die Herrschaft mastery; government; *pl.* master and mistress
der Kamerad comrade	die Kameradschaft comradeship, fellowship
der Kunde customer	die Kundschaft clientele
der Mann man	die Mannschaft team; crew
der Ort place	die Ortschaft town, village
der Student student	die Studentenschaft fraternity; student body

Other feminine suffixes

You have learned previously that nouns ending in **-in**, **-ung**, and many nouns ending in **-e** (those derived from adjectives and denoting a state or condition, such as **die Fläche** from **flach**) are feminines in Class IV [**-(e)n** ending for plural]. Also, the above nouns in **-heit**, **-keit**, and **-schaft** belong in this class of feminines. In addition, nouns ending in **-ei (die Polizei)**, **-ie (die Geographie)**, **-ion (die Tradition)**, **-kunft (die Zukunft)**, and **-tät (die Universität)** are all feminines in Class IV.

B. Inference

With the help of the clues provided guess the meanings of the words in boldface:

1 Mutti, es hat **jemand** für dich angerufen, aber ich weiß nicht, wer es war.
2 Obwohl alle die Geschichte schon kannten, hat er sie **abermals** erzählt.

3 A. Kennen Sie ein anderes Wort für: sehr stark?
  B. Wie ist es mit **heftig**?
4 Er fuhr viel zu schnell. Das war der **Grund** für den schweren Unfall. **der Grund, ⸚e**
5 Meine Eltern haben silberne **Hochzeit** gefeiert. **die Hochzeit, -en**
6 Tante Inge ist gestern unverhofft zu Besuch gekommen. Wir waren alle **überrascht**. **überraschen**
7 Bevor ich nach Deutschland fliege, muß ich noch einige **Dollars** in Mark **umwechseln**. **der Dollar, -s**
8 A. Wann hast du das schöne Buch gekauft?
  B. Es gehört mir nicht, ich habe es nur **geliehen**. **leihen: er leiht, lieh, hat geliehen**
9 Ein Quadrat hat vier Ecken, aber ein **Kreis** hat keine Ecken, er ist rund. **der Kreis, -e** · Das Flugzeug kreiste dreimal über der Stadt. **kreisen**
10 Die Mutter kocht das Essen in der **Küche**, aber wir essen natürlich im Eßzimmer. **die Küche, -n**
11 Er kann gut singen. Er hat eine warme, tiefe **Stimme**. **die Stimme, -n**
12 Wenn es einen netten Film gibt, gehe ich gern mal ins **Kino**. **das Kino, -s**
13 Sie ist eine arme, unglückliche Frau. Man muß sie **bedauern**. Das war ein **bedauernswertes** Unglück.
14 Jede Uhr hat wenigstens zwei **Zeiger**. Sie zeigen zusammen die genaue Zeit an. **der Zeiger, -**
15 A. Heike, bist du nun bald fertig?
  B. Ja, ich bin sofort **bereit**.
16 A. Essen Sie gerne Kuchen?
  B. Ja, aber ich kann frischen Kuchen nicht gut **vertragen**. Das letzte Mal war ich davon fast krank.
17 A. Kennst du ein anderes Verb für: aufhören?
  B. Ja: **einhalten**.
18 Man sagt „**Verzeihung**", wenn man sich entschuldigen will.
19 Er aß ein ausgezeichnetes Mittagessen und trank noch eine Flasche Wein **obendrein**.
20 Der Unfall sah zuerst scheußlich aus, nachher **jedoch** war es gar nicht so schlimm.
21 Es bildete sich sogleich eine **Gruppe** von Menschen um den Unfallplatz herum. **die Gruppe, -n**
22 Susi ist hingefallen, weil Hans sie **gestoßen** hat. **stoßen: er stößt, stieß, hat gestoßen**
23 Er hat alles gehört, was wir uns erzählt haben, denn er hat hinter der Tür gestanden und **gehorcht**. **horchen**
24 **Fühlst** du nicht, wie kalt es plötzlich geworden ist? · Sie ist heute nicht gekommen, sie **fühlt sich** nicht wohl. **fühlen**
25 Auf diesen rutschigen Straßen muß man vorsichtig und **langsam** fahren.
26 Kleine Kinder, die noch nicht gehen können, **kriechen** von einer Stelle zur anderen. **kriechen: er kriecht, kroch, ist gekrochen**
27 A. Was hast du in der Stadt gemacht?
  B. Ich bin nur herumgegangen und hab' **umher**geschaut.
28 Eben hat die Sonne noch geschienen, jetzt sieht es **auf einmal** nach Regen aus.

29 Er sagt nie die Wahrheit, er **lügt** immer.   **lügen: er lügt, log, hat gelogen**
30 Susi, die Kiste ist zu schwer für dich. Du kannst sie bestimmt nicht **heben**.   **heben: er hebt, hob, hat gehoben**
31 Ohne **Dach** würde der Regen direkt ins Haus fallen.   **das Dach, ⸚er**
32 Wer nicht gerade schläft, ist **wach**.
33 Er ist der Sohn meines Onkels, also ist er mein **Vetter**.   **der Vetter, -n**
34 A.   Kannst du deine alte Wunde noch fühlen?
   B.   Nein, ich **merke** sie kaum noch.   **merken**
35 Die Decke dieses Zimmers ist so **niedrig**, man kann sie mit der Hand erreichen.

Unit 33

READING

Vom Geist unserer Zeit: Rekorde*g*, Rekorde!

Unsere Zeit ist die Zeit der Rekorde: die schnellsten Autos, die höchsten Häuser, die schönsten Beine, die größten Bomben*g* ... Der Rekord gehört so sehr zu unserem Leben, daß man eigentlich nicht mehr genau weiß, ob nicht vielleicht unser Leben zum Rekord gehört. Ein konstruiertes*g* Wortspiel*g*?

Seit einiger Zeit schon weiß man es genau: Rauchen ist stark gesundheitsschädlich. Man sollte nun meinen, daß die Menschen jetzt also weniger rauchen als früher, etwas weniger jedenfalls, denn im allgemeinen liebt man heute ja sein bißchen Leben sehr. Aber im Gegenteil, die Raucher pfeifen auf das neue Wissen und rauchen sogar noch mehr als früher! Ein neuer Rekord!

In Deutschland hat man den alten Rekord sogar um gut 5% verbessern können. Die Experten*g* sind darüber zuerst aus allen Wolken gefallen, sie wollten es nicht glauben. Aber die Statistiker wissen noch mehr. In den ersten drei Monaten des neuen Jahres haben die deutschen Raucher dabei mehr als zwei Milliarden Mark „verraucht", zu „blauer Luft" gemacht. Das schöne Geld, was hätte sich damit alles tun lassen!

Die Zigarette ist des deutschen Rauchers liebstes Kind (86%). Nur 10% rauchten Zigarren. Die anderen steckten ihren Tabak in die Pfeife oder kauten ihn.

Nun kann und soll natürlich jeder machen, was er will. Wenigstens beim Rauchen. Es schmeckt eben einfach so gut, daß man jeden Preis bezahlen will. Warum nicht? Hier soll es auch nicht etwa Vorwürfe geben. Wir sprachen nur gerade von neuen Rekorden und davon, daß der

der Geist, -er spirit · **der Rekord,** -e [Reˈkɔrt]

die Bombe, -n [ˈbɔmbə] · **gehören zu** be part of **gehören** + *dat.* belong to

gesundheitsschädlich injurious to health
die Gesundheit health **der Schaden,** ⸚ damage, injury
im allgemeinen in general
pfeifen: er pfeift, pfiff, hat gepfiffen whistle **pfeifen auf** + *acc.* snap one's fingers at, not care about
um gut 5% by a good five percent
der Experte, -n, -n [ɛksˈpɛrtə]
die Wolke, -n cloud **aus allen Wolken fallen** be dumbfounded
die Luft air
kauen chew

etwa about, perhaps
der Vorwurf, ⸚e reproach

1 Was gehört zum Geist unserer Zeit?
2 Was wissen wir jetzt genau?
3 Was sollte man nun meinen?
4 Bedeutet das neue Wissen viel für die Raucher?
5 Wieviel haben die deutschen Raucher in drei Monaten zu „blauer Luft" gemacht?
6 Was rauchen die deutschen Raucher am liebsten?
7 Warum soll es hier keine Vorwürfe geben?

Rekord vielleicht uns hat, und nicht wir ihn. Man könnte zu diesem Thema ebensogut auch andere Geschichten erzählen, vielleicht noch eindringlichere. Aber dieses Beispiel ist auch klassisch[g]. Fast jeder weiß (oder glaubt doch zu wissen), was ,,richtig'' ist. Aber er tut es nicht. Er ,,wird getan'', und so gibt es plötzlich einen neuen Rekord des ,,Falschen''. Man braucht schon recht viel Galgenhumor, um das unwichtig zu finden, denn ganz sicher gibt es heute eine ganze Menge ,,Rekorde der Unvernunft'', viel zu viele.

Fortschritt oder der Weg nach oben

Die Meinungsforscher haben etwas Neues herausgefunden. Sie fragten die Leute einmal wieder, wieviel Geld eine Familie von vier Personen heute in der Bundesrepublik unbedingt zum Leben braucht. Hier ist das Ergebnis: 650,— Mark im Monat.

Nun, die Zahl allein sagt noch nicht viel. Sehen wir uns also einmal an, woher der Durchschnitt von 650,— Mark eigentlich kommt, und was die Leute in früheren Jahren dazu gesagt haben.

Zunächst gibt es erhebliche Unterschiede der Meinungen in den einzelnen Bundesländern. Die Bayern z.B. fanden im Durchschnitt 600,— Mark pro Monat genug, in Nordrhein-Westfalen aber meinte man, auch 700,— Mark monatlich sei für eine Familie von vier Personen noch nicht ausreichend. Zwischen den Meinungen der Städter und den Meinungen der Bauern gab es einen noch größeren Unterschied, nämlich 160,— Mark. Der größte Unterschied scheint

eindringlich urgent, forceful
der Galgenhumor grim humor   **der Galgen**, - gallows   **der Humor** [huˈmoːʀ]
die Unvernunft unreasonableness, folly, absurdity   **die Vernunft** reason, intelligence

8 Was glaubt jeder zu wissen?
9 Tut er es auch?
10 Wozu braucht man viel Galgenhumor?

---

der Fortschritt, -e progress   **fort** away, ahead   **der Schritt**, -e step, stride · **der Weg**, -e way, path, road · **nach oben** upward, to the top   **oben** up, above
das Ergebnis, -se result
die Zahl, -en number, figure
zunächst zuerst, hauptsächlich · **erheblich** groß, wichtig
der Bayer, -n, -n ein Mensch, der aus Bayern kommt oder dort wohnt · **z.B.** *abbr. for* **zum Beispiel** for example   **das Beispiel**, -e example
ausreichend genug, genügend

11 Was wollten die Meinungsforscher wissen?
12 Bedeutet die Durchschnittszahl allein sehr viel?
13 Warum soll man sich die Sache etwas näher ansehen?
14 Wieviel genügte den Bayern?
15 Was meinte man in Nordrhein-Westfalen?
16 Haben auch die Städter und die Bauern verschiedene Meinungen?

aber zwischen den Meinungen der jüngeren und der älteren Leute zu bestehen. Die Jüngeren waren davon überzeugt, eine Familie von vier Personen brauche 200,— Mark im Monat mehr, als der Durchschnitt der Älteren gemeint habe. Interessant, nicht wahr?

Aber es kommt noch besser. Vor einigen Jahren hatte man nämlich eine deutlich andere Meinung zu derselben Frage. 1951 hatte man noch gemeint, 325,— Mark im Monat seien eigentlich genug für vier Personen. 1958 waren es schon 465,— Mark geworden, und 1963 hatten die Leute immerhin noch 550,— Mark als Mindestbetrag genannt.

Das Leben ist in den letzten Jahren in Deutschland also erheblich teurer geworden. Die Frage ist nur, ob die Preise so sehr viel höher geworden sind, oder ob die Leute heute so viel höhere Ansprüche stellen. Oder gehören beide Tatsachen vielleicht zusammen? Jedenfalls geht auch in Deutschland heute alles tüchtig nach oben! Ist das der Fortschritt?

Die Interpretationen[g] der Tatsachen sind natürlich ganz und gar verschieden. Konservative[g] Kreise um die Rechtsparteien CDU (Christlich Demokratische Union) und FDP (Freie Demokratische Partei) schimpfen auf die Arbeiter und Angestellten, die immer noch mehr Geld haben wollen. Die viel zu hohen Ansprüche seien, so sagen sie, der wahre Grund dafür, daß alles immer teurer würde in Deutschland. Die mögliche, ja wahrscheinliche Folge sei eine gefährliche Wirtschaftskrise[g]. Die Kreise um die Linkspartei SPD (Sozialdemokratische Partei Deutschlands), hauptsächlich Arbeiter und Angestellte, sagen dagegen, sie bekämen immer erst nachher etwas mehr Geld, wenn die Preise schon höher seien; und auch dann noch lange nicht genug, um die (inzwischen) schon höheren Preise einfangen zu können.

Keine dieser beiden extremen Formulierungen[g] ist für sich allein korrekt[g]. So einfach sind die Dinge nun einmal nicht. Die Wahrheit wird irgendwo ziemlich in der Mitte zwischen den beiden Formulierungen liegen. Aber das macht die Gesamtsituation natürlich nicht weniger gefährlich. Inzwischen dauert die ebenso flotte wie gefährliche Entwicklung an: das Leben in Deutschland wird laufend teurer.

Wer allerdings amerikanische Dollars hat, der kann in Deutschland immer noch verhältnismäßig billig leben. Eine amerikanische Hausfrau kann nämlich für einen Dollar durchschnittlich ungefähr so viel kaufen, wie eine deutsche Hausfrau für 2,50 Mark kaufen kann. Für die Durchschnittsfamilie ist 1 Dollar also praktisch etwa 2,50 Mark wert. Wenn man aber einen amerikanischen Dollar offiziell in deutsche Mark umwechselt, bei einer Bank z.B., so bekommt man fast 4,— Mark für jeden Dollar. Leichter kann man sein Geld kaum verdienen.— Nun, wohin werden Sie im nächsten Sommer verreisen?

überzeugt sein sicher sein

deutlich klar, sicher zu erkennen
der Mindestbetrag, ⸚e minimal sum   mindest- wenigst-   der Betrag, ⸚e amount, sum
Ansprüche stellen make demands   der Anspruch, ⸚e demand, claim
die Interpretation, -en [ɪntɛʀpʀetatsiˈoːn] · konservativ [kɔnzɛʀvaˈtiːf]
demokratisch [demdˈkrɑːtɪʃ] · die Union, -en [uniˈoːn]

schimpfen auf + acc. scold · der Angestellte, -n adj. noun employee   anstellen employ
ja here indeed · die Folge, -n result, consequence
gefährlich dangerous · die Krise, -n
dagegen here on the other hand, however, on the contrary
einfangen catch, capture
extrem [ɛksˈtʀeːm] · die Formulierung, -en [fɔʀmuˈliːʀʊŋ] · für sich by itself · korrekt [kɔˈʀɛkt]
die Mitte, -n middle
gesamt whole
andauern continue, go on
verhältnismäßig relativ, ziemlich   das Verhältnis, -se relation, situation, condition
wert sein be worth
verreisen reisen, eine Reise machen

17 Wo scheint der größte Meinungsunterschied zu bestehen?
18 Hatte man zu derselben Frage schon immer dieselbe Meinung?
19 Sind die Preise in den letzten Jahren höher geworden?
20 Was ist aber auch höher geworden?
21 Wie heißen die zwei konservativen Parteien in Deutschland?
22 Wie erklären sie die hohen Preise?
23 Zu welchen Kreisen gehören hauptsächlich Arbeiter und Angestellte?
24 Wie erklären sie die hohen Ansprüche?
25 Welche von diesen beiden Erklärungen ist richtig?
26 Wer kann in Deutschland ziemlich billig leben?
27 Was ist 1 Dollar für die Durchschnittsfamilie praktisch etwa wert?
28 Was bekommt man, wenn man einen amerikanischen Dollar in deutsche Mark umwechselt?

PHONOLOGY

A. The Sounds for r and l

Read the following aloud at normal reading speed, concentrating on perfect sounds for r and l:

Jah r, k leine r, Angeste ll te r, du r ch, wa r m, Augenb lick, **R** est, **B** r ot, mo r gens, üb r ig, g l ück l ich, ein ä l te r e r He rr, Ähn l ichkeit, entschu l digen Sie, vie l meh r, F r au, F r emde, a ll e r dings, eigent l ich, b r auchen, B r ill e, r ichtig, **R** eko r de, schne ll sten, konst r uie r tes, so ll te, **R** auche r, f r ühe r, Gegentei l, aus a ll en Wo l ken fa ll en, zue r st, g l auben, ve rr aucht, b l aue r, L uft, d r ei Mi l ia r den Ma r k, vie l, Ge l d, a ll es, l assen, l iebsten, natü r l ich, wi ll, Vo r wü r fe, wa r um, vie ll eicht, e r zäh l en, eind r ing l iche r e, Beispie l, r ichtig, Ga l genhumor, vie l zu vie l e, Fo r sche r, Fami l ie, a l so, eigent l ich, Unte r schied, e r heb l ich, monat l ich, aus r eichend, g r öße r en, ä l te r en, inte r essant, besse r, Jah r en, näm l ich, gewo r den, F r age, P r eise, nu r, jedenfa ll s, Fo r tsch r itt, Inte r p r etation, **R** echts- pa r tei, meh r Ge l d, wo ll en, Sozia l demok r atische Pa r tei Deutsch l ands, ext r em, Fo r- mu l ie r ung, Wah r heit, ziem l ich, wenige r, gefäh r lich, f l otte Entwick l ung, L eben, l aufend, teu r e r, ve r hä l tnismäßig, bi ll ig, offizie ll, l eichte r, ve rr eisen

B. Consonants and Consonant Clusters

Read the following aloud at normal reading speed, concentrating especially on the consonants and consonant clusters in boldface:

Ho **chz** eit, **St** adtpa **rk**, ma **nch** mal, glückli **chst** en, du **rch**, en **tsch** uldigen, em **pf** in dl ich, hö **chst** en, kon **str** uiertes, Wo **rtsp** iel, gesundhei **tssch** ädlich, **Z** eit, bi **ßch** en, **pf** eifen, Deu **tschl** and, zue **rst**, **zw** ei, **Z** igarette, **st** eckt, lie **bst** es, **schm** e **ckt**, weni **gst** ens, viel- lei **cht**, ni **cht**, plö **tzl** ich, fa **lsch**, Unvernu **nft**, Fo **rtschr** itt, Du **rchschn** itt, zunä **chst**, **zw** ischen, übe **rz** eugt, Minde **stb** etrag, An **spr** üche, Re **chtsp** artei, Wi **rtsch** a **ftskr** ise, Li **nksp** artei, i **nzw** ischen, verhä **ltn** ismäßig, Hau **sfr** au, du **rchschn** i **ttl** ich, Du **rch**- **schn** i **ttsf** amilie, umwe **chs** elt, pra **kt** isch, nä **chs** ten

C. Vowel Quality and Quantity

Read the following aloud at normal reading speed, concentrating on perfect quality and quantity of the stressed and unstressed vowels in boldface:

M **a** nn, H **o** chzeit, v **o** m, Gesch **ä** ft, F **u** ß, St **a** dt, h **o** lt, Br **o** tes, T **a** sche, m **o** rgens, h **a** t, **e** s, z **u**, M **i** nuten, H **a** nd, j **e** mand, B **a** nk, **Ä** hnlichkeit, entsch **u** ldigen, v **ie** lmehr, f **a** st, d **o** ch, D **a** nk, d **e** nn, Br **i** lle, **i** st, d **e** r, d **ie**, Aut **o**, gr **ö** ßten, L **e** ben, m **a** n, eigentl **i** ch, k **o** nstr **u** iertes, schon, gesundheitsschädlich, daß, weniger, früher, etwas, Wissen, hat, alten, zuerst, wollten, aber, Monat, als, Mark, gemacht, schöne, lassen, Zigarette, Kind, natürlich, wenigstens, etwa, Vorwürfe, davon, das, uns, und, ebensogut, tut, getan, gibt, plötzlich, Galgenhumor, falsch, ganz, sicher, Unvernunft, Fortschritt, weg, oben, Forscher, etwas, wieviel, Personen, Bundesrepublik, unbedingt, zu, zum, Ergebnis, nun, noch, sehen, also, an, woher, Durchschnitt, erheblich, in, genug, zwischen, Städter, gab, nämlich, interessant, wahr, aber, Frage, waren, Betrag, genannt, Ansprüche, zusammen, alles, noch, Tatsache, natürlich, ganz, gar, Angestellten, noch, mehr, Grund, Folge, Wirtschaftskrise, erst, dann, einfangen, können, irgendwo, ziemlich, Mitte, liegen, ebenso, an, hat, kann, amerikanisch, ungefähr, praktisch, für, wert, offiziell, wohin, nächsten, Sommer

Copy the following, indicating with the symbol ‾ the long, close vowels in boldface and with the symbol ˘ the short open ones. Examples: schōn, ŭnsere, mēhr, ĭm.

braver, vorigen, nur, Wetter, Ende, durch, manchmal, gibt, Rest, er, abends, immer, übrig, wissen, saß, kam, Herr, sehr, gut, kenne, Gott, sagte, schönsten, gehören, ob, zum, sollte, nun, aber, bißchen, Leben, jedenfalls, denn, im, man, ja, nicht, haben, hat, als, tun, lassen, was, Zigarre, eben, jeden, bezahlen, sprachen, gerade, andere, fast, doch, richtig, viel, getan, finden, ganz, sicher, oder, nach, oben, Geld, unbedingt, Monat, Zahl, sagt, früheren, noch, von, Person, Familie, vor, derselbe, geworden, immerhin, Mindestbetrag, ist, erheblich, stellen, verschieden, konservativ, christlich, demokratisch, Union, Geld, wollen, möglich, bekämen, nachher, etwas, schon, lange, genug, um, nun, macht, leben, in, wer, allerdings, verhältnismäßig, durchschnittlich, kann, umwechselt, Bank

---

VOCABULARY

A. Singular and Plural of Nouns

der Angestellte, -n *adj. noun*
der Anspruch, ⸚e
der Bayer, -n, -n
das Beispiel, -e
der Betrag, ⸚e
die Bombe, -n
das Ergebnis, -se
der Experte, -n, -n
die Folge, -n
die Formulierung, -en

der Fortschritt, -e
der Galgen, -
der Geist, -er
die Interpretation, -en
die Krise, -n
der Mindestbetrag, ⸚e
die Mitte, -n
der Rekord, -e
der Schaden, ⸚
der Schritt, -e

die Union, -en
das Verhältnis, -se
der Vorwurf, ⸚e
der Weg, -e

die Wolke, -n
das Wortspiel, -e
die Zahl, -en

B. Inference

With the help of the clues provided, guess the meanings of the words in boldface:

1. Junge Mädchen sind oft **schüchtern**, manchmal sogar **scheu**.
2. Fast alle kleinen Kinder sind **niedlich**. Am **niedlichsten** sind sie, wenn sie schlafen.
3. Im Volkswagen ist der Motor hinten, nicht **vorn**.
4. Sogar Katzen und **Hunde** schließen manchmal miteinander Freundschaft.   **der Hund, -e**
5. Hunde haben manchmal **Flöhe**. Sie sitzen gern in langem **Haar** und beißen, wenn sie hungrig sind.   **der Floh, ⸚e · das Haar, -e**
6. Das Geld für das gebrauchte Auto hat **sich** nicht **rentiert**. Das Auto ist schon ganz kaputt. **sich rentieren**
7. Menschen essen mit dem **Mund**, Hunde **fressen** mit dem **Maul**.   **der Mund, ⸚er · das Maul, ⸚er · fressen: er frißt, fraß, hat gefressen**
8. Nach zwei Tagen **flaute** der starke Wind **ab**. Endlich **rollte** das Schiff nicht mehr.   **abflauen · rollen**
9. Er lacht fast immer, er hat ein sonniges **Gemüt**. Ich habe ihn noch nie **schwermütig** gesehen.   **das Gemüt → gemütlich**
10. Der kleine Motor **surrte** so leise, daß er kaum zu hören war.   **surren**
11. Zuerst gingen wir ins Kino und **hinterher** noch in ein nettes Kaffeehaus.
12. Nach den schönen Ferien im Schwarzwald hatte sie wieder frische, rote **Backen**.   **die Backe, -n**
13. Hans hatte sich seinen Kopf am Schrank gestoßen. Bald darauf **schwoll** die Stelle **an**.   **schwellen: er schwillt, schwoll, ist geschwollen**
14. Die Kinder **verbrennen** altes Papier im Garten. Das **Feuer** kann gefährlich werden.   **brennen: er brennt, brannte, hat gebrannt · das Feuer, -**
15. Wie kam es denn zu dem Unfall? Erzählen Sie mal den ganzen **Vorgang**.   **der Vorgang, ⸚e**
16. Der **Vorfall** passierte am Mittwoch um 10.30 Uhr.   **der Vorfall, ⸚e**
17. Die Reise nach Zentralafrika war ein echtes **Abenteuer**.   **das Abenteuer, -**
18. Es ist so heiß, und die Luft ist so schlecht hier, man kann kaum atmen, man **erstickt** fast.   **ersticken**
19. Sie schluchzte so stark, daß die **Tränen** nur so über ihr Gesicht rollten.   **die Träne, -n**
20. Er sagte kein Wort, er blieb **stumm** wie ein Fisch.
21. Trotz des Unglücks war die Frau ruhig und **gefaßt**.
22. Berlin ist von Hamburg ungefähr 300 km **entfernt**.
23. Die Sonne **strahlte** hell vom Himmel.   **strahlen**

24 In eine **Mausefalle** können **Mäuse** hineingehen, aber nicht wieder heraus!   **die Maus, ⸚e ·
 die Falle, -n**
25 Meine Schuhe sind mir zu eng. Besonders der rechte **drückt** meinen Fuß.   **drücken**
26 Der rücksichtslose Autofahrer bekam eine hohe **Geldstrafe.**   **die Strafe, -n**
27 Sie **wischte** sich die Tränen mit einem Taschentuch **ab.**   **abwischen**
28 A. Die Lampe funktioniert nicht mehr, Werner!
 B. Oh, wahrscheinlich ist nur die **Birne** kaputt.   **die Birne, -n**
29 Essen Sie lieber Äpfel oder **Birnen**?   **die Birne, -n**
30 A. Weißt du, wieviel **Briefmarken** ein Luftpostbrief in die Schweiz braucht?
 B. Wie schwer ist er denn?   **die Briefmarke, -n**
31 A, B, C sind die ersten drei **Buchstaben** des Alphabets [alfaˈbeːts].   **der Buchstabe, -n, -n**

C. Some Sets of Adverbs, Adjectives, and Prepositions

Many adverbs, adjectives, and prepositions with similar meanings have forms that are obviously related to each other. Some of the more common ones are listed below:

Adverb				*Adjective*	*Preposition*
Wo?	*Wohin?*	*Woher?*	*Verb prefix*		
unten	nach unten	von unten	unter-	unter-	unter
oben	nach oben	von oben	über-	ober-	über
vorn	nach vorn	von vorn	vor-	vorder-	vor
hinten	nach hinten	von hinten	hinter-	hinter-	hinter
innen	nach innen	von innen	ein-	inner-	in
außen	nach außen	von außen	aus-	äußer-	aus

Adverb: **Wo?**   Die Kinder sind **hinten** im Garten.
   The children are *in back* in the yard.

   Wohin?   Gehst du **nach oben**?
   Are you going *upstairs*?

   Woher?   Der Streifenwagen ist **von hinten** gekommen.
   The patrol car came *from behind*.

   Prefix   Ich ziehe mir die Schuhe **aus.**
   I'm taking my shoes *off*.

Adjective   Die **vorderen** Zimmer sind sonniger als die **hinteren.**
   The *front* rooms are sunnier than the *back* ones.

Preposition: Die Kinder spielen **hinter** dem Haus **in** der Sandkiste.
                          The children are playing *behind* the house *in* the sandbox.

The adverbs of location (**wo?**) are often combined with **da** or **dar-**; the latter, in turn, may be contracted to **dr-**: **da unten, drunten, da oben, droben, da vorn, da hinten, da innen, drinnen, da außen, draußen.**

Also related to **innen** and **außen** are the adverbs of destination **hinein, herein, hinaus,** and **heraus. Hinein** and **hinaus** imply that the direction of movement is away from the speaker; **herein** and **heraus** imply motion toward the speaker.

Some of these forms may occur as the first element in compound nouns: **die Oberschule** *secondary school,* **das Unterhemd** *undershirt,* **der Vorgarten** *front yard,* **die Hintertür** *back door,* **die Einführung** *introduction,* **die Ausnahme** *exception.*

WRITING

A. Dehydrated Sentences

Write complete sentences, using the tense suggested. The nominative singular masculine **der** is used to indicate that a form of the definite article is desired. The English expressions in boldface deserve special attention because most of them require unexpected idiomatic equivalents in German. Some rearrangement of word order will be necessary:

1   glauben / Sie / **in** / alle / neu / Theorie / der / Professor?   (*pres.*)
2   unser / Tante / ankommen / **not until** / **at** / Mitternacht   (*fut.*)
3   der / Schule / beginnen / wieder / **on** the / erst / Montag / **in** / Januar   (*pres.*)
4   unser / **oldest** / Bruder / sein / lange / **abroad** // **but** / wir / denken / oft / **of him**   (*first clause past, second clause pres. perf.*)
5   **since** / **when** / haben / dein / Vater / ein / Sportwagen?   (*pres.*)
6   der / Rekord (*pl.*) / gehören / **to the** / Geist / unser / Zeit   (*pres.*)
7   **although** / Rauchen / gesundheitsschädlich / sein // pfeifen / viel / Menschen (*pl.*) / auf / dieser / Tatsache   (*both clauses pres.*)
8   der / Experte (*pl.*) / fallen / darüber / aus / alle Wolke (*pl.*)   (*pres. perf.*)
9   nun / vier / Prozent / stecken / ihr / Tabak / in / der / Pfeife / **or** / kauen / er   (*both verbs past*)
10   stehen / der / Kirche / **on this side of** / oder / **on that side of** / dieser / Fluß?   (*pres.*)
11   der / beide / klein / Dorf (*pl.*) / liegen / **above** / dieser / Wald (*pl.*)   (*pres.*)
12   wir / arbeiten / der / ganz / Tag // **without** / etwas / essen   (*pres. perf.*)
13   er / arbeiten / gern // er / spielen / **rather** / aber / er / essen / **best of all**   (*all clauses past*)
14   wissen / ihr // daß / Susi / sein / schon / **as** / groß / **as** / Hans?   (*first clause pres. perf., second clause pres.*)

15. sein / Galgenhumor / gefallen / sein / Frau / nie (*pres. perf.*)
16. Susi / entgegenlaufen / ihr / Vater / **at noon** / immer (*pres. perf.*)
17. der / Tisch / stehen / zwischen / der / Lampe / und / der / Stuhl (*fut.*)
18. es / gelingen / er // der / Schrank / zusammenbauen / allein (*past*)
19. mein / Eltern / fliegen / trotz / der / schlecht / Wetter / **to Switzerland** (*pres. perf.*)
20. **when** / ich / studieren // ich / wohnen / **at the house of** / mein / Onkel (*both clauses past*)
21. der / Mantel // der / liegen / hier // gehören / der / jung / Student (*both clauses past*)
22. Onkel Richard / fahren / morgen / **with** / mein / Tante / zu / **them** (*fut.*)
23. bei / dies / tief / Schnee / der / Autofahren / sein / gefährlich (*pres.*)
24. **on** / Freitag / er / sein / gewöhnlich / schon / um vier / **at home** (*past*)
25. der / alt / Herr / **would like** / einige / gut / Flasche / rot / Wein
26. mein / klein / alt / Volkswagen / laufen / immer noch / ausgezeichnet (*pres.*)
27. ich / sein / überzeugt // daß / er / bleiben / nicht lange / **in Switzerland** (*both clauses pres.*)
28. statt / der / Buch / er / mitbringen / ein / Zeitschrift (*past*)
29. **when** / er / ziehen / nach / Kiel // wir / wohnen / schon / ein / ganz / Jahr / hier (*both clauses past*)
30. Herr Wirt // dürfen / haben / ich / ein / Tasse / schwarz / Kaffee? (*pres.*)
31. **if** / wir / gewinnen / im Lotto // wir / können / **take** / ein / Bildungsreise (*both clauses pres. subj.*)
32. der / **most beautiful** / Garten (*pl.*) / sein / **outside of** / der / Stadt (*pres.*)
33. **below** / dieser / Wald / ein / schön / klein / Kirche / stehen (*pres.*)
34. er / wollen / spazierengehen / mit / einige / klein / Kind (*pl.*) // aber / ich / glauben // alle / klein / Kind (*pl.*) / der / Dorf / gehen / mit / er (*first clause past, second clause pres., third clause pres. perf.*)

B. Free Composition

In about 200 words relate a story or an anecdote that can be told in German with the vocabulary and grammatical patterns that you know.

Unit 34

READING

Die Zimmervermieterin[g]

Fritz Frauenfeind ist Junggeselle. Und Untermieter[g] natürlich. Wie das so ist: wenigstens einmal im Jahr sucht ein Untermieter ein neues Zimmer bzw. eine neue Zimmervermieterin. Besonders wenn man Fritz Frauenfeind heißt.

In der Zeitung sieht das Zimmer ganz anständig aus. Also setzt Frauenfeind sich in die Straßenbahn[g] und fährt zum Schillerplatz. Die Gegend gefällt ihm. Die Villen[g] rund um den Platz sind alt, aber gut erhalten. Das ganze Stadtviertel[g] hat im Krieg Glück gehabt.

Fräulein Säuerlich, die Zimmervermieterin, ist Ende vierzig. Sie sieht nicht schlecht aus, aber das Beste ist zweifellos gewesen. Mit dem Zimmer ist es nicht viel anders, aber Frauenfeind hat die Gegend gern. Er will sofort mieten.

,,Ganz so schnell schießen die Preußen nicht, junger Mann. Da gibt es noch einiges zu besprechen. Zuerst: keine Damenbesuche, kein Radio[g]. Zigarrenrauch stört meine Katze Mitzi noch mehr als mich, und außerdem ist es nicht gut für meine neuen Gardinen. Um halb zehn muß das Licht spätestens ausgemacht[g] werden. Den Morgenkaffee müssen Sie sich schon selbst kochen, und natürlich müssen die Schuhe vor dem Betreten der Wohnung ausgezogen werden, nicht nur bei Regenwetter. Wie das mit dem Hausschlüssel wird, muß ich noch einmal sehen. Wenn Sie ein ordentlicher Mensch sind, können Sie ihn über das Wochenende bekommen. Natürlich nur, wenn Sie nicht später als zehn Uhr nach Hause kommen. Selbstverständlich haben Sie das Zimmer regelmäßig zu putzen, Fußboden, Fenster . . .''

der Junggeselle, -n, -n ein unverheirateter Mann
bzw. *abbr. for* **beziehungsweise** respectively, or as the case may be
anständig gut, recht ordentlich
die Villa, -llen ['vɪlɑ] · **rund** *adv.* around

säuerlich sourly · **Ende vierzig** fast fünfzig

der Preuße, -n, -n Prussian **Preußen** bis 1945 das größte deutsche Bundesland
die Gardine, -n curtain

der Schlüssel, - key

putzen clean **Sie haben das Zimmer zu putzen = Sie müssen das Zimmer putzen**

1 Ist Fritz Frauenfeind verheiratet?
2 Wie oft sucht ein Untermieter ein neues Zimmer?
3 Wie sieht das Zimmer in der Annonce aus?
4 Wer ist Fräulein Säuerlich?
5 Ist Herr Frauenfeind mit dem Zimmer zufrieden?
6 Warum darf man nicht rauchen?
7 Wann ist das Licht auszumachen?
8 Wer kocht für den Mieter den Morgenkaffee?
9 Wann muß man sich die Schuhe ausziehen?
10 Wann wird der Mieter den Hausschlüssel bekommen?
11 Was muß er auch noch regelmäßig tun?

,,Entschuldigen Sie, meine Dame'', unterbrach Frauenfeind Fräulein Säuerlich vorsichtig, ,,ich glaube, wir haben uns falsch verstanden. Ich komme nämlich auf eine Annonce für Zimmervermietung in der Tageszeitung von gestern, nicht auf ein Heiratsinserat.''

Eigener Herd ist Goldes wert

Seit drei Jahren hatte Paul im Wirtshaus ,,Zur Post'' gegessen, tagaus, tagein[g]. Immer dasselbe, Woche für Woche: Wiener Schnitzel[g], Gulasch[g], Schweinebraten[g] mit Sauerkraut, Pfannkuchen, gebratener Fisch, Frankfurter Würstchen[g] mit Kartoffelsalat, Roastbeef[g]. Natürlich hätte Paul schon längst das Gasthaus gewechselt, aber die anderen waren auch nicht besser. Er hatte sie schon alle probiert, eines nach dem andern. Jetzt war es genug. Es war nicht nur jede Woche genau dasselbe, es schmeckte auch alles gleich. Und das Gemüse war auch nicht besonders gut.

Paul war Junggeselle. Und er war es gern. Aber was zu weit geht, geht zu weit. Eines Mittags warf er die Gabel auf den Tisch und rief: ,,Eigener Herd ist Goldes wert. Das Opfer ist nicht zu umgehen. Ich brauche eine Frau!''

Gesagt, getan. Gleich nach dem Essen suchte Paul das nächste Ehevermittlungsinstitut auf. Er war kein gewöhnlicher Kunde. Er fragte nicht nach Schönheit. Er wollte weder Geld noch Gut. Er wollte eine Frau, die kochen kann. Nichts sonst.

,,Natürlich kann ich Ihnen helfen, lieber Herr. Ich habe sogar genau die richtige Frau für Sie. Sehen Sie hier, eine Köchin von Beruf.''

das Inserat, -e [ɪnzəˈʀɑːt] die Annonce

12 Warum glaubt Herr Frauenfeind, sie haben einander falsch verstanden?

der Herd, -e stove, hearth · **Goldes wert** worth gold
der Schweinebraten, - das Schwein, -e
das Würtchen, - die Wurst, ⸚e · **die Kartoffel, -n** potato · **das Roastbeef** [ˈʀoːstbiːf]
schon längst long ago
probieren versuchen
das Gemüse, - vegetable
werfen: er wirft, warf, hat geworfen throw · **das Opfer, -** sacrifice
umgehen: er umgeht, umging, hat umgangen avoid
aufsuchen besuchen
gewöhnlich usual, common · **weder ... noch** neither ... nor
das Gut, ⸚er property, possession

13 Was ist „Goldes wert"?
14 Wo hatte Paul schon seit drei Jahren gegessen?
15 Warum gefiel es ihm dort nicht?
16 Was hätte er schon längst getan?
17 Gab es Unterschiede zwischen den verschiedenen Wirtshäusern?
18 Wohin ging Paul gleich nach dem Essen?
19 Welche Qualifikationen mußte die Frau haben?

„Die oder keine", seufzte Paul, denn er dachte an seine Freiheit. Aber es mußte sein. Seine Zunge war schon ganz unempfindlich geworden. Wo er stand und ging, roch er Gasthausessen. Es war wie ein böser Traum. Sein Magen revoltierte[g]. Es mußte einfach etwas geschehen.

Luise war ein nettes Mädchen. Nun, genau genommen war sie kein Mädchen mehr. Ende dreißig schon und ein bißchen zu dick. Aber Paul sah über alles hinweg. Ihm lief trotzdem das Wasser im Mund zusammen, wenn er an die Zukunft dachte: Endlich gute Suppen, richtig gebratenes Fleisch, schmackhafte Saucen[g], selbstgebackene Kuchen zum Kaffee... Der Traum war fast zu schön, um wahr zu sein.

Das Ziel war erreicht. Es gab eine nette, kleine Hochzeit. Das erste Mittagessen kam auf den Tisch. Paul war ganz glückliche Erwartung.

„Sag mal, Luise, wo warst du eigentlich Köchin vor unserer Hochzeit?"

„Das wußtest du nicht, Paul? Seit mehr als drei Jahren war ich Köchin im Gasthof ‚Zur Post'."

Herr und Frau Neureich

Herr Neureich ist Kaufmann[g], ein sehr geschickter Kaufmann sogar. Natürlich geht er nicht von Tür zu Tür. Die Zeiten sind längst gewesen. So etwas hat Herr Neureich jetzt nicht mehr nötig. Er ist nämlich schon Millionär. „Schrott-Großhandel H. Neureich" heißt seine Firma[g]. Es wird wohl nicht mehr lange dauern, und Herr Neureich hat seine zweite Million zusammengebracht. Herr Neureich ist nämlich ein guter Kaufmann.

seufzen sigh
riechen: er riecht, roch, hat gerochen smell (*trans. and intrans.*)
der Magen, ≟ stomach · **revoltieren** [RevɔlˈtiːRən] · **geschen: es geschieht, geschah, ist geschen** happen
genau genommen strictly speaking
hinwegsehen über + *acc.* disregard
die Sauce, -n [ˈzoːsə]

die Erwartung, -en expectation

der Gasthof, ⸚e das Wirtshaus, das Gasthaus, die Gaststätte

20 Warum mußte einfach etwas geschehen?
21 Wie alt war Luise?
22 Sah sie gut aus?
23 Woran dachte Paul jetzt?
24 Was fragte Paul, als er hungrig vor seinem Teller saß?
25 Was war ihre Antwort?

---

reich rich

der Kaufmann, *pl.* **die Kaufleute** · **geschickt** tüchtig
nötig haben need · **der Schrott** scrap metal   **der Handel** trade, business · **die Firma, -men**

26 Was ist Herr Neureich von Beruf?
27 Was braucht Herr Neureich nicht mehr zu tun?
28 Scheint es ihm in seinem Geschäft gut zu gehen?

Manchmal^g (neuerdings immer häufiger) ist es sogar notwendig, daß Herr Neureich geschäftlich ins Ausland reist. In der vorigen Woche z.B. mußte er nach Rom: Internationale Konferenz der Schrott-Großhändler^g. Natürlich versuchte Herr Neureich, noch ein paar Geschäftchen nebenbei zu machen. Eines davon klappte besonders gut, es erfüllte Neureichs kühne Erwartungen. Und seine Erwartungen sind kühn!

Herr Neureich ist auch ein guter Ehemann. Von jeder Reise ins Ausland bringt er Lieschen, seiner Frau, ein kleines Geschenk mit. Lieschen ist eine geborene^g Müller und hat bis vor wenigen Jahren im Haushalt^g des Bürgermeisters^g geholfen. Inzwischen ist das natürlich anders geworden. Frau Neureich könnte nicht nur den ganzen Haushalt der Frau Bürgermeister, sondern sogleich die halbe Stadt aufkaufen, wenn sie wollte.

Aber Frau Neureich hat schon alles, was man haben kann, und deshalb interessiert sie sich neuerdings für Kunst und Kultur. Musik, Literatur^g, ganz besonders aber alte Meister^g der Malerei liebt sie über alles,— erzählt sie ihren Bekannten. So kauft Herr Neureich ihr eben einen Michelangelo. Herr Neureich ist ein wirklich guter Ehemann.

Frau Neureich platzte fast vor Stolz, als ihr Michelangelo im Wohnzimmer hing. Frau Neureichs Bekannte platzten auch—vor Neid. Das war eine Situation! Sogar einen Experten hatte man gebeten. Experten machen sich immer gut, sie verbessern das Ansehen einer jeden Gesellschaft. Beim Herrn Bürgermeister waren auch immer Respektspersonen zu Besuch.

Professor Schöngeist staunte, auf den ersten Blick jedenfalls. Dann inspizierte^g er das Gemälde näher. Schließlich sagte er ruhig: „Dieser Michelangelo ist höchstens zehn Jahre alt!"

„Ach, das macht nichts", antwortete Frau Neureich, geborene Müller, dem Professor lächelnd, „Hauptsache, es i s t ein Michelangelo."

Fanny[*]

Wir hatten ein Hausmädchen. Ein einfaches Kind vom Lande. Die Stadtluft tat ihr gut. Sie wurde von Tag zu Tag munterer. Am ersten Samstag kam sie zu meiner Frau.

„Ich möchte heute gern tanzen gehen."

„Gehen Sie, Fanny."

„Ich habe nichts anzuziehen."

„Sie haben doch Ihr Sonntagskleid."

[*] By permission of Jo Hanns Rösler, Feilnbach am Wendelstein, Germany.

neuerdings recently, lately · **notwendig** nötig
vorig previous, former · **international** [ɪntɛʀnatsioˈnɑːl]
nebenbei in addition, on the side
kühn bold, brave
das Geschenk, -e etwas, was man einer anderen Person gibt, besonders bei Festen (z.B. zu Weihnachten)
sogleich sofort
die Kunst, ⸚e art · **die Literatur, -en** [lɪtəʀaˈtuːʀ]
die Malerei, -en [mɑləˈʀaɪ] painting
Michelangelo [mɪkelˈandʒelo]
vor Stolz platzen burst with pride   **der Stolz**
der Neid envy
das Ansehen reputation, esteem · **ein jeder** jeder
staunen überrascht sein · **inspizieren** [ɪnspiˈtsiːʀən] · **das Gemälde, -** painting, picture
höchstens nicht mehr als
lächeln smile
die Hauptsache, -n main point

29 Was mußte Herr Neureich in der vorigen Woche tun?
30 Ist es ihm gelungen, ein paar Geschäftchen nebenbei zu machen?
31 Was bringt Herr Neureich von jeder Reise ins Ausland zurück?
32 Wo hatte Frau Neureich gearbeitet, bevor sie Frau Neureich wurde?
33 Was könnte sie jetzt tun, wenn sie wollte?
34 Wofür interessiert sie sich jetzt?
35 Was erzählt sie ihren Bekannten?
36 Welches Geschenk bekommt sie?
37 Waren Neureichs Bekannte auch stolz auf den Michelangelo?
38 Warum hatte man sogar einen Experten gebeten?
39 Was sagte der Experte, nachdem er das Gemälde näher ansah?
40 Wie antwortete Frau Neureich darauf?

Fanny [ˈfani]

munter lively, gay, bright

41 Woher kam Fanny?
42 Hat die Stadtluft ihr gut getan?
43 Wohin wollte sie am ersten Samstag gehen?

„Das ist mir zu zugeknöpft", sagte Fanny, „wenn Sie mir Ihr Abendkleid leihen möchten—"

Fanny bekam das Abendkleid. Geschenkt obendrein. Besser ohne Abendkleid, als ohne Hausmädchen. Jedoch, das war erst der Anfang. Am nächsten Samstag kam Fanny wieder.

„Ich brauche einen Mantel über das Kleid."

„Sie haben doch einen, Fanny."

„Für den Wochentag. Zum Einkaufengehen", sagte Fanny, „aber am Abend und zu dem schönen Kleid paßt er nicht. Könnten sie mir Ihren Mantel—?"

Fanny bekam den Mantel. Fanny bekam noch viel mehr. Jeden Samstag hatte sie einen neuen Wunsch. Sie bekam die Handtasche meiner Frau, den Schal^g meiner Frau, den Hut meiner Frau, die kurzen und die langen Handschuhe^g meiner Frau, eine Bluse^g für Sonntag, ein Twinset für wochentags, die Schuhe trug sie mit meiner Frau gemeinsam.

Ich machte meiner Frau heftige Vorwürfe. Sie zeigte mir nur die sieben Seiten Inserate in der Sonntagszeitung.

Sieben Seiten „Hausmädchen gesucht!" Da pflichtete ich ihr bei.

Am nächsten Samstag kam Fanny abermals.

Meine Frau hatte nichts mehr im Schrank.

Dafür hatte sie Galgenhumor.

„Nun, Fanny, was soll's denn heute sein?" fragte sie freundlich.

„Nichts, Madame."

„Was? Kein Kleid? Kein Hut? Kein Mantel?"

„Nichts", sagte Fanny, „ich möchte etwas ganz anderes."

„Was denn?"

„Ich möchte kündigen."

Meine Frau fiel aus allen Wolken.

„Kündigen? Warum?"

Fanny, ganz große Dame, sagte:

„Wissen Sie, Madame, wenn man so gut angezogen ist wie ich jetzt . . . dann macht man sich nicht gern die Hände schmutzig mit Hausarbeit."

Jo Hanns Rösler

zuknöpfen button up · **leihen** lend; borrow
schenken geben als Geschenk
erst only

der Schal, -s
die Bluse, -n · **das Twinset**, -s

beipflichten zustimmen, „ja" zu etwas sagen

die Madame [maˈdam]

kündigen sagen, daß man eine Stelle nicht mehr haben will

schmutzig dirty

44 Warum wollte sie ihr Sonntagskleid nicht tragen?
45 Was bekam sie?
46 Worum hat sie am nächsten Samstag gebeten?
47 Konnte sie nicht ihren eigenen Mantel tragen?
48 Was bekam Fanny auch noch?
49 Warum konnte die Frau nie „nein" sagen?
50 Warum hat Fanny doch gekündigt?

PHONOLOGY

Form a short oral sentence with each of the following expressions and watch the pronunciation carefully:

Junggeselle, Untermieter, Zimmer, Zeitung, Straßenbahn, Villen, Stadtviertel, Zimmervermieterin, besprechen, Radio, stören, Gardinen, Licht ausmachen, Morgenkaffee, Schuhe ausziehen, Hausschlüssel, putzen, falsch verstanden, Heiratsinserat, Herd, Frankfurter Würstchen und Salat, Gasthaus, Köchin, ein böser Traum, Luise, Zukunft, Hochzeit, Millionär, Ausland, Rom, kühne Erwartungen, Lieschen Müller, Michelangelo, platzen, Gesellschaft, Professor Schöngeist, Gemälde, Hauptsache, Hausmädchen, Stadtluft, kommen, tanzen, Sonntagskleid, zugeknöpft, brauchen, Wochentag, passen, Wunsch, Handtasche, Hut, gemeinsam, Vorwürfe, zeigen, abermals, Galgenhumor, heute, fragen, kündigen, schmutzig

---

VOCABULARY

A. Singular and Plural of Nouns

der Beruf, -e
die Bluse, -n
der Bürgermeister, -
die Erwartung, -en
die Firma, -men
die Gardine, -n
der Gasthof, ⸚e
das Gemälde, -
das Gemüse, -
das Geschenk, -e
das Gut, ⸚er
der Händler, -
der Handschuh, -e
die Hauptsache, -n
die Hausarbeit, -en
der Haushalt, -e
das Hausmädchen, -
der Herd, -e
das Inserat, -e
der Junggeselle, -n, -n
die Kartoffel, -n
die Köchin, -nen

die Kunst, ⸚e
die Literatur, -en
der Magen, ⸚
die Malerei, -en
das Opfer, -
der Preuße, -n, -n
das Radio, -s
die Sauce, -n
der Schal, -s
der Schlüssel, -
das Schnitzel, -
das Schwein, -e
der Schweinebraten, -
das Stadtviertel, -
die Straßenbahn, -en
der Untermieter, -
die Villa, -llen
der Wochentag, -e
die Wurst, ⸚e
das Würstchen, -
die Zimmervermieterin, -nen

B. Inference

With the help of the clues provided guess the meanings of the words in boldface:

1. Wenn man schon **gähnen** muß, hält man wenigstens die Hand vor dem Mund, Susi. Aber es ist ja auch schon spät, du solltest jetzt lieber zu Bett gehen.
2. Das Wasser des Flusses **wälzte sich** langsam dem Meere zu. Die Schweine wälzten sich im **Schmutz**. **sich wälzen · der Schmutz**
3. Als der kleine Hans sein Auto bekam, war er **selig** vor Glück.
4. Draußen am Schillerplatz war eine große **Kundgebung** gegen die Politik seiner Partei. **die Kundgebung, -en**
5. Goethe und Schiller sind die bekanntesten deutschen **Dichter**. **der Dichter, -**
6. Bücher und Zeitungen werden **gedruckt**, Hände aber werden gedrückt, wenn man jemanden begrüßt. **drucken**
7. Stell dir vor, Wegners haben zwölf Kinder, ein volles **Dutzend**. **das Dutzend**
8. Wir haben ein Dutzend frische **Eier** im Hause. Möchtest du zwei zum Frühstück, vielleicht gekocht oder gebraten? **das Ei, -er**
9. Vier Wochen allein in einem Waldhäuschen? Das wäre mir denn doch zu **einsam**!
10. A. Wenn unser **Opa** mein Großvater ist, was bin ich dann zu ihm, Mutti?
    B. Du bist Großvaters **Enkel**, mein Junge. **der Opa,-s · der Enkel, -**
11. Warum kann er sich nicht **entschließen**, ob er das Haus kaufen will oder nicht? **sich entschließen**
12. Zuerst hatte er nur ein **Fahrrad**, dann kaufte er sich ein **Motorrad**, aber jetzt fährt er einen dicken Wagen. Ein Fahrrad hat zwei **Räder**, ein Auto vier. **das Rad, ⸚er**
13. Du hast in deiner Hausarbeit viele **Fehler** gemacht, Werner, beinah alles ist falsch. **der Fehler, -**
14. Es hat heute nacht **gefroren**, hier ist Eis am Fenster. **frieren: es friert, fror, hat gefroren**
15. Die Polizisten haben den Dieb gefangen und ins **Gefängnis** gebracht. **das Gefängnis, -se**
16. Wenn es erst regnet und dann friert, sind die Straßen gefährlich **glatt**.
17. Das Schiff lief heute morgen in den New Yorker **Hafen** ein. **der Hafen, ⸚**
18. Schüler müssen ihre Hausarbeiten in **Hefte** schreiben. **das Heft, -e**
19. Es ist warm, die Sonne scheint, das Wetter ist **herrlich**.
20. Blau, grün und rot? Nein, die Bluse ist mir zu **bunt**.
21. Sein Waldhäuschen ist ganz aus **Tannenholz**. **das Holz**
22. England ist eine große **Insel**. **die Insel, -n**
23. In dieser Fabrik ist so viel **Lärm**, man kann kaum sein eigenes Wort verstehen. **der Lärm**
24. Nach Mitternacht wurde die Gesellschaft so **lustig**, daß die Nachbarn ihre Fenster schlossen.
25. Zwischen Ost- und Westberlin gibt es eine lange **Mauer**. **die Mauer, -n**
26. Sie stand fast dreißig Minuten vor dem **Spiegel**, um sich schön zu machen. **der Spiegel, -**
27. Im Herbst werden die Abende **kühl**, man muß etwas **überziehen**, wenn man nach draußen geht.
28. Sie haben sich für das neue Haus ganz moderne **Möbel** gekauft. Schön finde ich sie allerdings nicht, besonders die Stühle nicht. **die Möbel** (*pl.*)

29 Schweizer **Käse** schmeckt gut.   **der Käse**
30 Ich esse **Obst** gern, besonders Äpfel und Birnen.   **das Obst**
31 Der Zug lief auf die Minute **pünktlich** in den Bahnhof ein.
32 Hans ist ein **kluges** Kind. Er kann schon lesen, obwohl er erst vier Jahre alt ist.
33 Das Fleisch ist mir zu **roh**. Du hättest es etwas länger braten sollen.
34 Weil sie fast alle ihre Kleider mitnahm, brauchte sie drei große **Koffer** für die kurze Reise. **der Koffer**, -
35 Der Lehrer schrieb die neuen Wörter an die **Wandtafel**.   **die Tafel, -n**
36 Jeder Student in diesem Zimmer sollte nun den **Inhalt** dieses Buches kennen.   **der Inhalt**
37 Man **vollstreckte** die Strafe nicht, sondern ließ den Dieb wieder frei.
38 Er ist **zwar** alt, aber er kann immer noch zehn Stunden am Tag arbeiten.

WRITING

A. Syllabication

Some of the rules of German syllabication were introduced in Unit 2 (Writing §B). The following are more complete and inclusive:

1 A single consonant always belongs to the following syllable:

Die-be, Fra-ge, Gei-ge, da-mals, le-gen, schnei-den

In this connection **ch**, **sch**, and **ß** are regarded as single consonants:

Bü-cher, wa-schen, rei-ßen

2 In the case of clusters of several consonants the last one belongs to the following syllable:

Ham-mer, Gar-ten, Kell-ner, Städ-ter, Ap-fel

In this connection note that:

a. **ck** is considered a double consonant and is broken up into **k-k**:

schmek-ken, Unglük-ke

b. **st** is not divided:

We-sten, Pfo-sten, Fen-ster, ern-ste

3 Even suffixes which begin with a vowel have the preceding consonant included in syllabication:

Schneide-rin, Kun-din, Bäcke-rei, Rich-tung, Versiche-rung

4   A single letter cannot stand alone in German. Therefore the following are not divided:

    oder (*not* o-der), Abend (*not* A-bend)

5   Doubled vowels, diphthongs, and vowels plus signs of length (**h, e**) cannot be divided:

    wei-nen, oh-ne, die-se

6   Compounds are divided at the seam:

    Groß-vater, Herz-anfall, Oster-fest, Pfann-kuchen, entgegen-laufen

    Within the component parts, however, the above rules apply:

    Groß-va-ter, Herz-an-fall, Pfann-ku-chen, ent-ge-gen-lau-fen

7   Divide the following words into syllables:

    Junggeselle, natürlich, wenigstens, Zimmer, Stadtviertel, zweifellos, mieten, junger, Zigarrenrauch, Gardinen, kochen, Wohnung, Wochenende, Hause, Fenster, Dame, nämlich, gestern, tagaus, dasselbe, Woche, Kartoffeln, Gabel, Kunde, Schönheit, ihnen, helfen, lieber, sogar, Köchin, seufzte, Freiheit, mußte, Zunge, revoltierte, nettes, Mädchen, dreißig, bißchen, über, Hochzeit, erste, Gasthof, geschickter, Zeiten, Firma, lange, nämlich, manchmal, geschäftlich, Ausland, machen, Ehemann, Reise, Lieschen, Bürgermeister, geholfen, inzwischen, aufkaufen, Malerei, platzte, Experten, Gesellschaft, Professor, Gemälde, schließlich, Hauptsache, möchten, obendrein, ohne, jedoch, Anfang, wieder, über, Mantel, Handtasche, sieben, pflichtete, nächsten, abermals, hatte, Galgenhumor, freundlich, kündigen, allen, Wolken, große, sagte, wissen, Hände, Hausarbeit

B. Dehydrated Sentences

Write complete sentences, using the tense suggested. The nominative singular masculine **der** is used to indicate that a form of the definite article is desired. The English expressions in boldface usually require idiomatic German equivalents. Some rearrangement of word order will be necessary:

1   **one** / Tag / kommen / mein / Onkel / aus / Amerika / ganz / unverhofft / **for a visit**   (*past*)
2   er / wohnen / schon / **for** / ein / Jahr / in / dieser / Dorf   (*pres.*)
3   sie / erzählen / **about** / ihr / Reise / **through** / verschieden / fremd/ Land (*pl.*)   (*pres. perf.*)
4   wissen / du // **from** / wer / Alfred / bekommen / dieser / Geschenk?   (*first clause pres., second clause pres. perf.*)
5   wer / helfen / ich // Wagen / waschen?   (*fut.*)
6   sie / kommen / natürlich **for** / Kind / **sake**   (*past perf.*)
7   ich / danken / die Leute / **for** / ihr / Hilfe   (*pres. perf.*)
8   Günther / bringen / gestern / einige / alt / Freund / mit / **home**   (*pres. perf.*)

UNIT 34 · WRITING

9. wer / sehen / du / denn / **at** / Konzert? (*pres. perf.*)
10. mein / Tante / ankommen / ein / Stunde / **ago** (*past*)
11. **when** / ich / sehen / er / gestern // er / aussehen / noch / ziemlich / blaß (*first clause past, second clause pres. perf.*)
12. jeder / Mal // **when** / ich / besuchen / er // er / erzählen / derselbe / Geschichte (*pl.*) (*pres., both clauses*)
13. haben / ihr / ein / Ahnung // **when** / der Zug / sollen / einlaufen? (*pres., both clauses*)
14. wir / warten / ein / ganz / Stunde / **for** / er (*past perf.*)
15. ich / bitten / er / **for** / ein / Zigarette // **for** (*conj.*) / ich / vergessen / mein (*first clause past, second clause past perf.*)
16. der / fremd / Leute / fragen / **about** / dein / Eltern (*pres. perf.*)
17. **during** / der / Mittagessen / er / sein / **on account of** / der / Unfall / hier (*pres. perf.*)
18. Rolf / können / antworten / der / Lehrer / leider / nicht (*pres. perf.*)
19. der / Frau / tun / nichts / **against** / oder / **without** / ihr / Mann (*pres.*)
20. ich / begegnen / der / Kind (*pl.*) / **inside of** / der / Kaufhaus (*pres. perf.*)
21. **whose** / Hemd / liegen / hier / **on** / der / Stuhl? (*pres.*)
22. **except for** / der / drei / Angestellte / niemand / sein / **in** / der / Gebäude (*past*)
23. Günther / sein / **taller than** / Rolf // **but** / Fritz / sein / **tallest** (*pres., both clauses*)
24. der / Bild / **of the** / Dom / werden (*pass. aux.*) / aufnehmen / **on the occasion of** / der / groß / Feier (*past, pass. voice*)
25. **why** / du / wollen / glauben / der / Junge / nicht? (*pres.*)
26. hier / ein / schrecklich / Unfall / passieren / **one night** (*pres. perf.*)
27. der Frau // **whose** / Kind / sein / so / krank // heißen / Frau Jäger (*pres., both clauses*)
28. dort / der / Mann / stehen // **whom** / ich / wollen / verkaufen / mein / alt / Wagen (*pres., both clauses*)
29. wo / sein / der / Schraubenzieher // **with which** / ich / arbeiten / eben? (*first clause pres., second clause past*)
30. sehen / du / der / Dame // **who** / sein / eben / hier / **in the** / Geschäft? (*pres. perf., both clauses*)
31. ich / wünschen / **myself** / ein / neu / Hut / zu / Weihnachten (*fut.*)
32. du / müssen / anziehen / **yourself** / noch / **for** / der / Konzert (*pres.*)
33. du / **ought to** / anziehen / **yourself** / bei / dies / Wetter / wärmer (*pres.*)
34. ich / interessieren / sich / **in** / alt / Musik (*past perf.*)
35. ausmachen / Sie / der / Licht / **before** / zehn Uhr!
36. **sit down** (*familiar*) // und / geben / ich / ein / Zigarette!

C. Free Composition

In about 200 words report an incident or situation that you experienced recently, writing it as if it were for your diary.

Unit 35

READING

Wolfgang Borchert (1921-1947)

Zwei Erzählungen von Wolfgang Borchert beschließen dieses Buch. Das ist kein Zufall. Es war vielmehr beabsichtigt, die Studenten bis an deutsche Literatur heranzuführen, und Erzählungen von Wolfgang Borchert gehören zweifellos zum Besten, was die jüngere deutsche Literatur zu bieten hat.

Wolfgang Borchert wurde am 20. Mai 1921 in Hamburg geboren. Man nennt ihn Dichter der „verlorenen" Generation, denn wie keiner sonst hat er das Verbrecherische des Krieges erkannt und die Problematik^g seiner Generation in dichterische^g Form gekleidet.

Früh Soldat, saß Wolfgang Borchert schon mit zwanzig Jahren im Militär-Gefängnis: zum Tode verurteilt, weil er geschrieben hatte, was er über diesen Krieg dachte. Zwar wurde das Todesurteil dann nicht vollstreckt^g. Nach sechs Wochen, in denen er jeden Tag auf den Tod gewartet hatte, wurde er schließlich begnadigt. Aber gegen Ende des Krieges wurde er abermals für Monate ins Gefängnis geworfen. Diesmal wegen einiger politischer Witze, die er verbreitet hatte.

Krieg und Gefängnis hatten seine Gesundheit zerstört. Den Rest besorgte die Hungersnot der Nachkriegsjahre. Wolfgang Borchert, wohl die größte dichterische Begabung deutscher Zunge in seiner Zeit, starb am 20. November 1947, ganze sechsundzwanzig Jahre alt. Geblieben ist uns sein Werk^g, klein nur, aber stark und zeitlos, obwohl er fast alle Themen für seine Werke aus dem Geschehen seiner Tage nahm.

Das Brot*

Plötzlich wachte sie auf. Es war halb drei. Sie überlegte, warum sie aufgewacht war. Ach so! In der Küche hatte jemand gegen einen Stuhl gestoßen. Sie horchte nach der Küche. Es war still. Es war zu still, und als sie mit der Hand über das Bett neben sich fuhr, fand sie es leer. Das war es, was es so besonders still gemacht hatte: sein Atem fehlte. Sie stand auf und tappte durch die dunkle Wohnung zur Küche. In der Küche trafen sie sich. Die Uhr war halb drei. Sie sah etwas Weißes am Küchenschrank stehen. Sie machte Licht. Sie standen sich im Hemd gegenüber. Nachts. Um halb drei. In der Küche.

Auf dem Küchentisch stand der Brotteller. Sie sah, daß er sich Brot abgeschnitten hatte. Das Messer lag noch neben dem Teller. Und auf der Decke lagen Brotkrümel. Wenn sie abends zu Bett gingen, machte sie immer das Tischtuch sauber. Jeden Abend. Aber nun lagen Krümel auf

* By permission of Rowohlt Verlag, GMBH.

heranführen lead, bring

das Verbrecherische *adj. noun* the criminal aspect, that which is of a criminal nature
verurteilen sentence
das Urteil, -e judgment, verdict, sentence
begnadigen pardon
diesmal dieses Mal · **verbreiten** weiter erzählen

besorgen bringen, machen

aufwachen wach werden
mit der Hand fahren run the hand · **leer** empty
fehlen nicht da sein · **tappen** unsicher gehen, z.B. wenn es dunkel ist
gegenüber *prep. with dat.* opposite, facing
abschneiden: er schneidet ab, schnitt ab, hat abgeschnitten cut off
der Krümel, - crumb
sauber clean

dem Tuch. Und das Messer lag da. Sie fühlte, wie die Kälte der Fliesen langsam an ihr hoch kroch. Und sie sah von dem Teller weg.

,,Ich dachte, hier wäre was'', sagte er und sah in der Küche umher.

,,Ich habe auch was gehört'', antwortete sie, und dabei fand sie, daß er nachts im Hemd doch schon recht alt aussah. So alt wie er war. Dreiundsechzig. Tagsüber sah er manchmal jünger aus. Sie sieht doch schon alt aus, dachte er, im Hemd sieht sie doch ziemlich alt aus. Aber das liegt vielleicht an den Haaren. Bei den Frauen liegt das nachts immer an den Haaren. Die machen dann auf einmal so alt.

,,Du hättest Schuhe anziehen sollen. So barfuß[g] auf den kalten Fliesen. Du erkältest dich noch.''

Sie sah ihn nicht an, weil sie nicht ertragen konnte, daß er log. Daß er log, nachdem sie neununddreißig Jahre verheiratet waren.

,,Ich dachte, hier wäre was'', sagte er noch einmal und sah wieder so sinnlos von einer Ecke in die andere, ,,ich hörte hier was. Da dachte ich, hier wäre was.''

,,Ich hab auch was gehört. Aber es war wohl nichts.'' Sie stellte den Teller vom Tisch und schnippte die Krümel von der Decke.

,,Nein, es war wohl nichts'', echote[g] er unsicher.

Sie kam ihm zu Hilfe: ,,Komm man. Das war wohl draußen. Komm man zu Bett. Du erkältest dich noch. Auf den kalten Fliesen.''

Er sah zum Fenster hin. ,,Ja, das muß wohl draußen gewesen sein. Ich dachte, es wäre hier.''

Sie hob die Hand zum Lichtschalter. Ich muß das Licht jetzt ausmachen, sonst muß ich nach dem Teller sehen, dachte sie. Ich darf doch nicht nach dem Teller sehen. ,,Komm man'', sagte sie und machte das Licht aus, ,,das war wohl draußen. Die Dachrinne schlägt immer bei Wind gegen die Wand. Es war sicher die Dachrinne. Bei Wind klappert sie immer.''

Sie tappten sich beide über den dunklen Korridor[g] zum Schlafzimmer. Ihre nackten[g] Füße platschten auf den Fußboden.

,,Wind ist ja'', meinte er. ,,Wind war schon die ganze Nacht.''

Als sie im Bett lagen, sagte sie: ,,Ja, Wind war schon die ganze Nacht. Es war wohl die Dachrinne.''

,,Ja, ich dachte, es wäre in der Küche. Es war wohl die Dachrinne.'' Er sagte das, als ob er schon halb im Schlaf wäre.

Aber sie merkte, wie unecht seine Stimme klang, wenn er log. ,,Es ist kalt'', sagte sie und gähnte leise, ,,ich krieche unter die Decke. Gute Nacht.''

,,Nacht'', antwortete er und noch: ,,ja, kalt ist es schon ganz schön.''

die Fliese, -n tile

liegen an + *dat.* be due to, be because of

sinnlos senseless(ly), foolish(ly)

was etwas
schnippen flick

man *here an adverb* **nur** *This occurs frequently in north German colloquial speech, especially with familiar imperatives:* **Iß man** = just eat.

der Lichtschalter, - light switch   **das Licht, -er** light
die Dachrinne, -n (roof) gutter
klappern rattle

platschen plop

leise soft(ly)

schon ganz schön *adverbs for emphasis:* It sure is awfully cold, all right!

Dann war es still. Nach vielen Minuten hörte sie, daß er leise und vorsichtig kaute. Sie atmete absichtlich tief und gleichmäßig, damit er nicht merken sollte, daß sie noch wach war. Aber sein Kauen war so regelmäßig, daß sie davon langsam einschlief.

Als er am nächsten Abend nach Hause kam, schob sie ihm vier Scheiben Brot hin. Sonst hatte er immer nur drei essen können.

,,Du kannst ruhig vier essen", sagte sie und ging von der Lampe weg. ,,Ich kann dieses Brot nicht so recht vertragen. Iß du man eine mehr. Ich vertrag es nicht so gut."

Sie sah, wie er sich tief über den Teller beugte. Er sah nicht auf. In diesem Augenblick tat er ihr leid.

,,Du kannst doch nicht nur zwei Scheiben essen", sagte er auf seinen Teller.

,,Doch. Abends vertrag ich das Brot nicht gut. Iß man. Iß man."

Erst nach einer Weile setzte sie sich unter die Lampe an den Tisch.

Der Stiftzahn oder warum mein Vetter keine Rahmbonbon mehr ißt*

Es war ein niedliches kleines Kino. Und niedrig. Es roch nach Kindern, Aufregung, Bonbon. Es roch im ganzen Klub⁹ nach Rahmbonbon. Das kam davon, weil man vorne neben der Kasse welche kaufen konnte. Für zehn Pfennig fünf Stück. Deswegen roch es nach Rahmbonbon an allen Enden. Aber sonst war es ein niedliches Kino. Und niedrig. Es gingen kaum zweihundert Menschen hinein. Es war ein richtiges kleines Vorstadtkino. Eines von denen, die man gutmütig Flohkiste nennt. Ohne Gehässigkeit. Unser Kino hieß Viktoria-Lichtspiele⁹. Sonntagsnachmittags gab es Kindervorstellungen. Für halbe Preise. Aber die Rahmbonbon waren beinahe noch wichtiger. Sie gehörten dazu, zum Sonntag, zum Kino. Fünf Stück einen Groschen. So rentierte sich das auch für den Besitzer.

Leider besaß mein Vetter dreißig Pfennig. Das waren eine Unmasse Rahmbonbon. Wir waren mit die Glücklichsten unter den zweihundert Kindern. Ich nämlich auch. Denn ich saß neben ihm und dafür war er mein Vetter. Wir waren sehr glücklich. Das l e i d e r kam erst später.

Dann wurde es langsam und genießerisch dunkel. Das schmatzende Lutschgeräusch von zweihundert Mäulern flaute augenblicklich ab. Statt dessen wälzte sich ein Indianergeheul⁹, Fußgetrampel und anhaltendes Pfeifkonzert durch das kleine Kino. Selige Freundenkundgebung allsonntäglich zum Beginn der Vorstellung.

Dann war es dunkel. Die Leinwand wurde hell und hinten surrte etwas. Dann gab es auch noch Musik. Das Indianergeheul brach ab. Man hörte wieder das Lutschen an allen Enden. Und beinahe zweihundert Herzen schlagen. Der Film begann.

* By permission of Rowohlt Verlag, GMBH.

gleichmäßig uniform(ly)
einschlafen fall asleep

ruhig *here* it's all right, go right ahead

sich beugen *acc. refl.* bow, bend

die Weile, -n while

---

der Stiftzahn, ⸚**e** post crown   **der Zahn,** ⸚**e** tooth

die Kasse, -n cashier's booth
welche *here* einige · **deswegen** deshalb

die Vorstadt, ⸚**e** suburb
die Gehässigkeit, -en hatefulness, animosity, malice
die Vorstellung, -en performance
der Groschen, - das Zehnpfennigstück (—,10 DM)
die Unmasse, -n sehr große Menge
mit *adv.* together with others; **die Glücklichsten** *is nominative*
genießerisch enjoyable (-bly) · **das Geräusch, -e** noise
anhalten dauern

die Leinwand movie screen
abbrechen plötzlich aufhören
schlagen *infinitive with* **hörte**: Man hörte . . . zweihundert Herzen schlagen

Hinterher kann man das nie mehr so genau auseinanderhalten. Auf jeden Fall wurde sehr viel geschossen, geritten, geraubt und geküßt. Alles war in Bewegung. Und vor der Leinwand zweihundert lutschende Zungen. Wenn man nachher im Hause erzählen sollte, wußte man nur noch, daß geschossen, geritten und geraubt wurde. Das Küssen unterschlug man. Das war ja sowieso Quatsch.

Je mehr auf der Leinwand geritten und geschossen wurde, um so mehr wurden die Rahmbonbon von einer Backe in die andere geschoben. Und das konnte man alles hören. Eine wüste Flucht zu Pferde auf der Leinwand — und das Lutschgeräusch schwoll an wie ein Wasserfall[g].

Es roch nach Kindern, Aufregung, Bonbon. An allen Enden nach Rahmbonbon.

Plötzlich, gerade wurde der blonde heldenmütige Held auf seinem treuen Schimmel von sieben schwarzbärtigen Räubern über die Leinwandprärie gejagt — gerade sandte er einen dringenden Heldenblick zum düster bewölkten Tragödienhimmel — gerade zogen die verbrecherischen Verfolger ihre haarscharfen Trommelrevolver und verbargen sich hinter einer riesigen Hecke von glühenden Kakteen[g] — da schrie es!

Das war an sich nichts Besonderes, denn alle aufregenden Vorgänge auf der Leinwand wurden mitfühlend durch die Aufschreie von zweihundert Kindermäulern untermalt und kommentiert. Aber dieser Schrei war aus der Art gefallen. Er war zu groß und zu erschrocken. Es lief mir heiß den Rücken herauf. Und mir ganz besonders, denn der geschrien hatte, war mein Vetter.

hinterher später · **auf jeden Fall** jeden falls **der Fall, ⸗e** case, event
reiten: er reitet, ritt, ist geritten ride (a horse) · **rauben** plunder, rob · **die Bewegung, -en** movement
unterschlagen: er unterschlägt, unterschlug, hat unterschlagen suppress
sowieso anyhow
je mehr . . . um so mehr the more . . . the more
die Flucht, -en escape · **das Pferd, -e** horse **zu Pferde** on horseback
heldenmütig heroic
der Schimmel, - weißes Pferd
der Räuber, - robber · **die Prärie, -n** [pʀɛˈʀiː] · **senden: er sendet, sandte, hat gesandt** send (*also* **sendete, hat gesendet,** *meaning specifically* broadcast) · **dringen: er dringt, drang, ist gedrungen** penetrate
bewölkt clouded, cloudy
riesig sehr groß **der Riese, -n, -n** giant · **die Hecke, -n** hedge
glühen glow · **der Kaktus** [ˈkaktʊs], **die Kakteen** [kakˈteːən] · **da schrie es** *impersonal construction* = **man schrie schreien: er schreit, schrie, hat geschrien** scream
mitfühlen sympathize · **der Aufschrei, -e** scream, outcry **der Schrei, -e** scream ·
untermalen supply a background
aus der Art fallen be different **die Art, -en** kind, sort · **erschrecken: er erschrickt, erschrak, ist erschrocken** Angst bekommen
der Rücken, - back · **der geschrien hatte** = **derjenige, der geschrien hatte**

Und dann schrie er noch einmal. Laut und wehklagend wie ein getretenes Hündchen. Und dann zum dritten Mal: Entsetzt und nicht zu überhören. So schrie mein Vetter.

Er hatte Erfolg. Das, was über die Leinwand gelaufen war, blieb mitten im Laufen stehen und surrte nicht mehr. Die Musik machte auch nicht mehr mit und das Licht ging an.

Es war nicht leicht, aus dem Heulenden, Schimpfenden, Schluchzenden, das vorher mein Vetter gewesen war, herauszubekommen, was den Ansporn zu seinem dreiteiligen Schrei gegeben hatte. Aber dann verstand man ihn doch und der Kinobesitzer, der zugleich Kassierer[g] und Rahmbonbonverkäufer war, widmete seinen Rahmbonbon einen männlichen Fluch. Und insbesondere den Rahmbonbon, die er an meinen Vetter verkauft hatte.

Aber Schuld hatte er natürlich selbst, mein Vetter. Wie oft und eindringlich war ihm zu Hause und vom Zahnarzt eingeschärft worden, um Himmels willen nie und niemals Rahmbonbon zu essen. Er hatte es trotzdem getan. Dabei war es passiert. Der Stiftzahn—mein Vetter trug damals schon, und er wurde von uns allen bestaunt und daran geachtet, einen richtigen Stiftzahn—dieser Stiftzahn hatte sich von der Rahmbonbonmasse betören lassen und hatte seinen Stift heimlich verlassen. Und da mein Vetter bei den atemraubenden Vorfällen auf der Leinwand den Mund vor Atemnot weit aufsperrte, war der Stiftzahn heimtückisch und häßlich aus der Gemeinschaft seiner Brüder entflohen und abenteuersüchtig unter den Bänken des Kinos von dannen gerollt.

Nach zehn Minuten mußte das Suchen aufgegeben werden. Der Stiftzahn hatte zu viele Vorteile für sich. Wer hätte sich erkühnen wollen, unter den dunklen Bänken, auf denen zweihundert Kinder hin und her rutschten, einen Stiftzahn wiederzufinden? Pfeifen und Rufen half erst recht nichts. Vielleicht hatte er längst als herzklopfenmachende Beute in einer fremden Hosentasche Unterkunft gefunden. Jedenfalls war er weg.

Es wurde wieder dunkel, die Leinwand wurde wieder hell und bewegte sich da weiter, wo sie stehengeblieben war. Und die Musik machte auch wieder mit. Und neben mir schwiegen schwermütig die tränenerstickten Reste meines vorhin noch so stolz lutschenden Vetters.

Einmal geht alles zu Ende. Am ehesten eine Kindervorstellung im Vorstadtkino. Die Leinwand konnte nicht mehr, die Musik auch nicht. Sie waren auch überanstrengt, deswegen machten sie Schluß. Aber dafür gingen zwei immer wieder überraschende Seitentüren vorne auf und ließen weiß und blendend den hellen sonntäglichen Sonntagmittag in das Kino herein. In

laut loud · **wehklagen** lament, wail ·
treten: er tritt, trat, hat (ist) getreten
kick; step
entsetzt frightened, terrified · **überhören**
nicht hören
der Erfolg, -e success · **stehenbleiben**
come to a stop
herausbekommen erraten · **der Ansporn**
incentive
zugleich gleichzeitig, auch
widmen dedicate · **der Fluch, ⸚e** curse
die Schuld guilt   **er hatte Schuld** it was
his fault   **die Schulden** *pl.* debts
einschärfen eindringlich sagen
trotzdem nevertheless
bestaunen look at with astonishment
betören deceive, delude
heimlich secret(ly)
aufsperren open wide · **heimtückisch**
crafty, mischievous(ly) · **häßlich** unschön
entfliehen: er entflieht, entfloh, ist entflohen escape, flee · **die Bank, ⸚e** bench
von dannen von dort weg
aufgeben give up
sich erkühnen venture, dare
klopfen knock; beat · **die Beute, -n** loot,
prey
die Unterkunft, ⸚ Haus, Wohnung, Heim
sich bewegen move, be in motion
**schweigen: er schweigt, schwieg, hat
geschwiegen** be silent
**meines vorhin noch so stolz lutschenden
Vetters** = meines Vetters, der vorhin
noch so stolz lutschte
zwei immer wieder überraschende Seitentüren = zwei Seitentüren, die uns
immer wieder überraschten
blenden dazzle, blind

wenigen Minuten plapperten und klapperten die Zweihundert aus den Türen und ihrem sonntäglichen Abenteuer an die sonntägliche Luft.

Als allerletzte, mit verfinsterten Gemütern und dunklen Vorahnungen, mein zahnloser Vetter und ich. Wir sahen uns an. Stumm und gefaßt. Und beinahe männlich. Trotz unserer zwölf Jahre beinahe schon männlich. Mir kam es allerdings so vor, als ob in den Augen meines Vetters eine ungeheure Warnung für mich lauerte. Diese Warnung sagte: Wenn du jetzt anfängst zu lachen, hau ich dich tot!

Ich lachte nicht. Ich lachte erst fünf Minuten später. Dann aber um so ausführlicher.

Wir waren nur noch zwei—drei Schritte vom Ausgang entfernt und die Sonntagssonne kam uns, gänzlich unangebracht, freudestrahlend entgegen geblinzelt, da schrie es abermals. Diesmal war ich es, der schrie.

Ich stand und blieb stehen, als ob meine Zehen in einer Mausefalle säßen. Dann schrie auch ich zum zweiten Mal. Siegesbewußt:

Mensch, ich hab ihn!

Mein Vetter konnte nur dumm flüsternd fragen: Wen?

Da schrie ich zum dritten Mal: Mensch, den Stiftzahn! Ich stehe drauf!

Und damit nahm ich meinen Fuß von dem dicken, roten, dreckigen Teppich hoch. Da lag der Stiftzahn und tat, als ob nichts geschehen wäre! Das harte Steinchen, das gegen meine Sohle[g] gedrückt hatte, war der treulose Zahn. Vierhundert Füße hatten ihn wohl durch das ganze Kino vor sich hergestoßen. Allein hätte er sich kaum so weit gewagt.

Mein Vetter schrie nun auch noch einmal zum Abschluß.

Dann riß er den Stiftzahn an sich, strahlte ihn mit beiden Augen strafend aber doch selig an und beförderte ihn—ohne ihn wenigstens an der Jacke[g] abzuwischen—wieder an seinen Platz.

Und dann konnten wir endlich lachen. Bis uns die Tränen in den sauberen Sonntagskragen liefen. Denn auch mein Vetter hätte furchtbar gern gelacht, als der Zahn plötzlich nicht mehr da und weg war. Wenn es nur nicht gerade sein eigener Zahn gewesen wäre. Aber jetzt war er wieder an Ort und Stelle und wir sahen nicht ein, warum wir uns jetzt nicht halbtot lachen sollten.

Rahmbonbon hat mein Vetter nie wieder angesehen. Nicht mal angesehen. Ich kann das verstehen.

plappern babble, chatter
allerletzt last of all, the very last · **finster** dunkel, düster   **sich verfinstern** dunkel werden
vorkommen appear, seem   **mir kam es vor** mir schien es
ungeheuer sehr groß · **lauern** lurk
hauen: er haut, hieb, hat gehauen schlagen
ausführlich at length   **um so ausführlicher** all the more
der Ausgang, ⸚e exit
unangebracht unsuitable, inappropriate · **blinzeln** blink   **die Sonntagssonne kam uns . . . entgegen geblinzelt** the Sunday sun came blinking toward us
der Zeh, -en toe
siegesbewußt conscious of victory   **der Sieg, -e** victory
flüstern whisper
dreckig schmutzig · **der Teppich, -e** carpet
vor sich herstoßen kick ahead of oneself · **wagen** sich erkühnen
der Abschluß, ⸚e das Ende
reißen: er reißt, riß, hat gerissen seize; tear
befördern transport
der Kragen, - collar
furchtbar gern sehr gern   **furchtbar** schrecklich
an Ort und Stelle where it belongs, in place · **einsehen** verstehen

GLOSSARY

The Glossary is meant to be complete except for words of the following categories: **der**-words, possessive adjectives, articles, pronouns, diminutives, infinitive nouns, and numbers. Some literal compound nouns whose parts are familiar have not been included.

The plural forms of nouns are indicated unless they are nonexistent or rare. If the genitive singular of a masculine or neuter noun is not **-s** or **-es**, it is shown: **das Herz, -ens, -en**.

The principal parts of strong and irregular verbs are shown. If only a vowel change is involved, then only the stem vowels are given for the principal parts. Otherwise the entire form is spelled out. The 3rd person present indicative is shown if its vowel differs from that of the infinitive: **schlafen, ä, ie, a; gehen, ging, gegangen**.

Verbs that require a form of **sein** as the perfect tense auxiliary are indicated by (**s**): **gehen, ging, gegangen (s)**. Those that may take either **sein** or **haben**, depending on what they mean in the sentence, are designated by (**s, h**).

Verbs are accompanied by **sich** if they are reflexive, and by (**sich**) if they may be nonreflexive as well. The case of the reflexive pronoun is indicated as *acc. refl.* or *dat. refl.*

Separable (stressed) prefixes are shown by means of a hyphen between the prefix and the stem. The absence of a hyphen between a prefix and a stem means that the prefix is inseparable: **über-wechseln**, but **überzeugen**.

If the comparative and superlative forms of an adjective or adverb are irregular, then these forms are given along with the positive form.

Adjectives in **-en** that could be confused with verbs are designated as adjectives: **verschieden** *adj*. Similarly, where it might be possible to confuse conjunctions with prepositions, prepositions with adverbs, etc., these functions are indicated.

Following each entry in the Glossary is a reference to the place where that word occurs for the first time in the book. The *number* refers to the unit. The *first letter* refers to the part of the unit. The following abbreviations are used:

      D   Dialog, or notes to the Dialog
      S   Supplement, or notes to the Supplement
      A   Audiolingual Drills
      G   Grammar (excluding the Word-Formation section)
      W   Word-Formation
      L   Listening Practice
      R   Reading, or Reading Practice
      V   Vocabulary (excluding the Inference section)
      I   Inference

Words that appear for the first time in the reading selections of Units 31, 33, 34, and 35 are given two additional letters to identify the specific reading selection. These are:

Eh	Der Ehemann aus der Zeitung
De	Deutschland—Reiseland
Ge	Vom Geist unserer Zeit: Rekorde, Rekorde!
Fo	Fortschritt oder der Weg nach oben
Zi	Die Zimmervermieterin
He	Eigener Herd ist Goldes wert
Ne	Herr und Frau Neureich
Fa	Fanny
Bo	Wolfgang Borchert (1921–1947)
Br	Das Brot
St	Der Stiftzahn oder warum mein Vetter keine Rahmbonbon mehr ißt

Thus the designation (16S) refers to the Supplement of Unit 16; (34R Fa) refers to the reading selection **Fanny** in Unit 34.

ab-brechen, i, a, o break off, stop (35R St)
der **Abend, -e** evening (11S)
die **Abendgesellschaft, -en** evening party (23D)
abendlich evening, in the evening (14W)
abends evenings, in the evening (15S)
das **Abenteuer, -** adventure (33I)
abenteuersüchtig thirsty for adventure (35R St)
aber but, however (3D)
abermals again, once more (32I)
ab-fahren, ä, u, a (s) depart, leave (8S)
ab-flauen (s) die down, give way (33I)
abgemacht settled, agreed (2D)
ab-hangen von, i, a depend on (28R)
das **Abitur, -e** final secondary school examination, after thirteen years of school (19R)
ab-lehnen refuse (31R Eh)
der **Abschluß, ⸗sse** conclusion (35R St)
ab-schneiden, schnitt ab, abgeschnitten cut off (35R Br)
die **Absicht, -en** intention (31I)
absichtlich intentional, deliberate (31I)
das **Abteil, -e** section, compartment (21D)
ab-warten wait for, wait and see (3D)

ab-wischen wipe off (33I)
achten respect (22R)
ähnlich similar, like (23D)
die **Ähnlichkeit, -en** similarity (32W)
die **Ahnung, -en** presentiment; idea (18D)
der **Akademiker, -** academician (25R)
all all, every (3D); **alle** all gone (9D); **alles** everything (14D)
allein alone (12D)
allerdings certainly, to be sure; nevertheless (21D)
allerletzt last of all, the very last (35R St)
allgemein general, common (25R); **im allgemeinen** in general (33R Ge)
allsonntäglich every Sunday (35R St)
allzu too, far too (6D)
die **Alpen** pl. Alps (31R De)
als than (18A); when, as (21D); **als ob** as if (30D)
also well, then, thus, so, therefore (12D)
alt old (4D)
das **Alter, -** age (31R Eh)
die **Amateurgruppe, -n** group of amateurs (30R)
der **Amerikaner, -** American (22R)
amerikanisch American (30R)

Glossary 743

die **Ampel, -n** traffic light (31I)
an at; on; by; to (5D)
an sich by itself; basically (31I)
an-bauen build onto (24W)
an-bieten, o, o offer (22R)
an-braten, ä, ie, a begin to roast (24W)
an-dauern continue, go on (33R Fo)
ander- other, different; else (15D)
andererseits on the other hand (22R)
(sich) **ändern** change, become different (20D)
der **Anfall, ⸚e** attack (15D)
der **Anfang, ⸚e** beginning (3D)
an-fangen, ä, i, a begin (22R)
angeblich alleged, supposed (31R Eh)
angenehm pleasant, agreeable (31I)
der **Angestellte, -n** *adj. noun* employee (33R Fo)
an-grenzen be adjacent to (24W)
die **Angst, ⸚e** fear, fright; anxiety (1D); **Angst haben** be afraid (1D)
ängstlich frightened; anxious (14W)
die **Ängstlichkeit** anxiety (32W)
der **Angstschweiß** cold sweat, sweat of fear (6D)
an-haben, hatte an, angehabt have on (24W)
an-halten, ä, ie, a last; stop (35R St)
an-heizen begin to heat (24W)
an-hören listen to (24W)
an-kochen boil partially, parboil (24W)
an-kommen, kam an, angekommen (s) arrive (8S); **an-kommen auf** + *acc.* depend on (25R)
anläßlich *prep.* + *gen.* on the occasion of (17D)
an-laufen, äu, ie, au (s) run toward (24W)
an-lernen give initial training to (24W)
an-nehmen, nimmt an, nahm an, angenommen accept, take on (24W)
die **Annonce, -n** advertisement (31R Eh)
an-probieren try on (29S)
an-rauchen begin to smoke (24W)
die **Anregung, -en** stimulus; impulse (28R)
an-rufen, ie, u call up (21D)

an-schauen look at (24W); (sich) **an-schauen** *dat. refl.* look at (28R)
an-schwellen, i, o, o (s) grow, swell (35R St)
an-sehen, ie, a, e look at (17D)
das **Ansehen** reputation, esteem (34R Ne)
die **Ansicht, -en** view, opinion (17D)
die **Ansichtskarte, -n** picture postcard (17D)
der **Ansporn, -e** incentive (35R St)
an-sprechen, i, a, o address (a person) (24W)
der **Anspruch, ⸚e** claim, demand (33R Fo)
anständig proper, respectable (34R Zi)
an-stellen employ (33R Fo)
anstrengend strenuous (16D)
an-treffen, trifft an, traf an, angetroffen find, come across (16D)
die **Antwort, -en** answer (21W)
antworten answer (3S)
(sich) **an-ziehen, zog an, angezogen** *acc. refl.* get dressed; *dat. refl.* put on (21S)
die **Anziehungskraft, ⸚e** attraction (28R)
der **Anzug, ⸚e** suit (21S)
der **Apfel, ⸚** apple (19I)
die **Apotheke, -n** pharmacy (31I)
der **Apparat, -e** apparatus (25I)
der **Appetit** appetite (14D)
der **April** April (11S)
die **Arbeit, -en** work; (research) paper (12D)
arbeiten work (16S)
die **Arbeiterschaft** working class, workmen (32W)
arbeitslos out of work, unemployed (16W)
der **Architekt, -en, -en** architect (27R)
die **Art, -en** kind, sort (35R St)
der **Arzt, ⸚e** physician (31I)
die **Ärzteschaft** medical society (32W)
der **Assistent, -en, -en** (research) assistant (28R)
der **Atem** breath (31I)
die **Atemnot** shortness of breath (35R St)
atemraubend breathtaking (35R St)
atmen breathe (31I)

auch too, also; even (2D)
auf on, onto; upon, on top of (2D)
auf-bauen build up (30R)
der **Aufenthalt, -e** stop (31R De)
die **Aufgabe, -n** lesson, exercise (31I)
auf-geben, i, a, e give up (35R St)
auf-gehen, ging auf, aufgegangen (s) open (35R St)
auf-hören stop (30D)
auf-kaufen buy up (34R Ne)
die **Aufnahme, -n** picture, snapshot (17D)
auf-nehmen, nimmt auf, nahm auf, aufgenommen take a picture (17D)
auf-passen pay attention (13D)
auf-regen excite, agitate; **sich aufregen** *acc. refl.* get excited (29S)
die **Aufregung, -en** excitement (35R St)
der **Aufschrei, -e** scream, outcry (35R St)
auf-schreiben, ie, ie write down (21D)
auf-sehen, ie, a, e look up (35R Br)
auf-sperren open wide (35R St)
auf-stehen, stand auf, aufgestanden (s) get up (35R Br)
auf-suchen go and see, visit (34R He)
auf-wachen (s) wake up (35R Br)
das **Auge, -n** eye (12D)
der **Augenblick, -e** moment, instant (12D)
augenblicklich immediate, at the moment (35R St)
der **August** August (6D)
aus out of, of, from (11D)
aus-bilden train (28R)
die **Ausbildung, -en** education, training (25R)
auseinander-halten, ä, ie, a keep apart, distinguish between (30S)
ausfindig machen search out, trace (31R Eh)
ausführlich at length, in detail (35R St)
die **Ausführung, -en** explanation, comment; performance (27D)
der **Ausgang, ⸗e** exit (35R St)
ausgesprochen pronounced, distinct (24D)
ausgezeichnet excellent, distinguished (30R)

das **Ausland** foreign countries, abroad (21D)
der **Ausländer, -** foreigner (22R)
aus-machen switch off (22I)
die **Ausnahme, -n** exception (22R)
aus-reichen be sufficient (33R Fo)
aus-sehen, ie, a, e appear, look (6D)
außen outside (31I)
außer except (for) (12A)
äußer- *adj.* external, outside (33V)
außerdem moreover, besides (19R)
außerhalb outside of (17S)
aus-steigen, ie, ie (s) get out, off (8S)
die **Auswahl** assortment, selection (10D)
auswendig by heart (31I)
(sich) **aus-zeichnen** *acc. refl.* distinguish (oneself) (28R)
(sich) **aus-ziehen, zog aus, ausgezogen** *acc. refl.* get undressed; *dat. refl.* take off (21S)
das **Auto, -s** automobile (31R De)
die **Autobahn, -en** superhighway (31R De)
der **Autor, -en** author (30R)

die **Backe, -n** cheek (33I)
der **Bäcker, -** baker (23D)
das **Bad, ⸗er** bath (25I)
baden bathe; swim (31R De)
das **Baden** swimming (2D)
die **Bahn, -en** railroad; course, track (7D)
der **Bahnhof, ⸗e** railroad station (31I)
bald soon (12D)
der **Ball, ⸗e** ball (25I)
die **Banane, -n** banana (25I)
die **Bank, ⸗e** bench (35R St)
die **Bank, -en** bank (19I)
barfuß barefoot (35R Br)
der **Bart, ⸗e** beard (28I)
der **Bau, -ten** building, construction (21W)
der **Bauch, ⸗e** belly (31I)
bauen build (27R)
der **Bauer, -n** farmer; peasant (31I)
der **Baum, ⸗e** tree (31I)
der **Baumeister, -** architect, master builder (27R)
der **Bayer, -n, -n** Bavarian (33R Fo)

beabsichtigen intend (31I)
der **Beamte, -n** *adj. noun* civil servant; official (28R)
bearbeiten work up, over (26W)
sich **bedanken** *acc. refl.* thank; decline (26W)
bedauern regret, feel sorry for (32I)
bedauernswert regrettable, unfortunate (32I)
bedecken cover up (26W)
bedenklich doubtful; critical (28R)
bedeuten mean (22R)
die **Bedeutung, -en** meaning, significance (28R)
bedienen serve, wait on (31I)
die **Bedingung, -en** condition, restriction (25R)
beenden finish (28R)
befehlen, ie, a, o order (31I)
befördern transport (35R St)
befragen interrogate, consult (26W)
begabt gifted (25R)
die **Begabung, -en** gift, talent (25R)
begegnen (s) + *dat.* meet (31I)
der **Beginn, -e** beginning (35R St)
beginnen, a, o begin (4D)
begnadigen pardon (35R Bo)
begrenzen border (26W)
begrüßen greet (22R)
behalten, ä, ie, a keep (25R)
behandeln handle, treat (31I)
die **Behandlung, -en** treatment (31I)
bei near, beside, with, at the house of (2D)
beide both, two (8D)
das **Bein, -e** leg (15D)
beinah(e) almost (29D)
bei-pflichten agree (34R Fa)
das **Beispiel, -e** example; **zum Beispiel (z.B.)** for example (33R Fo)
beißen, biß, gebissen bite (26W)
der **Bekannte, -n** *adj. noun* acquaintance (8D)
die **Bekanntschaft, -en** acquaintance (31R De)
bekommen, bekam, bekommen receive, get (15D)

belachen laugh at (26W)
beleben enliven; resuscitate (26W)
belehren teach, inform (26W)
Belgien Belgium (12S)
das **Benzin** gasoline (28I)
bequem comfortable (31R De)
beraten, ä, ie, a give advice to (26W)
bereit ready (32I)
bereits already (21D)
der **Berg, -e** mountain (31R De)
bergig mountainous (31R De)
der **Bericht, -e** report (21W)
berichten report (21D)
der **Beruf, -e** profession; calling (25R)
berufen, ie, u appoint, call (28R)
die **Berufsausbildung, -en** professional training (25R)
das **Berufstheater, -** professional theater (30R)
beruhigen calm; reassure (16D)
die **Beruhigung, -en** calming (17W)
berühmt famous (31R De)
beschauen look over (26W)
beschließen, beschloß, beschlossen conclude, decide (26W)
der **Beschluß, ⸗sse** agreement (26D)
beschreiben, ie, ie describe (26W)
besehen, ie, a, e look over (26W)
besetzen occupy (26W)
besichtigen visit; inspect (26D)
die **Besichtigung, -en** visit; inspection (26D)
besitzen, besaß, besessen possess; sit upon (26W)
besonder- *adj.* special (28R)
besonders especially (22R)
besorgen provide, take care of (35R Bo)
besprechen, i, a, o discuss (26W)
bestaunen look at with astonishment (35R St)
bestehen, bestand, bestanden pass (a test) (21D); exist (25R); **bestehen aus** consist of (12D); **bestanden** covered (31R De)
bestimmt definite, certain (1D)

der **Besuch**, -e   visit   (15D)
betören   deceive, delude   (35R St)
der **Betrag**, ⸗e   amount, sum   (33R Fo)
betragen, ä, u, a   amount to; **sich betragen** *acc. refl.*   behave (oneself)   (26W)
betreffen, betrifft, betraf, betroffen   concern   (26W)
betreten, betritt, betrat, betreten   step on; enter   (26W)
das **Bett**, -en   bed   (15D)
sich **beugen** *acc. refl.*   bow, bend   (35R Br)
die **Beute**, -n   loot, prey   (35R St)
die **Bevölkerung**, -en   population   (31R De)
die **Bevölkerungsdichte**   population density   (31R De)
bevor *conj.*   before   (26S)
(sich) **bewegen** *acc. refl.*   move   (35R St)
die **Bewegung**, -en   movement   (35R St)
bewölkt   cloudy, clouded   (35R St)
bezahlen   pay   (25R)
beziehungsweise (bzw.)   respectively, or as the case may be   (34R Zi)
das **Bier**, -e   beer   (14S)
bieten, o, o   offer, bid   (26W)
das **Bild**, -er   picture   (17D)
bilden   form, shape   (28R)
die **Bildung**, -en   education   (25R)
die **Bildungsreise**, -n   educational trip   (29D)
billig   cheap, inexpensive   (10D)
die **Biologie**   biology   (25R)
die **Birne**, -n   pear; light bulb   (33I)
bis *prep.*   until, up to   (15S); *conj.* until   (28R)
bißchen: ein bißchen   a little (bit)   (15D)
die **Bitte**, -n   request   (21W)
bitten, bat, gebeten   ask, request   (7D); invite   (34R Ne); **bitten um**   ask for   (21D)
bitter   bitter   (25I)
blaß   pale   (16D)
die **Blässe**   paleness, pallor   (30W)
das **Blatt**, ⸗er   leaf; sheet (of paper)   (31I)
das **Blaulicht**, -er   blue light   (6D)
das **Blei**   lead   (21D)

bleiben, ie, ie (s)   remain, stay   (3D)
der **Bleistift**, -e   pencil   (21D)
blenden   dazzle, blind   (35R St)
der **Blick**, -e   look, glance; view   (12D)
blind   blind   (25I)
die **Blindheit**   blindness   (32W)
blinzeln   blink   (35R St)
blond   blond   (31R Eh)
blühen   bloom, blossom   (31I)
die **Blume**, -n   flower   (31I)
die **Bluse**, -n   blouse   (34R Fa)
das **Blut**   blood   (28I)
bluten   bleed   (28I)
der **Boden**, ⸗   floor, ground   (23S)
der **Bodensee**   Lake Constance   (12S)
die **Bombe**, -n   bomb   (33R Ge)
der **Bonbon**, - *or* -s   candy   (30S)
böse   angry; bad   (31I)
der **Bote**, -n, -n   messenger   (11D)
die **Botschaft**, -en   message   (32W)
der **Brand**, ⸗e   fire, burning   (27D)
braten, ä, ie, a   fry, roast, bake   (14S)
brauchen   need   (8D)
brav   good, honest   (15D)
brechen, i, a, o   break   (26W)
breit   broad, wide   (28I)
die **Breite**, -n   breadth, width; latitude   (30W)
brennen, brannte, gebrannt   burn   (26W)
das **Brett**, -er   board   (12D)
der **Brief**, -e   letter   (30D)
die **Briefmarke**, -n   postage stamp   (33I)
die **Brille**, -n   (eye)glasses   (31R Eh, 31I)
bringen, brachte, gebracht   bring   (20A); print   (31R Eh)
das **Brot**, -e   bread   (14S)
die **Brücke**, -n   bridge   (31I)
der **Bruder**, ⸗   brother   (4D)
die **Brüderschaft**, -en   brotherhood; fellowship   (32W)
das **Buch**, ⸗er   book   (9D)
der **Buchstabe**, -n, -n   letter of the alphabet   (33I)
der **Bund**, ⸗e   federation, union   (31R De)
das **Bundesland**, ⸗er   state (of the Federal

Republic of Germany) (33R Fo)
die **Bundesrepublik,** -en federal republic; **die Bundesrepublik Deutschland** Federal Republic of Germany (31R De)
bunt many-colored, colorful (34I)
der **Bürgermeister,** - mayor (34R Ne)
der **Bus,** -se bus (20D)
der **Busch,** ⸗e bush, shrub (22I)
die **Butter** butter (14S)

die **Chemie** chemistry (25R)
die **Christlich-Demokratische Union** Christian Democratic Union (33R Fo)
da *adv.* there (1D); then, in that case (4D); *conj.* since, because (31R De)
dabei with it (12D); among them (17D); with regard to this (22R)
das **Dach,** ⸗er roof (32I)
die **Dachrinne,** -n (roof) gutter (35R Br)
dagegen on the other hand (33R Ge)
damals at that time, then (20D)
die **Dame,** -n lady (27D)
damit *adv.* with it (14A); *conj.* so that (16D)
Dänemark Denmark (12S)
der **Dank** thanks, gratitude (6D)
dann then (2D)
dannen: von dannen away from there (35R St)
daran (glauben) in it (3D)
darauf (warten) for it (3D); afterwards (20D)
darin in it (7D)
dauern last (28R)
der **Daumen,** - thumb (25I)
davon from that, from it (9D)
dazu in addition (28R)
die **Decke,** -n tablecloth; blanket; ceiling (13D)
decken cover; set (a table) (13D)
demokratisch democratic (33R Fo)
denken think; **denken an** + *acc.* think of, about (16S); **sich denken** *dat. refl.* imagine (21S)

der **Denker,** - thinker (25I)
denn *adv.* anyway; tell me (1D); *conj.* for, because (19D)
derselbe the same (6D)
deshalb therefore, for that reason (31R Eh)
deswegen therefore, for that reason (35R St)
deutlich clear, distinct, evident (33R Fo)
deutsch German (10G)
das **Deutsch** German (language) (22R)
der **Deutsche,** -n *adj. noun* German citizen (22R)
Deutschland Germany (12S)
der **Dezember** December (11S)
der **Dialog,** -e dialog (9A)
der **Dichter,** - poet; writer (of fiction) (34I)
dichterisch poetic (35R Bo)
dick thick, fat (25I)
die **Dicke,** -n thickness, fatness (30W)
der **Dieb,** -e thief (25I)
der **Dienstag** Tuesday (11S)
diesmal this time (35R Bo)
diesseits this side of (17S)
das **Ding,** -e thing (12D)
diskutieren discuss (28R)
doch after all, but, nevertheless; do! oh yes! oh no! (2D)
der **Doktor,** -en doctor (19R)
die **Doktorarbeit,** -en doctoral dissertation (25I)
der **Dollar,** -s dollar (32I)
der **Dom,** -e cathedral (17D)
die **Domäne,** -n domain, area (30R)
der **Donnerstag** Thursday (11S)
das **Donnerwetter,** - thunderstorm; I'll be darned! (20D)
das **Dorf,** ⸗er village (17S)
der **Dorn,** -en thorn (25I)
dort there (5D)
das **Drama,** -men drama (19I)
draußen outside, outdoors (31I)
dreckig dirty, filthy (35R St)
dreijährig three-year, lasting three years (25R)

die **dreißiger Jahre** *pl.* the thirties (31R De)
dreiteilig three-part, consisting of three parts (35R St)
dringen, a, u (s) penetrate (35R St)
drinnen inside, indoors (31I)
das **Drittel, -** third (part) (30R)
drüben over there (31I)
drucken print (34I)
drücken press, push, clasp (33I)
dumm stupid, dull (31I)
dunkel dark (31I)
die **Dunkelheit** darkness (32W)
dünn thin (25I)
durch through, by (6D)
durchaus absolutely, positively (31R Eh)
durchlaufen, äu, ie, au run through, pass through (25R)
der **Durchschnitt, -e** average (31R Eh)
durchweg ordinarily; always (28R)
dürfen, darf, durfte, gedurft may, can, be permitted to; **nicht dürfen** must not (13D)
der **Durst** thirst (25I)
durstig thirsty (25I)
düster gloomy, dark; sad (30D)
das **Dutzend, -e** dozen (34I)
duzen address with **du** (22R)

eben just; even; exactly (7D)
ebensogut just as well (13D)
echoen echo (35R Br)
echt genuine, real (28R)
die **Ecke, -n** corner (6D)
die **Ehe, -n** marriage (31R Eh)
der **Eheanbahner, -** professional matchmaker (31R Eh)
die **Eheanbahnung, -en** professional matchmaking (31R Eh)
der **Ehemann, ⸗er** married man (31R Eh)
die **Ehevermittlung, -en** professional matchmaking (31R Eh)
das **Ehevermittlungsinstitut, -e** matrimonial agency (31R Eh)
das **Ei, -er** egg (34I)

eigenartig peculiar, special (22R)
eigentlich actually, really (4D)
eilig quick, urgent, in a hurry (7D)
einander each other (20D)
eindringlich urgent; forceful (33R Ge)
einfach simple (11D)
ein-fangen, ä, i, a catch, capture (33R Fo)
der **Einfluß, ⸗sse** influence, effect (28R)
ein-führen introduce (something) (17W)
die **Einführung, -en** introduction (3D)
ein-halten, ä, ie, a stop (32I)
einige a few (17D)
ein-kaufen shop (19R)
ein-laufen, äu, ie, au (s) arrive; pull in (7D)
einmal once (10D); **auf einmal** all of a sudden (32I); **nicht einmal** not even (20D)
ein-nehmen, nimmt ein, nahm ein, eingenommen take up, occupy (30R)
einsam lonely, alone (34I)
ein-schärfen impress (something upon someone) (35R St)
ein-schlafen, ä, ie, a (s) fall asleep (35R Br)
der **Einschreibbrief, -e** registered letter (30D)
ein-sehen, ie, a, e realize (35R St)
ein-steigen, ie, ie (s) get in, on; board (7D)
einzeln separate, individual (25R)
das **Einzelteil, -e** separate part (11D)
einzig only (28R)
das **Eis** ice; ice cream (1D)
das **Eisen** iron (31R De)
die **Eisenbahn, -en** train, railroad (31R De)
der **Eismann, ⸗er** ice-cream man (1D)
elektrisch electric (25I)
die **Eltern** *pl.* parents (21S)
der **Empfang, ⸗e** reception (27D)
empfangen, ä, i, a receive (27D)
empfinden, a, u feel (7D)
die **Empfindung, -en** feeling (17W)
das **Ende, -n** end (9D); **an allen Enden** all over the place (35R St)

das **Endexamen**, - final examination (19R)
   endlich finally, at last (4D)
   endlos endless (16W)
die **Energie**, -n energy (25R)
   eng narrow, small; crowded (31R De)
   England England (29L)
   englisch English (30R)
das **Englisch** English (language) (25R)
der **Enkel**, - grandson (34I)
das **Ensuite-Theater**, - theater in which a single production is performed repeatedly over a long period of time (30R)
   entdecken discover (26W)
   entfernen remove; **entfernt** distant, away (33I)
   entfliehen, o, o (s) escape, flee (35R St)
   entgegen-gehen, ging entgegen, entgegengegangen (s) go toward, go to meet (11D)
   entgehen, entging, entgangen (s) escape (26W)
(sich) **entkleiden** *acc. refl.* undress (26W)
   entkommen, entkam, entkommen (s) escape, get away (26W)
   entlassen, ä, ie, a dismiss, discharge (26W)
   entlaufen, äu, ie, au run away (26W)
sich **entschließen, entschloß, entschlossen** *acc. refl.* make up one's mind, decide (34I)
(sich) **entschuldigen** *acc. refl.* excuse (oneself) (3D)
die **Entschuldigung**, -en excuse, apology (17W)
   entsetzen frighten, terrify (35R St)
   entspringen, a, u (s) rise; escape (12D)
die **Entwicklung**, -en development (28R)
   entziehen, entzog, entzogen take away from (26W)
der **Epikureer**, - epicurean (29D)
   erarbeiten attain by hard work (26W)
   erbauen build up, construct (27D)
   erbitten, erbat, erbeten beg; obtain by begging (26W)
   erblicken catch sight of (26W)

die **Erde**, -n earth (31I)
das **Ereignis**, -se event, incident (22R)
   erfahren, ä, u, a find out, learn; experience (20D)
die **Erfahrung**, -en experience (4D)
   erfinden, a, u invent (26W)
der **Erfolg**, -e success (35R St)
   erfreuen bring joy to (26W)
sich **erfrischen** *acc. refl.* refresh oneself (26W)
   erfüllen fulfill (26W)
   ergänzen supplement, complete (26W)
   ergeben, i, a, e yield, produce (26W)
das **Ergebnis**, -se result, outcome (33R Fo)
   erhalten, ä, ie, a maintain; receive (26W)
   erheblich considerable (33R Fo)
   erhitzen heat (26W)
   erhoffen expect (26W)
   erhöhen raise (26W)
(sich) **erholen** *acc. refl.* recover (26W, 31R De)
sich **erkälten** *acc. refl.* catch cold (26W)
   erkennen, erkannte, erkannt recognize (23D)
   erklären explain (7D)
   erkranken become ill (26W)
sich **erkühnen** *acc. refl.* venture, dare; make bold (35R St)
   erleben experience (26W)
   erleichtern make easy, facilitate (26W)
   erlernen learn (25R)
   erliegen, a, e succumb (26W)
   ermöglichen make possible (26W)
   ermorden murder (27D)
   ernennen, ernannte, ernannt nominate, appoint (26W)
   erneue(r)n renew (26W)
   ernst serious (5D)
der **Ernst** earnestness, seriousness (3D)
   erraten, ä, ie, a guess correctly (26W)
   erreichen reach, attain (25R)
   errichten erect, establish (27D)
   erscheinen, ie, ie (s) make an appearance (26W)
   erschrecken, erschrickt, erschrak, er-

schrocken (s)   be startled   (35R St)
erschweren   make more difficult   (26W)
ersetzen   replace   (26W)
(sich) ersparen *dat. refl.*   save up; save (effort)   26W)
erst *adj.*   first   (3D); *adv.* only, not until, no sooner than, no more than   (4D);
erst recht   more than ever   (31I)
ersticken (s)   suffocate, smother   (33I)
ertragen, ä, u, a   endure   (26W)
ertrinken, a, u (s)   drown   (26W)
der Erwachsene, -n *adj. noun*   adult   (22R)
erwärmen   warm up   (26W)
erwarten   expect   (26W)
die Erwartung, -en   expectation   (34R He)
erzählen   tell   (4D)
die Erzählung, -en   story   (8D)
erziehen, erzog, erzogen   bring up, educate   (25R)
essen, i, a, e   eat   (1D)
etwa   about, perhaps   (33R Ge)
etwas   something, anything; somewhat; some; so etwas   such a thing   (7D)
der Europäer, -   European   (31R De)
europäisch   European   (31R De)
ewig   eternal   (20D)
das Examen, -   examination   (19R)
der Experte, -n, -n   expert   (29L, 33R Ge)
der Export, -e   export(s)   (29L)
extrem   extreme   (30R)

die Fabrik, -en   factory   (21D)
das Fach, ⸚er   subject (in school)   (25R)
fahren, ä, u, a (s,h)   drive, go, travel, ride   (8A)
der Fahrer, -   driver   (6D)
das Fahrrad, ⸚er   bicycle   (34I)
die Fahrt, -en   trip, excursion   (21W)
die Fakultät, -en   (university) faculty   (28R)
der Fall, ⸚e   case, event   (35R St)
die Falle, -n   trap   (33I)
fallen, fällt, fiel, gefallen (s)   fall   (25I)
falsch   false   (16D)
die Falschheit   falseness   (32W)
falten   fold   (28I)

die Familie, -n   family   (23D)
die Farbe, -n   color   (17D)
das Farbfoto, -s   color photograph   (17D)
fassen   grasp, get hold of; gefaßt   composed, calm   (33I)
fast   almost   (9D)
der Februar   February   (11S)
die Feder, -n   pen; feather   (25I)
fehlen   be absent   (35R Br)
der Fehler, -   mistake   (34I)
die Feier, -n   celebration   (17D)
die Feierlichkeit   festivity   (32W)
fein   fine   (1D)
die Feindschaft, -en   hostility   (32W)
die Feinheit, -en   fineness   (32W)
das Fenster, -   window   (10D)
die Ferien *pl.*   vacation   (31R De)
fertig   ready, finished   (11D)
das Fest, -e   holiday; feast; festival   (17D)
die Festlichkeit, -en   festivity   (32W)
der Festtag, -e   holiday   (17S)
der Festzug, ⸚e   festive procession   (17D)
das Feuer, -   fire   (33I)
der Film, -e   film, movie   (18D)
finanziell   financial   (28R)
finden, a, u   find   (3D)
der Finger, -   finger   (19I)
finster   dark, gloomy   (35R St)
die Firma, -men   firm   (34R Ne)
der Fisch, -e   fish   (19I)
flach   flat, level   (31R De)
die Fläche, -n   surface; area   (31R De)
die Flasche, -n   bottle   (18S)
das Fleisch   meat   (14S)
fleißig   industrious, diligent   (28R)
die Fleißigkeit   industriousness   (32W)
die Fliese, -n   tile   (35R Br)
der Floh, ⸚e   flea   (33I)
flott   free and easy, carefree   (15D)
der Fluch, ⸚e   curse   (35R St)
fluchen   swear   (29S)
die Flucht, -en   flight, escape   (35R St)
der Fluß, ⸚sse   river   (17S)
flüstern   whisper   (35R St)
die Flut, -en   flood   (28I)
der Föderalismus   federalism   (30R)

die **Folge**, -n   result, consequence, sequence (33R Fo)
  folgen (s)   follow (3D)
die **Form**, -en   form, shape (9D)
  formen   form, shape, mold (28R)
  förmlich   formal, ceremonial (14W)
die **Formulierung**, -en   formulation, precise wording (33R Fo)
  forschen   do research; investigate (31R Eh)
der **Forscher**, -   researcher; inquirer (31R Eh)
  fort-fahren, ä, u, a (s)   continue (27D)
der **Fortschritt**, -e   progress (33R Fo)
die **Fortsetzung**, -en   continuation (3D)
das **Foto**, -s   photograph (17D)
die **Frage**, -n   question (7D)
  fragen   ask, inquire (3S)
  Frankreich   France (12S)
der **Franzose**, -n, -n   Frenchman (27R)
  französisch   French (30R)
das **Französisch**   French (language) (25R)
die **Frau**, -en   Mrs.; woman, wife (5D)
das **Fräulein**, -   Miss; young lady (3D)
  frei   free; vacant (3D)
die **Freie Demokratische Partei (FDP)**   Free Democratic Party (33R Fo)
die **Freiheit**   freedom; **die Freiheiten** pl. liberties (32W)
der **Freitag**   Friday (11S)
  freiwillig   voluntary (25R)
  fremd   strange; foreign (22R)
  fremdartig   strange, unfamiliar (22R)
die **Fremde**   foreign country (30W)
der **Fremdenführer**, -   tourist guide (26D)
die **Fremdheit**   foreignness, strangeness (32W)
die **Fremdsprache**, -n   foreign language (25R)
  fressen, i, a, e   eat (*said of animals*) (33I)
die **Freude**, -n   joy, pleasure (35R St)
die **Freudenkundgebung**, -en   demonstration of joy (35R St)
  freudestrahlend   beaming with joy (35R St)
sich **freuen** *acc. refl.*   be glad, be happy (24D);

sich **freuen auf** + *acc.*   look forward to (24D); sich **freuen über** + *acc.* be happy about (25R)
der **Freund**, -e   friend (8D)
die **Freundin**, -nen   girl friend (8D)
  freundlich   friendly (14W)
die **Freundschaft**, -en   friendship (22R)
  frieren, o, o   freeze (34I)
  frisch   fresh (18S)
  fromm   religious, pious (31I)
  früh   early, in the morning (15D)
die **Frühe**   early morning (30W)
der **Frühling**, -e   spring (11S)
das **Frühstück**   breakfast (31I)
  fühlen   feel (something); **sich fühlen** *acc. refl.*   feel (well, bad, ill, etc.) (32I)
der **Führer**, -   guide, leader (26D)
  füllen   fill (13D)
  für   for; in (10D)
  furchtbar   awful, terrible; **furchtbar gern**   very much (35R St)
der **Fuß**, ⸗e   foot (23S)
der **Fußboden**, ⸗   floor (23S)
das **Fußgetrampel**   stamping with the feet (35R St)

die **Gabel**, -n   fork (13D)
  gähnen   yawn (34I)
der **Galgen**, -   gallows (33R Ge)
der **Galgenhumor**   grim humor (33R Ge)
  ganz   whole, entire; all; quite (5D)
  gänzlich   complete, total (35R St)
die **Ganzzeitschule**, -n   full-time school (25R)
  gar nicht   not at all (11D)
die **Gardine**, -n   curtain (34R Zi)
der **Garten**, ⸗   garden; yard (19I)
das **Gas**, -e   gas (22I)
der **Gast**, ⸗e   guest (31R De)
das **Gasthaus**, ⸗er   restaurant, inn (31R De)
der **Gasthof**, ⸗e   inn, small hotel (34R He)
die **Gaststätte**, -n   restaurant (31R De)
das **Gebäude**, -   building (29W)
  geben, i, a, e   give; **es gibt**   there is, there are (17R)

das **Gebiet**, -e   area, region   (31R De)
das **Gebirge**, -   mountains, mountain range   (31R De)
die **Gebirgslandschaft**, -en   mountain landscape   (31R De)
   geboren   born   (34R Ne)
der **Gebrauch**, ⸚e   use   (29W)
der **Gedanke**, -ns, -n   thought, idea   (21D)
das **Gedeck**, -e   cover, table setting   (29W)
das **Gedicht**, -e   poem   (10D)
   gefährlich   dangerous   (33R Fo)
das **Gefährt**, -e   vehicle   (29W)
das **Gefälle**, -   slope, grade   (29W)
   gefallen, gefällt, gefiel, gefallen   please; like   (11D)
der **Gefallen**, -   favor   (21W)
das **Gefängnis**, -se   prison   (34I)
   gefaßt   composed, calm   (33I)
das **Gefolge**, -   retinue   (29W)
das **Gefrage**   questioning   (29W)
das **Gefühl**, -e   feeling   (26D)
   gegen   against; toward; around   (2D)
die **Gegend**, -en   area, region   (23D)
das **Gegenteil**, -e   opposite; **im Gegenteil**   on the contrary   (3D)
   gegenüber *prep.* + *dat.*   opposite, facing   (35R Br)
das **Gehalt**, ⸚er   salary   (29W)
das **Gehänge**, -   garland, festoon   (29W)
die **Gehässigkeit**, -en   hatefulness, animosity, malice   (35R St)
   gehen, ging, gegangen (s)   go, walk   (2D); **wie geht's**   how are you?   (2D)
der **Gehilfe**, -n, -n   assistant; clerk   (29W)
das **Gehör**   (sense of) hearing   (29W)
   gehören   belong to   (11D); **gehören zu**   be a part of   (25R)
die **Geige**, -n   violin   (2D)
der **Geist**, -er   spirit   (33R Ge)
das **Geklapper**   clatter(ing)   (29W)
das **Gelächter**   laughter   (29W)
das **Gelaufe**   running around   (29W)
das **Geld**   money   (9D); *pl.* **Gelder**   funds
   geldsüchtig   greedy for money   (30S)
   gelingen, a, u (s)   succeed   (11D)
das **Gemälde**, -   painting, picture   (34R Ne)

   gemeinsam   together, joint   (26D)
die **Gemeinschaft**   community   (32W)
das **Gemüse**, -   vegetable   (34R He)
das **Gemüt**, -er   feeling, temper, disposition   (33I)
   gemütlich   comfortable, cozy   (24D)
   genau   exact, precise; just   (12D)
die **Genauigkeit**, -en   exactness, precision   (32W)
die **Generation**, -en   generation   (28R)
   genießen, genoß, genossen   enjoy   (26S)
   genießerisch   enjoyable   (35R St)
   genug   enough   (6D)
   genügen   suffice, be enough   (18D)
das **Geräusch**, -e   noise   (35R St)
   gern   gladly   (13S); **lieber**   (18G); **liebst-**   (18G)
das **Gerücht**, -e   rumor   (29W)
das **Gerufe**   calling, shouting   (29W)
   gesamt   whole; common, joint   (33R Fo)
das **Gesäß**, -e   seat   (29W)
das **Geschäft**, -e   business; shop, store   (11D)
   geschäftlich   commercial; on business   (14W)
   geschehen, ie, a, e (s)   happen   (34R He)
das **Geschenk**, -e   present   (34R Ne)
die **Geschichte**, -n   story; history; event, affair   (15D)
   geschickt   able, capable   (34R Ne)
der **Geschmack**, ⸚e   taste   (21W)
die **Gesellschaft**, -en   company; society; party   (23D)
das **Gesetz**, -e   law   (29W)
das **Gesicht**, -er   face   (29W)
das **Gespött**   mockery   (29W)
das **Gespräch**, -e   conversation   (21W)
das **Gestell**, -e   stand, rack   (29W)
   gestern   yesterday   (15S)
das **Gesuch**, -e   application (for a job)   (29W)
   gesund   healthy   (33R Ge)
   gesundheitsschädlich   injurious to health   (33R Ge)
das **Getränk**, -e   beverage   (29W)
   gewinnen, a, o   win   (29D)

gewiß   sure, certain   (16D)
das Gewissen   conscience   (29W)
die Gewißheit   certainty   (32W)
gewöhnlich   usual, common   (34R He)
das Gift, -e   poison   (1D)
das Glas, ⸚er   glass   (18S)
glatt   smooth; slippery   (34I)
der Glaube, -ns, -n   belief   (21W)
glauben   believe, think; glauben an + acc.   believe in   (3D)
gleich   same, like, alike; immediately   (8D)
die Gleichheit, -en   equality   (32W)
gleichmäßig   uniform, constant   (35R Br)
gleichzeitig   at the same time, simultaneous   (22R)
das Glück   happiness; luck   (10D)
glücklich   happy; lucky   (14W, 18D)
glühen   glow   (35R St)
gnädig   gracious; gnädige Frau   Madame   (10D)
das Gold   gold   (22I)
der Gott   God   (6D); der Gott, ⸚er   god, deity
göttlich   divine, godlike   (14W)
gottlos   godless   (16W)
der Grad, -e   degree, level   (28R)
das Gramm, -e (g)   gram   (22I)
das Gras, ⸚er   grass   (25I)
die Grenze, -n   border   (21W)
grenzen   border   (12S)
das Griechisch   Greek (language)   (25R)
der Groschen, -   ten-pfennig coin   (35R St)
groß   big, tall, grand, great   (10D); größer, größt-   (18A)
die Größe, -n   size   (27R)
die Großeltern pl.   grandparents   (21S)
der Großhandel   wholesale trade   (34R Ne)
die Großmutter, ⸚   grandmother   (21S)
der Großvater, ⸚   grandfather   (21S)
grün   green   (18S)
der Grund, ⸚e   reason, basis   (32I)
der Grundsatz, ⸚e   principle   (25R)
die Grüne   green(ness)   (30W)
die Gruppe, -n   group   (32I)

das Gulasch   goulash   (34R He)
gut   good, well, fine   (2D); besser   better   (8D); am besten   best of all   (1D)
das Gut, ⸚er   property, possession   (34R He)
die Güte   goodness; quality   (30W)
der Gymnasiast, -en, -en   student at a Gymnasium   (28R)
das Gymnasium, -sien   secondary school   (19R)

das Haar, -e   hair   (33I)
haarscharf   extremely accurate   (35R St)
haben, du hast, er hat, hatte, gehabt   have   (1D)
die Habilitation, -en   postdoctoral examination   (28R)
(sich) habilitieren acc. refl.   qualify for a position as university professor   (28R)
der Hafen, ⸚   harbor, port   (34I)
halb   half   (7S)
die Halbtagsarbeit   part-time job   (19R)
halten   endure, last, hold up   (31R Eh); Ruhe halten   stay quiet, stay calm   (15D)
die Haltestelle, -n   stopping place   (23D)
die Haltung, -en   posture; attitude   (17W)
der Hammer, ⸚   hammer   (19I)
die Hand, ⸚e   hand   (19I)
der Handel   trade, business   (34R Ne)
der Händler, -   dealer, merchant   (34R Ne)
der Handschuh, -e   glove   (34R Fa)
das Handtuch, ⸚er   towel   (24S)
der Handwerker, -   artisan, workman   (25R)
hängen, i, a   hang, be suspended   (23S)
hart   hard   (25I)
die Härte, -n   hardness   (30W)
häßlich   ugly, unpleasant   (35R St)
hauen, hieb, gehauen   beat   (35R St)
häufig   frequent   (8D)
die Häufigkeit   frequency   (32W)
das Hauptfach, ⸚er   major subject   (25R)
die Hauptsache, -n   main point   (34R Ne)
hauptsächlich   principally   (25R)
die Hauptstadt, ⸚e   capital   (30R)

das **Haus**, ⸚er   house, building   (6D); **nach Hause gehen**   go home   (12D); **zu Hause sein**   be at home   (12D)
die **Hausarbeit, -en**   housework   (34R Fa); homework   (34I)
der **Hausbesitzer, -**   house owner, landlord   (30D)
die **Hausecke, -n**   corner of a house or building   (6D)
der **Haushalt, -e**   household   (34R Ne)
der **Hausherr, -n, -en**   landlord   (30D)
häuslich   domestic   (14W)
das **Hausmädchen, -**   maid   (34R Fa)
der **Hauswirt, -e**   landlord   (30D)
heben, o, o   raise, lift   (32I)
die **Hecke, -n**   hedge   (35R St)
das **Heft, -e**   notebook, booklet   (34I)
heftig   intense, vigorous, violent   (32I)
heilen   cure   (31R De)
die **Heilquelle, -n**   mineral spring, spa   (31R De)
das **Heim, -e**   home   (22I)
die **Heimat**   native country, homeland   (31R De)
das **Heimatland,** ⸚er   native country   (31R De)
heimlich   secret   (35R St)
heimtückisch   crafty, mischievous   (35R St)
die **Heirat, -en**   marriage; wedding   (31R Eh)
heiß   hot   (1D)
heißen, ie, ei   be called   (11S)
heizen   heat   (22I)
der **Held, -en, -en**   hero   (3D)
heldenmütig   heroic   (35R St)
helfen, i, a, o   help   (4D)
hell   light, bright   (31I)
das **Hemd, -en**   shirt   (21S)
heran-führen   lead, bring   (35R Bo)
heraus-bekommen   solve, puzzle out   (35R St)
heraus-finden, a, u   find out   (31R De)
herbei-führen   pass (a resolution)   (26D)
der **Herbst, -e**   fall, autumn   (11S)
der **Herd, -e**   stove, hearth   (34R He)

herein   in (to this place)   (24D)
der **Herr, -n, -en**   Mr.; gentleman   (3D)
herrlich   magnificent, splendid   (34I)
die **Herrschaft**   mastery; government; *pl.* **die Herrschaften**   master and mistress   (32W)
her-stellen   manufacture   (17W)
die **Herstellung, -en**   production   (17D)
die **Herstellungskosten** *pl.*   production costs   (17D)
her-stoßen, ö, ie, o   kick forward   (35R St)
herum-kommen, kam herum, herumgekommen(s)   come around   (6D)
das **Herz, -ens, -en**   heart   (15D)
der **Herzanfall,** ⸚e   heart attack   (15D)
heulen   scream, weep, howl   (30D)
heute   today   (1D); **heute morgen**   this morning   (12D); **heute nachmittag**   this afternoon   (2D)
heutig   today's, of today   (31R De)
heutzutage   nowadays   (31R De)
hier   here   (3D)
die **Hilfe, -n**   help   (21W)
hilflos   helpless   (24R)
die **Hilfskraft,** ⸚e   helper, assistant   (28R)
der **Himmel, -**   sky, heaven   (12S)
die **Himmelsrichtung, -en**   point of the compass, direction   (12S)
hin   there, in that direction, to that place   (5D)
hinten *adv.*   behind, in back; in the distance   (5D)
hinter *prep.*   behind   (13D)
hinter- *adj.*   back, rear   (33V)
hinüber-gehen, ging hinüber, hinübergegangen(s)   go over, go across   (12D)
hinweg-sehen, ie, a, e über + *acc.*   disregard   (34R He)
die **Hitze**   heat   (22I)
hoch   high, tall; **höher**   higher   (17D); **höchst-**   (18A)
die **Hochschule, -n**   college; university   (28R)
der **Hochschullehrer, -**   professor   (28R)
höchstens   at the most   (34R Ne)

die **Hochzeit**, -en wedding, marriage (32I)
  hoffen hope (20D)
  hoffentlich it is to be hoped, I hope, let's hope (4D)
die **Höhe**, -n height (30W)
  holen get, go and get, fetch (12D)
das **Holz**, ⸗er wood (34I)
  horchen listen (32I)
  hören hear (24D)
die **Hose**, -n pants, trousers (23S)
das **Hotel**, -s hotel (31R De)
  hübsch nice; pretty (2D)
der **Humor** humor, sense of humor (33R Ge)
der **Hund**, -e dog (33I)
  hungrig hungry (14D)
der **Hut**, ⸗e hat (9D)

  ideal ideal (31R De)
die **Illustrierte**, -n *adj. noun* illustrated magazine (18D)
  immer always (7D)
  immerhin nevertheless (30D)
  in in, within, into (3D)
der **Indianer**, - (American) Indian (35R St)
das **Indianergeheul** howling of Indians (35R St)
die **Industrie**, -n industry (19I)
die **Information**, -en information (25R)
der **Ingenieur**, -e engineer (25R)
der **Inhalt**, -e contents, content (34I)
  innen *adv.* within, inside (31I)
  inner- *adj.* inner, inside (33V)
  innerhalb *prep.* inside of (17S)
  insbesondere in particular (35R St)
die **Insel**, -n island (34I)
das **Inserat**, -e advertisement (34R Zi)
  inspizieren inspect (34R Ne)
das **Institut**, -e institute (31R Eh)
das **Instrument**, -e instrument (19I)
  intelligent intelligent (25R)
  interessant interesting (19R)
das **Interesse**, -n interest; **Interesse haben an** + *dat.* be interested in (7D)
  sich **interessieren** *acc. refl.* be interested; sich **interessieren für** + *acc.* be interested in (19I)
  international international (29L)
die **Interpretation**, -en interpretation (33R Fo)
das **Interview**, -s interview (29L)
  inzwischen in the meantime (28R)
  irgendwo somewhere; anywhere (20D)
  Italien Italy (31R De)

  ja yes; indeed (1D)
die **Jacke**, -n jacket (35R St)
  jagen chase, hunt (30D)
der **Jäger**, - hunter (30D)
das **Jahr**, -e year (9D)
die **Jahreszeit**, -en season (11S)
das **Jahrhundert**, -e century (27R)
  jährlich yearly, annual (14W)
der **Januar** January (11S)
  Japan Japan (29L)
  je mehr ... um so mehr the more ... the more (35R St)
  jedenfalls anyway, in any case, at any rate (3D)
  jedoch but, however (32I)
  jemand somebody (32I)
  jenseits on the other side of, beyond (17S)
  jetzig- present, now (24R)
  jetzt now (5D)
der **Juli** July (11S)
  jung young (1D)
der **Junge**, -n, -n boy (1D)
der **Junggeselle**, -n, -n bachelor (34R Zi)
der **Junglehrer**, - junior teacher (28R)
der **Juni** June (11S)
die **Jurisprudenz** law, jurisprudence (4D)

der **Kaffee** coffee (14S)
der **Kaktus**, -teen cactus (35R St)
der **Kalender**, - calendar (22I)
die **Kalorie**, -n calorie (22I)
  kalt cold (14S)
die **Kälte** cold(ness), chilliness (30W)
der **Kamerad**, -en, -en comrade (23D)
die **Kameradschaft**, -en comradeship, fel-

lowship (32W)
Kanada Canada (29L)
der **Kandidat, -en, -en** candidate (28R)
der **Kapitän, -e** captain (22I)
kaputt broken; **kaputt-gehen, ging kaputt, kaputtgegangen(s)** get broken (13D)
die **Karte, -n** card; ticket; map (25I)
die **Kartoffel, -n** potato (34R He)
der **Käse** cheese (34I)
die **Kasse, -n** cashier's booth (35R St)
der **Kassierer, -** cashier (35R St)
der **Kasten, ⸚** box (12D)
der **Katalog, -e** catalog (12D)
die **Katze, -n** cat (22I)
kauen chew (33R Ge)
der **Kauf, ⸚e** purchase (17S)
kaufen buy (1D)
der **Käufer, -** buyer, customer (17D)
das **Kaufhaus, ⸚er** department store (17S)
kaum hardly (31R De)
kein no, not any (1D)
keinesfalls by no means, in no case (22R)
der **Kellner, -** waiter (23D)
kennen, kannte, gekannt know, be acquainted with (8D)
kennen-lernen get acquainted with, get to know (8D)
der **Kerl, -e** fellow (23D)
das **Kilogramm, -e (kg)** kilogram (22I)
das **Kilometer, - (km)** kilometer (22I)
das **Kind, -er** child (1D)
der **Kindergarten, ⸚** kindergarten (25R)
kinderlos childless (16W)
die **Kindheit** childhood (32W)
kindlich childlike (14W)
das **Kino, -s** movie, movie theater (32I)
die **Kirche, -n** church (17S)
die **Kiste, -n** box, crate (5D)
der **Klang, ⸚e** sound (21W)
klappen clap; **es klappt** it works (12D)
klappern rattle (35R Br)
klar clear, plain; of course (5D)
die **Klarheit, -en** clarity (32W)
die **Klasse, -n** class, grade (in school) (22R)

der **Klassenkamerad, -en, -en** classmate (23D)
klassisch classic(al) (33R Ge)
der **Klatsch** crash; smack (5D)
das **Kleid, -er** dress; *pl.* clothes (23D)
kleiden clothe, dress; disguise (23D)
klein small, little (10D)
das **Klima** climate (31R De)
klingen, a, u sound, ring (20D)
klopfen knock; beat (35R St)
der **Klub, -s** club (35R St)
klug intelligent, clever (34I)
knapp scarce (9D)
der **Koch, ⸚e** cook (22I)
kochen cook; boil (22I)
die **Köchin, -nen** (female) cook (34R He)
der **Koffer, -** suitcase (34I)
die **Kohle, -n** coal (22I)
der **Kollege, -n, -n** colleague (22I)
kommen, kam, gekommen (s) come (4D); **kommen von** be due to (16S)
der **Kommentar, -e** commentary (22I)
kommentieren comment (35R St)
das **Kompliment, -e** compliment (23D)
kompliziert complicated (22R)
die **Konferenz, -en** conference (19I)
die **Konfirmation, -en** confirmation (22R)
der **Konflikt, -e** conflict (22I)
der **König, -e** king (27D)
konkav concave (22I)
können, kann, konnte, gekonnt can, be able to (1D)
konservativ conservative (22I)
konstruieren construct (33R Ge)
der **Kontakt, -e** contact (22I)
das **Konzept** rough copy; **aus dem Konzept bringen** sidetrack, disconcert (26D)
das **Konzert, -e** concert (19R)
der **Kopf, ⸚e** head (6D)
kopflos headless; confused (16W)
die **Kopie, -n** copy, reproduction (22I)
korrekt correct (33R Fo)
der **Korridor, -e** hall, corridor (35R Br)
kosten cost (10D)
die **Kosten** *pl.* costs, expenses (17D)
der **Kragen, -** collar (35R St)

krank sick; **der Kranke**, -n *adj. noun* patient, sick person (16D)
der **Krankenbesuch**, -e visit with a sick person (16D)
die **Krankheit**, -en illness (31R De)
der **Kreis**, -e circle (32I)
   kreisen circle, revolve (32I)
   kreuzen cross (17W)
die **Kreuzung**, -en crossing (5D)
   kriechen, o, o (s) creep, crawl (32I)
der **Krieg**, -e war (27D)
die **Krise**, -n crisis (33R Fo)
   kritisch critical (22I)
der **Krümel**, - crumb (35R Br)
die **Küche**, -n kitchen (32I)
der **Kuchen**, - cake (14S)
der **Küchenschrank**, ⸚e kitchen cupboard (35R Br)
   kühn bold, brave (34R Ne)
die **Kultur**, -en culture (19I)
   kulturell cultural (30R)
der **Kunde**, -n, -n customer (10D)
die **Kundgebung**, -en demonstration, rally (34I)
   kündigen give notice (of leaving) (34R Fa)
die **Kundin**, -nen (female) customer (10D)
die **Kundschaft** clientele (32W)
die **Kunst**, ⸚e art (34R Ne)
das **Kupfer** copper (19I)
die **Kur**, -en cure (31R De)
der **Kurort**, -e health resort, spa (31R De)
der **Kurs**, -e course (of study) (28R)
   kurz short (20D)
die **Kürze** shortness, brevity (30W)
   küssen kiss (25I)

   lächeln smile (34R Ne)
   lachen laugh (5D)
die **Lage**, -n situation, position (21W)
die **Lampe**, -n lamp (22I)
das **Land**, ⸚er land; country, state (12S)
die **Landkarte**, -n map (25I)
die **Landschaft**, -en landscape (31R De)
   lang long (8D)

die **Länge**, -n length, tallness; longitude (30W)
   langsam slow (32I)
   längst long ago, for a long time (34R He)
   langweilig boring, tedious (4D)
der **Lärm** noise (34I)
   lassen, ä, ie, a leave; let; cause (12D)
das **Latein** Latin (language) (25R)
die **Laterne**, -n lantern, lamp, streetlight (5D)
   lauern lurk (35R St)
der **Lauf**, ⸚e current; track; career (21W)
   laufen, äu, ie, au (s) run, walk (5D)
   laut loud (28I)
   leben live (15D)
   lebenserfahren *adj.* experienced in life (31R Eh)
das **Leder**, - leather (25I)
   leer empty (35R Br)
   legen lay, put, place (13D)
die **Lehre**, -n apprenticeship; instruction; theory (22R)
   lehren teach (22R)
der **Lehrer**, - teacher (22R)
der **Lehrerberuf** teaching profession (28R)
die **Lehrerin**, -nen (female) teacher (22R)
die **Lehrerprüfung**, -en teacher's examination (28R)
der **Lehrling**, -e apprentice (22R)
   leicht easy; light (3D)
   leid painful, disagreeable; **es tut mir leid** I am sorry (21D)
das **Leid** sorrow; harm (21W)
   leiden, litt, gelitten suffer, endure (16D)
   leider unfortunately (24D)
   leihen, ie, ie borrow (32I); lend (34R Fa)
die **Leinwand** movie screen (35R St)
   leise soft, quiet (35R Br)
   lernen learn (5D)
   lesen, ie, a, e read (3D)
   letzt- last (6S)
die **Leute** *pl.* people (11D)
der **Leutnant**, -s lieutenant (31I)

das **Licht,** -er   light   (35R Br)
der **Lichtschalter,** -   light switch   (35R Br)
das **Lichtspiel,** -e   movie   (35R St)
   lieb-   dear; **liebst-**   favorite   (33R Ge)
   liegen, a, e   lie; be, be situated   (5D); **liegen an** + *dat.*   be due to, be because of   (35R Br)
der **Likör,** -e   liqueur   (25I)
   links   left   (14D)
die **Linkspartei,** -en   (political) party on the left   (33R Fo)
die **Liste,** -n   list   (31R Eh)
das (der) **Liter,** - (l)   liter   (28I)
die **Literatur,** -en   literature   (34R Ne)
der **Löffel,** -   spoon   (13D)
   los   loose; wrong, the matter   (14D)
   los-gehen, ging los, losgegangen (s)   start, begin   (4D)
das **Lotto,** -s   lottery   (29D)
die **Luft**   air   (33R Ge)
   lügen, o, o   tell a lie   (32I)
   lustig   merry, jolly; funny   (34I)
   lutschen   suck   (30S)
   Luxemburg   Luxemburg   (12S)

   machen   make; do   (2D); **das macht nichts**   that doesn't matter, that's all right   (5D); **es macht Spaß**   it's fun   (2D)
die **Madame**   madam   (34R Fa)
das **Mädchen,** -   girl   (2D)
der **Magen,** ⸗   stomach   (34R He)
der **Mai**   May   (11S)
das **Mal**   time, occurrence; **das nächste Mal**   next time   (14D)
   mal   once, just   (11D); times   (6S); sometime   (7D)
die **Malerei,** -en   painting   (34R Ne)
   man   one, somebody, they   (8D)
   manchmal   sometimes   (34R Ne)
der **Mann,** ⸗er   man; husband   (8D)
   männlich   masculine   (14W)
die **Mannschaft,** -en   team, crew   (32W)
der **Mantel,** ⸗   coat   (23S)
die **Mark**   mark (German monetary unit)   (10D)

der **Markt,** ⸗e   market   (22I)
die **Marmelade,** -n   jam   (14S)
   marschieren (s)   march   (31I)
der **März**   March   (11S)
die **Maschine,** -n   machine; engine   (22I)
das **Material,** -ien   material   (25I)
die **Mathematik**   mathematics   (25R)
   mathematisch   mathematical   (25R)
die **Mauer,** -n   wall   (34I)
das **Maul,** ⸗er   mouth (animal)   (33I)
die **Maus,** ⸗e   mouse   (33I)
der **Mechaniker,** -   mechanic   (25I)
die **Medizin,** -en   medicine   (15D)
das **Meer,** -e   sea   (31R De)
die **Mehrheit,** -en   majority   (32W)
   meinen   think; mean   (1D)
   meinetwegen   as far as I'm concerned, for all I care   (9D)
die **Meinung,** -en   opinion   (17W)
der **Meinungsforscher,** -   pollster   (31R Eh)
   meistens   most of the time   (25R)
der **Meister,** -   master   (27R)
die **Menge,** -n   quantity, amount; crowd   (24D)
der **Mensch,** -en, -en   person, human being   (5D)
die **Menschheit**   humanity   (32W)
   menschlich   human, humane   (14W)
   merken   notice   (32I)
das **Messer,** -   knife   (13D)
das **Metall,** -e   metal   (19I)
die **Miete,** -n   rent   (30D)
die **Milch**   milk   (5D)
der **Milchmann,** ⸗er   milkman   (5D)
der **Milchwagen,** -   milk truck   (5D)
   mild   mild   (31R De)
das **Militär**   military   (22I)
das **Millimeter,** - (mm)   millimeter   (31R De)
der **Millionär,** -e   millionaire   (30D)
der **Mindestbetrag,** ⸗e   minimal sum, lowest sum   (33R Fo)
die **Minute,** -n   minute   (7S)
   mit *prep.*   with   (2D); *adv.*   along   (2D)
   mit-fühlen   sympathize   (35R St)
   mit-helfen, i, a, o   help, assist   (19R)
   mit-kommen, kam mit, mitgekommen

(s) come along (2D)
mit-machen participate (35R St)
der **Mitmensch**, -en, -en fellow human being (31R Eh)
der **Mittag**, -e noon, midday (11S)
mittags at noon, noons (15S)
der **Mittagstisch**, -e dinner table (13D)
die **Mitte**, -n middle (33R Fo)
das **Mittelgebirge**, - highlands, uplands (31R De)
die **Mittelschule**, -n lower-grade secondary school (25R)
der **Mittelschüler**, - student at a **Mittelschule** (25R)
die **Mitternacht** midnight (11S)
der **Mittwoch** Wednesday (11S)
die **Möbel** pl. furniture (34I)
die **Mode**, -n fashion, vogue (30R)
mögen, mag, mochte, gemocht like to, want to (11D); möchte would like to (2D)
möglich possible (9D)
der **Moment**, -e moment (19I)
der **Monat**, -e month (9D)
monatelang for months (30R)
monatlich monthly (14W)
der **Montag** Monday (11S)
morgen tomorrow (15S)
der **Morgen**, - morning (11S)
morgens in the morning, mornings (15S)
der **Motor**, -en motor (25I)
das **Motorrad**, ⸗er motorcycle (34I)
die **Mühe**, -n effort, trouble (11D)
mühelos effortless, easy (16W)
der **Mund**, ⸗er mouth (33I)
munter lively, gay, bright (34R Fa)
das **Museum**, -seen museum (27R)
die **Musik** music (19I)
musisch artistic (25R)
müssen, muß, mußte, gemußt must, have to (2D)
das **Muster**, - pattern, model (24D)
der **Musterschüler**, - model student (24D)
die **Mutter**, ⸗ mother (12D)
mütterlich motherly (14W)
die **Mutti**, -s Mommy (1D)
die **Mütze**, -n cap (23S)

na well (8D)
nach prep. after; about; toward, to (4D)
der **Nachbar**, -n neighbor (12S)
das **Nachbarland**, ⸗er neighboring country (12S)
nachdem conj. after (26S)
nachher adv. afterward, later (26S)
nach-holen make up (a test) (25R)
der **Nachmittag**, -e afternoon (11S)
nachmittags in the afternoon, afternoons (15S)
der **Nachname**, -ns, -n last name, family name (22R)
die **Nacht**, ⸗e night (11S)
die **Nachtarbeit**, -en night work, night job (19R)
nächtlich nightly (14W)
nachts in the night, at night, nights (6D)
nach-weisen, ie, ie prove; point out (28R)
nackt naked, bare (35R Br)
die **Nadel**, -n needle (31I)
nah, näher, nächst- close, near (14D)
die **Nähe** nearness, vicinity (30W)
der **Name**, -ns, -n name (22R)
namenlos nameless (16W)
nämlich namely; you see (7D)
natürlich natural(ly); of course (6D)
die **Naturwissenschaft**, -en natural science (25R)
naturwissenschaftlich of natural science (25R)
neben beside, at the side of, next to (13D)
nebenbei in addition, on the side (34R Ne)
der **Neffe**, -n, -n nephew (21S)
nehmen, nimmt, nahm, genommen take; have (1D)
der **Neid** envy (34R Ne)
nennen, nannte, genannt name (22R)
nett nice, kind (1D)
das **Netz**, -e net, network (22I)
neu new (9D)
neuerdings recently, lately (34R Ne)
die **Neuigkeit**, -en something new; piece of news (32W)
nicht not (2D)

die **Nichte**, -n niece (21S)
  nichts nothing (5D)
  nie never (1D)
die **Niederlande** *pl.* Netherlands (12S)
  niedlich pretty, nice (33I)
  niedrig low (32I)
das **Niveau**, -s level (30R)
  noch still, in addition (2D); **noch nicht** not yet (2D)
der **Norden** north (12S)
  nördlich north, northern (12S)
die **Nordsee** North Sea (12L)
  normal normal (19I)
die **Not**, ⸗e need, necessity, privation (28I)
  notieren write down, note (19R)
  nötig necessary (34R Ne)
  notwendig necessary (34R Ne)
der **November** November (11S)
  null zero (6S)
die **Nummer**, -n number (21D)
  nun now (2D)
  nur only (3D)
die **Nuß**, ⸗sse nut (1D)
das **Nuß-Eis** walnut ice cream (1D)

  ob whether, if (2D); **als ob** as if (30D)
  oben up, above, upstairs (33R Fo)
  obendrein in addition, besides (32I)
  ober- *adj.* above, upper (33V)
  oberhalb above (17S)
die **Oberschule**, -n secondary school (19R)
der **Oberschüler**, - student at a secondary school (25R)
die **Oberstufe**, -n last three years in a **Gymnasium** (25R)
das **Obst** fruit (34I)
  obwohl although (21G)
  oder or (17D)
die **Öffentlichkeit** public; publicity (31R Eh)
  offiziell official (22R)
  oft often (28R)
  ohne without (10D); **ohne zu** . . . without . . .-ing (16S)

der **Oktober** October (11S)
das **Öl**, -e oil (25I)
der **Onkel**, - uncle (15D)
der **Opa**, -s grandpa (34I)
die **Oper**, -n opera (19I)
das **Opfer**, - sacrifice, offering; victim (34R He)
  ordentlich orderly; regular; proper (15D)
das **Organ**, -e organ (22I)
der **Organismus**, -men organism (22I)
der **Ort**, -e place; town (31R De)
die **Ortschaft**, -en town, village (32W)
der **Oscar** Oscar (18D)
  Ostdeutschland East Germany (German Democratic Republic) (12L)
der **Osten** east (12S)
das **Osterfest**, -e Easter holiday (17S)
das **Ostern** Easter (17S)
  Österreich Austria (12S)
  östlich east, eastern (12S)
die **Ostsee** Baltic Sea (12L)

  paar: ein paar a few, some (18D)
  pädagogisch pedagogic (28R)
das **Paket**, -e package (11D)
der **Papagei**, -en parrot (26D)
das **Papier**, -e paper (21D)
der **Park**, -s park (31R De)
die **Partei**, -en party (political) (22I)
der **Partner**, - partner (31R Eh)
  passen fit, be appropriate (31I)
  passieren (s) happen (6D)
die **Pause**, -n pause (28I)
die **Person**, -en person (19I)
der **Pfad**, -e path (25I)
der **Pfahl**, ⸗e post (19I)
die **Pfanne**, -n pan (19I)
der **Pfannkuchen**, - pancake (19I)
der **Pfeffer** pepper (19I)
die **Pfeife**, -n pipe (19I)
  pfeifen, pfiff, gepfiffen whistle; **pfeifen auf** + *acc.* not care about, snap one's fingers at (33R Ge)

der **Pfennig**, -e   pfennig   (10D)
das **Pferd**, -e   horse   (35R St)
die **Pflanze**, -n   plant   (19I)
   pflanzen   plant   (19I)
die **Pflaume**, -n   plum   (19I)
   pflegen   care for; **gepflegt sein**   be well groomed   (31R Eh)
die **Pflicht**, -en   duty   (25R)
der **Pfosten**, -   post   (19I)
das **Pfund**   pound   (19I)
die **Philosophie**, -n   philosophy   (3D)
die **Physik**   physics   (25R)
der **Plan**, ⸚e   plan, schedule   (25R)
   plappern   babble, chatter   (35R St)
   platschen   plop; splash   (35R Br)
der **Platz**, ⸚e   place, seat; square; room   (3D)
   platzen (s)   burst   (34R Ne)
die **Platzwunde**, -n   open wound   (6D)
   plötzlich   sudden, quick   (5D)
das **Podium**, -dien   platform, stage   (2D)
Polen   Poland   (12S)
die **Politik**   politics; policy   (21I)
die **Polizei**   police   (22I)
der **Polizist**, -en, -en   policeman   (22I)
die **Portion**, -en   portion; serving   (18S)
die **Post**   post office; mail   (11D)
der **Postbote**, -n, -n   postman   (11D)
das **Praktikum**   laboratory course; practical experience   (28R)
   praktisch   practical   (22I)
die **Prärie**, -n   prairie   (35R St)
der **Preis**, -e   price; prize   (17D)
der **Preuße**, -n, -n   Prussian   (34R Zi)
Preußen   Prussia   (34R Zi)
   prima   first-class, great   (14D)
die **Privatschule**, -n   private school   (25R)
   pro   per   (25R)
die **Probe**, -n   test, trial, rehearsal   (28R)
   probieren   try   (34R He)
das **Problem**, -e   problem   (19R)
der **Professor**, -en   professor   (3D)
das **Programm**, -e   program   (25R)
das **Prozent**, -e   percent   (9R)
die **Prüfung**, -en   examination   (25R)
   publizieren   publish, make public   (28R)
   pünktlich   punctual   (34I)

   putzen   clean, polish   (34R Zi)

das **Quadrat**, -e   square   (31R De)
das **Quadratkilometer**, - (km^2, qkm)   square kilometer   (31R De)
die **Qualifikation**, -en   qualification   (25R)
   qualifizieren   qualify   (28R)
die **Qualität**, -en   quality   (28R)
der **Quatsch**   nonsense   (6D)
die **Quelle**, -n   spring; source   (31R De)

das **Rad**, ⸚er   wheel; bicycle   (34I)
das **Radio**, -s   radio   (29L, 34R Zi)
der **Rahm**   cream   (30S)
der **Rahmbonbon**, - *or* -s   taffy   (30S)
der **Rang**, ⸚e   rank, class; row   (22R)
die **Rangordnung**, -en   scale, order of precedence   (30R)
der **Rat**   counsel, advice   (21W)
   raten, ä, ie, a   guess; counsel   (8D)
   rauben   plunder, rob   (35R St)
der **Räuber**, -   robber   (35R St)
der **Rauch**   smoke   (21W)
   rauchen   smoke   (21D)
der **Raucher**, -   smoker   (21D)
das **Raucherabteil**, -e   smoking section   (21D)
der **Raum**, ⸚e   room, hall; space   (31R Eh)
   recht   rather, very   (16D); **recht haben**   be correct, be right   (30D)
   rechts   right, to the right   (5D)
die **Rechtspartei**, -en   (political) party on the right   (33R Fo)
die **Regel**, -n   rule   (28R)
   regelmäßig   regular, normal   (28R)
der **Regen**   rain   (21W)
das **Regenwetter**   rainy weather   (30D)
   regnen   rain   (6D)
   reich   rich   (34R Ne)
   reif   ripe, mature   (25I)
die **Reife**   maturity; ripeness; **die Mittlere Reife**   examination after ten years of school   (25R)
die **Reifeprüfung**, -en   final examination in

762 Glossary

the **Gymnasium** (25R)
die **Reise,** -n trip (26D)
 reisen (s) travel (31R De)
 reißen, riß, gerissen seize; tear (35R St)
 reiten, ritt, geritten (s) ride (35R St)
der **Reiz,** -e charm, fascination (31R De)
 reizend charming, fascinating (18D)
 reizvoll attractive, charming (31R De)
der **Rekord,** -e record (33R Ge)
 relativ relative (28R)
das **Rendezvous,** - rendezvous, date (19R)
sich **rentieren** *acc. refl.* be profitable, pay (33I)
das **Repertoire-Theater,** - repertory theater (30R)
der **Reporter,** - reporter (29L)
die **Republik,** -en republic (31R De)
der **Rest,** -e rest, remainder (27R)
 revoltieren revolt (34R He)
der **Revolver,** - revolver (35R St)
 richten direct, turn; set right (17W)
 richtig right, correct (11D)
die **Richtung,** -en direction (12S)
 riechen, o, o smell (34R He); **riechen nach** smell like, smell of (35R St)
der **Riese,** -n, -n giant (31I)
 riesig huge, immense (35R St)
der **Ring,** -e ring (22I)
der **Rock,** ⸚ skirt; coat (23S)
 roh raw (34I)
 rollen (s,h) roll (33I)
die **Rose,** -n rose (19I)
 rot red (18S)
die **Röte** redness, blush (of shyness) (30W)
der **Rücken,** - back (35R St)
die **Rücksicht** regard, consideration; **Rücksicht nehmen auf** + *acc.* take into consideration, have regard for (22R)
 rücksichtlos careless (6D)
der **Ruf,** -e call; reputation (21W)
die **Ruhe** rest; quiet, calm, peace; **Ruhe halten** stay quiet, stay calm (15D)
 ruhlos restless (16W)
 ruhig quiet, calm (17D)
 rund round, around (34R Zi)

 rutschen (s) slide (5D)
 rutschig slippery (5S)

der **Saal, Säle** hall, large room (27D)
die **Sache,** -n thing; matter, affair (2D)
der **Saft,** ⸚e juice (14S)
die **Sage,** -n legend, fable (21W)
 sagen say, tell (1S)
der **Salat,** -e salad (5D)
das **Salz** salt (22I)
der **Samstag** Saturday (11S)
der **Sand** sand (31R De)
der **Sandstrand,** ⸚e sandy beach (31R De)
 sauber clean (35R Br)
die **Sauce,** -n sauce, gravy (34R He)
das **Sauerkraut** sauerkraut (34R He)
 säuerlich sourish (34R Zi)
der **Schaden,** ⸚ damage, injury, harm (33R Ge)
der **Schal,** -s shawl, scarf (34R Fa)
 scharf sharp (28I)
die **Schärfe,** -n sharpness (30W)
 schauen look (9D)
der **Scheck,** -s check (28I)
die **Scheibe,** -n slice (18S)
 scheiden, ie, ie divorce, separate (31R Eh)
die **Scheidung,** -en divorce, separation (31R Eh)
der **Schein,** -e shine, light (21W)
 scheinen, ie, ie shine (2D); seem, appear (31R Eh)
 schenken give (a present) (34R Fa)
 scheu shy (33I)
 scheußlich hideous, horrible, abominable (10D)
der **Schi,** -er ski (31R De)
 schieben, o, o push, shove (26S)
 schießen, schoß, geschossen shoot (26S)
das **Schilaufen** skiing (24R)
der **Schiläufer,** - skier (31R De)
das **Schild,** -er sign (21D)
der **Schillerplatz** Schiller Square (5D)
der **Schimmel,** - white horse (35R St)

schimpfen auf + *acc.* scold (33R Fo)
der **Schlaf** sleep (21W)
  schlafen, ä, ie, a sleep (15D)
  schlagen, ä, u, a beat (heart) (35R St)
  schlau cunning, clever (13D)
die **Schlauheit** cunning (32W)
der **Schlaukopf** cunning person, foxy person, "little fox" (13D)
  schlecht bad (6D)
  schließen, schloß, geschlossen close (26S)
  schließlich finally; after all (6D)
  schlimm bad (6D)
das **Schloß, ⸗sser** castle (26D)
  schluchzen sob (30S)
der **Schluß, ⸗sse** end; closing, conclusion (4D)
der **Schlüssel, -** key (34R Zi)
  schmackhaft tasty (34R He)
  schmatzen smack the lips (30S)
  schmecken taste (1D)
der **Schmutz** dirt, filth (34I)
  schmutzig dirty, filthy (34R Fa)
der **Schnee** snow (28I)
  schneiden, schnitt, geschnitten cut (28I)
  schnell quick, fast (5D)
  schnippen flick (35R Br)
der **Schnitt, -e** cut (31R Eh)
das **Schnitzel, -** cutlet (34R He)
die **Schokolade, -n** chocolate (22I)
  schon already; even; very well, all right (2D)
  schön nice, beautiful (2D)
die **Schöne, -n** *adj.noun* beautiful woman (18D)
der **Schrank, ⸗e** cabinet, cupboard (11D)
die **Schraube, -n** screw (12D)
der **Schraubenzieher, -** screwdriver (12D)
der **Schrei, -e** scream (35R St)
  schreiben, ie, ie write (21D)
  schreien, schrie, geschrien shout, scream (35R St)
  schriftlich written, in writing (28R)
der **Schritt, -e** step, stride (33R Fo)
der **Schrott** scrap metal (34R Ne)

  schüchtern shy, timid (33I)
der **Schuh, -e** shoe (23S)
die **Schulausbildung, -en** schooling, education (25R)
der **Schulbesuch** attending school (25R)
die **Schuld** guilt; **Schuld haben** be at fault (35R St); *pl.* **Schulden** debts
die **Schule, -n** school (19R)
  schulen school, teach, train (25R)
der **Schüler, -** pupil, student (22R)
der **Schulfreund, -e** school friend, friend from school (20D)
das **Schulgeld** school fees (25R)
die **Schulpflicht** compulsory education (25R)
das **Schulpraktikum** practice teaching (28R)
das **Schulwesen** educational system (25R)
die **Schulzeit, -en** schooldays (22R)
die **Schüssel, -n** bowl, tureen (13D)
  schwach weak (30W)
die **Schwäche, -n** weakness (30W)
  schwappen (s) splash, spill (5D)
  schwarz black (17D)
  schwarzbärtig having a black beard (35R St)
das **Schwarzweißbild, -er** black-and-white picture (17D)
  Schweden Sweden (29L)
  schweigen, ie, ie be silent (35R St)
das **Schwein, -e** pig (34R He)
der **Schweinebraten, -** roast pork (34R He)
der **Schweiß** sweat, perspiration (6D)
die **Schweiz** Switzerland (12S)
  schwellen, i, o, o (s) swell (33I)
  schwer heavy, difficult (3D)
  schwermütig sad, melancholy (33I)
die **Schwester, -n** sister (21S)
die **Schwierigkeit, -en** difficulty (22R)
  schwimmen, a, o (s,h) swim (28I)
der **See, -n** lake (12S)
die **See** sea, ocean (12S)
  sehen, ie, a, e see, look (1D)
  sehr very; very much (9D)
  sein, ist, war, gewesen be (1D)
  seit since (6D)

die **Seite**, -n   page; side   (18D)
die **Seitentür**, -en   side door   (35R St)
   selbst   self; even   (17D)
   selbständig   independent, autonomous   (30R)
   selbstgebacken   home-baked   (34R He)
   selbstverständlich   self-evident, obvious   (17D)
   selig   happy, blissful   (34I)
das **Semester**, -   semester   (19R)
die **Semesterarbeit**, -en   term paper   (24R)
das **Seminar**, -e   seminar   (28R)
   senden, sandte, gesandt (sendete, gesendet)   send   (35R St)
der **September**   September   (11S)
   setzen   set, place, put; **sich setzen** *acc. refl.*   sit down   (21D)
   seufzen   sigh   (34R He)
   sicher   sure, certain; safe   (15D)
   sichern   make safe, secure   (28R)
der **Sieg**, -e   victory   (35R St)
   siegesbewußt   conscious of victory, triumphant   (35R St)
   siezen   address with **Sie**   (22R)
das **Silber**   silver   (22I)
   singen, a, u   sing   (27D)
der **Sinn**, -e   sense; mind   (30D)
   sinnlos   senseless, foolish   (35R Br)
die **Sitte**, -n   custom, habit   (22R)
die **Situation**, -en   situation   (34R Ne)
der **Sitz**, -e   seat   (21W)
   sitzen, saß, gesessen   sit   (8D)
   sitzen-bleiben, ie, ie (s)   remain sitting; not pass to the next grade   (25R)
die **Sitzung**, -en   sitting; meeting   (17W)
   so   so; thus; then; in this way, in that way   (2D); **um so mehr**   the more, all the more   (35R St)
die **Socke**, -n   sock   (28I)
   sofort   immediately, right away, at once   (23D)
   sogar   even   (5D)
   sogenannt   so-called   (28R)
   sogleich   immediately, right away, at once   (34R Ne)
die **Sohle**, -n   sole   (35R St)

der **Sohn**, ⸚e   son   (20D)
   solange   as long as; meanwhile   (12D)
der **Soldat**, -en, -en   soldier   (22I)
   sollen   be supposed to; be said to   (3D)
der **Sommer**, -   summer   (11S)
   sondern   but, to the contrary   (21G)
der **Sonnabend**   Saturday   (11S)
die **Sonne**, -n   sun   (2D)
   sonnig   sunny   (29D)
der **Sonntag**   Sunday   (11S)
   sonntäglich *adj.*   Sunday   (35R St)
   sonntags   on Sundays, Sundays   (15S)
   sonst   otherwise, else, besides; **sonst noch etwas**   something else, anything else   (18D)
die **Sozialdemokratische Partei Deutschlands (SPD)**   Social Democratic Party of Germany   (33R Fo)
das **Spanisch**   Spanish (language)   (25R)
das **Sparbuch**, ⸚er   savings account book   (9D)
   sparen   save; **sich sparen** *dat. refl.*   spare   (25R)
die **Sparsamkeit**   thriftiness, frugality   (23D)
der **Spaß**, ⸚e   fun; joke   (2D)
   spät   late   (8S)
das **Spätbarock**   Late Baroque   (27R)
   spazieren-gehen, ging spazieren, spazierengegangen (s)   stroll, take a walk   (31R De)
   spezialisieren   specialize   (28R)
der **Spezialist**, -en, -en   specialist   (28R)
die **Spezialschule**, -n   special school   (25R)
   speziell   special; particular   (25)
der **Spiegel**, -   mirror   (34I)
das **Spiel**, -e   game; play   (25R)
   spielen   play   (24S)
der **Sport**   sport(s)   (29D)
der **Sportler**, -   sports enthusiast   (31R De)
der **Sportwagen**, -   sports car   (29D)
der **Spott**   mockery, ridicule   (21W)
   spotten   mock, ridicule; be sarcastic   (2D)
die **Sprache**, -n   language   (21W)
   sprechen, i, a, o   speak   (8D)
das **Sprichwort**, ⸚er   proverb   (3D)

springen, a, u (s) jump (26W)
der **Spruch,** ⸗e saying; verdict (21W)
der **Staat, -en** state (19R)
die **Stadt,** ⸗e city, town (7D)
die **Stadtbahn, -en** city commuter train (7D)
der **Städter, -** city dweller (31I)
das **Stadtviertel, -** quarter, district (municipal) (34R Zi)
der **Stamm,** ⸗e stem (28I)
stark strong (18S)
die **Stärke, -n** strength (30W)
die **Statistik, -en** statistics (25R)
der **Statistiker, -** statistician (31R Eh)
statt instead of (17S); **statt zu . . .** instead of . . .-ing (16S)
die **Stätte, -e** place (31R De)
staunen be astonished (34R Ne)
stecken stick, put, place (21D)
stehen, stand, gestanden stand; be (location) (2D)
stehen-bleiben, ie, ie (s) come to a stop; remain standing (35R St)
steigen, ie, ie (s) rise (29L)
der **Stein, -e** stone (29D)
die **Stelle, -n** place; position, job (6D)
stellen put, place (13D)
die **Stellung, -en** position; job (17W)
sterben, i, a, o (s) die (27D)
der **Stern, -e** star (18D)
der **Stichtag, -e** fixed day, deadline (22R)
der **Stift, -e** pencil; spike; peg (21D)
der **Stiftzahn,** ⸗e post crown (35R St)
der **Stil, -e** style (27D)
still still, quiet (28I)
die **Stille** stillness, silence (30W)
die **Stimme, -n** voice (32I)
stimmen be correct (4D)
die **Stimmung, -en** mood, atmosphere (17W)
das **Stipendium, -dien** scholarship (19R)
die **Stirn, -en** forehead (6D)
stolz proud (30D); **stolz auf** + *acc.* proud of (31R Eh)
der **Stolz** pride; vanity (34R Ne)
stören disturb (26W)

stoßen, ö, ie, o push, shove, kick (32I)
die **Strafe, -n** punishment; fine (33I)
strahlen radiate, beam, shine (33I)
der **Strand,** ⸗e shore (31R De)
die **Straße, -n** street, road (5D)
die **Straßenbahn, -en** streetcar (34R Zi)
der **Streifenwagen, -** patrol car, police car (6D)
der **Streik, -e** *or* **-s** strike (26D)
der **Strumpf,** ⸗e stocking (24S)
das **Stück, -e** piece (17D)
der **Student, -en, -en** university student (4D)
die **Studentenschaft, -en** fraternity; student body at a university (32W)
der **Studienassessor, -en** provisional teacher in a secondary school (after second state examination) (28R)
der **Studienrat,** ⸗e teacher in a secondary school (28R)
der **Studienreferendar, -e** provisional teacher in a secondary school (after first state examination) (28R)
studieren study (at a university) (4D)
das **Studium, -dien** studies (at a university) (19R)
die **Stufe, -n** stage, level (25R)
der **Stuhl,** ⸗e chair (23S)
stumm speechless, silent (33I)
die **Stunde, -n** hour; class period (12D)
stundenlang for hours (31R De)
der **Stundenplan,** ⸗e class schedule (25R)
stündlich hourly (14W)
suchen look for (24S)
der **Süden** south (12S)
südlich south, southern (12S)
die **Suppe, -n** soup (13D)
surren hum, buzz (33I)
süß sweet (26W)
die **Süße** sweetness (30W)
die **Süßigkeit, -en** sweetness; *pl.* sweets, candies (32W)

der **Tabak, -e** tobacco (28I)
die **Tablette, -n** tablet (19I)

die **Tafel**, -n   blackboard; bar (chocolate) (34I)
der **Tag**, -e   day (2D)
   tagaus   day out (34R He)
   tagein   day in (34R He)
die **Tagesfrage**, -n   current event(s) (7D)
   täglich   daily (14W)
   tagsüber   during the day (6D)
das **Tal**, ⸚er   valley (28I)
die **Tanne**, -n   fir (31I)
die **Tante**, -n   aunt (1D)
   tanzen   dance (27D)
   tappen (s)   grope (35R Br)
die **Tasche**, -n   pocket (24S)
das **Taschentuch**, ⸚er   handkerchief (24S)
die **Tasse**, -n   cup (18S)
die **Tatsache**, -n   fact (14W)
   tatsächlich   actual; matter-of-fact (5D)
   täuschen   deceive; **sich täuschen** *acc. refl.*   be mistaken (6D)
die **Technik**   technology (25R)
der **Tee**   tea (22I)
der (das) **Teil**, -e   part, section (3D)
das **Telefon**, -e   telephone (21D)
die **Telefonnummer**, -n   telephone number (21D)
der **Teller**, -   plate (13D)
der **Teppich**, -e   carpet (35R St)
   teuer   expensive (10D)
der **Teufel**, -   devil (28I)
das **Theater**, -   theater (19R)
der **Theaterspielplan**, ⸚e   program, repertory (30R)
das **Thema**, -men   theme, topic (25I)
die **Theologie**   theology (25I)
   theoretisch   theoretical (25I)
die **Theorie**, -n   theory (25I)
der **Therapeut**, -en, -en   therapist (25I)
die **Therapie**   therapy (25I)
das **Thermometer**, -   thermometer (25I)
der **Thermostat**, -e   thermostat (25I)
die **These**, -n   thesis (25I)
   tief   deep (28I)
die **Tiefe**, -n   depth (30W)
der **Tisch**, -e   table (13D)
der **Titel**, -   title (18D)

die **Titelseite**, -n   cover (of a magazine) (18D)
die **Tochter**, ⸚   daughter (20D)
der **Tod**, -e   death (25I)
das **Todesurteil**, -e   death sentence (35R Bo)
   tot   dead (28I)
die **Tradition**, -en   tradition (25R)
   tragen, ä, u, a   carry, wear (23D)
die **Tragödie**, -n   tragedy (19I)
   trampeln   stamp (with the feet), trample (30S)
die **Träne**, -n   tear (33I)
   tränenerstickt   choking from tears (35R St)
der **Traum**, ⸚e   dream (28I)
   träumen   dream (28I)
   treffen, trifft, traf, getroffen   meet; hit; **sich treffen** *acc. refl.*   meet, get together (21D)
   treten, tritt, trat, getreten (s)   step; **(h)**   kick (35R St)
   treu   faithful, loyal (30D)
die **Treue**   fidelity, loyalty (30W)
   treulos   faithless, disloyal (35R St)
   trinken, a, u   drink (18D)
die **Trommel**, -n   drum; cylinder (of a gun) (35R St)
der **Trommelrevolver**, -   revolver (with a cylinder) (35R St)
   trotz   in spite of (17S)
   trotzdem   nevertheless (35R St)
die **Tschechoslowakei**   Czechoslovakia (12S)
   tüchtig   hardworking, efficient, able; smart, clever (2D)
die **Tüchtigkeit**   ability; excellence (32W)
   tun, tat, getan   do (2D)
die **Tür**, -en   door (23S)
das **Twinset**, -s   twin-set (34R Fa)
der **Typ**, -en   type (25R)
   typisch   typical (31R Eh)

   üben   practice (2D)
   über   over, across; by way of; about;

above (5D)
überall everywhere (23D)
überallhin in every direction (31R De)
überanstrengt overworked, strained (35R St)
der **Überblick, -e** overall view, survey (25R)
überhaupt altogether; generally; at all; actually (23D)
überhören fail to hear (35R St)
(sich) **überlegen** *acc. refl.* consider, reflect (30D)
übermorgen day after tomorrow (15S)
überraschen surprise (32I)
übertreiben, ie, ie exaggerate; overdo (8D)
über-wechseln (s) change over (25R)
überzeugen convince (33R Fo)
über-ziehen, zog über, übergezogen put over (34I)
übrig left (over) (15D)
übrig-bleiben, ie, ie (s) be left, remain (15D)
die **Übung, -en** practice, exercise (19R)
die **Uhr, -en** clock, watch; o'clock (7S)
um around; at (4D); **um ... willen** for the sake of (17A); **um zu ...** in order to ... (16D)
umgehen, umging, umgangen go around, detour, avoid (34R He)
umher around, about (32I)
um-kippen (s) tip over (5D)
(sich) **um-schauen** *acc. refl.* look around (31R De)
um-wechseln exchange; change (money) (32I)
um-ziehen, zog um, umgezogen (s) move; change residences (20D)
sich **um-ziehen, zog um, umgezogen (h)** *acc. refl.* change clothes (21S)
unangebracht unsuitable, inappropriate (35R St)
unbedingt absolute, unconditional (25R)
unbestimmt indefinite; uncertain, undecided (16W)
und and (1D)

der **Undank** ingratitude (16W)
unecht false, insincere (35R Br)
unendlich endless, infinite (16W)
die **Unendlichkeit** infinity (32W)
der **Unfall, ⸚e** accident (5D)
unfrei not free (16W)
unfreundlich unfriendly (16W)
ungeachtet *prep. + gen.* notwithstanding, in spite of (31R De)
ungefähr approximately, about (25R)
ungeheuer huge, monstrous (35R St)
ungenau inaccurate, inexact (16W)
ungern reluctantly, unwillingly (16W)
ungewiß uncertain (16W)
das **Unglück, -e** misfortune, bad luck, accident (16W)
die **Union, -en** union (33R Fo)
die **Universität, -en** university (19R)
unkindlich unchildlike, precocious (16W)
unklar vague, not clear; muddy; misty (16W)
die **Unmasse, -n** vast quantity (35R St)
der **Unmensch** monster, brute (16W)
unmodern not modern, out of style (9D)
unmöglich impossible (9D)
unnatürlich unnatural (16W)
unpolitisch nonpolitical (22I)
die **Unruhe** uneasiness; trouble; anxiety (16W)
unsicher insecure; unsteady; unsafe; uncertain (16W)
der **Unsinn** nonsense (30D)
unten *adv.* below, down; downstairs (33V)
unter *prep.* under (14A)
unter- *adj.* lower (33V)
unterbrechen, i, a, o interrupt (27D)
unterhalb below (17S)
die **Unterkunft, ⸚e** shelter, lodging (35R St)
untermalen supply a background (35R St)
der **Untermieter, -** subtenant (34R Zi)
der **Unterricht, -e** instruction (25R)

768 Glossary

unterrichten instruct, teach (25R)
der **Unterschied**, -e difference, distinction (9D)
unterschiedlich different, distinct (14W)
unterschlagen, ä, u, a suppress (35R St)
unterwegs under way, on the way (12D)
unverhofft unexpected, not hoped for (20D)
die **Unvernunft** unreasonableness, folly, absurdity (33R Ge)
unversichert uninsured (16W)
unvollkommen *adj.* imperfect (16W)
unvorsichtig not cautious; inconsiderate; imprudent (16W)
unwahr untrue (16W)
unwichtig unimportant (16W)
die **Unwichtigkeit** unimportance (32W)
das **Urteil**, -e judgment, verdict, sentence (35R Bo)
die **USA** *pl.* (**die Vereinigten Staaten von Amerika**) the United States of America (29L)

der **Vater**, ∺ father (12D)
väterlich fatherly (14W)
der **Vati**, -s Daddy (14D)
verachten despise (26W)
veralten (s) become obsolete (26W)
(sich) **verändern** *acc. refl.* change (26W)
die **Veränderung**, -en change (31R De)
verarbeiten work up into; manufacture (26W)
verarmen (s) become poor (26W)
verbergen, i, a, o hide (26S)
verbessern improve (26W)
verbieten, o, o forbid, prohibit (26W)
verbilligen cheapen (26W)
verblassen (s) fade (26W)
verbrauchen use up, consume (26W)
verbrecherisch criminal (35R Bo)
verbreiten spread, circulate (35R Bo)
verbrennen, verbrannte, verbrannt burn up (26W)
verbringen, verbrachte, verbracht spend (one's time) (26W)
verdecken cover (tracks); hide (26W)
verdienen earn (28R)
der **Verdienst**, -e earnings, gain, profit (28R, 29L)
verdunkeln make dark (26W)
der **Verein**, -e association, club (26D)
vereinen unite (26W)
vereisen ice up; freeze (meat) (26W)
sich **verfahren**, ä, u, a *acc. refl.* get lost (while driving) (26W)
verfallen, verfällt, verfiel, verfallen (s) decay (26W)
verfilmen film (26W)
(sich) **verfinstern** *acc. refl.* grow dark (35R St)
vergeben, i, a, e forgive (26W)
vergeblich in vain, futile (24D)
vergessen, i, a, e forget (21D)
vergeßlich forgetful (21D)
vergiften poison (26W)
verglasen glaze (26W)
vergrößern enlarge (26W)
das **Verhältnis**, -se relation; situation; condition (33R Fo)
verhältnismäßig relatively, rather (33R Fo)
verheiratet married (18D)
verhören interrogate (26W); **sich verhören** *acc. refl.* misunderstand (26W)
verhungern (s) starve (26W)
verjüngen rejuvenate (26W)
der **Verkauf**, ∺e sale (17D)
verkaufen sell (21W)
der **Verkäufer**, - salesman, seller (17D)
der **Verkaufsstand**, ∺e sales booth (17D)
der **Verkehr** traffic (31R De)
das **Verkehrsnetz**, -e traffic system (31R De)
verkleinern make smaller (26W)
verkürzen shorten (26W)
verlachen laugh at, ridicule (26W)
verlängern lengthen (26W)
verlassen, ä, ie, a leave, abandon (25R)
verleben spend, pass (time) (26W)
verlegen misplace; remove (26W)

verlernen forget (26W)
verlieren, o, o *lose* (24D)
sich **verloben** *acc. refl.* become engaged; **verlobt** engaged (20D)
(sich) **vermehren** *acc. refl.* increase (26W)
vermitteln mediate; arrange (31R Eh)
der **Vermittler**, - mediator; agent (31R Eh)
die **Vermittlung**, -en mediation; arrangement (31R Eh)
vermutlich presumable; probable (15D)
vernehmen, vernimmt, vernahm, vernommen find out; cross-examine (26W)
verneinen decry; answer in the negative (26W)
die **Vernunft** reason, intelligence (33R Ge)
vernünftig reasonable (29D)
verraten, ä, ie, a betray (26W)
verrauchen go off in smoke; spend on tobacco (26W)
verreisen (s) go on a trip (33R Fo)
das **Versandgeschäft**, -e mail-order house (11D)
verschicken send off (26W)
verschieden *adj.* different (25R)
verschiedenartig varied (30R)
verschöne(r)n embellish, beautify (26W)
verschreiben, ie, ie prescribe (medicine) (31I)
versetzen transfer; advance (25R)
versichern insure (5D)
die **Versicherung**, -en insurance (17W)
versinken, a, u (s) sink out of sight (26W)
sich **verspäten** *acc. refl.* be late; be delayed (26W)
verspielen gamble away (26W)
verspotten mock, scoff at (26W)
versprechen, i, a, o promise (26W)
der **Verstand** intellect; understanding (21W)
verstärken strengthen (26W)
(sich) **verstecken** *acc. refl.* hide, conceal (26W)
verstehen, verstand, verstanden understand (10D)
versuchen try (26W)

versüßen sweeten (26W)
vertragen, ä, u, a tolerate, endure (26W)
vertraut intimate (22R)
verurteilen sentence (35R Bo)
verwirklichen realize, make real (26W)
verwunden wound (26W)
verwünschen curse; bewitch (26W)
Verzeihung! Excuse me! Pardon me! (32I)
der **Vetter**, -n (male) cousin (32I)
viel much, a lot (4D); **mehr** (12D); **meist-** (6D)
vielleicht perhaps, maybe (4D)
vielmehr rather, much more (31R De)
das **Viertel**, - quarter; **viertel** quarter (4D)
die **Villa, -llen** villa, mansion (34R Zi)
das **Volk**, ⸚er people; nation (19R)
die **Volksschule**, -n elementary school (19R)
der **Volksschüler**, - pupil at an elementary school (19R)
voll full; the full hour (4D); **voller** full of (25I)
vollkommen *adj.* perfect; complete, entire (9D)
vollstrecken put into effect, carry out, execute (34I)
von about; from; of; by (8D)
vor in front of; before; to; ago (7S)
die **Vorahnung**, -en premonition, foreboding (35R St)
vorder- *adj.* forward, front, in front (33V)
der **Vorfall**, ⸚e event, incident (33I)
der **Vorgang**, ⸚e procedure; event (33I)
vorgestern day before yesterday (15S)
vorher *adv.* before (26S)
vorhin *adv.* before (26S)
vorig- *adj.* previous, former (34R Ne)
vor-kommen, kam vor, vorgekommen (s) appear, seem (35R St)
vor-lesen, ie, a, e lecture, read aloud (17W)
die **Vorlesung**, -en lecture (3D)
der **Vorlesungsraum**, ⸚e lecture hall (3D)

der **Vormittag** forenoon (11S)
    vormittags in the morning, mornings (15S)
der **Vormonat**, -e last month, the preceding month (30D)
    vorn(e) *adv.* in front (33I)
der **Vorname**, -ns, -n first name (22R)
    vornehm fashionable, distinguished (29D)
    vor-schlagen, ä, u, a suggest (29D)
    vorsichtig cautious, careful (13D)
die **Vorstadt**, ⸚e suburb (35R St)
sich **vor-stellen** *dat. refl.* imagine (23D)
die **Vorstellung**, -en performance (35R St)
der **Vorteil**, -e advantage (31R De)
der **Vorwurf**, ⸚e reproach (33R Ge)

    wach awake (32I)
    wachsen, ä, u, a (s) grow (22R)
die **Waffe**, -n weapon (31I)
    wagen dare, risk (35R St)
der **Wagen**, - car, truck, wagon (5D)
    wahr true; **nicht wahr?** isn't it? is it? (10D)
    während during (17D)
die **Wahrheit**, -en truth (32W)
    wahrscheinlich probable, likely (11D)
der **Wald**, ⸚er forest (12S)
sich **wälzen** *acc. refl.* roll (34I)
die **Wand**, ⸚e wall (31I)
    wann when (2D)
    warm warm (18S)
die **Wärme** warmth (30W)
die **Warnung**, -en warning (35R St)
    warten wait; **warten auf** + *acc.* wait for (3D)
    warum why (3D)
    was what (1D); *rel. pron.* which (19R)
    waschen, ä, u, a wash (23S)
das **Wasser** water (28I)
der **Wasserfall** waterfall (35R St)
    waten (s,h) wade (28I)
    wechseln change, alternate (30R)

    weder...noch neither...nor (34R He)
der **Weg**, -e way, path, road (33R Fo)
    weg away, gone (16D)
    wegen because of, due to (17D)
    weg-gehen, ging weg, weggegangen (s) go away (16D)
    weh-klagen lament, wail (35R St)
die **Weihnachten** *pl.* Christmas (17S)
das **Weihnachtsfest**, -e Christmas festivity, celebration (17S)
    weil because (21G)
die **Weile**, -n while (35R Br)
der **Wein**, -e wine (14S)
    weiß white (17D)
    weit far, distant (29D); **und so weiter (usw.)** und so forth (5S)
    weitverzweigt with many branches (31R De)
die **Welt**, -en world (31R Eh)
der **Weltkrieg**, -e world war (30R)
    wenig little, a little bit; few; **weniger** (6S)
    wenigstens at least (14D)
    wenn if; whenever (2D)
    wer who (8D)
    werden, wird, wurde, geworden (s) become (13D)
    werfen, i, a, o throw (34R He)
das **Werk**, -e work (35R Bo)
das **Werkzeug**, -e tool(s) (11D)
der **Werkzeugkasten**, ⸚ toolbox (12D)
    wert valuable; worth (33R Fo)
    wesentlich considerable (17D)
    Westdeutschland West Germany, Federal Republic of Germany (12L, 29L)
der **Westen** west (12S)
    westlich west, western (12S)
das **Wetter** weather (30D)
    wichtig important (22R)
    widmen dedicate; devote (35R St)
    wie how (2D); like (2D); **so...wie** as...as (3D)
    wieder again (12D)

wieder-erkennen, erkannte wieder, wiedererkannt recognize (23D)
wieder-sehen, ie, a, e see again (20D)
das **Wiedersehen** reunion (20D)
wieso why, how so (14D)
wieviel how much, how many (8S)
wild wild (32W)
die **Wildheit** wildness; fury (32W)
willen: um . . . willen for the sake of (17G)
der **Wind, -e** wind (35R Br)
der **Winter, -** winter (11S)
wirklich real, actual (10D)
der **Wirt, -e** innkeeper, host (14D)
die **Wirtin, -nen** hostess (14D)
die **Wirtschaft, -en** domestic economy; economic system; inn (25R)
wirtschaftlich economic, economical (29L)
wissen, weiß, wußte, gewußt know (6D)
die **Wissenschaft, -en** science (25R)
wissenschaftlich scientific (25R)
der **Witz, -e** joke; wit (22I)
wo where (2S)
die **Woche, -n** week (9D)
wochenlang for weeks (30R)
der **Wochentag, -e** weekday (34R Fa)
wochentags on weekdays (34R Fa)
wöchentlich weekly (14W)
woher where from (14A); **wo . . . her** where from (20D)
wohin where to (2S)
wohl I wonder, do you suppose; probably; well (11D)
wohnen live, reside (6D)
das **Wohnhaus, ⸚er** dwelling house; apartment building (17R)
die **Wohnung, -en** apartment, dwelling (17W)
die **Wolke, -n** cloud (33R Ge)
wollen want to, desire to; intend to (13A)
die **Wollsocke, -n** woolen sock (28I)
womöglich probable; if possible (28R)

das **Wort, -e** word (in context) (3D)
das **Wort, ⸚er** word (out of context) (3D)
wörtlich literal, verbal (14W)
wortlos wordless, without saying a word (16W)
das **Wortspiel, -e** pun, play on words (33R Ge)
die **Wunde, -n** wound (6D)
der **Wunsch, ⸚e** wish (21W)
wünschen wish (12D)
die **Wurst, ⸚e** sausage (34R He)
wüst wild, riotous (30S)

die **Zahl, -en** figure, number (33R Fo)
zahm tame (22I)
der **Zahn, ⸚e** tooth (35R St)
der **Zahnarzt, ⸚e** dentist (35R St)
der **Zeh, -en** toe (35R St)
das **Zeichen, -** sign (16D)
der **Zeiger, -** pointer; hand (of a clock) (32I)
die **Zeit, -en** time (11S)
zeitlos timeless, eternal (35R Bo)
der **Zeitraum, ⸚e** period of time (31R Eh)
die **Zeitschrift, -en** magazine (16D)
die **Zeitung, -en** newspaper (7D)
die **Zelle, -n** cell (22I)
das **Zentrum, -ren** center (22I)
zerbeißen, zerbiß, zerbissen bite to pieces (26W)
zerbrechen, i, a, o break to pieces; smash (26W)
die **Zeremonie, -n** ceremony (22R)
zerlegen take apart (26W)
zerstören destroy (26W)
ziehen, zog, gezogen (s) move (21D); **(h)** pull
das **Ziel, -e** goal, end, aim (25R)
ziemlich rather (16D)
die **Zigarette, -n** cigarette (21D)
die **Zigarre, -n** cigar (22I)
das **Zimmer, -** room (12D)
die **Zimmervermieterin, -nen** landlady (34R Zi)
der **Zirkus, -se** circus (22I)

die **Zivilisation, -en** civilization (22I)
der **Zoll, ⁼e** toll, customs (22I)
zu to; at (2D); too (expensive, etc.) (10D)
der **Zucker** sugar (22I)
zuerst first, at first (13D)
der **Zufall, ⁼e** coincidence, chance event (23D)
zufrieden *adj.* satisfied (30D)
der **Zug, ⁼e** train (7D); procession (17D)
das **Zuhause** home (31R Eh)
zu-knöpfen button up (34R Fa)
zukünftig future (28R)
zumeist mostly, for the most part (25R)
zunächst first; chiefly (33R Fo)
zünden light, ignite (31I)
die **Zunge, -n** tongue (22I); language (35R Bo)
zurück-schicken send back (11D)
zusammen-bauen put together (11D)
zusammen-bringen, brachte zusammen, zusammengebracht bring together; amass (34R Ne)
zusammen-laufen, äu, ie, au (s) run together, join (34R He)
zusammen-trommeln call together (26D)
zu-sprechen, i, a, o award, grant; ascribe (28R)
zu-stimmen agree (31R De)
zuviel too much (29D)
zwanziger Jahre die *pl.* the twenties (31R De)
zwar indeed, to be sure, certainly (34I)
der **Zweifel, -** doubt (31R De)
zweifellos undoubted, certain (31R De)
der **Zweig, -e** branch, twig (22I)
zwingen, a, u force, compel (30D)
zwischen between (14A)

INDEX

Page numbers in *italics* refer to drills. German words are in **boldface** type.

Accusative case, 199–200
   as direct object, 199
   prepositions with, *212–213*, 221–222, *259*
   in time expressions, 199
Adjectival nouns, *406*, 414–415
Adjectives, 136
   comparison of, *406–410*, 415–418
   demonstrative, *501–503*, 509
   descriptive, 413–418
   endings of, *392–393*, *396–406*, 413–414
   limiting, 196–198, 381
   possessive, *186–187*, 197
   predicate, 413
Adverbs:
   comparison of, *406–410*, 415–418
   order of, 689–690
Affirmative answer pattern, *21–22*, *45–46*, *67–68*, *85*
Alphabet, 112
anstatt zu with infinitive, *354–355*, 359–360
Appositives, *394–395*, *410–411*, 418
Articles:
   definite, *86*, 87–88, 196, 381
   indefinite, 196–197, 381

Capitalization, 112–113
-chen, 215
Comma, 90–91, 113, 136–137
Commands, 24
Comparison of adjectives and adverbs, *406–410*, 415–418
Compound nouns, 88–89
Conditional sentences, *645–649*, 654–656
Conjunctions, 467–468
   coordinating, 474–475
   subordinating, 475–476
Consonants:
   combinations of, 105–107, 125–126, *704*
   fricatives, 19–21, 42–44
   l, 63–64, *672*, *704*

Consonants:
   r, 64–66, *672*, *704*
   stops, 18–19
   voiced and voiceless, 18
Contractions:
   preposition and definite article, *258*, 263
Coordinating conjunctions, 474–475
Countries, *252*, 266

da-compounds, *305*, 312–313
   anticipatory, *355–356*, 360
Dates, *122–125*
Dative case:
   as indirect object, *235–236*, 242
   of limiting adjectives, 240
   noun endings in, 241
   of personal pronouns, 241
   prepositions with, *254–259*, 262–265
   uses of, 242–243
   verbs with, *237–238*, 242–243
Days of week, *230–233*
Definite articles, *86*, 87–88, 196
   summary of cases of, 381
Demonstrative adjectives, *501–503*, 509
Demonstrative pronouns, *501–503*, 509–510
Dependent clauses, 70, *147–148*, 154
Dependent infinitive, 87, 282–283
   position of, *46–47*, 68
   with **sehen**, **helfen**, **lassen**, *281*, 286–287
   with **zu**, 277, 283, *524–525*, 531–532
   without **zu**, 283
der-words:
   accusative case, *191*, 193–194, 196
   nominative case, *190*, 193–194, 196
   summary of cases of, 381
Descriptive adjectives, *396–406*, 413–418
   after expressions of indefinite quantity, 685–686
Diphthongs, *488*, *547*, *607–608*
Direct object, 199
Directions, *250–253*, *259–260*, 265

Double infinitive, *525–529*, 532–534
du, 482–487

-e, 652
einander, *466*, 473
ein-words:
　accusative case, *192–194*, 197
　nominative case, *191–194*, 197
　as pronouns, *564–565*, 572
　summary of cases of, 381

Finite verb, 23
　position of, 70–71, *130–131*, 133–135
Fricatives, *547–548*, 607
Future perfect tense, *529*, 534
Future tense, *277–278*, 283–284
　for probability, *529*, 534

Ge-, 625–626
Gender of nouns, 195
Genitive case, *372–378*
　for indefinite time, *378*, 383–384
　noun endings in, 382–383
　prepositions with, *368–371*, *376–378*, 384–385
　to show possession, 383
　uses of, 383–385
gern, idiomatic uses of, 418
Glottal stop, 126–127

haben as tense auxiliary, 340–341
-heit, 693

Identification expressions, *186–189*, *194*, 200
-ieren, 412
Imperative, *169–171*, 176–178
　irregular, *466–467*, 473–474
Indefinite articles, 196–197
　summary of cases of, 381
Indefinite time, genitive case for, *378*, 383–384
Indicative mood, 626
Indirect discourse, 678–683
Indirect object, *235–236*, 242
Infinitive, 23
　double, *525–529*, 532–534
　as noun, 508
　perfect, *589*, 593–594

Infinitive:
　with sein, *587–588*, 592
　with um zu, ohne zu, (an)statt zu, *354–355*, 359–360
Inseparable prefixes, 565–569
Irregular weak verbs, 449, *501*

-keit, 693–694

lassen as passive substitute, *587*, 592
-lein, 215
-lich, 307–308
Limiting adjectives, 196–198
　dative case, 240
　summary of cases of, 381
Little words, 173–175
-los, 356–357

man, 684–685
　as passive substitute, *586–587*, 591–592
Masculine-feminine noun pairs, 172
Modal auxiliaries, *278–281*, 284–286
Months, *232–233*
Mood, 626

nach, nachher, nachdem, 573
nach Hause, 260
Negative answer pattern, *22*, *47*, *68*, *85–86*
Negators kein, nicht, nie, 50
nicht, 50, 690–691
Nominative case, 198–199
Noun plurals, 216–221
Nouns:
　adjectival, *406*, 414–415
　compound, 88–89
　dative endings of, 241
　feminine suffixes of, 693–694
　genitive endings of, 382–383
　infinitives as, 508
　masculine-feminine pairs, 172
　notes on, 512–514
　verbs related to, 469–470
Numbers, *128–129*, 133
　cardinal, *121–122*
　ordinal, *122*

INDEX 775

ob, omission of, *649–651*, 656
Objects:
   direct, 199
   indirect, 242
   order of, 689–690
ohne zu with infinitive, *354–355*, 359–360
Orthography, 25–26, 50–51, 71–72, 91
   ß and **ss**, 113

Passive, *561–564*, 570–572, *585–589*, 590–593
   agents of, *585*, 590–591
   dative objects with, *588–589*, 592–593
   without subject, *585–586*, 591
   substitutes for, *586–588*, 591–592
Past participle:
   with inseparable prefixes, 340
   of irregular weak verbs, 339
   with separable prefixes, 340
   of strong verbs, 338–339
   of verbs in **-ieren**, 340
   of weak verbs, 338
Past perfect tense, *445–447*, 454
Past tense, 448–451
   of strong verbs, *443–445*, 448–449
   of weak verbs, *441–442*, 448
Perfect infinitive, *589*, 593–594
Personal pronouns, *98–105*, 111–112
   accusative, *208–209*, 211–212
   agreement with nouns, *109–110*, *131*, *149*
   dative, 241
   nominative, *211–212*
   nominative and accusative, 221
   summary of cases of, 381
Phonology, 9–21, 37–44, 63–66, 83–84, 105–107, 125–127, 429–430, 487–488, 547–548, 607–608, 672, 704–705, 722
Possessive adjectives, *186–187*, 197
   summary of cases of, 381
Predicate, 48–50
Predicate nouns, 198
Prefixes:
   inseparable, 155, 565–569
   separable, *148–149*, 154–155, 530–531
Prepositions:
   with accusative, *212–213*, 221–222, 259
   with accusative or dative, 299–304, 309–312

Prepositions:
   with dative, *254–259*, 262–265
   with genitive, *368–371*, *376–378*, 384–385
Present participle, *354*, 359
Present perfect tense, *320–323*, *325–335*, 340–342, *353*, 449–450
   use of, 342
   word order with, 341
Present tense, *142–143*, *147*, 151–153, *168–169*
   forms of, 151–152
   idiomatic use of, *353–354*, 358
   of irregular verbs, 175–176
   uses of, 152–153
Prices, *208–209*, *214*, 222
Principal parts of verbs, 451–454
Probability, future tenses for, *529*, 534
Pronouns:
   agreement with nouns, *109–110*, *131*, *149*
   demonstrative, *501–503*, 509–510
   ein-words as, *564–565*, 572
   personal, *98–105*, 111–112
      summary of cases of, 381
   relative, *503–507*, 510–512

Question pattern, *22–23*, 46
Questions, 24–25
   with **wem**, *258–259*
   with **wer, wen, was**, *213–214*
Question-words, 69

Reflexive verbs, *464–466*, 471–473
   as passive substitutes, *587*, 592
Relative pronouns, *503–507*, 510–512

-schaft, 694
Seasons, *232–233*
sein:
   with infinitive, *587–588*, 592
   as tense auxiliary, 341
Sentences:
   structure of, 48
   types of, 23–25
Separable prefixes, *148–149*, 154–155, 530–531
Sie, 482–487
Statements, 24

statt zu with infinitive, *354–355*, 359–360
Strong verbs, *327–332*, *353*, 358, *443–445*, 448–449, *500–501*, *524*, *560*, *584–585*, *618*, *642*
  principal parts of, 451–454
Subject, 198
Subjunctive mood, 626–627
Subjunctive I:
  as first person imperative, 684
  in indirect discourse, 678–683
Subjunctive II, *619–624*, 626–632, *642–651*, 653–656
  als ob, **als wenn** with, *642–643*, 653
  conditional sentences with, *645–649*, 654–656
  past tense of, *621–623*, 629
  present forms of, *619–621*, 627–629
  uses of, 631–632, 653–656
  wishing-verbs with, *643–644*, 653–654
  würde-alternatives of, *623–624*, 629–630, 655–656
Subordinating conjunctions, 475–476
Syllabication, 51–52, 724–725
ß and **ss**, 113

Time:
  accusative case for, 199
  expressions of, *239*, 243, 336–337
  indefinite, *378*, 383–384
  telling, *144–145*, 155–156
  and travel expressions, *164–167*, *171–172*, 178–179
Times of day, *232–233*
Travel expressions, *164–167*, *171–172*, 178–179

um zu with infinitive, *354–355*, 359–360
Umlaut sounds, 41–42, *487*
un-, 357–358
-ung, 380

Verbs:
  with dative, *237–238*, 242–243

Verbs:
  finite, 23
  in **-ieren**, 412
  infinitive forms of, 23
  irregular, 175–176, *326*, 449, *500–501*
  nouns related to, 469–470
  principal parts of, 451–454
  reflexive, *464–466*, 471–473
  strong, *327–332*, *353*, 358, *443–445*, 448–449, *500–501*, *524*, *560*, *584–585*, *618*, *642*
  weak, *325–326*, *441–442*, 448
  and strong, 337–338
vor, **vorher**, **vorhin**, **bevor**, 572–573
Vowels, 12–18, 38–42, 83–84
  long and short, *429–430*, *487*, *547*, *607–608*
  quality and quantity, *704–705*
  umlaut sounds, 41–42, *487*

was:
  as question-word, *213–214*
  as relative pronoun, 512
Weak verbs, *325–326*, *441–442*, 448
  irregular, 449
wem, *258–259*
wen, *213–214*
wenn, omission of, *649–651*, 656
wer:
  as question-word, *213–214*
  as relative pronoun, 512
werden, functions of, 572
wessen, *378–379*
wissen, *299*, 308–309
wo, **wohin**, **woher**, *305–306*, 313
wo-compounds, *304–305*, 312–313
  in relative clauses, 511
Word order, 24–25, 49–50, 70–71, 133–135, 154, 341, 686–692

zu Hause, *260*

NORDSEE
Kiel
SCHLESWIG-HOLSTEIN
Lübeck
Hamburg
Bremerhaven
Bremen
Elbe
Ems
NIEDERSACHSEN
Hannover
Braunschweig
NIEDERLANDE
Münster
NORDRHEIN-WESTFALEN
Weser
Essen
Dortmund
Duisburg
Ruhr
Düsseldorf
Rhein
Ha
Leipzi
BELGIEN
Köln
Aachen
Bonn
BRD
HESSEN
Saale
Koblenz
Frankfurt
Mosel
Trier
LUX.
RHEINLAND-PFALZ
SAAR-LAND
Saarbrücken
Main
Nürnberg
Neckar
BAYERN
Rhein
Reg
Stuttgart
Donau
BADEN-WÜRTTEMBERG
FRANKREICH
Ulm
Isar
Augsburg
Freiburg
München
SCHWEIZ